WHO'S WHO

in the

JFK

Assassination

An A-to-Z Encyclopedia

Michael Benson

A Citadel Press Book
Published by Carol Publishing Group

For my grandmother, NAOMI LOPEZ

A Citadel Press Book
Published by Carol Publishing Group
Citadel Press is a registered trademark of Carol Communications, Inc.
Editorial Offices: 600 Madison Avenue, New York, N.Y. 10022
Sales and Distribution Offices: 120 Enterprise Avenue, Secaucus, N.J. 07094
In Canada: Canadian Manda Group, P.O. Box 920, Station U, Toronto, Ontario M8Z 5P9
Queries regarding rights and permissions should be addressed to Carol Publishing Group, 600 Madison Avenue, New York, N.Y. 10022

Carol Publishing Group books are available at special discounts for bulk purchases, for sales promotion, fund raising, or educational purposes. Special editions can be created to specifications. For details, contact: Special Sales Department, Carol Publishing Group, 120 Enterprise Avenue, Secaucus, N.J. 07094

Manufactured in the United States of America
10 9 8 7 6 5 4 3 2 1

Library of Congress Cataloging-in-Publication Data

Benson, Michael.
    Who's who in the JFK assassination : an A-to-Z encyclopedia / by Michael Benson.
        p.   cm.
    "A Citadel Press book."
    ISBN 0-8065-1444-2 (pbk.)
    1. Kennedy, John F. (John Fitzgerald), 1917-1963—Assassination—Encyclopedias.   I. Title.
E842.9.B46   1993
364.1'524'0973—dc20   93-27949
                                                                CIP

Contents

ACKNOWLEDGMENTS

The author wishes to express his deep gratitude to—and admiration for—the hundreds of witnesses, law enforcement officials, and journalists who, since day one, have worked tirelessly to share their message of truth and whose words have been so hungrily digested in this book. Thanks also to the truthseekers yet to come who might find this gathering of data helpful in solving the mystery that continues to haunt the world, and to the following persons and organizations without whose help the preparation of this work would have been impossible.

Research consultants: Mitch Highfill, David Henry Jacobs, and Richard Erickson.

And also: Sawnie Aldredge, Mr. and Mrs. Benny R. Benson, Michele Cohen, the Collector's Archives, Barbara Daigle, John H. Davis, Michael Gingold, Gary Goldstein, Mr. and Mrs. Anthony Grasso, Lisa M. Grasso, Larry Howard, David Hutchison, Norman Jacobs, Julie Jacobson, the JFK Assassination Information Center, Arlene Jones, Bill E. Kelly, Kimberly Lyons, David McDonnell, Pete McKenna, Jim McLernon, Mr. and Mrs. Raymond Merrow, George Napolitano, the New York Public Library, Rita Lascaro, Frank Rosner, Jo Anne Sanabria, Andrew Sexton, Martin Shackelford, Ruth Carol Stearns, Milburn Smith, Anthony Timpone, Carole B. Williams.

Introduction

A Trip Down the Rabbit Hole

Despite U.S. government assurances to the contrary, the crime of the century remains unsolved. The assassination of President John F. Kennedy on November 22, 1963, remains the greatest mystery of our time. It is a murder mystery with the final page torn out.

Investigators and researchers have been obsessed with the assassination—the sleazy slice of grotesque Americana, the labyrinth of characters and the deeply layered plot. It is a trip down the rabbit hole into a mirrored maze of corrupt power and greed, a story short on heroes. The men we most expected to respond gallantly to a national crisis either scrambled to cover themselves or stuck their heads in the sand.

Sorting out the evidence presents difficulties. People lie. Even some of those innocent in JFK's death did not want to see their dirty laundry aired out in the Warren Report or, to use a more modern example, in a Geraldo Rivera exposé. Plus, it was a glamorous crime, very high profile. Some people wanted to be a part of the action. How could their universe be disturbed without them playing a part? So they lied. Eyewitnesses—as is typical of their ranks, regardless of the crime—misperceived the happenings. In this case, normal misperception was exaggerated by trauma and shock. Nobody could witness a U.S. president's violent death without having his or her senses rattled. Published reports were biased, either steadfastly echoing the dubious "official facts," or advocating a tunnel-visioned yet commercially viable theory. Law-enforcement agencies were universally reluctant to pursue the truth. As there is evidence of intelligence activity surrounding JFK's death, disinformation has been purposefully circulated.

LSD hit the intelligence community twelve years before it got to Haight-Ashbury, so there may be a genuine chemical explanation for the hallucinatory nature of this case. Red herrings swim in schools. Reports conflict. A balanced weighing of the evidence is very difficult—yet the aim of this book is balance.

How to Use This Book

This is an alphabetical listing of essential people associated with JFK's death, those whose statements and/or reported activity illuminate (or cloud) the big picture. Most entries have been coded so that a quick scan of a page can categorize them. Coded entries include:

Assassination witnesses. These entries can be located by the code "a.w." following the name. These are eye- and ear-witnesses to the assassination of JFK at 12:30 P.M., on November 22, 1963, in Dealey Plaza in Dallas, Texas. Entries coded "a.w. (prelude)" are for those who witnessed pertinent happenings in and around Dealey Plaza before the assassination. The code "a.w. (aftermath)" refers to witnesses to the crime scene immediately following the shooting. The code "possible a.w." will be used sparingly. It refers to individuals who may have witnessed the shooting, but whose witness status cannot be confirmed. Witnesses who have made no statement will be listed anyway to establish their presence on the scene.

Witnesses to the murder of Officer J.D. Tippit ("t.k.w." for Tippit killing witness[es]) in the Oak Cliff section of Dallas 46 minutes or less after JFK was shot. As with assassination witnesses, "t.k.w. (prelude)" and "t.k.w. (aftermath)" codes will be used for those at the scene before and after the actual murder. The code "possible t.k.w." will be used for the same reasons as stated above.

Witnesses to the murder of Lee Harvey Oswald (hereafter referred to as Oswald) by Jack Ruby (hereafter referred to as Ruby) in the basement of the Dallas police station on the morning of November 24, 1963, are coded "o.k.w." for Oswald killing witness. Variations on this code are the same as for the other two groups of murder witnesses.

"Parkland witness" designates people who were at Parkland Hospital while JFK and/or Texas Governor John Connally were being treated there, as well as those who observed the removal of JFK's body.

"Texas Theatre witness" refers to those who saw Oswald's arrest at the Texas Theatre movie house.

"Bethesda witness" refers to those who either attended or observed activities surrounding JFK's autopsy at Bethesda Naval Hospital on the evening of November 22.

"Oswald witness" refers to people who had meaningful firsthand knowledge of the accused assassin at any time from his birth to his death. Entries will fall into this category whether or not they have made that knowledge public.

"Ruby witness" refers to those with firsthand knowledge of Oswald's killer.

"Possible murder victim" refers to those with knowledge of the assassination who perhaps died prematurely.

For eyewitnesses, all time references—unless otherwise noted—should be considered contemporaneous with the witnessed event. If it says that an a.w. is a fireman, it means he was a fireman on November 22, 1963.

Entries may be coded for more than one category.

Other entries are not coded, but include: (1) investigators, researchers, and theorists—those who have unearthed evidence, as well as those whose research has led to a publishable scenario of the events of November 22–24 (none of their opinions should be confused with those of this author); (2) principal players (i.e., suspects) in the major theories; and (3) JFK's enemies.

Entries have been cross-referenced to make it easier to weave complementary threads of evidence. The only entries not cross-referenced are Oswald, Ruby, and JFK. Use the coding system or the index to isolate references to these central entries. At the bottom of each entry is a list of the sources and relevant page numbers. The sources are abbreviated to save space and can be looked up in the "Key to Abbreviations and Terms" section, which follows.

Overview

Readers familiar with the events of the assassination weekend may want to dive right into the entries. Use the cross-referencing to explore the case's many nooks and crannies and piece together your own theoretical cabals. For neophytes, here is a *brief* overview of the events, a rundown of the major theories and an explanation of relationships and terms that will help you sort out the pieces of the puzzle.

JFK was killed by rifle fire at 12:30 P.M., on November 22, 1963, as he rode west in a motorcade down Elm Street, on the north side of symmetrical

Dealey Plaza in Dallas, Texas. He was riding in an open-top limousine, moving slowly downhill toward the mouth of a triple-underpass railroad bridge (hereafter referred to as the "triple underpass"). The motorcade had just completed a slow journey through downtown Dallas, heading from Love Field airport to the Trade Mart, where JFK was scheduled to deliver a luncheon speech. First Lady Jacqueline Kennedy was riding beside him on his left in the limo's backseat. The gunfire blew off a major portion of JFK's head. Which portion is still a matter of controversy, as we shall learn. Also seriously wounded in the ambush was Texas Governor John Connally, who was sitting in a jump seat in front of JFK, slightly below JFK and about eight inches to his left. Connally's wife Nellie was sitting at the governor's left. Many witnesses said that the shots came from in front of the president, from behind a wooden fence atop a grassy knoll on the north side of Elm Street, adjacent to the triple underpass. Others thought the shots came from the buildings to JFK's rear, at the northeast corner of Dealey Plaza. Some heard shots coming from both directions.

Special attention was drawn to the Texas School Book Depository (TSBD)—the building where Oswald worked—at the northwest corner of Elm and Houston streets, where some eyewitnesses had seen a man shooting from a sixth-floor window. A search of the sixth floor produced three shell casings and a rifle. It was discovered that the rifle had apparently been mail-ordered by Oswald under the pseudonym A. J. Hidell. Oswald had left the building following the shooting and was arrested later in the afternoon in the Texas Theatre in connection with the shooting murder of a police officer.

At Parkland Hospital a pristine bullet (a.k.a. "the magic bullet") was found on a stretcher in the vicinity of the emergency area where JFK and Connally were treated. The bullet ballistically linked the rifle found in the TSBD with the crime, even though the bullet didn't look as if it had actually struck anything. Officials almost immediately began to disregard all eyewitnesses who said that the shots came from anywhere other than the TSBD, including those who said that the shots came from behind—but not from the TSBD. Many thought the shots came from either the Dal-Tex Building or the County Records Building, which are on the east side of Houston Street facing Dealey Plaza. Still, dissenters continued to talk, keeping alive the now-accepted implausibility of the lone-gunman theory.

Because one eyewitness, Abraham Zapruder, made an 8mm film of the assassination from his position atop a pergola wall only a few feet east of the picket fence atop the knoll, we know that a lone gunman using the alleged assassination weapon had time to fire only three shots during the shooting sequence. Explaining all of JFK's and Governor Connally's wounds with three shots stretched credibility. When one considers that a bystander was wounded by the ricochet of a shot that missed, more than one gunman becomes a necessity to provide a reasonable explanation. The film also shows JFK's head being driven backward and to the left by the fatal shot, fueling suspicions that he had actually been killed by a rifleman in front of him and to his right.

Within minutes of the shooting, three vagrants were apprehended in a railcar behind the grassy knoll. The men were escorted across Dealey Plaza by police and, in the process, were photographed repeatedly. Who these three "tramps" were and what connection they had to the assassination remains a matter of controversy.

JFK and Connally were rushed to Parkland Hospital. The president was pronounced dead at 1:00 P.M. Connally survived. At Parkland, emergency personnel well experienced in the treatment of gunshot wounds were unanimous in their opinion that JFK had been shot from the front—once in the front of the throat and once in the right temple. The throat wound was enlarged so that a tracheotomy could be performed; this enlargement caused much confusion later. The emergency doctors never turned JFK over, so an alleged entrance wound in JFK's back wasn't seen until the autopsy.

Yet, that night, when JFK's body was autopsied at Bethesda Naval Medical Center in Bethesda, Maryland, by medical examiners unfamiliar with gunshot wounds, it was determined that JFK had been shot exclusively from the rear; once in the back (the throat hole, they said, was an exit wound) and once in the back of the head. All photos and X rays of the autopsy, though impossible to authenticate, agree with the autopsists. Is this a case of mass hallucination in Dallas or mass cover-up in Washington? It has to be one or the other.

Since one bullet—apparently the one that struck JFK in the head—had split apart and had been found inside the limo after the shooting, and the bullet that missed has never been found, the "magic bullet" had to account for all of the nonfatal wounds suffered in the limo. JFK's back wound and throat wound, as well as all of Governor Connally's wounds, had to be caused by a bullet that didn't look as if it had hit anything at all. Indeed, there was more metal left inside Governor Connally's body than was missing from the bullet.

Forty-six minutes or less after the assassination, Dallas Police Officer J. D. Tippit was gunned down near the corner of Tenth Street and Patton Avenue in the Oak Cliff section of Dallas. Again, eyewitnesses disagreed strongly on what happened. Still, most said that one man shot Tippit and that the man was Lee Harvey Oswald. Others saw two assailants, either fleeing in opposite directions on foot, or one fleeing on foot and one fleeing in a car. These witnesses were anonymously threatened and told to keep their mouths shut. One man (Warren Reynolds) refused to identify Oswald as the murderer, but was subsequently ambushed and shot in the head. After recovering miraculously, the man decided that, yes, it was Oswald he had seen fleeing the scene.

Less than an hour later, Oswald was arrested inside the Texas Theatre after police were alerted that a suspicious man had just snuck into the movie theater without buying a ticket. Oswald was reportedly arrested while in possession of the gun that had killed Tippit and fake I.D. linking him to the rifle found in the TSBD.

The Dallas Police Department (DPD), the Federal Bureau of Investigation (FBI), and the Secret Service (SS) interrogated Oswald for almost two days in the DPD station without allowing him a lawyer. According to all law-enforcement agencies, no stenographic or tape recordings were kept of these interrogations. All we know for certain about what Oswald said after his arrest are the statements he managed to scream to members of the press while being moved from one place to another within the station. Oswald said he "emphatically denied the charges." He called himself a "patsy." (The entry for Oswald in this book should be among the first read.) The accused assassin had a public persona created through a number of seemingly staged incidents in his life, which made him perfectly suited to a frame-up. His private persona, however—with his connections to organized crime, the Central Intelligence Agency (CIA), the FBI, Soviet intelligence (KGB), anti-Castro exiles, etc.—was so complex that it virtually assured that the crime would never be investigated adequately. This was a time when the world still hovered on the edge of nuclear holocaust, and the evil specter of conspiracy was frightening even to those whose own reputations and well-being were not protected by the cover-up.

On Sunday morning, November 24, 1963, Jack Ruby shot Oswald to death in the basement of the DPD station while Oswald was being transferred from the city jail to the county facility. Ruby, who claimed to have shot Oswald on the spur of the moment, was the owner of a Dallas strip joint called the Carousel Club. He was a man with organized crime ties that dated back to his childhood in Chicago working for Al Capone. Ruby was also a police-phile, whose chummy relationship with the DPD caused that department much embarrassment as it tried to explain how Ruby had walked right through supposedly stringent security to pump a single bullet into Oswald's abdomen.

Within days of JFK's death, Lyndon B. Johnson, the new president, appointed the Warren Commission (WC), helmed by Chief Justice Earl Warren. The official purpose of the WC was to "investigate" the assassination. The real reason for the WC, whose knowledge of the hard evidence in the case was limited to information supplied to it by the FBI, was to put an official government stamp of approval on the lone gunman/no conspiracy theory.

In 1966, controversial civil-rights attorney Mark Lane published the book *Rush to Judgment*, which strongly established the case that Oswald had been framed. In 1967, New Orleans District Attorney Jim Garrison started his own investigation into the assassination, based on the fact that Oswald had spent the summer of 1963 in New Orleans in the company of men who, according to reports received by Garrison, were plotting to kill JFK. Garrison's primary target was a bizarre, hairless, middle-aged man named David Ferrie, a CIA pilot, a private investigator for Carlos Marcello of the New Orleans mob, a soldier of fortune and a homosexual pedophile who had known Oswald since Oswald was a teenager. When Ferrie died under suspicious circumstances (officially suicide) just hours before Garrison was going to arrest him, Garrison instead arrested New Orleans import-export millionaire Clay Shaw who—using the name "Clay" or "Clem Bertrand"—had also been seen by witnesses in the company of Oswald and Ferrie discussing the assassination of JFK. Garrison immediately faced a seemingly organized media campaign to stop him. Other government agencies and elected officials refused to help Garrison, and several of his key witnesses died before they could take the stand at Shaw's trial. Shaw was acquitted. Read the entries for Garrison, Shaw, and Ferrie (as well as their cross-references) for more information on the New Orleans case.

In 1976, the people of the United States saw the Zapruder film for the first time and learned that earlier reports from Dan Rather of CBS News and from *Life* magazine, stating that JFK's head snapped forward at the time of the fatal head shot, were false. The opposite was true: JFK was rocketed backward by the fatal shot. The public outcry caused by the national telecast led directly to the formation of the House Select Committee on Assassinations (HSCA), which reopened the case, as well as that of the 1968 assassination of Dr. Martin Luther King Jr. in Memphis, Tennessee. The HSCA had to deal with internal squabbles, and with its own share of dying witnesses. The committee concluded that there were a number of organized crime figures (Carlos Marcello, Santos Trafficante, Jimmy Hoffa, and Sam Giancana) who had the motive, means, and opportunity to order JFK's assassination, but developed no evidence directly linking these men with the crime. Using acoustic evidence seemingly recorded at the assassination scene, the HSCA concluded that there had been a fourth shot and that it had come from the grassy knoll. However, because the autopsy showed no signs of a shot hitting JFK from the front, the HSCA determined that the knoll shot had missed. All wounds, they concluded, had been caused by Oswald's firing from the TSBD. Having run out of time and money, the HSCA disbanded, recommending that the Justice Department continue the investigation. The Justice Department did no such thing, but it did issue a statement discrediting the HSCA's acoustic evidence and repeating the official conclusion of the WC: one gunman, three bullets, no conspiracy.

Although many assassination theories and variations of theories will be examined in the entries, there are four basic groups which are considered primary suspects: organized crime, the CIA, the military-industrial complex, and an international web of Fascists. Many theories involve a combination of these groups. Mobsters hated JFK because his brother, Attorney General Robert Kennedy, was at war against the mob. Many CIA agents wanted JFK dead because they considered him soft on Communism and felt betrayed by what they perceived as his failure to give them adequate air support during the CIA/Cuban exile Bay of Pigs invasion of Cuba. (The Mafia, the CIA, and anti-Castro Cubans had been working hand in hand in attempts to assassinate Fidel Castro, so it is feasible that these same groups collaborated to change U.S. leadership.) The military-industrial complex hated JFK because, so the story goes, he was resisting its attempts to start a long, profitable (for them) war in Vietnam.

To study the Mafia theory, first read the entries for Marcello, Trafficante, Hoffa, Giancana, and Ruby. To study the CIA theory, read the entries for Oswald associate George DeMohrenschildt, CIA Agent E. Howard Hunt, CIA asset (i.e., employed by the CIA on a freelance basis) Marita Lorenz, and their cross-references. For the military-industrial complex theory, read the entries for Oswald associate Michael Paine, former Nazi general Walter Dornberger, and Texas oil billionaires H. L. Hunt and Clint Murchison. For the international Fascist theory, read the entries for researcher William Torbitt, alleged espionage broker L. M. Bloomfield, and Clay Shaw. This theory involves a Swiss corporation called

HOS   *A Heritage of Stone*, book by Jim Garrison
HSCA   House Select Committee on Assassinations
HT   *High Treason*, book by Robert J. Groden and Harrison Edward Livingstone (Berkley edition)
HT2   *High Treason 2*, book by Harrison Edward Livingstone
HURT   *Reasonable Doubt*, book by Henry Hurt
JAF   *JFK Assassination File*, book by Jesse Curry
KANTOR   *Who Was Jack Ruby?*, book by Seth Kantor
KKK   *Khrushchev Killed Kennedy*, book by Michael H.B. Eddowes
LEGEND   *The Legend of Lee Harvey Oswald*, book by Edward Jay Epstein
LEWIS   *The Scavengers and Critics of the Warren Report*, book by Richard Warren Lewis and Lawrence Schiller
ME   *Mortal Error*, book by Bonar Menninger
MEAGHER   *Accessories After the Fact*, book by Sylvia Meagher
MOORE   *Conspiracy of One*, book by Jim Moore
MORROW   *First Hand Knowledge*, book by Robert D. Morrow
NORTH   *Act of Treason*, book by Mark North
OAS   French Secret Army Organization
OGLESBY   *Who Killed JFK?*, book by Carl Oglesby
o.k.w.   Oswald killing witness(es)
ONI   Office of Naval Intelligence
OSS   Office of Strategic Services
OTT   *On the Trail of the Assassins*, book by Jim Garrison
PD   *Plausible Denial*, book by Mark Lane
PROUTY   *JFK*, book by L. Fletcher Prouty
PWW   *Photographic Whitewash*, book by Harold Weisberg
RC   Rockefeller Commission, 1975 (Commission on CIA Activities Within the United States, Vice President Nelson Rockefeller, chairman)
RTJ   *Rush to Judgment*, book by Mark Lane
RUSSELL   *The Man Who Knew Too Much*, book by Dick Russell
SHAW   *Cover-up*, book by J. Gary Shaw
SPOT   *JFK: The Mystery Unraveled*, special booklet excerpted from *The Spotlight* (Liberty Lobby)
SSID   *Six Seconds in Dallas*, book by Josiah Thompson (1976 revised edition)
SUMMERS   *Conspiracy*, book by Anthony Summers
TEX   *The Texas Connection*, book by Craig I. Zirbel
t.k.w.   Tippit killing witness(es)
TSBD   Texas School Book Depository
UPI   United Press International
USMC   United States Marine Corps
UTM   *Unsolved Texas Mysteries*, book by Wallace O. Chariton
WC   Warren Commission
WCD   Warren Commission Document

WCE   Warren Commision Exhibit

WCH   Warren Commission Hearings (refers to the 26 volumes of hearings and exhibits published with the Warren Report)

WR   *Warren Report* (*New York Times* Edition)

WHO'S WHO
in the
JFK Assassination

A

AASE, JEAN (aka West, Jean; Ann), Ruby witness. Described by Ruby associate Larry Meyers as a "rather dumb, but accommodating broad," Aase accompanied Meyers, a married sporting-goods salesman from Chicago, to Dallas on the eve of the assassination. Together, the pair checked into the Teamster-financed Cabana Hotel in Dallas for a series of business meetings. Also staying at the hotel, checking in on the same day, was a.w. Eugene Hale Brading, traveling under the name Jim Braden. Braden was arrested the following day for suspicious behavior in Dealey Plaza after the shooting. On the eve of the assassination, Meyers had a meeting in Dallas' Egyptian Lounge with Ruby and Dallas mobster Joseph Campisi. According to her phone records, obtained by New Orleans District Attorney Jim Garrison, Aase received a phone call from assassination suspect David Ferrie two months before the assassination. (See also Brading, Eugene Hale; Campisi, Joseph; Ferrie, David; Meyers, Lawrence)
SOURCES: COA 263, OTT 111–13 • HT 319 • SUMMERS 454 • BLAKEY 313 • EVICA 163–4, 166 • KANTOR 37 • NORTH 313, 373

ABADIE, WILLIAM, Ruby witness. Abadie, Ruby's slot machine/juke box mechanic for seven weeks during March and April of 1963, told the FBI of illegal gambling on Ruby's property.
SOURCES: COA 87–88, 90–91, 115, 118 • DAVIS 159, 285, 452, 457 • NORTH 472

ABLES, DON R., Oswald witness; DPD jail clerk. Ables was in the police lineup when t.k.w. Helen Markham identified Oswald as Officer J. D. Tippit's killer. Ables was #4 in the lineup, Oswald #2.
SOURCES: WCH VII, 239 • Bishop 290, 387

ABRAMS, GUS, possible a.w. JFK assassination files released by the DPD in February 1992 indicate that Abrams was the oldest of the three tramps apprehended moments after the assassination in a railroad car behind the grassy knoll and photographed as they were escorted across Dealey Plaza. The files said that Abrams was 53 years old and that the other two tramps were John F. Gedney, 38, and Harold Doyle, 32. Checking into this matter, the FBI discovered that Abrams is dead. Doyle and Gedney are still alive and have been located. The FBI has now concluded, according to the *New York Daily News* (March 4, 1992), that these three men were indeed the tramps and that they were, contrary to long-time beliefs, actually vagrants.

Other men who previously had been "positively" identified as one of the tramps include Charles V. Harrelson, Charles Frederick Rogers, Chauncy Marvin Holt, E. Howard Hunt, and Frank Sturgis. (See also Doyle, Harold; Gedney, John Forrester; Harrelson, Charles V.; Holt, Chauncy Marvin; Hunt, E. Howard; Rogers, Charles Frederick; Sturgis, Frank)

ABT, JOHN J., New York City attorney whom Oswald sought to represent him after his arrest. "If I can't get him, then I may get the [ACLU] to get me an attorney," Oswald said reportedly. Oswald used a DPD pay phone to call Abt's office collect, but his call was refused. Abt was out of town for the weekend.

SOURCES: WR 189, 268 • WCH X, 95–107, 116 • WCE 1145, 1937, 2073, 2144, 2152, 2165 • BISHOP 233–35, 307, 352, 466, 506, 528 • DOP 427 • SUMMERS 101 • NORTH 202, 405, 415, 417, 419, 426

ADAMCIK, JOHN P., DPD detective. Adamcik was one of the men who searched the home of Ruth Paine in Irving, Texas, where Marina Oswald lived, during the mid-afternoon of November 22, 1963, then again the following day. It was during the second search-and-seizure process that the reportedly doctored photos of Oswald holding the alleged murder weapons were found in a cardboard box in the Paines' garage. The day before, a conically rolled blanket that Marina said usually hid her husband's rifle was found.

Adamcik was also one of the first policemen to question Buell Wesley Frazier regarding his "curtain rods" story and among those who questioned Oswald late into the night of November 22 and early morning November 23. (See also Frazier, Buell; Oswald, Marina; Paine, Ruth)

SOURCES: WCH VII, 202 • BISHOP 275–8, 367, 378, 419, 462, 471

ADAMS, FRANCIS W. H., WC assistant counsel; senior partner of WC General Counsel Arlen Specter. Adams, a former New York City police commissioner, who was 59 years old when appointed to the WC, was originally assigned, with Specter, to write the WR chapter regarding the number and direction of bullets fired in Dealy Plaza—which included the

"magic bullet theory." Adams resigned de facto, however, forcing Specter to write the chapter himself. (See also Specter, Arlen)
SOURCES: WCH II, 347; IV, 101; VII, 457-71

ADAMS, JOEY, Ruby witness. Now the *New York Post* funnyman columnist, Adams was then the New York City AGVA official to whom Ruby spoke via long-distance telephone before the assassination. Ruby's accelerated number of long-distance phone calls in the preassassination weeks were explained by problems that Ruby was having with the union. (Ruby complained that his Dallas competitors were being allowed to use amateur (i.e., nonunion) strippers. However, witnesses have stated that Ruby used "amateurs" as well.) There were too many calls to powerful men with mob ties for the excuse to be real. Perhaps Ruby called men like Adams to legitimize the other calls.
SOURCES: COA 247 • BLAKEY 306

ADAMS, ROBERT L., Oswald witness; placement interviewer, Texas Employment Commission. Adams interviewed Oswald and sent him on two job interviews: (1) Solid State Electronics Co. and (2) Burton-Dixie Co. (October 7 and 9, respectively). Oswald went on both interviews but was hired for neither job. By the time Adams got Oswald a third interview, Oswald was already employed at the TSBD.
SOURCE: WCH XI, 480

ADAMS, VICTORIA ELIZABETH, a.w. Adams, on the fourth floor of the TSBD, watched the motorcade with coworkers Sandra Styles, Elsie Dorman, and Dorothy May Garner. She told the FBI she thought the shots came from below and to the right, from the direction of the grassy knoll. After the shooting, she saw a man who looked "very similar" to Ruby—whom she later saw on TV but did not know—questioning people at the corner of Houston and Elm as if he were a policeman.
SOURCES: WR 144 • WCH VI, 386 • WCE 1381; 2, 90 • RTJ 110, 262–3 • GERTZ 526 • BISHOP 130 • CF 44, 53, 325 • PWW 51–2 • HOS 52

AKIN, DR. GENE COLEMAN, Parkland witness; anesthesiologist. Akin told the WC: "the back of the right occipital-parietal portion of [JFK's] head was shattered, with brain substance extruding...I assume that the right occipital parietal region [right rear] was the exit." Akin believed initially that JFK was shot from the front.
SOURCES: WR 66 • WCH VI, 63 • HT 44–5, 52 • BE 43, 274, 313, 317 • BISHOP 156 • ME 53

ALBA, ADRIAN THOMAS, Oswald witness; acquaintance of Oswald in New Orleans. According to Jim Garrison, Alba—who operated the

Crescent City Garage in New Orleans, next door to the Reily Coffee Company, where Oswald worked theoretically from May 14 to July 19, 1963—said Oswald spent a lot of time in the garage when he should have been working. (Interestingly, four of Oswald's colleagues at Reily quit within weeks of him, and all four went on to work for NASA.) Alba told the WC that Oswald paid a lot of attention to the garage's plentiful "rifle magazines."

SOURCES: WCH X, 219 • WCE 1933, 1934, 3119 • HSCA Report 146, 191, 193–4, 617–8 • OTT 27 • FLAMMONDE 181 • NORTH 276

ALCOCK, JAMES, assistant district attorney in New Orleans under Jim Garrison at the time of the Clay Shaw trial. Because of the media campaign to smear Garrison, the D.A. kept a low profile during the trial, leaving Alcock to do most of the examining and cross-examining.

SOURCES: FMG III, 61–4 • OTT, many • FLAMMONDE, many • HOS 7, 242

ALEKSEEV, ALEXANDR I. (see SHITOV, ALEXANDR I.)

ALEMAN, JOSE BRAULIO, JR., wealthy Cuban exile; FBI informant. Aleman had a meeting with Florida mobster Santos Trafficante in September 1962 at the Scott Byron Hotel in Miami Beach. According to Aleman, as reported by the *Washington Post* in 1976, Trafficante was angry about the way the Kennedys were treating Jimmy Hoffa and said: "[JFK] doesn't know that this kind of encounter is very delicate. Mark my words, this man Kennedy is in trouble, and he will get what is coming to him." To the HSCA on March 12, 1977, Aleman quoted Trafficante as saying: "He's not going to be reelected, he's going to be hit." According to a right-wing periodical called the *Spotlight*:

> Aleman's fortunes took a turn for the worse in 1978 when he testified [before the HSCA] about the alleged role of the Mafia and the CIA in the plot to kill JFK. He fingered Florida mob boss Santos Trafficante... By July of 1983, Aleman was almost penniless and hiding in Miami. Suddenly—for no apparent reason—he went berserk, shooting and killing one relative and wounding three others. Police were called to the scene and a shoot-out ensued. During the exchange of gunfire, Aleman allegedly put his weapon to his head and blew his brains out.

SOURCES: HSCA Report 173–5 • HSCA V, 314 • COA 59–60 • SPOT 80 • SUMMERS 254–5 • BLAKEY 246 • EVICA 221–2, 283, 288–91, 311, 315–7, 327 • KANTOR 136 • DAVIS 124–5, 240, 255, 284–5, 428, 445–7, 571 • NORTH 196, 226, 410, 524

ALEXANDER, OFFICER (first name unknown), DPD member. Os-

wald's housekeeper, Earlene Roberts, told the WC that, about 30 minutes after the assassination, Oswald entered the house at 1026 North Beckley, went to his room, put on a jacket and left. While Oswald was in his room DPD squad car #207 pulled up in front of the house. Roberts testified, "Yes—it stopped directly in front of my house and it just 'tip-tip' [imitates sound of a car horn] and that's the way Officer Alexander and George Burnley would do when they stopped, and I went to the door and looked and saw it wasn't their number." The WC did not ask her Officer Alexander's first name. There was no one in the DPD at that time named George Burnley, but there was a Charles Burnley. (See also Alexander, Olen, below)
SOURCES: WCH VI, 434 • FMG I, 172, 174, 183

ALEXANDER, OLEN, possible Ruby witness. Bertha Cheek, the sister of Oswald's housekeeper Earlene Roberts, testified before the WC because she had met with Ruby a few days before the assassination. Ruby had asked to meet with her at the Carousel Club to propose that she invest $6,000 in the club, since Cheek invested in real estate. Cheek told the WC that Ruby had gotten her name from "Olen Alexander." The WC offered no information concerning this person. Since one possible connection between Ruby and Cheek is Officer Harry Olsen of the DPD, who was friends with Ruby and had once rented from Cheek, it is conceivable that Olen Alexander is a product of a transcription error at the WC hearings. (See also Alexander, Officer; Cheek, Bertha; Olsen, Harry)
SOURCES: WCH VI, 434 • FMG I, 95

ALEXANDER, STEVEN L., o.k.w.; NBC photographer. According to a December 2, 1963, FBI report:

> On November 22, 1963, Alexander was on vacation at Waco, Texas, when he heard the President had been shot... He immediately drove to Dallas, arriving about 3:30 P.M. the same day. He stayed in Dallas until 6:10 P.M. on November 24, 1963, during which time he was working for NBC... to cover the incident... [On] Sunday, November 24, 1963, Alexander entered City Hall, Dallas, at 7:30 A.M. He immediately went to the basement.... No one asked for his identification.... Alexander... walked in various parts of the basement... until the shooting of Oswald... [at] 11:30 A.M. He was carrying a camera but wore no identification of any kind.

Much time and attention has been spent trying to figure out how Ruby got into the basement to shoot Oswald, the theory being that security down there was so stringent that someone must have purposely allowed Ruby to enter. Alexander's experience adds feasibility to Ruby's story that he "just walked in."

SOURCES: PWW 121, 271–3 • WCE 2037

ALEXANDER, WILLIAM F. "BILL," Oswald witness; Ruby witness; Dallas assistant district attorney. Alexander talked briefly with Ruby on November 23. According to Alexander, the meeting was set up to discuss bad checks Ruby had received. Alexander was the assistant district attorney who most vigorously presented the case against Oswald to the public immediately following the assassination. According to HT, "It has been suggested that Alexander was in the car that stopped in front of Oswald's house around 30 minutes after the assassination." (See the entry for Roberts, Earlene, for more on this incident.) After the arrest of Oswald, at which he had been present, Alexander said, "Yes, he's a goddamned Communist." Again, according to HT, "[Alexander] was waiting with a group of policemen in the alley behind the theater. It is believed that someone intended to murder Oswald there, but was foiled when Oswald didn't run out of the theater." According to Penn Jones, Jr., "Three policemen and... Alexander were waiting for him at the back door. Had Oswald run out that door, his execution would have been quick and painless, and the lone-gunman theory would have been intact completely." By November 23, Alexander said he was ready to prosecute Oswald "as part of an international Communist conspiracy."

Alexander later prosecuted Ruby for Oswald's murder. During the Louisiana trial of Clay Shaw for conspiracy to assassinate the president, Alexander helped witness Sergio Arcacha Smith successfully resist extradition.

Alexander's permanent pass to Ruby's Carousel Club, bearing Alexander's signature, was found among Ruby's belongings following Ruby's arrest. WCE 1322 describes all of the cards found and lists the names on them, including Alexander's. However, a microfilm of the actual cards shows all of them except Alexander's.

When Ruby was in jail, he repeatedly requested that he be taken away from Dallas, where his life was in danger, so that he could take a polygraph examination. The WC agreed to allow Ruby to take the lie detector test, but only in Dallas. The test was administered in the presence of Bill Alexander, who told the WC that there was no evidence that Ruby had any connections with organized crime.

Alexander participated vigorously in Ruby's prosecution. According to attorney/author Elmer Gertz, who was on the defense team that successfully appealed Ruby's death sentence:

> There were eighty people in the [Dallas District Attorney's] office in 1963...and it would be hard to find a more dedicated, and indelicate, lieutenant than... "Bill" Alexander.... If Alexander had been elected to the U.S. Presidency—God forbid!—he would have signed treaties and public documents "Bill." He was Bill even to those whose lives he was intent on taking—in a legal way, of course. The gun which he carried was a symbol to him of the strength of the law...For years Ruby had regarded Alexander as his friend; Alexander did not deny it, but friendship did not deter him in the least from his grim task. He was determined to "fry" his friend, and to that end he would devote his shrewd, resourceful, and remorseless mind...Whether or not Alexander mourned the assassination of the President, he could not resist a typical crack when a St. Patrick's Day parade was held in 1964 on the street of the President's death, "Don't you think we're pushing our luck a little having another parade for an Irishman around here?" In the same manner he described his political philosophy as being "just to the left of Little Orphan Annie and just to the right of the John Birchers."

According to Penn Jones Jr., "[Alexander] is alleged to have threatened to kill a man in the Court House by jamming a pistol to the man's head and saying, 'You son of a bitch, I will kill you right here.'...In view of the close relationship attested to by both Ruby and Alexander, and in view of a visit to Alexander's office by Ruby on the day before the assassination, we feel it is necessary to ask Alexander if he was the 'officer Alexander' making the [according to Earlene Roberts's WC testimony] periodic visits to the rooming house in which Oswald was living."

Dr. William Robert Beavers was the psychiatrist called by the WC to testify that Ruby was mentally unstable. One of the points Beavers used to illustrate his instability was the fact that Ruby had said, before his polygraph examination was administered, that he would rather have Bill Alexander in the room than his own defense attorney, Joe Tonahill. Anyone who preferred an assistant district attorney's presence in such a situation to his own defense lawyer, Beavers argued, is not aware of the situation.

(Psychologically speaking, however, Ruby's behavior can be explained without insanity or conspiracy. Tonahill was trying to get people to believe that Ruby was insane, to keep him out of the electric chair. Alexander, who was Jack's friend, wanted to see Ruby fry—nothing personal, of course, but that was his job. Ruby's mother had died in a mental institution. It is entirely possible that Ruby had considered his possible future scenarios, and had come to the conclusion that the electric chair was his best bet.)

After Beavers's statements to the WC, Alexander was allowed by WC counsel Arlen Specter to ask Beavers a few questions. Immediately, Bill's ego got into the thick of his query: "Did it appear to you that Ruby [during his polygraph examination] was looking to me for aid in framing some of the questions because of my peculiar knowledge of the case, in that I was in on it from the moment of the assassination of the President?"

Beavers replied, "I noticed that he did look to you in terms of getting some sort of support or information or possibly framing questions."

Alexander, who should have been among the first to testify before the WC, was instead allowed to ask questions. (See also Garrison, Jim; Hill, Gerald; Roberts, Earlene; Smith, Sergio; Shaw, Clay)

SOURCES: WR 312 • WCH XIV, 504–79 • WCE 1322, 1571, 1628, 1686, 1788, 2003, 2245, 2405–13 • HT 139, 237–8, 289 • RTJ 261 • COA 111, 163, 259, 330, 455 • GERTZ, many • BISHOP 364, 452, 473, 504 • DOP 287 • FMG I, 12, 14, 16–17, 19–20, 51–3, 77, 175–82; III, 18, 102 • SUMMERS 58, 94–6, 98, 202, 409 • BLAKEY 326, 328–9 • KANTOR 57, 113–6, 119, 125–6, 182 • NORTH 434–5, 506

ALKANA, IRVING, Ruby witness; owner, before Ruby, of Dallas's Vegas Club. Ruby purchased one-third of the club in the early 1950s. In April or May of 1954, according to Alkana, Ruby attacked him and beat him severely. Two months later, Alkana sold the remainder of the club to Ruby.
SOURCE: COA 84-5

ALLEN, ROSEMARY. A note reading "Rosemary Allen...Deputy Sheriff Decker's secretary" was found among Jack Ruby's belongings following Ruby's arrest. Some statements from assassination eyewitnesses given to the Dallas County Sheriff's office, including that given by Julia Ann Mercer, were notarized by Allen. (See also Mercer, Julia Ann)
SOURCES: COA 111 • FMG I, 26

ALLEN, WILLIAM, a.w.; news photographer for the *Dallas Times Herald*. With Joe Smith of the *Fort Worth Star* and Jack Beers of the *Dallas Morning News*, Allen was one of three photographers to take photos of the three "tramps" as they were led by police away from a railroad car near Dealey Plaza, presumably to be questioned. Ten minutes after the assassination, Allen also took photos of Deputy Sheriff Buddy Walthers and

an unidentified man on the south side of Dealey Plaza while the man, wearing a plastic earpiece, picked something out of the grass and put it in his pocket. (See also Walthers, Buddy)
SOURCE: OTT 207–9

ALLMAN, PIERCE, a.w. Oswald told police that he had directed an SS agent to a telephone as he left the TSBD, minutes after the assassination. Though it is generally assumed that this was NBC reporter Robert MacNeil, WCD 354 says that the man entering the building as Oswald was leaving was WFAA-TV reporter Pierce Allman. (See also MacNeil, Robert)
SOURCES: WCD 354 • MOORE 53 • MEAGHER 74

ALTGENS, JAMES W. "IKE," a.w.; standing on the south side of Elm, between the TSBD and the grassy knoll; AP photographer who took a famous picture of Kennedy as he was shot. Altgens told WC counsel that, because of the direction of flying brain matter, he thought the bullet had exited the left side of JFK's head. Altgens told researcher David Lifton on November 1, 1965, that he remembered, just before the motorcade arrived, that a number of people appeared behind the wall on the knoll "to the right of the stairs as you face the knoll." There were police among them. He told the WC: "I made one picture at the time I heard a noise that sounded like a firecracker... the sound was not of such a volume that it would indicate to me it was a high-velocity rifle... It sounded like it was coming up from behind the car." That Altgens saw people to the right of the stairs on the north side of Elm is physically impossible in Dealey Plaza. Because those stairs curve right after disappearing from view, what appears from the south side of the street to be on the right of the stairs is actually to the left of the stairs and behind them.

The photo also shows that the SS agents assigned to protect LBJ reacted more quickly than JFK's guards. While the presidential SS agents had merely turned to look back at the TSBD, LBJ's protectors were already leaving their car.

Altgens also took this book's cover photo, showing the presidential limo moments after the fatal head shot. (See also Lovelady, Billy; Taylor, Warren)
SOURCES: WR 109–10, 137 • WCH VII, 515 • WCE 203, 369, 900, 1407–8 • HT 218–9 • RTJ 55, 353–4, 355 • BE 29, 285 • FMG III, 17 • PWW, many • MOORE 89–90, 98, 120 • ME 82–3, 106, 116, 214

ALVARADO, GILBERTO UGARTE, Nicaraguan informant. Evidence shows that someone—or some group—tried to make Oswald look like part of a Communist conspiracy both before and after the assassination. Perhaps part of the conspirators' plan included igniting worldwide anti-Communist tension. According to HT, Alvarado told personnel at the American embassy in Mexico City on November 24, 1963, that he had seen Oswald paid $6,500 by Cubans on September 17, 1963, and overheard Oswald and the Cubans discussing the assassination. The story turned out to be false. The activities of anyone quick to proclaim Oswald part of a Communist conspiracy should be scrutinized closely.

According to Summers, Alvarado was "handled and debriefed by David [Atlee] Phillips, CIA Chief of Cuban Operations in Mexico." (See also Phillips, David Atlee)
SOURCES: HT 192 • SUMMERS 415–9, 518

ALVAREZ, LUIS, acoustics expert. Alvarez served on a panel of the National Academy of Sciences, commissioned by the Department of Justice, that reported on May 14, 1982: "The acoustic analyses do not demonstrate that there was a shot from the grassy knoll." This report refutes the conclusion of the HSCA and ostensibly preserves the feasibility of the WR.
SOURCES: COA 27 • MOORE 183 • ME 201-2

ALYEA, TOM, a.w. (aftermath); WFAA-TV cameraman who entered the TSBD immediately after the assassination, before the DPD sealed off the building. Alyea told researcher Gary Mack in 1985 that federal agents on the scene were "bent on getting me out of the place" but that local cops allowed him to stay. When he had trouble filming the three shells on the sixth floor because of the boxes that surrounded them, Captain Will Fritz picked up the shells and held them in his hand so that they could be photographed, then threw them back down. This occurred before the crime-scene search unit had arrived. This means that, according to Alyea, the official photographs of the three shells do not show them as they were found, but as they were after Fritz tossed them down. (See also Fritz, Will)
SOURCES: WCE 2594 • CF 437–8 • PWW 39–40, 121–3, 274–5

ANDERSON, ALICE, coauthor, with Diana Hunter, of the book *Ruby's Girls* (Hallux, Inc., 1970). Both Anderson and Hunter claim to have worked for Jack Ruby. The book sticks carefully to the official version of the facts: "Suddenly, as if on impulse, Ruby got up from his seat and hurried to the telephone. He put in a call to his sister in Chicago... 'Isn't it terrible!' he shouted when she came on the line. 'How could anybody kill the President? What will happen to the country? What will happen to Jackie and those poor kids?... If they catch that guy, they'll have the trial here. They'll make

Jackie come back and testify. She shouldn't have to do that. It just isn't fair.'"

ANDERSON, EUGENE D., major, USMC marksmanship expert. Anderson defended Oswald's shooting ability despite Oswald's miserable marine marksmanship scores.
    SOURCES: WR 177, 179, 183 • WCH XI, 301 • RTJ 124

ANDERSON, JACK, investigative reporter/syndicated columnist. Anderson was told by mobster Johnny Roselli that the CIA/Mafia plans to assassinate Castro backfired, resulting in JFK's death. Roselli was later found murdered. Anderson reported that an intelligence agent using the code name "Maurice Bishop" (see Phillips, David Atlee) had bribed certain individuals to say they saw Oswald at the Cuban embassy in Mexico City in September 1963 (see Alvarado, Gilberto). Anderson reported that, as early as 1946, Richard Nixon had received substantial campaign funds from organized-crime figures in Los Angeles. In 1959, Anderson reported that Nixon's political manager, Murray Chotiner, had in his legal career handled the defenses of 221 organized crime figures. Reportedly Anderson was once an assassination target of E. Howard Hunt, a man involved in assassination attempts on Castro and later arrested for his involvement in the Watergate burglary. The *Washington Post* reported that Hunt had been ordered to kill Anderson with an untraceable poison, but that the plan had been dropped at the last second. Other than Roselli, Anderson's souce of information concerning CIA/Mafia/assassination matters was CIA agent Frank Sturgis. When Sturgis was arrested for the Watergate break-in, it was Anderson who bailed him out and asked that Sturgis be released in his custody. Anderson once wrote that Castro's expulsion of the casinos from Cuba "hit the mob as hard as the 1929 stock market crash rocked Wall Street."

Anderson reported in 1988 that two unnamed waitresses had reported to him that they had seen Ruby and Oswald together at 2:30 A.M. on the morning of the assassination at the Lucas B&B Restaurant in Dallas. (See also Castro, Fidel; Hunt, E. Howard; Nixon, Richard M.; Roselli, John; Sturgis, Frank)
    SOURCES: HSCA Report 107, 114 • HT 141, 193, 293, 306, 317, 355–7, 379 • COA 38, 103, 189, 219, 239, 397 • FLAMMONDE 111–2 • BLAKEY 52, 152–3, 155, 383, 385–7 • EVICA, many • ME 185 • KANTOR 5, 211–2 • DAVIS 367, 474, 484–5, 580, 599–600, 604–8 • PD 113–4, 124, 205–6

ANDREWS, DEAN ADAMS, JR., Oswald witness; New Orleans attorney. During the summer of 1963, Oswald asked Andrews to have his

USMC discharge changed from "undesirable" to "honorable." On November 23, Andrews received a call from a lawyer named "Clay Bertrand" (see Shaw, Clay) who asked him to represent Oswald in Dallas. Andrews told the WC that on the day after the assassination, while a patient at Hotel Dieu Hospital, he'd received a call from a man identifying himself as "Clay Bertrand," asking him to fly to Dallas to represent Oswald—and, although Andrews said "Bertrand" was a client of his, he had never seen him in person.

Andrews, whom Jim Garrison described as a "roly-poly lawyer who spoke in a hippie argot all his own," met with Garrison in 1967 at Broussard's Restaurant in New Orleans's French Quarter to explain his story—which kept changing. When first interviewed by the FBI following the assassination, he said that Bertrand was 6'2". He told the WC Bertrand was 5'8". He told Garrison he'd never met Bertrand. In the FBI interview, Andrews said that Bertrand had called him occasionally, always to request help getting a young male friend out of some sort of legal jam. This was how Andrews first met Oswald. Bertrand asked Andrews to help Oswald with problems concerning Marina Oswald's citizenship. Oswald had subsequently visited Andrews repeatedly in his office. (During the FBI interview, it became obvious that the feds did not want to hear about this Bertrand, prompting Andrews to tell them it was okay if they said he was nuts. In their report, the FBI stated that Bertrand was a "figment of Andrews' imagination.") In 1967, Garrison had known Andrews for years. They had attended Tulane Law School at the same time, although they had graduated in different years. According to Garrison, "[Andrews] appeared to obtain much of his business from his regular presence in some of the more off-beat bars in [New Orleans]." When Garrison asked Andrews about Bertrand in Broussard's Restaurant in 1967, Andrews reportedly said:

God almighty, you're worse than the FeeBees. How can I convince you that I don't know this cat? I don't know what he looks like and I don't know where he's at. All I know is that sometimes he sends me cases. So, one day, this cat Bertrand's on the phone talkin' to me about going to Dallas and representing Oswald. Scout's honor, man. That's all I know about the guy . . . Is this off the record, Daddy-o? In that case, let me sum it up for you quick. It's as simple as this. If I answer that question you keep asking me, if I give you that name you keep trying to get, then it's goodbye Dean Andrews. It's bon voyage, Deano. I mean like permanent. I mean like a bullet in my head—which would make it hard to do one's legal research, if you catch my drift.

There is evidence that Andrews and Shaw knew one another. Edward Whalen, a professional criminal from Philadelphia, told Garrison that Shaw introduced him to Andrews in Shaw's apartment in early 1967.

Andrews appeared on an NBC *White Paper* special called "The Case of Jim Garrison," saying that Clay Shaw was definitely not Clay Bertrand, and—contradicting himself—that he wouldn't know Shaw if he "fell across him lying dead on the sidewalk." When Andrews repeated that latter statement to the New Orleans grand jury deciding whether or not to indict Clay Shaw for conspiracy to assassinate the president, Garrison filed perjury charges against Andrews and earned a conviction in court. Andrews never served time on the perjury conviction. He died soon thereafter of complications from a longtime heart condition. (See also Garrison, Jim; Shaw, Clay)

SOURCES: WR 303 • WCH XI, 325 • WCE 1931, 2899, 2900–1, 3094, 3104 • RTJ 389–90 • OTT 79–84, 123–4, 169–70, 241, 243, 250 • FMG III, 50, 61–3 • PWW 110 • SUMMERS 303, 309 • FLAMMONDE, many • BLAKEY 45–8, 81 • ME 90 • DAVIS 143, 448–9

ANGEL, J. LAWRENCE, forensic expert; curator of physical anthropology at the Smithsonian Institution. Angel was the HSCA pathology-panel member assigned to explain how a piece of JFK's skull, found in Dealey Plaza by a.w. Billy Harper, appears to come from the back of JFK's head, while JFK's autopsy photos and X rays show no loss of skull from that area. "I'm puzzled," Angel said. (See also Harper, Billy)

SOURCES: HSCA VII, 247 • BE 530–1

ANGLETON, JAMES JESUS, CIA counterintelligence chief. According to former Nixon aide H. R. Haldeman, in his book *The Ends of Power*, "The CIA literally erased any connection between Kennedy's assassination and the CIA... in fact... Angleton... called Bill Sullivan of the FBI [#3 man under J. Edgar Hoover, who died later of a gunshot wound] and rehearsed the questions and answers they would give to the WC investigators."

When KGB agent Yuri Nosenko defected to the United States on January 20, 1964 and told the CIA that he had handled the Oswald case during Oswald's stay in the USSR, the CIA subjected Nosenko to 1,277 days of "intense interrogation." During that time Nosenko, though failing multiple lie-detector tests, maintained that the KGB had given Oswald two mental examinations and found that, along with not being too bright, Oswald was "mentally unstable." Nosenko said that Oswald was not used as an agent and was not even debriefed concerning his military background. The respective heads of the FBI and the CIA, J. Edgar Hoover and Richard Helms, believed Nosenko. Angleton did not. He, along with the rest of the CIA's counterintelligence faction, believed Nosenko had been sent to the U.S. by the KGB to stifle suspicions that the Soviets had JFK killed and to cover for KGB agents working within U.S. intelligence. After his retirement, according to CF, Angleton wrote: "The... official decision that Nosenko is/was bona fide is a travesty... The ramifications for the U.S. intelligence community, and specifically the CIA, are tragic." (See also Haldeman, H.R.; Helms, Richard; Hoover, J. Edgar; Nixon, Richard M.; Nosenko, Yuri)

SOURCES: HT 333 • BELIN 141, 148 • CF 130–4 • SUMMERS 112–3, 132–3, 163, 168–9, 522 • BLAKEY 79, 117, 125–6 • EVICA 131, 325–6 • OGLESBY 77 • DAVIS 296 • PD, many

ANSON, ROBERT SAM, author of *They've Killed the President* (Bantam, 1975).

SOURCES: HT 190–1, 413 • COA 51, 53, 185, 274 • BELIN 29–31, 223, 226 • FMG III: 101 • MOORE 35, 37, 66, 71, 79, 111, 215 • EVICA 207, 210 • KANTOR 14, 210

APPLE, TOM, Ruby witness. Apple saw Ruby for 45 minutes on November 23 around 3:00 P.M. in Sol's Turf Bar on Commerce Street in Dallas. Apple says Ruby showed him photos of the "IMPEACH EARL WARREN" road sign he had taken the night before and defended Dallas against others in the bar who were bad-mouthing the city.

SOURCE: WR 324

APPLIN, GEORGE JEFFERSON, JR., Texas Theatre witness; possible Ruby witness. Applin told the WC that Oswald fought with four or five policemen before he was handcuffed. One of the policemen, Applin said, struck Oswald in the back with the butt end of a shotgun. According to the WR, Applin is the only witness who saw Oswald struck by a gun. Applin claims to have seen Ruby inside the theater at the time. (See also Gibson, John)

SOURCES: WR 166 • WCH VII, 85

ARCE, DANNY G., a.w.; TSBD employee. Arce, who was standing in front of TSBD, told FBI agents that he thought shots came from the direction of the railroad tracks—from in front of JFK and to his right.

SOURCES: WCH VI, 363 • RTJ 111 • BISHOP 45, 100, 121, 127 • CF 27

ARCHER, DON RAY, Ruby witness; DPD officer. Archer told Jack Ruby, in his jail cell, that Oswald had died and said Ruby seemed "greatly

relieved" at the news.
SOURCES: WCH XII, 395 · HT 462 · GERTZ 47, 57, 71, 76, 87, 90–4, 98–9, 415 ·
BLAKEY 331

ARMSTRONG, ANDREW, JR., Ruby witness; ex-convict and handy-
man who worked in Ruby's Carousel Club. Armstrong originally told the
FBI that he had called stripper Karen Carlin on Friday night, November
22, 1963, to tell her that, because of JFK's death, Ruby's clubs would be
closed for the next three nights. When testifying to the WC, Armstrong
denied calling Carlin at all. (Carlin told the WC that Armstrong called her
on Friday night, but that he'd said the clubs would be closed for only one
night.) Armstrong told the HSCA that Ruby wasn't having the problems he
said he was having with AGVA, thus throwing further doubt on Ruby's cover
story to explain his extraordinary number of long-distance phone calls
during the weeks leading up to the assassination. He told the WC that Ruby
was visited at the Carousel Club by Mickey Ryan on the afternoon of
November 21, 1963. Ryan told the WC that he had last seen Ruby two
weeks before the assassination. (See also Carlin, Karen; Ryan, Mickey)
SOURCES: WR 314–5, 322, 325 · WCH XIII, 302 · WCE 2275, 2430, 2439, 2783,
2793, 2984, 3069 · RTJ 251 · COA 141–2, 249, 260 · GERTZ 104–5, 110, 112, 522 ·
FMG I, 23, 109–10 · EVICA 110–1 · KANTOR 41–4, 189, 202

ARNETT, CHARLES OLIVER, o.k.w.; reserve captain, DPD. Arnett,
53 years old; did not see Ruby enter the basement. He struggled with Ruby
after Ruby shot Oswald. (See also Harrison, William)
SOURCES: WR 206 · WCH XII, 128

ARNOLD, CAROLYN (MRS. R. E.), a.w., Oswald's TSBD coworker.
Arnold testified: "About a quarter of an hour before the assassination, I
went into the lunchroom on the second floor for a moment... Oswald was
sitting in one of the booth seats on the right-hand side of the room as you go
in. He was alone as usual and appeared to be having lunch. I did not speak
to him, but I recognized him clearly."

By 12:15, when Arnold saw Oswald on the second floor, a.w. Arnold
Rowland was already seeing a gunman on the sixth floor. If Mrs. Arnold
and Rowland are both correct about the time, Oswald could not have been
the sixth-floor guman. Mrs. Arnold was standing in front of the TSBD at
the time of the shooting. (See also Henderson, Ruby; Rowland, Arnold;
Walther, Carolyn)
SOURCES: HT 175 · CF 49 · PWW 74–6, 210–1 · SUMMERS 77–80 · OGLESBY 52 ·
DAVIS 432–3 · NORTH 377–8, 438

ARNOLD, GORDON, a.w. Arnold tried to film the motorcade from
behind the wooden fence atop the grassy knoll but was chased away by a

man showing SS credentials. Instead, he filmed the assassination from in front of the fence. Arnold says that the first shot "whistled by" his left ear. He hit the dirt and covered his head. Arnold was in the military at the time and knew how to duck and cover. He says the next shot went over him. According to author Henry Hurt, in his book *Reasonable Doubt*, Arnold said he felt "as if he were standing there under the muzzle." Arnold then claims he was confronted by a hatless man with dirty hands in a policeman's uniform. The man, who was "shaking and crying," kicked him and took the film out of his camera.

Arnold told Earl Golz of the *Dallas Morning News* in 1978: "The shot came from behind me, only inches over my left shoulder. I had just got out of basic training. In my mind, live ammunition was being fired. It was being fired over my head. And I hit the dirt... you don't exactly hear the whiz of a bullet, you hear just a shock wave. You *feel* it... you feel something and a shock wave comes right behind it."

Recent computer enhancements of the Mary Moorman photograph substantiate Arnold's statements. In the Moorman photograph, the man directly behind Arnold firing a rifle over the fence appears to be wearing a policeman's uniform and has long been referred to as "Badge Man." Senator Ralph Yarborough, who rode with LBJ in the motorcade, remembers seeing Arnold up on the knoll diving to the ground, thinking, "Now, there's a good soldier." Two days after the assassination, Arnold was transferred to Alaska. He did not return for several years. (See also Moorman, Mary; White, Jack)

SOURCES: HT 462 • COA 23 • CF 78–9, 320 • SUMMERS 24–7, 50–1 • OGLESBY 36

ARONSON, LEV, Oswald witness. Aronson, first cellist of the Dallas Symphony Orchestra, attended a party at Katherine N. Ford's house in Dallas in 1962, along with many members of the Dallas Russian-speaking community and Lee and Marina Oswald. Aronson's date for the evening was a Japanese woman named Yaeko Okui, with whom Oswald "spoke at length." (See also Ford, Katherine; Okui, Yaeko)

SOURCE: WR 643

ARTIME, MANUEL, Cuban exile leader. At the time of JFK's death, according to an article called "The Curious Intrigues of Cuban Miami" by Horace Sutton in the September 11, 1973, edition of the *Saturday Review/ World*, Artime was living in Nicaragua, where he maintained two military bases, a 300-man armed force and a huge "arsenal of equipment." Artime was a friend of assassination suspect E. Howard Hunt and worked with

Hunt on CIA and Mafia schemes to assassinate Castro. Artime later delivered, for Hunt, the first "hush money" payments to the Watergate burglars.
SOURCES: HT 312 • EVICA, many • FLAMMONDE 254–5 • SUMMERS 322, 418 • BLAKEY 158 • DAVIS 408 • PD 253

ASCHKENASY, ERNEST, acoustics expert; associate of Professor Mark Weiss and Dr. James Barger, the latter being the chief acoustical scientist for Bolt, Beranek and Newman. The three men analyzed a DPD Dictabelt recording, which seemed to have inadvertently recorded the assassination and designed an "acoustical reconstruction in Dealey Plaza." According to author Anthony Summers: "Early one morning in 1978, guns boomed once again at the scene of President Kennedy's murder. The results showed that impulses on the police recording matched sound patterns unique to the scene of the crime. Certain impulses, the scientists firmly decided, were indeed gunshots. They were distinguishable as rifle fire, rather than the noises produced by, say, a pistol or a car's backfire. The scientists were able to say that the sounds had been picked up by a microphone moving along at about eleven miles per hour at the time of the assassination."
Aschkenasy testified to the HSCA on December 29, 1978, that he was "95 percent" certain that a police Dictabelt recording of the assassination showed oscillating waves, i.e., "sound fingerprints," indicating a fourth shot from the grassy knoll. His key testimony was broadcast live by PBS Television. (See also McLain, H.B.)
SOURCES: HSCA Report 69, 486, 495, 507 • HSCA V, 588 • BE 563 • HT 249, 261–2 • COA 26–8 • BELIN 191 • MOORE 141 • BLAKEY 95, 101–2, 104 • ME 182 • OGLESBY 44

ATKINS, THOMAS, a.w.; White House photographer. Austin rode in the motorcade six cars behind JFK's limo. In 1977, Atkins told *Midnight* magazine, "The shots came from below and off to the right from where I was... I never thought the shots came from above. They did not sound like shots coming from anything higher than street level."
SOURCE: CF 16–7

AUSTIN, EMORY, t.k.w. Austin says that he did not see Helen Markham, the WC's star witness to the Tippit killing, at the scene during the minutes immediately following the shooting.
SOURCE: CF 341

AUSTIN, HORACE, Oswald witness; New Orleans police sergeant. Austin saw and heard Oswald after his arrest on August 9, 1963, for getting into a fight on Canal Street while passing out pro-Castro leaflets.

According to author Anthony Summers, Austin said that Oswald "appeared as though he is being used by these people and is very uninformed," but he didn't say who "these people" were.

SOURCE: SUMMERS 272

AYCOX, JAMES THOMAS, Ruby witness; drummer at Ruby's Vegas Club. Aycox quit about a week before JFK's death because he couldn't get along with the band, The Players.

SOURCE: WCH XV, 203

AYNESWORTH, HUGH, a.w., o.k.w., Texas Theatre witness; *Newsweek* reporter. In the May 15, 1967, issue of *Newsweek* Aynesworth wrote: "Jim Garrison is right. There has been a conspiracy in New Orleans—but it is a plot of Garrison's own making." Aynesworth claimed Garrison had invented a conspiracy for his own politically opportunistic reasons.

SOURCES: WCE 831 • RTJ 161–2 • MOORE 80, 83–4 • OTT 161–2 • FLAMMONDE 290–1 • EVICA 176, 194

AYRES, JOSEPH C., suspicious death; chief steward aboard Air Force One on November 22, 1963. David Lifton, author of *Best Evidence* (Macmillan, 1981), theorizes that JFK's body might have been altered on this plane to make it appear as if it had been shot only from behind. According to CF, Ayres died in an August 1977 "shooting accident," just prior to the HSCA investigation. (See also Lifton, David)

SOURCES: DOP, many • CF 565

AZCUE, EUSEBIO, possible Oswald witness; Cuban consul in Mexico City in September 1963, at the time Oswald supposedly visited there. When Oswald (or an Oswald impersonator, hereafter referred to as Oswald) found out from consulate employee Silvia Duran that it would take a week for him to get a visa to travel to Cuba, Oswald had a temper tantrum until Azcue, the consul himself, was forced to step in. According to author Anthony Summers, Azcue

> laboriously repeated the formalities, but still the stranger fumed. Now the consul lost patience too, finally telling the American that "a person of his type was harming the Cuban revolution more than helping it." That was still not the end of the saga. There was yet another visit and another row with the consul. Azcue and a colleague were suspicious of a card Oswald produced showing membership in the American Communist Party. It looked strangely new and unused. The officials were justifiably doubtful; Oswald had never joined the Party. According to Azcue, the final straw was when [Oswald] mocked him and Silvia Duran as "mere bureaucrats." At this the consul

ordered him out of the building. The man who called himself Lee Harvey Oswald had made an unforgettable impression.

Azcue was shown a photograph of Oswald and was asked if this were the man who visited him in September 1963. He said, "This gentleman... is not the person who went to the consulate... the man... was... over 30 years of age and very, very thin faced... He was... dark blond... He had a hard face. He had very straight eyebrows, cold, hard, and straight eyes. His cheeks were thin. His nose was very straight and pointed." No one has ever described Oswald as having "straight eyes." Azcue was not questioned by the WC. He did, however, testify before the HSCA. The committee showed Azcue photographs of Oswald, and he said this was not the man at the consulate. (See also Duran, Silvia)

SOURCES: WR 279–80 • HSCA Report 123, 125–6, 250–1 • HT 182, 377, 395 • OTT 64–5 • BLAKEY 34, 143, 147 • DAVIS 164–5

B

BADEN, MICHAEL, pathologist and forensics expert; chairman of the HSCA's Forensic Pathology Panel. Baden, who was then New York City's Chief Medical Examiner, concluded that there was a possibility, although highly remote, that JFK was struck in the head by a bullet fired from the grassy knoll. He said that the medical evidence of this shot, however, was obliterated by another shot's striking JFK in the head from behind a fraction of a second later. Baden maintains that there is no medical evidence indicating that JFK was shot from the front. He told the HSCA in September 1978, regarding the competency of JFK's autopsy, "Some people assume authority and upon others authority is thrust as happened to Dr. [James] Humes... A well-experienced hospital pathologist... he had not been exposed to many gunshot wounds and had not performed autopsies in deaths due to shooting previously: neither had the other autopsy pathologists present." Although Baden's panel concluded that the autopsist's report did not jibe with the photographic evidence of the autopsy, both the autopsy and the photos indicated that JFK had been shot twice, both times from the rear.

SOURCES: HSCA Report 80 • HSCA I, 311 • HT 101, 219, 375–6, 453 • BE 418, 453, 461, 531, 538, 549, 555, 663, 669 • MOORE 189, 191–3, 204, 215 • SUMMERS 9, 11, 38–9 • ME 160, 162, 182, 228–9

BAGANOV, IGOR (See VAGANOV, IGOR)

BAGERT, BERNARD. With Orleans Parish Criminal District Court Judges Matthew Braniff and Malcolm O'Hara, Bagert was one of three judges who presided as a panel over Clay Shaw's preliminary hearing on conspiracy to assassinate JFK and who decided that New Orleans District Attorney Jim Garrison had presented enough evidence for Shaw to be held over for trial.

SOURCES: OTT 156–8 • FLAMMONDE, many

BAGSHAW, THOMAS, Oswald witness; USMC acquaintance. Bagshaw was present at the incident in Atsugi, Japan, during which Oswald supposedly shot himself in the arm—an incident believed by some to have been staged to covertly separate Oswald from the marines who knew him. He told author Edward Jay Epstein that he believed Oswald had faked shooting himself and that the bullet had actually struck the ceiling.
SOURCES: SUMMERS 125

BAILEY, JOHN D., Ruby witness; Dallas City Hall official. Bailey's signed permanent pass to the Carousel Club was found among Ruby's belongings after Ruby's arrest. He was not questioned by WC.
SOURCES: WCE 1322 • COA 111

BAKER, MARRION L., a.w.; DPD officer. With TSBD superintendant Roy Truly, Baker saw Oswald in the second-floor lunchroom of the TSBD between 75 and 90 seconds after the assassination. Baker was a motorcyle patrolman in the motorcade and was assigned to flank the right rear of JFK's limo. However, he straggled behind the car before the shots were fired. Baker says that he approached the TSBD immediately after seeing pigeons fly off its roof. Unlike other earwitnesses to the assassination, Baker did not say that he thought the first report was a firecracker or a car backfiring. He said that he had just returned from a deer-hunting trip and immediately recognized the sound of a powerful rifle.

At the sound of the shots, Baker rode toward the north curb of Elm Street. With revolver drawn, he ran up the front steps of the TSBD. He was met at the entrance by TSBD manager Roy Truly, who identified himself. "Come with me," Baker said. Truly led Baker to the elevators, which were both on one of the upper floors. Not willing to wait, Baker ran up the stairs, Truly close behind him. On the second floor, Baker caught a movement out of the corner of his eye that stopped him from proceeding up the stairs. Through a glass door he could see an empty-handed man (Oswald), standing near a Coke machine in the building's lunchroom. Baker entered the room and said, "Come here." Oswald approached slowly. Truly entered the room and Baker asked him, "Do you know this man?" Truly replied that he did. "Does he work here?" Baker asked. "Yes, he works for me," Truly answered, at which time Baker and Truly left the lunchroom and continued up the stairs. Since both TSBD elevators were on the upper floors just after the assassination, the official scenario has Oswald using the stairs to get from the sixth to the second floor. In Baker's original written report to the FBI (dated November 23, 1963), he wrote that Oswald was "drinking a

Coke." The words "drinking a Coke" were scratched out, and the WC did not probe the matter. Moments after Oswald was seen by Baker, he was seen drinking a Coke by Mrs. Elizabeth Reid. Did Oswald have time to get down the stairs (eight flights, 72 steps), and get a Coke from a machine and start drinking it? Tests indicate yes—but barely. Reid and Baker reported that Oswald was not breathing hard. (See also Truly, Roy)

SOURCES: WR 23–4, 139, 141–5, 151, 235 • WCH III, 242; VII, 592 • HSCA Report 58 • HT 152, 175 • BE 350, 365 • BISHOP 136, 140–1, 224 • CF 14, 50–1 • PWW 29 • MOORE 51–3, 82 • SUMMERS 80 • BLAKEY 16 • HOS 52 • OGLESBY 15–6, 19, 53

BAKER, ROBERT B. "BARNEY," Ruby witness; strong-arm man for Jimmy Hoffa. Baker made a 17-minute collect call to Ruby from Chicago on November 7, 1963. Ruby called Baker in Chicago on November 8, 1963. According to WC Exhibit #1763, the name "Barney" was found in Ruby's notebook, followed by three of Baker's phone numbers.

SOURCES: HSCA Report 154–5, 177 • COA 93–4, 106–7, 119, 240–1, 253, 390 • SUMMERS 246, 440, 447–8 • BLAKEY 304–5 • EVICA 199, 311–2 • KANTOR 20, 22–3, 30–4, 37–8 • DAVIS 182–3, 190, 299 • NORTH 352

BAKER, ROBERT G. "BOBBY," LBJ aide for eight years, resigned October 7, 1963. Baker made $2 million in those eight years, and his influence peddling (including deals with the mob) had been exposed by the *Washington Post*. As a result of the scandal, it was rumored that JFK would dump LBJ as vice president for the 1964 election. Penn Jones Jr. reported in the *Midlothian* (Texas) *Mirror* on July 31, 1969:

> Bobby Baker was about the first person in Washington to know that Lyndon Johnson was to be dumped as the Vice-Presidential candidate in 1964. Baker knew that President Kennedy had offered the spot on the ticket to Senator George Smathers of Florida... Baker knew because his secretary, Miss [Nancy] Carole Tyler, roomed with one of George Smathers' secretaries. Miss Mary Jo Kopechne had been another of Smathers' secretaries. Now both Miss Tyler and Miss Kopechne have died strangely.

(See also Johnson, Lyndon B.; Kopechne, Mary Jo; Torbitt, William; Tyler, Nancy Carole)

SOURCES: HT 158, 282, 321 • COA 183, 219, 223–5, 282, 385, 400 • FMG III, 83 • EVICA 185, 222–4, 284, 295–7 • OGLESBY 6 • DAVIS 300–2, 347, 475, 483 • NORTH, many

BAKER, MRS. DONALD "VIRGIE" (née RACHLEY), a.w.; TSBD bookkeeper. Standing in front of TSBD at the time of the shooting, Baker then ran 50 yards westward to see what was happening over on the grassy knoll. She saw the first shot miss, striking on southmost lane of Elm Street just behind JFK's limo. Baker told WC: "I thought it was firecrackers because I saw a shot or something hit the pavement... you could see the sparks from it and I just thought it was a firecracker." She said she thought the firecrackers came from "down below or standing near the underpass or back up here by the [Stemmons Freeway] sign." Her statement, corroborated by a.w. Royce Skelton and Harry Holmes, indicates it was the first shot that missed. During her testimony, WC counsel Wesley Liebeler tried to talk Mrs. Baker out her belief that the shots had come from the front, explaining that "the shots actually came" from the TSBD. Could that jibe with what she had actually heard? Mrs. Baker replied, "Well, I guess it could have been the wind, but to me it didn't [sound that way]."

SOURCES: WCH VII, 507 • RTJ 111 • BISHOP 133 • CF 27 • PWW 211 • MOORE 198, 201, 204 • BE 20 • ME 72–4, 77

BAKER, T. L., a.w.; o.k.w.; DPD motorcycle patrolman. Baker rode in the Dallas motorcade. Two days later, he was involved in Oswald's aborted transfer from DPD headquarters to the county jail.

SOURCES: WR 200 • WCH IV, 248 • HT 152, 175 • RTJ 211

BALL, JOSEPH A., WC counsel; California attorney; 61 years old when appointed. Ball evaluated evidence leading to the WC's conclusion that Oswald was the murderer of JFK and Officer J. D. Tippit. (See also Epstein, Edward Jay)

SOURCES: HT 122, 135, 187, 329 • BE 10, 98, 121, 207, 222–3, 349 • COA 154 • OTT 18–9 • BELIN 14–5, 32, 59, 62, 72 • DOP, many • FMG III, 31–2 • PWW 18, 43, 53–6, 58–60, 120, 142 • SUMMERS 7–17, 73–4, 87–90 • BLAKEY 333 • OGLESBY 61 • KANTOR 4, 84 • DAVIS 412 • PD 52

BALLEN, SAMUEL B., Oswald witness; acquaintance of Oswald in Texas. Self-employed financial consultant and senior officer for several corporations, including High Plains Natural Gas Co. and Electrical Log Services, Inc.; studied geology and petroleum engineering as well as banking. He met Oswald in autumn 1962 through Oswald associate George DeMohrenschildt; interviewed Oswald for a job doing photo reproduction with Electrical Log, but said "he was too much of a hardheaded individual... and probably wouldn't fit in." Ballen said DeMohrenschildt told him "this is a fellow with no hatred." Ballen also said that DeMohrenschildt befriended "another stray dog" around the same time, this one from Hungary or Bulgaria, who disappeared after being around DeMohrenschildt for five or six weeks. Ballen told the *Washington Post* (December 1, 1963) that Oswald was "the kind of person I could like... He had a kind of Gandhi, far off look about him." (See also DeMohrenschildt, George; Vaganov, Igor)

SOURCES: WCH IX, 45 • PD 353

BANISTER, WILLIAM GUY, Oswald witness; former head of the Chicago FBI offfice; worked closely with the CIA and the ONI; closely associated with assassination suspects David Ferrie and New Orleans mob boss Carlos Marcello. Banister died within 10 days of the conclusion of the WC's hearings, of a heart attack. According to Jim Garrison, he was seen in 1963 in his New Orleans office having meetings with Ferrie and Oswald. Oswald used the address of Banister's office on his FPCC leaflets. According to HT, "Banister was clearly running Oswald as an *agent provocateur.*" According to author Peter Noyes, in *Legacy of Doubt*, Banister was "a bigwig in the ultraright Minutemen."

At the time of the assassination, according to Garrison, Banister was a deputy superintendant of police in New Orleans and "a man who had a lifetime reputation as a rigid exponent of law and order." Garrison described Banister as "a ruddy-faced man with blue eyes which [sic] stared right at you, he dressed immaculately and always wore a small rosebud in his lapel."

Garrison says Banister had an occasional drink but was not known to drink to excess. Other sources have called Banister an alcoholic. Whatever the case, he drank to excess on November 22, 1963. When Banister got the word that JFK had been assassinated in Dallas, he "made a noble effort to polish off all of the liquor in the Katzenjammer Bar in the 500 block of Camp Street."

With Banister on the binge was Jack Martin, an occasional private detective who frequented Banister's Camp Street office. After leaving the bar, the pair returned to Banister's office, where they got into a heated argument. The row ended with Banister pistol-whipping Martin so severely that Martin had to be hospitalized (New Orleans Police Department report # K-12634-63, November 22, 1963).

Soon thereafter, Martin began to tell his friends that he suspected that David Ferrie, another frequenter of Banister's office, had "driven to Dallas on the day of the assassination to serve as the getaway pilot for the men involved in the assassination."

The fact that the first batch of pro-Castro pamphlets that Oswald handed out in New Orleans had the 544 Camp Street address of Guy Banister Associates stamped on them was Garrison's first indication that Oswald might not have been a Communist after all, but rather an *agent provocateur* who might infiltrate and eventually expose New Orleans's Communist community—which was no doubt a populous tribe in the fertile imaginations of Cold Warriors. Oswald put the 544 Camp Street address only on the first batch of pamphlets. Thereafter, Oswald showed the address of the FPCC, New Orleans Chapter (of which Oswald was the only member), as a New Orleans post-office box number. The number on the pamphlets did not correspond to any real post-office box number. Oswald really had rented a post-offfice box, using the alias Hidell (just as he would later do in Dallas). Except when Oswald wrote the number down in his notebook, he transposed two of the numbers, inadvertently creating a nonexistent number. Might Oswald's dyslexia have been his fatal flaw?

When Jack Martin got out of the hospital, Garrison interviewed him to find out why Banister had beaten him. "I told him that I remembered the people I had seen around the office that summer," Martin is reported to have said. "And that's when he hit me." Garrison asked him who the people were. "There were a bunch of them," Martin replied. "There were all those Cubans...They all looked alike to me...There was David Ferrie...He practically lived there...[Oswald] was there, too. Sometimes he'd be meeting with Guy Banister with the door shut. Other times he'd be shooting the bull with David Ferrie...[Banister] was the one running the circus." Martin ended the meeting by telling Garrison that he should stop his investigation because he was going to "bring the goddamned federal government down on our backs" and get them both killed.

Banister died only nine months after JFK's assassination, reportedly of a heart attack. In 1967, Banister's widow told Garrison that, when cleaning out his office after his death in 1964, she had found boxes of leftover pamphlets, the same as the ones handed out by Oswald. She also told Garrison that by the time she got to her late husband's office, representatives of the federal government (FBI or SS, she couldn't be sure) had already been there and had removed all of the locked file cabinets.

Banister's secretary, Delphine Roberts, corroborated Martin's statements that Oswald and Banister had engaged in closed-door meetings in Banister's office and added that Banister had allowed Oswald to use a third floor office, just one flight up.

Banister's partner Hugh Ward and New Orleans Mayor Chep Morrison were killed in a plane crash within 10 days of Banister's death. According to Penn Jones Jr. in the *Midlothian* (Texas) *Mirror* (January 23, 1969),

Mayor Morrison's secretary had once attempted to rent an apartment in New Orleans for Guy Banister's "business use." The man she tried to rent the apartment from was Rev. Abraham Khrushevski, who at the time was the landlord of Nancy and Robert Lee Perrin. According to author Anthony Summers:

> Banister was an old-fashioned American hero who had refused to go gracefully. He had been a star agent for the FBI, a tough guy whose long career covered some of the Bureau's most famous cases, including the capture and killing of "Public Enemy Number One," murderer and bank robber John Dillinger. He was commended by FBI Director [J. Edgar] Hoover and rose to become Special Agent-in-charge in a key city, Chicago. In World War II—according to his family—he distinguished himself with Naval Intelligence [ONI], a connection he reportedly maintained all his life. Banister came to New Orleans in the Fifties, at the request of the mayor, to become Deputy Chief of Police. This was the high point of a flawed career. In 1957, at the age of fifty-eight, Banister was pushed into retirement after an incident in New Orleans's Old Absinthe House, when he allegedly threatened a waiter with a pistol.

It was at this time that he set up Guy Banister Associates on Camp Street. Along with being a member of the John Birch Society, the Minutemen, and Louisiana's Committee on Un-American Activities, Banister published a racist magazine called the *Louisiana Intelligence Digest* and helped to organize the anti-Castro organizations Friends of a Democratic Cuba and the Cuban Revolutionary Democratic Front. He served as a supplier of arms for the 1961 Bay of Pigs invasion. In 1963, he did investigative work for assassination suspect and New Orleans crime boss Carlos Marcello.

A New Orleans crime commissioner said that it was not alcohol that caused Banister's downfall, but rather a "serious brain disorder which led him increasingly into irrational, erratic conduct."

Banister's offices were in the same building as those of the Cuban Revolutionary Front, which counted among its members Carlos Bringuier, the man whose street scuffle with Oswald led to Oswald's arrest during the summer of 1963. Banister's offices were also right around the corner from the William Reily Coffee Company, where Oswald was employed that summer. (See also DeBrueys, Warren; Ferrie, David; Gatlin, Maurice; Johnson, Guy; Maheu, Robert; Martin, Jack; Morrison, DeLesseps; Morrow, Robert; Nagell, Richard; Novel, Gordon; Quiroga, Carlos; Roberts, Delphine; Rodriguez, Manuel; Ward, Hugh)

SOURCES: HSCA Report 143–6, 219 • HSCA X, 123 • HT 144, 154, 171, 181, 288, 309, 421 • COA 40, 42 • OTT, many • CF 99–100, 235–7, 494, 499 • FMG III, 46–7 • FLAMMONDE 23–4, 102, 115–9, 180–1 • SUMMERS 290–8, 384, 444, 489 • WEISBERG, *Oswald in New Orleans*, 51, 327, 337, 364, 380, 391, 410 • BLAKEY 46, 165–9 • HOS 92, 107–16, 119, 122, 138, 142, 164, 169, 242 • EVICA 58–9, 208, 315 • ME 90 • OGLESBY 64, 71 • DAVIS 145–7, 173, 175, 205, 231, 336, 407, 615 • NORTH, many)

BARBEE, EMMETT CHARLES, JR., Oswald witness; coworker at the William B. Reily Company; Oswald's immediate supervisor. Barbee quit within weeks of Oswald's leaving and went to work for NASA, as did three other Reily employees who worked with Oswald. (See also Branyon, John; Claude, Alfred; Marachini, Dante; Reily, William)

SOURCES: WCH XI, 473 • OTT 116 • HOS 150

BARBER, STEVE, musician. Using a plastic record of the HSCA's acoustic evidence that he got in a copy of *Gallery* magazine, Barber noticed crosstalk that seems to indicate that the recorded gunfire and words spoken over a minute after the assassination appear simultaneously. Some, including WC counsel David Belin, have said that this crosstalk discredits the evidence. But Barber's discovery does not account for the "sound fingerprints" of gunfire on the Dictabelt recording. More likely, Barber's discovery indicates the tape was tampered with (perhaps there was an error in dubbing), rather than that the evidence is erroneous. (See also Barger, James)

SOURCES: HT 252, 254–5, 259, 463 • BELIN 198–200 • SUMMERS 474–5 • ME 184–5 • OGLESBY 45

BARCLAY, MALCOLM JAMES "MIKE," a.w.; friend of Ruby's roommate George Senator. Standing on the corner of Main and Houston streets, Barclay heard "one or more" shots, but couldn't determine their source.

SOURCE: WCE 3015, 3024

BARGAS, TOMMY, Oswald witness; superintendent of the Leslie Welding Company in Fort Worth, Texas; knew Oswald when he worked for Louv-R-Pak Weather Co., which merged with Leslie Welding Co. in 1962. Bargas recruited Oswald as a sheet-metal worker through the Texas Employment Agency. Oswald interviewed for the job on July 17, 1962, got the job, and worked there until October 8, 1962, when he stopped coming to work.

SOURCE: WCH X, 160

BARGER, JAMES, physicist; HSCA acoustics expert; chief scientist at

Bolt, Beranek and Newman of Cambridge, Massachusetts. Barger converted the Dictabelt acoustic evidence into digitized waveforms and discovered six sounds that could have been shots. The HSCA eventually admitted to four of them. They occurred at intervals of 1.65, 7.56, and 8.31 seconds after the first.

SOURCES: HSCA Report 66, 69, 71–5, 485–6, 505–7 • OGLESBY 45–6 • ME 181–2 • HT 241, 244, 247–9, 253, 381 • BE 560 • COA 26–8 • SUMMERS 14–5, 475 • BLAKEY 93–102, 104–5

BARKER, BERNARD, possible a.w.; worked with assassination suspects David Ferrie, E. Howard Hunt, and Frank Sturgis, as well as General Charles Cabell and Richard M. Nixon, in the CIA planning of the Bay of Pigs operation. Barker was the leader of the Watergate burglars and was once associated with the Miami mob, headed by Santos Trafficante. Assassination witness Seymour Weitzman identified Barker as the man on the grassy knoll who was showing SS identification and ordering people out of the area. (See also Cabell, Charles; Hunt, E. Howard; Marchetti, Victor; Nixon, Richard M.; Sturgis, Frank; Weitzman, Seymour)

SOURCES: HT 292, 320 • EVICA 138, 255, 305, 309, 313–6, 320, 328 • DAVIS 401–2, 410 • PD 108, 273

BARNES, GENE, o.k.w.; NBC cameraman. Barnes arrived at the DPD basement at 9:30 A.M., November 24, 1963; was covering Oswald's transfer, with KTAL-TV (Shreveport, Louisiana) cameraman Steven L. Alexander. An FBI report filed in Los Angeles by agents Eugene P. Pittman and John C. Oakes said that Barnes had told them that a colleague of his, Bob Mulholland of NBC's Chicago bureau, had "talked in Dallas to one Fairy, a narcotics addict now out on bail on a sodomy charge in Dallas. Fairy said that Oswald had been under hypnosis from a man doing a mind-reading act at Ruby's 'Carousel.' Fairy was said to be a private detective and the owner of an airline who took young boys on flights 'just for kicks.'" (See also Crowe, William D., Jr.; Ferrie, David)

SOURCES: PWW 273 • FLAMMONDE 27

BARNES, TRACY, assassination suspect, Barnes was an ex-CIA agent and author Robert Morrow's CIA case officer who allegedly ordered Morrow to purchase four Mannlicher-Carcano rifles in 1963, rifles which were later used in the assassination. (See also Diggs, Marshall; Kohly, Mario; Morrow, Robert)

SOURCES: MORROW, many • RUSSELL many

BARNES, WILLIE E., t.k.w. (aftermath); DPD sergeant. Barnes was called to the site of the Tippit shooting and took photographs of Tippit's car

that showed the driver's window rolled up, thus contradicting t.k.w. Helen Markham's Oswald-damaging testimony that Oswald had spoken to Tippit before the shooting through that open window. Barnes initialed two shell cartridges that he received from Officer J. M. Poe at the scene of the Tippit killing. He was later unable, as was Poe, to identify the cartridges. (See also Markham, Helen)
SOURCES: WCH VII, 270 • RTJ 187, 198 • OTT 201

BARNETT, WELCOME EUGENE, a.w. (aftermath); DPD officer. Barnett was one of the first policemen to report a shooter in the TSBD, having heard this info from a construction worker, presumably a.w. Howard Brennan. (See also Brennan, Howard)
SOURCES: WR 145, 235 • WCH VII, 539 • RTJ 88, 108 • BISHOP 75 • PWW 37, 168–9

BARNUM, GEORGE A., Bethesda witness; member of the U.S. Coast Guard. With six others, Barnum attended JFK's body from the time it arrived in Washington, D.C., until it was buried. He served as a security guard at Bethesda during the autopsy.
SOURCES: BE 398 • *Dallas Morning News,* November 26, 1963, p. 15

BARR, CANDY (See SAHAKIAN, JUANITA SLUSHER DALE PHILLIPS)

BARRIGAN, JAMES C., Ruby witness; Dallas nightclub owner; competitor of Ruby. According to the WC, Barrigan said that Ruby served drinks at the Carousel illegally after midnight, even with policemen present.
SOURCES: WCE 1756 • RTJ 236 • COA 113

BARSON, PHILLIP, WC staff member; Internal Revenue Service agent; with Edward A. Conroy and John J. O'Brien, analyzed Oswald's finances in Appendix XIV of the WR.

BASHOUR, FOUAD, Parkland witness; associate professor of medicine in cardiology. Bashour was present when JFK was treated. When shown the purported JFK autopsy photos in 1979, he shook his head. He had seen a big hole in the back of JFK's head, a hole that does not appear in the photos. "Why do they cover it up?" he asked. "This is not the way it was!"
SOURCES: WR 66–7 • WCH VI, 61 • HT 45 • BISHOP 156 • SUMMERS 481

BATCHELOR, CHARLES, Ruby witness; Dallas assistant chief of police. Batchelor testified to the WC concerning security—or lack thereof—at the time of the Oswald killing. He was in charge of security for Oswald's transfer. According to HT, it has been suggested that it was Batchelor who allowed Ruby into police headquarters before Ruby killed

Oswald, taking him down in an elevator. After losing Kennedy and Oswald, Batchelor was "punished" by promotion to police chief after Jesse Curry retired. Batchelor told the WC, "Ruby's operation has not been a troublesome one for the [DPD]." According to DPD chief Jesse Curry's WC testimony, Batchelor was among those who accompanied the SS along the motorcade route several days before the assassination to determine the best locations to place security officers. (See also Fischer, N.T.; Niell, James)
SOURCES: WR 52, 54, 191–2, 194, 199–200, 214, 423 • WCH XII, 1 • HT 155, 157, 188, 236–7, 393 • COA 330 • RTJ 213 • GERTZ 81, 84 • BISHOP 40, 59, 89, 196, 280, 450, 481 • FMG I, 45, 152 • BLAKEY 93, 316 • KANTOR 60, 63–4, 69, 73, 143, 151

BATES, JOHN, JR., ballistics expert; member of the HSCA's ballistics panel; senior firearms examiner for the New York State Police Academy. The panel determined that JFK had been shot twice, both times from above and to the rear.
SOURCE: ME 229

BATES, PAULINE VIRGINIA, Oswald witness; public stenographer in Fort Worth, Texas. Bates met Oswald on June 18, 1962, when he hired her to transcribe some notes he "smuggled out of Russia." After eight hours together over three days, Oswald ran out of money to pay her. During that time she typed the first ten pages of an intended article titled "Inside Russia." She was called to testify before the WC because of reports that Oswald had told her that "he had become a 'secret agent' of the U.S. government and that he was going back to Russia 'for Washington.'" She testified that none of this was true, but admitted that she had a thought when she first learned Oswald had been in the USSR that "maybe he was going under the auspices of the State Department—as a student or something."
SOURCES: WR 303 • WCH VIII, 330

BAUMAN, ROGER, mobster business associate of Eugene Hale Brading, who, according to Peter Noyes in *Legacy of Doubt*, met with Texas oil billionaire Lamar Hunt on November 21, 1963.
SOURCES: COA 47, 260 • EVICA 166

BAXTER, CHARLES R., physician; Parkland witness. Baxter told the WC that it was "unlikely" that JFK's throat wound was one of exit, and that JFK had a "large, gaping wound at the back of the skull." Baxter assisted Dr. Malcolm Perry in performing JFK's tracheotomy, thus obliterating the wound in JFK's throat. (See also McClelland, Robert; Patman, Ralph)
SOURCES: WR 66–7, 70 • WCH VI, 39 • WCE 392 • RTJ 52, 54, 59 • HT 45, 459 • BE 40, 67, 272, 274–6, 322, 330 • BISHOP 219, 271

BEARD, JAMES, Ruby witness. According to an August 18, 1978, *Dallas Morning News* article written by Earl Golz, Beard claimed that Ruby had been heavily involved in shipping weapons to Cuba as early as 1957. Ruby stored guns and ammunition in a house on the southern coast of Texas. The material was then ferried to Cuba aboard a military-surplus boat. Beard said that he "personally saw many boxes of new guns, including automatic rifles and handguns...each time the boat left with guns and ammunition, Jack Ruby was on it." According to Beard, the munitions were destined for Castro's followers for their still-active war against the forces of Batista, the theory being that when Castro won the Mafia would be in his good graces.
  SOURCE: SUMMERS 436

BEATY, BUFORD LEE, o.k.w.; member DPD (narcotics bureau). Beaty was stationed at the Trade Mart when JFK was shot. He says he didn't see Ruby in the DPD station at all during that weekend; he went to the basement for the Oswald transfer out of "curiosity" and helped keep an aisle clear to let Oswald through.
  SOURCES: WCH XII, 158

BEAUBOEUF, ALVIN, friend of David Ferrie. On the afternoon of November 22, 1963, Ferrie, Beauboeuf, and Melvin Coffee drove in a heavy rainstorm from New Orleans—where Ferrie's employer, Carlos Marcello, had just been acquitted in his deportation case—to Texas. The men said they were going goose-hunting and ice-skating. They brought no guns and did no skating. When talking with the FBI on November 25, 1963, Beauboeuf spoke openly about Ferrie until asked about the ride in the rain, when he clammed up and asked for his lawyer. According to Jim Garrison, Ferrie later admitted that his job was to pick up the Dallas assassins and provide them with their getaway, but the assassins never showed up at the meeting place. (See also Ferrie, David; Martens, Layton)
  SOURCES: HSCA Report 144 · COA 40–1 · OTT 162, 320–1 · BLAKEY 50 · FLAMMONDE, many · DAVIS 204

BEAVERS, WILLIAM ROBERT, Ruby witness; Dallas psychiatrist. On May 27, 1964, Beavers wrote to Judge Joseph Brown, who was presiding over Jack Ruby's murder trial, strongly recommending a "formal sanity hearing for him." Ruby insisted that Dallas assistant district attorney Bill Alexander be in the room—rather than Joe Tonahill, his own lawyer—during his polygraph examination while he made statements that indicated his murder of Oswald was done with malice. Beavers used this point to impress upon the WC that Ruby lacked an "awareness and appreciation of

reality."
  SOURCES: WCH XIV, 570 • GERTZ 133, 188 • FMG I, 176 • BLAKEY 337 • KANTOR
  176, 179, 181–4

BECKER, EDWARD, businessman/private investigator. Becker had met with assassination suspect Carlos Marcello in 1962. When Robert F. Kennedy came up in conversation, Becker quoted Marcello, in his 1978 HSCA testimony, as saying, *"Take the stone out of my shoe!* Don't worry about that little Bobby son of a bitch. He's going to be taken care of!" Becker's testimony went on to say, "[Marcello] clearly stated that he was going to arrange to have President Kennedy murdered in some way." Marcello reportedly said, "Cut off the dog's tail and the dog keeps biting. Cut off the head and the dog dies," meaning that a hit on JFK was preferable to one on RFK.

Marcello's plan included the using of a "nut" to deflect blame from the mob. Becker says he told the FBI about the plot a year before the assassination. In 1978, Becker repeated the story to the HSCA, who found him credible. (See also Marcello, Carlos)
  SOURCES: COA 56–8, 202, 217–8, 225, 231 • SUMMERS 258–61 • BLAKEY 244–6 •
  DAVIS, many • NORTH 189, 200–1, 203, 214, 218, 220, 607

BEERS, IRA J. "JACK," JR., a.w. (aftermath); o.k.w.; *Dallas Morning News* photographer who took one of the famous photographs of Ruby shooting Oswald. With William Allen of the *Dallas Times Herald* and Joe Smith of the *Fort Worth Star,* Beers was one of three photographers who photographed the three "tramps" moments after the assassination as they were led by Dallas police from a railcar near Dealey Plaza, presumably to be questioned.
  SOURCES: OTT 207 • WCH XIII, 102 • GERTZ 512 • PWW 273

BEHN, GERALD A. "JERRY," SS agent. Behn spoke with Forrest Sorrels, head of the Dallas SS, ten hours after the assassination. "It's a plot," Behn said. "Of course," Sorrels replied.
  SOURCES: WR 50, 71 • WCD 7 • HSCA Report 228 • ME 233 • HT 148 • BISHOP 30–2,
  59, 154, 168, 179, 189, 294, 320, 376 • DOP, many • BE 250, 489, 614, 641–2, 650,
  679, 685, 687 • BLAKEY 7, 22 • NORTH 103

BELIN, DAVID W., WC counsel; Des Moines, Iowa, attorney; 35 years old when appointed. Belin assisted Joseph A. Ball in establishing Oswald's guilt. Since then he has been a staunch WC defender. Belin is author of *Final Disclosure* and *November 22, 1963: You Are the Jury.* Penn Jones Jr. writes of Belin: "Along with Gerald Ford, Assistant Counsel to the Warren Commission David W. Belin emerges as one of the most responsible for the methods and conclusions of the Warren whitewash...."

SOURCES: HSCA Report 500 • EVICA 197 • ME 129, 131–2, 183–4 • BE 98, 222, 349, 366 • OTT 19–20 • PWW 18, 32–3, 51–3, 55–6, 120, 142 • SUMMERS 97 • FMG I, 33; III, 32–5, 93 • BLAKEY 336 • KANTOR 3, 68, 84, 154, 177–8, 204–5, 209 • NORTH 495 • PD 324

BELKNAP, JERRY BOYD, a.w. (prelude); *Dallas Morning News* employee. Fifteen minutes before the motorcade passed through Dealey Plaza, a very strange thing happened in front of the TSBD. Belknap, dressed in army fatigues, had an apparent epileptic seizure that managed to draw everybody's attention. Because of the timing, the seizure resembles a diversion, to keep witnesses from noticing other things that might have been going on in the vicinity. Belknap later claimed to have had a history of seizures since childhood. He was picked up in Dealey Plaza by an ambulance, taken to Parkland Hospital's emergency area and was subsequently forgotten because of the mass hysteria and confusion caused by the arrival of JFK and Governor Connally. Without saying anything to anyone, Belknap left Parkland and took a bus back to downtown Dallas. (See also Harkness, D.V.; Rike, Aubrey)
SOURCE: CF 42–3

BELL, AUDREY, Parkland witness; supervising operating-room nurse when Governor Connally was treated. Bell removed "four or five" bullet fragments from Connally's wrist, placed them in an envelope and gave them to government agents. She said that "the smallest was the size of the striking end of a match and the largest at least twice that big. I have seen the picture of the 'magic bullet,' and I can't see how it could be the bullet from which the fragments I saw came." Bell corroborates the multitude of evidence that there was a large gaping wound in the back of JFK's skull when he was brought into Parkland.
SOURCES: HT 73, 453, 456 • BE 558–9 • BISHOP 188 • SUMMERS 546 • OGLESBY 30–2

BELL, JACK, a.w.; AP correspondent; rode in the press-pool car.
SOURCES: DOP 134, 168–9, 190–1, 220–1

BELLAH, S.C., a.w., DPD sergeant. Eyewitnesses have said that JFK's limo slowed down on Elm Street during the shooting sequence because one of the motorcycle patrolman in front of the car swerved from its flank directly in front of it, forcing the driver to put on his brakes. The three motorcycle patrolmen in front of the limo were Bellah (# 190), J. B. Garick (132) and G. C. McBride (133).
SOURCES: WCH XX, 489 • FMG III, 54

BELLI, MELVIN M., Ruby witness; famous California trial attorney; member of Ruby's defense team; author of *Dallas Justice: The Real Story of*

Jack Ruby and His Trial (David McKay Co., 1964); friend of California mobster Mickey Cohen. Instead of concentrating on showing that Ruby had murdered Oswald without malice (premeditation), Belli put all of his eggs in one basket, attempting to prove that Ruby was temporarily insane because he suffered from "psychomotor epilepsy" due to head injuries he had received throughout his life. The jury didn't buy it. Belli was fired by the Ruby family after Jack was sentenced to death.

SOURCES: COA 154 • GERTZ, many • CF 414 • FMG I, 37, 89, 180–1 • BLAKEY 322, 324–33 • FLAMMONDE 290 • EVICA 194 • KANTOR 115–20, 122–5, 152, 169, 188, 215, 217 • NORTH 479, 482, 490, 501

BELLOCCHIO, FRANK, Ruby witness; jewelry designer. Bellocchio saw Ruby in Sol's Turf Lounge on the evening of November 22, 1963. He testified for the defense at Ruby's murder trial that, on that occasion, Ruby was incoherent.

SOURCES: WR 323–4 • WCH XIV, 466 • GERTZ 61, 111

BELMONT, ALAN H., FBI agent; assistant to the director. One of the methods used to link Oswald with the Mannlicher-Carcano rifle that was purportedly used to kill JFK, was a palm print found inside the rifle by DPD Lieutenant J. C. Day several days after the assassination—and *not* found by FBI experts immediately following the assassination. On August 28, 1964, Belmont received a memo that expressed FBI doubts as to the authenticity of the palm print. The memo read: "[WC General Counsel J. Lee] Rankin advised because of the circumstances that now exist there was a serious question in the minds of the Commission as to whether or not the palm print impression that has been obtained from the Dallas Police Department is a legitimate latent palm impression removed from the rifle barrel or whether it was obtained from some other source..."

SOURCES: WR 304, 412, 418, 438 • WCH V, 1 • HSCA Report 185 • HT 170 • BE 302, 362, 484, 503 • BISHOP 361, 402, 476, 492, 520 • FLAMMONDE 159 • BLAKEY 23, 27, 210, 215, 238 • DAVIS 276–7 • NORTH, many

BENAVIDES, DOMINGO, t.k.w.; automobile repairman. According to the WR:

> [Benavides] heard the shots and stopped his pickup truck on the opposite side of the street about 25 feet in front of Tippit's car. He observed the gunman start back toward Patton Avenue, removing the empty cartridge cases as he went. Benavides rushed to Tippit's side. The patrolman, apparently dead, was lying on his revolver, which was out of its holster. Benavides promptly reported the shooting to police headquarters over the radio in Tippit's car. The message was received shortly after 1:16 P.M.

***

Although Benavides had a clear view of the fleeing assailant, he wasn't asked by the DPD to view a lineup because, according to WC counsel Belin, "he didn't think he was very good at identifying people." Benavides said that, at the time of the shooting, there was a man between 25 and 30 years old sitting in a red 1961 Ford Falcon, parked about six cars from Tippit's car. This man has never been located. Benavides was anonymously threatened after the Tippit killing. His brother Edward was murdered by an unknown assailant in 1964. (See also Mather, Carl; Vaganov, Igor; White, T. F.)

SOURCES: WR 25, 156, 160 • WCH VI, 444 • HT 278 • RTJ 172–3, 177–8, 186, 190, 198, 285 • BELIN 17–9, 21, 29, 31 • BISHOP 199–200 • OTT 194, 201 • SUMMERS 88–9, 92 • FLAMMONDE 191–2 • HOS 41, 66 • OGLESBY 61

BENAVIDES, EDWARD, brother of Domingo (see above); murdered in February 1964; shot in head by unknown assailant.

SOURCE: HT 143

BENNETT, GLENN, a.w.; SS agent. Bennett rode in the car directly behind the presidential limo. He said, "I looked at the back of the President. I heard another firecracker noise and saw the shot hit the President about four inches down from the right shoulder." This location for JFK's back wound agrees with the observations of the doctors at Parkland and places the entry wound too low for it to have been caused by the "magic bullet."

SOURCES: WR 60, 108 • HT 90 • BE 77, 284, 510 • BISHOP 102, 139, 151 • DOP 134, 229 • CF 14 • ME 60, 71, 101, 218, 220, 248, 253

BENNETT, KAREN (See CARLIN, KAREN)

BENTLEY, PAUL, Texas Theatre witness; DPD member. Officially, it was Officer Bentley who, while going through Oswald's wallet following his arrest in the Texas Theatre, discovered the "Hidell" identification that linked Oswald with the purported murder weapons of JFK and Tippit. However, Bentley did not report the Hidell I.D. in his written report of the arrest, nor did Sergeant Gerald Hill, who was also in the squad car at the time the wallet was searched. Hill and Bentley claim that they radioed in the Hidell information at the time the I.D. was discovered, but the transcript of the Dallas police tapes shows no record of such a call. (See also Hill, Gerald Lynn)

SOURCES: WR 165 • HT 184 • BISHOP 216 • DOP 513

BENTON, JOSEPH NELSON, Ruby witness; Parkland witness; CBS-TV reporter. Benton was at radio station KRLD in Dallas when JFK was

shot. He spent the next two hours at Parkland, where he did not see Ruby. He saw Ruby that night in the DPD station for Oswald's midnight "press conference."
SOURCE: WCH XV, 456

BERTRAM, LANE, SS agent. Bertram filed a report on December 2, 1963, stating that Ruby had been seen by five witnesses on the 400 block of Milam Street in Houston for "several hours" on November 21, 1963, while JFK was in town. Ruby was seen one block from JFK's "entrance route to and from the Rice Hotel where he [JFK] stayed."
SOURCES: WCE 2399 • COA 260–2

BERTRAND, CLAY (See SHAW, CLAY)

BERTRAND, CLEM (See SHAW, CLAY)

BETHELL, TOM, one of several traitors on Jim Garrison's staff during the trial of Clay Shaw. According to Penn Jones Jr. in the March 13, 1969, edition of the *Midlothian* (Tex.) *Mirror,* "Bethell, an Englishman with a rather strange background, had a meeting with one of Clay Shaw's defense attorneys. After this meeting Bethell made the entire trial plan, a complete list of State's witnesses and their expected testimony and other materials available to the Shaw defense team... Bethell has admitted his guilt and signed a confession of his crimes." (See also Garrison, Jim)
SOURCES: FMG III, 42, 99 • FLAMMONDE 139, 198

BETZNER, HUGH WILLIAM, JR., a.w. Betzner stood near the corner of Houston and Elm, then ran west, following JFK's limo. Twenty-two years old. He told the Dallas sheriff's department that there were "at least" four shots and that, during the shooting sequence, the limousine came to a stop. Betzner took three photos of JFK's limo as it passed his position, but these photographs were not used as evidence by the WC.
SOURCES: WCE 2003 • CF 23–4, 73 • PWW 42–5, 47, 57–8, 174–5

BEWLEY, T. F., t.k.w. Bewley was driving to pick up his wife when he saw the body of Officer Tippit in the street. He looked at his watch as he got out to help; it read 1:10 P.M. This would further indicate that either Oswald did not shoot Tippit, or that he was given a ride from his rooming house to the scene of the Tippit killing. The official version of the facts, which has Oswald walking to the site from his home, depends on the fact that the shooting took place at 1:15 or later, which barely allows Oswald enough time to arrive on foot.
SOURCES: SUMMERS 92 • RTJ 171–73, 186, 195 • OTT 196

BICKERS, BENNY H., Ruby witness; owner of Dallas nightclub one

block from Ruby's Carousel Club. Bickers told FBI that Ruby visited the DPD "almost every day." He said that Ruby received favors from policemen (including light and suspended sentences following arrests) and that Ruby often beat and refused to pay his strippers.
SOURCES: RTJ 236 • COA 101, 115, 202 • FLAMMONDE 172

BIEBERDORF, FRED A., Ruby witness; Oswald witness; physician, first-aid attendant, Dallas Health Department. Bieberdorf examined Ruby at approximately 2:00 P.M. on Sunday, November 24, 1963, a few hours after Ruby shot Oswald. He also attended to Oswald after he was shot.
SOURCES: WCH XIII, 83 • GERTZ 51, 513–4

BIGGIO, WILLIAM S., member DPD (Special Service Bureau, Criminal Intelligence section). A woman who was a friend of his wife's called Biggio at work and said that "a friend of hers had been into a restaurant in the downtown area and a mechanic had come in and made mention of the fact that Oswald drove Ruby's car for approximately a two-week period that he knew of, and that Oswald had brought the car there for repairs to his garage." On callback, she found out that the garage was on Lover's Lane. The friend of a friend was Bill Chesher, who died several days later of a heart attack before Biggio had a chance to interview him. Since the story was thirdhand, Biggio disregarded it, as did the WC. (See also Chesher, Bill)
SOURCE: WCH XIV, 48

BILLETT, MYRON, organized-crime-conspiracy witness. According to John Edgington and John Sergeant in their article "The Assassination of Martin Luther King, Jr." (*Covert Action Information Bulletin*, Summer 1990):

> In early 1968, Myron Billett was the trusted chauffeur of Mafia chief Sam Giancana. Giancana asked Billett to drive him, and fellow mobster Carlos Gambino, to a meeting at a motel in upstate New York. Other major Mafia figures from New York were there as well as three men who were introduced as representatives from the CIA and FBI. There were a number of subjects on the agenda, including Castro's Cuba... According to Billett, one of the government agents offered the mobsters a million dollars for the assassination of Martin Luther King Jr. Billett stated that Sam Giancana replied, "Hell no, not after you screwed up the Kennedy deal like that." As far as Billett knows, no one took up the offer.

Billett relayed the information in June 1989, a week before he died of emphysema.

BILLINGS, RICHARD, author of the HSCA report; coauthor, with G. Robert Blakey, of *The Plot to Kill the President* (New York Times Books, 1981). Billings believes that the Mafia was responsible for JFK's death.
SOURCES: HT 221, 245–6, 387–8 • BE 382 • COA 62–3, 225 • OTT 114, 163–4, 300–1 • BELIN 195–6 • FLAMMONDE 6, 56, 114–5 • BLAKEY 82, 90 • ME 181

BINTLIFF, RUSSELL, CIC agent. Bintliff told the *Washington Star* in 1976 that Pepsico had set up a bottling plant in Laos in the early 1960s that did not make Pepsi, but rather converted opium into heroin. If true, this is pertinent because Richard M. Nixon was counsel for Pepsico at the time and, theoretically, one of the immediate consequences of the JFK killing was the escalation of American involvement in Vietnam, in theory providing the alleged Pepsico plant with fresh customers.
SOURCE: COA 274, 303

BIRD, SAMUEL R., Bethesda witness; U.S. Army first lieutenant. With six others, Bird attended JFK's body from the time it arrived in Washington, D.C., until it was buried. He served as a security guard at Bethesda during the autopsy.
SOURCES: BE 398 • *Dallas Morning News*, November 26, 1963,˙ p. 15

BISHOP, JIM, author of *The Day Kennedy Was Shot* (Funk & Wagnalls, 1968).
SOURCES: HT 21 • BE 12, 476 • GERTZ 300 • FMG III, 98 • ME 109–10

BISHOP, MAURICE. "War name" for U.S. agent seen with Oswald by Antonio Veciana soon before the assassination in Dallas. (See also Phillips, David Atlee; Mertz, Michael Victor)
SOURCES: HT 192–4, 286–8, 303 • BLAKEY 175 • DAVIS 439 • EVICA, many

BISHOP, WILLIAM C. (aka Garcia, Oscar del Valle), possible Parkland witness; U.S. Army colonel and confessed political assassin; CIA contract agent. Bishop was a military intelligence aide under Major General Charles Willoughby during the Korean War. He was an associate of assassination suspect Rolando Masferrer in anti-Castro activities. In 1990, Bishop told assassination researchers Dick Russell and J. Gary Shaw that among his CIA assignments was the assassination of Dominican Republic dictator Rafael Trujillo in 1961. "I hit Trujillo," he said. Bishop also said that he had been to Mexico City two or three times in 1963, and once to New Orleans in August or September 1963. The New Orleans trip, he said, was to function as a liaison between the mob and Alpha 66, an anti-Castro group linked to the Kennedy assassination by ex-CIA agent and author

Robert D. Morrow. Bishop said, "[Jimmy] Hoffa gave Masferrer $50,000. Expense money. To partially set up the assassination team... [On the morning of November 21, 1963] I was flown to Dallas by military aircraft... I was to make sure the press had proper credentials at the Trade Mart when Kennedy came to speak the next afternoon. I was in position and waiting for his arrival, when I heard... that shots had been fired in Dealey Plaza. I commandeered a police car and ordered the driver to take me directly to Parkland... There the [SS] instructed me to secure the area outside the Trauma Room and make myself available to the First Lady or medical staff." (See also Masferrer, Rolando; Rodriguez, Manual Orcarbero; Trafficante, Santos; Willoughby, Charles)

SOURCE: RUSSELL, many

BISSELL, RICHARD M., JR., CIA agent; "Father of the U-2 Program." With Sheffield Edwards, Bissell was the top planner of the CIA/Mafia assassination plots against Castro. Both Bissell and Edwards have testified that they were ordered to develop these plans by CIA Director Allen Dulles and Deputy CIA Director General Charles Cabell, the brother of the Dallas mayor. According to the *U.S.-Senate Intelligence Report on Foreign Assassinations*, Bissell, with Edwards, initiated the recruitment of underworld figures for the Castro hit in August 1960. Along with Dulles and Cabell, Bissell was fired by JFK following the Bay of Pigs. (See also Edwards, Sheffield)

SOURCES: HSCA Report 107 • HT 311, 410, 427, 434, 439 • OTT 291–2, 304, 328 • BELIN 102, 104, 107, 109, 113, 123 • DUFFY 74 • SUMMERS 226, 238 • BLAKEY 53–5, 159 • EVICA, many • OGLESBY 7 • DAVIS 97–8, 282, 406–7 • NORTH 133–4 • PD 95, 98, 332

BLAHUT, REGIS, HSCA's liaison with the CIA; once worked for James McCord, the man suspected of entrapping E. Howard Hunt in the Watergate scandal. During the HSCA hearings, Blahut broke into the committee's safe and stole the JFK autopsy photos.

SOURCES: HT 107, 124, 385, 395 • SUMMERS 12

BLALOCK, VANCE DOUGLAS, Oswald witness. The 16-year-old Blalock met Oswald in Carlos Bringuier's store in New Orleans in August 1963, the only time Blalock ever went into the store. Blalock says that Oswald talked about blowing up bridges and derailing trains; says Oswald offered to give him and his pal, Philip Geraci, a copy of the USMC manual. (See also Geraci, Philip)

SOURCE: WCH X, 81

BLAKEY, G. ROBERT, chief counsel to and director of the HSCA, replacing Richard A. Sprague; coauthor, with Richard Billings, of *The Plot to Kill the President* (New York Times Books, 1981). Blakey believes that the Mafia killed JFK. He told journalist Jack Anderson in 1988: "We knew... that... Oswald was in fact involved with the mob, in the sense that his uncle [his mother's brother-in-law] was 'Dutz' Murret, who is a gambler and was connected, if only loosely, with the Carlos Marcello family of the mob." (See also Sprague, Richard A.)

SOURCES: HSCA Report 483–4, 491, 495 • BE 527, 549, 561, 563–4, 592 • OTT 299–308 • BELIN 187, 189–92, 195–97, 202–3, 215, 222 • CF 524–30 • SUMMERS, many • ME 136, 147–8, 152–6, 165, 181–3, 185–6, 226, 237 • KANTOR 214 • DAVIS, many • PD 34–6

BLANCH, ANTONIO VECIANA (See VECIANA, ANTONIO)

BLEDSOE, MARY E., Oswald witness. Bledsoe told the WC that she saw Oswald board a bus near Dealey Plaza ten minutes after the assassination. When the bus became stuck in traffic four minutes later, she said, Oswald left the bus at Lamar and Elm Streets, four blocks from the TSBD. Bledsoe had rented a room to Oswald for a week in October 1963, so she knew what he looked like. She said that Oswald, while on the bus, "looked like a maniac... and his face was so distorted." It's likely that Bledsoe was describing the Oswald she saw on TV later in the day—after his face was bruised by police battering—rather than the man she saw on the bus.

Bledsoe died on March 27, 1969, at age 72. The *Midlothian* (Tex.) *Mirror* (April 10, 1969) reported, "...we have learned that her son was acquainted with [assassination suspect] David Ferrie." Like Oswald, Bledsoe's son was trained by Ferrie when Ferrie was a captain in the Civil Air Patrol. (See also Ferrie, David)

SOURCES: WR 24, 34, 119, 148, 150, 152, 235 • WCH VI, 400 • RTJ 162–5, 174 • BELIN 57, 72 • BISHOP 163 • FMG III, 48, 70 • BLAKEY 360

BLOOMFIELD, LOUIS MORTIMER, Montreal resident; with assassination suspect Clay Shaw, a board member of Permindex, the shady Swiss corporation suspected of involvement in assassination attempts upon Charles de Gaulle. According to a 1967 article in the Canadian newspaper *Le Devoir*, Bloomfield was not only a major stockholder in Permindex, but in its sister corporation CMC as well. The paper reported that Bloomfield had been involved in "espionage" missions for the U.S. government. As for CMC and Permindex, *Le Devoir* wrote:

...[CMC] was the creature of the CIA... set up as a cover for the transfer of CIA... funds in Italy for illegal political-espionage activities. It still remains to clear up the presence on the administrative

Board of the [CMC] of Clay Shaw and ex-Major [of the OSS] Bloomfield...[CMC is] the point of contact for a number of persons who, in certain respects, have somewhat equivocal ties whose common denominator is anti-communism...

According to Jay Pound, in his article "Who Told the TRUTH About JFK?" in *Critique* (Spring/Summer 1986), the real purposes of CMC and Permindex were fourfold:

(1) To fund the direct assassinations of European, Mid-East, and world leaders considered to be threats to the Western World and to petroleum interests of the backers.

(2) To furnish couriers, agents and management in transporting, depositing and re-chanelling funds through Swiss banks for Las Vegas, Miami, Havana, and the international gambling syndicate.

(3) To coordinate the espionage activities of the Solidarists and Division 5 of the FBI with groups in sympathy with their objectives.

(4) To receive and channel funds and arms from the financiers to the action groups (assassination teams).

All parenthetical interjections are Pound's, who continues:

The Swiss corporation Permindex was used to head five front organizations that were responsible for furnishing personnel and supervisors to carry out the assigned duties. These five groups and their supervisors were:

(1) The Czarist, Russian, Eastern European, and Middle East exile organization known as Solidarists; headed by Ferenc Nagy, ex-Hungarian premier and John [Jean] DeMenil, Russian exile from Houston, Texas—a close friend and supporter of Lyndon Johnson for 30 years.

(2) A section of the American Council of Christian Churches, headed by H. L. Hunt of Dallas, Texas, working with [Rev.] Carl McIntire.

(3) A Cuban exile group called the Free Cuba Committee, headed by Carlos Prio Socarras, ex-Cuban President; he worked closely with Jack Ruby and Frank (Fiorino) Sturgis of Watergate fame.

(4) An organization of the United States, Caribbean, and Havana, Cuba gamblers called The Syndicate, headed by Clifford Jones, ex-lieutenant Governor of Nevada and National Committeeman, and Bobby Baker of Washington, D.C., also a close friend of Lyndon

Johnson. This group worked closely with the Mafia family headed by Joseph (Joe Bananas) Bonanno.

(5) The Security Division of the National Aeronautics and Space Administration (NASA) headed by: Wernher von Braun, head of the German Nazi rocketry program from 1932 through 1945, when he was recruited by the USA in Operation Paper Clip. Headquarters for this group were: the Defense Industrial Security Command located at Muscle Shoals Redstone Arsenal in Alabama, and also housed on East Broad Street in Columbus, Ohio.

Both Permindex and CMC lost their charters (in Switzerland and Italy, respectively) after Charles de Gaulle learned they had been involved in plots to assassinate him in 1961 and 1962. According to *Le Devoir* (March 16, 1967):

> ... the [CMC] and Permindex got into difficulties with the Italian and Swiss governments. They refused to testify to the origins of considerable amounts of money, the sources of which are, to say the least, uncertain, and they never seemed to engage in actual commercial transactions. These companies were expelled from Switzerland and Italy in 1962 and then set up headquarters in Johannesburg.

(See also D'Amelio, Carlo; DiSpadaforo, Gutierrez; Nagy, Ferenc; Torbitt, William; von Braun, Wernher; Zigiotti, Giuseppi)
SOURCES: OTT 88–9, 118 • FLAMMONDE 31, 218–9, 221

BOERDER, FRANK, Ruby witness; interior decorator. Boerder was present in Ruby's Carousel Club on November 18, 1963, four days before the assassination, for a meeting between Ruby and Bertha Cheek, during which the possibility of Cheek's investing in the nightclub was discussed. This meeting was investigated because Cheek is the sister of Oswald's housekeeper Earlene Roberts and might have represented a link between Oswald and Ruby. (See also Cheek, Bertha)
SOURCE: WR 339

BOGARD, ALBERT GUY, possible Oswald witness; suspicious death; Dallas automobile salesman at Downtown Lincoln-Mercury. Bogard said that on November 9, between 1:30 and 2:00 P.M., a man claiming to be "Lee Oswald" came in and test-drove a Mercury Comet recklessly on Stemmons Freeway. After the test drive, "Oswald" said he would have to come back in two or three weeks to put a down payment on the car as "he had some money coming in." Many feel this "Oswald" was a fake, since the real Oswald did not know how to drive a car. After testifying for the WC, Bogard was beaten so badly by a group of men that he had to be hospitalized for a long time. Bogard was found dead at the age of 41 in his car in a Hallsville, Louisiana, cemetery on February 14, 1966. A hose had been connected to his exhaust pipe and run into the car, which had all of its windows rolled up. Officials called Bogard's death a suicide.

At the time of the assassination, Downtown Lincoln-Mercury also employed the suspicious Jack Lawrence. (See also Lawrence, Jack; Pizzo, Frank; Wilson, Eugene)

SOURCES: WR 297 • WCH X, 352 • RTJ 331 • HT 129, 132–3, 190 • COA 36–7 • OTT 67 • SUMMERS 377 • ME 24 • DAVIS 169 • PD 367

BOGGS, REPRESENTATIVE HALE, member of the WC; suspicious death; Louisiana Democrat and majority party whip. Boggs was among those on the WC who never accepted the single-bullet theory. Boggs's plane disappeared without a trace while flying over Alaska in the early 1970s.

SOURCES: HSCA Report 256 • ME 12 • HT 67, 68, 129, 134, 371 • RTJ 23, 154, 196, 200, 313, 367, 373 • BE 78, 85, 298, 380 • COA 211, 395 • OTT 14 • BELIN 13 • DOP 13–4, 35, 60, 142, 206, 254, 384, 402 • SUMMERS 1, 36, 139 • BLAKEY 24–5, 27–8, 74, 77, 232, 266 • KANTOR 80, 82 • DAVIS 290–1, 295–7, 302–3, 344, 368 • NORTH 432, 434, 465, 507–8, 519 • PD 48

BOLDEN, ABRAHAM, first black member of the SS. Bolden reported in early November 1963, that there was a plot by "four Cuban gunmen" to kill JFK in Chicago. He received this info from the FBI, who detailed the plot to kill the president with "high-powered rifles." No records exist of the ensuing investigation (if there was one). After the assassination, Bolden charged the SS with laxity in protecting JFK. Soon thereafter, Bolden was indicted by the federal government and charged with trying to sell government files. Bolden claimed the charges were "retaliation." He was convicted in August 1964 and served a six-year sentence. (See also Vallee, Thomas)

SOURCES: HSCA Report 231–2, 636 • HT 13–4, 157–9 • RTJ 275 • RUSSELL 635 • SUMMERS 403

BOND, WILMA, a.w. Bond was among those who photographed the assassination scene from the south side of Elm Street. She was with a.w. Mary Muchmore at the corner of Elm and Houston and took 35mm slides of the motorcade as it headed north on Houston and then of the scene following the shooting sequence. Although she gave the slides to the FBI, they were not entered into evidence before the WC.

SOURCES: FMG III, 59–60 • PWW 42, 46–9, 82, 176

BONDS, JOE (aka Joe Locurto), Ruby witness; former Ruby business partner. Bonds told the FBI that Ruby often "made women available to [police] officers."

SOURCES: RTJ 234 • COA 85, 90, 112, 329–30 • FLAMMONDE 172 • BLAKEY 291–2

BOOKHOUT, JAMES W., Oswald witness; FBI agent. Bookhout interrogated Oswald after his arrest in Dallas. He says that Oswald told him that the pictures of him holding the murder weapons were composites, with Oswald's face superimposed over someone else's body.

SOURCES: WR 188 • WCH VII, 308 • RTJ 361 • BISHOP 231, 233, 250, 258, 447 • FMG I, 157 • OGLESBY 19–20 • NORTH 409

BOONE, EUGENE, a.w. (aftermath), Dallas deputy sheriff. With Deputy Constable Seymour Weitzman, Boone discovered the alleged assassination weapon poorly hidden on the sixth floor of the TSBD. The rifle was identified at the scene as a German Mauser rather than as an Italian Mannlicher-Carcano. (See also Craig, Roger; Day, J.C.; Weitzman, Seymour)

SOURCES: WR 27, 85 • WCH III, 291 • HSCA Report 50 • RTJ 114 • HT 144, 232–3 • OTT 98 • EVICA 16–20, 22, 50, 54, 58 • BELIN 9 • DOP 282 • PWW 43, 174

BOSCH, ORLANDO AVILA, assassination suspect; Cuban-exile leader. Marita Lorenz, a former undercover operative for the CIA and the FBI, told the *New York Daily News* that a few days before the JFK assassination, she drove from Miami to Dallas, and that her companions on the trip were "Oswald," CIA contact agent Frank Sturgis, Bosch, and his fellow Cuban exile Pedro Diaz Lanz, and two Cuban brothers named Novis—all members of Operation 40, a CIA guerrilla group that had been formed three years earlier in preparation for the Bay of Pigs invasion. Lorenz said that Operation 40 was an "assassination squad" that killed JFK because they blamed him for the Bay of Pigs fiasco. Lorenz also said that she saw "Oswald" at an Operation 40 training camp in the Florida Everglades and that he was at a meeting at Bosch's home in Miami with the above-mentioned men. During the meeting, she said, the men spread out street maps of Dallas and studied them.

Years later, Bosch would become friends with Jeb Bush, son of former President George Bush. (See also Lanz, Pedro Diaz; Lorenz, Marita)

SOURCES: HSCA Report 237 • HT 347–8 • PD 301 • BLAKEY 175 • EVICA 143, 252, 267, 269, 271, 315, 320, 327

BOSWELL, J. THORNTON, Bethesda witness; U.S. navy commander. Boswell assisted Dr. James J. Humes in performing JFK's autopsy. He told author Josiah Thompson that JFK's back wound was explored by Humes at the autopsy, who found only "a penetration of one or two inches." If this is true, then it is impossible for this wound to be caused by the same bullet that caused JFK's throat wound. (See also Finck, Pierre A.; Humes, James J.; O'Connor, Paul)

SOURCES: WR 89–90 • WCH II, 376 • RTJ 77 • HT 29, 34, 56–60, 64, 77, 80, 99, 108, 232, 267 • BE, many • OTT 245 • BISHOP 348–9, 365, 384–5, 397, 410, 431, 440, 449–50 • ME 32–3, 53, 62–3

BOTELHO, JAMES ANTHONY, Oswald witness; USMC acquaintance. Botelho told the WC:

> I shared a room with Oswald [in Santa Ana, California] for about two months before his discharge. He was unusual in that he generally would not speak unless spoken to, and his answers were always brief. He seldom associated with others... It was common knowledge that Oswald had taught himself to read Russian... [Some] kidded him by calling him "Oswaldkovich"... My impression is that, although he believed in pure Marxist theory, he did not believe in the way Communism was practiced by the Russians... We both enjoyed classical music... Oswald played chess with both me and [Richard] Call. Oswald was not a very good chess player, although he was better than I was... My impression was that Oswald was quite intelligent... [His] clearance was taken away from him... I believe he was made company clerk... Before Oswald requested his hardship discharge, the Sergeant Major was planning to take steps to "straighten Oswald out."... I remember Oswald's having a date with a girl who spoke Russian. I believe Oswald liked the girl a great deal, but he was for some reason unable to get in touch with her thereafter...

(See also Quinn, Rosaleen)

SOURCES: WCH VIII, 315 • AO 97

BOUCK, ROBERT, employee of the Protective Research Section of the Treasury Department. After the JFK autopsy, Bouck signed a receipt that read "One receipt from FBI for a missile removed during the examination of the body." This corroborates the memo written by FBI agents Francis O'Neill and James Sibert that a bullet was removed from JFK's body during the autopsy. Officially, no such bullet exists. (See also O'Neill, Francis; Sibert, James)

SOURCES: WR 404, 407–8, 434 • WCH IV, 294 • HSCA Report 233 • HT 235 • BE 136, 427, 503, 600, 648–9 • BLAKEY 9

BOUDREAUX, ANNE, Oswald witness. Boudreaux knew Oswald in his youth in New Orleans and lived in a house once occupied by Marguerite Oswald and her sons. She knew Oswald's childhood baby-sitter, who said Lee was a bad child who "wouldn't listen."

SOURCE: WCH VIII, 35

BOUHE, GEORGE A., Oswald witness; acquaintance of the Oswalds in Texas; member of Dallas's Russian-speaking community. According to the WR, "[Bouhe] attempted to dissuade Marina from returning [to Oswald] in November 1962, and when she rejoined him, [as he did not like Oswald]... became displeased with her as well." In the latter part of 1962 "relations between Oswald and his wife became such that Bouhe wanted to 'liberate' her from Oswald." Among other things, Bouhe is involved in the mystery of how Oswald met his Dallas mentor George DeMohrenschildt. DeMohrenschildt said that Bouhe introduced him to Oswald. Bouhe denied it. (See also Gregory, Peter)

SOURCES: WR 260–1, 376–7 • WCH VIII, 355 • FMG I, 186 • FLAMMONDE 154 • SUMMERS 196–7 • EVICA 296

BOWEN, JACK LESLIE (See BOWEN, JOHN)

BOWEN, JOHN (aka OSBORNE, ALBERT ALEXANDER; GROSSI, JOHN CAESAR), Oswald witness; supposedly rode on the bus to Mexico City with Oswald in September 1963. Known as Osborne, this man later told the FBI that his name was really John Bowen.

When Oswald was arrested in Dallas, he was carrying a library card with the name Jack L. Bowen on it. The card, which appears in Michael H. B. Eddowes book *Khrushchev Killed Kennedy*, reads (in part):

Name Oswald, Mr. Lee Harvey
M. Address 602 Elsbeth
City Dallas[...]
School or Business Jaggers-Chiles-Stovall
Name Jack L. Bowen
Home Address 1916 Stevens Forest Dr.
Phone WH8-8997 Expire 12-7-65

"Jack" Bowen worked with Oswald at the firm of Jaggers-Chiles-Stovall, a defense contractor that did photographic work in Dallas. Jack Bowen has a son named Howard, who researcher Penn Jones Jr. claims is the same Howard Bowen who worked for the CIA and was named by former CIA director Richard Helms in the Watergate hearings. Oswald himself is said to have used the name Osborne when he ordered his FPCC pamphlets in New Orleans. To further muddy the issue of who's who, HT reported that one of the three tramps arrested following the assassination in the railroad yards behind the grassy knoll told police that his name was Albert Alexander Osborne. Recently released DPD files indicate this is not true.

According to Michael H. B. Eddowes in *Khrushchev Killed Kennedy*, Jack Leslie Bowen is aka John Caesar Grossi, Oswald's coworker at Jaggers-Chiles-Stovall. John Howard Bowen is aka Albert Osborne, the man who traveled with Oswald (or an Oswald impersonator) by bus to Mexico City in September 1963.

Regarding Osborne/Bowen, author Anthony Summers writes:

> Questioned about his use of two identities, Bowen-Osborne said he had been doing so for fifty years. He claimed that he was a "missionary" who travelled extensively and that his most recent trip, begun just before the Kennedy assassination, had included France and Spain. Intensive frontier checks revealed no record of entrance to either country, and Bowen-Osborne did not reveal how his frequent travels were financed. Not surprisingly, there has been speculation that he was in some way connected with intelligence. If so, we may hazard a guess as to which side of the political fence he was on. During World War II Bowen-Osborne was a fanatical supporter of Nazi Germany.

(See also Grossi, John; Osborne, Albert; Stovall, Robert)
SOURCES: WR 733 • WCH XI, 220; XXIV, 576; XXV, 42 • HT 180–1 • SUMMERS 344

BOWERS, LEE E., JR., a.w.; suspicious death; railroad towerman for the Union Terminal Company. Bowers says that he watched the assassination from a 14-foot tower behind the wooden fence atop the grassy knoll near the railroad tracks. Of all of the assassination witnesses, Bowers reportedly had the best view of the spot from which at least one shot—and probably more—was fired. During the hour before the assassination, Bowers observed three cars enter the parking lot behind the TSBD and the knoll, one at a time. The first car was a blue-and-white 1959 Oldsmobile station wagon with an out-of-state license plate. This car, which had a "Goldwater for President" sticker on the bumper, was splattered with dirt. It circled the lot, then left. The second car was a black 1957 Ford, driven by a man who appeared to be speaking into a microphone. It, too, circled the lot before leaving. The third car was a 1961 white Chevy Impala and entered the lot about ten minutes before the shooting. It also had a Goldwater sticker.

At the time of the shooting, Bowers saw two men near the wooden fence. One was middle-aged and heavy-set. The other was in his mid-twenties and wore a plaid shirt. They were the only two strangers in the area. Bowers recognized everyone else he saw as railroad employees. As the shots rang out, Bowers's attention was drawn to the area. He said there was a "flash of light or smoke or something." Bowers's description of the men behind the wooden fence corroborates the statement of a.w. Julia Mercer.

Bowers told the WC, "I heard three shots. One, then a slight pause, then two very close together. Also reverberations from the shots... The sounds came either from up against the School Depository Building or near the mouth of the triple underpass... I had worked this same tower for some 10 to 12 years... and had noticed at that time the similarity of sounds occurring in either of these locations... There is a similarity of sound, because there is a reverberation which takes place from either location."

According to the *Midlothian* (Texas) *Mirror*, Bowers received death threats after the assassination. Bowers died on August 9, 1966, in a one-car crash. Bowers apparently drove his car off the road into a concrete abutment in Midlothian, Texas. No autopsy was performed. His body was cremated.

According to a.w. Ed Hoffman, the man in the railworker uniform, whom Hoffman saw with a rifle after the shooting, was last seen by Hoffman walking toward Bowers's tower. (See also Hoffman, Ed; Mercer, Julia A.)
SOURCES: WR 81–3 • WCH VI, 284 • WCE 2003 • HT 129, 134–5 • RTJ 30–3, 36–7, 39, 43 • BE 18 • COA 24, 35 • OTT 16, 18–9, 207 • BISHOP 142 • CF 75–8, 82, 332 • SUMMERS 28–9, 49 • BLAKEY 91 • ME 22–3, 51 • OGLESBY 36, 46–7 • DAVIS 196 • NORTH 379

BOWIE, JIM, Ruby witness; Dallas assistant district attorney. Bowie was present at Ruby's police questioning following the shooting of Oswald.
SOURCES: RTJ 243 • GERTZ 6–7, 65, 175, 219, 232, 264, 524 • FLAMMONDE 174 • BLAKEY 328

BOWLES, JAMES C., DPD member (head of Radio Division); first to transcribe the DPD radio tape made at the time of the assassination, the transcription used by the WC. On the recordings one can hear the Morse code signal for "V" (victory). Bowles told author Harrison Edward Livingstone that this was merely a coincidence. "It's just a heterodyning," he said. In his opinion, the open mike that reportedly recorded the assassination was at the Dallas Trade Mart and could not have recorded the shots. Bowles later became the sheriff of Dallas County.
SOURCES: HT 126, 248, 250, 253, 260 • BELIN 192

BOWRON, DIANA HAMILTON, Parkland witness; nurse. Bowron saw JFK arrive at Parkland and helped wheel him into the emergency room. She told the WC that JFK "was moribund... lying across Mrs. Kennedy's knee and there seemed to be blood everywhere. When I went around to the other side of the car, I saw the condition of his head... the back of his head... it was very bad... I just saw one large hole." Bowron was among the nurses who, after JFK died, washed the body and prepared it for the coffin. (See also Hinchliffe, Margaret)

SOURCES: WCH VI, 134 • HT 41–2, 454 • BE 40, 192, 312, 599 • BISHOP 152, 156, 180, 208, 228 • DOP 183–4, 294, 304

BOYD, ELMER L., Oswald witness; DPD detective (Homicide and Robbery). At the time of the assassination, Boyd was at the Trade Mart with Captain Will Fritz. He went to the sixth floor of the TSBD with Fritz and was present during interrogations of Oswald on November 22. Boyd escorted Oswald to and from police lineups. He found five .38 shells on Oswald and marked them for evidence. He said Oswald was calm except for when he was questioned by FBI Agent James Hosty. (See also Fritz, Will; Hosty, James).

SOURCE: WCH VII, 119

BOXLEY, BILL (See WOOD, WILLIAM)

BRADEN, JIM (See BRADING, EUGENE HALE)

BRADING, EUGENE HALE (aka Braden, Jim), a.w.; "suspicious behavior." Following the assassination, a man named Jim Braden was arrested and taken in for interrogation because he had been in the Dal-Tex Building, overlooking Dealey Plaza, without a good excuse. Braden told the police that he was in Dallas on oil business and had gone into the building to make a phone call. He was released. Although Braden claimed that he had not entered the building until after the shooting, eyewitnesses place him inside the building when the shots were fired. Braden visited the offices of Texas oil billionaire Lamar Hunt the day before the assassination (as would be appropriate if he were on "oil business"). Ruby visited Hunt's offices at the same time.

That night Braden stayed at the Cabana Motel in Dallas. Ruby visited there, too, around midnight. According to author Peter Noyes, Braden had an office in New Orleans at the time in Room 1701 of the Pere Marquette Building. At the time assassination suspect David Ferrie was working for organized crime boss Carlos Marcello's attorney G. Wray Gill on the same floor, in room 1707. It was later discovered that Jim Braden was actually

Eugene Hale Brading, an ex-convict suspected of having ties with organized crime in Southern California. He had a new driver's license made for him, in the name of Jim Braden, on September 9, 1963. On parole at the time JFK was shot, Brading's rap sheet showed 35 arrests. He had previously been convicted of burglary, bookmaking, and embezzlement. Some of Brading's arrest records later disappeared from the National Archives. Brading didn't testify at the 1967 Clay Shaw trial because his extradition was refused by later U.S. Attorney General Edwin Meese III.

Brading was a charter member of Moe Dalitz's La Costa Country Club, which was Teamster-financed, and once lived in a Palm Springs mansion that had been owned by Bing Crosby. In 1968, the Los Angeles Police Department interviewed Brading about his presence in Los Angeles, far from his home, on the night of Robert Kennedy's murder. (See also Aase, Jean; Bauman, Roger; Brown, Morgan; Dalitz, Moe; Dolan, James; Hunt, H.L.; Lewis, Clint; Meyers, Lawrence; Powell, James)

SOURCES: WCE 2003 • HT 121, 185, 305, 319 • COA 45–7, 50, 168, 229, 259, 263, 267, 284, 329 • OTT 205–6, 286 • CF 337–40 • SUMMERS 452–3 • BLAKEY 306, 396–7 • EVICA 164–6 • OGLESBY 50 • KANTOR 32–7, 111 • DAVIS 208, 212, 583 • NORTH 192, 308–10, 372, 390, 516

BRADLEY, EDGAR EUGENE, suspected a.w.; California right-wing preacher. Bradley was identified in October 1967 by former Deputy Sheriff Roger Craig as a man in Dealey Plaza after the assassination who was posing as a SS agent. During Jim Garrison's assassination investigation, Garrison wanted to charge Bradley with conspiring to kill the president, but California Governor Ronald Reagan refused to extradite Bradley. Bradley gave Reagan an affidavit stating that he was in El Paso at the time of the assassination.

On December 20, 1967, Garrison filed a bill of information in New Orleans, charging that Bradley did "willfully and unlawfully conspire with others to murder John F. Kennedy."

According to Paris Flammonde, "Bradley was originally from Arkansas, moving to Los Angeles in 1936, after serving in the United States Navy. Five feet eight inches tall, with dark hair, graying a little at the temples," he was married, with a grown son and daughter. Bradley had a "special assignment" during World War II about which nothing is known.

According to the *New Orleans States-Item* (December 22, 1967), Garrison replied to Bradley's alibi, saying, "Our evidence indicates that he was in Dallas. Furthermore, I think I can say with assurance that the Federal government and the Federal investigative agencies know he was in Dallas, and know precisely what he was doing." Garrison refused to discuss specifics.

In Los Angeles, District Attorney Eville J. Younger ordered Bradley's arrest on December 26, 1967, adding "this does not indicate any opinion on our part as to the validity of the charge or the guilt or innocence of Mr. Bradley" (*New York Post*, December 27, 1967).

Contemporaneous with these events, Flammonde spoke with an unnamed source within the Garrison investigation who said Bradley had been an OSS officer, probably still had intelligence connections and was a member of an elite Minuteman-like group. The source said that Bradley knew assassination suspect Loran Hall and had been involved in anti-Castro activities. Flammonde writes: "On January 15, 1968, Court Clerk Max Gonzalez asserted he had observed 'meetings at New Orleans's Lakefront Airport in either June or July 1963 between... Bradley of North Hollywood and the late David W. Ferrie.'" Garrison claimed to possess an affidavit from former Dallas County Deputy Sheriff Roger Craig, whom he did not name, stating that Bradley had impersonated an SS agent in front of the TSBD after the assassination.

While Bradley successfully fought extradition attempts, researcher Mark Lane said, in May 1968, that he had a copy of a letter written by Bradley to a young woman, in which he had written that he knew "facts about the [assassination] that the public will never know about...," that "his life had been threatened many times," and that "another patriotic friend of [his] has just been shot and killed." Lane reported in the *Los Angeles Free Press* (May 3–9, 1968) that the recipient of that letter had been asked by Bradley to lie, with a prepared affidavit, to provide him with an alibi for November 22, 1963. Lane claimed that the woman showed him her diary, and that it indicated that, although she had seen Bradley on November 20, she had not seen him on November 22.

That same month, Garrison interviewed Loran Hall, who told him that he knew Bradley, having met him at a "house that was noted for their anti-Semitic and paramilitary feelings and thinkings," and that, in his mind, he figured Bradley for a CIA man. By 1969, Bradley was a sheriff in Los Angeles and part-time assistant to Reverend Carl McIntire. According to Penn Jones Jr., at this time, Bradley "hounded" Craig "almost daily."

SOURCES: FMG III, 29, 33, 36, 73–4, 86, 88 • FLAMMONDE 198–202, 204–5, 282

BRADLEY, MARSHALL, Ruby witness. According to SS agent Lane Bertram, Bradley saw Ruby in Houston on November 21, 1963, when JFK

was in town. Ruby was seen "one block from the President's entrance route and from the Rice Hotel where he stayed." Bradley was one of five witnesses who saw Ruby on the 400 block of Milam Street from 2:30 to 7:15 P.M.
    SOURCE: COA 261

BRANCH, JOHN HENRY, Ruby witness; manager of Dallas's Empire Room. Though Ruby's tax statements and living quarters reflect a modest income, Branch told the WC that Ruby regularly came into his establishment and handed out five-dollar bills to random customers. Branch said that Ruby even did this on the night of November 23, 1963.
    SOURCES: WCH XV, 473 • COA 118, 127

BRANIFF, MATTHEW, Orleans Parish Criminal District Court Judge. With Judges Bernard Bagert and Malcolm O'Hara, Braniff was one of three judges who presided as a panel over Clay Shaw's preliminary hearing for conspiracy to assassinate JFK and who determined that Jim Garrison had presented enough evidence for Shaw to be held over for trial.
    SOURCES: OTT 156–8 • FLAMMONDE, many

BRANTLY, ROY, Ruby witness. Ruby says that he got the .38 used to kill Oswald from Brantly, with whom he may have run guns to Cuba in 1959. Ruby says that he merely relayed a phone call to Brantly in 1959 concerning the running of the guns. Brantly denies receiving the call.
    SOURCES: HT 237 • GERTZ 46, 184, 188

BRANYON, JOHN, Oswald witness; one of the four men who worked at the Reily Coffee Company in New Orleans with Oswald. All four quit within weeks of Oswald's departure and later went on to work for NASA. (See also Barbee, Emmett; Claude, Alfred; Marachini, Dante; Reily, William)
    SOURCES: OTT 116 • HOS 150

BREEN, JAMES, Ruby witness. With his girlfriend, Eileen Curry, Breen jumped bond on narcotics charges and moved to Dallas, where (as Curry told the FBI) Breen had to get the okay from Ruby before working in the Dallas narcotics trade. (See also Curry, Eileen)
    SOURCE: COA 89, 90

BREHM, CHARLES, a.w. Brehm was standing on the south curb of Elm Street only 20 feet from JFK at the time of the fatal shot. He told Mark Lane that he saw a portion of the president's skull fly toward the rear and left, indicating that the final shot came from in front and to the right. He was not called to testify before the WC.
    SOURCES: WCE 1425, 2003 • RTJ 56 • HT 231 • BE 17, 44, 96, 316, 331 • CF 34 •

SUMMERS 19, 23

BREMER, ARTHUR. Bremer attempted to assassinate George Wallace in 1972, thus taking Wallace out of the running for president and assuring Richard Nixon's reelection. After the Wallace shooting, Charles Colson ordered JFK assassination suspect E. Howard Hunt to break into Bremer's apartment, but Hunt balked, so Nixon ordered Bremer's apartment sealed. (See also Colson, Charles; Hunt, E. Howard; Nixon, Richard M.)
SOURCE: HT 120, 384

BRENGEL, MARY, secretary for Guy Banister Associates during the summer and fall of 1963. In 1979, Brengel was interviewed by author Anthony Summers, who writes, "She recalls that one day, as she was taking dictation from Banister, he openly referred in a letter to his work in helping [Carlos] Marcello fight deportation. [She] expressed surprise that her employer was involved with organized crime, and Banister responded curtly, 'There are principles being violated, and if this goes on it could affect every citizen in the United States.' He left no doubt that he was firmly on Marcello's side."
SOURCE: SUMMERS 309–10

BRENNAN, HOWARD LESLIE, a.w. Brennan was standing on the southwest corner of Houston and Elm, facing the TSBD. He claims to have seen Oswald in the "sniper's nest" window, 120 feet away. Brennan was later found to have poor eyesight, but the WC took him at his word anyway. It was supposedly Brennan's description of Oswald ("slender white male, 5'10", early thirties") that was broadcast over police radio minutes after the assassination. But Brennan could not possibly have known how tall the assassin was, since any rifleman shooting from the sniper's nest would have had to kneel to get into position. (See also Harkness, D.V.; Haygood, Clyde; Sawyer, J. Herbert; Speaker, Sandy)
SOURCES: WR 23, 75–6, 80, 133–6, 145, 232 • WCH III, 140, 184, 211 • WCE 2003, 2006 • RTJ, many • BE 355 • BELIN 6–10, 31, 33, 49, 73, 214, 220 • BISHOP, many • DOP 49, 150–1, 157, 159, 280, 447, 638 • CF 25–7, 319 • PWW 92, 125 • SUMMERS 41, 52, 78–9 • DAVIS 195, 209

BREWER, E. D., a.w. (aftermath); member DPD. Brewer was told that the shots came from the TSBD, but couldn't remember by whom. Brewer's number that day was 137. According to the WC, Brewer was one of the motorcycle patrolmen in the motorcade, traveling one-half block ahead of JFK's limo.
SOURCES: WCH VI, 302; XX, 489 • FMG III, 54

BREWER, JOHNNY CALVIN, Oswald witness; Texas Theatre witness;

manager of a Hardy's shoe store on Jefferson Boulevard in Oak Cliff. After hearing a news flash that a policeman had been shot nearby, Brewer saw a man acting suspiciously (turning his face toward the window when a police car drove by), then sneaking into the Texas Theatre. Brewer asked the ticket taker to call the police and then identified Oswald when the lights went up in the theater. (See also Postal, Julia)

SOURCES: WR 26, 164, 166 • WCH VII, 1 • BELIN 23–8, 30, 32, 212, 220 • BISHOP, many • SUMMERS 53

BRIAN, V. J., a.w. (aftermath); member DPD. Brian was involved in the search of the TSBD immediately following the assassination. He discovered acoustical tiles on the second-floor ceiling, and he and another policeman began ripping them out when someone suggested that an assassin might be hiding behind them.

SOURCES: WR 417 • WCH V, 47 • BISHOP 232

BRIGHT, H. R., wealthy Dallas businessman who, along with Edgar R. Crissey and Nelson Lamar Hunt, contributed to pay for the full-page, black-bordered anti-JFK advertisement that ran in the *Dallas Morning News* on the day of the assassination.

SOURCES: WR 276 • FMG I, 130

BRILL, STEVEN, author of *The Teamsters* (Simon & Schuster, 1978). Brill reports that Harold Gibbons, a top Jimmy Hoffa aide, overheard Hoffa discussing the option of having RFK murdered.

SOURCE: BLAKEY 204–8

BRINGUIER, CARLOS, Oswald witness; anti-Castro activist; author of *Red Friday: November 22, 1963* (C. Hallberg, 1969). On August 5, 1963, Oswald visited the store in New Orleans that anti-Castro activist Bringuier managed and expressed interest in joining the anti-Castro struggle. When Oswald was arrested in New Orleans on August 9, 1963, for disturbing the peace, he was handing out pro-Castro FPCC leaflets. He got into an argument with Bringuier. Oswald reportedly told Carlos to hit him, and Carlos did. Oswald was arrested and was later released after speaking with FBI Agent John Quigley. Later, on August 21, 1963, Bringuier took the anti-Castro viewpoint in a New Orleans radio debate on a show called "Conversation Carte Blanche." His opponent, representing the FPCC, was Oswald.

Many researchers suspect that these two men were actually playing on the same team and "staged" their confrontations. This is how Bringuier described his association with Oswald in his WC testimony:

...on August 9 [1963]...I was sure that [Oswald] was a pro-Castro and not an FBI. ...[O]n August 5,...Mr. Oswald came into the store...He told me that he was against Castro and that he was against Communism...and he told me that he will bring to me next day one book as a present, as a gift to me, to train Cubans to fight against Castro...August 6, Oswald came back...and he left with my brother-in-law a Guidebook for Marines...on August 9, one of my two friends, Miguel Cruz...told me that the guy [Oswald] was another time in Canal Street...I was surprised when I recognized that the guy [outside Ward Discount House] with the sign hanging on his chest, said "Viva Fidel" and "Hands Off Cuba" was Lee Harvey Oswald...I became angry...he recognized me...immediately he smiled at me and he offered the hand to shake hands with me. I became more angry...The people in the street became angry and they started to shout to him, "Traitor! Communist! Go to Cuba! Kill him!" ...When we were in the first District of Police...some of the policemen start to question Oswald as if he was a Communist...and Oswald at that moment...was really cold blood. He was answering the questions that he would like to answer, and he was not nervous, he was not out of control...On August 16, another friend of mine left a message in the store that Oswald was another time handing out pro-Castro propaganda for the [FPCC], this time in front of the International Trade Mart...The leaflet [on] August 9 didn't have his name of Oswald...they have the name A. J. Hidell and one post office box here in New Orleans and the address and leaflets that he was handing out on August 16 have the name L. H. Oswald, 4907 Magazine Street...my friend [Carlos Quiroga] asked to me if I think it would be good that he would go to Oswald's house posing as a pro-Castro and try to get as much information as possible from Oswald. I told him yes; and that night [August 16] he went to Oswald's house...My friend...was talking to Oswald for about one hour...in the porch of the house, and there was where we found that Oswald had some connection with Russia...because the daughter came to the porch and Oswald spoke to her in Russian, and my friend...asked Oswald if that was Russian and Oswald told him yes, that he was attending Tulane University and that he was studying the language...my friend came back from Oswald's house and told me what had happened over there...We also discussed this conversation in front of Ed Butler...[of] the Information Council of the Americas...the matter that Oswald spoke in Russian...that he was married to a Russian girl. We gave all that information to Butler and he was trying to contact some person, somebody in Washington, to get more the background of Oswald before the debate... The last day that I saw Oswald was August 21, the day of the debate. I went to WDSU radio... They were already there—[broadcaster] Bill Stuckey and Lee Harvey Oswald... before the debate started.... [Oswald] saw my guidebook for the Marines that I was carrying... and he told me, "Well, listen Carlos, don't try to do an invasion with that guidebook for the Marines, because that is an old one and that will be a failure." That was his joke in that moment...

According to author Anthony Summers, Bringuier "certainly had contact with the CIA. He was New Orleans's delegate to the *Directorio Revolucionario Estudiantil*, the outgrowth of a militant Cuban student group. The group had naturally been involved with the CIA at the time of the Bay of Pigs invasion and continued to receive funds afterward. The [HSCA] found that Bringuier had reported his contact with Oswald to his group's headquarters in Miami and that the information had in turn been relayed to the CIA. A document obtained from the agency reveals that the CIA had 'past contact with... Bringuier... Contact was limited to Domestic Service activities.'"

Bringuier gave a letter to the FBI that he had written to a friend (identified as Jose Antonio) sometime after the assassination. It read, in part:

The police here are looking for a certain "Clay Bertrand" who is a pervert. They say Ruby is also a pervert. One of these individuals that was distributing handbills with Oswald has a face that appears to me to indicate that he is also a pervert... I advised the [SS] that one of those who was distributing handbills with Oswald was working in Pap's Supermarket located on Mirabeau Avenue and who, last year, had attended Delgado Trade School. He mentioned that his name might possibly be Charles and that he regularly got off of the bus at Paris Avenue and Filmore Street.

(See also Butler, Edward; Easterling, Robert; Stuckey, William)
SOURCES: WR 384, 395 • WCH X, 32 • HSCA Report 141–2, 145, 236 • HSCA X, 81 • SUMMERS 271–4, 278, 318, 421 • HT 309 • BELIN 210 • DUFFY 183–4 • AO 120–2 • FLAMMONDE 22, 116, 121, 123–5, 251 • BLAKEY 162, 167, 169–70, 177, 358–9, 364 • HOS 140 • EVICA, many • KANTOR 199 • DAVIS 141–2 • NORTH 294–5, 300, 405, 414, 446

BROCK, ALVIN R., o.k.w. (prelude); DPD patrolman; 25 years old. On the morning of Oswald's aborted transfer Brock was assigned to guard the elevator the prisoner would eventually come down on, but by the time Oswald was moved, Brock had been reassigned to traffic duty at a nearby intersection. Brock told the WC he saw nothing suspicious during his time in the DPD basement. At 11:30 A.M., Brock was assigned to Parkland Hospital, where Oswald was dying.

SOURCE: WCH XII, 171

BROCK, MARY, t.k.w.; wife of a mechanic who worked at a Jefferson Blvd. gas station. Brock saw a man fleeing the scene of the Tippit shooting and described the man as white, 5'10", wearing light clothing and a light-colored jacket and walking fast with his hands in his pockets. She last saw the man in the parking lot directly behind the gas-station parking lot where a light-colored jacket was later found. During an FBI interview conducted on January 21, 1964, she positively identified the man she had seen as Oswald.

SOURCES: WR 163 • WCH VII, 593

BRONSON, CHARLES L., a.w. Bronson made a motion picture of Dealey Plaza just before the shooting. In it, some independent researchers (including Robert Groden) say that one or more figures can be seen on the sixth floor of the TSBD. The HSCA called the movement "random photographic artifact." The film is still being studied. Groden told the HSCA, regarding the Bronson film, "You can actually see one figure walking back and forth hurriedly. I think what was happening there is the sniper's nest was actually being completed just prior to the shots being fired."

SOURCES: HSCA Report 49, 86, 480–1, 485, 487 • HT 228 • CF 21–2 • SUMMERS 44–5 • OGLESBY 67–8 • DAVIS 196, 459–61, 613

BROOKS, DONALD E., Oswald witness; employment counselor, Texas Employment Commission. Brooks counseled Oswald on October 9, 1962, and says that Oswald told him he didn't want to do industrial work anymore.

SOURCE: WCH X, 143

BROOKS, JACK S., Parkland witness; U.S. Representative (D-Texas). Brooks was among the members of the presidential party in Dallas who were assigned to protect LBJ in Parkland during the chaotic first few moments following the assassination.

SOURCE: WR 70–1

BROSHEARS, RAYMOND, informant; minister. In 1965, Broshears gave New Orleans District Attorney Jim Garrison a statement that he had met and spoken to assassination suspects David Ferrie and Clay Shaw together on a number of occasions and that, when Ferrie drank, he liked to talk about his role in the JFK assassination. Broshears shared an apartment with Ferrie in 1965. In August 1968, he said on a Los Angeles television program, and was quoted in the August 15, 1968, issue of the *New York Free Press*, that, "David admitted being involved with the assassins. There's no question about that. [Ferrie] was in Houston at the time. Mr. Garrison has him in Houston with an airplane waiting." He also said that Ferrie's job was to pilot two of the actual assassins on the second stage of an escape flight which would eventually take them to South Africa via South America. Author Paris Flammonde points out that the U.S. had no extradition treaties with South Africa, and that it was here that "the CIA front operation Permindex moved when it was asked to leave Europe."

Broshears said that Ferrie told him the plan had fallen apart when the assassins, flying in a light plane, had decided to skip the Houston stop and "make it all the way to some point in Mexico non-stop." The assassins reportedly crashed off the coast of Corpus Christi, Texas, and died. In the television interview, Broshears also said that it was his opinion that Ferrie had been murdered, since Ferrie had once told him that "no matter what," he would never commit suicide. (See also Ferrie, David)
SOURCES: OTT 120 • FLAMMONDE 39–40

BROWDER, EDDIE, possible Ruby witness. An FBI informant claimed that Ruby was active in the late 1950s smuggling weapons from Miami to Castro's forces in Cuba, and that Browder was his pilot. Browder is known to have engaged in gun-running with Havana mobster Norman Rothman, a close associate of mobster and assassination suspect Santos Trafficante.
SOURCE: SUMMERS 437, 440–1, 469

BROWN, ARNOLD J., Oswald witness; FBI special agent. With John W. Fain, Brown interviewed Oswald in the back seat of Fain's car (which was parked outside Oswald's home) on August 16, 1962. According to Brown, Oswald was cold, arrogant, uncooperative, and evasive. (See also Fain, John W.)
SOURCES: HSCA Report 190, 250 • DUFFY 189

BROWN, CHARLES W., o.k.w.; DPD detective. On November 22, 1963, Brown and his partner, Detective J. R. Leavelle accompanied t.k.w. Helen Markham to the DPD station because she had several emotional breakdowns before tentatively identifying Oswald in a lineup. On November 24, Brown was the driver of the car that was to receive Oswald during the aborted transfer. Brown's car was not in position when it was supposed to be.

SOURCES: WR 200 · WCH VII, 246 · RTJ 211–2 · BISHOP 122, 290 · KANTOR 67, 72

BROWN, EARLE V., a.w.; DPD officer. Brown was standing on the railroad trestle just north of the triple underpass. He told the WC, "The first I noticed [JFK's] car was when it stopped [after turning onto Elm]." He saw the pigeons flying off the roof of the TSBD when the shots were fired. Several minutes after the shooting, Brown says he smelled gunpowder.

Those seeking to discredit the HSCA's acoustic evidence note that no motorcycle siren is audible following the shots. Brown offers a possible explanation: The motorcade stopped shortly after the shooting on the entrance ramp to the Stemmons Freeway (with JFK's limo speeding ahead to Parkland). The motorcycle with the stuck mike would have had to stop, too, and the siren may not have been turned on until the motorcade started again.

SOURCES: WCH VI, 321 · HT 249 · BISHOP 142, 351–2 · CF 59–60 · SUMMERS 29 · ME 77

BROWN, JOSEPH B. Ruby witness; judge who presided over Ruby's murder trial and eventual death sentence. Brown eventually had to disqualify himself from the case, and a retrial was ordered when it was learned that he had been working on a book during the trial, the sales of which would have been enhanced by a quick conclusion of the proceedings.

Brown granted columnist Dorothy Kilgallen permission to interview Ruby alone for 30 minutes during Ruby's murder trial. According to author Penn Jones Jr., even Ruby's guards left the room during the interview. Kilgallen died suspiciously before she had an opportunity to publish what she had learned. (See also Beavers, William)

SOURCES: GERTZ, many · BISHOP 530 · DOP 634 · FMG I, 22, 24 · FLAMMONDE 295 · BLAKEY 326, 328–9 · KANTOR 120–2, 179

BROWN, MADELEINE, possible Oswald witness; Ruby witness; advertising businesswoman; former LBJ mistress. Brown admits drinking in the Carousel Club and claims to have met Ruby through one of LBJ's lawyers. She told Jack Anderson in 1988, "In the fall of 1963 I was in the Carousel Club with other advertising people and Jack Ruby was saying that Lee Harvey Oswald had been in the club and he had been bragging that he had taken a shot at Major General Edwin Walker."

On the television show *A Current Affair* (February 24, 1992), Brown said that LBJ had foreknowledge of the assassination but did nothing to stop it because of his intense desire to be president and his hatred of JFK. (See also Zirbel, Craig I.)

SOURCE: TEX 242

BROWN, MAGGIE, a.w.; *Dallas Morning News* employee. Brown was standing on the north side of Elm Street "in the grassy knoll area." She said that the shots came from behind her and to the right—i.e., from the direction of the wooden fence atop the knoll. She was not questioned by the WC.
SOURCE: SUMMERS 27

BROWN, MORGAN, associate of assassination suspect, Eugene Hale Brading; with Roger Bauman and Brading, visited the offices of oil billionaire Lamar Hunt on November 21, 1963, according to the FBI. The next day, Brown checked out of Dallas's Cabana Motel at 2:00 P.M., while his colleague Brading was still being held by Dallas sheriffs for questioning because of suspicious behavior in Dealey Plaza. (See also Brading, Eugene Hale)
SOURCES: SUMMERS 453 • NORTH 372

BROWN, ORAN, possible Oswald witness; Dallas car salesman (at Downtown Lincoln-Mercury). Brown's testimony corroborates that of Albert G. Bogard. After Bogard was beaten nearly to death following his WC testimony, Brown told an independent investigator on April 4, 1966, "You know, I am afraid to talk...I think we may have seen something important, and I think there are some who don't want us to talk." When Brown spoke these words, he did not know that Bogard was already dead, of an apparent suicide. (See also Bogard, Albert G.; Lawrence, Jack; Willis, Philip)
SOURCES: WR 297 • RTJ 331–3 • COA 37

BROWN, PETER MEGARGEE, counsel for Community Service Society, New York. Brown maintained a file on Lee and Marguerite Oswald following Oswald's truancy problem in the Bronx. Brown turned his file on Marguerite Oswald over to the WC.
SOURCE: WCH XI, 470

BROWN, TOM, Ruby witness; Dallas garage attendant. Brown told FBI that around midday on November 23, Ruby made a phone call from his garage (Nichols Garage, adjacent to Ruby's Carousel Club), during which he discussed "the whereabouts of Chief of Police Curry."
SOURCES: WR 323–4 • RTJ 270 • COA 134 • BLAKEY 319

BRUNEAU, EMILE (appears in some sources as Bruno, Emile), Oswald witness; alleged member of Carlos Marcello's New Orleans crime organization. Bruneau paid Oswald's bail after his New Orleans arrest for disturbing the peace.
SOURCES: OTT 304 • COA 42 • BLAKEY 342, 359 • SUMMERS 312–3

BRUNER, FRED (possibly aka BRUNNER, ED), Ruby witness; attorney. Fred represented Ruby at the time he shot Oswald; Ed is reported to have met with Ruby three times in 1961 to discuss the sale of arms to Cuba. Are they the same person?
SOURCE: KANTOR 157, 307

BRUNER, PABLO, received a phone call in Mexico City at 12:52 P.M. on November 22, 1963, from a Riverside 8 exchange in Dallas. The caller said only, "He's dead, he's dead." JFK's death had yet to be announced.
SOURCE: CRENSHAW 91

BRYANT, BAXTON, Duncanville, Texas, Methodist minister. According to Penn Jones Jr., Bryant "was a leader of a group that insisted President Kennedy make a downtown detour of Dallas 'in order to be seen by more voters.'...Shortly after the assassination Bryant's lifestyle changed completely. He left his church, grew a full beard, grew long, flowing red hair and went to work for the Federal Government." According to Jones, Bryant has bragged that he was "in the area" at the time of the assassinations of JFK, RFK, and Martin Luther King Jr.
SOURCE: FMG III, 104

BUCHANAN, THOMAS G., author of the book *Who Killed Kennedy?* (Secker & Warburg, 1964). Reportedly, Ruby read this book, which theorizes about a conspiracy, and praised it.
SOURCES: RTJ 115 · BE 29 · PWW 127–9, 235 · FLAMMONDE 121, 126, 166 · OGLESBY 70

BUCKNELL, DAVID, Oswald witness; USMC acquaintance. Bucknell told author Mark Lane that Oswald had told him, while stationed in Atsugi, that he had been alone in a bar when he was approached by a woman who was curious about the details of his "top secret" work. Oswald reported the incident to his superior officer, who arranged for Oswald to meet a civilian. The civilian told Oswald that the woman was a known KGB agent. The man gave Oswald money and told him he could do his country a great service by feeding the woman false information regarding the U-2 spy plane flown out of Atsugi. This would explain how Oswald contracted a venereal disease "in the line of duty."
SOURCE: CF 104

BUNDY, McGEORGE "MAC," military adviser to JFK. According to Colonel Fletcher Prouty, Bundy radioed Air Force One while it was flying from Dallas to Washington carrying JFK's body and LBJ, saying that the assassination was not the result of a conspiracy, but had been the act of a lone gunman. Prouty also claims that it was Bundy who ordered the air support for the Bay of Pigs invasion to be canceled. (See also Hallet, Oliver)

SOURCES: HT 20, 427–8 • BELIN 114, 121–6, 140, 156, 159 • BISHOP, many • DOP, many • SUMMERS 395, 400, 407 • FLAMMONDE 256–7, 262 • BLAKEY 18–9, 60–1, 159 • EVICA 257 • KANTOR 132, 164 • DAVIS 270 • NORTH 102, 368, 443–4 • PD 105–6

BUNDY, VERNON, Oswald witness; inmate of the New Orleans Parish prison at the time of Jim Garrison's conspiracy investigation. Bundy told one of his prison guards that he had information regarding Oswald. Garrison was contacted, and Bundy ended up on the witness stand during Clay Shaw's preliminary court hearing. He testified that he had gone to the seawall at Lake Pontchartrain in July 1963 "to get a fix" of heroin and while there saw Shaw and Oswald have a 15-minute meeting. He testified, "The older fellow gave the guy what I'm not sure, but it looked like a roll of money. The young guy stuck it in his back pocket." Bundy also testified effectively at Shaw's trial, at one point volunteering that the factor that convinced him beyond a shadow of a doubt that Shaw was the man he had seen at the waterfront was Shaw's distinctive gait; a slight limp, a twisting of his foot when he walked. (Shaw later explained that the limp was a result of a back injury suffered in the army.)

SOURCES: OTT 156–9, 169, 235–6, 275 • FLAMMONDE 5, 60, 94–5, 109, 118–20, 184, 305–6, 312–3

BURCHAM, JOHN W., Chief of Unemployment Insurance, Texas Employment Commission. Burcham testified to the WC regarding Oswald's Intrastate Unemployment Compensation case.

SOURCE: WCH XI, 473

BURKE, YVONNE BRATHWAITE, member HSCA (D-California).

SOURCES: HSCA XI, 79, 143, 263

BURKLEY, GEORGE G., Parkland witness; Bethesda witness; admiral, U.S. Navy; JFK's personal physician. Burkley rode at the tail end of the Dallas motorcade. Burkley was the only physician present at both Parkland and Bethesda. He was never asked to sort out the dicrepancies between descriptions of JFK's wounds at those two locations. Autopsy witnesses say that Burkley was at least partially responsible for the procedure's incompleteness, since he constantly interrupted and ordered that certain standard procedures not be performed because "the Kennedy family would not approve." Burkley's death certificate for JFK (first made public in 1975) says simply that JFK was "struck in the head." He also says that JFK was shot "in the posterior back at about the level of the third thoracic vertebra." This places the back wound well below where the WC insisted it had to be to preserve the "magic bullet" theory. There is evidence that a bullet was removed from JFK's body at the autopsy, that Burkley turned this bullet over to the FBI and that he received a receipt for it. The Treasury Department still has the receipt; the bullet hasn't been seen since. (See also Keeton, Stanley)

SOURCES: WR 60, 66, 68 • HT 87, 98, 110–1, 235 • BE, many • BISHOP, many • DOP, many • ME 10

BURLESON, PHIL, Ruby witness. Burleson was a member of Ruby's defense team during his murder trial.

SOURCE: GERTZ, many

BURLEY, WILLIAM B., III. Burley was one of four men responsible for the writing and placing of the full-page, black-bordered anti-JFK advertisement that ran in the *Dallas Morning News* on the day of the assassination. Two of the other men involved, Bernard W. Weissman and Larrie H. Schmidt, had served with Burley in Munich, Germany, in the U.S. Army in 1962. The fourth man was Joseph P. Grinnan. (See also Grinnan, Joseph P.; Schmidt, Larrie; Weissman, Bernard W.)

SOURCES: WR 273, 275 • FMG I, 122, 132, 136, 139–43, 146

BURNS, DORIS, a.w.; TSBD employee. Burns was on the third floor. She heard one shot and says it sounded as if it came from the west. She looked out the window, but didn't see anything of interest. Once worked for a geologist.

SOURCE: WCH VI, 397

BURROUGHS, WARREN "BUTCH," Texas Theatre witness; theater employee. Burroughs recalled seeing Oswald's hands being brought up high and tight against his spine as he was led from the theater.

SOURCES: WCH VII, 14 • BISHOP 211–2, 215

BURT, JIM, t.k.w.; soldier on leave. Burt was standing in front of his house at the corner of Denver and Tenth, about a block east of the scene of the Tippit killing, talking to a friend, when he noticed a man walking west on Tenth Street. Moments later, he saw the same man talking with Officer Tippit, then heard gunfire and saw the man run away. This statement is important because, officially, the assailant was walking east on Tenth Street (or, generally, from the direction of Oswald's rooming house) when he encountered Tippit. Burt's observations are corroberated by those of cabdriver William Scoggins, who also says the gunman was walking west. (See also Scoggins, William)

SOURCE: SUMMERS 94

BUSH, GEORGE HERBERT WALKER, possible CIA agent; later CIA director; former vice president and 41st president of the United States. While CIA director, Bush wrote on November 17, 1976, that a reported FBI memo stating that Oswald had been in touch with Cuba just before the assassination did not exist. Bush admitted that the CIA had been guilty in the past of "abuses of power" but said that there was no evidence the agency was involved in the JFK assassination or its cover-up. He then reaffirmed his belief that an intelligence-gathering agency working in other countries was necessary.

Bush claims to have had no association with the CIA before he was named director in 1976. There is evidence this is not true. According to the *Nation* (July 1988), there is an FBI memo—acquired through the Freedom of Information Act—dated November 29, 1963, from J. Edgar Hoover, stating that "George Bush of the CIA" would be assessing reaction to the assassination by the Cuban-exile community.

Although there is no evidence that Bush was involved in the Bay of Pigs operation, there is a series of thought-provoking coincidences. According to Fletcher Prouty, who was the CIA/Pentagon liaison during the Bay of Pigs attack and in charge of ordering supplies for the invasion, "The CIA had code-named the invasion 'Zapata.' Two boats landed on the shores of Cuba. One was named Houston, the other Barbara. They were Navy ships that had been repainted with new names. I have no idea where the new names came from." At the time of the Bay of Pigs invasion, George Bush lived in Houston, had a wife named Barbara, and owned a company named Zapata.

In a memo dated September 15, 1976, from CIA Director Bush to his deputy director of central intelligence, Bush stated: "A recent Jack Anderson story referred to a November 1963 CIA cable, the subject matter of which had some U.K. journalist observing Jack Ruby visiting [Santos] Trafficante in jail [in Cuba]. Is there such a memo? If so, I would like to see it."

In 1992, while visiting Australia, President Bush was asked by NBC News correspondent John Cochran whether he had ever gone back and read the CIA's findings regarding the assassination to satisfy his curiosity.

"No," Bush said, apparently forgetting about the memo he had written in 1976. "I didn't have any curiosity because I believed the Warren Commission...I saw no reason to question it. Still see no reason to question it." (See also Rather, Dan)

SOURCES: HT 355 • COA 453 • PD 329–33

BUTLER, CLAYTON, t.k.w. (aftermath); Dallas ambulance driver.

Butler drove the ambulance that picked up the body of Officer J. D. Tippit.
SOURCE: RTJ 194

BUTLER, EDWARD, Oswald witness; executive director of the Information Council of the Americas. Butler appeared on the New Orleans WDSU radio debate arranged by William Stuckey and broadcast on August 21, 1963, between Oswald and anti-Castro Cuban Carlos Bringuier. (See also Bringuier, Carlos; Stuckey, William)
SOURCES: WR 385 • SUMMERS 273, 279

BUTLER, GEORGE, o.k.w.; DPD lieutenant; former head of the Dallas Policeman's Union; associate of Dallas oil billionaire H. L. Hunt; member of the Ku Klux Klan. Butler once told author Penn Jones Jr. that one-half of the DPD members were also members of the KKK. Butler was in immediate charge of Oswald's aborted transfer. He gave the "all-clear" sign in spite of the fact that the car assigned to pick up Oswald had not yet completely backed into position. He was not called as a WC witness.

According to the WC testimony of o.k.w. Thayer Waldo of the *Fort Worth Star Telegram*, throughout most of the assassination weekend Butler seemed to be a man of extraordinary poise who was constantly in on inside information and was willing to share it with the press. Butler's poise, however, deserted him on the morning of November 24, when the transfer of Oswald became imminent. Waldo testified that Butler "was an extremely nervous man, so nervous that when I was standing asking him a question after I had entered the ramp and gotten down to the basement area, just moments before Oswald was brought down, he was standing profile to me and I noticed his lips trembling as he listened and waited for my answer. It was simply a physical characteristic. I had by then spent enough time talking to this man so that it struck me as something totally out of character."
SOURCES: WCH XV, 585 • WCE 1184, 1265, 1709, 2002, 2249, 2416, 2887 • HT 188 • COA 453 • BISHOP 481 • FMG I, 91, 160–1, 165–7, 169; III, 7 • BLAKEY 286 • EVICA 170–1 • KANTOR 66–7, 104–6, 149, 216

C

CABELL, CHARLES P., brother of Earle, mayor of Dallas (see below); former Air Force general; former deputy director of the CIA (fired by JFK after the Bay of Pigs disaster). After his dismissal, Cabell worked for Howard Hughes. According to HT, Cabell was involved with Robert Maheu in plots to kill Castro. (See also Barker, Bernard; Bissell, Richard; Cabell, Earle; Edwards, Sheffield; Hughes, Howard; Hunt, E. Howard; Maheu, Robert; Marchetti, Victor)

SOURCES: HT 154, 292, 305–6, 311, 313–5, 425, 434 • FMG III, 87 • OTT 103–4, 176, 178, 182, 273, 327 • EVICA 134, 209–10, 245, 247 • OGLESBY 6–7 • DAVIS 98, 369 • NORTH 121 • PD 95, 98

CABELL, EARLE, brother of Charles (see above); mayor of Dallas. According to UPI correspondent H. D. Quigg, Cabell was under police protection in the days following the assassination because of death threats. (See also Cabell, Charles; Curry, Jesse)

SOURCES: WR 55, 77 • WCH VII, 476 • *Four Days*, 39 • GERTZ 34 • BISHOP 103–4, 153, 239, 254–5, 407, 422–3, 465 • DOP 45, 180, 287, 299–300, 331, 569, 637 • FMG III, 87 • OTT 102–3, 176, 273 • ME 77, 102, 111, 220 • KANTOR 73 • HT 154, 161, 285, 305

CABELL, ELIZABETH "DEARIE," a.w.; wife of the Dallas mayor. Mrs. Cabell presented Jackie Kennedy with the bouquet of red roses at Love Field that Mrs. Kennedy held right up until the shooting. (All the other ladies in the motorcade were given the traditional Texas yellow roses.) She was in a car, still on Houston Street, at the time of the shooting, and says that she jerked her head toward the TSBD with the sound and saw something sticking out of one of the windows. (See also Roberts, Ray)

SOURCES: WR 77–8 • WCH VII, 485 • BISHOP 137, 208 • DOP 45, 111, 130, 290, 328–9 • CF 16 • SUMMERS 29 • ME 77

CADIGAN, JAMES, FBI questioned-document expert; WC witness.

Cadigan didn't get a chance to testify for the HSCA. He died in August 1977 after an accident in which he fell in his home.
SOURCES: WR 128, 162, 171 • WCH IV, 89; VII, 418 • RTJ 143

CAIN, RICHARD, assassination suspect; murder victim; trusted lieutenant of Chicago crime boss Sam Giancana. According to Charles and Sam Giancana (the late crime boss's half-brother and nephew) in their book *Double Cross,* Cain was part of an assassination team sent to Dallas by Giancana, and it was Cain who fired the fatal shot from the sixth floor window of the TSBD. Cain was murdered in 1973, "gangland style." Author G. Robert Blakey calls this accusation "absurd," adding, "Cain's eyesight was so poor he had trouble driving an automobile."
SOURCE: FATAL xlii

CALL, RICHARD DENNIS, Oswald witness; USMC acquaintance. Call lived in the ensign hut next to, and was on the same radar crew as Oswald with MACS-9 from December 1958 to December 1959. He told the WC:

> I estimate that I talked with Oswald each day during the period we were stationed together... It was very difficult to evaluate Oswald's personality because he never talked about his life prior to joining the Marine Corps... [B]y usual standards I was just an acquaintance. I was probably one of his best friends... I played chess with him about once a week... [He] was studying Russian... [We] kidded him about being a Russian spy; Oswald seemed to enjoy this sort of remark... I had a phonograph record of Russian classical pieces entitled "Russian Fireworks." When I would play this record Oswald would come over to me and say, "You called?" I had a chess set which contained red and white chessmen; Oswald always chose the red chessmen... he preferred the "Red Army."... It was my opinion that the Staff Non-Commissioned Officers did not think Oswald was capable... a result of the fact that Oswald did not try to hide his lack of enthusiasm... it is difficult to tell how intelligent Oswald was, because of his refusal to communicate. It was clear, however, that Oswald wanted to be thought of as intelligent... Oswald's reactions to everything were subdued and stoic... I do not recall Oswald's making serious remarks with regard to the Soviet Union or Cuba.

(See also Botelho, James)
SOURCES: WCH VIII, 322 • AO 95 • OTT 46

CALLAWAY, TED, t.k.w. Callaway reported murder to DPD over Tippit's car radio and helped put Officer Tippit's body in the ambulance. He saw a man fleeing the scene with a gun in his hand; later that day he identified Oswald as the man. Callaway said that he did not see Helen Markham (the WC's star witness to the Tippit killing) at the scene immediately following the murder. (See also Hulse, Clifford; Searcy, B.D.)

SOURCES: WR 26, 158–9, 161, 164 • WCH III, 351 • WCE 2003 • BELIN 19–21, 28, 31–2 • RTJ 192, 201 • BISHOP 200, 353, 355–6 • CF 341

CALVERY, GLORIA, a.w.; TSBD employee. Calvery stood next to a.w. John Chism and Karen Westbrook near the "Stemmons Freeway" sign on the north side of Elm Street. She was not questioned by the WC about the direction of the shots.

SOURCES: WR 144 • CF 28, 46 • SSID 61–3 • NORTH 380

CAMARATA, DONALD PETER, Oswald witness; USMC acquaintance. Camarata told the WC, "I have no recollection of any remarks on [Oswald's] part concerning Communism, Russia, or Cuba."

SOURCES: WCH VIII, 316 • OTT 46

CAMPBELL, ALLEN and DANIEL, Oswald witnesses; brothers; former marines recruited by New Orleans private investigator and Oswald associate Guy Banister during the summer of 1963 to help identify pro-Castro sympathizers among New Orleans college students. Daniel told author Anthony Summers in 1979 that Oswald came into the Guy Banister Associates offices on the day he was arrested and used Daniel's desk phone to make a call. Allen told the New Orleans District Attorney's office in 1969 that Banister usually had a temper tantrum when notified of Communist activity, but when he was told about Oswald's pro-Castro demonstration, he just laughed. (See also Banister, William Guy)

SOURCE: SUMMERS 293, 297

CAMPBELL, DON J., Ruby witness; advertising employee of the *Dallas Morning News.* Campbell was the last man to see Ruby before the assassination (12:20 P.M.). Ruby was in the *News* building, a short distance from Dealey Plaza. Ruby was not seen again in the *News* building until 12:40. Ruby claimed he was in the building during the shooting, but several witnesses said they saw him in Dealey Plaza immediately following the shooting.

SOURCES: RTJ 261–2 • GERTZ 43, 526 • BISHOP 118 • BLAKEY 313, 315

CAMPBELL, GARY, a.w.; Campbell, a junior high school student skipping school to watch the motorcade, was standing near the corner of Main and Houston. Campbell claims he recognized one of the shots as having come from a 30.06 rifle. During the shooting sequence, Campbell claims, he looked up and saw a man with a rifle run behind the west side of

the pergola. (See also Hill, Jean; Moorman, Mary)
SOURCES: FMG IV, 95 • SHAW 155

CAMPBELL, JUDITH (See EXNER, JUDITH)

CAMPBELL, OCHUS V., a.w.; TSBD vice-president. Campbell, who was standing in front of the TSBD, said, "I heard shots being fired from a point which I thought was near the railroad tracks..."
SOURCES: WR 144, 312 • RTJ 41, 111 • BISHOP 121, 127, 176 • CF 27 • PWW 211 • OTT 16–7 • NORTH 338

CAMPISI, JOSEPH, Ruby witness; owner of the restaurant where Ruby and his business partner Ralph Paul ate on the night of November 21, 1963. Campisi, who reportedly had organized crime connections, later visited Ruby in jail. (See also Aase, Jean; Meyers, Lawrence)
SOURCES: WCE 2259, 2274, 3039 • HSCA Report 171 • COA, many • SUMMERS 451–2 • BLAKEY 291, 299, 313–4, 335 • DAVIS 155–8, 181, 194–5, 228, 299, 331, 449–51, 586 • NORTH, many

CAMPLEN, CHARLES, possible Oswald witness. Camplen was among those who say they saw a rude man who resembled Oswald firing a rifle at the Sports Drome Rifle Range in Dallas in the weeks preceding the assassination.
SOURCE: RTJ 334

CANADA, CAPTAIN ROBERT O., Bethesda witness; commanding officer of Bethesda Naval Hospital; purposefully misled the press so that JFK's body could be taken into the hospital in secret.
SOURCES: BE 298, 395, 418, 476, 491

CANFIELD, MICHAEL, coauthor, with A.J. Weberman, of *Coup d'Etat in America* (Third Press, 1975). Canfield maintains that assassination suspects E. Howard Hunt and Frank Sturgis were two of the three mysterious "tramps" detained after the assassination. Before writing the book, Canfield was the art director of George McGovern's presidential campaign, an editor of two tabloids in Wisconsin and Florida, and resident manager of a state drug rehabilitation center in Florida.
SOURCES: EVICA 147, 168, 198, 204–5, 216 • KANTOR 14 • PD 130–1, 187

CANNING, THOMAS N., HSCA ballistics trajectories expert; engineer, NASA, Space Project Division. Canning concluded in 1978 that all shots came from the TSBD.
SOURCES: ME 230, 241

CARLIN, BRUCE RAY, husband of "Little Lynn" (aka Carlin, Karen Bennett, see below), stripper at Ruby's Carousel Club.
SOURCES: WR 325, 334–5 • WCH XIII 201; XV, 641 • RTJ 251 • GERTZ 524–5 • FMG III, 102 • BLAKEY 38 • HOS 116–7

CARLIN, KAREN BENNETT (aka "Little Lynn"; Bennett, Karen; Norton, Teresa), Ruby witness; Carousel Club stripper; 20 years old. It was Carlin to whom Ruby was wiring money a scant three minutes before he shot Oswald. This split-second timing helped Ruby convince the WC that he murdered without malice. On November 24, 1963, SS agent Roger C. Warner interviewed Carlin. His written report reads in part: "Mrs. Carlin was highly agitated and was reluctant to make any statement to me. She stated to me that she was under the impression that Lee Harvey Oswald, Jack Ruby, and other individuals unknown to her, were involved in a plot to assassinate President Kennedy and that she would be killed if she gave any information to the authorities." Carlin reportedly died in August 1964 of a gunshot wound in Houston, Texas. She was using the name Teresa Norton at the time. Author Harrison Edward Livingstone believes that Carlin's death may have been staged and she may still be alive. (See also Reeves, Huey)

SOURCES: WR 314, 324–6, 330–1, 334, 336 • WCH XIII, 205; XIV, 656 • RTJ 251 • COA 137–8 • GERTZ 14–17, 50, 113–4, 455, 525 • DOP 521, 523 • FMG I, 23, 174 • BLAKEY 37–8, 320, 329 • KANTOR 59, 64–5, 68, 189 • HT2 84–6 • NORTH 361, 490

CARLSON, ALEX E. According to author James Hepburn in *Farewell America:*

> [Carlson], a Spanish-speaking lawyer from Miami Springs who fought in the Philippines and Okinawa, is President of the Double-Chek Corporation, a Brokerage firm that serves as a CIA cover for the recruitment of pilots employed in Central America and the Caribbean...FBI agents Regis Kennedy and Warren de Brueys knew David Ferrie well. De Brueys was based in New Orleans, where he was involved in the CIA's anti-Castro activities. After the assassination, the FBI interrogated David Ferrie and Gordon Novel. Novel was a buddy of Ferrie's who had been working with the CIA since 1959. He worked through the Double-Chek Corporation and the Evergreen Advertising Agency and he had carried out several missions in the Caribbean, was involved with arms purchases, and knew both Ruby and Oswald. The FBI questioned him on five separate occasions, but Novel didn't scare easily, and he didn't talk...In 1969 New Orleans District Attorney Jim Garrison subpoenaed Novel, but Novel left Louisiana for Ohio, and Garrison never succeeded in obtaining his extradiction [sic].

Jay Pound writes in *Critique* (Spring/Summer 1986): "Carlson was the

Miami Springs manager for the CIA's Double-Chek operation. He turned the entire organization [over] to Division 5 of the FBI to work for Permindex in executing the assassination, thus causing many researchers to believe that the CIA carried out the assassination." (See also deBrueys, Warren; Ferrie, David; Kennedy, Regis; Novel, Gordon; Torbitt, William

CARNES, WILLIAM H., pathology expert; member of 1968 Justice Department pathology panel. Dr. Carnes was allowed access to JFK's autopsy photos and X rays. Panel concluded JFK was shot exclusively from the rear. (See also Fisher, Russell)

SOURCE: ME 63–4

CARR, RICHARD RANDOLPH, a.w. Carr watched from a perch on a girder on the new Courts Building at the northeast corner of Main and Houston Streets, then under construction. He saw a heavyset man wearing a hat, a tan sportscoat and horn-rimmed glasses on the sixth floor of the TSBD before the shooting. After climbing down from his perch, Carr saw the man in the tan sportscoat and two other men hurrying away from the scene on Commerce Street. Carr told the FBI, "This man, walking very fast, proceeded on Houston Street south to Commerce Street to Record Street, which is one block from Houston Street. The man got into a 1961 or 1962 gray Rambler station wagon which was parked just north of Commerce Street on Record Street. The station wagon, which had Texas license plates and was driven by a young Negro man, drove off in a northerly direction." Carr's claims corroborate those of Roger Craig, Carolyn Walther, and James R. Worrell.

Authorities did not want to hear his story. The FBI told Carr, "If you didn't see Lee Harvey Oswald in the School Book Depository with a rifle, you didn't see it." Later twelve Dallas policemen and detectives raided his home in the middle of the night. They took away his sons and held one of them overnight, claiming they had found stolen goods. Carr received threatening phone calls, telling him to leave Texas. Carr moved to Montana. In Montana, he once found dynamite taped to his car ignition. He was about to testify in the New Orleans trial of Clay Shaw when someone took a shot at him. Carr captured the gunman with the help of a policeman neighbor.

Carr went through with his testimony in New Orleans, by this time confined to a wheelchair because of a construction accident, and was later attacked again by two men in Atlanta. This time he was stabbed but managed to kill one of his attackers by shooting him three times. After

being shot, the assailant said, "Doodle Bug, he has killed me." In 1975, as the HSCA was gearing up, Carr again began to get threatening calls. (See also Craig, Roger; Robinson, Marvin; Walther, Carolyn; Worrell, James)
SOURCES: CF 21, 318–9 • FMG III, 64, 86, 88 • OTT 95–6, 238–9, 281 • HOS 43, 177–80 • ME 23

CARR, WAGGONER, Texas attorney general. Carr reported to the WC that Oswald had been a hired undercover agent for the FBI, had been assigned number 179 and had received $200 a month from September 1962 right up until his death. J. Edgar Hoover denied it and the WC chose to believe him.

Carr told the WC that, at 8:00 or 9:00 P.M., November 22, 1963, he received a phone call from somebody at the White House. ("I can't for the life of me remember who it was," Carr testified.) The caller asked Carr whether he had heard a rumor that Oswald's indictment for JFK's murder was to include an allegation that Oswald had acted as part of an "international conspiracy." Carr testified:

> the concern of the caller was that because of the emotion or the high tension that existed at that time that someone might thoughtlessly place in the indictment such an allegation without having the proof of such a conspiracy... There was no talk or indirect talk or insinuation that the facts, whatever they might be, should be suppressed. It was simply that in the tension someone might put something in an indictment for an advantage here or a disadvantage there, that could not be proved, which would have a very serious reaction, which the local person might not anticipate since he might not have the entire picture of what the reaction might be.

(See also Hoover, J. Edgar)
SOURCES: WCH V, 258 • RTJ 367, 369 • COA 225 • GERTZ 499–500 • BISHOP 84, 404–5, 475 • DOP 70, 85, 299, 319, 568 • OTT 224–5 • FLAMMONDE 158–9, 285 • FMG I, 38, 43, 47–8, 52–3, 60–2, 73 • BLAKEY 23, 26 • HOS 135, 204 • KANTOR 4, 78–9, 90, 162–3, 203

CARRICO, CHARLES JAMES (also listed in some sources as James Carrico), Parkland witness; first physician to attend JFK. Carrico signed a hospital report on the afternoon of November 22 stating that the wound in JFK's throat was one of entrance. Like the other Parkland doctors, Carrico saw a large gaping wound in the back of JFK's head, a wound which does not appear on the official autopsy photographs. Although Carrico says he did a "brief manual examination" of JFK's back, he found no sign of a wound there. No one at Parkland saw JFK's back wound.

SOURCES: WR 66–9, 91–2 • WCH III, 357; VI, 1 • RTJ 47, 54 • BISHOP 149, 156, 176, 286, 386 • DOP 183, 222 • BE, many • HOS 182 • ME 31, 34

CARRO, JOHN, Oswald witness; probation officer, New York City, 1952–54. During this time, Oswald—while living in the Bronx—was taken to Youth House for truancy problems. According to the WR, "Carro reported that Lee was disruptive in class after he returned to school on a regular basis in the fall of 1953. He had refused to salute the flag and was doing very little, if any, work..." Carro reported that when questioned about his mother, Lee said, "Well, I've got to live with her. I guess I love her."

SOURCES: WR 357–8 • WCH VIII, 202

CARROLL, BOB K., Texas Theatre witness; DPD officer. Carroll drove the car that carried Oswald from the theater to the DPD station. Sgt. Gerald Hill told the WC that Carroll got into the car with the handgun reportedly taken from Oswald. Carroll handed the gun to Hill, who held the gun until they got to the police station.

SOURCES: WR 166 • WCH VII, 17 • BISHOP 215–6

CARSON, VINCE (see VAGANOV, IGOR)

CARSWELL, ROBERT, special assistant to the secretary of the treasury. Carswell told the WC that, following JFK's death, SS protection was offered to Speaker of the House McCormack, who refused it.

SOURCE: WCH IV, 299; V, 486

CARTER, B. THOMAS, Oswald witness; FBI agent. With John W. Fain, Carter interviewed Oswald on June 26, 1962, in the Fort Worth FBI office. The interview dealt with Oswald's experiences while in the Soviet Union. Oswald denied any dealings with the KGB and refused to take a polygraph test. (See also Fain, John W.)

SOURCES: WR 410 • DUFFY 188

CARTER, CLIFTON C., a.w.; LBJ aide. Carter rode in the motorcade, in the middle of the front seat of the SS's vice-presidential follow-up car, three cars behind JFK's limo.

SOURCES: WR 59, 65, 70 • WCH VII, 474 • BISHOP, many • DOP, many • FMG III, 3, 17–8, 83

CARTER, JOHN, Oswald witness; possible preassassination link between Oswald and Ruby. Carter was a boarder at 1026 North Beckley in Oak Cliff (where Oswald lived), was friends with longtime friend and ex-employee of Ruby, Wanda Joyce Killam, and worked with Wanda's husband Hank as a house painter. (See also Killam, Hank)

SOURCES: WR 338–9 • HSCA Report 148 • COA 33 • FMG I, 7–8

CASON, FRANCES, DPD telephone clerk. Cason called the ambulance after Oswald was shot.
SOURCE: WCH XIII, 89

CASON, JACK CHARLES, president, TSBD. Cason submitted an affidavit to the WC that described the TSBD and its history.
SOURCE: WCH VII, 379

CASTILLO, LUIS ANGEL, possible a.w.; reportedly stated under hypnosis that "he was on the parade route with a rifle that day...[with] instructions to shoot at a man in a car with red roses." Mrs. Kennedy was the only person in the parade with red roses. All of the other women were given yellow roses.
SOURCE: FMG III, 94

CASTRO, FIDEL, Cuban premier. Castro once said that, if CIA attempts on his life did not cease, U.S. leaders should expect payback in kind. Some Cuban nationalists, as well as CIA agents, who attempted to overthrow Castro's government—both through assassination attempts and the botched Bay of Pigs invasion—are suspects in the JFK assassination. They blamed Kennedy for the failure at the Bay of Pigs and may have turned on JFK because they felt betrayed. (See also Giancana, Momo; Lorenz, Marita; Morgan, Edward)
SOURCES: WR, many • HSCA Report 25, 30, 103, 122–3, 126, 152 • ME 21, 62, 90, 128, 131–2, 183 • OGLESBY 6–7, 23, 78–9 • BELIN 10, 13, 50, 61, 93, 95, 99, 103–34, 163, 174–5 • RTJ 131, 290–1, 298–301, 303, 324, 336–7, 339 • COA, many • GERTZ 473, 529 • BISHOP 12, 416, 452, 522 • DOP 141, 208, 249, 353, 447 • CF 138–54 • OTT 77, 153–4, 285–6, 292, 327–8 • SUMMERS, many • BE 31 • FMG I, 42; III, 40 • FLAMMONDE, many • BLAKEY, many • EVICA, many • KANTOR, many • DAVIS, many • NORTH 54, 86, 92, 640 • PD, many

CAVAGNARO, JOSEPH R., Ruby witness and close friend; manager of the Sheraton Dallas Hotel. Cavagnaro told FBI agents that Ruby "knew all of the policemen in town." The WC claimed Ruby knew only 30 to 50 of the 1,200 Dallas policemen.
SOURCES: RTJ 232–3, 235 • COA 111 • GERTZ 31

CERAVOLO, MARIO, Christian Democrat and charter member of the CMC's board of directors, upon which he served with assassination suspect Clay Shaw. Because of its close association with Permindex, the CMC is suspected of involvement in the JFK assassination. Ceravolo, apparently an honest man, resigned from the board in 1962, when he tried and failed to determine exactly what business CMC engaged in. (See also Bloomfield, Louis; Shaw, Clay; Torbitt, William

CHAMPAGNE, DONALD E., member, HSCA ballistics panel; member, Florida Department of Law Enforcement. The panel determined that JFK was shot twice, both times from above and to the rear.
SOURCE: ME 229

CHANEY, JAMES M., a.w.; DPD motorcycle patrolman. Chaney rode to the side and just behind the presidential limo. The first shot, he said, came from over his right shoulder—i.e., from the direction of the TSBD. Describing the fatal shot, Chaney said JFK was "struck in the face." On November 23, 1963, Chaney told reporters that the first shot had missed.
SOURCES: GERTZ 110 • DOP 155 • CF 14 • SUMMERS 23

CHARLES, PEDRO, possible non-person. After Oswald's death, Oswald received two pieces of mail from Havana, each stating that a man named Pedro Charles had paid Oswald $7,000 for an unnamed killing. The WC considered the letters a hoax.
SOURCE: HT 192

CHEEK, BERTHA, Ruby witness and acquaintance; sister of Oswald's housekeeper, Earlene Roberts. Cheek had once considered investing in Ruby's Carousel Club and had visited the club on November 18, 1963, four days before the assassination. She was also the former landlady of Officer Harry N. Olsen, the only member of the DPD on record who doesn't remember precisely where he was at the time of the assassination (although his best guess places him in close proximity to the scene of the Tippit killing). She probably met Ruby through Olsen, who later married one of Ruby's strippers. In 1968, Cheek purchased a hotel in Dallas for more than $900,000. (See also Boerder, Frank; Olsen, Harry N.; Roberts, Earlene)
SOURCES: WR 339 • WCH XIII, 382 • HSCA Report 148 • FMG I, 79, 85, 89, 91–8, 144; III, 79 • SUMMERS 457 • EVICA 112

CHEEK, TIMOTHY, Bethesda witness; USMC lance corporal. With six others, Cheek attended JFK's body from the time it arrived at Andrews Air Force Base until it was buried. He served as a security guard at Bethesda during the autopsy.
SOURCES: BE 398 • *Dallas Morning News*, November 26, 1963, p. 15

CHERAMIE, ROSE (aka Marcades, Melba Christine), possible Oswald witness; Ruby witness; suspicious death; prostitute and drug addict who once worked for Ruby. On November 20, 1963, Cheramie was found battered and bruised lying next to a road near Eunice, Louisiana, and was taken to Louisiana State Hospital (near Jackson, Louisiana), where she hysterically tried to convince doctors that JFK was to be killed. According to Dr. Victor Weiss, in a deposition for the HSCA, Cheramie said "the word in the underworld" was that JFK would be hit. She claimed that it had been two of Ruby's employees—Latin men—who had dumped her on the road. She also said that Oswald and Ruby had been "bedmates." On September 4, 1965, Cheramie was reportedly struck and killed by a car near Big Sandy, Texas. The driver said that Cheramie was lying in the road and, although he tried, he couldn't avoid running over her head. Although her death certificate reads "DOA," official hospital records indicate she was operated on for eight hours after she arrived. Those records say she had a "deep punctate stellate" wound to her right forehead, which could indicate a gunshot wound at point-blank range.

SOURCES: HSCA X, 199 • COA 34, 156 • CF 401–2 • SUMMERS 591–2 • FLAMMONDE 167 • OGLESBY 72 • DAVIS 194, 254, 571–2, 586, 606 • NORTH 192, 411

CHESHER, BILL, possible Oswald witness; possible Ruby witness; suspicious death. According to author Sylvia Meagher, Cheshire had information linking Oswald and Ruby. He died of a heart attack in March 1964. (See also Biggio, William)

SOURCE: HT 129, 135

CHETTA, NICHOLAS, suspicious death; New Orleans coroner during the Garrison investigation. Chetta supposedly performed autopsies on assassination suspect David Ferrie, Ferrie associate Dr. Mary Sherman, and Ruby connection Robert Perrin, all of whom died before they had a chance to testify for Garrison. He died soon thereafter of a heart attack, at 10:20 P.M., Saturday, May 25, 1968, before Garrison had finished his investigation. On January 26, 1969, Professor Henry Delaune, Chetta's brother-in-law, who worked in his coroner's office, was murdered. (See also DeLaune, Henry; Ferrie, David; Perrin, Robert; Sherman, Mary)

SOURCES: FMG III, 28, 57 • OTT 156, 163 • FLAMMONDE 34, 36, 55, 60, 84, 90–1, 289–91 • DAVIS 370–1

CHISM, JOHN ARTHUR and MARY, a.w. Standing with their three-year-old son directly in front of the "Stemmons Freeway" sign on the north side of Elm Street; the Chisms looked behind them in the direction of the grassy knoll to see whether they could see the shooter. Karen Westbrook stood next to Mr. Chism.

SOURCES: CF 29 • SUMMERS 27 • BE 17 • NORTH 379 • SSID 61–3

CHURCH, COLONEL and MRS. GEORGE B., JR., Oswald witnesses. The Churches were two of three passengers with Oswald on S.S. *Marion Lykes,* which started Oswald on his journey to the USSR, September/October 1959.

SOURCES: WCH XI, 115, 116 • DUFFY 30

CIRELLO, JOSEPH (See CIVELLO, JOSEPH)

CIVELLO, JOSEPH (aka Cirello, Joseph), Ruby witness; reputed Dallas crime boss. Civello was the reported liaison between his friend Ruby and his employer, New Orleans crime boss Carlos Marcello. According to author Anthony Summers, Civello was "widely acknowledged to have been Texas representitive for...[assassination suspect Carlos] Marcello." Civello was also reportedly friendly with Sergeant Patrick Dean of the DPD who was one of those responsible for security in the DPD basement when Ruby shot Oswald. Summers writes, "Civello had invited...Dean to dinner as far back as 1957, not long after Civello's arrest at the famous Apalachin meeting of organized crime figures." (See also Davis, John H.; Lee, Ivan)
  SOURCES: HSCA Report 171 • COA, many • SUMMERS 452, 467–8 • BLAKEY, many • EVICA 171, 182 • KANTOR 8–9 • DAVIS, many

CLAASEN, FRED, Texas businessman; suspicious death. Claasen was told via phone in 1975 by Mafia figure John Martino that Martino had been a CIA contact agent and had personal knowledge of the plot to kill JFK. According to Earl Golz of the *Dallas Morning News*, Claasen quotes Martino as saying, "The anti-Castro people put Oswald together. Oswald didn't know who he was working for—he was just ignorant of who was really putting him together. Oswald was to meet his contact at the Texas Theatre. They were to meet Oswald in the theater and get him out of the country, then eliminate him. Oswald made a mistake...There was no way we could get to him. They had Ruby kill him." Martino died soon thereafter and, according to his widow, the CIA or "the government" picked up the body. The cause of death was determined to be a heart attack.
  SOURCE: SUMMERS 427

CLARDY, BARNARD, Ruby witness; DPD detective. Clardy was one of the policemen who guarded Ruby immediately following the shooting of Oswald. He stated, as did his DPD colleagues, that Ruby said he entered the basement via the Main Street ramp. SS agent Forrest Sorrels, also present at the interrogation, remembered Ruby's saying no such thing.
  SOURCES: WCH XII, 403 • GERTZ 71, 76, 91–2 • SUMMERS 463

CLARK, COMER, British reporter; now deceased. Clark claimed to have interviewed Fidel Castro in July 1967. Clark claims Castro said:

Lee Oswald came to the Cuban Embassy in Mexico City twice. The first time, I was told, he wanted to work for us. He was asked to explain, but he wouldn't. He wouldn't go into details. The second time he said something like "Someone ought to shoot that President Kennedy." Then Oswald said—and this is exactly how it was presented to me—"Maybe I'll try to do it." This was less than two months before the U.S. President was assassinated... Yes, I heard of Lee Harvey Oswald's plan to kill President Kennedy. It's possible I could have saved him. I might have been able to—but I didn't. I never believed the plan would be put into effect... I thought the visits [by Oswald to the Cuban Embassy] might be something to do with the CIA... Then, too, after such a plot had been found out, we would be blamed—for something we had nothing to do with. It could have been an excuse for another invasion try... I think he was killed by U.S. fascists—right-wing elements who disagreed with him.

In 1978, Castro told members of the HSCA that he had never made the statements attributed to him by Clark. Castro's denial is supported by Clark's widow, who says that if her husband had ever interviewed Castro, he never mentioned it to her.

SOURCES: HSCA Report 122–3 • HSCA III, 283 • SUMMERS 363–5

CLARK, HUBERT, Bethesda witness; naval officer on duty at Bethesda at the time JFK's body arrived. Clark said that two ambulances arrived, one a decoy. With six others, he attended JFK's body from the time it arrived in Washington, D.C., until it was buried.

SOURCES: BE 398 • *Dallas Morning News*, November 26, 1963, p. 15 • SUMMERS 483

CLARK, MAX E., Oswald witness; Texas acquaintance of the Oswalds; retired Air Force colonel, attorney and former security officer for General Dynamics. Clark's wife Katya was born Princess Sherbatov, a member of the Russian royal family. The Clarks were once dinner guests at the Oswalds' apartment in Dallas, at which Marina prepared the meal.

SOURCES: WCH VIII, 343 • HSCA Report 217 • OTT 54

CLARK, RICHARD L., Oswald witness; member DPD. Clark participated in the police lineup at which Mrs. Helen Markham identified Oswald as the man who shot Tippit. Clark was #3 in the lineup, Oswald was #2.

SOURCES: WCH VII, 235 • BISHOP 290–1

CLARK, WILLIAM KEMP, Parkland witness; chief of neurosurgery. Clark officially pronounced JFK dead. Later he told the press that one bullet struck Kennedy at about the necktie knot. "It ranged downward in his chest and did not exit," he said. Kemp is reported to have said in the emergency room, "My God, the whole back of his head is shot off."

SOURCES: WR 66–8, 92 • WCH VI, 18 • RTJ 47, 53, 58–9 • BISHOP 156, 166, 176, 189, 219, 286, 386 • DOP 186, 188–9, 213, 227, 243, 293, 299–300, 303–4 • SUMMERS

480 • BE, many • BLAKEY 16 • OGLESBY 29, 39

CLAUDE, ALFRED, Oswald witness. Claude was one of four of Oswald's coworkers at the William Reily Coffee Company in New Orleans who started work around the same time as Oswald and left around the same time he did during the summer of 1963. All four went on to work for NASA. The other three were Dante Marachini, Emmett Barbee, and John Branyon.
SOURCES: OTT 116 • HOS 149

CLAUNCH, MAX, aide to Major General Edwin A. Walker. Claunch says that several days before someone took a shot at Walker (a crime of which Oswald has been accused), he saw a dark-skinned, possibly Cuban, man in a 1957 Chevy suspiciously circling the general's house.
SOURCES: SUMMERS 214

CLAY, BILLIE P., a.w. Mrs. Clay stood on north sidewalk of Elm Street in front of the pergola. She told author Josiah Thompson, "Just a few seconds after the car. . . passed the location where I was standing, I heard a shot."
SOURCES: SSID 61–3 • NORTH 379

CLEMENTS, MANNING C., Oswald witness; FBI agent. Clements interrogated Oswald during the evening of November 22, 1963. He described Oswald as "angry," particularly hostile toward FBI agents, for whom he refused to answer questions.
SOURCES: WR 207 • WCH VII, 318 • BISHOP 447, 462

CLEMONS, ACQUILLA, t.k.w. Clemons watched the shooting from her house on the north side of Tenth Street, four houses west of Patton Avenue. She told several independent investigators that she saw two men talking with Tippit just before he was shot. One of the men shot Tippit; then both men fled the scene in opposite directions. The gunman, she said, was "kind of a short guy and kind of heavy." The other man, she claimed, was tall and thin in khaki trousers and a white shirt. Clemons was warned by DPD members not to say what she saw because if she did, "she might get hurt." Clemons was not called as a WC witness. (See also Vaganov, Igor; White, Roscoe)
SOURCES: BELIN 31 • RTJ 176, 190, 193–4, 200, 274, 280–1, 384 • COA 36 • GERTZ 528 • CF 319, 342 • OTT 197–8 • SUMMERS 90–1 • HOS 41, 67–8

CLEWIS, WALTER C., Ruby witness; manager of the Municipal Auditorium in Mobile, Alabama; Ruby acquaintance for several years. Clewis told FBI that Ruby had said that he could not be prosecuted in Dallas because he "had enough information on the Dallas Police Department and judges" so that he could not be convicted. Ruby's criminal record (many arrests but no convictions) tends to bear out the truth of this statement.

SOURCES: RTJ 238 • FLAMMONDE 172

CLICK, DARRYL, probable nonperson; originally identified as the cabdriver who drove Oswald from the Greyhound Bus Station in downtown Dallas to the vicinity of his rooming house in the Oak Cliff section of Dallas following the assassination. According to the WR, Click does not exist but stems from a transcription error of Dallas District Attorney Henry Wade saying, "In Oak Cliff."

SOURCES: WR 218 • PD 345–6

CLIFTON, CHESTER V. "TED," a.w.; major general U.S. army, military aide to JFK. Clifton rode in the motorcade in a station wagon with Godfrey McHugh. He was still on Main Street at the time of the shooting. He said to McHugh, "That's crazy, firing a salute here." Author William Manchester describes Clifton as a "realist" who adjusted quickly to the change in power that occurred in Dallas.

SOURCES: DOP, many • BE 681, 684, 686–7

CLINTON, SAM HOUSTON, JR., Ruby witness; Texas counsel for the ACLU. Clinton joined Jack Ruby's defense team following his murder conviction.

SOURCES: GERTZ, many • FLAMMONDE 177

CODY, JOSEPH, Ruby witness; DPD homicide detective; reported directly to Captain Will Fritz; assigned to the CIC during the Korean War. Cody says he knew Ruby for 13 years. He ran into Ruby repeatedly at the Fair Park Skating Rink, as they shared an interest in skating. Cody had a pilot's license and was not in Dallas on November 24 because "while flying low, had hit a high wire with the wing of the plane and had been forced down on Lake Bisteneau near Shreveport, Louisiana." Author Seth Kantor called Cody one of Ruby's "special pals."

SOURCES: WCE 1736 • KANTOR 148

CODY, JULIE ANN (See RICH, NANCY PERRIN)

COFFEY, MELVIN, friend of assassination suspect David Ferrie who accompanied Ferrie and Alvin Beaubouef on November 22, 1963, on a road trip from New Orleans to Texas. The trip, if it took place when they said it did, must have occurred during a violent thunder and lightning storm. The trip was said to have been a combination ice-skating and duck-hunting expedition, yet the men brought neither skates nor weapons. Ferrie later admitted while drunk that he had gone to Texas to serve as the getaway pilot for JFK's assassins, but the gunmen had not shown up. Coffey later went on

to work for the Aerospace Operation at Cape Canaveral. (See also Beauboeuf, Alvin; Ferrie, David)
  SOURCES: OTT 116 • FLAMMONDE 15, 28 • HOS 152

COHEN, MICKEY, Los Angeles organized crime leader. Among Cohen's rackets was sexually compromising famous movie actresses using his "stable of Italian studs," then blackmailing the actresses or selling the black-market films of their activities. According to author John H. Davis, "It was this activity that unexpectedly resulted in the killing of Lana Turner's Cohen-planted lover, Johnny Stompanato, by Miss Turner's teenage daughter one night in the actress's bedroom." Cohen reportedly gave "substantial support" to Richard M. Nixon's campaign for the House of Representatives in 1946. Cohen was among the mobsters "having trouble with RFK." Records show that, during the weeks before the assassination, Ruby repeatedly called the number of Cohen's girlfriend, Juanita Sahakian (Candy Barr). (See also Belli, Melvin; Sahakian, Juanita)
  SOURCES: COA 62, 100, 120, 154, 256, 293, 296, 303 • SUMMERS 448 • BLAKEY, many • EVICA 260, 264 • KANTOR 21–2, 116 • DAVIS 71, 182–3, 262, 385–8, 392–8, 421

COLBY, WILLIAM E., future director of the CIA. As late as 1976, Colby insisted that the CIA had no contact with Oswald after his return from the USSR.
  SOURCES: SUMMERS 189–90, 354, 359 • EVICA 131–2 • PD 75, 78, 85–6, 110, 374

COLE, ALWYN, Treasury Department; expert on questioned documents/handwriting. Cole told the WC that the handwriting on the coupon ordering the Mannlicher-Carcano rifle, reportedly the assassination weapon, was Oswald's. He also "testified that the false identification found on Oswald upon his arrest could have been produced by employing elementary techniques used in a photographic printing plant...to perform the necessary procedures would have been difficult without the use of expensive photographic equipment... Cole testified that the cards in Oswald's wallet did not exhibit a great deal of skill, pointing out various errors that had been committed." Oswald had access to expensive photographic equipment when he worked at Chiles-Jaggers-Stovall in Dallas (October 12, 1962–April 6, 1963).
  SOURCES: WR 162, 290 • WCH IV, 358; XV, 703

COLEMAN, KAY HELEN (See OLSEN, KAY HELEN)

COLEMAN, WALTER KIRK, witness to the aftermath of the assassination attempt on Major General Edwin A. Walker on the evening of April 10, 1963. Walker says he narrowly escaped death when a bullet was fired into

his home. WC claimed the shot was fired by Oswald. Coleman saw two men in separate cars drive from the scene immediately following the shooting and that "neither man looked like Oswald."
SOURCES: RTJ 384 • SUMMERS 213–4 • OGLESBY 59 • NORTH 253, 469, 475

COLEMAN, WILLIAM T., JR., WC counsel; Philadelphia attorney. Coleman investigated every aspect of possible foreign conspiracy regarding JFK's death. Officially he found none. However, when he developed information supporting Sylvia Odio's claim that she had been paid a visit by a "Leon Oswald" when "Lee Harvey Oswald" was supposed to be in Mexico, WC General Counsel J. Lee Rankin became angry, saying, "At this stage we are supposed to be closing doors, not opening them." (See also Walker, Edwin A.)
SOURCES: HSCA Report 130, 134 • BELIN 47 • FLAMMONDE 151–2 • BLAKEY 78, 115–6, 131, 161, 363–4

COLEY, JERRY, a.w. (aftermath); Ruby witness; *Dallas Morning News* employee (advertising department). According to UTM, he was with fellow DMN workers "soon" after the assassination in Dealey Plaza when he saw a mysterious pool of blood on a sidewalk near the pergola; later he was told by the FBI that, as far as the pool of blood was concerned, "it never happened, you didn't see it." Knew Ruby. Still alive. (See also Couch, Malcolm; Hood, Jim; Mulkey, Charles)

COLLINS, CORRIE, Oswald witness; local chairman of the Clinton, Louisiana, Congress of Racial Equality. Collins organized a registration drive for black voters at the beginning of September 1963. Only one white person showed up to register: Oswald, who arrived at the drive in a black Cadillac. Its the other occupants were identified by eyewitnesses as assassination suspects David Ferrie and Clay Shaw. (See also Ferrie, David; Shaw, Clay)
SOURCE: SUMMERS 305

COLSON, CHARLES. According to HT, Colson was known in Washington as the "assassin-master." Colson was assassination suspect E. Howard Hunt's boss during the Watergate era and was an aide to Richard M. Nixon with possible mob ties. Within hours of the attempted assassination of George Wallace by Arthur Bremer, Colson ordered Hunt to break into Bremer's apartment. The orders were canceled after Hunt objected. After the Watergate scandal, Colson became a born-again Christian. (See also Hunt, E. Howard; Nixon, Richard M.)
SOURCES: HT 293, 327–8, 384, 418 • COA 301–3, 448 • EVICA 235 • DAVIS 409, 411 • PD 50, 188, 202, 204, 206, 258, 260, 263

COMBEST, B. H. "BILLY," o.k.w.; DPD detective who shouted, "Jack, you son-of-a-bitch, don't!" Combest was standing on the Commerce Street side of the passageway from the jail-office door at the time of the shooting, facing Ruby's position, which was on the Main Street side. He told the WC:

Almost the whole line of people pushed forward when Oswald started to leave the jail office, the door, the hall—all the newsmen were poking their sound mikes across to him and asking questions, and they were everyone sticking their flashbulbs up and around and over him and in his face...Ruby was bootlegging the pistol like a quarterback with a football...I knew what he was going to do...but I couldn't get at him.

SOURCES: WCH XII, 176 • GERTZ 59, 513–4 • SUMMERS 461

CONFORTO, JANET ADAMS BONNEY CUFFARI SMALLWOOD (aka Jada), Ruby witness; 27-year-old Carousel Club stripper. Conforto told reporters on November 23, 1963, that Ruby knew Oswald. That was one day before Ruby shot Oswald. According to Beverly Oliver ("The Babushka Lady"), Conforto died a mysterious death. Ruby hired Jada in June 1963, in New Orleans, where she was working in a club run by Harold Tannenbaum and at least partially owned by assassination suspect Carlos Marcello. Author Seth Kantor described Jada as "supercharged with animalism." According to G. Robert Blakey, Jada got Ruby into "considerable trouble with her 'x-rated' act." Reportedly, Ruby once asked Jada to live with him platonically, to help stifle rumors he was homosexual—a proposition that infuriated the libidinous dancer. (See also Oliver, Beverly)
SOURCES: RTJ 236 • COA 113, 129, 251–2, 258, 439 • FLAMMONDE 172 • BLAKEY 303 • KANTOR 21–2, 139, 171–2, 174 • DAVIS 257, 362, 452, 603

CONNALLY, JOHN BOWDEN, JR., a.w.; governor of Texas, severely wounded in the JFK assassination. Connally was sitting directly in front of the president when the shots were fired. During the shooting sequence, he said, "My God, they are going to kill us all!" His wounds included the back, the chest, the thigh and the wrist. In order for the WC to pin the assassination on Oswald as the lone assassin, all of Connally's wounds had to be caused by the same bullet that supposedly caused the wounds to Kennedy's back and neck (the so-called "magic bullet"). This theory is supported neither by the Zapruder film, which shows Connally holding onto his Stetson hat after Kennedy has been hit and after his wristbone supposedly has been shattered, nor by Connally himself who claimed he heard the first shot and responded to it before he was hit. According to Connally, "They talk about the 'one-bullet' and the 'two-bullet theory,' but as far as I am concerned, there is no 'theory.' There is my absolute knowledge, and my wife's too, that one bullet caused the President's first wound, and that an entirely separate shot struck me." If Kennedy's and Connally's wounds were caused by separate bullets, then more than one gunman had to have been firing from the rear. This likelihood, along with eyewitness evidence of shots coming from the front, would indicate that at least three shooters were on the scene.

Many researchers have felt for a long time that the shot (or shots) that struck Governor Connally were fired from the roof of the Dallas County Records Building at the southeast corner of Elm and Houston Streets. Metal traces in the threads of Governor Connally's coat at the point of entry may have helped determine the source of the shots. Unfortunately, his coat was cleaned and pressed before it was delivered to the WC.

In 1969, while Jim Garrison was trying Clay Shaw in New Orleans for conspiracy to kill JFK, he sought to question Sergio Arcacha Smith, who was in Dallas. Connally refused to extradite Smith.

Connally's first campaign manager, Eugene Locke, was also Mrs. J. D. (Marie) Tippit's attorney before the assassination.

Connally died on June 15, 1993, at age 76 at Methodist Hospital in Houston, Texas, from complications of pulmonary fibrosis. A day later, several JFK assassination researchers—including James H. Lesar, the head of the non-profit Assassination Archives and Research Center, and Cyril Wecht, a forensic pathologist and longtime vocal critic of the "magic bullet" theory—asked the U.S. Justice Department to try to recover the bullet fragments from Connally's wrist before the body was buried. They asked that neutron activation analysis and other tests be performed on the bullets to determine conclusively whether or not the fragments came from WCE 399 (the magic bullet). If the fragments did not come from that particular bullet, there would be proof for the first time that more than one gunman fired upon the Dallas motorcade. U.S. Attorney General Janet Reno forwarded the request to the FBI's Dallas Field office for a determination.

On June 17 in what must been a bizarre scene, the FBI—after determining that it favored the removal of the bullet fragments—decided to approach the Connally family about the matter *during* the funeral. The FBI was angrily rejected by the family, who told the press through a representative that it was deeply offended by the FBI's methods. Connally's burial was held as planned. The following day the FBI requested permission to exhume Connally's body. Again they were rejected by the family who promised to "resist vigorously any efforts to disturb the body of John Connally." (See also Connally, Nellie; Greer, William; Gregory, Charles; Jimison, R.J.; Kirkwood, Pat; Locke, Eugene; Parker, John; Shaw, Robert; Shires, George; Smith, Sergio Arcacha; Tippit, Marie; Tomlinson, Darrell; Zirbel, Craig)

SOURCES: WR, many • WCH IV, 129 • HSCA Report 36–40, 44, 46, 48, 82, 182–3 • BELIN 1–2, 4, 16, 27, 29, 45, 73, 187 • RTJ, many • COA 19, 125, 140, 166, 212–3, 233, 264, 434 • GERTZ 5, 337, 339, 347, 421 • BISHOP, many • DOP, many • CF 6, 8–9, 12–3, 362–5 • PWW, many • OTT 222, 240–1 • SUMMERS 3–4, 13, 19, 22 • BE 68, 73, 122, 288, 556–7, 671 • FMG I, 27, 36, 39, 55, 153, 185–7; III, 2–3, 5, 13–6, 21–2, 80 • BLAKEY 3–6, 10–3, 15–6, 28–9, 88–90, 106–7, 326 • FLAMMONDE 100, 105–6, 108–9, 120, 151, 284 • HOS 19, 162, 176 • ME 14–5, 26, 31, 38–43, 47, 49, 69–70, 82, 159–60 • OGLESBY 9, 13, 32–3 • KANTOR 19, 41, 80, 155, 191–4, 206–8 • DAVIS 209, 220, 323, 411, 434, 604–5, 608–9 • NORTH, many • PD 30, 354–8

CONNALLY, NELLIE, a.w.; wife of John. Mrs. Connally sat on her husband's left. Her statements corroborate his: that he was not struck by the first shot. (See also Connally, John; Greer, William)

SOURCES: WR 57–8, 61–3, 70, 83, 100, 108 • WCH IV, 146 • BELIN 4–5, 16, 27 • RTJ 67, 72–3, 383–4 • COA 19, 21, 166 • BISHOP, many • DOP, many • CF 11–3 • FMG III, 13, 15 • SUMMERS 3, 19 • BLAKEY 14–5, 106 • HOS 176–7 • ME 14–5, 74, 159 • OGLESBY 9, 13, 32–3 • PD 356

CONNEL, MRS. C. L., FBI informant. Mrs. Connel was an acquaintance of Oswald witness Sylvia Odio. She told the FBI that Odio claimed to know Oswald and that Odio "personally considered Oswald brilliant and clever." Mrs. Connel also told the FBI that Major General Edwin A. Walker, a man Oswald allegedly attempted to kill, had been involved in arousing Cuban exiles in Dallas against the Kennedy administration.

SOURCES: WCE 3108 • HT 308

CONNOR, PETER FRANCIS, Oswald witness; USMC acquaintance. Connor, stationed in Atsugi, Japan, with Oswald, told the WC:

When the fellows were heading out for a night on the town, Oswald would either remain behind or leave before they did. Nobody knew what he did... Oswald had a reputation of being a good worker. I observed he was not personally neat... He often responded to the orders of his superiors with insolent remarks... I was of the opinion that Oswald was intelligent... I never heard Oswald make any anti-American or pro-Communist statements. He claimed to be named after Robert E. Lee, whom he characterized as the greatest man in history.

Regarding the Atsugi incident in which Oswald was supposed to have shot himself in the arm accidentally with an unauthorized weapon, Connor has said that, in his opinion, the bullet missed Oswald altogether and struck the ceiling.
SOURCES: WCH VIII, 317 • BISHOP 412 • AO 93 • OTT 46 • SUMMERS 125

CONROY, EDWARD A., WC staff member; Internal Revenue Service agent. With Phillip Barson and John J. O'Brien, analyzed Oswald's finances in Appendix XIV of the WR.
SOURCE: EPSTEIN 602

COOK, AUSTIN, member, John Birch Society; owner of Austin's Barbeque, which employed J. D. Tippit part-time as a security guard on weekends. Cook once sold a business to Ruby's business partner, Ralph Paul. According to researcher Larry Harris, Tippit had a long affair with one of Cook's waitresses, a blonde, who was also married. At the time of Tippit's death, this waitress was pregnant, perhaps with Tippit's child. (See also Paul, Ralph; Tippit, J. D.)
SOURCES: HSCA XII, 41–2 • HT 279 • SUMMERS 487

COOKE, LEON, Ruby witness; secretary-treasurer of the Waste Handlers' Union in Chicago; murdered in December 1939. A suspect in the murder was Jack Rubenstein, who later moved to Dallas and changed his name to Ruby.
SOURCES: BLAKEY 284 • EVICA 148–50, 153–6, 184, 219 • HT 413

COOLEY, SHERMAN, Oswald witness; USMC acquaintance. According to Edward Jay Epstein, Cooley said Oswald was a "shitbird"—that is, he couldn't qualify with his weapon because he was a poor shot. Cooley said, "It was a disgrace not to qualify, and we gave him holy hell."
SOURCES: AO 90 • LEGEND 63

COOPER, JOHN SHERMAN, WC member; Republican senator from Kentucky; former U.S. ambassador to India. Cooper objected strongly to the "magic bullet" theory, saying, "there is no evidence that both men [Connally and JFK] were hit by the same bullet."
SOURCES: HSCA Report 256 • ME 12 • OGLESBY 12, 27 • BELIN 79 • RTJ 23, 367, 371 • OTT 14 • SUMMERS 36 • BE 85 • FMG I, 50, 125 • BLAKEY 24, 71, 266

COOPER, MARION, CIA informant. Cooper attended a meeting in Honduras on January 1, 1955, to discuss the assassination of Panama President Jose Antonio Remon. Present at the meeting, according to Cooper, were the hired team of assassins and Vice President Richard M. Nixon. The following day, Remon was killed by machine-gun fire.

SOURCES: WCE 279 • HT 317

CORNWELL, GARY, HSCA deputy chief counsel. Questioned JFK autopsist Dr. James J. Humes regarding the location of JFK's wounds.
SOURCES: HSCA Report 484 • HSCA I, 324–5 • BE 550

CORPORON, JOHN, Oswald witness; head of the news department at WDSU-TV and radio in New Orleans, the radio station upon which Oswald debated Carlos Bringuier on August 21, 1963. Oswald had earlier appeared on the station for a straight interview on August 17. (See also Bringuier, Carlos; Stuckey, William)
SOURCE: WCH XI, 471

COUCH, MALCOLM O., a.w.; WFAA-TV cameraman. Couch rode in the motorcade in an open press car still on Houston Street during the shooting. He and Robert Jackson, the fellow photographer with whom he was riding, saw a rifle barrel being withdrawn from the "sniper's nest" window. Five minutes after the assassination, Couch saw a pool of blood, 8 to ten inches in diameter on a sidewalk 10 to 15 feet from the southwest corner of the TSBD. He saw nothing else suspicious in the area that might explain why the blood was there. The blood was also seen, and verified as blood, by three *Dallas Morning News* employees. Couch told WC that Wes Wise, a KRLD employee, saw Ruby near the TSBD soon after the assassination. The WC refused to consider this testimony because it was hearsay, yet did not call Wise as a witness. (See also Coley, Jerry; Darnell, James; Dillard, Thomas; Hood, Jim; Jackson, Robert; Mulkey, Charles; Underwood, James)
SOURCES: WR 77 • WCH VI, 153 • RTJ 263, 382 • PWW 29, 53–8, 95, 107, 119–20

COULTER, HARRIS, State Department interpreter. Coulter interpreted for Marina Oswald during the WC Hearings. (See also Oswald, Marina)
SOURCES: WCH V, 408

COX, ROLAND A., o.k.w.; DPD reserve. Cox directed traffic on the morning of November 24, 1963, outside the Commerce Street ramp entrance to the DPD station. He did not see Ruby enter the building, but was told that Ruby had sneaked in pushing a TV camera. Cox had worked as a security man at Ruby's Vegas Club "eight or nine years" before.
SOURCE: WCH XV, 153

CRAFARD, CURTIS LaVERNE "LARRY," Ruby witness; Carousel Club employee; lived in a back room at Ruby's Carousel Club; theoretic Oswald lookalike (according to the WC). Crafard was under Ruby's employ from mid-October until November 23, 1963. He fled Dallas following the assassination. Before coming to Dallas, Crafard worked as a carnival barker with small-time freak-show acts like "the two-headed baby" and "the snake girl." He met Ruby while working with some of Jack's strippers in a carnival sideshow called "How Hollywood Makes Movies" at the 1963 Texas State Fair.

At 5:00 A.M., November 23, Crafard met with Ruby and his roommate George Senator in a Dallas garage. The three remained there for about an hour. Later that morning, Crafard left Dallas and hitchhiked to Michigan with only seven dollars on him. Ruby returned to the garage later that morning where he was overheard on the phone discussing security for Oswald's transfer.

The WC said that Crafard's sudden departure from Dallas following the assassination was not indicative of Ruby's involvement in a conspiracy. The WR states:

> [Crafard] made no attempt to communicate with law enforcement officials after Oswald's death; and a relative in Michigan recalled that Crafard spoke very little of his association with Ruby. When finally located by the FBI six days later, he stated that he left Ruby's employ because he did not wish to be subjected to further verbal abuse by Ruby and that he went north to see his sister, from whom he had not heard in some time...

While many researchers were searching for men who might have impersonated Oswald during the weeks preceding the assassination, the WC used Crafard's supposed resemblance to Oswald to diffuse rumors of conspiracy: "The testimony of a few witnesses who claim to have seen Ruby with a person who they feel may have been Oswald warrants further comment... Ruth Paine testified that Crafard's photograph bears a strong resemblance to Oswald..." However, photos of Crafard in WCH show no resemblance. After the assassination, according to *Time*:

> the FBI followed Crafard to Michigan and questioned him repeatedly; he had to go back to Dallas for Ruby's trial; he never found the wife he'd lost. And then in the early '80s, just when his life seemed to have settled down, renewed interest in the JFK case made his name the object of speculation again: it appeared in a book on the organized-crime connections to Ruby and the assassination. His new wife read the book and began to get a little paranoid. She wondered about the serious car accident they had had: Was it really an accident?

Eventually, things began to go awry: His marriage broke up, he lost his job." When last contacted, Crafard was working "as a night security guard in a mill, boarding with some people," without a traceable phone number of his own.

According to author David E. Scheim, "There is no possibility that Crafard could have been mistaken for Oswald since Crafard had 'no front teeth,' was 'creepy,' looked 'like a bum,' and had 'sandy hair,' as witnesses described him, whereas Oswald was good looking, had all of his front teeth, and had brown hair." (See also Patterson, Robert; Rocco, Eddie)

SOURCES: WR 312–7, 332, 335, 337, 345–6 • WCH XIII, 402; XIV, 1 • WCE 451, 453–6, 2250, 2275, 2281, 2429–30, 2403, 2432, 2792–3 • RTJ 18, 250–1, 270 • COA 118, 132–3, 141, 148, 157, 255–6, 331, 442 • GERTZ 60, 104, 109–10, 522, 525, 527 • BISHOP 268–9, 329, 371 • FMG III, 41 • BLAKEY 319 • KANTOR 24, 41–2, 49–53

CRAIG, ROGER D., a.w.; suspicious death; Dallas County deputy sheriff. Craig said that 15 minutes after the shots he heard someone whistle, so he turned and saw a man run down the grassy slope in front of the TSBD and get into a white Nash station wagon, with a luggage rack on top, which had come to a stop on Elm Street. The driver of the station wagon, he said, was a black or dark-skinned Latin man.

The man running down the knoll, Craig said, was Oswald. Craig positively identified the man as Oswald after the alleged assassin's arrest. Craig told Captain Fritz his story, and Fritz asked Oswald, "What about the car?"

Oswald replied, "That station wagon belongs to Mrs. Paine [Marina Oswald's housemate, and the woman who got Oswald his job at the TSBD]. Don't try to tie her in with this. She had nothing to do with it."

Ruth Paine did own a white station wagon with a luggage rack on top, although it was a Chevrolet. The WC paid attention to none of this. When Craig testified before the WC, he was questioned by David Belin. Later Craig was shocked to read the WCH and find his testimony changed 14 times.

Craig was also with Deputy Sheriff Eugene Boone and Deputy Constable Seymour Weitzman when a rifle was found on the sixth floor of the TSBD. Like the other two, Craig said the rifle was a 7.65 Mauser. Craig became *persona non grata* after testifying for the WC about what he saw, including the Nash station wagon. He was eventually fired from the Dallas sheriff's department.

In 1967, Craig traveled to New Orleans to be a prosecution witness at

Clay Shaw's assassination-conspiracy trial. Later that year, back in Dallas, a bullet grazed his head while he was walking to a parking lot. In 1973, a car forced Craig's car off the road, and he severely injured his back. In 1974, he was shot again, this time by a shotgun in Waxahachie, Texas. Craig was told that the Mafia had put a price on his head. He died on May 15, 1975, soon after appearing on a series of radio talk shows to discuss the assassination, of a "self-inflicted" gunshot wound. Shortly before his death, he was seriously injured when his car engine exploded. (See also Boone, Eugene; Bradley, Edgar; Carr, Richard; Ingram, Hiram; Paine, Ruth; Robinson, Marvin; Weitzman, Seymour)

SOURCES: WR 150–1, 233–5 • WCH VI, 260 • BELIN 71–2 • RTJ 18, 96, 98, 173–4, 384 • COA 37–8, 156 • CF 20, 328–33 • PWW 168 • FMG I, 25, 29–31, 33–5, 67, 74; III, 15, 29–31, 33–7, 64, 79–80, 86–8, 90, 93 • OTT 94–6, 98, 194, 202, 204–5, 239, 273–4, 281, 326–7 • OGLESBY 68 • DAVIS 207

CRAIG, WALTER E., president of the American Bar Association. Craig was chosen by the WC to represent Oswald's interests at the WC hearings, which were nonetheless conducted with an absolute assumption of Oswald's guilt.

SOURCES: COA 215, 385 • PD 362

CRAWFORD, JAMES N., a.w. Crawford was standing on the southeast corner of Elm and Houston with fellow Dallas County Deputy District Clerk Mary Ann Mitchell. According to the WR:

> After the President's car turned the corner, Crawford heard a loud report, which he thought was a backfire coming from the direction of the triple underpass. He heard a second shot seconds later, followed quickly by a third. At the third shot, he looked up and saw a "movement" in the far east corner of the sixth floor of the Depository, the only open window on that floor. He told Miss Mitchell, "that if those were shots they came from that window."

Asked to describe the "movement" by the WC, Crawford testified, "I would say it was a profile, somewhat from the waist up, but it was a very quick movement and rather indistinct and it was very light colored... When I saw it, I automatically in my mind came to the conclusion that it was a person having moved out of the window... " (See also Mitchell, Mary Ann)

SOURCES: WR 78 • WCH VI, 171

CRAWFORD, JOHN M., possible murder victim; possible Ruby witness; pilot; lifelong friend of a.w. and Oswald witness Buell Wesley Frazier. The pair grew up together in Huntsville, Texas. According to Penn Jones Jr., "Crawford was a homosexual and a close friend of Jack Ruby." Crawford died in a plane crash near Huntsville on April 15, 1969. The circumstances surrounding the crash were most strange. At the time, Crawford was living in a trailer home at the Huntsville airport. Investigators found the stereo still playing in his trailer. Six other people died in the crash: three men, a woman, and two children. All three men had left their keys in their cars and the woman had left her purse on the car seat. (See also Frazier, Buell)

SOURCES: FMG III, 56 • HT 291

CREEL, ROBERT J., Louisiana Department of Labor employee in New Orleans. Creel told the WC that the written record of Oswald's unemployment record was accurate.

SOURCE: WCH XI, 477

CRENSHAW, CHARLES, Parkland witness; surgeon; author, with Jens Hansen and J. Gary Shaw, of *JFK Conspiracy of Silence* (Signet, 1992). Crenshaw told Geraldo Rivera on the *Now It Can Be Told* TV program on April 2, 1992, "The bullet [that killed JFK] entered from the right side, [pointing to the right temple] coming down and coming across. It was a huge, blown-out hole [toward the back of JFK's head]...If the bullet had come from the back, the cerebellum [in the front] would have been destroyed." Crenshaw indicated that he believed that the fatal shot came from the direction of the grassy knoll.

CRIMALDI, CHARLES, Government informant. Crimaldi claims that Jimmy Hoffa was the "original liaison" between the CIA and the Mafia for their plots to murder Fidel Castro. Crimaldi has said that Hoffa (along with Sam Giancana) was killed to protect the secrets of those plots. (See also Giancana, Sam; Hoffa, James)

SOURCE: SUMMERS 493, 495

CRISSEY, EDGAR R., one of three wealthy Dallas businessmen who, according to the WR, helped finance a full-page, black-bordered anti-JFK advertisement that ran in the *Dallas Morning News* on the day of the assassination. (See also Bright, H. R.; Hunt, Nelson Bunker)

SOURCES: WR 276 • FMG I, 130

CRONKITE, WALTER, CBS News anchor. Cronkite broke the news of the shooting and of JFK's death to those watching CBS-TV. In 1970, Cronkite interviewed LBJ. Of that interview, Cronkite said to the AP in 1992: "He said he'd never been sure the [WC] was right, that he'd always thought there was a possibility of a conspiracy in Kennedy's death. He just tossed it off and then he wouldn't talk any more about it. He indicated that he thought [the conspiracy] was international, but he wouldn't go into it. He seemed to be a little embarrassed about having brought it up, as if he didn't have anything to back it up. It seemed it was just a feeling he had." (See also Johnson, Lyndon B.)

SOURCES: BE 60 • HOS 59 • ME 9, 128 • PD 13, 25, 45, 49, 73–4, 236, 325

CROWE, WILLIAM D., JR. (aka DeMar, Bill), Ruby witness; possible Oswald witness. The 22-year-old Carousel Club performer, ventriloquist and "mind reader," whose repertoire consisted of a "memory act," appeared in the exploitation film *Naughty Dallas*, which contained several scenes shot in Ruby's Carousel Club. Crowe told a *Dallas Morning News* reporter on November 25, 1963, that he remembered seeing Oswald and Ruby drinking and talking in the Carousel "a little more than a week" before JFK's death. (See also Barnes, Gene; Hoy, David; McClendon, Gordon; Rocco, Eddie)

SOURCES: WR 335 • WCH XV, 96 • COA 442 • FLAMMONDE 24, 166 • KANTOR 206

CROWLEY, JAMES D., Oswald witness; State Department intelligence specialist. Crowley stated in an affidavit: "The first time I remember learning of Oswald's existence was when I received copies of a telegraphic message from the [CIA] dated October 10, 1963, which contained information pertaining to his current activities." Crowley said he reviewed the file briefly on November 14, 1963; he offered no further details regarding this potentially fascinating message.

SOURCE: WCH XI, 482

CROY, KENNETH HUDSON, o.k.w.; DPD reserve. Croy was among the policemen who stood in front of Jack Ruby, with his back to the gunman, just before Ruby moved past to shoot Oswald. (See also Harrison, William)

SOURCE: WCH XII, 186

CRULL, ELGIN E., Dallas city manager. Crull told the WC that he had spoken to Dallas Chief of Police Jesse Curry on the morning of Saturday, November 23, 1963, regarding the madhouse being created in police headquarters by all of the newsmen covering the assassination. Curry told him that he "felt it necessary to cooperate with the media representatives, in order to avoid being accused of Gestapo tactics in connection with the handling of Oswald." (See also Curry, Jesse)

SOURCES: WR 223 • WCH XV, 138 • FMG I, 50

CRUMP, RAYMOND, JR. Crump was tried and acquitted for the 1964 murder of JFK mistress Mary Pinchot Meyer, whose body was found along a towpath that paralleled a canal on one side and the Potomac River on the other. She had been shot to death during the noon hour. A detective of the Metropolitan Police Department responded to the scene where an eyewitness told him that Crump, a black man who had just consumed a six-pack of beer, had been seen bending over the body of Mrs. Meyer. Crump accounted for his presence in the area by saying he had been fishing in the river. His clothing was water-soaked, a result, he claimed, of falling in the river. No fishing gear was found in the area, nor were police successful in their search for a gun. Says author Leo Damore, "Two shots were fired within eight seconds—one behind her ear so that it traversed her brain, and one behind her shoulder blade so it severed her aorta." These are earmarks of a professional hit. (See also Meyer, Mary Pinchot)

CUBELA, ROLANDO, CIA assassin. Cubela was given equipment to kill Castro by CIA agent Desmond FitzGerald, who claimed that he was a U.S. senator, representing Attorney General Robert F. Kennedy. (See also FitzGerald, Desmond)
SOURCES: HSCA Report 113 • SUMMERS 321–4, 398, 400–2, 411

CUNNINGHAM, CORTLANDT, ballistics expert; member of the FBI Laboratory's Firearms Identification Unit. Cunningham told the WC that it was impossible to ballistically match the bullets recovered at the scene of the Tippit shooting with the gun allegedly belonging to Oswald, but that he could match the four shell casings found near the scene with "Oswald's" handgun, "to the exclusion of all other weapons."
SOURCES: WR 160 • WCH II, 251 • RTJ 122, 195–7, 199–200 • OTT 199 • ME 203–5

CUNNINGHAM, HELEN P., Oswald witness; employment counselor for the Texas Employment Commission. Cunningham referred Oswald to a job opening for a messenger at Harrell & Huntington Architects on October 10, 1962, but Oswald was not hired. She then referred him to the photo job at Jaggers-Chiles-Stovall, where Oswald started work on October 15, 1962.
SOURCE: WCH XI, 477

CURRY, EILEEN, Ruby witness; informant for the Federal Narcotics Bureau. Curry told the FBI that anyone seeking to sell narcotics in Dallas had to obtain clearance first from Ruby. The WC said it found "no evidence" that Ruby had underworld connections.
SOURCES: RTJ 301 • COA 89–91 • KANTOR 110

CURRY, JESSE EDWARD, a.w.; Dallas chief of police. Curry drove the presidential motorcade's lead car, an enclosed sedan. Moments after the shooting, he called into his microphone, "Get a man on that overpass and see what happened up there." He guarded LBJ at Love Field and was aboard Air Force One when the new president was sworn in. The next day, Curry told reporters that he could tell by the sound of the shots that they had come from the TSBD, a reversal of his original opinion. This was not the last time that Curry was forced to flip-flop, as the evidence seemed to change beneath him. He later wrote that the WR had "yielded to political pressure." After viewing the Zapruder film, Curry agreed with Governor Connally that Connally and JFK had been struck by separate bullets.

Curry attended the meetings that determined the motorcade route and later wrote that most of the decisions were made by SS agent Winston G. Lawson.

Just before Ruby shot Oswald, Curry was taken out of the security picture. "I was called to take a phone call from Dallas Mayor [Earle] Cabell in my office," Curry wrote.

Curry's book about the assassination (*JFK Assassination File*, American Poster and Publishing Co., 1969) was the first to publish photos of an official-looking man picking something up out of the grass in Dealey Plaza following the shooting (a bullet perhaps) and marks made on curbstones by bullets that are unaccounted for in the official version of the facts.

Curry did not believe that Oswald acted alone—or acted at all, for that matter. "We don't have any proof that Oswald fired the rifle, and never did. Nobody's yet been able to put him in that building [the TSBD] with a gun in his hand," he once said to interviewer Tom Johnson. Curry died in June 1980, of a heart attack. (See also Crull, Elgin; Decker, J. E.; Duff, William; Fisher, N. T.; Henslee, Gerald; King, Glen; Lawson, Winston; Thornberry, Homer)

SOURCES: WR, many • WCH IV, 150; XII, 25; XV, 124, 641 • HSCA Report 38, 66–7, 76 • EVICA 18–9, 24, 44–5, 49–50, 78–9, 81 • ME 104, 130 • BELIN 62 • RTJ, many • COA 23, 29, 111, 134 • GERTZ 71, 74, 78, 84, 106, 286–7, 519–20 • BISHOP, many • DOP, many • CF 9, 14, 47, 324, 361–2 • PWW 264, 271, 274 • OTT 95 • SUMMERS 51, 58, 98, 145, 215, 458 • BE 354 • FMG I, 45, 71, 90, 149, 155–6, 162–6, 175; III, 87–8 • FLAMMONDE 231 • BLAKEY 11–5, 17, 92–3, 316, 318–20 • HOS 76 • KANTOR, many • DAVIS 223–5 • NORTH, many • PD 342

CURTIS, DON TEEL, Parkland witness; oral surgeon. Curtis was one of 12 doctors called to the emergency area as JFK was rushed to the hospital.
SOURCES: WR 66 • WCH VI, 57 • BISHOP 156

CUSHMAN, ROBERT, major general, USMC; Richard M. Nixon's military liaison when Cuban exiles were receiving covert CIA training. As president, Nixon made Cushman the CIA's deputy director. Cushman

played a large role in the Watergate case. According to Cushman, presidential aide John Ehrlichman called him in July 1972, and requested CIA assistance for E. Howard Hunt's upcoming "security" work. (See also Nixon, Richard M.)
SOURCE: HT 292, 317

CUSTER, JERROL F., Bethesda witness; with Edward Reed, one of two technicians who X-rayed JFK's body at the autopsy. Like so many other eyewitnesses, Custer insists that there was a massive wound in the back of JFK's head. He said, "I could put both my hands in the wound." Describing JFK's wounds to author David Lifton via telephone on September 30, 1979, Custer said, "Let me tell you one thing. If you have ever gone hunting, you know as well as I do, when a bullet goes into a body, it goes in small and comes out big. Okay? Well, that is exactly how the skull looked. Okay?...from the front to the back." Custer says that he never saw the small entrance wound in the back of JFK's head that is visible in the autopsy photos.
SOURCES: SUMMERS 481 • BE 592, 619, 623, 626, 656, 696

CUTCHSHAW, WILBUR JAY, o.k.w.; DPD detective (Criminal Division, Juvenile Bureau). Cutchshaw saw three men from Dallas's Channel 5 moving a TV camera into the basement before the shooting, but only two men moved it out. Was Ruby the third man?
SOURCE: WCH XII, 206

CUTLER, ROBERT B., author of *The Umbrella Man* (self-published, 1975); coauthor, with W. R. Morris, of *Alek James Hidell, Alias Oswald* (self-published, 1985). Cutler theorizes that the Umbrella Man's umbrella was used to fire a paralyzing pellet into the front of JFK's throat, thus explaining the extremely small size of the throat wound and JFK's lack of evasive movements during the shooting sequence. (See also Morris, W. R.)
SOURCES: CF 30–1 • ME 158–9

D

DALITZ, MORRIS BARNEY "MOE," Las Vegas investor; later builder and proprietor of Rancho La Costa Country Club, the magnificent California retreat frequented by members of organized crime (such as assassination suspect Eugene Hale Brading, who was a charter member), as well as Earl Warren and Richard M. Nixon. The *HSCA Report* discusses Jimmy Hoffa and other Teamsters gathering at Dalitz's golf resort, near San Clemente, California. "Here they no doubt reflected that, as long as John Kennedy was President, Robert Kennedy was unassailable." Dalitz died peacefully in bed on August 31, 1989, at age 89. (See also Brading, Eugene Hale; Hoffa, James; Nixon, Richard M.; Warren, Earl)
  SOURCES: HSCA Report 34, 176–7 • DUFFY 160 • SUMMERS 249 • HT 318 • COA 120, 309, 311, 394 • BLAKEY 207, 230, 250 • EVICA 220, 227–30, 235, 244, 260–1, 276, 281, 318

DALZELL, WILLIAM, international petroleum engineer; adviser to the Ethiopian government; with Guy Banister, one of the incorporators in 1961 of the militant, right-wing anti-Castro group Citizens for a Free Cuba. Dalzell had a post-office box during the summer of 1963 in the same building as Oswald, Kerry Thornley, Jules Kimble, and Jack Martin. According to author Paris Flammonde: "On June 30, 1967 [Jim] Garrison issued a subpoena for Dalzell to appear for questioning in his probe of the Kennedy assassination, but the subpoena was subsequently withdrawn after Dalzell volunteered to testify in secret." (See also Banister, William Guy; Kimble, Jules; Martin, Jack; Thornley, Kerry)
  SOURCE: FLAMMONDE 116

D'AMELIO, CARLO, one of the directors of CMC, Permindex's sister corporation, and the attorney for members of the Italian royal family. D'Amelio was the first president of CMC, founded in Italy in 1961.

Previously, he had been the lawyer and administrator of the former Italian royal family's interests. According to the Italian newspaper, *Paesa Sera* (March 4, 1967), which exposed CMC and Permindex as little more than espionage brokers: "The farce... reached the point of the grotesque when the lawyer D'Amelio, praising Permindex as a 'capillary organization located in the principal centers of production, with its head office [CMC] in Rome (an organization, all the while, virtually nonexistent), brought all of Italian civilization into play by affirming that thanks to the Centro [CMC], 'Rome will recover once again the position as *caput mundi*, as center of the civilized world.'" Three days later, that same newspaper said that D'Amelio had admitted that Clay Shaw, freshly under arrest as an assassination conspirator, had been a member of CMC's administrative board during the time D'Amelio was president. (See also Bloomfield, Louis M.; Shaw, Clay)
SOURCES: OTT 88 • FLAMMONDE 215–6, 222

DANIELS, GODFREY JEROME "GATOR," Oswald witness; USMC acquaintance; met Oswald aboard the USS *Bexar*, on the way to Japan. Daniels told author Edward Jay Epstein, "He was simple folk, just like I was... we were a bunch of kids—never been away from home before—but Oswald came right out and admitted that he had never known a woman... It was real unusual that a fellow would admit that... but he never was ashamed to admit it... He was just a good egg."
SOURCES: AO 93 • LEGEND 68–71

DANIELS, JOHN J., Dallas parking-lot employee; 32 years old. Daniels worked at the Norton parking lot, across the street from the downtown Western Union office. After the shooting of Oswald, Daniels witnessed the DPD taking away Ruby's car.
SOURCE: WCH XIII, 296

DANIELS, NAPOLEON J., o.k.w. (prelude); former DPD officer. Daniels told the WC that just before the shooting of Oswald, he saw a man greatly resembling Ruby walk down the Main Street ramp into the DPD basement with his right hand in his suit pocket. He said the man entered the secured area in full view of DPD Officer Roy E. Vaughn, who made no effort to stop him. (See also Vaughn, Roy E.)
SOURCES: WR 204 • WCH XII, 225 • RTJ 221–6, 384

DANN, SOL, Ruby witness. Dann was a member of Ruby's defense team during his murder trial.
SOURCES: WR 212 • GERTZ, many • FLAMMONDE 294–5 • KANTOR 178–9

DANNELLY, MRS. LEE, possible Oswald witness; employee of the Selective Service System in Austin, Texas. Dannelly says that on Septem-

ber 25, 1963, a man calling himself "Harvey Oswald" came to her asking if it were possible to have his "other than honorable" discharge upgraded. He told her he lived in Fort Worth. She couldn't find a Harvey Oswald listed in her files and suggested that he try the Fort Worth office. He left. Officially, Oswald was on his way from New Orleans to Mexico City on that date.
SOURCE: SUMMERS 376

D'ANTONIO, EMILE, coproducer, with Mark Lane, of the 1966 film *Rush to Judgment*, based on Lane's book of the same title. If Oswald had lived to stand trial, this film would have been a representation of the case for his defense. (See also Lane, Mark)
SOURCES: BELIN 31–2 • PD 4

DARNELL, JAMES, a.w.; television newsreel cameraman. Darnell rode in a press car in the motorcade with *Dallas Times Herald* staff photographer Robert H. Jackson, James Underwood of Dallas TV-station KRLD, *Dallas Morning News* chief photographer Thomas Dillard and fellow newsreel cameraman Malcolm O. Couch. The car was midway between Main and Elm Streets on Houston Street when the first shot was fired. (See also Couch, Malcolm O.; Dillard, Thomas; Jackson, Robert H.; Underwood, James)
SOURCE: WR 77

DAVID, CHRISTIAN, jailed French mobster. David named fellow French gangster Lucien Sarti, now deceased, as one of the men who shot JFK. According to Nigel Turner's 1988 British television documentary, *The Men Who Killed Kennedy*, David said there were three Corsican assassins in Dealey Plaza but named only Sarti because he is no longer living. He has written his entire knowledge of the assassination on a piece of paper and has sealed it inside an envelope. He gave the envelope to his lawyer, who is not to open it until David has been given his freedom. The information revealed in the documentary was originally discovered by assassination researcher Steve Rivele, who is currently living in hiding.

David says that the three assassins were all members of the Corsican Mafia, hired in Marseilles in the fall of 1963. They were flown from Marseilles to Mexico City, where they spent two or three weeks in the house of a contact. They were then driven from Mexico City to Brownsville, Texas, where they crossed the border and were picked up in Texas by a representative of the Chicago Mafia, with whom they conversed in Italian. They were then driven to Dallas and put up in a safe house. They spent several days photographing Dealey Plaza, carefully planning a crossfire.

David says that two of the assassins were in buildings to the rear of the president, one high and one low (almost on the horizontal). There were four shots: the first from the rear, striking Kennedy in the back; the second from the rear, causing Governor Connally's wounds; the third shot, fired by Sarti from behind the wooden fence atop the grassy knoll, causing JFK's fatal wound; the fourth shot, fired from the rear, missing the car entirely. Earwitnesses heard only three shots because two of the shots were fired almost simultaneously. In the panic that followed the assassination, the three gunmen had no trouble getting out of Dealey Plaza. They returned to their safe house, where they remained for 10 days, before flying from Dallas to Montreal. From Montreal they returned to Marseilles.

David says that the assassins were paid in heroin. David's publicly disclosed information has been corroborated by former mobster turned U.S. government informant Michel Nicoli, who says that he and David received the information contemporaneously. (See also Nicoli, Michel; Rivele, Steve; Sarti, Lucien)
SOURCE: SUMMERS 523–7

DAVID, DENNIS DUANE, Bethesda witness; E6, Petty Officer; Chief of the Day for the Bethesda Medical Center on November 22, 1963. David supervised the unloading of JFK's body from the casket in the autopsy room. David says that, immediately following the autopsy, an SS agent had him type a memo stating that four pieces of lead were removed from JFK during the procedure. These were not separate bullets, but had ragged edges like shrapnel. "There was more material than would have come from one bullet," David said, "but not enough for two." David told author David Lifton that the ornamental casket that arrived at Bethesda with the former First Lady was a decoy, and that JFK's body was already in the hospital when it arrived, carried into the back entrance in a plain coffin. (See also Pitzer, William)
SOURCES: SUMMERS 482–3 • BE, many

DAVIS, MRS. AVERY, a.w. Stood in front of TSBD. Mrs. Davis thought the shots came from the triple underpass.
SOURCE: RTJ 112, 262

DAVIS, BARBARA JEANNETTE and VIRGINIA R., t.k.w.; sisters-in-law who lived in a house at the southeast corner of Tenth Street and Patton. They heard shots and ran to the door, where they saw a man crossing their lawn 20 feet away. They found two shells in the bushes on their front lawn and handed the shells over to a Dallas police officer. Virginia Davis testified that she ran to the police car seconds after the shooting and that the passenger side window was rolled up. This is in contrast to Helen Markham's testimony that the officer chatted through the open window with his killer moments before he was shot. Both women positively identified the man they had seen as Oswald.

Since Oswald was supposed to have killed Tippit with a revolver, and revolvers do not automatically eject shells, why would a killer empty shells from his gun and "hide" them close to the crime scene?

SOURCES: WR 25, 157, 160, 163 • WCH III, 342; VI, 454 • BELIN 18–21, 28–32 • RTJ 187, 198, 201 • BISHOP 372, 387–8 • CF 346

DAVIS, BENJAMIN J., leader of Communist Party U.S.A.; with Gus Hall and Arnold Johnson, one of three extreme-leftist leaders to whom Oswald presented "honorary membership cards" to his one-man New Orleans chapter of the FPCC. (See also Hall, Gus; Johnson, Arnold)

SOURCE: WR 386

DAVIS, EUGENE C., New Orleans bar owner; identified at one time by Dean Andrews as "Clay Bertrand," thus, in theory, getting Clay Shaw off the hook as an assassination conspirator. Andrews named Davis as the real "Clay Bertrand" in an interview with NBC-TV's Frank McGee for the TV special "The Case of Jim Garrison," which was broadcast on June 19, 1967.

Immediately thereafter, Davis denied Andrews's charges in an affidavit prepared in the offices of New Orleans District Attorney Jim Garrison.

Andrews was indicted in New Orleans for perjury after his testimony at the Clay Shaw trial. He was convicted but never served time because he died first. Davis testified at Andrews's trial.

Meanwhile, Davis threatened a defamation suit against Andrews and NBC. By this time, Davis's lawyer was G. Wray Gill, the man who had gotten assassination suspect Carlos Marcello acquitted of immigration-fraud charges in 1963, and also the same attorney who in 1963 had employed assassination suspect David Ferrie as a private investigator. (See also Andrews, Dean; Ferrie, David; Gill, G. Wray; Shaw, Clay)

SOURCES: FLAMMONDE 56–9, 65–7, 235, 307–8

DAVIS, FLOYD GUY and VIRGINIA LOUISE, possible Oswald witnesses. The Davises told the WC that they saw a man who resembled Oswald firing a rifle at the Sports Drome Rifle Range in Dallas in the weeks preceding the assassination. Floyd Davis operated the range.

SOURCES: WCH X, 356, 363 • RTJ 334

DAVIS, JOHN H., author of *Mafia Kingfish* (McGraw-Hill, 1988), a book suggesting that New Orleans crime boss Carlos Marcello ordered the assassination. Davis, a first cousin of Jackie Kennedy, told journalist Jack

Anderson in 1988: "An informant witnessed Oswald in Marcello's head-quarters, the Charles Guthrie Hotel, in New Orleans receiving what appeared to be a payment from a Marcello lieutenant. This is a scandalous story because Oswald's relationship with organized crime was completely withheld from the American people and the Warren Commission."

Addressing the JFK Assassination Symposium in Dallas on November 16, 1991, Davis said:

Since Dallas was under the Mafia jurisdiction of Carlos Marcello—who operated out of New Orleans, but who also controlled Dallas and Houston—Jack Ruby would not have been allowed to operate in those areas without Marcello's permission. So we may assume that Marcello was fully aware of the existence and activities of Jack Ruby at the time of the assassination... As the [HSCA] discovered in 1978, Ruby was closely connected in Dallas with at least three associates of Carlos Marcello. One was Joseph Civello, who represented Marcello at the Apalachin Crime Conference in 1957... Then there were the Campisi brothers, Joe and Sam. Joe ran the Egyptian Lounge in Dallas and Ruby ate at Joe's restaurant on the night before the assassination. Joe was one of the first people to visit Ruby in jail after he killed Oswald... Ruby, we have found out, also knew several members of the Marcello organization in New Orleans. One of them was Carlos Marcello's brother, Pete, who also ran a nightclub in the French Quarter... He knew one of Ruby's chief lieutenants, Nofio Pecora. He phoned him about a month before the assassination. He also knew two French Quarter operators—one of whom, Frank Caracci, inciden-tally, is running the rackets now in the French Quarter.

But Ruby's mob connections extended all over the nation. He knew Mickey Cohen in California. He knew Johnny Roselli, the front man in Las Vegas. He knew Santos Trafficante, the mob boss in Florida. And he knew several henchmen of Sam Giancana and Jimmy Hoffa, who, of course, was under the influence of Giancana... Phone records indicate that he called *all* of these people in the months leading up to the assassination. Ruby actually met with Roselli in Miami about a month before the assassination.

One of Ruby's activities was cultivating the Dallas police. He was what is called a "police buff." It has been estimated that Jack Ruby was on a first-name basis with more than 50 officers on the Dallas police force. It's hard to believe. He bought the men on the night watch deli sandwiches. He arranged loans for certain officers in need of financial assistance. He introduced officers to the sexiest striptease dancers in his nightclub, acting, in a sense, as a pimp. Many members of the Dallas police force were beholden to Jack Ruby in one way or another. This, of course, made Ruby extremely useful to the conspirators once Oswald was arrested and jailed by the Dallas police.

At the time of the assassination he owed upwards of $40,000 to the IRS...he was desperate for money...This is why we believe he allowed himself to become an instrument in a conspiracy to assassinate President Kennedy....

Apparently, at least six members of the [SS] who were assigned to protect Kennedy in Dallas attended a raucous party at the Cellar Door nightclub in Fort Worth on the night before the assassination. The son of the proprietor of the Cellar Door, a man by the name of Pat Kirkwood, said that Jack Ruby had sent his striptease dancers over to the party, to make sure the Secret Servicemen got bombed out of their minds and were not able to function properly the following day.

SOURCES: SUMMERS 501 • ME 211–3 • NORTH 370

DAVIS, JOSEPH H., HSCA medical expert; chief medical examiner for Dade County, Florida. Some assassination researchers have suggested that the difference in behavior of the two bullets that officially struck JFK (one exploded while the other remained intact and near-pristine) is evidence that there were two shooters in Dealey Plaza. Davis says this is not necessarily so: "It's all a matter of happenstance. There is no rule of thumb that a jacketed bullet is going to behave in a certain specific way and a nonjacketed bullet is going to behave in a totally different way."
SOURCE: ME 228–31

DAVIS, THOMAS ELI, III, Ruby witness; suspicious death. Davis ran guns and jeeps to Cuba with Ruby. In December 1963, Davis was jailed in Tangiers for running guns but was released through the efforts of a CIA agent code-named QJ/WIN (see Souetre, Jean). After Ruby's arrest, his lawyer asked Ruby if there was anyone who could hurt his defense that he had killed Oswald spontaneously to save Jackie the ordeal of a trial. Davis's was the only name Ruby mentioned. Davis died on September 9, 1973, electrocuted while stealing wire from a warehouse.
SOURCES: SUMMERS 470–1 • NORTH 441

DAVISON, ALEXIS, captain, U.S. Air Force; known contact man for at least one CIA spy within the USSR. In 1962, Davison was the assistant air attaché and doctor at the U.S. embassy in Moscow. He admitted to the FBI that he spoke to Lee and Marina Oswald at the end of May 1962, just before they left the Soviet Union. Davison's hometown in the United States was Atlanta, Georgia. When the Oswalds flew from New York City to Texas, they took a flight that made a stop in Atlanta. After Oswald's death, the name and address of Davison's mother were found in Oswald's address book.

SOURCES: WCH XVI, 37 • WCD 87, 235, 409, 1115 • HSCA Report 215 • SUMMERS 185, 188

DAY, J.C., a.w. (aftermath); DPD lieutenant. Day was among the first to examine the rifle discovered on the sixth floor of the TSBD, which belonged at the time to the DPD's Crime Scene Search Section Identification Bureau. When the rifle was discovered hidden—but not very well— between boxes, Day was summoned immediately. Day photographed the rifle, noted its serial number (C–2766) and scratched his name on the stock—the standard police procedure for "marking evidence." Later in the day, Dallas authorities told reporters the rifle was a 7.65 German Mauser, different from the 6.5 Italian Mannlicher-Carcano eventually linked to Oswald. Later, while testifying to the WC about the palm print reportedly found on the rifle, Day said, "No, sir, I could not make a positive identification of these prints."

SOURCES: WR 27, 84, 117, 127, 131 • WCH IV, 249; VII, 401 • BELIN 9–10 • RTJ 114–7, 120, 154–8, 386 • BISHOP 197, 268, 342, 370, 378–80, 420–1, 476, 496 • PWW 122 • EVICA 18, 20, 22, 24–5, 37, 42–5, 48, 50–1, 54

DEALEY, GEORGE BANNERMAN, founder of the *Dallas Morning News* in 1885. JFK was assassinated in the plaza named for him.

DEAN, HARRY. According to researcher W. R. Morris, Dean is the "war name" of a man currently living in hiding. Morris writes:

His knowledge of the true facts behind the President's assassination has caused him and his family to live in constant hell... Born in Cuba, Dean joined Castro's guerillas in the revolution against Batista and kept U.S. Intelligence informed as to the Cuban leader's activities. On returning to the U.S. he monitored the [FPCC], becoming secretary of local committees in Chicago, Detroit, and Los Angeles. Later, he joined the John Birch Society where, in 1962, he learned of a conspiracy to assassinate the President.

Dean told Morris (and later Tom Snyder on the *Tomorrow* show on NBC-TV on an episode that never aired) that two of the gunmen hired by the John Birch Society to kill JFK were Eladio del Valle and Loran Hall. (See also Hall, Loran; Del Valle, Eladio)

SOURCE: AO, many

DEAN, PATRICK TREVORE, Ruby witness; DPD sergeant; interviewed Ruby on November 26, 1963. Dean told the WC that Ruby had told him he had entered the DPD basement to shoot Oswald via the Main Street ramp and that he had decided to kill Oswald two days before the event. This second statement is in direct contrast to Ruby's later claim (and the WC's conclusion) that Ruby had spontaneously decided to shoot Oswald. Dean said that all the basement entrances were locked and guarded, so that— contrary to some claims—Ruby must have entered via the ramp the way he said he did. A longtime friend of Ruby, Dean failed a polygraph examination about Oswald's death, despite permission to write his own questions. According to author Anthony Summers, "Years earlier [Dean] had been on good terms with Joe Civello, the Dallas Mafia figure widely acknowledged to have been the Texas representative for [assassination suspect] Carlos Marcello." (See also Civello, Joe; Marcello, Carlos)

SOURCES: WR 196, 198, 205–6 • WCH V, 254; XII, 415 • HSCA Report 158 • RTJ 18, 227, 392–5 • COA 148 • GERTZ, many • DOP 50, 633 • PWW 40, 56 • BE 99 • SUMMERS 463–4, 467–8 • FMG I, 37, 67–73, 78 • BLAKEY 320–4, 330, 333 • KANTOR, many

DeBRUEYS, WARREN, FBI agent. According to Jim Garrison, De-Brueys was heavily involved in the activities of Guy Banister, David Ferrie, and anti-Castro Cubans during the summer of 1963. According to author Anthony Summers, DeBrueys also monitored Oswald's activities during that same period. He was also the agent who took Oswald's possessions from Dallas to Washington for analysis. Garrison subpoenaed DeBrueys, but he pleaded executive privilege and refused to testify at the conspiracy trial of Clay Shaw under instructions from the Justice Department. Garrison said in his October 1967 *Playboy* interview:

> DeBrueys was involved with anti-Castro activities in New Orleans... I'd like to find out the exact nature of DeBruey's relationship with Lee Oswald. As long as Oswald was in New Orleans, so was DeBrueys. When Oswald moved to Dallas, DeBrueys followed him. After the assassination, DeBrueys returned to New Orleans. This may all be coincidence, but I find it interesting that DeBrueys refuses to cooperate with our office—significant and frustrating, because I feel he could shed considerable light on Oswald's ties to anti-Castro groups.

(See also Banister, William Guy; Carlson, Alex; Ferrie, David; Shaw, Clay)

SOURCES: OTT 182 • FLAMMONDE 26, 118 • DAVIS 130 • NORTH 294–5, 301 • PD 55–6

DECKER, J. E. "BILL," a.w.; Dallas county sheriff. Decker rode in the backseat of the motorcade's lead car. With him were the driver, Police Chief Jesse Curry, Winston G. Lawson, sitting in the front passenger seat, and Forrest Sorrels, who sat to Decker's right in the backseat. After the shooting, Decker ordered, "Move all available men out of my office into the railroad yard...and hold everything secure until Homicide and other investigators should get there."

DPD Captain Will Fritz's initial interrogation of Oswald on the afternoon of November 22 was interrupted by a phone call from Sheriff Decker. Whatever Decker's message for Fritz, it couldn't be discussed on the phone. Fritz left the interrogation room and walked 15 blocks from City Hall to Decker's office. The pair had a meeting, topic unknown, and Fritz returned to resume the questioning.

Crack shot and Deputy Sheriff Harry Weatherford, who had received a custom-made silencer for his rifle several weeks before the assassination, had been ordered by Sheriff Decker to stand atop the Dallas County Jail during the presidential motorcade—which is very suspicious indeed, since this spot is suspected by some assassination researchers of being the source of the shots that struck Governor Connally. (When Decker died in 1970, Weatherford was at his death bed.) Further suspicion is added by the fact that, on the morning of November 22, Decker had ordered his deputies to "take no part whatsoever in the security of the presidential motorcade." (See also Fritz, Will; Henslee, Gerald; Weatherford, Harry)

SOURCES: WR 58, 195 • WCH XII, 42 • RTJ 43, 243 • COA 23, 110–1, 148, 153–7, 431 • GERTZ, many • BISHOP, many • DOP 133 • CF 9, 14 • PWW 32, 45 • SUMMERS 24, 474–5 • BE 15 • FMG I, 35, 158; III, 7, 30–1, 35–7, 76, 90 • BLAKEY 11, 322, 334–5 • FLAMMONDE 127, 174 • HOS 234 • ME 73–4, 184 • OGLESBY 17 • KANTOR 4–5, 32–3, 36, 53, 60, 124, 166, 178, 187 • PD 356

DeGAULLE, CHARLES, general and president of Fifth French Republic. After several attempts on his life were traced to the Swiss corporation Permindex, de Gaulle saw to it that the company was booted out of Switzerland, forcing it to relocate in South Africa. (See also Gatlin, Maurice; Shaw, Clay; Torbitt, William)

SOURCES: HSCA Report 28 • BISHOP 515 • DOP, many • KANTOR 16 • NORTH 79, 155, 179–80, 186, 194, 201–3, 236, 283

DeLAPARRA, EUGENE, employee of assassination suspect Carlos Marcello; FBI informant. DeLaparra once quoted Marcello's brother Anthony as saying in the spring of 1963, "The word is out to get the

Kennedy family." DeLaparra also worked for Marcello associate Bernard Tregle at his New Orleans restaurant and says that in April 1963 he saw Tregle and two friends looking at an advertisement for a cheap foreign rifle. Tregle reportedly said that the rifle would be good to "get the President... Somebody will kill Kennedy when he comes down south." Officially, Oswald ordered the cheap foreign rifle used to kill JFK through a magazine advertisement.
    SOURCES: SUMMERS 502 • DAVIS, many • NORTH 239, 444

DELAUNE, HENRY, murder victim; brother-in-law and coworker of Dr. Nicholas Chetta, the New Orleans coroner who performed autopsies on some of Jim Garrison's dead witnesses, including assassination suspect David Ferrie, Ferrie associate Dr. Mary Sherman, and Ruby connection Robert Perrin. Chetta died of a heart attack on May 25, 1968. Delaune was murdered on January 26, 1969. (See also Chetta, Nicholas)
    SOURCE: FMG III, 57

DELGADO, NELSON, Oswald witness; USMC acquaintance. Delgado bunked "next door" to Oswald for almost a year (November 1958 to September 1959) at the El Toro Marine Base in California. He told the WC that Oswald's proficiency with a rifle was minimal: "It was a pretty big joke because he got a lot of 'Maggie's drawers,' you know, a lot of misses, but he didn't give a darn... [Oswald] wasn't as enthusiastic as the rest of us. We all loved—liked, you know—going to the range... He was mostly a thinker, a reader. He read quite a bit." Oswald once told him that the best way to escape United States law enforcement, should that become necessary, was to flee to Russia, via Mexico and Cuba. Delgado testified:

> We got to know each other quite well... before Christmas, before I took my leave [1958]... He liked Spanish and he talked to me... in Spanish... I was kind of a loner myself... at the time he was commenting on the fight Castro was having at Sierra Madres [sic]... When I went on leave... coincided with the first of January [1959], when Castro took over. So when I got back, he was the first to see me... [He said,] "Well, you took a leave and went there and helped them, and they all took over." It was a big joke... He had trouble in one of the huts and he got transferred to mine... [The] way I understand it... came time for a cleanup... he didn't want to participate... griping all the time... the sergeant in charge of that hut asked to have him put out... they put him into my hut. He was a complete believer that our way of government was not quite right... he was for, not the Communist way of life, the Castro

way . . . the way he was going to lead his people . . . he never said any subversive things or tried to take any classified information . . .

Delgado testified that there had been an evening when Oswald was allowed to stand down from guard duty so he could meet for two hours with a stranger in an overcoat who appeared "Cuban." Of his unit, including Oswald, Delgado said, "We all had access to classified information. I believe it was classified 'secret.'" After the WC hearings, Delgado took his family to England, because he was fearful that ". . . the conspirators might think I know more than I do."
SOURCES: WC VIII, 228 • BELIN 214 • RTJ 387–9 • CF 102, 109 • AO 102–3 • BE 101 • FLAMMONDE 136–37 • SUMMERS 118, 122, 127 • HOS 58 • KANTOR 205

DeLOACH, CARTHA D. "DEKE," FBI assistant director. DeLoach wrote an internal memo to J. Edgar Hoover's close friend and assistant Clyde Tolson that "the President [LBJ] felt the CIA had something to do with this plot."
SOURCES: COA 218 • BISHOP 402, 530 • BE 116, 302, 304–6 • BLAKEY 77 • EVICA 172 • DAVIS 330, 362 • NORTH, many

DEL VALLE, ELADIO CEREFINE (sometimes shown as Aladio), murder victim; Cuban exile; close friend of assassination suspect David Ferrie; occupation unknown (possibly freelance pilot). Del Valle died just hours after Ferrie on February 22, 1967; he was found with a split-open head and a gunshot to the heart. Del Valle's head wound appeared to have been caused by a machete. At the time of Del Valle's death, Jim Garrison was searching for him to testify against Clay Shaw.

According to Harry Dean (the "war name" of a man who claims to be an ex-CIA agent, as quoted by W. B. Morris and R. B. Cutler in their book *Alias Oswald*), the JFK assassins were Loran Hall and Eladio del Valle, who were hired to do the job by the John Birch Society.

According to author Anthony Summers, del Valle was the leader of Florida's Free Cuba Committee in Florida who had "links" with Floridian mobster and assassination suspect Santos Trafficante, who was also later murdered. (See also Dean, Harry; Ferrie, David; Hall, Loran; Wade, Henry)
SOURCES: AO, many • SUMMERS 319, 491 • DAVIS 372

DeMAR, WILLIAM (See CROWE, WILLIAM D., JR.)

DEMARIS, OVID, coauthor, with Garry Wills, of *Jack Ruby* (New American Library, 1968).

DeMENIL, JEAN, in 1963 the president of the international Schlumberger Corporation, which had close CIA ties. According to Gordon Novel, Schlumberger was used as a front to store arms for the Bay of Pigs invasion. Among DeMenil's close friends was Oswald associate George DeMohrenschildt. (See also Bloomfield, Louis; DeMohrenschildt, George; Novel, Gordon)

SOURCES: OTT 53 • HOS 112

DeMOHRENSCHILDT, ALEXANDRA (See GIBSON, MRS. DONALD)

DeMOHRENSCHILDT, GEORGE SERGEI, Oswald witness; suspicious death; close friend of the Oswalds following their return from the Soviet Union; White Russian count with a background in intelligence; enjoyed ice skating. DeMohrenschildt was involved in CIA training for the Bay of Pigs invasion in Guatemala. At the time of JFK's death, he lived in Haiti where he was representing the interests of Dallas oil billionaire Clint Murchison.

The Oswalds originally moved to Fort Worth following their return to the U.S., and on October 7, 1962, they were visited by DeMohrenschildt, who convinced them to move to Dallas, which they did. He urged the Oswalds to mingle with the Dallas Soviet émigré community, many of whom were right-wing "solidarists" who had sided with the Nazis against the Communists. He apparently worked for the Nazis during WW II. DeMohrenschildt said that Oswald spoke "almost flawless Russian." He wrote that Oswald's handgun was a "Beretta," not at all like the gun reportedly found on him in the Texas Theatre. DeMohrenschildt once worked for a Murchison oil company, Three States Oil and Gas. He was friends with Ruth Paine's father.

The fact that DeMohrenschildt was an educated man of foreign nobility who has been linked to the Bay of Pigs operation, had ties to Dallas oil billionaire H. L. Hunt, had ties with the Bouviers (Jacqueline Kennedy's family), was suspected of being a spy, and was a close friend of Oswald, casts serious doubt on the WC's portrait of Oswald as a "lone nut."

According to Cindy Adams in the *New York Post* (February 12, 1992), DeMohrenschildt was once engaged to Jacqueline Bouvier's Aunt Michele and "nearly married [Jackie's mother] Janet Auchincloss...President Kennedy's widow called him Uncle George."

Jackie's first cousin Edie Beale is quoted by Adams as saying, "We all knew George. He was a regular visitor. As a child, Jackie played on the lawn with Uncle George."

According to Adams, Jackie's brother Jack said, "George took Janet out

during the time she was divorcing Jackie's father. George was very much a
potential stepfather to Jackie. He wanted to marry Janet, but Janet wanted a
very rich man."

In 1976 he wrote a manuscript titled *I Am a Patsy! I Am a Patsy!*, which
he claimed named names. Later he said, "That's when disaster struck. You
see, in that book I played devil's advocate. Without directly implicating
myself as an accomplice in the JFK assassination, I still mentioned a
number of names, particularly of FBI and CIA officials who apparently may
not be exposed under any circumstances. I was drugged surreptitiously. As
a result I was committed to a mental hospital . . . "

On the day he agreed to an interview with the HSCA, he was found dead
of a gunshot through his mouth. His death was ruled a suicide. George's
wife Jeanne said that, before he was committed to Parkland Hospital for
mental problems, he was under the medical care of Dr. Charles Mendoza, a
"shadowy" Dallas doctor who gave him two or three hours of therapy at a
time that included injections.

Jeanne believes her husband was the subject of a mind-control experi-
ment, and that his suicide death was triggered by a telephoned command.
Near the end, he was ranting and raving about his WW II experiences,
saying, "The Jews have finally caught up with me." (See also DeMenil,
Jean; Epstein, Edward Jay; Ferrie, David; Fonzi, Gaeton; Gregory, Peter;
Hunt, H. L.; Hyde, William; Lancelot, Jacqueline; McDonald, Hugh;
Mendoza, Charles; Moore, J. Walton; Murchison, Clint; Oswald, Marina;
Prio Socarras, Carlos; Voshinen, Igor)

SOURCES: WR 238–9, 261–2, 371, 376–7, 393 • WCH IX, 166 • HSCA Report 56, 180,
217–8 • COA 38 • CF 199–202, 278–9 • OTT 51–6, 62, 70, 176, 273, 286 • SUMMERS
104, 192–200, 206–12, 492 • FMG I, 186; III, 8, 80 • BLAKEY 33, 349–53, 355–7 •
FLAMMONDE 146, 154–5, 192–8 • HOS 112, 132–3 • EVICA, many • OGLESBY 73–4
• NORTH 156, 205, 235, 238, 604 • PD 32

DeMOHRENSCHILDT, JEANNE, wife of George S.; enjoyed ice
skating. (See also DeMohrenschildt, George; Oswald, Marina)

SOURCES: WR 261–2, 376–7, 394, 638–40, 642, 645 • WCH IX, 166 • CF 122–3,
278–9 • SUMMERS 195–8, 209–10 • BLAKEY 33, 352, 356 • FLAMMONDE 146,
194–5 • EVICA 11, 291–2

DENSON, R. B., Ruby witness; Ruby defense investigator. Denson
researched Jack's long-distance telephone calls during the months preceding the assassination. He wrote in a memo to Ruby defense attorney Melvin
Belli, "These calls clearly indicate some very undesirable connections with
underworld characters."

SOURCE: GERTZ 15–21, 26, 104

DEVINE, SAMUEL L., member of the HSCA (R-Ohio).
SOURCES: BLAKEY 66, 77

DHORITY, CHARLES N., o.k.w.; DPD member. Dhority was involved in Oswald's aborted transfer. He drove the follow-up to the car that was to receive Oswald and also helped administer the paraffin test to Oswald to determine whether he had recently fired a gun. The tests were positive for Oswald's hands and negative for his face, indicating that he had fired a handgun, but not a rifle. The WC called the tests "inconclusive."
SOURCES: WR 200 • WCH VII,149, 380 • RTJ 211 • BISHOP 351–2, 399 • EVICA 25, 50–1

DIETRICH, EDWARD C., Armored Motor Service guard. Dietrich rode to the DPD station on the morning of November 24 with driver Don Goin and parked outside the Commerce Street entrance to the basement. He told the WC that he didn't hear any shots when Ruby murdered Oswald.
SOURCE: WCH XV, 269

DIGGS, MARSHALL, assassination suspect; attorney and one-time comptroller of the United States. Diggs was, according to former CIA agent and author Robert Morrow, a "major player" in the plot to kill JFK. (See also Barnes, Tracy; Kohly Mario)
SOURCE: MORROW, many

DILLARD, THOMAS C., a.w.; Dallas photojournalist; chief photographer for the *Dallas Morning News*. Dillard rode in a motorcade press car—the sixth car, five behind JFK's limo. He was about 50 yards away from the TSBD on Houston Street at the time of the shooting sequence. He heard three shots, equally spaced, and smelled gunpowder at the corner of Houston and Elm. According to researcher Jim Bishop, Dillard claims to have snapped two pictures of the TSBD after the third shot, after a.w. Robert H. Jackson—who was in the same car—said, "There's a rifle barrel up there." Dillard's photo of the sniper's-nest window immediately after the shooting shows boxes and shadows in that window. Comparing this photo with one taken 30 seconds later by James Powell gives the impression that the boxes in the sniper's-nest window were rearranged after the shooting. Because Oswald was seen 90 seconds after the shooting on the second floor of the TSBD, composed and not out of breath, this photographic evidence supports the implausibility of Oswald's lone guilt. (See also Couch, Malcolm O.; Darnell, James; Jackson, Robert H.; Underwood, James)
SOURCES: WR 77 • WCH VI, 162 • BISHOP 140 • CF 53 • PWW 53, 57–60, 82, 85, 95, 131–2 • HOS 56

DILLON, C. DOUGLAS, RC member; former secretary of the treasury under JFK; in charge of the SS at the time of the assassination. Before the WC, Dillon discussed the failure of the SS to adequately protect JFK and methods of improving presidential protection in the future.
SOURCES: WR 360, 400, 441, 443, 445 • WCH V, 573 • BELIN 79–80, 163–4 • BISHOP 107, 474

DINKIN, EUGENE. Among the WCDs comprised of "top secret" CIA documents still sealed in the National Archives is WCD 943, which is titled, "Allegations of Pfc. Eugene Dinkin re Assassination Plot."
SOURCE: FLAMMONDE 162

DiSPADAFORO, GUTIERREZ, Italian prince; member of the House of Savoy. With assassination suspect Clay Shaw and L. M. Bloomfield, DiSpadaforo was a member of the board of directors of CMC. (See also Bloomfield, Louis; Shaw, Clay; Torbitt, William)
SOURCES: FLAMMONDE 215, 217 • OTT 87–88

DOBBS, FARRELL, International secretary of the Socialist Workers Party. Dobbs told the WC that Oswald was not a member of his organization.
SOURCES: WR 268 • WCH XI, 208

DODD, CHRISTOPHER, HSCA member (D–Connecticut). Dodd dissented from the committee's opinion that all of the rear shots were fired by Oswald, since the acoustic evidence showed that only 1.66 seconds separated two of them. He pointed out that, assuming the evidence found on the sixth floor of the TSBD was not planted, three shell casings do not necessarily indicate three shots. One of the casings could have come from a shot taken well before the assassination and ejected only before the first shot at the motorcade. Ballistics tests can show that those shells had been fired in the Mannlicher-Carcano rifle reportedly owned by Oswald, but they cannot show when the shots were fired.
SOURCES: SUMMERS 47, 73 • BLAKEY 128–9, 142 • ME 136, 244

DODD, RICHARD C., a.w. Dodd stood atop the triple underpass. He told Dallas reporter Jim Marrs that he, like other witnesses who watched the shooting from that vantage point, saw smoke coming out of the bushes atop the grassy knoll after the shots were fired.
SOURCES: CF 58–9 • RTJ 40 • COA 21–2, 24 • BE 16

DOLAN, JAMES HENRY, Ruby witness and friend. According to the HSCA, Dolan knew suspicious a.w. Eugene Hale Brading in 1951, when Brading was using the name James Bradley Lee. According to the HSCA, Dolan was also an associate of assassination suspects Santos Trafficante and Carlos Marcello. According to author G. Robert Blakey, Dolan was present when Ruby hit Breck Wall's assistant Joseph Patterson over the last-minute scrub of a business deal. According to author Anthony Summers, in "the period before the assassination, Dolan... committed acts of violence on Trafficante's behalf." (See also Brading, Eugene; Marcello, Carlos; Peterson, Joseph; Trafficante, Santos; Wall, Breck)

SOURCES: HSCA Report 156, 173 • HSCA IX, 424 • COA 246, 250, 329–30 • SUMMERS 442, 452 • BLAKEY 288, 305–6

DOLCE, JOSEPH, wound ballistics expert. Dolce reported, with Dr. F. W. Light in April 1964, that Governor Connally must have been struck by two bullets—the basis of this conclusion being that the "magic bullet" (WCE 399) could not have shattered Connally's wrist bone yet emerged pristine. (See also Light, F. W.)

SOURCE: WR 106

DONABEDIAN, GEORGE, captain, U.S. navy; staff medical officer, U.S. Navy Medical Corps, USMC Headquarters. Donabedian interpreted Oswald's USMC medical records for the WC.

SOURCE: WCH VIII, 311

DONAHUE, HOWARD, Maryland ballistics expert; one of the eleven marksmen hired by CBS in 1967 to duplicate the three-shot feat attributed to Oswald; assassination theorist. Donahue claims to have put 25 years of research into the assassination, and this work is now the basis of *Mortal Error* by Bonar Menninger. The book says JFK was killed by accident by SS agent George Hickey, who was riding in the presidential follow-up car. When Oswald began to shoot at JFK from the TSBD, Hickey turned, reached for his rifle and slipped off the safety. As he tried to stand up on the backseat of the car, he lost his balance and accidentally pulled the trigger of his AR-15 (now called an M-16). The theory states that Oswald fired only twice, missing the first shot and delivering all of the nonfatal wounds with the second shot. *Mortal Error* claims that the third and fatal shot was fired by Hickey.

SOURCE: ME, many

DONALDSON, ANN, a.w.; *Dallas Morning News* employee. Donaldson watched the motorcade "from the grassy knoll area" (i.e., from the north side of Elm Street west of the TSBD) with coworkers Mary Woodward, Maggie Brown, and Aurelia Lorenzo. Like the women she was with, she said the shots came from behind her and to her right—the direction of the wooden fence atop the grassy knoll.

SOURCES: SUMMERS 27 • *Dallas Morning News,* November 23, 1963

DONOVAN, JOHN E., Oswald witness; USMC acquaintance; first lieutenant in charge of Oswald's radar crew at El Toro Marine Base in California from November 1958 to September 1959. Before joining the USMC, Donovan earned a B.S. degree in foreign service at Georgetown University and graduated in 1956. He told the WC that Oswald read a Russian-language newspaper while in the marines, that he believed it to be a Communist paper and that Oswald had a subscription to it. Donovan was asked whether he recalled a man named Thornley. Donovan replied, "I don't recall the name at all."

He told author Edward Jay Epstein that he clearly remembered discussing the U-2's radar blips with Oswald—although the conversation took place at the Cubi Point base in the Philippines instead of in Japan. Although, officially, Oswald had a "confidential" clearance, Donovan says that it must have been higher than that. "He must have had 'secret' clearance to work in the radar center, because that was the minimum requirement for all of us," Donovan said. (See also Thornley, Kerry W.)

SOURCES: WR 361, 365 • WCH VIII, 289 • HSCA Report 219 • DUFFY 22 • AO 98–100 • OTT 46 • FLAMMONDE 136–8 • SUMMERS 115, 117, 127 • LEGEND 280

DORFMAN, PAUL, Ruby witness; had links with both Ruby and assassination suspect Jimmy Hoffa. In 1939, Dorfman was Ruby's union boss in the Scrap Iron & Junk Handlers Union. At the time of the assassination, Dorfman was a key henchman for Hoffa, who was then president of the International Brotherhood of Teamsters.

SOURCE: SUMMERS 246, 433

DORMAN, ELSIE, a.w. Dorman watched the shooting with Victoria Adams, Sandra Styles, and Dorothy May Garner from an open TSBD fourth-floor window. She told the FBI on November 24, 1963, that she "thought at the time that the shots or reports came from a point to the west of the building."

SOURCES: BISHOP 131 • CF 44 • PWW 42, 49-52, 83, 177

DORNBERGER, WALTER, ex-Nazi general. According to *Standard and Poor's 1963*, Dornberger was the overall supervisor of classified projects for Bell Aerospace. Working in Dornberger's division at defense contractor Bell Helicopter at the time of the assassination was Oswald-acquaintance Michael Paine, the estranged husband of Marina Oswald's housemate Ruth. One man responsible for Dornberger's migration from Nazi Germany to the American security force was future CIA director and Warren Commissioner Allen Dulles. (See also Paine, Michael; Paine, Ruth; Torbitt, William; von Braun, Wernher)

SOURCE: *Critique*, #21/22, p. 82

DOUGHERTY, JACK EDWIN, Oswald witness; TSBD employee. Dougherty saw Oswald enter the TSBD on the morning of the assassination. He told the WC that he didn't think Oswald was carrying anything.
SOURCES: WR 126, 143 • WCH VI, 373 • RTJ 145–6 • CF 42

DOWE, KENNETH LAWRY, Ruby witness; KLIF radio disc jockey in Dallas. On the night after the assassination, Ruby helped arrange an interview for the station with Dallas District Attorney Henry Wade and later visited the station to deliver sandwiches. (See also Wade, Henry)
SOURCES: WR 370 • WCH XV, 430 • COA 90, 134 • GERTZ 61

DOWLING, ADA, Oswald witness; waitress at the Dobbs House restaurant on North Beckley Street in Dallas, the street where Oswald lived. Dowling said that Officer J. D. Tippit came into the restaurant every morning and, on at least one occasion, Tippit and Oswald were in the restaurant at the same time, although she didn't know whether they knew each other. (See also Tippit, Jefferson Davis)
SOURCE: HT 276

DOWNEY, WILLIAM, a.w. Downey stood at the corner of Main and Houston. He said he heard "one or more" explosions and "thought they were firecrackers." Downey told the WC that George Senator, Ruby's roommate at the time of the assassination, called him and his wife on the morning of Sunday, November 24—the morning that Ruby shot Oswald—saying that Jack had left their apartment and offering to visit their home and make them breakfast. Downey declined the offer and Senator said he would probably go downtown for breakfast. Oddly, Senator firmly denied ever making this phone call, explaining that he and the Downeys were no longer friends. (See also Senator, George)
SOURCES: WR 347–8 • WCH XXVI, 551

DOWNING, THOMAS N., first HSCA chairman (D–Virginia). A few months before assuming the chair of the committee, Downing wrote that he was "convinced...there was more than one assassin." (See also Gonzalez, Henry; Stokes, Louis)
SOURCES: BELIN 188 • CF 518–24 • BLAKEY 62–5, 68 • DAVIS 422–3

DOX, IDA, artist who made hair-by-hair tracings of the JFK autopsy photos. These drawings were available to the public before the actual photographs, which still, though widely published, have not been officially released.
SOURCE: BE 548, 550, 662, 669

DOYLE, HAROLD, possible a.w.; suspected "tramp." According to Ray and Mary La Fontaine in the *Houston Post*, JFK assassination files released by the DPD in February 1992 name Doyle, 32 years old at the time of assassination, as one of the three tramps apprehended in a railroad car near Dealey Plaza moments after the assassination. The files name the other two tramps as Gus Abrams, 53, and John F. Gedney, 38.

At the time of this writing, Doyle is a 61-year-old pool-hall worker in Klamath Falls, Oregon. When interviewed by Steve Dunleavy of the TV program *A Current Affair* (February 25, 1992), Doyle said that the three tramps were just what they appeared to be—hoboes, who were on their way to Fort Worth and were looking to catch a ride, and that they made themselves scarce after that for fear that they would be blamed for something they knew nothing about.

Initial reports on the tramps said that they were released immediately without their names ever being taken, but new DPD records and Doyle's statements show that this is not true. Doyle says that the three were arrested for vagrancy and had an opportunity to see Oswald while in the police station. Dunleavy commented, "The tale of these three reveals what appears to be shocking laxity on the part of assassination investigators... Why police or anyone else couldn't locate this man is a mystery." Neighbors of Doyle's when he lived in Amarillo, Texas, confirmed that Doyle had, on occasion, mentioned the fact that he was one of the tramps. They said that he didn't seem proud of the fact, but that he wasn't ashamed of it either. According to the *New York Daily News* (March 4, 1992), the FBI has confirmed that the three men named in the DPD were the real tramps and are not suspects in the case. They have discovered that Abrams is dead and Gedney was located in Melbourne, Florida, and interviewed.

Other men "positively" identified as the "tramps" are Charles Frederick Rogers, Chauncy Marvin Holt, Charles V. Harrelson, E. Howard Hunt, and Frank Sturgis. (See also Abrams, Gus; Gedney, John Forrester; Harrelson, Charles V.; Holt, Chauncy; Hunt, E. Howard; Rogers, Charles; Sturgis, Frank

DRAIN, VINCENT, FBI special agent. Drain transported the Mannlicher-Carcano rifle from Dallas to Washington on the morning of November 23, 1963, so that it could be examined by the FBI laboratory. In a 1984 interview with researcher Henry Hurt, Drain said that he didn't think the discovery, by the DPD, of Oswald's palm print on the Mannlicher-Carcano rifle was legitimate. Drain said, "All I can figure is that [the print] was some kind of cushion because they [the DPD] were getting a lot

of heat by Sunday night. You could take the print off Oswald's card and put it on the rifle." The FBI examined the rifle and found no prints. They sent it back to Dallas, where the palm print was discovered. (See also Day, J. C.)
SOURCES: FMG III, 65 • OTT 64 • BE 354 • EVICA 45 • KANTOR 186

DROBY, C. A., Dallas attorney. Droby arranged the meeting between Ruby's roommate George Senator, Ruby's lawyer Tom Howard and two journalists, Bill Hunter, and Jim Koethe in Ruby's apartment on the evening of November 24, 1963, the day Ruby shot Oswald. The meeting is noteworthy because Howard, Hunter, and Koethe all died soon thereafter.
SOURCE: FMG I, 5

DUFF, WILLIAM McEWAN, possible Ruby witness; employee of Major General Edwin A. Walker. Duff told DPD chief Jesse Curry and the FBI that he saw Ruby go to Walker's house. He later denied it without offering an explanation why he had lied. According to author Paris Flammonde, Duff was "an Englishman of shadowy background who served for some time as General Walker's personal secretary." Duff was not called as a WC witness. (See also Curry, Jesse; Walker, Edwin A.)
SOURCES: WR 344 • WCE 2931

DUFFY, JAMES R., author of *Who Killed JFK?* (Shapolski Publishers, 1988).

DUGGER, ROBERT E., Parkland witness; DPD sergeant. Dugger was stationed at the Trade Mart during the shooting. Later, he stood guard outside Trauma Room #1 as JFK was treated. Author William Manchester describes Dugger as a "bespectacled...towering bullock of a cop, with a beefy face and piercing eyes; to Jacqueline Kennedy he looked rather ugly. [She wondered] whether he could be a Bircher." (See also Bishop, William)
SOURCES: DOP 149, 179, 185, 187–8, 211, 213, 217, 294

DULANY, RICHARD B., Parkland witness; first-year resident in surgery on call in the emergency room. When shown the JFK autopsy photos, Dulany said, "...that's not the way I remember it." However, Dulany primarily treated Governor Connally.
SOURCES: WR 69 • WCH VI, 113

DULLES, ALLEN WELSH, member of the WC; former CIA director. Ironically, Dulles had been fired by JFK. He had been a master spy during WW II, supervising the penetration of the Abwehr (Hitler's military intelligence agency) and the subsequent absorption of many of its undercover agents into the CIA. Dulles was a known enemy of JFK. During Jim Garrison's assassination probe, Garrison subpoenaed Dulles. Dulles ignored the subpoena. Dulles was the younger brother of John Foster

Dulles, former secretary of state (1953 to 59) under Eisenhower, who employed a strong anticommunist "cold war" policy. (See also Billings, Richard; Dornberger, Walter; Edwards, Sheffield; Hunt, E. Howard; von Braun, Wernher)

SOURCES: HSCA Report 33, 104, 257 • OGLESBY 6, 12 • EVICA, many • BELIN 13, 104, 124, 137–8, 169 • RTJ 23, 73, 187, 367, 369–71, 373, 392 • COA 192, 210, 225 • GERTZ 75 • OTT 14, 49, 104, 176–8, 273, 282, 291, 327 • SUMMERS 106–7, 131, 133, 139–40, 238 • BE, many • FMG I, 138; III, 78 • BLAKEY 24, 27, 52–5, 59, 77–8, 116, 159, 266 • FLAMMONDE 242 • HOS 18, 81, 84, 86–9, 99 • KANTOR 80, 82, 93, 162 • DAVIS 97–8, 282–3, 290–1, 295, 302–3, 404, 406 • NORTH, many • PD 48–9, 53, 67, 98, 165, 210, 362

DUNCAN, WILLIAM GLENN, JR., Ruby witness; KLIF radio newsman in Dallas. Duncan says that Ruby called him around midnight, 11½ hours after the assassination, and asked whether Duncan was interested in interviewing Dallas District Attorney Henry Wade. Duncan said yes, and a few moments later Ruby put Wade on the phone. Between 1:30 and 1:45 A.M. on November 23, 1963, Ruby showed up at the KLIF studios with sandwiches and soda pop for the staff. At that time Ruby told the men that he had been in the DPD station when they had brought Oswald down for his press conference and had been standing "close" to Oswald. Ruby left the radio station at approximately 2:00 A.M.

SOURCES: WR 319 • WCH XV, 482 • GERTZ 44 • BISHOP 495, 501–2 • DOP 88, 116

DUNN, WILLIAM, Oswald witness; member of the Clinton, Louisiana, Congress of Racial Equality. Dunn organized a voter-registration drive in early September 1963. Only one white man attempted to register that day; that man was later identified by eyewitnesses as Oswald. Dunn saw the man arrive in a black Cadillac. One of the passengers in the car was identified by eyewitnesses as David Ferrie. According to author Anthony Summers, ". . . some of the Clinton witnesses thought [Clay Shaw] could have been the driver. . . In the light of all the other evidence, many investigators now favor the theory that the car's driver was in fact Guy Banister."

SOURCES: HSCA Report 142 • SUMMERS 305

DURAN, SILVIA TIRADO DE, possible Oswald witness; secretary at the Mexico City Cuban consulate when Oswald supposedly visited there in September 1963. She said that the Oswald she saw was "35 years old."

Duran was arrested twice in Mexico after the assassination, apparently on CIA orders, and told not to say anything more about "Oswald." The first order to arrest Duran (November 23, 1963) read, in part; "With full regard for Mexican interests, request you ensure that her [Duran's] arrest is kept absolutely secret, that no information from her is published or leaked, that all such info is cabled to us... " Duran was not released until she identified Oswald as the man she had seen. In a 1978 interview with Anthony Summers, Señora Duran said that the man she had seen was only her height—5'3"—at least six inches shorter than Oswald. (See also Navarro, Horacio Duran)

> SOURCES: WR 267, 280–2, 285–6 • HSCA Report 123–5, 250–1 • CF 193–5 • SUMMERS 345–51, 521 • BLAKEY 33–4 • DAVIS 164–5 • NORTH 316 • PD 46, 49, 54, 58–60, 313

DURHAM, GRADY C., right-wing activist. With Guy Banister, Durham was one of the incorporators, in 1961, of the militant right-wing anti-Castro group, Citizens for a Free Cuba. (See also Banister, William Guy; Hunt, E. Howard)

> SOURCE: FLAMMONDE 242

DYMITRUK, LYDIA, Oswald witness. Dymitruk was a resident of Fort Worth, Texas; a member of the "Dallas Russian-speaking community." She was born in Russia; raised in Belgium and divorced a White Russian who brought her to the U.S. from Belgium. She was a friend of Anna Meller, whom she met through George Bouhe and met Marina Oswald through Meller and Bouhe. She took Marina and her newborn daughter Rachel to the hospital when the baby had a high temperature and later witnessed a fight between Lee and Marina. (See also Bouhe, George; Meller, Anna; Oswald, Marina)

> SOURCE: WCH IX, 60

DYMOND, F. IRVIN. Clay Shaw's chief defense attorney during his trial for conspiracy to assassinate the president. (See also Shaw, Clay)

> SOURCES: FMG III, 61 • OTT 157, 231–3, 236–7, 246, 249 • FLAMMONDE, many

DZIEMIAN, ARTHUR J., U.S. Army wounds ballistics expert, chief of the Army Wound Ballistics Branch. Dziemian told the WC, regarding JFK's and Governor Connally's nonfatal wounds, "I think the probability is very good that... all the wounds were caused by one bullet."

> SOURCES: WR 105 • WCH V, 90

E

EASTERLING, ROBERT WILFRED (aka Taylor, George; "Hardhat"), possible Oswald witness; possible Ruby witness; confessed assassination conspirator. Easterling was diagnosed ten years after the assassination as a psychotic and schizophrenic. He called author Henry Hurt on September 29, 1981, and gave him a detailed confession of his knowledge of, and participation in, a plot to kill JFK. He had previously attempted to tell his story to the FBI and the SS, who didn't pay much attention; he said he was confessing because he believed he was dying and wanted to clear his conscience.

Because of his mental state, his confession might be easy to dismiss if it weren't for the key items in his scenario that have been corroborated independently. Here is Easterling's story:

In February 1963, Easterling was working as a diesel engine mechanic near New Orleans and frequently drank at the Habana Bar at 117 Decatur Street in New Orleans (see PEÑA, OREST). It was here that Easterling met a CIA/Castro double agent whom Hurt calls Manuel (not his real name). Easterling described Manuel as being of medium height, with a stocky build, heavy body hair, a receding hairline, and a visible birthmark on the side of his neck. Manuel enlisted Easterling in a scheme to kill JFK. Manuel explained that their group wanted JFK dead because they were betrayed at the Bay of Pigs invasion. Easterling says that other members of the conspiratorial group included David Ferrie and Clay Shaw, whom he also saw in the same bar, and a Cuban named Joe who had a deformed hand and who sometimes tended bar. Orest Peña, owner of the bar, admits that Ferrie and Shaw had both been known to drink there, but denies ever employing a bartender with a deformed hand. Manuel, who drove a gray

121

Volkswagen, explained that JFK was going to be shot by a 7mm Czech weapon, the design of which he had supervised personally. This weapon fired bullets that disintegrated on impact and left no ballistic evidence. The cover story was going to involve a patsy (Oswald) and fake ballistic evidence. The cover assassination weapon was to be a Mannlicher-Carcano. To create the phony ballistic evidence, Manuel went to a field (behind the trailer park where Easterling lived with his wife) and fired the weapon into a barrel of water. He then collected the shell casings and the fired bullets—which would be planted at the appropriate time to incriminate Oswald. Manuel then lined up three coconuts and fired his Czech weapon into each of them, to show off. This story is partially corroborated by Easterling's wife (now remarried and requesting anonymity), who remembers that, before the shooting started, Easterling came into their trailer to borrow dishcloths. When Hurt told Easterling of this, Easterling frowned and then recalled that he and Manuel had tried for a time to suspend the dishcloths in the barrel so that the bullets could be retrieved without completely emptying the barrel. Mrs. Easterling also recalled that, later that day, Easterling had brought her three coconuts with bullet holes in them. She made coconut pie.

In late February, Easterling says that a large white car with several Cubans in it parked outside his trailer. Easterling telephoned Manuel, who told him that the Cubans were afraid Easterling would talk and planned to kill him and his wife and burn his trailer. Manuel showed up and talked the Cubans out of it. This story is corroborated by Mrs. Easterling and a neighbor, both of whom clearly remember the incident.

Later, Easterling claims, he was blindfolded and taken to the group's headquarters. There Manuel showed Easterling a heavy wooden box with a false bottom, in which a rifle could be hidden. The box, Manuel explained, would be placed at the assassination site. After the shooting, the Czech weapon would be hidden in the box's false bottom while the false evidence would be planted. The box would be removed at some later date. Easterling met Oswald, who spoke little, and quickly figured out that Oswald was the patsy. Manuel explained that he had met Oswald in Czechoslovakia, where the weapon had been built. (Oswald was officially in the USSR at that time.)

Easterling says that he knew a New Orleans businessman (whom Hurt does not name) who laundered cash for a Dallas oilman. One of the legmen for this operation was Ruby. Easterling learned that the Dallas oilman was paying for the assassination effort, having once heard him on tape saying, "Don't pay the bastards too much, because it will drive up the price on Bobby and the rest of them."

On September 24, 1963, at about 9:00 A.M., Manuel assigned Easterling to pick up Oswald and sneak him from New Orleans to Houston. The mission was touchy because at the time Oswald was under constant surveillance by the FBI. The conspirators started a fire in what Easterling believed to be a "wooden church in a black neighborhood" and used the confusion to get Oswald out of town. Even with the diversion, says Easterling, the FBI was still on their tail and it took a 100 mph chase through New Orleans streets to lose their pursuers. Hurt checked on this story and found that there was a suspicious fire in a wooden building (2011 Melpomene) in a black neighborhood (albeit an apartment building across the street from a church) that was reported at 9:22 A.M., on September 24.

In Houston, says Easterling, he and Manuel stayed in the car while Oswald got out at the bus station. When Oswald returned, he was with a man introduced as "Carlo," who greatly resembled Oswald. Easterling says that Carlo, Manuel, and Oswald spoke to one another in Russian. Soon thereafter, Easterling said good-bye to the three men and drove home alone.

Easterling's next assignment was to drive to Monterrey, Mexico, where he was to wait for Oswald in a motel. After Oswald arrived, he was to drive him to Fort Worth. Easterling waited for ten days, but Oswald never showed up, so he drove back to Baton Rouge.

On November 19, Easterling called Manuel, and David Ferrie answered the phone. Ferrie told him that Manuel had gone on to Dallas. Ferrie gave Easterling his next assignment, which was to pick up Oswald at 10:30 A.M. on November 22 at the Greyhound Bus Station in Dallas. From there they were to go to Mexico City, where Manuel would meet them.

At this point, Easterling's conscience (as well as his fear that he would be rubbed out for knowing too much) began to get the better of him. He called the FBI and explained his situation. He says that the FBI told him, "You're in too deep. You're going to get killed. We have lines open to Dallas now...We know all about it. We're going to catch them red-handed...Whatever you do, don't go to Dallas."

Easterling didn't go to Dallas. Instead, he tried to rob a store on the day of the assassination. He was eventually caught (February 1964) and was sentenced to five years in the Louisiana State Penitentiary in Angola. He

was later told by Manuel's brother that the conspirators didn't get around to retrieving the Czech weapon from the TSBD until seven months after the assassination.
SOURCE: HURT 346–91

EBERHARDT, AUGUST MICHAEL "MIKE," Ruby witness; DPD detective. Eberhardt told the WC that he saw Ruby in the third-floor hallway, near the Burglary and Theft Office of the DPD station, between 6:00 and 7:00 P.M. on November 22, 1963. He knew Ruby through the Carousel Club and asked him what he was doing at the police station. Ruby told him that he had brought some "nice lean corned beef" sandwiches to the reporters and that he himself was acting as a reporter, functioning as a translator for the Israeli press. According to Eberhardt, Ruby said of Oswald, "It is hard to realize that a complete nothing, a zero like that, could kill a man like President Kennedy."
SOURCES: WR 318 • WCH XIII, 181 • COA 126 • BISHOP 371 • DOP 334–5 • BLAKEY 317 • EVICA 120

EDDOWES, MICHAEL, author of *Khrushchev Killed Kennedy* (self-published, 1975), later retitled *The Oswald File* (Clarkson N. Potter, 1977), and *November 22, How They Killed Kennedy* (Neville Spearman, 1976). Eddowes's first book was financed by ultra-right-wing Dallas oil billionaire H. L. Hunt. His theory is that Oswald was captured while in the USSR and that a KGB agent was substituted for him. Eddowes brought a suit in Texas to exhume Oswald's body. The body was exhumed, and the official proclamation was that it "was Oswald." However, the exhumed body showed no sign of the craniotomy, which reportedly was performed at Oswald's autopsy in 1963. (See also Hunt, H. L.; Ivanov, Yevgenni; Kostikov, Valeri; Kostin, Valeri; Nosenko, Yuri; Shitov, Alexandr; Yatskov, Paul)

EDGAR, ROBERT W., member HSCA (D-Pennsylvania), which concluded that "because of the acoustic evidence of a fourth shot from the grassy knoll," there was a "high probability" that two gunmen fired at JFK. Edgar wrote the dissenting views for the committee, agreeing with the WC. He felt that the committee had put too much weight on the acoustic evidence.
SOURCES: BELIN 194, 197 • BE 563 • BLAKEY 99 • ME 184

EDWARDS, ROBERT EDWIN, a.w.; Dallas City Courthouse employee. Edwards watched from the southwest corner of Elm and Houston. His statements (that he saw a man leaning out of the TSBD "transfixed" on the triple underpass ten minutes before the shooting) corroborate those of his

companion that day, Ronald B. Fischer. At the sound of the first shot, Edwards laughed, thinking that it was a backfire. (See also Fischer, Ronald B.)
SOURCES: WR 135–6 • WCH VI, 200 • WCE 2003 • BISHOP 129 • DOP 150–1, 155 • CF 23

EDWARDS, SHEFFIELD, CIA agent. With Johnny Roselli, Sam Giancana, Robert Maheu, and Richard Bissell, Edwards claims, he plotted to assassinate Castro in 1961 using a "botulism pill." The plan did not work, obviously, because the assassin assigned to actually give the pill to Castro lost nerve at the last second. Edwards claims that Attorney General Robert F. Kennedy was fully briefed on the plan and had approved it. According to Edwards, he was authorized to plan the murder by CIA Director Allen Dulles and Deputy Director General Charles Cabell. (See also Bissell, Richard; Cabell, Charles; Dulles, Allen; Giancana, Sam; Houston, Lawrence; Lorenz, Marita; Maheu, Robert; Roselli, John)
SOURCES: HSCA Report 107 • BELIN 102–10, 113–5 • COA 192 • OTT 304 • BLAKEY 53–5, 57–9, 385 • EVICA 208–10, 248–9, 256–7, 261, 289 • KANTOR 25)(DAVIS 97–8, 282, 361

EISENBERG, MELVIN ARON, WC counsel. Eisenberg took testimony from experts, predominantly from the FBI, regarding the ballistic evidence against Oswald.
SOURCES: FMG III, 66 • BE 89 • BLAKEY 72 • EVICA 37–9, 41, 44 • ME 51–2 • MEAGHER 53–4, 108, 109, 118–9, 123, 125, 203, 259 • PD 53–4, 56

EISENHOWER, DWIGHT DAVID, 34th president of the United States (1953–1961). On January 17, 1961, during his final speech as president, Eisenhower said, "The conjunction of an immense military establishment and a large arms industry is new in the American experience. We must guard against the acquisition of unwarranted influence, whether sought or unsought, by the military-industrial complex."
SOURCES: WR 360 • HSCA Report 25, 104–5, 131, 213, 228 • BELIN 94, 103–4, 143, 162, 169, 171 • RTJ 383 • COA 185, 298 • BISHOP 106–7, 126, 285, 350, 412, 428, 444 • DOP, many • FMG III, 85 • OTT 177 • FLAMMONDE 61, 278 • BLAKEY 109–10, 136, 147, 195 • EVICA 208, 247–8, 273, 307 • ME 4 • KANTOR 81, 131 • DAVIS 97–8, 398, 404, 417 • NORTH 143, 156 • PD 41, 124

EKDAHL, EDWIN A., Oswald witness; geologist. Ekdahl was Oswald's stepfather from the time Oswald was 5½ until he was almost 9.
SOURCES: WR 28, 353–4 • BELIN 207 • BLAKEY 341

ELLIS, STARVIS, a.w.; DPD motorcycle patrolman. Ellis rode alongside the lead car in the motorcade. He told the HSCA that he looked back and "saw" a bullet bounce off the Elm Street pavement.
SOURCE: HT 22

ELLSWORTH, FRANK, Treasury agent. Ellsworth was one of two

Treasury agents present on the sixth floor of the TSBD at the time the rifle was found and allegedly was involved in Oswald's interrogation. In 1976, Ellsworth told *Village Voice* writer Dick Russell that he had knowledge of an "Oswald double" who had been associating with the Dallas Minutemen (a right-wing organization) in 1963. He told Russell that the Oswald double was still alive and resided in Dallas. He said that this man (whom he did not name) was the man mistaken for Oswald repeatedly in and around Dallas during the weeks and months before the assasination. This "twin" was a frequent traveler to Mexico, had associations with the family of oil billionaire H. L. Hunt, and had been convicted of a federal arms violation. (According to a WC memo, the member of the Minutemen whom Ellsworth had been investigating was a "local gun-shop owner.") Ellsworth said that the "twin" associated with anti-Castro Cuban exiles, was associated with the anti-Castro group known as Alpha 66 and had admitted to supplying arms to a terrorist Cuban organization. Major General Edwin Walker was among other associates of the "twin." Ellsworth told. Russell that he had gone undercover, posing as a criminal involved in Mexican smuggling, to track the Oswald twin—and had eventually gotten the twin convicted on a gun violation. (See also Masen, John; Walker, Edwin A.; Hunt, H. L.)
  SOURCES: HSCA Report 184 • EVICA 98–104, 123, 144

ELY, JOHN HART, WC staff member. Ely was a Supreme Court law clerk assigned to help WC staffers Albert E. Jenner and Wesley Liebeler develop Oswald's biography.
  SOURCE: EVICA 25

EPSTEIN, EDWARD JAY, author of *Inquest* (Viking, 1966), one of the first criticisms of the WR. *Inquest* was highly criticized in the 1960s, especially by members of the WC. According to A. L. Goodhart in the *Law Quarterly Review*:

> In Mr. Epstein's book there is a section entitled "The Staff's Image of the Commission"; he begins by quoting Joseph Ball, a leading practitioner at the California Bar, and a professor of criminal law at the University of Southern California, as saying that the Commission "had no idea what was happening, we did all the investigating, lined up the witnesses, solved the problems, and wrote the report." I have heard from Mr. Ball that all the quotations in the Epstein book attributed to him are "wrong, or false." He has protested to the publishers. He saw Epstein only once for about ten minutes in the lobby of the Regent Hotel in New York.

Goodhart writes that Wesley Liebeler, another WC staffer, had a similar reaction to the book and denies making many of the statements attributed to him in Epstein's book.

Epstein located George DeMohrenschildt and scheduled an interview with him on the day that DeMohrenschildt committed suicide. One of Epstein's theories was that the real Oswald had been captured in the Soviet Union and had been replaced by a Russian spy. Epstein was among those who wanted Oswald's body exhumed. The body was exhumed in 1981 and was offically declared to be Oswald, despite the fact that a craniotomy performed at Oswald's autopsy was not visible on the body.

During his research for his book, Epstein used the Freedom of Information Act to obtain CIA documents stating that the Company was not in agreement about whether or not KGB defector Yuri Nosenko was telling the truth about having no interest in Oswald. (See also Fonzi, Gaeton)
SOURCES: HSCA Report 220 • BELIN 27 • COA 48 • DUFFY 72 • FMG III, 49–50 • SUMMERS 112, 141, 155, 163–4, 171–2 • BE, many • FLAMMONDE 26, 159, 330–1 • BLAKEY 42–3, 49, 51, 117, 130, 133 • HOS 241 • KANTOR 163–4

EUINS, AMOS LEE, a.w. Euins was standing across Elm Street from the TSBD. The 15-year-old said he saw a black man with a rifle in the southeast corner window before the shooting. After his family received threatening phone calls, Euins said he "couldn't tell" whether the man was white or black. In his testimony to the WC, Euins left out his description of the rifleman altogether: "...I seen this pipe sticking out of the window. I wasn't paying too much attention to it. Then when the first shot was fired, I started looking around, thinking it was backfire... Then I looked up at the window, and he shot again... I got behind this little fountain... and then, after he shot again, he pulled the gun back in the window." (See also Harkness, D.V.; Underwood, James)
SOURCES: WR 76, 137, 146 • WCH II, 201 • BELIN 8–9, 31, 49, 73, 220 • RTJ 92, 281 • GERTZ 528–9 • BISHOP 133, 137, 140, 150, 195, 343, 356, 452 • CF 26 • OTT 20, 93–4 • SUMMERS 41

EVANS, JULIAN and MYRTLE, acquaintances of Marguerite Oswald during Lee's youth. Myrtle Evans told the WC that Lee was a spoiled child. Julian Evans added, "I thought he was a psycho. I really did."
SOURCES: WCH VIII, 45, 66

EVANS, SIDNEY, JR., Ruby witness; 37-year-old truck driver; resident of Ruby's apartment building. Evans told WC that he thought he saw Ruby doing his laundry in their building at 10:00 A.M. on November 24, 1963, the morning that Ruby shot Oswald. However, Ruby's roommate George

Senator said that Ruby never did his laundry in the building, and other witnesses place Ruby at that time lurking about the DPD station inquiring about the time of Oswald's transfer.

SOURCES: WCH XIII, 195

EVICA, GEORGE MICHAEL, author of *And We Are All Mortal: New Evidence and Analysis in the Assassination of John F. Kennedy* (University of Hartford Press, 1978).

EWELL, JIM (See WELL, JIM E.)

EWING, MICHAEL, HSCA staff member; coauthor, with Bernard Fensterwald Jr. of *Coincidence or Conspiracy?* (Kensington Publishing Corp., 1977).

SOURCES: BELIN 190 • BE 542, 561, 592

EXNER, JUDITH (aka Campbell, Judith), mistress to both JFK and assassination suspect Sam Giancana. In 1988, Exner told *People* magazine, "I lied when I said that President Kennedy was unaware of my friendship with mobsters. He knew everything about my dealings with Sam Giancana and Johnny Roselli because I was seeing them *for* him."

According to author Anthony Summers, "For 18 months in 1960 and 1961, Exner said, she repeatedly carried envelopes from the president to Giancana and Roselli. There were, she calculated, some ten meetings between the president and [Giancana], one of them in the White House."

Exner offered her opinion on why these meetings were held: "...I was probably helping Jack orchestrate the attempted assassination of Fidel Castro with the help of the Mafia."

SOURCES: SUMMERS 248–9, 527 • COA 63, 170 • BLAKEY 276, 377–82, 393 • ME 132, 144 • DAVIS 406–7, 415

F

FAIN, JOHN W., Oswald witness; FBI agent. Fain interviewed Oswald twice following Oswald's return from the USSR—on June 6, 1962, in the Fort Worth FBI office and on August 16, 1962, in the backseat of Fain's car, parked outside Oswald's home. Oswald was not cooperative. He denied any dealings with the KGB and refused to take a polygraph examination. (See also Brown, Arnold; Carter, B. Thomas)

SOURCES: WR 303, 409 • WCH IV, 403 • HSCA Report 185, 190, 194, 250 • DUFFY 188–9 • NORTH 177

FARRINGTON, FENELLA, possible Oswald witness. Farrington was in the Mexican consulate in New Orleans in September 1963 with her friend Lillian Merilh when a rude young man asked her, "What do you have to do to take firearms or a gun into Mexico?" At this point, according to the FBI, a hidden camera began to film the scene. The FBI located and questioned Farrington on November 26, 1963. They told her that the man she had seen was Oswald. The FBI also told her that she had seen Oswald in Mexico City and that she had seen Ruby in New Orleans on the same day she saw Oswald. Farrington denied all of this. During the Clay Shaw investigation, Farrington was questioned by attorney Mark Lane at the request of New Orleans District Attorney Jim Garrison. During that interview, Lane showed her 17 photos and asked if any were the man she had seen. She chose two photos: one of Oswald and another of suspected Oswald impersonator Kerry W. Thornley.

SOURCE: OTT 65–7, 281

FATTER, ESMOND, prosecution witness at the preliminary court hearing of Clay Shaw; physician and hypnotist. A little background is necessary to understand Dr. Fatter's role. One of New Orleans District Attorney Jim Garrison's key witnesses at the Shaw hearing was Perry

Raymond Russo, who said that he had attended a party at which Shaw, David Ferrie, and Oswald had plotted the murder of JFK. In order to verify Russo's story, Garrison asked Russo to be hypnotized and given sodium pentothal (truth serum). When Shaw's defense team learned of the hypnosis and truth serum—which had indicated that Russo was telling the truth— they argued in court that the techniques had been used to suggest in Russo's mind the story Garrison wanted him to tell. Fatter, who had hypnotized and examined Russo, was then called to explain what he had done and insist that, in his opinion, Russo was telling the truth. (See also Garrison, Jim; Russo, Perry; Shaw, Clay)
    SOURCES: OTT 155–6, 163 • FLAMMONDE 55, 60, 84, 90–4, 289, 291, 302, 322

FAUNTROY, WALTER E., HSCA member (D–District of Columbia). Black caucus leader in Congress.
    SOURCES: HSCA Report 495 • BLAKEY 63, 66–7

FEHRENBACH, GEORGE WILLIAM, resident of Ashland, Oregon; jewelry shop owner. Fehrenbach told the WC that, while he was living in Muncie, Indiana, a group of "communists" attempted to recruit him into their "cell." He stole a list of 150 names from one of their meetings and submitted it to the FBI. The name Jack Rubenstein was on that list.
    SOURCE: WCH XV, 289

FEISST, ERNEST, Swiss minister and, in 1961, a member of the board of directors of the CMC. The CMC is believed by some to be behind JFK's death, due to the Fascist nature of their directors, their links to espionage, and the inclusion among their numbers of assassination suspect Clay Shaw. (See also Torbitt, William)
    SOURCES: FLAMMONDE 215

FELDER, JAMES L., Bethesda witness; former army sergeant; member of the Bethesda security guard on the night of November 22, 1963. Felder corroborates the multitude of evidence indicating that there was deception regarding the movements of JFK's body. He said, "There were two ambulances. One was supposed to be the decoy."
    SOURCES: BE 398 • SUMMERS 483 • *Dallas Morning News*, November 26, 1963, p. 15

FELDSOTT, LOUIS, president of Crescent Firearms, Inc. Author George Michael Evica writes:

What type of Mannlicher-Carcano did Klein's possess and have available for sale on February 22, 1963 [when Oswald reportedly mail-ordered the assassination weapon]? In 1959, Louis and Irving Feldsott of Folsom Arms, in connection with Adam Consolidated, won the competitive bidding on approximately 570,000 6.5-mm. Model 91 and $^{91}/_{38}$ Mannlicher-Carcanos offered in 1958 by the Italian Ministry of Defense. Consolidated acted as importer and financier. A new distributing entity, Crescent Firearms, was created on December 29, 1959.

Feldsott told the WC he sold the Mannlicher-Carcano 6.5-mm. rifle, serial number C2766 (the TSBD rifle) to Klein's Sporting Goods Inc. of Chicago on June 18, 1962.
SOURCES: WCH XI, 205 • EVICA 27

FENLEY, ROBERT GENE, *Dallas Times Herald* reporter. Fenley told the WC about his interview with possible Oswald witness C. A. Hamblen, who says that Oswald came into his Western Union office to receive a money order. (See also Hamblen, C. A.)
SOURCE: WCH XI, 314

FENNER, NANNY, Oswald witness; receptionist at the FBI's Dallas office. On November 6, 1963, Oswald left a note with Fenner for James Hosty, the agent in charge of Oswald's case after Oswald's return from the Soviet Union. Hosty was at lunch when Oswald dropped off the note. Fenner read the note, which said: "Let this be a warning. I will blow up the FBI and the Dallas Police Department if you don't stop bothering my wife. [signed] Lee Harvey Oswald." The note was destroyed by Hosty after the assassination, and the existence of the note did not become public knowledge until 1975. Hosty remembers a more mildly worded note, and has described Fenner as "excitable" and "unreliable." (See also Hosty, James)
SOURCES: HSCA Report 195 • SUMMERS 370

FENSTERWALD, BERNARD "BUD," JR., suspicious death; Washington, D.C. attorney; founder, Committee to Investigate Assassinations; founder, Assassination Archives Research Center; coauthor, with Michael Ewing, of *Coincidence or Conspiracy?* (Kensington Publishing Corp., 1977).

Fensterwald—whose clients have included Watergate figure and CIA agent James McCord, convicted Martin Luther King assassin James Earl Ray, and an admitted intelligence agent with foreknowledge of the JFK assassination, Richard Case Nagell—died April 2, 1991, cause of death officially unknown. On November 19, 1992, in New York City, author Robert D. Morrow told this author, "Bud Fensterwald was the man who started the Assassination Archives in Washington, D.C. Bud was a friend of mine. In February 1991, he asked me to go down to interview an Air Force colonel, who is still alive, who I had identified to the [HSCA] as the possible bagman [responsible for paying the conspirators] for the [JFK] assassination. I told Bud at the time—and I told Gus Russo, who is an independent researcher who had interviewed the man himself—that Bud is going to get himself killed. I will make the arrangements and I will do all that, but Bud is never going to make the interrogation of this man. Eleven days before we were to meet in the Miami area, Bud died, was cremated almost immediately; no autopsy was performed on the body. His wife says nothing happened. I happen to believe he was deliberately killed." (See also Paisley, John)

SOURCES: FMG III, 39, 105 • BLAKEY 64 • EVICA 135, 140, 168 • ME 134 • KANTOR 132–3 • DAVIS 390, 410–2, 422, 616–7 • PD 29 • MORROW 292, 300 • RUSSELL, many

FERRELL, MARY, independent assasination researcher. DPD Captain Will Fritz told Ferrell that, the day after the assassination, LBJ called him and said, "You've got your man, the investigation is over." It was private citizen Ferrell who brought the DPD Dictabelt recording of the assassination to the HSCA's attention. (See also Fritz, Will)

SOURCES: BLAKEY 91–2 • SUMMERS 14 • HT 188 • OGLESBY 42–4 • KANTOR 197 • NORTH 349

FERRIE, DAVID WILLIAM (aka Ferris, David), assassination suspect; Oswald witness; suspicious death; CIA asset; pilot; employee (private detective) of assassination suspect Carlos Marcello. Reportedly born in Ohio in 1918, Ferrie died on February 22, 1967, of a "brain hemorrhage" just before he could be indicted and tried by Jim Garrison. With Ferrie right up until the time of his death was *Washington Post* reporter George Lardner Jr., son of Ring Lardner. Ferrie's close friend Eladio del Valle was murdered the same hour that Ferrie died.

Ferrie first met Oswald when he was Oswald's leader in the Civil Air Patrol in New Orleans. Ferrie once wrote, in a letter to the commander of the United States 1st Air Force, "I want to train killers. There is nothing I would enjoy better than blowing the hell out of every damn Russian, Communist, Red or what-have-you."

Beverly Oliver, who worked next door to Ruby's Carousel Club, claims that she saw Ferrie in the Carousel so often that she thought he was one of the managers. The HSCA developed strong evidence that Ferrie once accompanied Oswald to an anti-Castro training camp in Lacombe, Louisiana, not far from New Orleans.

Ferrie was a bizarre individual who was once fired as a pilot for Eastern Airlines because of his homosexual pedophilia. He had no hair on his body, reportedly because he suffered from the rare disease *alopecia praecox* (total early baldness) and wore a piece of rug as a toupee, and painted-on eyebrows. Ferrie's appearance was so strange that he would have been a perfect master of disguise. All he would have to do was make himself up to appear "normal" and no one would recognize him. Conversely, all someone would have to do was paint on eyebrows and wear a goofy wig and he could pass himself off as Ferrie. As Captain David Ferrie of the Civil Air Patrol, Ferrie counted among his students Oswald and the son of Mrs. Mary Bledsoe, Oswald's onetime landlady, who told the WC that she recognized Oswald on a city bus moments after the assassination.

When Jim Garrison began his assassination investigation, he had met Ferrie only once, a meeting Garrison, in *On the Trail of the Assassins*, calls "casual but unforgettable." The incident took place in 1962, as Garrison was walking across Carondelet Street, near Canal Street in New Orleans. Garrison recounted:

> Just then, a man grabbed me by both arms and stopped me cold. The face grinning ferociously at me was like a ghoulish Halloween mask. The eyebrows plainly were greasepaint, one noticeably higher than the other. A scruffy, reddish homemade wig hung askew on his head as he fixed me with his eyes. The traffic was bearing down on us as he gripped me, and I hardly could hear him amidst the din of the horns... he was shouting congratulations on my recent election [to New Orleans District Attorney]. As I dodged a car, at last escaping his clutch, I recall his yelling that he was a private investigator... I remembered Ferrie's reputation as an adventurer and pilot... the legend that he could get a plane in and out of the smallest fields... his involvement in the abortive 1961 Bay of Pigs invasion of Cuba, his anti-Castro activities, and his frequent speeches to veterans' groups about patriotism and anti-communism... [Ferrie's] name... was well known in New Orleans.

Prompted by Oswald's presence for much of the summer of 1963 in New Orleans, Garrison's jurisdiction, Garrison first became interested in Ferrie during the initial stages of his investigation. Garrison learned that Oswald and Ferrie had been seen together that summer. The D.A. later learned that Jack Martin, who was in the hospital because of a pistol-whipping he'd received from Guy Banister on November 22, 1963, was telling friends that

Ferrie's role in the assassination was to go to Houston to serve as "getaway" pilot for the assassins. Garrison called Ferrie into his office on November 25, 1963, and Ferrie appeared as if "he'd been shot by cannon through a Salvation Army clothing store." At that time, Ferrie denied knowing Oswald but admitted to an odd "ice-skating" trip through a horrible storm to Houston on the day of the assassination. Garrison's staff discovered that Ferrie had deposited more than $7,000 in cash to his bank accounts during the weeks leading up to JFK's death. (Around the same time, Carlos Marcello gave Ferrie a successful gas-station franchise.)

Garrison first linked Ferrie to Clay Shaw (whom Garrison would later unsuccessfully prosecute for conspiracy to assassinate the president) through the statements of Jules Ricco Kimble, a right-wing fanatic who told Garrison that Ferrie had introduced him to Shaw in 1960 or 1961. The relationship between Ferrie and Shaw was corroborated by the statements of David Logan, who had been introduced to Shaw by Ferrie in a Bourbon Street bar, and those of Nicolas and Mathilda Tadin, who met Shaw through Ferrie when arranging to have Ferrie give their son flying lessons.

But the most damaging link was provided by Raymond Broshears, who told Garrison in 1965 that he had seen and talked to Ferrie and Shaw on a number of occasions together and that Ferrie, when drunk, liked to discuss his connection with the assassination. Ferrie told Broshears that his job in Houston was to pick up two members of the assassination team—one of whom Ferrie knew fairly well and was named Carlos—who were to arrive from Dallas in a single-engine plane. Ferrie was then to fly the men to a never-specified distant location. Ferrie did as he had been instructed, but Carlos and his companion never showed up. Ferrie told Broshears that Carlos was a Cuban exile, as were the other members of the assassination team, who believed JFK had "sold them out to the communists."

Edward Whalen, a professional criminal from Philadelphia, Pennsylvania, told Garrison's staff in 1967 that recently Ferrie and Shaw (who was using his usual alias, Clay Bertrand) had met him in a Bourbon Street bar and had offered him $25,000 to "hit" Garrison. Ferrie had told Whalen that "Bertrand had done a lot for. . . Oswald and it was only because Oswald had fouled up that he had been killed."

On February 22, 1967, Garrison was about to arrest Ferrie when he learned that Ferrie was dead. He had been found in his apartment lying on the couch with a sheet pulled up over his head. By the time Garrison received the news, the coroner had already picked up the body and removed it from the scene. In Ferrie's apartment, Garrison found two typed suicide notes, many empty cages that still reeked from the white mice they had once held, stacks of books, a big map of Cuba, and overall filthy conditions. Along the bathroom's medicine cabinet mirror were globs of purple glue presumably used to hold on Ferrie's wig. The suicide notes read, in part. "To leave this life is, for me, a sweet prospect. I find nothing in it that is desirable and on the other hand, everything that is loathsome," and "When you read this I will be quite dead and no answer will be possible." In the medicine cabinet were several empty bottles of Proloid, a thyroid medicine, with their covers off. Garrison did not actually see Ferrie's body, but was shown a photo of it. The photo showed the scar on Ferrie's stomach caused by a knife wound while working as a soldier-of-fortune pilot in Cuba.

Regarding Ferrie's suspicious postassassination activities, registration cards at the Alamotel in Houston, an inn owned by assassination suspect Carlos Marcello, show that D. W. Ferrie and his young companions, Melvin Coffey and Alvin Beauboeuf, checked into room #19 at 4:30 P.M. on November 23, 1963, and checked out the following day. Oddly, records at the Driftwood Motel in Galveston, Texas, show that the same trio checked in there at 11:00 P.M. on November 23 and checked out at 10:00 A.M. on November 24. In both establishments, registration indicates the trio were traveling in a car with Louisiana license plate #784-895.

FBI reports regarding Ferrie—which fell into the hands of author David Lifton through WC staffer Wesley Liebeler—indicated that Ferrie flew to Guatamala aboard Delta Airlines twice during the fall of 1963, evidence that Ferrie's detective work for G. Wray Gill was related directly to his defense of Carlos Marcello's immigration-fraud charges. (Marcello was acquitted on November 22, 1963. Ferrie said that he was in court when JFK was shot.)

This is what Ferrie's friend, prosecution witness Perry Raymond Russo, said during cross-examination at the assassination-conspiracy trial of Clay Shaw:

Dave Ferrie talked about so many things. When he would talk to me, he would give me advice or make statements and he would refer to certain books—certain pages—and advise that I read them...there was some talk of the assassination last summer, but we talked about many things. He talked about a cure for cancer. You name it, he talked about it. I learned not to argue with him. I knew that he knew everything. I believed him. People say to me about Ferrie, "What was he like?" To me, he was a walking encyclopedia...he knew it all...all the answers...why should I question him? That was the way it was,...later, after being around David for some time, you didn't question him, he gave you all the answers before a question was necessary. You got out of the habit of asking questions.

Earlier, during direct examination at the Shaw trial, Russo described the meeting he had attended in September 1963 in Ferrie's apartment. Present were Russo, Ferrie, Shaw (using the name Clem Bertrand), and a man who was introduced as "Leon Oswald":

...Ferrie took the initiative in the conversation, pacing back and forth as he talked...[He said] an assassination attempt would have to involve diversionary tactics...there would have to be a minimum of three people involved. Two of the persons would shoot diversionary shots and the third...would shoot the "good shot."...[You would have to create] a triangulation of crossfire...If there were three people, one of them would have to be sacrificed.

According to author Paris Flammonde:

A low requiem mass was said for David William Ferrie at St. Matthas' Church on March 1, 1967. Only two mourners attended. Interment followed in near solitude at St. Bernard's Memorial Cemetery. His body was claimed by Parmalee T. Ferrie of Rockford, New York, understood to be a brother. Two weeks later the press reported in an isolated three-inch item that attorney John P. Nelson Jr., representing J. T. Ferrie of Rockford, Illinois, also identified as a brother (the same or another?) had petitioned for a search for a will...Among Ferrie's final possessions were found four rifles, an assortment of shotgun shells and .22 rifle blanks, a radio transmitter tuning unit, two Signal Corps field telephones, a 100-pound aerial-type practice bomb and—a sword.

In an interview published in the October 1967 *Playboy*, Jim Garrison said:

I had nothing but pity for Dave Ferrie when he was alive, and I have nothing but pity for him now that he is dead. Ferrie was a pathetic and tortured creature, a genuinely brilliant man whose twisted drives locked him into his own private hell. If I had been able to help Ferrie, I would have; but he was in too deep and he was terrified. From the moment he realized we had looked behind the facade and established Lee Oswald was anything but a Communist, from the moment he knew we had discovered the role of the CIA and anti-Castro adventurers in the assassination, Ferrie began to crumble psychologically... yes, I suppose I may have been responsible for Ferrie's death. If I had left this case alone, if I had allowed Kennedy's murderers to continue to walk the streets unimpeded, Dave Ferrie would be alive today. I don't feel personally guilty about Ferrie's death, but I do feel terribly sorry for the waste of another human being. In a deeper sense, though, David Ferrie died on November 22, 1963. From that moment on, he couldn't save himself, and I couldn't save him.

Ferrie was known to use the alias "Ferris," a name that appears in Jack Ruby's last address book. (See also Banister, William Guy; Barker, Bernard; Beauboeuf, Alvin; Bledsoe, Mary; Bringuier, Carlos; Carlson, Alex; Chetta, Nicholas; Coffey, Melvin; Craig, Roger; DeBrueys, Warren; Del Valle, Eladio; Broshears, Raymond; Gill, C. Wray; Kimble, Jules; Lardner, George; Lewallen, James; Logan, David; Manchester, John; Marcello, Carlos; Marchetti, Victor; Martens, Layton; Martin, Jack; Moffett, Sandra; Morgan, Reeves; Nagell, Richard; Novel, Gordon; Oliver, Beverly; Quiroga, Carlos; Russo, Perry; Sherman, Dr. Mary; Spiesel, Charles; Tadin, Nicolas; Thornley, Kerry; Whalen, Edward)
SOURCES: WCH XXIII, 455 • WCE 2038, 3119 • HSCA Report 142–5, 147, 170, 180 • OTT, many • COA 39–42, 44–5, 47–8, 50, 57, 167, 194, 229, 284 • CF 99–100, 188–9, 338, 494–6, 501–3 • FMG III, 28, 46, 70 • SUMMERS 299–304, 453–4, 459–60, 489–91 • FLAMMONDE, many • BLAKEY 46–50, 166–70, 177–8, 275, 313, 346–8, 365, 396 • HOS, many • EVICA 163–4, 166, 236 • ME 61, 90 • OGLESBY 64, 72 • DAVIS, many • NORTH, many

FINCK, PIERRE A., Bethesda witness; lieutenant colonel, U.S. Army; chief of the Wound Ballistics Pathology Branch of the Armed Forces Institute of Pathology and a doctor at Bethesda Naval Hospital. Finck was the only one of the autopsists to have had previous experiences with gunshot wounds. He told the WC that the "magic bullet" could not have caused Governor Connally's wrist wound because there were more metal fragments in Connally's wrist than were missing from the bullet.

Finck testified as a defense witness at the Clay Shaw trial in New Orleans that the autopsy "strongly" suggested that JFK had been killed by a lone gunman shooting from the rear and above. It was upon cross-examination that Finck revealed some illuminating facts about JFK's autopsy: "I was called as a consultant to look at these wounds...I heard Dr. Humes stating that—he said, 'Who's in charge here?' and I heard an army general, I don't remember his name, stating, 'I am.' You must understand that in those circumstances, there were law-enforcement officers, military people with various ranks and you have to coordinate the operation according to directions."

Finck then admitted that the army general in question was not, to his knowledge, a qualified pathologist. Finck continued:

> The autopsy room was quite crowded. It is a small autopsy room, and when you are called in circumstances like that to look at the wound of the President of the United States who is dead, you don't look around too much to ask people for their names and take notes on who they are. I did not do so. The room was crowded with military and civilian personnel and federal agents, Secret Service agents, FBI agents, for part of the autopsy ... there were [also] admirals, and when you are a lieutenant in the Army you just follow orders, and at the end of the autopsy we were specifically told—as I recall it, it was by Admiral Kinney, the surgeon of the Navy—this is subject to verification—we were specifically told not to discuss the case... We did not dissect the neck... I was told that the [Kennedy] family wanted an examination of the head, as I recall, the head and chest, but prosectors in this autopsy didn't remove the organs in the neck, to my recollection... I looked at the trachea, there was a tracheotomy wound the best I can remember, but I didn't dissect or remove these organs... I was told not to, but I don't remember by whom.

Finck said that autopsists did not dissect JFK's neck wound because they were ordered not to, "perhaps" by an army general. He also said that it is essential in a firearms case to examine the victim's clothing, but in this case the doctors were ordered by "another official" *not* to examine JFK's clothing. (See also Humes, James J.; Boswell, J. Thornton; Kellerman, Roy)

SOURCES: WR 88–90 • WCH II, 377 • HSCA VII, 13, 192 • RTJ 77 • BISHOP, many • COA 434 • HOS 20, 195–201, 243 • ME 32, 36, 206, 232

FIORINI, FRANK (See STURGIS, FRANK)

FISCHER, RONALD B., a.w.; Dallas County auditor. Fischer stood on the southwest corner of Elm and Houston. Ten minutes before the shooting, Fischer saw a man in a white T-shirt or a light sport shirt leaning out of a TSBD window, surrounded by boxes, staring "transfixed" in the direction of the triple underpass. Fischer later said that he thought the shots came from "just west" of the TSBD. Fischer's observations are corroborated by his companion, a.w. Robert Edwards. At the sound of the first shot, both men laughed, thinking it was a backfire.

Fischer later told researcher Larry Harris that he did not think the man in the window was Oswald, insisting that the man in the window had "light-colored hair." (See also Edwards, Robert)

SOURCES: WR 135–6 • WCH VI, 191 • WCE 2003 • BISHOP 129, 141 • DOP 49, 150–1, 155, 447 • CF 23 • FMG III, 92

FISHER, N.T., DPD deputy chief. Fisher was one of the three DPD members (Jesse Curry and Charles Batchelor were the others) who spoke with the SS about the selection of the site for JFK's speech in Dallas and possible motorcade routes. He testified to the WC about the lack of security in DPD headquarters while Oswald was being held there and said that, at least as late as Saturday, November 23, "anybody could come up with a plausible reason for going to one of the third-floor bureaus and was able to get in." (See also Batchelor, Charles; Curry, Jesse)

SOURCES: WR 52, 192 • NORTH 359

FISHER, RUSSELL S., Maryland medical examiner and head of a panel of doctors who reviewed the JFK autopsy photos and X rays for Attorney General Ramsey Clark in 1968, in response to the Garrison case. On February 26 and 27, 1968, Fisher was allowed access to 45 autopsy photos, 14 X rays, JFK's clothes, the Zapruder film, and the "magic bullet." Other members of the panel were Drs. Alan Mortiz, William H. Carnes, and Russell Morgan. They determined that neither of JFK's rear wounds were where the autopsists said they were. The photos showed no massive wound in the back of JFK's head, and the smaller entry wound had moved upward 4 to 5 inches from the hairline to the cowlick, in the center of where the larger wound had once been. Afterward, Fisher told researcher Howard Donahue, "...the bullet that hit [JFK] in the head disintegrated completely. We saw nearly 40 fragments throughout the right cerebral hemisphere and imbedded in the interior of the skull." Fisher also found a bullet fragment near the entrance in JFK's head that was imbedded in the skull *from the outside*, leading Fisher to believe that JFK had been wounded by the ricochet of a shot that missed.

SOURCES: EVICA 92 • ME 60–1, 63–8, 76–7, 82–5, 87–9, 125, 160–2, 167, 198–200

FITHIAN, FLOYD J., HSCA member (D–Indiana). Fithian was a firm believer in the "Mafia did it" theory.

SOURCE: SUMMERS 251

FITZGERALD, DESMOND, CIA special affairs staff chief. In late 1963, FitzGerald met with members of AM/LASH (an anti-Castro covert operations organization) to discuss how to start a Cuban coup. He replaced William Harvey as the CIA's head of covert operations in Cuba, and held that position at the time of the JFK assassination. JFK supposedly loathed this operation, which continued busily if ineffectively for at least three years after JFK's death. FitzGerald's daughter, Frances, author of the anti-Vietnam book, *Fire in the Lake*, was Daniel Ellsberg's girlfriend at the time of the Pentagon Papers controversy in 1971.

FitzGerald was known to pose as a U.S. senator representing Robert Kennedy when giving assassination supplies to Cuban Rolando Cubela. (See also Cubela, Rolando; Harvey, William)
SOURCES: HSCA Report 112 • DUFFY 128 • SUMMERS 322, 400–1, 497–8 • BLAKEY 61, 151

FLAMMONDE, PARIS, author of *The Kennedy Conspiracy* (Meredith Press, 1969).
SOURCE: OTT 88

FLEMING, HAROLD J., corporate counsel and general operations manager of Armored Motor Service, Inc.; Fleming provided the armored trucks that were to be used as decoys for the aborted transfer of Oswald. (See also Dietrich, Edward)
SOURCE: WCH XV, 159

FLORER, LAWRENCE HUBER "LARRY," a.w. (aftermath). Florer, a 23-year-old, was apprehended by Dallas County sheriffs 10 to 15 minutes after the assassination exiting the County Records Building, where he says he had been on the third floor looking for a pay phone. He told the sheriffs he was at a Bar-B-Q place on Pacific Street at the time of the shooting and heard about it on the radio.
SOURCE: WCE 2003, p. 208

FLYNN, CHARLES W., Ruby witness; Dallas FBI agent. Starting in March 1959, Flynn had a series of meetings with Ruby to recruit him as an informant. According to William Scott Malone in his article "Rubygate" (*New Times*, January 23, 1978): "After the first FBI contact Ruby went on an electronic shopping spree. He purchased...a wristwatch [sic] with a built-in microphone, a telephone bug, a wire tie clip and bugged attaché case." Ruby spent more than $500 on sophisticated spy equipment.
SOURCES: HSCA Report 151 • HSCA V, 218 • WCD 732 • SUMMERS 442–3 • NORTH 261

FOLSOM, ALLISON G., JR., Oswald witness; commander, U.S. Navy.

Folsom told the WC that Oswald was given the Practical Russian Test #21 by the U.S. Army—thus implying that they had taught him Russian as well. The WR says that Oswald taught himself Russian while in the marines.

SOURCES: WCH VIII, 303 • RTJ 123 • OTT 22–3

FONZI, GAETON, HSCA investigator. Along with Edward Jay Epstein, Fonzi discovered the whereabouts of Oswald associate George DeMohrenschildt approximately one hour before DeMohrenschildt committed suicide.

SOURCES: SUMMERS 506–7, 512, 517–8, 535 • BE 138, 224, 333, 508 • ME 134

FORD, MR. and MRS. DECLAN P. and KATHERINE N. Oswald witnesses; acquaintances of the Oswalds in Texas. The Fords were members of the Dallas Russian-speaking community. He was a self-employed consulting geologist for various oil companies. Marina Oswald stayed at their home for several days after a fight with Lee. Both told the WC that, because of Oswald's boorish behavior, as of January 1963, "Marina and her husband" were "dropped" from their social scene. Declan Ford told the WC that Oswald was "really a screwy nut."

SOURCES: WCH II, 295, 322 • NORTH 156

FORD, GERALD R., WC member; chairman of the House Republican Conference; later became 38th president of the United States (1974 to 1977). His book, *Portrait of the Assassin*, staunchly defends the WC's methods and conclusions. Still, Ford's writings indicate that the WC was more concerned with preserving national unity and tranquillity than it was with finding the truth. (See also Hunt, H. L.)

SOURCES: HSCA Report 256 • BELIN 13, 27, 37–9, 59, 79–80, 98–100, 126–7, 162–3, 165, 167, 171–2 • RTJ, many • COA 151–2, 156, 161, 211, 395 • FMG I, 47–8, 61; III, 92, 102 • OTT 14 • SUMMERS 22, 419, 430 • BE 196, 298, 380, 383 • FLAMMONDE 157–60, 175, 284 • BLAKEY 24, 71, 77, 192, 266, 333, 336 • EVICA 48–50, 131 • ME 12, 127–8, 132, 216 • OGLESBY 12, 69 • KANTOR, many • NORTH 397, 400, 448–9, 478, 480 • PD 30, 43, 48, 268, 374

FORD, HAROLD, member HSCA (D–Tennessee).

FOREMAN, PERCY, Ruby witness; Houston trial attorney. Foreman was Ruby's defense attorney for four days, then quit because of "meddling by the Ruby family." Later, Foreman defended convicted Martin Luther King assassin James Earl Ray.

SOURCE: BLAKEY 326

FOSTER, J. W., a.w.; DPD member. Foster, standing atop the triple underpass, thought the shots came from the TSBD. He immediately ran to that building and guarded the rear exits until relieved by a sergeant. He then moved to a spot where he thought a bullet might have struck, in the turf near a manhole cover on the south side of Elm Street—very close to where a.w. Jean Hill had been standing at the time. There, Foster found a tear in the grass—and guarded the spot until an unidentified man, who seemed official, came by and removed the evidence. (See also Holland, Sam)

SOURCES: WR 80–2, 111 • WCH VI, 248 • WCE 1358 • CF 55–6

FOWLER, CLAYTON, Ruby witness; Fowler was a defense attorney during Ruby's murder trial. During Ruby's lie detector test for the WC, he was asked, "Is Mr. Fowler in danger for defending you?" Ruby failed to answer the question. (See also West, Louis Jolyan)

SOURCES: BELIN 40 • FMG I, 12, 14–17, 19, 176–78, 180 • GERTZ, many • KANTOR 339–40, 346, 350

FOX, SYLVAN, Pulitzer Prize-winning journalist; author of *The Unanswered Questions about the Kennedy Assassination* (Award, 1965), the first U.S. book published in response to the WR and its 26 volumes of hearings and exhibits. The slender paperback was published with three "bullet" holes punched into its cover.

SOURCE: BE 26, 32, 306

FRANZEN, MRS. JACK, a.w. Mrs. Franzen stood with her small son on south side of Elm, across from the TSBD and thought the first shot was a firecracker. She saw "dust or small particles of debris" fly from JFK's limo and later saw blood come from JFK's head. Her son noticed SS in follow-up car with guns. (See also Donahue, Howard)

SOURCES: WCE 1358, 2090

FRAZIER, BUELL WESLEY, a.w.; Oswald witness; TSBD employee and Oswald coworker; neighbor of Mrs. Ruth Paine (Marina Oswald's housemate). Frazier often gave Oswald a ride to work on Monday mornings after Lee had spent weekends with his family in Irving. The only time he ever gave Oswald a ride to work on a Friday was on the day of the assassination. Frazier, along with his sister, Linnie Mae Randle, were the only two WC witnesses to testify that Oswald carried a "long and bulky package" to work that day. Oswald claimed it contained curtain rods. Both Frazier and Randle testified that the package was too short to have contained a rifle, even if broken down. Garland G. Slack, who testified that he had seen a man who looked like Oswald practicing with a rifle at a firing range on November 10, 1963, told the WC that the man had been driven to the driving range by "a man named Frazier from Irving." The first broadcasts about the assassination said that the weapon found in the TSBD was a British .303 rifle, which was the type of rifle Frazier owned. Frazier's lifelong friend was John M. Crawford, who was also a friend of Ruby's.

Has pockmarks on the right side of his chin. (See also Adamcik, John; Crawford, John; Lewis, R. D.; Litchfield, Wilbyrn; McCabe, J. A.; Paine, Ruth; Randle, Linnie Mae; Slack, Garland)

SOURCES: WR 34, 123, 125–7, 130, 149, 169, 229, 332, 397 • WCH II, 210; VII, 531 • WCE 1381, 1980, 2003, 2009, 2454, 2936, 3077 • BELIN 58–60, 64, 68 • RTJ 112, 142–7, 335, 384 • BISHOP, many • DOP 94, 101, 111–2, 114–5, 248, 278 • CF 40–2, 44–5 • FMG III, 56 • BLAKEY 31 • SUMMERS 57, 70–1 • DAVIS 194–5 • NORTH 325–6, 329–31, 333, 352, 357, 371, 374–5

FRAZIER, ROBERT A., FBI firearms identification expert. Frazier testified, following the WC's re-creation of the assassination in Dealey Plaza (supposedly based on the Zapruder film), that with regard to the damage attributed to the "magic bullet": "They [JFK and Connally] both are in direct alignment with the telescopic site at the ['Oswald'] window. The Governor is immediately behind the President in the field of view." His testing with the Mannlicher-Carcano rifle determined it took a minimum of 2.3 seconds to work the bolt and refire. Therefore, a lone assassin could have fired only three shots during the shooting sequence, thus creating the necessity of the "magic bullet." Frazier testified at the Clay Shaw trial (February 22, 1969). (See also Shaw, Clay)

SOURCES: WR 83, 86–8, 94, 102–3, 160, 173, 177, 182 • WCH XII, 52 • BELIN 53 • RTJ 62–3, 67, 76, 115 • BISHOP 362, 492–4, 497–8, 520 • FMG III, 65 • PWW 79 • BE 74, 76, 89, 524 • EVICA, many • ME 34

FRAZIER, W. B., DPD captain. Frazier was the first to tell Captain Will Fritz on the morning of November 24 on the telephone that there had been threats on Oswald's life. (See also Fritz, Will)

SOURCE: WR 211

FREEMAN, H. D., a.w.; DPD motorcycle patrolman. Freeman was one of the lead motorcycles in motorcade. According to the WC, Freeman was number 135 that day.

SOURCES: WCH XX, 489 • HT 153 • FMG III, 55

FREEMAN, LUCY, coauthor, with Dr. Renatus Hartogs, of *The Two Assassins* (Thomas Y. Crowell Co., 1965), a book about Oswald and Ruby.

FRITZ, JOHN WILL, Oswald witness; o.k.w.; DPD captain. Fritz was involved in the discovery of the rifle on the sixth floor of the TSBD and led the interrogation of Oswald following his arrest. Just after Oswald was brought in for interrogation, Fritz was called away from the prisoner by Sheriff Bill Decker for a private meeting (they didn't want to use the phone) a mile away, despite their having just seen each other. Officially, Fritz made no tapes or transcripts of Oswald's interrogation. He says he based his written report on rough notes, but these notes have never been made available. Independent researcher Mary Ferrell says that Fritz later told a friend at a luncheon that, the day after the assassination, he received a phone call from LBJ, the new president, saying, "You've got your man, the investigation is over." On June 9, 1964, Fritz wrote a letter to the WC regarding the spent shells found on the sixth floor of the TSBD. That letter is now missing. (See also Alyea, Tom; Craig, Roger; Ferrell, Mary; Frazier, W. B.; Hill, Gerald; Hosty, James; Olds, Gregory)

SOURCES: WR, many • WCH IV, 202; VII, 403; XV, 145 • BELIN 9, 41–2, 62, 71–2 • RTJ, many • COA 112, 126, 147 • GERTZ 14, 46, 81, 83, 97, 106, 514, 517 • BISHOP, many • DOP 281–2, 284, 332, 425, 427, 456, 458–9, 513, 520, 522–3 • CF 314 • FMG I, many; III, 30–3, 87–8, 101 • PWW 265, 274 • OTT 22, 95, 98–100, 202, 205 • SUMMERS 54, 58, 64 • BE 351, 354, 356 • BLAKEY 316, 319–20, 324 • FLAMMONDE 132 • OGLESBY 17, 19, 55 • KANTOR, many • DAVIS 223, 225 • NORTH 393, 409, 412, 417, 427–8 • PD 16

FUQUA, HAROLD R., parking attendant in the basement of the DPD station. Fuqua told the WC that police ordered him out of the basement and up to the first floor before Oswald's transfer—testimony apparently intended to confirm the DPD's stringent security measures.

SOURCE: WCH XIII, 141

G

GADASH, CLYDE, Ruby witness. Gadash was foreman at the *Dallas Times-Herald*, where Ruby visited between 4:00 and 4:30 A.M. on November 23, 1963. While there, according to the WR:

> Ruby displayed to the composing room employees a "twistboard" he had previously promised to Gadash. The twistboard was an exercising device consisting of two pieces of hardened materials joined together by a lazy susan bearing so that one piece could remain stationary on the floor while a person stood atop it and swiveled to and fro. Ruby had been trying to promote sales of the board in the weeks before President Kennedy was killed. Considerable merriment developed when one of the women at the *Times-Herald* demonstrated the board, and Ruby himself put on a demonstration for those assembled. [Ruby] later testified: "...not that I wanted to get in with the hilarity of frolicking, but he [Gadash] asked me to show him, and the other men gathered around." Gadash agreed that Ruby's general mood was one of sorrow.

SOURCE: WR 320

GALLAGHER, JOHN F., ballistics expert; FBI spectographer. Gallagher examined WCE 399 (the "magic bullet") and the bullet fragments found in JFK's limo.
SOURCES: WCH XV, 746 • PWW 79 • EVICA 76–7 • ME 122

GALLOWAY, CALVIN, Bethesda witness; admiral, U.S. Navy; navy doctor; commanding officer of the National Naval Medical Center at Bethesda. As the autopsists' commanding officer, Galloway observed JFK's autopsy and later handled much of the autopsy's paper work.
SOURCES: BE, many • HOS 201

GANGL, THEODORE FRANK, Oswald witness; Padgett Printing Corp. plant superintendent. Gangl interviewed Oswald for a job on October 4, 1963. He told the WC that Oswald made a favorable impression but was not hired because of a poor recommendation from his previous employer, Robert Stovall, who said Oswald had "communistic tendencies." (See also Stovall, Robert)
SOURCE: WCH XI, 478

GANNAWAY, W. PATRICK, DPD captain; officer in charge of the DPD Special Service Bureau. Gannaway said that Oswald's description was broadcast following the shooting of JFK because he was missing from a "roll call" at the TSBD. There is evidence, however, that no such roll call ever took place. Besides, Oswald was already under arrest by the time he was a named suspect. (See also Revill, Jack)
SOURCES: RTJ 82 • BISHOP 248–9 • BLAKEY 313–4

GARCIA, OSCAR DEL VALLE (See BISHOP, WILLIAM)

GARNER, DARRELL WAYNE, suspicious death. Warren Reynolds, a t.k.w., originally stated that he could not identify the gunman as Oswald, despite the fact that he had followed the man for a block after the shooting. Before Reynolds could testify to this effect, on January 23, 1964, he was shot through the head in the darkened basement of his used-car-lot office. Reynolds survived the attack and later told the WC that the man he saw was Oswald. The primary suspect to the Reynolds shooting was Garner, who was arrested after drunkenly claiming that he shot Reynolds. He later said that "Reynolds got what he deserved" and confessed to being on the scene at the time of Reynolds's shooting. Garner was released after he was provided an alibi by Nancy Jane Mooney, who claimed she was with Garner at the time of the shooting. Mooney, a former employee of Ruby at the Carousel Club, was arrested for "disturbing the peace" by Dallas police eight days after providing the alibi. She was later found hanged in her cell with her pants tied around her neck, presumably a suicide. Garner died in 1970 at age 30 of an alleged heroin overdose. (See also Mooney, Nancy; Reynolds, Warren; Tippit, J. D.)
SOURCES: FMG IV, 4 • RTJ 278 • COA 35

GARNER, DOROTHY ANN (also shown as Dorothy May Garner), a.w. Garner was on the fourth floor of the TSBD with coworkers Victoria Adams, Elsie Dorman, and Sandra Styles. She claims the shots "came from the west." (See also Adams, Victoria; Dorman, Elsie; Styles, Sandra)
SOURCES: RTJ 111 • BISHOP 131 • CF 44 • PWW 42, 51

GARNER, JESSE J. and NINA, Oswald witnesses; neighbors and landlords of the Oswalds when he lived at 4905 Magazine Street in New Orleans beginning May 10, 1963. According to author Anthony Summers, Nina Garner said, "FBI agent Milton Kaack questioned her about Oswald within three weeks of his arrival in New Orleans." She later learned that her lodger was under heavy surveillance by "FBI" men in "a car which used to park there at night and watch him and the house, round the corner by the drugstore." Mrs. Garner told the WC she had seen "a Cuban" looking for Oswald when he wasn't home. Jesse Garner told the WC that when Oswald moved out, he skipped out on 15 days' rent. (See also Kaack, Milton)
SOURCES: WCH X, 264, 276 · SUMMERS 281 · NORTH 319

GARRICK, J. B., a.w.; DPD motorcycle patrolman who, according to the WC, was one of the three patrolmen who rode directly in front JFK's limo. Garrick's number that day was 132. (See also Freeman, H. D.)
SOURCES: WCH XX, 489 · FMG III, 54

GARRISON, EARLING CAROTHERS "JIM," New Orleans district attorney who indicted and unsuccessfully prosecuted Clay Shaw for conspiracy to assassinate JFK; author of *Heritage of Stone* (G. P. Putnam's Sons, 1970) and *On the Trail of the Assassins* (Sheridan Square, 1988), both of which deal with his attempts to solve the crime of the century. Garrison was born in 1921 in Denison, Iowa and moved to New Orleans in 1930. He was a WW II artillery observation pilot in Europe (1944 to 1945); graduated from Tulane University Law School; spent four months as an FBI agent; and was elected New Orleans district attorney in 1961.

One of the reasons Clay Shaw was acquitted by his jury so rapidly was that many of the witnesses and suspects subpoenaed by Garrison were not extradited. Garrison commented on this problem in an October 1967 interview in *Playboy* magazine:

> The reason we are unable to extradite *anyone* connected with the case is that there are powerful forces in Washington who find it imperative to conceal from the American public the truth about the assassination. And as a result, terrific pressure has been brought to bear on the governors of the states involved to prevent them from signing the extradition papers and returning the defendants to stand trial. I'm sorry to say that in every case, these Jell-O-spined governors have caved in and "played the game" Washington's way.

***

On May 24, 1968, Garrison was quoted by the *Los Angeles Free Press* as saying:

> The assassination of President Kennedy... was precipitated by the Fascists and the rightist anarchists [who] are one and the same. I firmly believe that the rightist anarchists and the CIA can take over our country right now and it would be a Fascist state except for two things. They would have to demolish and destroy the conservative movement by the radical right. They would have to destroy organizations such as the John Birch Society... [and] the other thing that is in their way is... Jim Garrison.

Garrison became an appeals judge and ironically played Chief Justice Earl Warren in the 1991 Oliver Stone film *JFK*, which was partially based on his second book.

Garrison died on October 21, 1992 at age 70, from a lengthy heart ailment. (See also Aase, Jean; Alcock, James; Andrews, Dean; Aynesworth, Hugh; Bundy, Vernon; Carlson, Alex; DeBrueys, Warren; Del Valle, Eladio; Farrington, Fenella; Fatter, Esmond; Ferrie, David; Gaten, Carver; Gurvich, William; Hicks, James; Ivon, Louis; Kimble, Jules; Klein, Frank; Kohlman, Herman; Lardner, George; Leemans, Fred; Long, Richard; McCarthy, Elizabeth; Moffett, Sandra; Nagell, Richard; Novel, Gordon; Oser, Alvin; Ray, Ellen; Russo, Perry; Spiesel, Charles; Tadin, Nicolas; Thornley, Kerry; Torbitt, William; Torres, Miguel; Whalen, Edward; Williams, D'Alton; Wood, William)

SOURCES: HSCA Report 142, 170 • COA 34, 37, 39, 47–50, 168, 287 • GERTZ 515 • CF 68, 230–1, 494–8 • FMG III, many • PWW 6, 80 • SUMMERS 292, 306, 469, 490–1 • BE 386, 428 • FLAMMONDE, many • BLAKEY 45–51, 166, 168–70, 178, 275 • EVICA, many • ME 60–3, 84, 87, 89–90, 127, 131, 213, 248 • FATAL xviii • DAVIS, many • NORTH 44, 192, 226, 229, 234, 239, 278 • PD 25, 138–9, 220–3, 325

GARRO DE PAZ, ELENA, possible Oswald witness; Mexican author. According to the HSCA:

> Garro de Paz... claimed that Oswald and two companions had attended a "twist" [1960s dance] party at the home of Ruben Duran, brother-in-law of Silvia Duran, the secretary of the Cuban consul [Eusebio] Azcue who dealt with Oswald [or an Oswald impersonator] when he applied at the consulate for a Cuban visa... The significance of the Elena Garro allegation, aside from its pointing to Oswald associations in Mexico City that the Warren Commission did not

investigate, lay in her description of one of [Oswald's] companions [at the party] as gaunt and blond-haired. These are the characteristics that both Azcue and Duran attributed to the visitor to the Cuban consulate who identified himself as Lee Harvey Oswald... The committee was unable to obtain corroboration for the Elena Garro allegation, although Silvia Duran did confirm that there was a "twist" party at her brother-in-law's home in the fall of 1963 and that Elena Garro was there. She denied, however, that Oswald was there, insisting that she never saw Oswald outside of the Cuban consulate. The committee was unable to check the story with official U.S. investigative agencies because they failed to pursue it, even though they were aware of it in 1964.

(See also Azcue, Eusebio; Duran, Silvia)
SOURCES: HSCA Report 123, 125, 251, 256 • HSCA III, 300

GATEN, CARVER, FBI agent. According to Jim Garrison, Gaten told Milwaukee resident Jim Gechnour that he knew James Hosty (the FBI agent in charge of Oswald's case following Oswald's return from the USSR) and Hosty told him that "Oswald had been paid regularly for information but provided little." Hosty expressed bitterness because he had been criticized by his superiors for not prying more out of Oswald.
SOURCE: OTT 225

GATLIN, MAURICE BROOKS, SR., suspicious death; CIA. With Ruby, Gatlin sold army surplus Jeeps to Fidel Castro in 1959. Gatlin was an associate of Guy Banister and general counsel of the Anti-Communist League of the Carribean. He died in 1964 after a fall from the sixth-floor window of the El Panama Hotel in Panama during the middle of the night.
SOURCE: OTT 24–5

GAUDET, WILLIAM GEORGE, CIA operative; now deceased. According to author Anthony Summers, Gaudet obtained a visa to accompany an alleged Oswald to Mexico City on September 17, 1963. Gaudet's and Oswald's entry papers into Mexico dated September 17, 1963, have consecutive serial numbers. Gaudet admitted to working for the CIA but denied any contact with Oswald south of the border. Bizarrely, in 1978 Gaudet admitted to Summers that he had seen Oswald on several occasions in New Orleans, handing out leaflets.
SOURCES: HSCA Report 218–9 • SUMMERS 336–8, 444 • HT 181

GAUTHIER, LEO J., FBI agent. Gauthier constructed 3D scale models of Dealey Plaza for the WC.
SOURCE: WCH V, 135

GEDNEY, JOHN FORRESTER, suspected a.w. According to JFK assassination files released by the DPD in February 1992, Gedney—reportedly 38 years old at the time of the assassination—was one of the three "tramps" apprehended in a railroad car near Dealey Plaza moments after the shooting. The files name the other two tramps as Harold Doyle, 32, and Gus Abrams, 53. According to the *New York Daily News* (March 4, 1992), Abrams, Doyle, and Gedney were indeed the tramps—actual vagrants—and are not considered suspects in the case. The most recent information indicates that these three men were held for four days by the DPD on vagrancy charges, rather than interviewed briefly and released, as was reported previously. According to the FBI, Gedney has been located in Melbourne, Florida, where he was interviewed and cleared of suspicion.

Other men who have previously been "positively" identified as some of the tramps include: Charles Frederick Rogers, Chauncy Marvin Holt, Charles Voyd Harrelson, E. Howard Hunt, and Frank Sturgis. (See also Abrams, Gus; Doyle, Harold; Harrelson, Charles; Holt, Chauncy Marvin; Hunt, E. Howard; Rogers, Charles; Sturgis, Frank)

GEFFNEY, WILLIAM, possible o.k.w. Geffney was arrested on November 24, 1963, after he was seen fleeing the DPD station following the shooting of Oswald. He was questioned and released. He said that he was on the first floor "sightseeing" when Oswald was shot.
SOURCE: WCE 2003, p. 366

GEMBERLING, ROBERT P., one of the FBI agents who interviewed assassination witnesses on November 22, 1963. When, on November 23, 1963, Gemberling submitted a list of names found in Oswald's notebook, he deleted the name of FBI agent James P. Hosty. (See also Hosty, James P.)
SOURCES: PWW 33, 40, 68, 160, 170, 194, 199 • NORTH 519

GEORGE, M. WALDO, Oswald witness; landlord of the Oswalds when they lived at 214 Neely Street in Dallas. (Rent was $60 per month.) George told the WC that Oswald beat Marina and said he tried to convince the Oswalds to go to church with him, to no avail.
SOURCE: WCH XI, p. 155

GERACI, PHILIP, III (shown some places as Gerici and Garaci), Oswald witness; suspicious death. Geraci, a 16-year-old New Orleans resident, met Oswald while in Carlos Bringuier's dry-goods store on August 5, 1963, when Oswald came in "pretending" to be an anti-Castro activist. Geraci was with his friend Vance Blalock at the time. According to Geraci, Oswald said "the thing he liked best of all [about rightist activism] was learning about how to blow up the Huey P. Long Bridge." That bridge spans the Mississippi River outside New Orleans and, according to author Paris Flammonde, "may have been used by Cuban exiles as a training run for actual sabotage within Cuba." Friend of Perry Russo, who testified against Clay Shaw. Died by electrocution in August 1968. (See also Blalock, Vance; Russo, Perry)

SOURCE: WCH X, p. 74 • FLAMMONDE 121 • BUCHANAN 127

GERASIMOV, VITALIY, employee at the Soviet embassy in Washington, D.C., in 1962. According to CIA records: Gerasimov was "known to have participated in clandestine meetings in [the U.S.] and to have made payments for intelligence information of value to the Soviets." In July 1962, Marina Oswald wrote Gerasimov, informing him and the embassy of her address in the United States. The letter was intercepted and read by the FBI.

SOURCE: SUMMERS 163

GERTZ, ELMER, Ruby witness; member of Ruby's defense team following his murder conviction; author of *Moment of Madness: The People vs. Jack Ruby* (Follett Publishing, 1968).

GERVAIS, PERSHING, New Orleans district attorney; Jim Garrison's friend and chief investigator during that office's investigation of JFK's death. Gervais later testified against Garrison, saying the D.A. had taken bribes from mobsters to allow the operation of pinball machines. Garrison was acquitted.

SOURCE: OTT 126–9, 256–60, 264–70, 275

GIANCANA, MOMO SALVATORE "SAM," Chicago mob boss; murder victim; alleged assassination conspirator. Giancana had been talking to a Senate Intelligence Committee and was under police protection when he died in June 1975. He was shot with a .22 pistol once in the back of his head and six times around his mouth—mob symbolism for "talks too much." In the early 1960s Giancana helped the CIA, with money and personnel, in covert operations within Cuba to rid that country of Castro.

Giancana was not known for his ability to keep a secret. When the CIA/ Mafia teams were planning to assassinate Castro in 1960, J. Edgar Hoover got wind of the plan because Giancana "told several friends."

According to Giancana's half-brother Charles (Chuck) and his nephew Sam in their book *Double Cross* (Warner Books, 1992), JFK was murdered by a team of Chicago hit men sent to Dallas by Giancana. The fatal shot, they claim, was fired by Giancana lieutenant Richard Cain, from the sixth

floor of the TSBD. Cain himself was murdered in 1973, "gangland style." The book states that the assassination was orchestrated by LBJ, Richard M. Nixon and others, and funded by Texas oil money. The book also claims that Giancana ordered the murder of his mistress Marilyn Monroe, who was killed by Giancana henchmen with a poisoned suppository. (See also Billett, Myron; Edwards, Sheffield; Maheu, Robert; Marcello, Carlos; Monroe, Marilyn; Trafficante, Santos)
    SOURCES: HSCA Report 114–5, 150, 164, 166, 173 • OGLESBY 5–6, 73 • EVICA, many
    • ME 132 • BELIN 104, 106, 108–11 • COA, many • DUFFY 123 • CF 175–9 • OTT 77,
    301 • SUMMERS 238–9, 248–51, 435, 494–5, 527–8 • BLAKEY, many • KANTOR 25,
    32–3, 135–6, 211–2 • FATAL xlii • DAVIS, many • NORTH, many • PD 328

GIBSON, MRS. DONALD (née DeMohrenschildt, Alexandra; formerly Taylor, Mrs. Gary), Oswald witness; daughter of Oswald associate George DeMohrenschildt. Gibson, formerly married to Oswald witness Gary Taylor; once baby-sat for June Oswald (August 1962). She told the WC that she and her husband (Taylor) spent a lot of time with the Oswalds at her father's encouraging. Gibson said of Oswald, "I don't think he knew what he wanted." She said Oswald "strongly" disliked Governor Connally. When Oswald rented PO Box 2915 in Dallas, he received the Taylors' permission to use their address on the application. (See also DeMohrenschildt, George; Oswald, Marina; Taylor, Gary)
    SOURCES: WR 289 • WCH XI, 123 • FLAMMONDE 196

GIBSON, JOHN, Texas Theatre witness. According to the WR: "[Gibson], another patron in the theater, saw an officer grab Oswald, and he claims he heard the click of a gun misfiring. He saw no shotgun in the possession of any policemen near Oswald." This last comment comes because of the statement of witness George Jefferson Applin Jr., who testified that a DPD member struck Oswald in the back with the butt end of a shotgun. (See also Applin, George)
    SOURCES: WR 166 • WCH VII, 70

GIBSON, LOIS, forensic artist used by the FBI and the Houston Police Department. In November 1991, in Dallas, Gibson—with private investigator John R. Craig and researcher Phillip A. Rogers—positively identified the "three tramps" as professional killer Charles Harrelson, confessed "tramp" and former CIA freelancer Chauncy Holt and wanted murderer Charles Frederick Rogers. (See also Craig, John R.; Harrelson, Charles; Holt, Chauncy Marvin; Rogers, Charles Frederick; Rogers, Philip A.)
    SOURCE: OGLESBY 48

GIESBRECHT, RICHARD, conspiracy witness. In 1964 Giesbrecht was a 35-year-old Mennonite businessman and father of four. He told the FBI of a conversation he had overheard in the Horizon Room cocktail lounge at Winnipeg International Airport on February 13, 1964, between a man he later identified as David Ferrie and a man in his middle or late 40s, with reddish blond hair, a badly pockmarked neck and jaw, who wore a hearing aid, and spoke with an accent, possibly Latin. Giesbrecht told the FBI that it didn't take him long to realize that the men he was eavesdropping on had knowledge of the plot to kill JFK. Both men, he said, wore light tweed suits and loafers. He assumed that both were homosexuals.

According to author Paris Flammonde:

> Ferrie indicated that he was concerned over how much Oswald had told his wife about the plot to kill Kennedy. Additionally, they discussed a man named Isaacs, his relationship with Oswald, and how curious it was that he would have gotten himself involved with a "psycho" like Oswald... Isaacs seemed to have allowed himself to be caught on television film near the President when Kennedy arrived in Dallas, and, at the time the conversation was taking place, was under the surveillance of a man named Hoffman, or Hochman, who was to "relieve" him and destroy a 1958 model automobile in Isaac's possession... [Ferrie said,] "We have more money at our disposal now than at any other time."... The conversation moved to another area and the two began speaking of a meeting to take place at the Townhouse Motor Hotel in Kansas City, Missouri, on March 18. They mentioned that the rendezvous would be registered under the name of the textile firm. It was noted that no meeting had been held since November 1963... Ferrie mentioned that an "aunt" (or "auntie"—gay [slang] for an older homosexual) would be flying in from California. A name which Giesbrecht thought sounded like "Romeniuk" was mentioned several times; Ferrie inquired about some paper, or merchandise, coming out of Nevada and the other man replied that things had gotten too risky and that the house, or shop, at a place called Mercury had been closed down, but that a "good shipment" had reached Caracas from Newport... It was also agreed that the Warren Commission would not stop its investigation, even if it did decide that Oswald was guilty.

At this point, Giesbrecht realized that a third man, sitting at another table, was staring at him as he eavesdropped. He described the man as 35 years old, light-haired and red-cheeked with a "slightly deformed" nose.

He weighed about 200 pounds, stood 6'0", and had either a scar or a tattoo on his left hand. Extremely frightened at this point, Giesbrecht headed for the airport's Royal Canadian Mounted Police office. He was followed. His entrance to the RCMP was blocked by two men. He ran to a phone booth and tried to call the RCMP, but was forced to hang up before getting his message across when his pursuers approached. He finally managed to lose the men elsewhere in the airport and called his lawyer, who called the U.S. consulate, which called the FBI.

At first the FBI was enthusiastic about Giesbrecht's information. "This looks like the break we've been waiting for," Special Agent Merryl Nelson reportedly told him. Within two months, however, the bureau had cooled considerably. They told him to forget what he had heard. "It's too big," an agent told him. "We can't protect you in Canada." (See also Isaacs, Harold; Isaacs, Martin)
SOURCE: FLAMMONDE 29–32

GIESECKE, ADOLPHE H., JR., Parkland witness; anesthesiologist. Giesecke told researcher Harrison Livingstone that, when JFK was brought in, the back of his head "was missing."
SOURCES: WR 66–7 • WCH VI, 72 • RTJ 58 • BISHOP 156, 176, 188, 289 • BE 40

GILL, G. WRAY, attorney to Carlos Marcello, who employed David Ferrie during the summer and fall of 1963. According to reporter Jim Marrs, Gill "had come to Ferrie's home [shortly after the assassination] and mentioned that when Oswald was arrested in Dallas, he was carrying a library card with Ferrie's name on it." If such a card actually existed, its existence has been thoroughly covered up. (See also Ferrie, David; Marcello, Carlos)
SOURCES: HSCA Report 143–5, 170 • FLAMMONDE 27–9, 65, 73 • CF 100 • COA 40–1, 47, 50 • OTT 109–10, 304 • SUMMERS 309, 489–90 • BLAKEY 46, 166, 168, 203, 396 • DAVIS, many • NORTH, many

GIVENS, CHARLES DOUGLAS, Oswald witness; TSBD employee. According to author Josiah Thompson, Givens was one of the last people to see Oswald before the assassination. He says that Oswald was on the sixth floor with a clipboard at 11:55 A.M. Oswald's clipboard was found on the sixth floor on December 2, 1963, ten days after the assassination, not far from where the Mannlicher-Carcano rifle had been hidden.

According to Penn Jones Jr., Givens originally said that he had seen Oswald on the first floor of the TSBD about a half hour before the assassination, but—by the time he testified for the WC—he had changed his story to seeing Oswald on the sixth floor.

Givens was considered a suspect immediately following the assassination. Not only was he missing from the TSBD after the shooting (contradict-ing the official version of the facts which says that Oswald was the only TSBD employee to miss a roll call taken after the assassination), but police records showed that he had a police record involving narcotics. (See also Kaiser, Frankie)

SOURCES: WR 132-3, 232 • WCH VI, 345; XXIII, 873 • BELIN 56 • BISHOP 98–9, 176, 225 • FMG III, 93 • SUMMERS 75

GOCHNOUR, JIM, informant. Gochnour told New Orleans District Attorney Jim Garrison of a story related to him by former FBI agent Carver Gaten. Gaten, an acquaintance of James Hosty, the FBI agent in charge of Oswald's case following Oswald's return from the Soviet Union, told Gochnour that Oswald had been an FBI contact agent and, although the alleged assassin had been paid regularly, he had been stingy in his supply of information. (See also Hosty, James)

SOURCE: OTT 225

GOIN, DONALD EDWARD, armored-car operator. Goin drove the armored truck that was to be used as a decoy during Oswald's transfer. He was parked outside the Commerce Street ramp to the DPD station with Edward C. Dietrich when Ruby shot Oswald, but heard no shots.

SOURCE: WCH XV, 168

GOLDBERG, ALFRED, WC staff member, U.S. Air Force historian. Goldberg wrote the WR's "Speculation and Rumor" appendix.

SOURCES: WCH II, 384; III, 1; IX, 166 • PWW 114–6, 143, 265, 267, 269 • BE 98, 368

GOLDSTEIN, DAVID, owner of Dave's House of Guns. Goldstein told the WC that he had no record of selling a gun to Oswald.

SOURCE: WCH VII, 594

GOLDSTEIN, RUBIN "HONEST JOE," Ruby witness. "Best friends" with Ruby; known as a "Dallas extrovert"; advertised himself as "Honest Joe Goldstein, the Loan Ranger"; owned a "gaudily painted Edsel with a plugged .50 caliber machine gun mounted on the top" which, according to SS agent Forrest Sorrels, was parked outside the DPD station on Commerce Street during the early evening of Saturday, November 23. A. J. Millican, an a.w., told sheriff's deputies he saw "a truck from 'Honest Joe's Pawn Shop' park close to the TSBD, then drive off five to ten minutes before the assassination." Assassination witness Jean Hill told Dallas reporter Jim Marrs that, before the assassination, she had seen a van with writing on the side that said "Uncle Joe's Pawn Shop." The van drove past police lines and down the service road in front of the TSBD, and behind the pergola. The FBI interviewed Goldstein and he told them the DPD had allowed him to

drive his Edsel sedan, which had cardboard covering the windows, around the motorcade route area for advertising purposes. (See Hill, Jean; Millican, A.J.)
SOURCES: WCH XIX, 486 • DOP 513–4 • PWW 36–37, 164, 166, 169

GOLOVACHEV, PAVEL, Oswald witness; son of Hero of the Soviet Union General P. Y. Golovachev. Pavel reportedly traveled in Minsk's "highest social circles" and was a friend of Oswald during the latter's stay in the USSR.
SOURCES: CF 122 • BLAKEY 147

GOLUB, GREGORY, Oswald witness; Soviet consul in Helsinki at the time Oswald entered the USSR; suspected by U.S. Intelligence of being a KGB agent. Golub issued Oswald a tourist visa in 48 hours, which was unusually fast. Golub, unlike other Soviet consuls, had the authority to grant visas without checking first with Moscow if he thought the individual was "all right." Oswald applied for his visa on October 12, 1959 and received it on October 14. (See also Shirakova, Rima)
SOURCES: HSCA Report 211–2 • DUFFY 32–3

GOLZ, EARL, *Dallas Morning News* reporter. In Dealey Plaza following the assassination, there was a piece of sidewalk with a bullet mark on it. The mark indicated that the shot had come from the south manhole (since paved over) atop the triple underpass. To avoid obliteration of the evidence, Golz had the piece of sidewalk with the mark removed.
SOURCES: BE 558 • DAVIS 459, FMG IV, 121 • HT 118, 248–9 • SHAW 86

GONZALES, PEDRO VALERIANO, president of the Abilene, Texas, Cuban exile organization, the Cuban Liberation Committee. According to Abilene photographer Harold Reynolds, as reported by the *Dallas Morning News* on June 10, 1979, Gonzales received a November 17, 1963, note slipped under his apartment door which said, "Call me immediately. Urgent." The note was signed "Lee Oswald." Reynolds says that Gonzales became very nervous upon reading the note and went down to the street to make a phone call from a pay phone, despite having a telephone in his apartment. Gonzales left Abilene soon after the assassination and moved to Venezuela. (See also Reynolds, Harold)
SOURCES: CF 152 • SUMMERS 382

GONZALEZ, HENRY B., a.w.; Parkland witness; Representative from San Antonio, Texas; rode in motorcade. Gonzalez had warned JFK "not to come to Dallas." In early 1977, Gonzalez replaced Congressman Thomas Downing as the chairman of the HSCA—and was subsequently replaced by Louis Stokes. (See also Downing, Thomas; Stokes, Louis)

SOURCES: WR 70 • BLAKEY 62–3, 65–8 • BELIN 188 • RTJ 263–4 • BISHOP 80, 97, 157, 259 • DOP, many • CF 518–24 • FMG III, 2–3

GOODSON, CLYDE FRANKLIN, DPD member. On the evening of November 22, 1963, Goodson, 29 years old, was assigned to guard the door to Captain Will Fritz's office, where Oswald was being interrogated. He told the WC that the man seen trying to get into that office only looked like Ruby, but was not him. He said he didn't see Ruby at all that night.
SOURCE: WCH XV, 596

GOPADZE, LEON I., Russian-speaking SS agent. Gopadze interrogated Marina Oswald extensively following the assassination and reported that Marina didn't know that Oswald had ever used the alias "Alek Hidell." Six months later, when Marina testified for the WC, she not only remembered Oswald's using the name, but said that she had personally signed that name, at Lee's request, on FPCC membership cards. (See also Oswald, Marina)
SOURCE: RTJ 132

GRAEF, JOHN G., Oswald witness; Oswald's supervisor in the photographic department at Jaggars-Chiles-Stovall in Dallas. Graef hired Oswald in October 1962. He told WC that Oswald's work performance started out well, but that he couldn't handle detail work. He said that Oswald didn't get along with his peers.
SOURCE: WCH X, 174

GRAF, ALLEN D., Oswald witness; USMC acquaintance; Oswald's platoon sergeant while stationed in Santa Ana, California. Graf told the WC: "Oswald seemed to me to resent all military authority. He also seemed narrow-minded, refused to listen to the views of others... with regard to his job... Oswald learned quickly... and kept his temper—if, indeed he had a temper—in check... Oswald never gave to me any indication of favoring Communism or opposing capitalism."
SOURCES: WCH VIII, 317 • AO 95 • OTT 46

GRAMMER, BILLY, Ruby witness; former member of the DPD. Grammer was answering the phone in the police station the night after the assassination when he received a call from a man he later realized was Ruby. The voice on the phone said, "If you move Oswald the way you are planning, we are going to kill him."
SOURCE: HT 461

GRANT, DAVID B., SS agent. Just after completing advance work for JFK's trip to Tampa, Grant joined Agent Winston G. Lawson to do advance work on JFK's Texas trip. (See also Lawson, Winston G.)

SOURCE: WR 421

GRANT, EVA, Ruby witness and sister. As a rule, Grant ran the Vegas Club for her brother, but at the time of the assassination, she was home, due to a recent illness. She told the New York *Herald Tribune* by telephone on December 5, 1963, that Jack and Officer Tippit knew each other. "Jack knew him and I knew him...Jack called him 'buddy.'" Grant also confirmed that Ruby owned clothes exactly like those he was seen wearing at Parkland Hospital after the assassination. (See also Larkin, Robert; Tippit, J. D.)
SOURCES: WR 312, 314, 316, 324, 327, 329 • BLAKEY 282–4, 286–7, 290–1, 305, 317 • WCH XIV, 429; XV, 321 • RTJ 252, 267 • COA, many • GERTZ, many • BISHOP 77–8, 118, 217, 270, 327–9, 358, 434–5, 507 • KANTOR, many • DAVIS 158, 182 • NORTH 450

GRAVES, JEAN, Oswald witness; secretary at the Leslie Welding Company. Graves supplied for the WC Oswald's time cards for when he worked for that company.
SOURCE: WCH XI, 479

GRAVES, L. C., o.k.w.; DPD detective. Graves was standing immediately to Oswald's left when Ruby shot him.
SOURCES: WR 157, 201 • WCH VII, 251; XIII, 1 • RTJ 211, 214 • GERTZ 46, 71, 98–9, 513 • BISHOP 257

GRAVITIS, DOROTHY, 74-year-old member of Dallas's Russian-speaking community; acquaintance of Marina Oswald's housemate Ruth Paine. Born in Latvia; Gravitis came to the U.S. in 1949 and taught Russian at the Berlitz School, where Ruth was both a friend and student. She never met Lee or Marina, but discussed Marina with Ruth on the phone. (See also Paine, Ruth)
SOURCE: WCH IX, 131

GRAY, L.E., a.w.; DPD motorcycle patrolman. According to the WC, Gray was one of five motorcycle patrolmen who rode half a block ahead of the presidential motorcade during the Dallas motorcade. Gray's number that day was 156.
SOURCES: WCH XX, 489 • FMG III, 54

GRAY, VIRGINIA, Assistant curator of manuscripts at the Duke University Library; specialist on Socialist Party of America records. Gray gave the WC a copy of a letter written October 3, 1956, by Oswald to that party, seeking information.
SOURCE: WCH XI, 209

GREENER, CHARLES W., Oswald witness. Greener owned the Irving Sports Shop in Irving, Texas—the same Dallas suburb where Marina

Oswald was living with Ruth Paine at the time of the assassination, and where Lee Harvey Oswald had been spending his weekends. The shop gained attention on November 25, 1963, when an undated repair tag was found bearing the name "OSWALD" in the handwriting of Dial D. Ryder, one of Greener's employees. The tag indicated that "three holes had been drilled in an unspecified type of rifle and a telescopic sight had been mounted on the rifle and boresighted." Since the Mannlicher-Carcano found after the assassination on the sixth floor of the TSBD already had a telescopic sight when it was shipped, this indicated that the work had been done for another "Oswald" or that Oswald had another rifle. Neither Greener nor Ryder recalled Oswald coming into the store. (See also Ryder, Dial)

SOURCES: WR 291–2 • WCH XI, 245 • RTJ 326

GREER, WILLIAM ROBERT, a.w.; SS agent. Greer was the driver of JFK's limo, a Lincoln Continental convertible sedan, designation SS Car No. 100-X. The Zapruder film shows that, after the first shot struck the president, the limo's brake lights went on, so that the car had almost come to a stop at the time the fatal shots were fired. The Zapruder film shows that Greer looked back over his shoulder at JFK after the sound of the first shot and did not turn his head back to look forward until after he had seen the results of the final shot. Greer has been severely criticized for being slow to react to the crisis. This diagram shows the seating arrangements in the presidential limousine at the time of the shooting:

William Greer	Roy Kellerman
Secret Service	Secret Service
driver	
Nellie Connally	Gov. John Connally
Jackie Kennedy	JFK

Greer was photographed laughing after he finished giving his WC testimony. Less suspicious behavior was exhibited by Greer at Parkland Hospital immediately following the shooting. According to William Manchester, Greer burst into tears when he saw Mrs. Kennedy at Parkland. He squeezed her head with both hands and said, "Oh, Mrs. Kennedy, oh my God! Oh my God! I didn't mean to do it, I didn't hear, I should have swerved the car, I couldn't help it! Oh, Mrs. Kennedy, as soon as I saw it I swerved the car. If only I'd seen it in time!" He then wept on the former First Lady's shoulder.

SOURCES: WR 20, 22, 58–9, 62–3, 66 • WCH II, p. 112 • HSCA Report 40 • ME 110, 218, 222 • OGLESBY 37 • BELIN 4, 16, 27 • BISHOP, many • DOP, many • CF 9, 12 • FMG III, 93–4 • SUMMERS 19, 21–2 • BE, many • BLAKEY 10 • HOS 175

GREGORY, CHARLES, Parkland witness; surgeon who treated Governor Connally. Gregory told the WC, in a statement unknowingly critical of the "single-bullet theory," that the bullet that struck Connally "behaved as if it had never struck anything except him."

SOURCES: WR 69, 96, 98 • WCH IV, 117; VI, 95 • HT 64 • SSID 97 • BISHOP 187–8 • ME 40, 42

GREGORY, DICK, entertainer and political activist. One of the first— and loudest—of those who have said that the CIA participated in the JFK assassination. According to HT, "They tried to kill him [Gregory], and they murdered his driver."

SOURCES: HT 409 • BELIN 177 • COA 283 • ME 128 • PD 28–9, 70, 187, 284

GREGORY, PAUL RODERICK, Oswald witness; son of Peter Paul Gregory (below) and an acquaintance of the Oswalds in Texas.

SOURCES: WR 260 • WCH IX, 141

GREGORY, PETER PAUL, Oswald witness; member of Dallas's Russian-speaking community. Gregory was a consulting petroleum engineer and part-time Russian instructor at the Fort Worth Public Library. He was born in Chita, Siberia; came to the U.S. in 1923; and attended the University of California at Berkeley. He said that Oswald spoke with a Polish accent.

When Gregory was contacted by Oswald in June 1962, soon after Lee and Marina returned from the USSR, he noted that Oswald was wearing a wool suit, inappropriate garb for summer in Dallas. Oswald got Gregory's name from the Texas Employment Commission in Fort Worth because Oswald was seeking a "letter certifying to his proficiency in the Russian language." It was through Gregory that the Oswalds entered the Dallas Russian-speaking community's social scene. Marina became a Russian tutor for Gregory's son, Paul.

Gregory introduced the Oswalds to George Bouhe and Anna Meller. Soon the Oswalds were acquainted with 30 Russian-speaking Texans, including Ruth Paine and George and Jeanne DeMohrenschildt. Sometime before the assassination, Marguerite Oswald, Lee's mother, signed up for and attended Gregory's Russian classes, presumably so that she would be able to communicate better with Marina.

Gregory was Marina Oswald's initial translator during her interrogation by the SS following the assassination. He died in January 1982 of natural causes. (See also Meller, Teofil; Torbitt, William)

SOURCES: WR 260, 376 • WCH II, 337 • FLAMMONDE 154–5 • EVICA 8–9)

GRIFFIN, BURT W., WC counsel; Cleveland attorney. Griffin was 31 years old when appointed. With Leon D. Hubert Jr., he investigated Ruby's life and activities. According to HT, Griffin "tried to get Police Sergeant Patrick Dean to change his story about how Ruby got into the basement to shoot Oswald, and Griffin threatened him." Later Griffin became a judge. (See also Hubert, Leon, Jr.)

SOURCES: HSCA Report 158–9, 168, 259 • EVICA 98–9, 103, 112, 158, 160–3, 204, 223, 302 • HT 281 • SHAW 23–4 • BELIN 46 • RTJ 18, 296–7, 392–5 • COA 158, 200, 204, 210, 259 • Gertz 76–7, 80, 89, 498–9, 511, 513 • PWW 56, 256–7, 260, 269 • SUMMERS 431, 463, 469, 531–2 • BE 12, 99, 109, 229, 288, 373 • FMG I, 2, 4, 67–73, 92, 96 • BLAKEY, many • KANTOR, many • DAVIS 285–6, 611

GRIFFIN, WILL HAYDEN, FBI agent. Griffin said Oswald was "definitely an [FBI] informant." He died in August 1982 of cancer.

Griffin interviewed Oswald's housekeeper, Earlene Roberts, on November 29, 1963. She told him that the Dallas police car that honked its horn outside her rooming house about a half hour after the assassination—while Oswald was in his room putting on his jacket—was #207. When Roberts testified before the WC, she said she wasn't sure about the number of the car—that it might have been #106. (See also Roberts, Earlene)

SOURCES: HSCA Report 194–5 • RTJ 103 • FMG I, 75

GRINNAN, JOSEPH P., Dallas independent oil operator; John Birch Society coordinator. With Bernard W. Weissman, William B. Burley, and Larrie H. Schmidt, Grinnan was one of four men who wrote and placed the full-page, black-bordered advertisement in the November 22, 1963, edition of the *Dallas Morning News*. It was also Grinnan's job to recruit the necessary funds for the ad ($1,465) on behalf of "The American Fact-Finding Committee," of which Weissman was the chairman. Grinnan's three primary contributors were Edgar R. Crissey, Nelson Bunker Hunt (son of H. R. Hunt) and H. R. Bright. (See also Bright, H. R.; Burley, William; Crissey, Edgar; Hunt, Nelson; Schmidt, Larrie; Weissman, Bernard)

SOURCES: WR 275–6 • FMG I, 128–32, 135–8, 140–1, 143–4)

GRODEN, ROBERT J., creator of the optically enhanced version of the Zapruder film which, after being shown on ABC-TV's *Goodnight America* program on March 6, 1975, was instrumental in the formation of the HSCA. Groden was coauthor of two books about the JFK assassination,

JFK: The Case for Conspiracy (1976) and *High Treason* (1990).
    SOURCES: HSCA Report 75, 487 • EVICA 68 • ME 53–4 • BELIN 178–81, 183, 188, 190,
    200–1, 223 • CF 22 • FMG III, 93, 96–7 • OTT 75 • SUMMERS 30, 44–5, 484 • BE 36,
    527, 539

GROSS, R.L., DPD patrolman. Just following the assassination, Gross
said into Channel Two on the Dallas police radio, "Dispatcher on Channel
One seems to have his mike stuck." It is more likely that it was a
motorcycle patrolman (most probably Officer H. B. McLain) who had his
mike stuck. The Dictabelt recording made by that open mike became a
crucial piece of evidence because it recorded more than three supersonic
sounds, said to represent shots, during the shooting sequence, thus—
according to the HSCA—proving the existence of a second gunman. (See
also McLain, H. B.)
    SOURCE: BISHOP 138

GROSSI, JOHN CAESAR, Oswald witness. Grossi, alleged by author
Michael H. B. Eddowes in his book *Khrushchev Killed Kennedy* to be aka
Jack Leslie Bowen, Oswald's coworker at Jaggars-Chiles-Stovall. This is
noteworthy because of the similarity of the pseudonym to John Howard
Bowen, the false name reportedly used by Albert Osborne when he traveled
via bus to Mexico City with Oswald (or an impersonator) in September
1963. (See also Bowen, John; Osborne, Albert)
    SOURCE: KKK 76

GROSSMAN, ROBERT G., Parkland witness; neurosurgeon. Grossman
told Ben Bradlee Jr., of the *Boston Globe*, soon after the assasssination that
JFK had a large wound, separate from his temple wound, in the back of his
head—much too large to be an entrance wound. This is the wound that
does not show up on the official autopsy photographs.
    Grossman is now a professor and chairman of the Neurosurgery
Department at the Baylor College of Medicine in Houston. Grossman was
new at Parkland at the time of the assassination; he had just joined the
teaching staff as an instructor of neurosurgery.
    Did not testify for the WC or the HSCA.
    SOURCE: HT 30, 36, 51, 53, 459

GRUBER, ALEX, Ruby witness; boyhood friend of Ruby's from Chicago;
associate of one of Jimmy Hoffa's "key officials." Gruber lived in Los
Angeles at the time of the assassination. According to the WR, Ruby called
Gruber at 2:37 P.M. on the afternoon of the assassination. The conversation
lasted for three minutes and reportedly consisted of discussions about: (1) a
dog Ruby had promised to send Gruber; (2) Gruber's plans to start a car-

wash business; and (3) the assassination. As soon as JFK's death came up, Ruby reportedly broke down and had to hang up.

Gruber met with Ruby ten days before the assassination and later told the FBI conflicting stories regarding the length of his stay in Dallas at that time and the number of meetings he had had with Ruby.

SOURCES: WR 315–6 • WCH XXII, 302 • WCD 1262, p. 10 • HSCA IX, 431 • KANTOR 22 • SUMMERS 447, 456

GUERINI, ANTOINE, Corsican Mafia boss in Marseilles. According to Christian David—an imprisoned criminal who claims to know full details of the plot to kill JFK and is willing to trade his secrets for freedom—it was Guerini who accepted the contract to kill JFK, then sent a team of assassins, including Lucien Sarti, to make the hit. (See also David, Christian; Sarti, Lucien)

SOURCE: SUMMERS 524

GUINN, VINCENT, HSCA ballistics expert; head of the activation analysis program of the general atomic division of General Dynamics Corporation. Guinn performed neutron activation analysis on the "magic bullet" (WCE 399) and bullet fragments reportedly taken from Governor Connally's wrist. He stated that his tests "established that it was highly likely that the injuries to the Governor's wrist were caused by the bullet found on the stretcher at Parkland Hospital."

According to HT, "The main problem with this test was that Dr. Guinn stated afterwards that none of the fragments he tested weighed the same as any listed as evidence by the Warren Commission. That is, along with many missing fragments, it would appear that the evidence had been switched before he got it." When Guinn opened up the can that was supposed to hold bullet fragments that had struck the limo's windshield, he found the can empty.

SOURCES: WCE 841 • HSCA Report 515 • HT 69, 73–4, 118, 233, 383 • RTJ 152–3 • SUMMERS 33–4, 37 • BE 556–8 • ME 164–5, 227

GUINYARD, SAM, t.k.w.; porter at a used-car lot at Patton Avenue and Jefferson Boulevard. Guinyard heard gunshots and saw a man run south on Patton. He said he saw the gunman stick his handgun in his belt and then untuck his sports shirt to cover it up. He positively identified the man as Oswald.

SOURCES: WR 158–9, 164 • WCH VII, 395 • BELIN 19–21, 28, 31–2 • BISHOP 353, 355–6

GUN, NERIN, author of *Red Roses from Texas* (Frederick Miller, 1964), the first book published about the assassination to question the three-bullet, lone-gunman theory. Published in London.

GURVICH, WILLIAM, private detective who, along with his brother Leonard, volunteered to help New Orleans District Attorney Jim Garrison's investigation into the assassination. Gurvich disappeared soon thereafter.

According to Garrison, Gurvich reemerged on a June 1967 NBC-TV special called *The Case of Jim Garrison,* a program seemingly designed to discredit Garrison, claiming that he was the district attorney's chief investigator. (See also Garrison, Jim)
SOURCES: OTT 169 · FLAMMONDE 60, 62, 84, 119, 235, 240, 306, 315–8, 323

GUSTAFSON, PATRICIA (née HUTTON), Parkland witness; nurse who helped wheel JFK from the limo into the emergency room. Gustafson told the WC that there was a "massive opening in the back of the head." In 1981, she told Ben Bradlee Jr., of the *Boston Globe* that she was given instructions to apply a pressure bandage to JFK's head. "I tried to do so but there was really nothing to put a pressure bandage on. [The wound] was too massive. So he told me to just leave it be... [The wound was] in the back of the head." She was also one of the nurses who washed JFK's body in preparation for the coffin.
SOURCES: WR 69 · HT 43, 454, 459 · BISHOP 207–8 · BE 193, 312, 599

GUTHRIE, STEVE, former Dallas sheriff. In 1946 Mafia emissary Paul Jones of Chicago offered the Dallas district attorney and the Dallas sheriff's department $1000 a week if they allowed a nightclub/gambling casino to operate in Dallas unhindered. No deal was made, and Jones faced bribery charges. In 1963, after Oswald's death, Guthrie admitted that the man Jones intended to run the illegal Dallas operation was Ruby, who arrived in Dallas in 1947. (See also Jones, Paul)
SOURCES: WCH XXII, 360 · HSCA Report 149 · HSCA App. IX, 516 · SUMMERS 434

GUTIERREZ, PEDRO, Oswald witness; Mexico City credit investigator. On December 2, 1963, Gutierrez wrote to LBJ, telling him that he had seen Oswald in the Mexico City Cuban embassy in September, and that Oswald had been passed a large wad of money. Research into Gutierrez's background revealed that he was a politically active anticommunist.
SOURCES: WCD 564 · SUMMERS 419

H

HABIGHORST, ALOYSIUS, New Orleans police officer who, while booking assassination suspect Clay Shaw, asked Shaw if he used any aliases. Shaw said, "Clay Bertrand," and this information was written on Shaw's fingerprint card. At Shaw's trial, Judge Haggerty would not allow this fact to be placed in evidence, saying that Shaw's rights had been violated. Habighorst has died, and his widow has publicly defended his integrity after it was attacked in "reviews" of Oliver Stone's film, *JFK*. (See also Shaw, Clay)
SOURCES: OTT 145–6, 242, 325 • FLAMMONDE 245

HAGEMANN, MAX, Swiss professor, owner-editor of the newspaper *Nazional Zeitung*, and charter member (1961) of the board of directors of CMC—a board that included assassination suspect Clay Shaw. (See also Bloomfield, Louis; Shaw, Clay)
SOURCE: FLAMMONDE 215, 219

HAIG, ALEXANDER, allegedly a member of Special Group 54-12, a committee, chaired in the 1950s by then-Vice President Richard M. Nixon. Designed to control the actions of the CIA and military intelligence. Others connected to 54-12 include E. Howard Hunt and Frank Sturgis. 54-12 allegedly sanctioned assassination plots against Fidel Castro. Haig was promoted from colonel to four-star general under the Nixon administration and later became secretary of state under Ronald Reagan.
SOURCES: SUMMERS 254 • HT 316–7 • COA 324, 453

HAGGERTY, EDWARD ALOYSIUS, JR., judge who presided over the Clay Shaw trial in New Orleans. According to Jim Garrison, Haggerty was "born and bred in the...Irish Channel of New Orleans." When the trial was over, Haggerty told a reporter that, in his opinion, Shaw had "lied

through his teeth" when he denied involvement in the JFK assassination. (See also Shaw, Clay)
SOURCES: FMG III, 61–2 • OTT 230–1, 242

HALDEMAN, H. R., President Richard Nixon's chief of staff who went down in the Watergate scandal. In his book *The Ends of Power*, Haldeman wrote about the Watergate tapes:

In all of those Nixon references to the Bay of Pigs, [Nixon] was actually referring to the Kennedy assassination... After Kennedy was killed, the CIA launched a fantastic cover-up... The CIA literally erased any connection between Kennedy's assassination and the CIA... in fact, Counter Intelligence Chief James Angleton of the CIA called Bill Sullivan of the FBI and rehearsed the questions and answers they would give to the Warren Commission investigators.

(See also Nixon, Richard M.)
SOURCES: EOP 68–9 • HT 328, 333, 344–5, 417 • COA 300, 302 • EVICA 229, 312, 317 • DAVIS 403–4 • PD 110–1

HALL, C. RAY, Ruby witness; FBI agent. Hall interviewed Ruby following Oswald's murder. Ruby told him that he was able to sneak down the Main Street ramp to the basement of police headquarters unmolested because he waited until Officer Roy Eugene Vaughn, who was guarding that entrance, was busy watching traffic while helping to guide the patrol car of Officer Rio "Sam" Pierce.

Hall said that Ruby initially refused to discuss when and where he had entered the building. It was only a full month after the shooting that Ruby told his story of entering via the Main Street ramp minutes before the shooting. (See also Pierce, Rio; Vaughn, Roy)
SOURCES: WCH XV, 62 • HSCA IX 137 • GERTZ 519 • BLAKEY 321, 324 • SUMMERS 462–3 • NORTH 425

HALL, GUS, longtime leader of the Communist Party U.S.A. Hall was one of three men who received honorary membership cards from Oswald to Oswald's fictitious New Orleans chapter of the FPCC. Hall testified voluntarily for the WC that he had never had any association with Oswald. (See also Davis, Benjamin; Johnson, Arnold)
SOURCES: WR 385 • FMG I, 75 • NORTH 214, 224 • PD 351

HALL, HARRY (aka Sinclair, Harry, Jr.), Ruby witness. Hall ran a bet-and-run swindle out of Dallas hotels. He claimed that Ruby provided the cash and the "likely victims" for the swindle, and that one of the victims was Texas oil magnate H. L. Hunt. (See also Hunt, H. L.)

SOURCES: RTJ 237–8 • COA 88–91, 115, 118, 128, 417

HALL, JOHN RAYMOND and ELENA A., Oswald witnesses; members of Dallas's Russian-speaking community. During October and November 1962, Marina Oswald lived in the houses of several of her new Dallas-area Russian-speaking friends, including the Halls, in October, while Lee looked for work. (See also Oswald, Marina)

SOURCES: WR 260, 306 • WCH VIII, 391, 406 • BLAKEY 350–1 • FLAMMONDE 154

HALL, LORAN EUGENE (aka Hall, Lorenzo; Pascillio, Lorenzo; "Skip"); anti-Castro Cuban activist. Hall is thought by the WC to be one of the three men who visited Cuban exile Sylvia Odio (one of whom identified himself as Leon Oswald) on either September 25 or 26, 1963, when, officially, Oswald was on his way by bus to Mexico City. The FBI claimed Hall was "Leon Oswald." J. Edgar Hoover said there was sufficient "phonetic resemblance" between the two names to cause the confusion. However, Hall was wearing a full beard at the time he visited Odio and could not have been mistaken for Oswald.

The WR says:

> On September 16, 1964, the FBI located Loran Eugene Hall in Johnsandale [sic], Calif. Hall had been identified as a participant in numerous anti-Castro activities. He told the FBI that in September of 1963 he was in Dallas, soliciting aid in connection with anti-Castro activities. He said he had visited Mrs. Odio. He was accompanied by Lawrence Howard, a Mexican-American from East Los Angeles and one William Seymour from Arizona. He stated that Seymour is similar in appearance to Lee Harvey Oswald; he speaks only a few words of Spanish, as Mrs. Odio had testified one of the men did... [T]he Commission has concluded that Lee Harvey Oswald was not at Mrs. Odio's apartment in September of 1963.

Both Howard and Seymour denied visiting Sylvia Odio when traced and questioned by the FBI.

According to Harry Dean (the "war name" of a man who claims to be an ex-CIA agent), as quoted by authors W. B. Morris and R. B. Cutler, the shooters of JFK were Hall and Eladio del Valle, who were hired to do the job by the John Birch Society.

Hall admits to having been both jailed and released in Cuba in 1959 at the same time as assassination suspect Santos Trafficante. Hall worked with a Cuban-exile/CIA anti-Castro group called INTERPEN (Intercontinental Penetration Force) with Marine veteran Gerry Patrick Hemming—who, in turn, was identified under oath by Marita Lorenz as one of the men who rode in a gun-toting caravan from Miami to Dallas, arriving on the eve of the assassination. Hall and Hemming also worked together in the International Anti-Communist Brigade, a group which included suspects David Ferrie and Frank Sturgis, and reportedly maintained a paramilitary training camp on Lake Pontchartrain near New Orleans, where Oswald had reportedly been seen with Ferrie.

According to the *Dallas Morning News* (September 17, 1978), Hall claims that, a month before the assassination, he was approached by ultra-right-wing activists working with CIA operatives, who wanted him to take part in the JFK hit. When testifying for the HSCA, Hall refused to divulge his whereabouts before and at the time of the assassination until he was granted immunity from prosecution. Blakey writes:

> In September 1963 Hall and Howard drove from Los Angeles for Miami with a trailer-load of arms, but they were forced to leave the trailer in Dallas for lack of a hiding place in Florida. In October Hall and Seymour, back in Dallas to retrieve the trailer, were arrested for possession of drugs; but with the help of an influential financial supporter, they were released. They took the arms back to Miami, but the mission for which they were intended, Hall told us, was aborted in late October when he, Howard, Seymour, and some Cubans were arrested by customs officials as they were driving to their embarkation point south of Miami. No charges were filed, but their arms and equipment were confiscated so they returned to Miami, frustrated, and in early November, headed west. All three swore they were at their respective homes—Hall and Howard in California, Seymour in Arizona—on November 22, 1963.

According to author Paris Flammonde, however, Seymour "claimed—with some proof—to have been in Miami at the time [of JFK's death]."

After New Orleans District Attorney Jim Garrison concluded a long interview with Hall in connection with his assassination investigation, Garrison issued a press release:

> It is apparent that Hall is in no way connected with the events culminating in the assassination... on the other hand, it is equally apparent that other individuals and agencies caused Mr. Hall's name to be injected into exhibits of the Warren Commission and into other

statements so that any effort to investigate the assassination would cause his name to appear... Mr. Hall proved to be a helpful witness for our inquiry.

Physical description at the time: Mexican, 6'0", 40 to 45 years old and, according to the FBI, a "loud mouth." (See also Dean, Harry; Del Valle, Eladio; Howard, Lawrence; Odio, Sylvia; Seymour, William; Rodriguez, Manuel)
SOURCES: WR 301 • WCH XXVI, 834 • WCD 1553 • HSCA Report, 138–9 • HSCA X, 22; XI, 600 • RTJ 339–42 • AO, many • BLAKEY 164, 174–5 • SUMMERS 319, 390–3, 491–2 • FLAMMONDE 112, 114–5, 201–6, 209 • EVICA, many

HALL, MARVIN E. "BERT," city manager of the Armored Motor Service in Dallas. Hall arranged to have two armored trucks sent to the DPD station on the morning of November 24, 1963, to act as decoys during the transfer of Oswald.
SOURCE: WCH XV, 174

HALLET, OLIVER S., commander, U.S. Navy. With McGeorge Bundy, Hallet manned the White House Situation Room at the time of the assassination. When Air Force One was en route from Dallas to Washington carrying JFK's body and the new president, either Bundy or Hallet sent a message saying that there was no conspiracy and that the assassination had been determined to be the act of a lone gunman. (See also Bundy, McGeorge)
SOURCES: HT 20 • DOP 223

HALLMARK, GARNETT CLAUD, Ruby witness; Dallas garage attendant. Hallmark told the FBI that Ruby made a phone call from his garage at 3:00 P.M. on November 23. He heard Ruby discussing the transfer of Oswald planned for the following morning and quoted Ruby as saying, "You know I'll be there."
SOURCES: WR 323–4 • WCH XV, 488 • RTJ 270 • GERTZ 45 • BLAKEY 319

HAMBLEN, C. A., possible Oswald witness; early night manager, Dallas Western Union Telegraph Co. According to the WR:

Five days after the assassination... Hamblen... told his superior that about two weeks earlier he remembered Oswald sending a telegram from the office to Washington, DC, possibly to the Secretary of the Navy, and that the application was completed in an unusual form of hand printing. The next day Hamblen told a magazine correspondent who was in the Western Union office on other business that he remembered seeing Oswald in the office on other occasions collecting money orders for small amounts of money. Soon thereafter, Hamblen signed a statement relating to both the telegram and the money orders, and specifying two instances in which he had seen the person he believed to be Oswald in the office; in each instance the man behaved disagreeably and one other Western Union employee had become involved in assisting him.

Federal investigators could find no record of any of the telegrams or money orders. The coworker implicated in Hamblen's story denies that it happened. During his WC testimony, Hamblen became uncertain about his story's details. The WR sums it up: "Hamblen's superiors have concluded 'that this whole thing was a figment of Mr. Hamblen's imagination,' and the Commission accepts this assessment."
SOURCES: WR 310–1 • WCH XI, 311 • OTT 222–3 • SUMMERS 378

HAMLIN, CECIL, Ruby witness. Hamlin received a phone call from Ruby at 5:00 P.M., November 22, 1963. According to Jim Bishop, Ruby wept freely during the call, told Hamlin that he had closed both of his clubs for the weekend and expressed his sorrow for the Kennedy "kids."
SOURCE: BISHOP 328

HANKAL, ROBERT L., o.k.w.; 32-year-old KRLD-TV director in Dallas. Hankal filmed Ruby shooting Oswald from between the guardrails separating the transfer point from the main basement parking lot.
SOURCE: WCH XIII, 112

HANSEN, TIMOTHY M., JR., Ruby witness; member DPD. Hansen told the WC that he saw Ruby between 9:00 and 9:30 A.M., November 22, 1963, standing outside the Harwood Street entrance to the DPD station with "four or five others."
SOURCES: WCH XV, 438 • COA 265–6, 447

HARBISON, CHARLES, Parkland witness; Texas state patrolman. Harbison told the HSCA that three bullet fragments fell from the wound in Governor Connally's leg, three or four days after the shooting, while he helped move Connally to another hospital room. He says the fragments were turned over to the FBI—thus casting further doubt on the plausibility of the "magic bullet." Officially, the fragments do not exist.
SOURCE: OGLESBY 32

HARDEE, JACK, JR., Ruby witness; runner of a Dallas numbers operation. Hardee told the FBI that Officer J. D. Tippit was "a frequent visitor to Ruby's nightclub." The FBI deposed Hardee on December 26, 1963—at the Mobile County Jail, Mobile, Alabama—where he was incarcerated at the time in federal custody. The FBI reported:

> Hardee stated that he has spent some time in Dallas, Texas, and he
> had met Jack Ruby during the course of his contacts in Dallas. He
> stated that approximately one year ago, while in Dallas, Texas, he
> attempted to set up a numbers game, and he was advised by an
> individual, whom he did not identify, that in order to operate in Dallas
> it was necessary to have the clearance of Jack Ruby. He stated that
> this individual... told him Ruby had the "fix" with the county
> authorities, and that any other fix being placed would have to be done
> through Ruby... Hardee stated that he did not like Ruby upon their
> first contact, and this, coupled with a change in his plans, which was
> unrelated to this, caused him to change his mind about operating the
> numbers game, and the plan fell through... During the period that
> Hardee was in Dallas approximately one year ago, he was in Ruby's
> presence on several occasions. He stated that Ruby impressed him as
> the type of individual who would kill without much provoca-
> tion... Hardee also stated that the police officer whom Harvey Lee
> Oswald [sic] allegedly killed after he allegedly assassinated the
> president was a frequent visitor to Ruby's night club, along with
> another officer who was a motorcycle patrol in the Oaklawn [sic]
> section of Dallas. Hardee stated from his observation there appeared
> to be a very close relationship between these three individ-
> uals... Hardee stated that he knows of his own personal knowledge
> that Ruby hustled the strippers and other girls who worked in his
> club. Ruby made dates for them, accepting the money for the dates in
> advance, and kept half, giving the other half to the girls. The dates
> were filled in the new hotel in downtown Dallas and the Holiday Inn
> in Irvington, where Ruby had an associate, whom Hardee could only
> identify as a Negro who drove a big Cadillac.

SOURCES: WCH XXIII, 372 • FMG I, 87, 99–100 • RTJ 251–2 • COA 88, 90–1, 116, 417
• NORTH 261, 491

HARDIE, JULIUS, a.w. (prelude). Hardie told the *Dallas Morning News*
long after the assassination that before noon on November 22, 1963, he'd
seen three men with longarms (he couldn't tell if they were rifles or
shotguns) standing atop the triple underpass.
SOURCE: CF 19

HARDIN, MICHAEL, o.k.w. (aftermath); Dallas City ambulance driver.
Hardin drove the dying Oswald from the DPD station to Parkland. He told
the WC that he received the call that Oswald had been shot at 11:21 A.M.,

arrived on the scene at 11:23, and was at Parkland by 11:30.
SOURCES: WCH XIII, 94 • GERTZ 54

HARGIS, BOBBY W., a.w.; DPD motorcycle patrolman. Hargis rode just behind and to the left of JFK's limo and was splattered with blood and brain tissue by the final shot (so much so that he thought he, himself, had been hit at first), indicating it came from the right front. There was a piece of JFK's brain and skull clinging to his lip. According to William Manchester, Hargis was "doused in a red sheet." According to Jesse Curry in his book, *JFK Assassination File*, Hargis parked his motorcycle immediately following the shooting and ran up the grassy knoll.
SOURCES: HSCA Report 88 • JAF 30 • HT 19, 231 • WCH VI, 293 • RTJ 41, 57 • COA 29 • BISHOP 104 • DOP 137, 160 • SUMMERS 32 • BE 18, 44, 365 • BLAKEY 15, 88, 267

HARKER, DANIEL, AP correspondent. Harker interviewed Fidel Castro at a reception at the Brazilian embassy in Havana on September 7, 1963. According to Harker, Castro said JFK was "a cretin...the Batista of his times...the most opportunistic American President of all time..." Regarding Cuban exile invasions such as the Bay of Pigs (and to attempts on his own life) Castro said, "We are prepared to fight them and answer in kind. United States leaders should think that if they are aiding terrorist plans to eliminate Cuban leaders, they themselves will not be safe." (See also Castro, Fidel)
SOURCES: SUMMERS 410–3, 426 • DAVIS 150–1

HARKNESS, D. V., a.w.; sergeant, DPD. Harkness summoned an ambulance to the front of the TSBD moments before the assassination to help Jerry B. Belknap, who apparently was having an epileptic seizure. Some have suspected the "seizure" was meant as a diversion.

Immediately following the assassination, Harkness searched "the area behind" the TSBD. He then moved to the front of the building where he overheard a.w. Howard Brennan telling policemen that he had seen a man shooting from an upper floor of the TSBD. Harkness then spoke to Amos Euins, a "little colored boy," who had also seen a rifleman (although not one who was alone) in the TSBD. At that point Harkness began to seal off the building. Moving back to the building's rear he saw two men "lounging." The men verbally identified themselves as SS agents, and Harkness did not ask for written I.D. (According to the SS, all real SS agents accompanied the motorcade to Parkland. This is not the only report of spurious SS agents on the assassination scene.)

Following this encounter, Harkness moved into the rail yards where he discovered and arrested three "hoboes" on a freight train that was about to leave. (Harkness never did seal off the TSBD. This was not done until seven minutes following the assassination under the orders of Inspector Herbert Sawyer.) For years it was believed these hoboes were released without any permanent record of their identities—very interesting since the three men were photographed being escorted by men in DPD uniforms across Dealey Plaza, reportedly on their way to the police station. The hoboes all had hair that had been recently cut, and their shoes were of good leather. DPD records released in 1992, however, say the hoboes were really hoboes, and were held four days for vagrancy.

Harkness testified at Ruby's murder trial that at approximately 3:00 P.M. on November 23, 1963, he saw Ruby in the crowd while clearing the entrance to the DPD station in preparation for a planned transfer of Oswald at 4:00 P.M. The transfer was eventually postponed until the following morning. (See also Abrams, Gus; Belknap, Jerry; Brennan, Howard; Doyle, Harry; Euins, Amos; Gedney, John; Sawyer, Herbert)
SOURCES: WR 76, 145 • WCH VI, 308 • GERTZ 45 • BISHOP 150–1, 161 • CF 42, 320 • OTT 19–21, 93, 207 • HOS 180, 190 • KANTOR 54

HARPER, WILLIAM "BILLY," a.w. Harper found a piece of JFK's skull 25 feet southeast of JFK's limo's position at the time the fatal bullet was fired. Harper turned the bone (commonly referred to as the "Harper fragment") over to the chief pathologist at Methodist Hospital. It was identified as the occipital bone, i.e., from the back of JFK's head. The fragment is significant because, officially, the back of JFK's skull was left intact by the shooting. (See also Weitzman, Seymour)
SOURCES: SSID 130 • HT 231 • SUMMERS 32 • BE 316, 503, 530 • DAVIS 390

HARRELSON, CHARLES VOYD, suspect. Jack Anderson, and other assassination researchers have suggested that the "tall tramp" photographed in Dealey Plaza after the assassination, was, in fact, Charles Harrelson, an organized crime hit man. The tramps had been arrested after they were discovered in a rail car near Dealey Plaza, on a train that was about to leave moments after the assassination. Until 1992, it was believed that the three tramps were released before any permanent record was made of their names. But DPD records released in 1992 and verified by the FBI say that the tramps really were tramps. Harrelson has been serving a life sentence in federal prison since 1979 for the murder of U.S. District Court Judge John H. Wood Jr. Harrelson is the father of actor Woody Harrelson who starred in ABC-TV's *Cheers*.

Harrelson told British documentary filmmaker Nigel Turner ("The Men Who Killed Kennedy," 1988), "On November 22, 1963, at 12:30, I was having lunch with a friend in a restaurant in Houston, Texas... I did not kill John Kennedy."

Independent forensic anthropologists, using the photographic evidence, have stated that there is a 90 to 95% chance that Harrelson is the "tall tramp." In November 1991, Lois Gibson, a forensic artist for the Houston Police Department, positively identified Harrelson as the tall tramp.

According to researcher Phillip A. Rogers:

Harrelson was born near Huntsville, Texas. As a young man he went on to California, where he became the salesman of the year as an encyclopedia salesman and soon turned to a life of crime. He was convicted of armed robbery in 1960. He turned probation and was cleared of probation in 1965. This is kind of a shady period of his life. Not too much is known about where he went or what he did during that time. In 1968 he became a public figure when he faced several trials, two of which he was acquitted for, then, at a re-trial he was convicted of his first murder for hire in South Texas. He served time and was released. He then quickly became involved in the Judge Wood assassination. He went on the run and ended up in El Paso. A funny thing happened: He borrowed a Corvette. He was high on cocaine, when he thought the muffler was making too much noise. He shot out the back tires trying to remove the muffler with a .44 magnum. He was arrested after a six-hour stand-off during which time he held a gun to his head and confessed to shooting President Kennedy. He later recanted that, saying that he was high at the time—although he continued to drop hints about the matter for a while. He was convicted of the Judge Wood assassination and was sent to the Marion Federal Penitentiary in Marion, Illinois.

(See also Abrams, Gus; Doyle, Harry; Gedney, John; Gibson, Lois; Holt, Chauncy; Mathews, Russell; Rogers, Charles; Rogers, Phillip A.)
    SOURCES: HT 142 • CF 85, 333–7 • OGLESBY 47–8 • DAVIS 208–9, 523–5, 579

HARRIS, LARRY, cowriter, with J. Gary Shaw, of *Cover-up* (Collector's Editions, 1992). As a young researcher, Harris once took a job at the TSBD for a few weeks, just to have access to the sixth floor. Harris is perhaps the leading expert on the Tippit killing.
    SOURCES: FMG III, 92 • SUMMERS 487)

HARRISON, WILLIAM J. "BLACKIE," o.k.w.; member DPD. With Captain Glen King and reserve officers Captain C. O. Arnett and Patrolman W. M. Croy, Harrison was one of the men who stood in front of

Ruby, with their backs to him, on the Main Street side of the basement entrance to the DPD headquarters, before Ruby lunged forward to shoot Oswald. With Louis Miller, Harrison is suspected by author Seth Kantor of informing Ruby of the precise time of Oswald's transfer. (See also Arnett, C. O.; Croy, W. M.; King, Glen; Miller, Louis)

SOURCES: WR 206 • WCH XII, 234 • SUMMERS 465 • DAVIS 226–7

HARTMAN, WAYNE and EDNA, a.w. The Hartmans stood on Main Street, east of Houston Street (around the corner from Dealey Plaza). After hearing shots, they ran onto the grassy area on the south side of Elm. Edna told reporter Jim Marrs, "There were not many people in this area at the time, but a policeman was there. He pointed to some bushes near the railroad tracks on the north side of the street and said that's where the shots came from... Then I noticed these two parallel marks on the ground that looked like mounds made by a mole. I asked, 'What are these, molehills?' and the policeman said, 'Oh no, ma'am, that's where the bullets struck the ground.'"

At the JFK Assassination Symposium in Dallas on November 15, 1991, Edna said that the bullet mark she had seen pointed southeast, consistent with a shot from the grassy knoll, rather than a shot from the TSBD.

SOURCE: CF 315–6

HARTOGS, RENATUS, Oswald witness; New York City psychiatrist. While 13-year-old Lee Harvey Oswald was living in the Bronx, he was detained at Youth House from April 16 to May 7, 1953, because of truancy. While there, he was examined by Hartogs, the institution's chief psychiatrist. According to the WR, Hartogs found Oswald to be a "tense, withdrawn and evasive boy who intensely disliked talking about himself and his feelings. [Hartogs] noted that Lee liked to give the impression that he did not care for other people but preferred to keep to himself, so that he was not bothered and did not have to make the effort of communicating. Oswald's withdrawn tendencies and solitary habits were thought to be the result of 'intense anxiety, shyness, feelings of awkwardness and insecurity.'"

Oswald was further quoted as saying, "I don't want a friend and I don't like to talk to people... I dislike everybody." Hartogs wrote that Oswald had a "vivid fantasy life, turning around topics of omnipotence and power, through which he tries to compensate for his present shortcomings and frustrations." Hartogs concluded:

This 13-year-old well built boy has superior mental resources and functions only slightly below his capacity level in spite of chronic truancy from school which brought him into Youth House. No findings of neurological impairment or psychotic mental changes could be made. Lee has to be diagnosed as "personality pattern disturbance with schizoid features and passive-aggressive tendencies." Lee has to be seen as an emotionally quite disturbed youngster who suffers under the impact of a really existing emotional isolation and deprivation, lack of affection, absence of family life and rejection by a self-involved and conflicted mother.

Dr. Hartogs is the coauthor, with Lucy Freeman, of *The Two Assassins* (Thomas Y. Crowell Co., 1965).

SOURCES: WR 355–6 • WCH XIII, 214 • HOS 57

HARVEY, WILLIAM K., CIA agent. Harvey was the commander of Cuban exiles and head of the CIA "assassination unit" (code name ZR/ RIFLE) in charge of CIA-Mafia plots to kill Fidel Castro. (See also FitzGerald, Desmond)

SOURCES: HT 312–3 • BELIN 112–6, 118–9, 123, 125–6, 132 • OTT 292 • SUMMERS 137, 226–7, 240, 471, 528–31 • BLAKEY 54–6, 58–61, 79, 155 • EVICA, many • DAVIS 422

HATHAWAY, PHILIP B., a.w. (prelude). Before noon on November 22, 1963, Hathaway was walking with coworker John Lawrence on Akard Street toward Main Street to find a place to watch the motorcade. According to Dallas reporter Jim Marrs, Hathaway saw a big man (6'5", 250 lbs.) with thick hair on his chest, carrying a rifle in a leather-and-cloth case. The man had "dirty blond hair in a crew cut" and wore a gray business suit. Lawrence, who saw the man but, because of the crowd, not the gun, said that the man resembled a "professional football player." Both witnesses assumed that the man was an SS agent. (See also Lawrence, John; McDonald, Hugh)

SOURCES: WCE 2003 • CF 17

HAUSER, JOSEPH, FBI agent. Hauser went undercover in 1979 to investigate the crime organization of assassination suspect Carlos Marcello. He claims that Marcello admitted to knowing Oswald and his uncle, Charles "Dutz" Murret, and that Oswald worked for him in 1963 as a runner for his betting operation. In 1980, when Ted Kennedy was running for president, Hauser commented to Carlos's brother, Joseph Marcello, about the way the Kennedys had hassled him and his brother during the early sixties. Joseph Marcello reportedly said, "Don't worry, we took care of them, didn't we?"

SOURCES: SUMMERS 503 • DAVIS, many

HAWKINS, RAY, Texas Theatre witness; member DPD. Hawkins was involved in Oswald's arrest. At the time of the arrest there were 16 policemen and 14 customers in the theater. With Patrolmen M. N. McDonald, T. A. Hudson, and C. T. Walker, Hawkins entered the theater through the rear entrance. Among Ruby's possessions found after his arrest was Hawkins's signed permanent pass to the Carousel Club. (See also Hutson, Thomas; McDonald, M. N.; Walker, C. T.)

SOURCES: WR 165–6 • WCH VII, 91 • COA 111 • BISHOP 213–4

HAYGOOD, CLYDE A., a.w.; DPD motorcycle patrolman. Haygood was assigned to protect the right rear of JFK's limo during the motorcade. However, Haygood "straggled" before the shots were fired, further weakening the already less-than-stringent security. After the shots were fired, Haygood parked his motorcycle at the base of the grassy knoll and ran into the parking lot behind the wooden fence, but saw "nothing suspicious." He was then told by an unidentified witness that the shots had come from the TSBD. Haygood then radioed in (using the code number 142) and called for the TSBD to be sealed off.

Haygood went on the air at 12:35, five minutes after the shooting, saying, "I just talked to a guy up here who was standing close to it and the best he could tell it came from the Texas School Book Depository. It is believed the shots came from there. If you're facing it on Elm Street looking toward the building, it would be the upper-right-hand window, the second window from the end." (See also Brennan, Howard)

SOURCES: WR 83 • WCE 1974, p.166 • HSCA XI, 526–9 • CF 60–1 • BE 365–6 • BLAKEY 16

HEBERT, ARTHUR, Oswald witness; ninth-grade classmate of Oswald. In Oswald's ninth-grade personal history record, in the blank space for "close friends," Oswald originally wrote "Arthor Abear," but erased this and wrote that he had no close friends. Hebert, when contacted after the assassination, indicated that he had not known Oswald well. Oswald's chronically poor spelling may have been a symptom of dyslexia.

SOURCE: WR 359

HEINDEL, JOHN RENE, Oswald witness; USMC acquaintance. Officially, Oswald purchased his rifle by mail order under the pseudonym Alek Hidell. The WC said that Oswald made the name up, that it was just a variation of "Fidel." This may not be the case. John Heindel and Oswald had been stationed together in Atsugi, Japan. Heindel's nickname was "Hidell." At the time of JFK's death, Heindel was living in New Orleans.

Heindel told the WC that Oswald:

...was often in trouble for failure to adhere to the rules and regulations and gave the impression of disliking any kind of authority...I was often referred to as "Hidell"—pronounced so as to rhyme with Rydell rather than Fidel...indeed he may himself have called me Hidell...Although I generally regarded Oswald as an intelligent person, I did not observe him to be particularly interested in politics or international affairs...did not often talk back to his superiors, but was likely to complain about their orders when he was alone with his fellow Marines...I do not recall Oswald's being called by any nicknames. Although our Air Marine Group was sent to Formosa...I am unable to remember Oswald's being there...

Neither the WC nor the HSCA investigated the possibility that there might have been a relationship between Oswald and Heindel after they left the marines.

SOURCES: WCH VIII, 318 • RTJ 131–2 • AO 94 • SUMMERS 59–60

HELMICK, WANDA YVONNE (aka Sweat, Wanda), Ruby witness; waitress at Ruby associate Ralph Paul's restaurant. Helmick testified that she overheard Paul speaking with Ruby on Saturday evening, November 23, 1963, and that, in response to Ruby, Paul said, "Are you crazy? A gun?" Paul admits to speaking with Ruby on the phone at that place and time, but denies that the conversation had anything to do with either a gun or Oswald. (See also Paul, Ralph)

SOURCES: WCH XV, 396 • RTJ 18, 271, 384 • COA 134 • GERTZ 527 • KANTOR 108

HELMS, RICHARD M., CIA deputy director for plans; liaison between the CIA and the WC. A memo from the WC to Helms dated February 24, 1964, suggests that the WC strongly suspected Ruby of being an assassination conspirator because of his association with "gamblers," "Dallas oil millionaires" and an "official of the John Birch Society." The WC, of course, later decided to ignore all associations between Ruby and enemies of JFK.

Helms told the WC that no one connected with the CIA had ever interviewed or "communicated in any way" with Oswald. MK-ULTRA, the CIA's LSD/mind control program, was Helms's brainchild. (See also Angleton, James; Helperan, Sammy; Hunt, E. Howard; Karamessines, Tom; Marchetti, Victor)

SOURCES: HSCA Report, many • HT 189, 341 • WCH V, 120; XI, 469 • BELIN 115–6, 118, 130, 134, 137, 140–1, 144–6, 148–9, 152–4 • RTJ 302–3 • DOP 12 • OTT 49, 178,

234, 251, 275–6, 290 • SUMMERS 131–2, 140, 322, 356, 471, 508 • BLAKEY, many • FLAMMONDE 161 • EVICA 158, 256, 310, 312–3, 325 • KANTOR 93–4, 133, 139, 161 • NORTH 133 • PD, many

HELPERAN, SAMMY, CIA agent. Helperan reportedly read and initialed an internal CIA memo allegedly written by Tom Karamessines (Richard Helms's assistant) stating that the CIA was concerned about the possibility that assassination suspect E. Howard Hunt's presence in Dallas at the time of the assassination would be discovered. (See also Helms, Richard; Hunt, E. Howard; Karamessines, Tom)

SOURCE: HT 346

HELPERN, MILTON, former NYC chief medical examiner. Helpern told author Josiah Thompson:

The original pristine weight of this bullet [WCE 399] before it was fired was 160–161 grains. The weight of the bullet recovered on the stretcher at Parkland Hospital was reported by the Commission as weighing in at 158.6 grains. The bullet wasn't distorted in any way. I cannot accept the premise that this bullet thrashed around in all of that bony tissue and lost only 1.4 to 2.4 grains of its original weight. I cannot believe either that this bullet is going to emerge miraculously unscathed, without any deformity, and with its lands and grooves intact.

SOURCES: HT 66 • SSID 206 • SUMMERS 8–9, 35–6 • BE 278

HEMMING, GERRY PATRICK (aka Patrick, Jerry), former marine; ONI operative; operative for INTERPEN (the International Penetration Force), the CIA/Cuban exile anti-Castro force. Hemming was named by Marita Lorenz, under oath, as one of the men who participated in a gun-toting caravan from Miami to Dallas that arrived on the eve of the assassination. Others in the caravan, according to Lorenz, were assassination suspect Frank Sturgis and Oswald (who, officially, was working at the TSBD at that time).

Hemming also worked for the International Anti-Communist Brigade, which trained anti-Castro Cuban-exile paramilitary troops at a camp on Lake Pontchartrain near New Orleans, where Oswald had reportedly been seen repeatedly in the company of assassination suspect David Ferrie. Hemming's association with INTERPEN and the International Anti-Communist Brigade, would have made him a colleague of assassination suspect Loran Hall.

According to author Harrison Edward Livingstone, Hemming claims that

"Frenchy," the shortest of the three tramps arrested in Dealey Plaza soon after the assassination, was a "mercenary working from a yacht owned by anti-Castro sympathizer Larry LaBorde." (See also Bosch, Orlando; Ferrie, David; Hall, Loran; Hunt, E. Howard; Lanz, Pedro Diaz; Lorenz, Marita; Sturgis, Frank)

SOURCES: WCD 1179 • SUMMERS 268 • SPOT 42 • EVICA 122–3, 242, 319 • BLAKEY 173, 175 • HT2 392 • PD 129, 300

HENCHLIFFE, MARGARET (See HINCHLIFFE, MARGARET)

HENDERSON, RUBY (referred to as "Toney" Henderson by Jim Garrison), a.w. Like witnesses Carolyn Walther and Arnold Rowland, Henderson saw two men on the sixth floor of the TSBD five minutes before the shooting, one of whom had a rifle. Like the others, Henderson thought the men were SS agents.

We can set the time of her sighting because Henderson recalled seeing the men in the window after the ambulance left the front of the TSBD, taking away a man who apparently had an epileptic seizure. Ambulance records show that the ambulance left for Parkland at 12:24, six minutes before the shooting.

Henderson told the FBI that one of the men had dark hair, dark skin, and was wearing a white shirt. She said he was "possibly a Mexican, but could have been a Negro." She said the other man was the taller and lighter of the two, but was unable to give a description of him. (See also Belknap, Jerry; Rike, Aubrey; Rowland, Arnold; Walther, Carolyn)

SOURCES: WCH XXIV, 524 • WCE 2089 • HT 175, 228 • CF 21 • OTT 93–4 • SUMMERS 42–3 • DAVIS 459

HENSLEE, GERALD D., DPD dispatcher at the time of the assassination. At 12:30 P.M., November 22, 1963, Henslee participated in this exchange on Channel Two:

Henslee: 12:30 P.M. KKB 364.

Chief Curry: Go to the Hospital—Parkland Hospital. Have them stand by. Get a man on top of that triple underpass and see what happened up there. Have Parkland stand by.

Sheriff Decker: I am sure that it's going to take some time to get your men in there. Pull every one of my men in there.

Henslee: Dallas One. Repeat. I didn't get all of it. I didn't quite understand all of it.

Decker: Have my office move all available men out of my office into the railroad yard to try to determine what happened in there and hold everything secure until homicide and other investigators should get there.

Henslee: Ten four. Dallas One will be notified... One. Any information whatsoever?

Curry: Looks like the President has been hit. Have Parkland stand by.

Henslee: They have been notified.

(See also Curry, Jesse; Decker, Bill; Hulse, Clifford)
SOURCES: WCH VI, 325 • HSCA Report 77 • BISHOP 88–9, 138, 150, 172, 174 • DOP 177 • BLAKEY 97

HEPBURN, JAMES (real name, Hervé Lamarr), author of *Farewell America* (Frontier, 1968); member, French intelligence. Hepburn's book alleges: "Ten hours after the assassination, Secret Service Chief James Rowley knew that there had been three gunmen, and perhaps four, firing in Dallas that day... Robert Kennedy... learned that evening from Rowley that the Secret Service believed the President had been the victim of a powerful organization."
SOURCE: HT 479

HERNDON, BILL P., Ruby witness; FBI polygraph operator. On July 18, 1964, Herndon administered a lie-detector test for the WC to Ruby at Ruby's insistence. The machine said Ruby was telling the truth when he said that he killed Oswald under his own volition and that it was a spontaneous act caused by sympathy for Jackie Kennedy.
SOURCES: WCH XIV, 579 • BELIN 40–1 • FMG I, 13, 19, 76–7

HESS, JACQUELINE, HSCA chief of research, "in charge of the 'mysterious deaths' project." Hess's report states: "... the available evidence does not establish anything about the nature of these deaths which would indicate that the deaths were in some manner, either direct or peripheral, caused by the assassination of President Kennedy or by any aspect of the subsequent investigation."
SOURCES: HSCA IV, 467 • HT 128–31, 146

HESTER, CHARLES and BEATRICE, a.w. Sitting on the grass on the north side of Elm Street, the Hesters heard two shots. They thought the shots came from the TSBD and told John Wiseman of the sheriff's department to check out the TSBD because all the police were running toward the railroad tracks.
SOURCE: WCE 2003, p. 211; 2088

HESTER, ROBERT, commercial photographer who worked for the DPD and the FBI. In an interview given to Jim Marrs (*Fort Worth Star-Telegram,*

September 20, 1978), Hess claimed that he had seen a version of the famous backyard photos showing Oswald holding a rifle before the DPD says they were discovered. He says he saw the photo on November 22, 1963, and that it was in the form of a color transparency—which is impossible if the original—as claimed—was a black-and-white print.
SOURCES: SUMMERS 67

HICKEY, GEORGE W., JR., a.w.; SS agent. Hickey sat in the backseat of the SS presidential follow-up car, directly behind JFK's limousine. At the sound of gunfire, Hickey rose to his feet with his AR-15 machine gun, but he saw nothing to shoot back at.

In a statement written several days after JFK's death, Hickey said that the first shot sounded to him like a firecracker. He wrote:

> I stood up and looked to my right and rear in an attempt to identify it. Nothing caught my attention except people shouting and cheering... [When Kennedy] was almost sitting erect I heard two reports which I thought were shots and appeared to me completely different in sound than the first report and were in such rapid succession that there seemed to be practically no time element between them... the last shot seemed to hit his head and cause a noise at the point of impact which made him fall forward and to his left again.

According to Bonar Menninger's book *Mortal Error* (St. Martin's Press, 1992)—based on 25 years of research by Howard Donahue, a Maryland ballistics expert—Hickey accidentally killed JFK while attempting to respond to the first reports of gunfire. When Oswald began to shoot at JFK from the TSBD, Hickey turned, reached for his rifle and slipped off the safety. As he tried to stand up on the backseat of the car, he lost his balance and accidentally pulled the trigger of his AR-15 (now called an M-16). The theory states that Oswald fired only twice, missing the first shot and delivering all of the nonfatal wounds with the second shot. The third and final shot was fired by Hickey.

The book bases its theory on these points:

(1) Hickey was seen with an AR-15 at the instant of the fatal shot;
(2) One witness (S. M. Holland) saw Hickey lose his balance during the shooting sequence;
(3) AR-15 rounds are encased in thin copper and tend to break up upon impact, as did the shot that struck JFK in the head;
(4) A Mannlicher-Carcano round would tend not to break up in this

fashion;

(5) Several people in the motorcade, including Senator Ralph Yarborough, smelled gunpowder during and after the shooting sequence, indicating that at least one shot had been fired from street level;

(6) Two witnesses (Austin Miller and Royce Skelton) thought the shot came from "around the President's car";

(7) According to Donahue, the bullet's trajectory, leads right to Hickey;

(8) The entrance wound in the back of JFK's head was 6mm in diameter, yet a Mannlicher-Carcano bullet is 6.5mm in diameter, making it physically impossible for the "Oswald" weapon to have caused the fatal wound.

Hickey told the WC that he didn't even pick up his weapon until after the fatal shot.

SOURCES: WR 64 • DOP 134, 159 • CF 83 • BE 43, 510 • ME, many

HICKS, J. B., Oswald witness; member DPD. At 8:00 P.M. on November 22, 1963, Hicks took Oswald's fingerprints and palm prints on an inkless pad.

SOURCES: WCH VII, 286 • BISHOP 400

HICKS, JAMES, a.w.; surveyor from Enid, Oklahoma. Hicks reported seeing a bullet hole in the Elm Street "Stemmons" traffic sign soon after the shooting. The sign was removed almost immediately by men he presumed to be members of the DPD. According to the January 12, 1968, edition of the *New Orleans Times-Picayune*, on the day before he was to testify for Jim Garrison before the New Orleans Grand Jury to indict Clay Shaw, Hicks was pushed through a plate-glass window and beaten severely. According to author Paris Flammonde, "In the early morning prior to his grand jury appearance [in the Clay Shaw case], Hicks reported, his hotel room was invaded by two Negro men who roughed him up and tossed him through French doors leading to a balcony outside his sixth-floor room. However, the witness said he did not believe the assault was related to the investigation."

Hicks is believed by some assassination researchers, including the late Bernard Fensterwald and Robert Sam Anson, to be the radio-communications coordinator for the assassins. Photographs taken immediately after the assassination appear to show Hicks in Dealey Plaza with some sort of radio. (See also Garrison, Jim; McDonald, Hugh)

SOURCES: HT 121 • FLAMMONDE 208 • ANSON 216 • HT 182, 248

HIDELL, ALEK JAMES, supposed pseudonym of Oswald and the name under which he was to have mail-ordered the assassination rifle. A photo I.D. with Oswald's picture under the name Hidell was found in Oswald's wallet immediately after his arrest. (See also Heindel, John Rene

HIGGINS, MR. and MRS. DONALD R., t.k.w. The Higginses lived at 417 East Tenth Street, across the street from the Tippit murder site. They heard the shots and saw activities following the flight of the assailant. The WC did not call upon them to testify, perhaps indicating that their observations did not conform with the "official version" of the facts.
SOURCE: RTJ 194

HILL, CLINTON J., a.w.; SS agent. Hill rode on the running board of the SS presidential follow-up car, directly behind JFK's limo. He climbed onto the back of the limousine and pushed Mrs. Kennedy back into the backseat after she had crawled out of the car to retrieve a portion of JFK's head.

In his WC testimony, Hill recalls the assassination as he rushed toward the rear of the presidential limo, just reaching it:

> ...there was another sound, which was different from the first sound...as though someone was shooting a revolver into a hard object—seemed to have some type of an echo...the second noise that I had heard had removed a portion of the President's head, and he had slumped noticeably to his left. Mrs. Kennedy had jumped up from the seat and was, it appeared to me, reaching for something coming off the right rear bumper of the car, the right rear tail, when she noticed that I was trying to climb on the car. She turned towards me and I grabbed her and put her in the back seat and lay there. I noticed a portion of the President's head on the right rear side was missing and he was bleeding profusely. Part of the brain was gone...His brain was exposed...one large gaping wound in the right rear portion of the head.

(See also Landrigan, Steve)
SOURCES: WR 21–2, 60, 63–4, 66, 71, 109, 429 • WCH II, 132; VI, 290 • HSCA Report 235 • HT 17–9, 55, 148, 231, 448 • RTJ 57, 64, 66 • BISHOP, many • DOP, many • CF 13, 15 • BE, many • BLAKEY 15 • EVICA 65, 67 • ME 56, 60, 101, 110–2, 116, 218–9, 222–3, 248 • KANTOR 195–6

HILL, GERALD LYNN, a.w. (aftermath); t.k.w. (aftermath); Texas Theatre witness; DPD sergeant. If one assumes that Oswald was guilty, then Sergeant Gerald Hill had one of the greatest days in law-enforcement history. Hill found—or was in the vicinity of—most of the hard evidence that would have been used against Oswald had he gone to trial. Hill was at the DPD station when he heard about the assassination, was working in plainclothes in personnel that day and rode from the DPD station to the TSBD in car #207, driven by Officer Jim M. Valentine. Also in the car was *Dallas Morning News* reporter Jim E. Well. Hill briefly searched the TSBD's sixth floor. He said that he hadn't been on the sixth floor for but a minute when someone shouted, "Here it is!" The sniper's nest had been found. Hill then promptly left the building. He told the WC: "I went over . . . west to another window . . . on the south side and yelled down to the street for them to send up the crime lab." He says that nobody could hear him, so he went down to tell them in person, just as Captain Will Fritz was arriving. Fritz, says the WR, arrived at the TSBD "shortly before 1:00 P.M."

While outside the TSBD, Hill encountered Assistant District Attorney Bill Alexander, and together they heard the call on the police radio that an officer was down in Oak Cliff. This call came at 1:18. Hill does not account for the missing 20 or so minutes. Hill, Alexander, and Sergeant Bud Owens drove together to Oak Cliff. It is not specified in which car they went. Hill was in the second car to arrive at the scene of the Tippit killing—yet Tippit's body had already been removed.

Soon after arriving, Hill, Owens, and Alexander, now joined by Officer C. T. Walker, left the scene to chase the shooter and "shake down vacant houses on the north side of Jefferson." Not finding anything, they returned to Tenth and Patton, where Officer J. M. Poe handed Hill an empty Winston cigarette pack containing shells. Hill says that he was talking to accident investigator Bob Apple when the call came in that a suspect had been seen entering the Texas Theatre. Hill and Apple traveled together in Apple's car to the theater, where Hill was involved in the arrest of Oswald, whereupon the revolver said to be the Tippit murder weapon was seized. After the arrest, in Hill's presence, an I.D. for "Alek Hidell" was found in Oswald's wallet, thus linking Oswald to the murder weapons. Hill later said, "I never did have the billfold in my possession."

With the exception of the pristine bullet found on a stretcher at Parkland Hospital, ballistic evidence found in JFK's limo, and the apparently doctored photos of Oswald holding the murder weapons "found" at the Paines' home following the assassination, Hill found or was near every piece of Oswald-incriminating evidence.

Oswald's housekeeper Earlene Roberts said that DPD car #207 stopped outside when Oswald was in his room around 1:00 P.M., tooted the horn twice and then drove off.

It is odd that Hill did not mention the "Hidell" pseudonym on the day of the assassination. He was interviewed on the afternoon of November 22, 1963, by NBC-TV and was asked to comment on the arrest. Hill said, "Oswald did not volunteer any information to us at all... The only way we found out what his name was was to remove his billfold and check it ourselves. He wouldn't tell us what his name was." Hill said the billfold's I.D. revealed that the suspect's name was "Oswald. O-S-W-A-L-D." According to the FBI, this wallet contained only one photo identification of the man and that I.D. bore the name "Alek James Hidell," although there were non-photo identification cards in the wallet that bore Oswald's true name. Why didn't Hill mention the pseudonym on November 22?

While Hill sat in the front seat of a patrol car outside the Texas Theatre, it was Officer Bentley who reached into Oswald's pocket to pull out his wallet. Hill told the WC: "...the name Lee Oswald was called out by Bentley from the backseat... and he also made the statement that there was some more identification in this other name, which I don't remember, but it was the same name that later came in the paper that he bought the gun under." It is remarkable that these men distinguished so rapidly between the suspect's real name and pseudonym, especially considering the fact that the best I.D.—the only one with a photo of the suspect—was under the pseudonym. Hill spelled the real name for reporters later that day, yet forgot about the pseudonym all together. Then, later, he still couldn't remember the pseudonym, although on this occasion he remembered that there was one.

T.k.w. Domingo Benavides says he picked up two shells at the scene of the crime, in shrubbery on the southeast corner lot of Tenth Street and Patton Avenue. He placed them in an empty pack of Winston cigarettes and handed them to a police officer, apparently Officer J. M. Poe. Hill later testified to WC counsel: "Poe showed me a Winston cigarette package that contained three spent jackets from shells... I told Poe to maintain the chain of evidence as small as possible, for him to retain these at that time, and to mark them for evidence." If Benavides discovered two shells, why were there three in the cigarette pack by the time Hill saw it?

In a taped radio interview with Hill recorded during the afternoon of November 22, Hill says: "[The Tippit murder weapon was] a .38 snub-nose that was fired twice, and both shots hit the officer in the head." How did

Hill know the gun had been fired twice? It was later learned that Tippit had been shot four times. Yet, when the gun was found on Oswald in the Texas Theatre, it was fully loaded. Hill wrote in his arrest report: "When the pistol was given to me, it was fully loaded and one of the shells had a hammer mark on the primer." The hammer mark supposedly indicated that Oswald had attempted to resist arrest by shooting one of his arresting officers. It is interesting that Hill refers to the gun on November 22 as a pistol when it was actually a .38 revolver—a distinction that *Hill* first pointed out from his squad car over the police radio at 1:40, about a half hour after Tippit was shot. He said, "Shells at the scene indicate the suspect is armed with an automatic .38 rather than a pistol."

Eight minutes elapsed between the time the first call for help came from the scene of the Tippit killing and Hill's first call-in from the area. At 1:26, Hill said, "I'm at 12th and Beckley now, have a man in the car that can identify the suspect if anyone gets him."

Among the items the WC says were found on the sixth floor of the TSBD was the paper bag in which Oswald allegedly brought his rifle into the building. During his testimony, Hill told the WC that he saw a chicken leg bone and a paper sandwich bag on top of the cartons near the "sniper's nest." Hill said, "That was the only sack I saw. If it [the long paper bag] was found up there on the sixth floor, if it was there, I didn't see it."

Hill, Alexander and the other law-enforcement officials who swarmed into the Texas Theatre to arrest Oswald nabbed the alleged assassin before he was officially a suspect. Hill described for the WC what happened after Oswald was brought to police headquarters for questioning: "Captain Fritz walked in. He walked up to [Detectives] Rose and Stovall and made the statement to them, 'Go get a search warrant and go out to some address on Fifth Street...' and '...pick me up a man named Oswald.' And I asked the captain why he wanted him, and he said, 'Well, he was employed down at the Book Depository and he had not been present for a roll call of the employees.' And we said, 'Captain, we will save you a trip,' or words to that effect, 'because there he sits.'" (See also Bentley, Paul; Carroll, Bob K.; Ewell, Jim; Poe, J. M.; Valentine, Jim)

SOURCES: WR 111, 167 • WCH VII, 43 • WCE 1502, 1547, 2003, 2160 • RTJ 135, 197 • GERTZ 522 • BISHOP 161, 215–6, 221, 224 • CF 342 • PWW 71, 207 • OTT 198, 201 • SUMMERS 89–90

HILL, JEAN LOLLIS, a.w. Hill was standing on the south side of Elm Street directly across from the grassy knoll with her friend Mary Moorman. She later said, "I frankly thought they [the shots] were coming from the

knoll... I did think there was more than one person shooting." Hill, a
Dallas schoolteacher, is easily identifiable in color photographs taken at
the time of the assassination because of her red coat. We can see her run
across Elm Street and up the grassy knoll to watch the chase of the
assailants behind the wooden fence toward the railroad yards. She was later
intimidated by the FBI because she insisted on giving a story that didn't
conform with the official version of the facts.

Hill told Dallas reporter Jim Marrs that, before the assassination, she
had seen a van with writing on the side that said UNCLE JOE'S PAWN
SHOP. The van drove past police lines and down the service road in front of
the TSBD, and behind the pergola atop the knoll just east of the wooden
fence. She told Marrs, "I saw a man fire from behind the wooden fence. I
saw a puff of smoke and some sort of movement on the grassy knoll where
he was. Then I saw a man walking briskly in front of the Texas School Book
Depository Building. He was the only person moving." That Sunday, after
Oswald was shot, Hill recognized Ruby as the man she had seen walking in
front of the TSBD.

In November 1991, Mrs. Hill told her story in Dallas to an assassination
symposium:

> In 1963 I was a teacher in the Dallas school system, having recently
> moved here from Oklahoma City. I didn't yet know my way around
> Dallas, so a friend of mine, Mary Moorman, had said that we should
> play hooky that day and head down to the motorcade. There were
> some policemen in that motorcade that we were particularly inter-
> ested in, so we went to see the President as well. The [policeman]
> friend of mine was riding on the President's wheel and I think that is
> one reason that Mary got the picture she got at the moment of the head
> shot. We had gotten down to the area in Dealey Plaza about an hour
> before the motorcade came around. We had been on the opposite side
> of the street, just out in front of the School Book Depository and
> people were filing in and it was getting—there were too many people
> there, and we were afraid that these policemen weren't going to see
> us. We started across the street toward the triangle. We were stopped
> by a policeman on the corner and he told us that there was no one
> allowed in that area. After some flirting, though, Mary and I got him
> to let us go down there. Mary was rather short and we wanted to get a
> picture of this police officer's motorcycle as it came around. That area
> is sloping so when Mary reached up to take the picture, we did get a
> picture of the School Book Depository. We knew that, because we had

a Polaroid camera, we were going to have to be quick if we wanted to take more than one picture. So what we planned was, Mary would take the picture, I would pull it out of the camera, coat it with fixative and put it in my pocket. That way we could keep shooting. When the head shot came, Mary fell down and the film [i.e., the famous photograph] was still in the camera. When the motorcade came around, there were so many voters on the other side [of Elm Street] that I knew the President was never going to look at me, so I yelled, "Hey Mr. President, I want to take your picture!" Just then his hands came up and the shots started ringing out. Then, in half the time it takes for me to tell it, I looked across the street and I saw them shooting from the knoll. I did get the impression that day that there was more than one shooter, but I had the idea that the good guys and the bad guys were shooting at each other. I guess I was a victim of too much television, because I assumed that the good guys always shot at the bad guys. Mary was on the grass shouting, "Get down! Get down! They're shooting! They're shooting!" Nobody was moving and I looked up and saw this man, moving rather quickly in front of the School Book Depository toward the railroad tracks, heading west, toward the area where I had seen the man shooting on the knoll. So, I thought to myself, "This man is getting away. I've got to do something. I've got to catch him." I jumped out into the street. One of the motorcyclists was turning his motor, looking up and all around for the shooter, and he almost ran me over. It scared me so bad, I went back to get Mary to go with me. She was still down on the ground. I couldn't get her to go, so I left her. I ran across and went up the hill. When I got there a hand came down on my shoulder, and it was a firm grip. This man said, "You're coming with me." And I said, "No, I can't come with you, I have to get this man." I'm not very good at doing what I'm told. He showed me I.D. It said Secret Service. It looked official to me. I tried to turn away from him and he said a second time, "You're going with me." At this point, a second man came and grabbed me from the other side, and they ran their hands through my pockets. They didn't say, "Do you have the picture? Which pocket?" They just ran their hands through my pockets and took it. They both held me up here [at the shoulder near the neck] someplace, where you could hurt somebody badly—and they told me, "Smile. Act like you're with your boyfriends." But I couldn't smile because it hurt too badly. And they said, "Here we go," each one holding me by a shoulder. They took me to the Records Building and we went up to a room on the fourth floor. There were two guys sitting there on the other side of a table looking out a window that overlooked "the killing zone," where you could see all of the goings on. You got the impression that they had been sitting there for a long time. They asked me what I had seen, and it became clear that they knew what I had seen. They asked me how many shots I had heard and I told them four to six. And they said, "No, you didn't. There were three shots. We have three bullets and that's all we're going to commit to now." I said, "Well, I know what I heard," and they told me, "What you heard were echoes. You would be very wise to keep your mouth shut." Well, I guess I've never been that wise. I know the difference between firecrackers, echoes, and gunshots. I'm the daughter of a game ranger, and my father took me shooting all my life.

(See also Foster, J. W.; Goldstein, Joe; Moorman, Mary; Wiseman, John)
SOURCES: WCH VI, 205; XIX, 479; XXIV, 212; XXV, 853, 875 • WCE 2003, 2582, 2594 • CF 37–9, 56, 322–4 • RTJ 41, 262, 285, 345, 389 • GERTZ 526 • BISHOP 128, 137, 140 • PWW 24, 30–3, 35–7, 39–40, 45, 158–61, 164–9 • OTT 18, 21 • BE 18, 29, 373 • SUMMERS 20, 23, 28, 50–1 • ME 51 • NORTH 386 • PD 17

HILL, L. L., DPD member. About 10 minutes after the assassination, Hill said into his police mike, "Get some men up here to cover this School Depository Building. It's believed the shots came from, as you see it on Elm Street, looking toward the building, it would be the upper-right-hand corner—second window from the end... I have one guy [James Tague] that was probably hit by a ricochet from the bullet off the concrete and another one saw the President slump."
SOURCES: WR 111 • BISHOP 171–2

HINCHLIFFE, MARGARET M. (later, Margaret Hood; shown in WR as Henchcliffe), Parkland witness; nurse. Hinchliffe helped wheel JFK from the limousine into the emergency room and later helped prepare the body for the coffin. She told *Boston Globe* reporters in 1981 that JFK had a gaping wound in the back of his head and an entrance wound in his throat. With nurse Diana Bowron, she used surgical shears to cut off JFK's clothes upon his arrival, removing everything except his underwear and his back brace. (Someone else removed the brace later, but the underwear remained on throughout the procedure, out of deference to JFK's position.)

After JFK's death, Hinchliffe was ordered to clean the body. According to author Jim Bishop, "The body was sponged carefully, the legs and arms still pliant. The cart drapes on the right-hand side were heavy with brain matter. This was cleaned up and the edges of the massive wound in the head were wiped. The brown hair was slicked back. The body was lifted off the carriage and white sheets were placed underneath. Enough loose material

was allowed to hang off the left side so that, when the President was placed in the box, his head and neck wounds would not soil the white satin interior." (See also Bowron, Diana)
SOURCES: HT 45, 68–9, 454 • WCH VI, 139 • BISHOP 156, 176, 179–80 • DOP 183, 290, 304 • BE 57, 192

HINE, GENEVA L., a.w.; TSBD employee. Hine, who worked on the second floor, was looking out the window when she heard three shots. She told WC they made the building "vibrate."
SOURCE: WCH VI, 393

HOCH, PAUL, California assassination researcher and physicist. Hoch is coauthor, with Peter Dale Scott and Russell Stetlet, of *The Assassinations: Dallas and Beyond* (Random House, 1976).
SOURCES: PWW 78, 145 • SUMMERS 475 • BE 15, 101, 137, 155, 541, 554 • HOS 235 • DAVIS 422, 441

HODGE, ALFRED DOUGLAS, Ruby witness. Hodge, owner of the Buckhorn Trading Post, a gun shop, which was right next door to his other establishment, the Buckhorn Bar; had sold several rifles during the weeks before the assassination. He gave the FBI a list of those who had purchased rifles from him and visited the DPD station at 11:45 P.M. on the day of the assassination to see whether he could identify the discovered weapons, but could not. While at the station, he ran into Ruby in the elevator, and they spoke.
SOURCE: WCH XV, 494

HODGES, FRED J., III, HSCA medical expert; professor of radiology at Johns Hopkins School of Medicine. Hodges was part of a medical panel that examined the JFK autopsy photographs and X rays and concluded that JFK was shot exclusively from the rear.
SOURCE: BELIN 181

HOFFA, JAMES RIDDLE "JIMMY," assassination suspect; suspicious death; president of the International Brotherhood of Teamsters from the late 1950s to the mid-1960s. Hoffa's closest ties in organized crime were with Santos Trafficante and Carlos Marcello. At the time of the assassination, Hoffa had been under investigation by Attorney General Robert F. Kennedy for six years. In 1963, Hoffa was under indictment. He once threatened to break Robert Kennedy's back and later said that JFK would make a better target because "when you cut down the tree, the branches fall with it." Hoffa vanished in July 1975 while on his way to meet Anthony Provenzano, a mob-connected Teamster official.
For 27 years Frank Ragano was the lawyer for Florida mob boss Santos

Trafficante and for 15 years he represented Hoffa. In the January 14, 1992, edition of the *New York Post*, Ragano revealed knowledge of a plot involving Hoffa, Trafficante, and New Orleans mob boss Carlos Marcello to assassinate the president. Hoffa, Marcello, and Trafficante are all dead. (See Marcello, Carlos, for more details on Ragano's story.)

According to the HSCA: "The long and close relationship between Hoffa and powerful leaders of organized crime, his intense dislike of John and Robert Kennedy dating back to their role in the McClellan Senate investigation, together with his other criminal activities, led the committee to conclude that the former Teamsters Union president had the motive, means, and opportunity for planning an assassination attempt upon the life of President Kennedy." (See also Baker, Robert B. "Barney"; Dalitz, Morris; Marcello, Carlos; Partin, Edward; Ragano, Frank; Scheim, David; Trafficante, Santos)

SOURCES: HSCA Report 34, 154, 174, 176–9 • BELIN 23 • COA, many • BISHOP 71 • DOP 89 • CF 171–5 • OTT 300 • SUMMERS 243–55, 260, 433, 448–9, 493 • BLAKEY 192–4, 201–8, 269, 304, 326 • FLAMMONDE 303, 322 • EVICA, many • KANTOR 20, 22, 28, 30, 101, 136, 218 • DAVIS, many • NORTH, many

HOFFMAN, ED, a.w. Hoffman stood on the shoulder of the Stemmons Expressway, 200 yards west of the TSBD parking lot and the railroad tracks behind the grassy knoll. The 26-year-old deaf-and-dumb witness saw men with a rifle moments after the shots were fired. The first man, who wore a dark suit and a tie, with an overcoat, ran west along the wooden fence with a rifle and tossed it to a second man who was dressed like a railroad worker. The second man hid behind a railroad switchbox, disassembled the rifle and put it in a soft brown bag. When last seen by Hoffman, the "railroad worker" was walking toward the tower in which Lee Bowers was posted. Hoffman tried in vain to communicate to authorities what he had seen. His story was not made public until 1985, when he related his tale to Dallas reporter Jim Marrs. In 1991, Hoffman claimed the FBI tried to pay him not to say anything more about what he saw. (See also Bowers, Lee)

SOURCES: HT 462 • CF 81–6

HOLLAND, LOUIS, Ruby witness. Holland was the judge who presided over Ruby's *habeas corpus* hearing on September 9, 1965, as well as at his sanity hearing on June 13, 1966.

SOURCE: GERTZ, many

HOLLAND, SAM M., a.w.; Union Terminal Company employee. Holland stood atop the triple underpass directly in front of a.w. J. W. Foster and says he heard four shots, one of which, he said, hit JFK on "part of his face," and afterward saw "a puff of smoke" come from "six or eight feet above the ground right out from under those trees" near the wooden fence at the top of the grassy knoll. He watched as "12 or 15 policemen and plainsclothesmen" looked for "empty shells" behind the wooden fence. Holland said there was a station wagon parked near the fence and it looked like somebody had been standing between it and the fence for some time. He said there was "mud up on the bumper" of the station wagon "in two spots" and described the footprints this way: "They didn't extend further [sic] than from one end of the bumper to the other. That's as far as they would go. It looked like a lion pacing a cage...Just to the west of the station wagon there were two sets of footprints that left...They could've gotten in the trunk compartment of this car and pulled the lid down, which would have been very, very easy." The trunks of cars parked in the area were never searched.

In the 1966 film *Rush to Judgment*, based on Mark Lane's book, Holland said, "I know where the third shot came from—behind the picket fence. There's no doubt whatsoever in my mind." Holland said in a 1967 interview that after JFK was shot "I noticed that this [SS] man stood up in the car...He jumped up in the seat...I actually thought he was shot too, because he fell backwards just like he was shot...He pointed this machine gun right towards that grassy knoll, behind that picket fence." This statement is used by Bonar Menninger to support the theory that JFK was killed accidentally by SS agent George Hickey. (See also Foster, J. W.; Hickey, George)

SOURCES: WR 81–2 • WCH VI, 239 • WCE 2003 • HSCA Report 89, 496–7, 606 • BLAKEY 90, 267 • CF 56–9, 320–1 • HT 232 • RTJ 33–4, 36–7, 40, 285 • COA 21–2, 24–5, 28, 409 • BISHOP 134, 136 • OTT 16 • SUMMERS 27–8 • BE 15, 35 • FMG I, 27, 29 • OGLESBY 36 • ME 102, 104–5, 220 • LEWIS 32–33

HOLLINGSWORTH, BOB, a.w.; *Dallas Times Herald* managing editor. Hollingsworth rode in the motorcade in the press-pool station wagon.
SOURCE: EPSTEIN 219

HOLLY, HAROLD B., JR., o.k.w. (aftermath). Holly, a 47-year-old member of the DPD Reserve Force, reported for duty five minutes after Oswald was shot. He later went to Parkland, where a fellow reservist told him that he had seen Ruby enter the basement. He told the WC: "They were trying to find out how in the world Ruby ever got down in the basement. And I said, 'Well, my Lord, one of the reserves let him in.'"
SOURCE: WCH XII, 261

HOLMES, HARRY D., a.w. Holmes, a 57-year-old postal inspector, watched through binoculars from his office window on the fifth floor of the Terminal Annex Building at the southwest corner of Houston and Commerce, directly across Dealey Plaza from the TSBD. He thought someone was throwing firecrackers because he saw dust fly up from Elm Street with the first report. He saw JFK's limo come to a halt and figured that the driver was trying to dodge something that was being thrown.

Holmes helped FBI trace the money order Oswald purchased to order his rifle as well as ownership of the post office box used to receive the alleged murder weapons. Holmes interrogated Oswald for the first time at 6:00 P.M., November 22, 1963. Holmes had records indicating that Oswald, while in New Orleans, had rented PO Box #30061 and that the application listed Marina Oswald and A. J. Hidell as the only others entitled to receive mail at that box. Oswald told Holmes that it was natural to put his wife's name on the application. When questioned about Hidell, Oswald reportedly said, "I don't recall anything about that." Because he dropped in on police headquarters to give his report moments before Oswald was to be transferred, Holmes was the last man to interrogate Oswald before his death.

SOURCES: WR 115, 169, 189, 288 • WCH VII, 289, 525 • BELIN 41–3, 62, 215 • RTJ 136–41 • BISHOP 136, 364 • HOS 239, 241 • EVICA 6–7, 51 • ME 73

HOLMES, KEN, JR., law-enforcement official. With his friend and fellow researcher Larry Harris of Dallas, Holmes is one of the leading experts in the murder of Officer J. D. Tippit.

SOURCE: SUMMERS 487

HOLT, CHAUNCY MARVIN, possible a.w. Holt is a confessed "tramp," i.e., one of the three men who were apprehended by the DPD in the railroad yard near Dealey Plaza moments after the assassination. Recent identification by the DPD and the FBI of another man as Holt's "tramp" has led some researchers to believe that Holt is a fraud, but if so, for what purpose?

At the Kennedy Assassination Symposium in Dallas on November 17, 1991, Holt was identified photographically as the tramp by Houston police forensic artist Lois Gibson, private detective John R. Craig, and researcher Phillip A. Rogers.

Holt has admitted to being the eldest tramp; he said the other two tramps were assassination suspect Charles Harrelson and a man known to him as Richard Montoya, whom the Houston police believe to be a wanted murderer named Charles Frederick Rogers. According to Craig, Holt is a career criminal, a genius, a pilot who has worked for organized crime, a master forger, and a man who has been tried and acquitted of murder.

Holt was born in Kentucky in 1921, enlisted in the army before World War II, and was incarcerated after a court-martial. After the war, he did time as a civilian as well, and through prison friends met mobster Peter Lacavoli who, in turn, introduced him to Meyer Lansky. According to Craig:

Holt went to Florida where he was an accountant for Lansky. After some years there in Miami, the Kefauver Hearings began. He was transferred away from there because he knew what was coming. Lansky arranged for him to work as a controller for an outfit called the International Rescue Corporation Committee, which was a proprietary of the CIA. After a time he realized what he was involved in. He forged documents for the CIA. He was transferred to California and in 1963 he provided Oswald with his Hidell I.D. and his [FPCC] leaflets. He claims he was in Dealey Plaza that day delivering the [SS] pins and other I.D. to individuals who were up in the Plaza. Subsequent to his release from there, he encountered Eugene Hale Brading, and together they went to Lacavoli's Grace Ranch.

According to Phillip A. Rogers:

Holt was under the impression that some sort of incident was to be staged in Dallas that would be blamed on pro-Castro forces. When the shots rang out he says he was behind the pergola and he did not see Kennedy or Connally get hit. He immediately ran to the box car as instructed, the ninth box car from the engine. There he met the other two tramps who identified themselves as agents. Together, they were escorted from the scene. It has occurred to Holt that they might have been alternative patsies in case Oswald had escaped.

Craig adds:

Holt runs an art studio in San Diego. He also operates a shooting school. Even at the age of 70 he is still a master marksman. For many years, he taught at a shooting school for a proprietary of the CIA ... Holt arrived at a parking lot [behind the grassy knoll] in an Oldsmobile station wagon. This fits with the observations of Lee Bowers. The parking lot was supposed to have been secured. Holt says that he had a key. The Secret Service identification bars have a color of the day, which is why Holt had to forge the I.D. at the last minute, because he did not know until then what color would be valid for that day.

(See also Craig, John R.; Gibson, Lois; Harrelson, Charles; Rogers, Charles Frederick; Rogers, Phillip A.)
SOURCE: OGLESBY 48

HOLT, JEANNIE, a.w. Holt stood on the north side of Elm, midway between the TSBD and the triple underpass with Stella Jacob and Sharon Nelson. None of these three were called as WC witnesses, most likely indicating that their observances didn't jibe with the "official" facts.
SOURCE: RTJ 110

HOOD, JIM, a.w. (aftermath); *Dallas Morning News* employee (advertising department). According to UTM, Hood was with fellow DMN workers "soon" after the assassination in Dealey Plaza when he saw and photographed a mysterious pool of blood (more than a pint of it) on a sidewalk near the pergola; later he was told by FBI that, as far as the pool of blood was concerned, "it never happened, you didn't see it." Now deceased. (See also Couch, Malcolm; Coley, Jerry; Mulkey, Charles)

HOOD, MARGARET (See HINCHLIFFE, MARGARET)

HOOVER, J. EDGAR, FBI director. Despite evidence to the contrary— Waggoner Carr, the attorney general of Texas said he had information that Oswald was an "undercover" agent for the FBI—Hoover denied that Oswald was ever an agent or a paid informant for his agency. According to author John H. Davis, "Hoover had no interest in uncovering the truth behind the assassination or in bringing the guilty to justice; he was only interested in protecting his reputation and that of the FBI."
According to author Mark North:

> In September 1962, as a result of data obtained through covert surveillance programs against the Mafia... Hoover learned that a subcomponent of that organization, the Marcello family of New Orleans... had, in order to prevent its own destruction... put out a contract on the life of [JFK]... Hoover did not inform his superiors within the Justice Department [i.e., RFK] or warn the [SS]... He withheld the data in part because he felt Kennedy was an indecisive, immoral liberal who... would destroy the nation. But most important, he did this because JFK... intended... to retire the Director and replace him with a man of his own, more liberal political philoso-

phy...[B]y the fall of 1962 [Hoover] held sufficient information to control [LBJ], a longtime friend, were he to become President. Through data gleaned (and withheld from the Justice Department) from investigations of the Billy Sol Estes and soon-to-break Bobby Baker/Mafia scandals, Hoover had hopelessly compromised [LBJ]. Johnson, a man tremendously dissatisfied with his position in government, knew this... As a result of Hoover's traitorous act, [JFK] was assassinated, Johnson became President, and the Director obtained an Executive Order, on May 8, 1964, waiving his compulsory retirement.

According to Penn Jones Jr., a conference was held November 21, 1963, at the home of Texas oil billionaire Clint Murchison. Present were Richard M. Nixon and J. Edgar Hoover. Jones writes, "...Hoover, the task force commander, was present to confer with his troops, to issue last minute instructions, to review the final plans and to give the word to 'go' or to cancel as necessary."

On November 24, 1963, Hoover wrote, in a memo to LBJ: "The thing I am concerned about...is having something issued so we can convince the public that Oswald is the real assassin." Soon thereafter, Hoover's FBI would become the primary source of information for the WC.

Among the HSCA's findings were that the FBI's initial investigation of the assassination had been conducted improperly and that it had issued a distorted report of its results. For example, while arguing that Ruby was, like Oswald, a lone nut, they omitted the fact that Ruby had acted as an FBI informant in the late 1950s. (See also Angleton, James; Carr, Waggoner; Giancana, Momo; Hall, Loran; Jones, Penn; Kennedy, Regis; Nagell, Richard; O'Donnell, P. Kenneth)

SOURCES: WR, many • WCH V, 97 • HSCA Report 33, 138, 176–7, 185, 238, 241, 243–5, 250, 260 • OGLESBY 12, 80 • BELIN 76, 109–11 • RTJ, many • COA, many • GERTZ 103 • BISHOP, many • DOP, many • CF 213–26 • PWW, many • OTT 50, 185, 197–8, 222, 229, 239, 282, 293 • SUMMERS, many • BE, many • FMG I, 38, 55, 187; III, 6, 85, 88 • BLAKEY, many • HOS 18, 45, 235 • FLAMMONDE 149, 156, 159, 200, 206, 273 • EVICA, many • ME 123–4, 133 • KANTOR, many • DAVIS, many • NORTH, many • PD, many

HOPKINS, LOUIS, Oswald witness; travel agent. Hopkins booked Oswald's passage from New Orleans to Le Havre, France, aboard the SS *Marion Lykes*, departing on September 20, 1959. This was the first step in Oswald's journey to the Soviet Union, which Hopkins did not know. Hopkins said that Oswald wasn't well versed in European travel—surprising, considering the sophisticated and efficient manner in which

Oswald penetrated the Iron Curtain.

According to the WC, Hopkins's address—as of December 3 and 4, 1963, when he was interviewed by the FBI—was Travel Consultants, Inc., International Trade Mart, 124 Camp Street, New Orleans, Louisiana. At that time, the director of the International Trade Mart was Clay Shaw, the man indicted, tried, and acquitted for conspiracy to assassinate JFK.

SOURCES: WCH XXVI, 29 • HSCA Report 211 • DUFFY 31 • FMG III, 55–6

HOPSON, MRS. ALVIN, a.w.; TSBD employee. Hopson watched through the glass of a fourth-floor TSBD window (the window would not open) and heard "two or more loud sounds." She thought they were firecrackers that had "been set off on the street below" and told the FBI that the shots "did not sound to her like [they] were coming from her building."

SOURCES: WCH XXIV, 521 • BE 17

HORN, JOHN T., Oswald witness. Horn was the 18-year-old member of the November 22, 1963, police lineup at which cabdriver William Whaley positively identified Oswald as the man he had driven from the Greyhound bus station in downtown Dallas to Oak Cliff. Horn was suspect #1, Oswald #3.

SOURCE: WR 152

HOSTY, JAMES P., JR., FBI agent in charge of Oswald's case in Dallas (now retired). According to the WR, on November 6, 1963, Oswald wrote a note to Hosty, which Hosty later ripped up and flushed down the toilet, under the orders of FBI office chief J. Gordon Shanklin. According to Hosty, the note read, in effect, "Dear Mr. Hasty [sic]: If you want to talk to me, talk to me. Do not talk to my wife when I am not around. If you do not cease and desist, I will have to take the matter up with the proper authorities."

Hosty was involved in the early interrogation of Oswald following Oswald's arrest in the Texas Theatre. According to Captain Will Fritz, Oswald became angered at Hosty's presence in the interrogation room, saying that Hosty had "accosted" his wife.

According to author J. Gary Shaw, Hosty was seen in the company of an Army Intelligence man on Main Street 45 minutes before the parade passed. Hosty's name (spelled "Hasty") and license-plate number appear in Oswald's notebook. According to Penn Jones Jr., Hosty was the bridge-playing partner of Major General Edwin A. Walker's aide, Robert Surrey. The WR tells us that Surrey was the printer and distributor of the anti-JFK "Wanted for Treason" leaflets prevalent in Dallas on November 22, 1963.

On the 1988 British television documentary *The Men Who Killed Kennedy*, Hosty said, "I feel there was, based on what I know now, a benign cover-up. [The government] was concerned about Oswald's connections to the Soviet Union and to Castro. They were fearful that, if the public were to find this out, they would become so incensed that it could possibly have led to an atomic war." Hosty also said in that documentary that he was told by an FBI counterintelligence agent, not long after the assassination, that he was to halt all FBI investigations of Oswald and all cooperation with the DPD regarding Oswald's background. Hosty said, "I have since determined that those orders came directly from Assistant Director William Sullivan, who was in charge of foreign counterintelligence and direct liaison to the National Security Council."

In his book *Oswald in New Orleans* (New York: Canyon Books, 1967, pp. 47–8), Harold Weisberg says that Hosty supplied the WC with the following memo regarding an October 1963 meeting of Carlos Bringuier's DRE *(Directorio Revolucionaro Estudiantil)* organization, at which both Major General Edwin A. Walker and Lee Harvey Oswald were in attendance. The memo read, in part:

> EDWIN L. STEIG, 713 Winifred Street, Garland, Texas, advised he attended a meeting of the Student Directorate of Cuba held on a Sunday evening at 8:00 P.M. some time during the month of October, 1963. There were about seventy-five persons present at this meeting which was held at the First Federal Savings and Loan Association Conference Room in the North Line Shopping Village in Dallas, Texas. [Steig said that he] sat in the back of the room and listened to several speakers who talked about the situation in Cuba...Steig stated that another individual sat in the back of the room who [sic] he believes is identical with...Oswald. This individual spoke to no one but merely listened and then left.

(See also Bringuier, Carlos; Fritz, Will; Gochnour, Jim; Gaten, Carver; Shanklin, J. Gordon)

SOURCES: WR 298, 304–5, 394–6, 413–9 • WCH I, 48, 56; II, 15; III, 92, 96; IV, 440 • HSCA Report 184–6, 189, 194–6, 250 • BLAKEY 36, 63, 76, 361–2 • SHAW 194 • BISHOP, many • DOP 32–3, 152, 206, 284, 332, 631 • OTT 223–7, 275, 324 • SUMMERS 369–74, 496 • BE 270 • FMG I, 156–7; III, 33 • HOS 136 • FLAMMONDE 125, 155 • EVICA 58, 125, 140, 321–7 • ME 130 • OGLESBY 19–20, 22–3 • KANTOR 87 • DAVIS 270–1 • NORTH, many • PD 56, 78

HOUSTON, LAWRENCE, CIA general counsel. Houston corroborated the testimony of Sheffield Edwards that CIA/Mafia plots to kill Castro were

known of and approved by RFK. JFK once said to Houston, "If you ever try to do business with organized crime again—with gangsters—you will let the Attorney General [RFK] know." (See also Edwards, Sheffield)
  SOURCES: HT 326 • SUMMERS 241–2, 355 • BLAKEY 58–9

HOWARD, LAWRENCE J., JR., East Los Angeles Mexican-American. Howard was thought by the WC to be one of the three men who visited Cuban exile Sylvia Odio (one of whom identified himself as Leon Oswald) on either September 25 or 26, 1963, when, officially, Oswald was on his way by bus to Mexico City. The WR identified Howard's companions as Loran Eugene Hall of Johnsondale, California, and William Seymour of Arizona.

Attempts by New Orleans District Attorney Jim Garrison to extradite Howard from California for the investigation and trial of Clay Shaw were refused by a California judge. On December 29, 1967, Garrison issued a subpoena for Howard in El Monte, California. Author Paris Flammonde writes: "The subpoena contended that Howard had associated with David Ferrie in New Orleans in 1963, that he participated in CIA-supported guerrilla-raid training in Florida, and that he was active in the militant Free Cuba movement in Florida, Louisiana, and Texas... Howard appeared in California Supreme Court on January 16, 1968, in response to a show cause order, and protested that returning to New Orleans would impose hardships upon him."

Howard explained that he was in Louisiana on November 22, 1963 and that, although he "helped train guerilla forces for a proposed invasion of Cuba," he had "no knowledge of any conspiracy concerning the assassination of President Kennedy." Howard later traveled voluntarily to New Orleans, where he was interviewed by Garrison. (See also Hall, Loran; Odio, Sylvia; Seymour, William)
  SOURCES: WR 301 • EVICA 314

HOWARD, THOMAS HALE, Ruby witness; suspicious death; attorney. According to assassination researcher Mark Lane, Howard met with Ruby's roommate George Senator and two members of the press at Ruby's apartment on the evening of November 24, hours after Ruby shot Oswald. What was discussed at the meeting is unknown. None of those three men Senator met at the meeting lived past 1965. On March 27, 1965, soon after Ruby's trial began, Howard died at 48 of a heart attack in Dallas.

According to A. L. Goodhart in the *Law Quarterly Review*, "The connection between Howard's heart attack and the conspiracy seems to be...remote because he was not at Ruby's apartment that night."

Howard was the first lawyer to represent Ruby after Ruby shot Oswald. He had been asked to handle the case by Ruby's friend and business associate Ralph Paul. Author Elmer Gertz writes: "Like Ruby himself, [Howard] was a 'little' man of great aspirations. The striking difference between the two was that Howard was highly successful in his small way, whereas Ruby was a spectacular flop in all that he did. Howard's clients were pimps and prostitutes and murderers and unimportant people. He lost no clients to the electric chair, however, and he was reasonably certain that he would not lose Ruby either."

By the time Ruby was convicted of murder with malice and sentenced to death, Howard was no longer involved in the case. Ruby believed Howard had "no class." (See also Hunter, William; Koethe, James; Paul, Ralph; Senator, George)

SOURCES: HSCA Report 158 • HT 129, 137 • RTJ 284 • COA 32, 128, 133, 147–8 • GERTZ, many • SUMMERS 461–3 • FMG I, 3–6, 22, 24 • BLAKEY 324–7, 333–4 • KANTOR, many • DAVIS 450 • PD 350

HOWLETT, JOHN JOE, SS agent. To see whether Oswald could have done in the first few seconds following the assassination what the WC claimed he did, the SS conducted a test using Howlett:

> [Howlett] carried a rifle from the southeast corner of the sixth floor along the east aisle to the northeast corner. He placed the rifle on the floor near the site where Oswald's rifle was actually found after the shooting. Then Howlett walked down the stairway to the second-floor landing and entered the lunchroom. The first test, run at normal walking pace, required 1 minute, 18 seconds; the second test, at a 'fast walk' took 1 minute, 14 seconds. The second test followed immediately after the first. The only interval was the time necessary to ride the elevator from the second to the sixth floor and walk back to the southeast corner. Howlett was not short winded at the end of either test run.

SOURCES: WR 142 • WCH VII, 592; IX, 425 • PWW 35, 161, 170 • ME 221

HOY, DAVID, referred to by the WR as a "news media friend" of sometime Carousel Club emcee William D. Crowe Jr. Crowe did a memory act during his performances and thought he remembered seeing Oswald in the Carousel. Although Crowe mentioned this to others, he reportedly did not discuss it when he called Hoy in Evansville, Indiana, "less than 20 minutes" after Oswald was shot. (See also Crowe, William)

SOURCE: WR 336

HUBER, OSCAR, Parkland witness; priest who administered the last rites of the Catholic church to JFK. As reported by the *Philadelphia Sunday Bulletin* on November 24, 1963, Huber said that JFK had a terrible wound over his left eye. Huber is probably referring to the wound over JFK's right eye. (See also Landrigan, Steve)
SOURCES: WR 68 • HT 231 • RTJ 60 • BISHOP 90, 119, 158–9, 172–4, 205, 333–4, 514, 531 • DOP 109–10, 136, 213–9, 221, 243–4, 254–5, 281, 283 • BE 46

HUBERT, LEON D., JR., WC counsel; New Orleans attorney; former Tulane law professor; former New Orleans district attorney. With Bert W. Griffin, Hubert investigated Ruby's life and activities. However, neither Griffin nor Hubert was involved in taking Ruby's testimony. Hubert died in 1977. According to author Seth Kantor, Hubert served only four years as New Orleans district attorney because he and assassination suspect Carlos Marcello couldn't "do business." (See also Griffin, Burt W.)
SOURCES: BELIN 46 • RTJ 225, 296 • COA 158, 200, 204, 259 • GERTZ 81–5, 91–5, 498, 511, 520 • FMG I, 2; III, 40 • PWW 256, 269 • OTT 271 • SUMMERS 431, 469 • BE 229 • BLAKEY 79, 81–2, 84, 293, 302, 315, 333 • FLAMMONDE 60 • EVICA, many • KANTOR, many • DAVIS 303

HUDSON, EMMETT JOSEPH, a.w.; Dealey Plaza groundskeeper. Hudson stood on the steps leading up to the top of the grassy knoll. With Hudson, according to photographic evidence, were two men, neither of whom was ever identified. Hudson told the WC:

> Well, there was a young fellow, oh, I would judge his age in his late twenties. He said he had been looking for a place to park...he finally [had] just taken a place over there in one of them parking lots, and he came on down there and said he worked over there on Industrial [Boulevard] and me and him both just sat down there on those steps. When the motorcade turned off of Houston onto Elm, we got up and stood up, me and him both...and so the first shot rung out and, of course, I didn't realize it was a shot...the motorcade had done got further on down Elm...I happened to be looking right at him when that bullet hit him—the second shot...it looked like it hit him somewhere along about a little bit behind the ear and a little above the ear...this young fellow that was...standing there with me...he says, "Lay down, Mister, somebody is shooting the President."...he was already lying down one way on the sidewalk, so I just laid down over on the ground and was resting my arm on the ground...when that third shot rung out...you could tell that the shot was coming from above and kind of behind.

Hudson was standing with his back to the picket fence atop the grassy knoll when the shots began. No mention of the third man on the steps (visible in photographs and film) is made by Hudson in his WC testimony.
SOURCES: WR 110 • WCH VII, 558 • WCE 2003, 2508 • HSCA Report 605–6 • CF 71–3 • PWW 31, 156–7 • BE 18

HUFF, LARRY, HSCA witness. Huff's wife told the HSCA that her husband had learned of a JFK assassination investigation team sponsored by the military and run out of Camp Smith in Hawaii. The man in charge of the investigation was reportedly Lieutenant General Carson A. Roberts. This report is interesting because no record of such an investigation exists. According to the HSCA:

> Huff stated under oath on December 14, 1963 that he departed Kaneohe Base in Hawaii in a C-54-T aircraft, serial number 50855, for Wake Island, with Chief Warrant Officer Morgan as pilot... Huff stated that there were ten to twelve CID military investigators on that flight [for which Huff was navigator]... Huff said that he learned the purpose of the trip by the CID investigators through conversations on the plane during the flight... On the return flight, he had spoken with the investigators about their work in Japan and was told that they had spent the entire stay investigating Oswald. Huff said that during that flight he was allowed to read the report prepared by the investigators. He described the report as being typewritten, about 20 pages, and classified "Secret—For Marine Corps Eyes Only." Huff recollected that the substance of the report dealt with interviews of individuals and that it contained a psychological evaluation of Oswald. Huff remembered the conclusion being that Oswald was incapable of committing the assassination alone.

The Defense Department told the HSCA that it had no record of any such flight or any such investigation. The department said that Huff was confusing his story with an actual military investigation of John Edward Pic, Oswald's half-brother. Why was the military investigating Oswald's half-brother? (See also Pic, John Edward; Roberts, Carson)
SOURCES: HSCA XI, 541–9 • HT 273–5 • SUMMERS 566

HUFFAKER, ROBERT S., JR., o.k.w.; 27-year-old KRLD radio and TV newsman in Dallas. Huffaker told WC that he was in front of the doors leading from the interior basement into the parking area when they brought Oswald out.

SOURCE: WCH XIII, 116

HUGHES, HOWARD, famous aviator, eccentric, and one of the richest men in the world. Hughes was an employer of General Charles Cabell. According to HT, JFK's death was the result of "the Dallas-Hughes-CIA-Mafia-Anti-Castro Cuban connection." According to Jack Anderson in the *New York Times* (February 25, 1977), who obtained his information from mobster Johnny Roselli (who was later murdered for talking too much), the first CIA plot to kill Castro was hatched when the CIA "spoke secretly to Howard Hughes's chief honcho in Las Vegas, Robert Maheu, about the project. Maheu recruited Roselli, then the Chicago Mob's debonair representative in Las Vegas... Roselli looked upon the assassination mission as an opportunity to gain favor with the U.S. government." According to Fletcher Prouty, in his book *The Secret Team* (Prentice-Hall, 1973), "Howard Hughes... had a huge empire which largely lived on CIA money. He was their chief cover in many operations." (See also Cabell, Charles; Maheu, Robert; Roselli, John)
SOURCES: HT 154, 306, 312, 314, 379, 435 • COA 302 • BLAKEY 384 • EVICA, many

HUGHES, ROBERT J., a.w. Hughes stood at the southwest corner of Houston and Elm Streets and took motion pictures which showed the TSBD moments before the shooting. The film seems to show two silhouettes in the "sniper's-nest" window. The FBI was the first to examine the film and claimed that there were no men visible in the photo, merely shadows. In 1975, CBS asked the Itek Corporation to examine the film, and its experts also concluded that there were no moving images in the window. Later on the same film there are scenes of the near-stampede of eyewitnesses as they run up the grassy knoll to see what is going on back by the railroad yards. (See also Selzer, Robert)
SOURCES: WCH XXV, 873 • WCD 205, 158 • WR 644 • WCE 2585 • HT 228–9 • CF 21 • RTJ 346–8 • PWW 57–8, 86, 125–30, 132–3, 278–81, 283 • SUMMERS 44–5 • DAVIS 196, 460 • NORTH 378, 395, 398, 451, 504, 511–2

HUGHES, SARAH, judge. Hughes swore in LBJ as the 36th president of the United States aboard Air Force One at Love Field, Dallas, at 2:38 P.M., November 22, 1963. (See also Johnson, Lyndon B.)
SOURCES: WR 22, 72 • BLAKEY 18 • GERTZ 172 • BISHOP 231, 239–44 • DOP, many • BE 588, 675

HULEN, RICHARD LEROY, Ruby witness; associate director of the health club of the YMCA in Dallas. Hulen told the WC that Ruby was a short-term member of the club. He used YMCA records to confirm that Oswald stayed there for a short time, but said Oswald never used the club

facilities since he was not a member and added that Oswald was never in the health club in the company of Ruby.
SOURCE: WCH X, 277

HULSE, CLIFFORD E., DPD member, one of the dispatchers (with Gerald Henslee) at the time of Officer Tippit's death. Hulse answered the frantic call from t.k.w. Ted Callaway at the scene of the Tippit shooting. (See also Callaway, Ted; Henslee, Gerald; Tippit, J. D.)
SOURCES: WCH XIII, 99 • RTJ 206 • BISHOP 174, 200

HUMES, JAMES J., Bethesda witness; commander, U.S. Navy. With two other naval doctors (Commander J. Thornton Boswell and Lt. Col. Pierre A. Finck), Humes performed the autopsy on JFK at Bethesda Naval Hospital in Maryland. He was unfamiliar with gunshot wounds. Humes's report bears little relation to the reports of doctors at Parkland Hospital in Dallas who saw the president's wounds immediately after the shooting. Humes saw a large wound to the right front of Kennedy's head and a small entrance wound in the back of the head. The Parkland doctors saw a large opening at the back of the head, indicating an exit wound. The Parkland doctors saw a small hole in Kennedy's throat, seemingly an entrance wound. Unfortunately, that wound was enlarged for a tracheotomy performed on the president in the emergency room, so Humes did not know that this was a wound at all. He saw a small wound in Kennedy's back but failed to trace the path of this entrance wound upon the orders of an unnamed general who was in the autopsy room.

When Humes learned that the wound in the throat was not just a tracheotomy but a bullet wound as well, he burned his original autopsy notes and rewrote his conclusions, saying that the throat wound was an exit wound and had been caused by the same bullet that entered JFK's back. Since the bullet, if fired from the TSBD, had to have a downward slope to its path, Humes moved the back wound in his report up into the back of Kennedy's neck, thus setting the framework for the WC's infamous "single-bullet theory."

To add further intrigue to the macabre discrepancies between the observations of doctors at Parkland and Bethesda, Humes's first impression was that "surgery" had been performed on Kennedy's head, leading some to believe that JFK's body had been altered somewhere between Texas and Maryland, perhaps on Air Force One while LBJ was being sworn in as the new president. This is another indication that official government alterations of the evidence were performed following the assassination to create the illusion that Oswald had been the lone gunman. (See also Boswell, J. Thornton; Lifton, David; Loquvam, George)

SOURCES: WR 89, 91 • WCH II, 347 • HT, many • RTJ 51, 59–64, 66, 74, 76–7, 385 • COA 212 • BISHOP, many • DOP 433 • OTT 244, 247, 325 • SUMMERS 10, 478 • BE, many • HOS 36, 189–90, 195–6, 201 • EVICA 86, 92 • ME, many • NORTH 467

HUNLEY, BOBB, Oswald witness; employee of the Louisiana Department of Labor in New Orleans. Hunley handled Oswald's interstate unemployment claims and told the WC: "I recall nothing unusual about...Oswald."

SOURCE: WCH XI, 476

HUNT, E. HOWARD, JR. (aka Warren, Edward; Hamilton, Edward J.; St. John, David, et al.), assassination suspect; CIA agent; later a Nixon henchman arrested and convicted in connection with the Watergate burglary. Photographs of the "three tramps" who were arrested in a railroad car behind the grassy knoll minutes after the assassination show that one of the three looks a great deal like Hunt. However, disclosures in 1992 by the DPD and FBI would seem to indicate that Hunt was not one of the photographed tramps.

To this day, Hunt remains the prime assassination suspect for attorney Mark Lane, whose book *Plausible Denial* (Thunder's Mouth Press, 1991), according to Lane, "definitely proves" that the CIA killed JFK. Lane's book arises from his successful defense of the Washington tabloid the *Spotlight* against a $1 million lawsuit by Hunt. The newspaper published an article by former CIA agent Victor Marchetti, which placed Hunt in Dallas on the day of the assassination and strongly suggested that a CIA memo indicated that Hunt had played a substantial role in the JFK killing.

Hunt claimed that allegations against him were causing his family stress, that his children were starting to fear that he might really have been involved in JFK's death. However, when asked under oath where he was when JFK was shot, Hunt said he was home watching TV with his children. This obvious discrepancy cost Hunt his case. (As far as courtroom battles go, this one between Lane and Hunt reminds us of the second Clay-Liston bout.) The jury at the trial ruled against Hunt and ordered him to pay the publisher of the *Spotlight*, the ultra-right-wing Liberty Lobby, $25,000 in court costs. In Lane's book, the strongest piece of evidence against Hunt involves the statements of Marita Lorenz who, according to Lane, "placed Hunt in Dallas days before the assassination with a group of people, one of whom [Frank Sturgis] subsequently admitted to her that he'd been involved in the assassination."

Hunt began his wild career as a *Life* war correspondent in 1943. He joined OSS that same year, serving in Kunming and Shanghai, China with the 202 detachment. After the war, Hunt tried to resume his writing career. He wrote a novel in Mexico, then attempted to write screenplays in Hollywood. His life needed excitement. In 1948 he became the press aide for U.S. ambassador to Mexico Averell Harriman—although it has been suggested by journalist Tad Szulc that this position was, already, a cover for Hunt's CIA activities.

Author Jim Hougan writes in his book *Spooks* (William Morrow, 1978) that Hunt and his Cuban plumbers were actually entrapped in the Watergate scandal by James McCord. Gore Vidal wrote in the *Saturday Review of Books* (December 13, 1973) that Hunt may have forged the diaries of Arthur Bremer, the man who shot George Wallace, and then adds snidely, "Although H.H. is a self-admitted forger of state papers, I do not think that he actually had a hand in writing Bremer's diary on the ground that the journal is a brilliant if flawed piece of work, and beyond H.H.'s known literary competence." That crack refers to Hunt's side career as a writer of spy novels (which he wrote both under his own name and under a series of pseudonyms). It has been suspected, of course, that Hunt is a Company man through and through and works as a scribe merely as a medium for the dissemination of CIA disinformation.

Hunt worked closely with General Charles Cabell, deputy director of CIA and active Cold Warrior whose brother was the mayor of Dallas in 1963. According to HT, Hunt's "good friend and idol" was Richard Helms, He was also close friends with former CIA director and WC member Allen Dulles, and even ghostwrote *The Art of Intelligence* for Dulles. Hunt was the political officer for the Bay of Pigs operation, in charge of coordinating the Cuban-exile warriors. He worked for many years for Richard Nixon— and not just prior to the Watergate break-in. According to HT, Hunt had "helped run operations for Nixon against Aristotle Onassis in the late '50s, when Nixon was Vice President under Eisenhower."

A note presented to the HSCA, which the FBI says was written by Oswald, reads. "Dear Mr. Hunt, I would like information concerding [sic] my position. I am asking only for information. I am suggesting that we discuss the matter fully before any steps are taken by me or anyone else. Thank you, Lee Harvey Oswald." Is this letter to E. Howard, H. L., Lamar, or some other Hunt? We'll never know. We do know that Nixon aide Charles Colson ordered Hunt to break into Arthur Bremer's apartment after Bremer was arrested for the attempted assassination of Wallace in 1972. Those orders were withdrawn after Hunt objected. (Nixon then ordered the FBI to seal off Bremer's apartment.)

In 1975, the *Washington Post* reported: "E. Howard Hunt, the former CIA agent who helped engineer the Ellsberg and Watergate burglaries, told associates that he was ordered to kill [Jack] Anderson with an untraceable poison obtained from a former CIA doctor, but that the scheme was dropped at the last minute." If Hunt and the doctor were "former" CIA agents, then who was giving them their orders?

Hunt's lawsuit against A. J. Weberman and Michael Canfield (which he lost), authors of *Coup d'Etat in America* (Quick American Archives, 1992), stems from their publication of a memo allegedly written by Richard Helms's aide Tom Karamessines, stating that Hunt was in Dallas on the day of the assassination. The memo allegedly expresses fear that this fact will be discovered. HSCA chief counsel G. Robert Blakey, who later wrote a book (*The Plot to Kill The President*, Times Books, 1981) about the assassination that points a guilty finger at organized crime, has repeatedly and vehemently defended Hunt, saying that the Karamessines memo does not exist. Weberman and Canfield were the first two to name Hunt and CIA colleague Frank Sturgis as two of the tramps.

Other dirty tricks that Hunt might have pulled in his career include the possible forging of cables accusing JFK of ordering the murder of South Vietnamese president Ngo Dinh Diem. Hunt's wife, who also had a background in intelligence work, died mysteriously when the airliner she was riding in blew up over Chicago.

According to Sturgis, "Howard was in charge of other CIA operations involving 'disposal' and... some of them worked."

According to Jim Hougan in his Watergate exposé, *Secret Agenda* (Ballantine, 1984), Hunt was a GS-15 CIA staff officer in 1969 when he began to pester Nixon staffer and fellow Brown University alumnus Charles Colson to get him a consultancy with the Nixon White House. (See also Blahut, Regis; Bremer, Arthur; Cabell, Charles; Colson, Charles; Lane, Mark; Lorenz, Marita; Marchetti, Victor; Nixon, Richard M.; Helms, Richard; Helperan, Sammy; Hougan, Jim; Karamessines, Tom; Phillips, David Atlee; Thornley, Kerry; Weberman, A. J.)

SOURCES: HSCA Report 91 • HT 107, 120, 154, 186, 191, 281, 384, 420 • COC 526 • COA 185, 302 • SUMMERS 224–5, 233–4, 319, 418–9, 424, 498, 626 • PD, many • EVICA, many • OGLESBY 47 • CANFIELD 199 • DAVIS 403–4, 407–11 • PD, many

HUNT, H. L. (Haroldson Lafayette), right-wing Dallas oil billionaire. According to Jeanne DeMohrenschildt in an article in the *Fort Worth Star-*

Telegram (May 11, 1978), George DeMohrenschildt was "friendly" with Hunt. According to former FBI agent William Turner in *Ramparts* (January 1968), Hunt was frequently escorted to public engagements by extreme right-winger Lieutenant George Butler of the DPD, the man who prematurely gave the "all clear" to transfer Oswald, moments before Ruby shot him. According to a report by Earl Golz in the *Dallas Morning News* (February 6, 1977), Hunt financed the publication of the book *Khrushchev Killed Kennedy* by Michael Eddowes (self-published, 1975). According to COC, Hunt was a longtime financial backer of Richard M. Nixon and had pushed to have former WC member Gerald Ford run as Nixon's vice-presidential candidate in 1968.

According to James Hepburn in *Farewell to America* (Frontiers, 1963), Hunt's personal bodyguards were composed almost entirely of ex-FBI men, and he employed his own intelligence staff. Through his riches, Hepburn writes, Hunt was able to subsidize many of the men in Congress, including LBJ. Hunt was the financial backer of witch-hunter Senator Joseph R. McCarthy, whose paranoiac attempt to purge the United States of an imaginary Red Menace became a national disgrace. Through McCarthy, Hunt grew to like attorney Roy Cohn's cutthroat methods and ended up employing Cohn long after the McCarthy era had burned itself out. In the 1950s, according to Hepburn, Hunt was spending upwards of $2 million a year for an anti-Communist broadcast campaign. And Hunt's son Lamar's offices were visited on the day before the assassination by two assassination suspects: Eugene Hale Brading and Jack Ruby.

Then there is the matter of the note turned over to the HSCA by the FBI, reportedly written by Oswald to a "Mr. Hunt." (For a full transcript of the note, see the entry for Hunt, E. Howard). Was this note written to H. L.?

Hunt told the UPI after the assassination, "Every American, whatever the faith of his views or his political affiliations, suffers a personal loss when a President dies...freedom is in fearful danger when a President dies by violence." According to Penn Jones Jr., "The FBI, who could not protect the President, could take the time and effort to hustle H. L. Hunt out of Dallas on Delta flight 44 on that November 22 afternoon." Hunt had claimed to have received death threats. (See also Artime, Manuel; Baker, Bernard; Bloomfield, Louis; DeMohrenschildt, George; Eddowes, Michael; Ellsworth, Frank; Brading, Eugene Hale; Johnson, Lyndon B.; Kirkwood, Pat; Torbitt, William)

SOURCES: WR 343 • HT 130, 151, 188, 237, 305–8, 318, 384 • COC 573 • RTJ 237, 249,

261 • *Four Days* 61 • COA 89, 158, 188, 204–5, 259 • GERTZ 108, 215 • DOP 45, 49, 109, 151, 204 • FMG III, 5, 8, 22–7, 68 • OTT 206 • FMG I, 130, 160; III, 5, 8, 22–7, 68 • BLAKEY 5 • SUMMERS 2, 507–8, 627 • EVICA 98–9, 101, 109, 165 • KANTOR 35, 37, 111–2, 161–2

HUNT, JACKIE H., Parkland witness; anesthesiologist. Hunt told author Harrison Edward Livingstone that the massive wound in JFK's head had to be in the rear portion of the head because she couldn't see it and, because of the way they were positioned in the Parkland Emergency Room, the back of JFK's head was the only part she couldn't see.
SOURCES: WR 66 • WCH VI, 76 • HT 52 • BISHOP 156, 175

HUNT, LAMAR, son of H. L. Hunt. On Thursday, November 21, 1963, Ruby and assassination suspect Eugene Hale Brading visited Lamar Hunt's Dallas office. (See also Trammel, Connie)
SOURCES: WR 344 • RTJ 261 • COA 46–7, 205, 259–60 • GERTZ 526 • EVICA 165, 167 • KANTOR 35, 37

HUNT, NELSON BUNKER, son of H. L. Hunt. Hunt donated $1,465 toward a full-page ad that ran in the *Dallas Morning News* on the day of JFK's visit. The black-bordered ad denounced JFK for having "scrapped the Monroe Doctrine in favor of 'The Spirit of Moscow.'"
SOURCES: WR 276 • COA 47, 188, 205, 259–60 • DOP 109 • FMG I, 130 • KANTOR 35, 37, 39

HUNTER, DIANA, coauthor, with Alice Anderson, of the book *Ruby's Girls* (Hallux, 1970). Both Hunter and Anderson claim to have worked for Ruby at the time of the assassination. Their book hews carefully to the official version of the facts. (See also Anderson, Alice)

HUNTER, GERTRUDE, possible Oswald witness. With Edith Whitworth, Hunter was in the Furniture Mart in Dallas when Oswald and his family reportedly visited there, seeking rifle repair, in early November 1963. (See also Whitworth, Edith)
SOURCES: WR 294–5 • RTJ 327–30 • WCH XI, 253, 275)

HUNTER, WILLIAM, suspicious death; reporter for the *Long Beach Independent Press Telegram*. Hunter was one of three men who met with Ruby roommate George Senator the evening after Ruby shot Oswald; the subject of the meeting is unknown. All three of the men who met with Senator died shortly thereafter. Hunter was shot to death in a police station on April 23, 1964. (The day before Hunter's death, George Senator had testified before the WC and had said that he did not remember the meeting in question.) According to A. L. Goodhart in the *Law Quarterly Review* (January 1967), "Hunter was shot accidentally by a detective he had known closely for years while the latter 'was clowning foolishly' with a revolver in the station pressroom. It may be remembered that at that time the dangerous game 'Quick on the draw' was popular in the West." (See also Koethe, James; Senator, George; Howard, Thomas)

SOURCES: HT 129, 137 • RTJ 284 • COA 32, 133 • FMG I, 5–7, 22, 24

HURT, HENRY, author of *Reasonable Doubt* (Holt, Rinehart, 1986).

SOURCES: BELIN 20–1, 69–72, 223, 226 • OTT 16, 52, 97

HUTCHISON, LEONARD EDWIN, owner of Hutch's Market, a grocery store in Irving, Texas. According to the WR: "[Hutchison]... has testified that on a Friday during the first week in November [1963], a man he believes to have been Oswald attempted to cash a 'two-party,' or personal check for $189, but that he refused to cash the check since his policy is to cash personal checks for no more than $25. Oswald is not known to have received a check for this amount from any source."

SOURCES: WR 309–10 • WCH X, 327 • SUMMERS 377

HUTSON, THOMAS ALEXANDER, Texas Theatre witness; DPD member. With patrolmen M. N. "Nick" McDonald, Ray Hawkins, and C. T. Walker, Hutson entered the Texas Theatre through the rear entrance.

SOURCES: WR 165 • WCH VII, 26 • BISHOP 213

HUTTON, BILL, a.w.; Dallas County Sheriff's Department deputy constable. Hutton stood at the corner of Main and Houston with fellow deputy constable Seymour Weitzman. As far as we know, no one ever asked Hutton what he heard or saw. (See also Weitzman, Seymour)

SOURCE: CF 74

HUTTON, PATRICIA (See GUSTAFSON, PATRICIA)

HYDE, MARIE, Oswald witness. Hyde was an elderly American woman who, while touring the USSR in August 1961, encountered and photographed Oswald in Minsk. She says this was coincidence. Author Anthony Summers argues that Hyde could have been an American agent sent to the USSR to check up on Oswald. For one thing, she told her traveling companions—Rita Naman and Monica Kramer, whom she had just met—that she had gotten separated from her tour group and was seeking company—an unlikely scenario, considering Intourist's tight restrictions on Americans traveling in the USSR at that time. (See also Naman, Rita; Kramer, Monica)

SOURCE: SUMMERS 183–5

HYDE, RUTH (See PAINE, RUTH)

HYDE, WILLIAM AVERY, father of Marina Oswald's friend Ruth Paine; possible associate of Oswald's friend George DeMohrenschildt. Were the Oswalds' social lives manufactured?
SOURCE: HT 300, 302

I

INGRAM, HIRAM, suspicious death; Dallas sheriff. According to Penn Jones Jr., Ingram had knowledge of an assassination conspiracy. He fell and broke his hip on April 1, 1968—and died of "cancer" three days later at the age of 53. Ingram was a friend and former colleague of Roger Craig, who also suffered because of what he knew. (See also Craig, Roger)
SOURCES: HT 142 • FMG III, 15

ISAACS, HAROLD R., possible CIA agent; died 1988. In 1963 Isaacs was a research associate specializing in international youth movements at the Massachusetts Institute of Technology's Center for International Studies. According to David Wise and Thomas B. Ross's book, *The Invisible Government* (Random House, 1964, p. 243), the Center was a CIA think tank. According to author Dick Russell, in the 1930s Isaacs was the editor of a "radical English-language weekly" in Shanghai. Two books about the Far East written at the time describe Isaacs as a "Trotskyist." Isaacs covered the Far East for *Newsweek* during World War II.

After the assassination, the FBI investigated a possible connection between Isaacs and Oswald's favorite cousin, the globetrotting Marilyn Murret, who was 12 years older than Oswald and who was herself suspected of being a CIA agent. The FBI vaguely concluded that Murret "was linked in some manner with the apparatus of Professor Harold Isaacs." (See also Giesbrecht, Richard; Murret, Marilyn)
SOURCES: WCD 942 • RUSSELL 28, 38, 119–23, 128, 132–33, 141, 145

ISAACS, MARTIN, Oswald witness; employee of the Special Services Welfare Center, New York City. After Oswald returned from the Soviet Union in June 1962, he appealed to the center to help his family. Isaacs granted the Oswalds a loan, put them up overnight in a Times Square hotel,

and then booked them on a commercial flight to Dallas, via Atlanta.
    SOURCES: WCH VIII, 324 • BISHOP 317

IVANOV, YEVGENNI M., clandestine GRU officer stationed at the Soviet embassy in London, England, 1959 to 1963. According to author Michael H. B. Eddowes, this man—along with Soviet premier Nikita Khrushchev—was part of the plot to assassinate JFK.
    SOURCE: KKK iii

IVON, LOUIS, assistant district attorney under Jim Garrison in New Orleans during the investigation and trial of Clay Shaw. Ivon was the investigator who initially gathered information about assassination suspect David Ferrie. (See also Garrison, Jim; Shaw, Clay)
    SOURCE: OTT, many

J

JACKS, HURCHEL, a.w.; Texas highway patrolman. Jacks was the driver of the motorcade's fourth car, a four-door Lincoln convertible carrying LBJ. After the shooting, Jacks was assigned to guard JFK's limo. He said on November 28, 1963, "We were assigned by the [SS] to prevent any pictures of any kind to be taken of the President's car on the inside." It is hoped that these orders came out of sensitivity to the Kennedy family—to prevent morbid souvenirs.

SOURCES: WCE 1024 • HT 86 • BISHOP 103 • DOP 129, 136, 145, 153, 161, 166 • CF 9

JACKSON, C. D., suspicious death; *Life* magazine publisher; alleged CIA propagandist. Jackson purchased and suppressed the Zapruder film. He died in September 1964 of unknown causes. HT called Jackson a "Cold-Warrior." *Life* magazine, in its original publication of frames from the Zapruder film, reversed the order of those frames so that it appeared as if JFK's head had snapped forward rather than rearward with the impact of the final shot. (Dan Rather also reported to the American people that JFK's head snapped forward, and the CBS correspondent reportedly had seen the film. (See also Rather, Dan; Zapruder, Abraham)

SOURCES: HT 284 • CF 66–7 • OGLESBY 72

JACKSON, MURRAY JAMES, DPD officer; friend of Officer J. D. Tippit for 20 years. Jackson was the radio dispatcher who instructed Tippit to patrol the Oak Cliff section of Dallas—where Tippit met his death—when virtually all other mobile personnel had been ordered to Dealey Plaza. (See also Tippit, Jefferson)

SOURCES: HSCA XII, 36 • HT 276 • RTJ 206 • BISHOP 200

JACKSON, ROBERT HILL, a.w.; o.k.w.; *Dallas Times-Herald* photographer. Jackson rode in the convertible press car near the end of the motorcade with fellow photographer Malcolm Couch. He saw a rifle being withdrawn from the "sniper's-nest" window in the TSBD and screamed, "There is the gun!" He is one of the few known witnesses to see a rifle or a pipe protruding from that window. Jackson was criticized by WC counsel David W. Belin for not immediately contacting a policeman, so the TSBD could have been sealed off immediately, rather than after several minutes. That way Oswald would not have been able to escape and Officer J. D. Tippit's life would have been saved, says Belin.

Jackson's photo of Ruby shooting a grimacing Oswald won a Pulitzer Prize. (See also Couch, Malcolm; Dillard, Thomas; Darnell, James; Underwood, James)

SOURCES: WR 76–7 • WCH II, 155 • WCE 2002 • BELIN 8, 31, 63, 73 • DOP 159

JACKSON, THEODORE, WC witness. Attendant at the All State parking lot, 2305 Main Street in Dallas. Jackson told the WC he saw policemen searching Ruby's car after the shooting of Oswald. Jackson was not a fruitful witness. Perhaps the WC didn't know ahead of time that Jackson had come on duty after Oswald was already shot.

SOURCE: WCH XIII, 299

JACOB, STELLA, a.w. Jacob stood on the north side of Elm midway between the TSBD and the triple underpass, with Jeannie Holt and Sharon Nelson. None of these three was called to testify for the WC. This probably indicates that they didn't think the shots came from the TSBD.

SOURCE: RTJ 110

JADA (See CONFORTO, JANET ADAMS)

JAMES, ROSEMARY, author, with Jack Wardlaw, of *Plot or Politics?* (Pelican Publishing, 1967), a look at New Orleans District Attorney Jim Garrison's investigation into JFK's death.

JAMES, VIRGINIA H., international relations officer, Office of Soviet Affairs, State Department. James told the WC that she received a telegram from the U.S. embassy in Moscow dated October 31, 1959, saying that Oswald had tried to renounce his U.S. citizenship. On October 3, 1961, James sent a cable to the same embassy authorizing Marina Oswald's visa. She sent another memo to the same destination on March 16, 1962, advising the embassy to get the Oswalds back to the United States, and explained to the WC that the policy was to keep husbands and wives together.

SOURCE: WCH XI, 180

JANUARY, WAYNE, possible Oswald witness. January ran a plane-rental

business at Redbird Airport near Dallas. He told FBI after the assassination that, on November 20, 1963, he was approached by two men who wanted to rent a plane for a flight to Mexico on the afternoon of the assassination. He said he "didn't like the look of them" and refused to rent the plane. (See also White, Roscoe)
SOURCE: NORTH 369.

JARMAN, JAMES, JR. "JUNIOR," a.w. Jarman was one of three men who watched from the fifth floor of the TSBD, one floor below where Oswald allegedly fired the shots. When Jarman heard the shots, his first reaction was that the shots had come from below. (See also Norman, Harold; Williams, Bonnie Ray)
SOURCES: WR 78–80, 134–5, 143, 170, 232 • WCH III, 198 • BELIN 11, 15, 57, 60, 73–4, 220 • RTJ 89–90, 100–2, 104–8, 113 • BISHOP 45, 58–9, 121, 136, 141, 150 • CF 47–9 • PWW 132 • SUMMERS 76

JARNAGIN, CARROLL, Ruby witness; possible Oswald witness; Dallas attorney. On December 5, 1963, the FBI received the following letter/ statement from Jarnagin:

> Dear Mr. Hoover,
>   On Oct. 4, 1963 I was in the Carousel in Dallas, Texas, and while there I heard Jack Ruby talking to a man using the name H.L. Lee. These men were talking about plans to kill the Governor of Texas. This information was passed on to the Texas Department of Public Safety on Oct. 5, 1963 by telephone. On Sunday Nov. 24, 1963 I definitely realized that the picture in the Nov. 23, 1963 Dallas Times Herald of Lee Harvey Oswald was a picture of the man using the name of H.L. Lee, whose conversation with Jack Ruby I had overheard back on Oct. 4, 1963.

According to Jarnagin, Ruby was plotting to kill Connally because the governor would not cooperate with organized crime. The FBI sent a copy of Jarnagin's document to Dallas County District Attorney Henry Wade, who dismissed it with the statement: "It didn't ring true to me." Jarnagin was not called as a witness by the WC. Wade told the WC that Jarnagin had been given a polygraph examination, which indicated that he had been in the Carousel but had not heard a suspicious conversation.
SOURCES: WCD 2821 • KANTOR 206–7, 209

JENKINS, JAMES CURTIS, Bethesda witness; Navy laboratory technician. Jenkins assisted Paul O'Connor in moving JFK's body from the coffin to the autopsy table. (See also O'Connor, Paul)

SOURCES: SUMMERS 76 • BE, many

JENKINS, MARION T., Parkland witness; chief anesthesiologist. Jenkins attended to JFK and told the WC that he did not see an entrance wound in the back of Kennedy's head, thus supporting allegations that the autopsy evidence (both written and photographic) has been doctored to conform with the official version of the facts. Jenkins said, "There was a great laceration on the right side of the head... even to the extent that the cerebellum had protruded from the wound... I would interpret it [as] being a wound of exit."

When author Harrison Edward Livingstone showed the purported JFK autopsy photos to Jenkins, he disagreed with what they showed. Jenkins said, beating at the back of his head with his fingertips, "Well, that picture doesn't look like it from the back... You could tell at this point with your fingers that it was scored out, that the edges were blasted out."

In Jenkins's written report, he noted that JFK had chest damage, a fact the WC had to disregard to sell the "single-bullet" theory. That theory involved raising the wound in JFK's back to the back of his neck so that it would correspond to JFK's throat wound, which in turn was changed from an entrance wound into an exit wound.

After years of having his own opinions differ so strongly with the official version of the facts, Jenkins did the natural thing: he began to believe that he was mistaken. Jenkins later said, "The first day I had thought that the one bullet must have... gotten into the lung cavity, I mean, from what you say now, I know it did not go that way. I thought it did." Jenkins's waffling opinion does not alter the fact that, while JFK was in the Parkland Hospital Emergency Room, a tube was inserted into his chest for drainage.

Today Jenkins is chairman of the Southwestern Medical School's Department of Anesthesiology.

SOURCES: WR 66–7 • WCH VI, 45 • HT 46, 48–50, 63–4, 88, 230, 453 • WCE 392 • BISHOP 156 • DOP, many • RTJ 59 • FLAMMONDE 268

JENKINS, RONALD LEE, Ruby witness; 27-year-old news editor for KBOX radio in Dallas. Jenkins saw Ruby just outside Captain Will Fritz's office where Oswald was being interrogated on Saturday afternoon, November 23, 1963—as well as at other times during the weekend within the DPD station.

SOURCE: WCH XV, 600

JENNER, ALBERT E., JR., WC counsel; former Northwestern University professor; Chicago attorney. Jenner investigated Oswald's life in the United States. His chapter was called "Area III: Oswald's Background

History, Acquaintances and Motives." Later, during the impeachment investigation of the House Judiciary Committee under Peter Rodino, Jenner was approved by President Nixon to serve as minority counsel for the Republican Party.
SOURCES: HT 331 • BELIN 46 • FMG III, 14, 78 • OTT 46, 68–9, 73 • FLAMMONDE 20, 138–9 • EVICA 8, 11, 296, 298 • DAVIS 412

JIMISON, R. J., Parkland witness; orderly. Jimison helped lift Governor Connally off the gurney and onto the operating table. He then pushed the empty gurney back into the hallway. (See also Connally, John)
SOURCES: WCH VI, 125 • BISHOP 187

JOESTEN, JOACHIM, frequently published assassination researcher (see bibliography). Joesten died at the age of 68 in 1976. Joesten writes in his book *Marina Oswald* (Peter Dawnay Ltd., 1967) (pp. 36–37):

The Russians never pay any foreign Communists, even the truest and most tested ones, for coming to the Soviet Union and extolling the virtues of communism from that safe sanctuary. Indeed, they only grant asylum to those most conspicuously in grave danger in their homelands and those who, exceptionally, are allowed to stay in the Soviet Union and are immediately put to work as translators, interpreters, analysts, economists or workers. They never receive a red Kopek just for expressing belief in communism as supposedly... Oswald did. In Minsk, where he lived for more than two years, doing unskilled work in a factory at the lowest pay rates, Oswald was never in a position to hold a press conference, to speak over the radio, to write for publication, or in any other way to make even a modest contribution to Communist propaganda. Why on Earth, then, should the Soviet secret police subsidize him to the tune of 700 rubles a month, putting him on a par, financially, with the director of the plant where he worked? Why, moreover, should the Soviet authorities make available to Oswald a comfortable apartment, one of the rarest and most eagerly sought-after amenities of life in the Soviet Union? Just because, in Moscow, upon his arrival, he had been ranting a bit about the "great Soviet Union"? Does it make any kind of sense?

SOURCES: FMG III, 100 • PWW 89 • FLAMMONDE 144, 146–8 • PD 72

JOHNS, THOMAS L. "LEM," a.w.; SS agent. Johns rode in the right rear of the SS vice-presidential follow-up car, three cars behind JFK's limo. In his written report, Johns said, "On the right hand side... a grassy area sloped upward... I was looking to the right and saw a man standing and

then being thrown or hit to the ground... " (See also Arnold, Gordon)
SOURCES: HSCA Report 184, 235 • DOP, many • FMG III, 17 • ME 305

JOHNSON, ARNOLD SAMUEL, Oswald witness; director of the Information and Lecture Bureau of the Communist Party, U.S.A. In 1962, according to the WR:

> Oswald... attempted to initiate... dealings with the Communist Party USA [with regard to his New Orleans chapter of the FPCC]... the organization was not especially responsive... [Johnson informed Oswald] that although the Communist Party had no "organizational ties" with the [FPCC], the party issued much literature which was "important for anybody who is concerned about developments in Cuba." In September 1963 Oswald inquired how he might contact the party when he relocated in the Baltimore-Washington area, as he said he planned to do in October, and Johnson suggested in a letter of September 19 that he "get in touch with us [in New York] and we will... [get]... in touch with you in [Baltimore]." However, Oswald had also written asking whether, "handicapped as it were, by... [his] past record" he could "still... compete with antiprogressive forces, above ground or whether in your opinion... [he] should always remain in the background, i.e. underground," and in the September 19 letter received the reply that "often it is advisable for some people to remain in the background, not underground."

Oswald wrote in one letter to Johnson: "On October 23, I had attended a [sic] ultra-right meeting headed by General Edwin a. [sic] Walker, who lives in Dallas... This meeting preceded by one day the attack on a.e. [sic] Stevenson at the United Nations Day meeting at which he spoke... As you can see, political friction between 'left' and 'right' is very great here." Oswald mailed Johnson, Gus Hall, and Benjamin J. Davis "honorary membership cards" to his New Orleans chapter of the FPCC. (See also Davis, Benjamin; Hall, Gus)
SOURCES: WR 266–7, 272, 385–6, 390–1

JOHNSON, MR. and MRS. ARTHUR CARL, Oswald witnesses. The Johnsons are the estranged couple who owned the house maintained by Earlene Roberts (1026 North Beckley), where Oswald was living, separated from his wife Marina, at the time of the assassination. Mrs. Johnson testified to the WC before Roberts did, and her statements were used to discredit Roberts's later claims. Roberts testified that about a half hour after the assassination, while Oswald was inside the rooming house putting on a jacket, a DPD squad car stopped directly outside, honked its horn twice, then drove on. Mrs. Johnson said she fired Roberts because she "had a lot of handicaps" like "talking, just sitting down and making up tales... have you ever seen people like that? Just have a creative mind, there's nothing to it, and just make up and keep talking until she makes a lie out of it." (See also Roberts, Earlene)

SOURCES: WR 123, 154, 574, 583, 656 • WCH X, 292, 301 • BISHOP 27, 181, 217, 240–1, 426 • FMG I, 174

JOHNSON, CLEMON E., a.w. Johnson stood atop the triple underpass and observed smoke coming from the grassy knoll following the shooting.

SOURCES: RTJ 40 • COA 22 • CF 58

JOHNSON, CLYDE, Ruby witness; Oswald witness; suspicious death. Johnson was a Kentwood, Louisiana, preacher who once ran for Louisiana governor on an anti-JFK platform. On the day before Johnson was scheduled to testify in New Orleans against Clay Shaw (February 18, 1969) regarding the personal relationship between Clay Shaw and Oswald, he was severely beaten. He never testified. Previously he told Jim Garrison that on September 2, 1963, from 2:00 to 9:00 P.M., he had spoken with Ruby, Clay Shaw, and Oswald at the Jack Tar Capital House in Baton Rouge, Louisiana. Soon thereafter (July 23, 1969), Johnson was killed at age 37 in a shotgun attack near Greensburg, Louisiana.

SOURCES: HT 129, 136 • FMG III, 81

JOHNSON, GUY P., attorney; ONI reserve officer. Johnson was the first attorney to defend Clay Shaw after he was arrested in New Orleans for conspiracy to assassinate the president. Johnson also knew former G-man and Oswald associate Guy Banister, and successfully recommended Banister's services to the ONI.

SOURCES: HSCA X, 123–32 • HT 289 • OTT 26 • FLAMMONDE 74, 77

JOHNSON, JOSEPH WELDON, JR., Ruby witness; bandleader at Carousel Club for six years. Johnson told author Mark Lane that Ruby knew at least half of the 1,200 Dallas policemen and that cops visited the Carousel "all the time" and were "treated royally."

SOURCES: WCH XV, 218 • RTJ 235

JOHNSON, "LADY BIRD," (née Taylor, Claudia Alta) a.w.; future First Lady; rode in motorcade next to her husband, LBJ, two cars behind JFK's limo.

SOURCES: WR 57, 59, 65, 70–2 • WCH V, 564 • RTJ 44 • GERTZ 202 • BISHOP, many • DOP, many • FMG III, 89, 97 • BLAKEY 11, 17, 262)

JOHNSON, LYNDON BAINES, a.w.; U.S. vice president before the assassination, 36th president afterward; former Texas senator. Johnson rode in the presidential motorcade with Senator Ralph Yarborough, two cars behind JFK. According to Yarborough, during the shooting sequence, LBJ had his ear pressed against a walkie-talkie that was "turned down real low." Johnson went to Parkland, where there were initial erroneous rumors that he had been wounded in the arm. He was kept in hiding at the hospital and then taken to Love Field, where his departure for Washington was delayed while they waited for JFK's body and the former First Lady to arrive. On the plane, still on the ground in Dallas, LBJ was sworn in as president, a mere technicality since the U.S. Constitution gave him complete powers of the presidency the instant JFK died. LBJ addressed the nation as president for the first time from Andrews Air Force Base in Washington, immediately after deplaning from Air Force One: "This is a sad time for all people. We have suffered a loss that cannot be weighed. For me it is a deep personal tragedy. I know the world shares the sorrow that Mrs. Kennedy and her family bear. I will do my best. That is all I can do. I ask for your help—and God's."

It has been alleged that, during his time in Congress, LBJ's career was subsidized largely by Dallas oil billionaire H. L. Hunt. According to author Craig I. Zirbel, "If [JFK] had not been murdered the [Bobby] Baker investigation would not have ended... [it] would have either destroyed or tarnished Johnson's image so completely that he would not have been on the 1964 ticket... the truth about LBJ may have put him in prison... rather than into the White House."

Immediately following the assassination, LBJ decided that—for the good of the country—it was best if all rumors, true or otherwise, concerning a conspiracy to kill JFK were squelched. He formed the WC largely to "prove" that Oswald and Ruby were a pair of lone nuts, each working alone.

That doesn't mean that LBJ believed it was true. On a *CBS Reports* special called "The American Assassins (Part II)," broadcast on November 26, 1975, LBJ said, "[Oswald] was quite a mysterious fellow, and he did have a connection that bore examination, and the extent of the influence of those connections on him I think history will deal with more than we're able to now."

In 1970, Walter Cronkite interviewed LBJ. Of that interview, Cronkite said to the AP in 1992: "He said he'd never been sure the Warren Commission was right, that he'd always thought there was a possibility of a conspiracy in Kennedy's death. He just tossed it off and then he wouldn't talk anymore about it. He indicated that he thought [the conspiracy] was international, but he wouldn't go into it. He seemed to be a little embarrassed about having brought it up, as if he didn't have anything to back it up. It seemed it was just a feeling he had." LBJ later made a personal request to CBS chairman William Paley that his comments regarding the assassination be deleted from the broadcast of the Cronkite interview.

According to Madeleine Brown, who claims to have been LBJ's mistress at the time of the assassination, LBJ had foreknowledge of the assassination but did nothing to prevent it because of his lust for power and his hatred for JFK. (See also Baker, Bobby; Brooks, Jack; Brown, Madeleine; Califano, Joseph; Carter, Clifton; Cronkite, Walter; Ferrell, Mary; Hughes, Sarah; Kirkwood, Pat; Kopechne, Mary Jo; Putnam, James; Thornberry, Homer; Tyler, Carole; Zirbel, Craig)
SOURCES: WR, many • WCH V, 561 • HT 17, 20, 40, 151, 282, 307, 310, 315, 357 • BELIN 1, 12–3, 122, 140, 143, 146, 149 • RTJ 7, 23, 44, 128, 304, 307, 340 • *Four Days* 38–39, 60 • COA, many • GERTZ 172, 388, 470, 473–4, 507, 538 • BISHOP, many • DOP, many • CF 9, 289–98 • FMG I, 64–5, 150, 186; III, 2–4, 9–13, 16–8, 22, 24, 72, 83, 89, 94, 97–9, 103, 106 • PWW, many • OTT 14, 273, 282, 293 • SUMMERS 101, 408, 410, 428, 532–3 • BLAKEY, many • DAVIS, many • NORTH, many • PD, many • TEX, many

JOHNSON, MARVIN, a.w. (aftermath); 43-year-old DPD detective (Homicide & Robbery). Johnson was assigned to guard the "sniper's nest" on the sixth floor of the TSBD on the afternoon of November 22, 1963.
SOURCES: WCH VII, 100

JOHNSON, PRISCILLA MARY POST (aka McMillan, Priscilla), Oswald witness; journalist and author. Johnson interviewed Oswald in the Soviet Union on November 16, 1959, for the North American Newspaper Alliance. She was impressed that, while Oswald was outspoken about his desire to renounce his American citizenship, he never bothered to follow through with the necessary paperwork. She wrote the book *Marina and Lee* (Harper & Row, 1977).
SOURCES: WR 242, 247–8 • WCH XI, 442 • BELIN 47 • DUFFY 38 • CF 120 • MOORE 216 • SUMMERS 571 • BLAKEY 345, 348–9, 351–5, 358 • PD 48, 51, 67–71, 312, 354

JOHNSON, SPEEDY, Ruby witness; Houston aircraft broker and manufacturer's agent. Johnson met Ruby in June or July 1963 in the Carousel Club and told the WC that Ruby picked up his tab despite never having met him before. He saw Ruby at Sol's Turf Bar on November 23. Ruby complained about the anti-JFK ad that had run the previous day in the *Dallas Morning News* and about the IMPEACH EARL WARREN sign he had photographed the previous night. Ruby said, "We ought to shoot all of them sonsofbitches." Johnson was under the impression that Ruby was advocating the shooting of Earl Warren. Johnson legally had his name changed to "Speedy."

SOURCE: WCH XV, 607

JOHNSON, TOM, Ruby witness; former aide to LBJ. Johnson interviewed Ruby, who said, "It is the most bizarre conspiracy in the history of the world. It'll come out at a future date... I walked into a trap when I walked down there. I wasn't clean enough. It was my destiny. I'd taken 30 antibiotic and Dexedrine pills. They stimulate you."

Johnson also interviewed Dallas Chief of Police Jesse Curry, who told him, "We don't have any proof that Oswald fired the rifle, never did. Nobody's yet been able to put him in that building with a gun in his hand." (See also Curry, Jesse)

SOURCES: HT 237 • FMG III, 106–7 • EVICA 155, 320

JOHNSTON, DAVID L., Oswald witness; Dallas justice of the peace. Johnston presided over the 7:10 P.M. (November 22, 1963) arraignment of Oswald for the Tippit murder in Captain Will Fritz's office on the third floor of the Dallas police station and the 1:30 A.M. (November 23, 1963) arraignment for the JFK assassination (murder with malice) held in the Dallas police station's fourth-floor identification bureau. The judge later said, "Oswald was very conceited. He said sarcastically, 'I guess this is the trial' and denied everything."

SOURCES: WR 186, 189, 366 • WCH IV, 155, 221; XV, 503 • DOP 426

JONES, JANICE N., Ruby witness; former waitress at the Carousel Club. Jones told FBI agents that Ruby never charged policemen who came into his club and that sometimes he would give them bottles of liquor.

SOURCES: RTJ 160–3 • COA 112

JONES, ORVILLE A., o.k.w.; DPD captain, member of the DPD's Criminal Investigations Division. Jones was involved in the badly botched security precautions made before Oswald's aborted transfer and subsequent death. On November 23, 1963, Jones told a *New York Post* reporter that the DPD had a "conclusive case against Oswald."

SOURCES: WR 198–9, 212–3 • WCH XII, 58 • RTJ 210 • FLAMMONDE 132

JONES, PAUL ROWLAND, Ruby witness; Chicago mobster. In 1946, Jones tried to bribe the Dallas sheriff's department and the Dallas district attorney into allowing the mob to operate a nightclub/gambling casino in Dallas unhindered. He offered the Dallas officials $1,000 a week—and was promptly arrested and charged with attempted bribery. According to former Dallas sheriff Steve Guthrie in a 1963 statement, the man the mob planned to put in charge of their Dallas operation was Jack Ruby, who arrived in Dallas in 1947 and promptly set up a nightclub. Jones later became known as the mob's "paymaster in Dallas" and met with Ruby only days before the assassination.

SOURCES: WR 793 • WCH XXII, 360 • HSCA IX, 513 • SUMMERS 434–5, 447–8 • DAVIS 184, 227 • NORTH 357–8, 487

JONES, PENN, JR., editor of the *Midlothian* (Texas) *Mirror* (circulation less than 1,000); author of *Forgive My Grief* (Volumes I–IV). Jones has been a breakthrough researcher concerning the mysterious deaths that followed the assassination. He claims to have taken a photograph that shows Ruby on the grounds of Parkland Hospital immediately following the assassination of JFK. (Unfortunately, the photo shows the man's back.) Jones reported that, at Parkland, one hospital employee had the nerve to ask Mrs. Kennedy if he might keep the president's T-shirt. (Author Josiah Thompson suggests that this "souvenir hunting" may be responsible for the location of the "magic bullet" at the time it was discovered. Perhaps, Thompson suggests, someone picked up the bullet and then, realizing its importance, placed it on the nearest empty stretcher.) Jones claims that, on the eve of the assassination, J. Edgar Hoover and Richard M. Nixon were both at the house of Texas oil billionaire Clint Murchison. Every year, on the anniversary of the assassination, Jones holds a memorial service at Dealey Plaza. (See also Hoover, J. Edgar; Murchison, Clint; Nixon, Richard M.)

SOURCES: HT 132, 155–6, 282, 464 • COA 33 • GERTZ 125, 528 • FLAMMONDE 177, 331

JONES, R. MILTON. Part of the reason the WC believed that Oswald had gotten on a bus immediately following the assassination were the statements of bus driver Cecil J. McWatters, who said that Oswald was on his bus following the shooting and grinned when told of the assassination. The next day, McWatters was driving the same bus along the same route when Milton Jones got on. McWatters immediately realized that it was Jones and not Oswald who was on the bus. He tried to withdraw his previous statements, but was ignored—probably because the appropriate bus transfer was found in Oswald's pocket hours after his arrest. (See also McWatters, Cecil)

SOURCE: WR 148

JONES, ROBERT, lieutenant colonel, U.S. Army, operations officer for the 112th Military Intelligence Group, San Antonio, Texas. Jones received a report from Dallas hours after JFK's death that an "A. J. Hidell" had been

arrested; he claims there was no mention in the report of Oswald's name. Jones looked up Hidell in his files and found it cross-referenced to Oswald.
SOURCES: HSCA Report 221 • SUMMERS 60–1

JONES, RONALD COY, Parkland witness; chief resident in surgery. Jones treated JFK and gave a detailed written description of JFK's throat wound as an entrance wound. He told the WC:

> The hole was very small and relatively clean cut, as you would see in a bullet that is entering rather than exiting a patient. If this were an exit wound, you would think that it exited at a very low velocity to produce no more damage than this had done, and if this were a missile of high velocity, you would expect more of an explosive type of exit wound, with more tissue destruction than this appeared to have on superficial examination... [there] appeared to be an exit wound in the posterior portion of the skull... There was a large defect in the back side of the head as the President lay in the cart with what appeared to be brain tissue hanging out of this wound with multiple pieces of skull noted next with [sic] the brain and with a tremendous amount of clot and blood.

Years later, when Jones was shown the JFK autopsy photos by the *Boston Sun*, he said, "the wound was not the same as what he saw in 1963." Jones was interviewed in 1988 on KRON-TV in San Francisco, at which time he said that the official JFK autopsy X rays, reportedly taken at Bethesda Hospital, do not accurately represent JFK's wounds. According to HT, those X rays show a head with severe facial damage—an eye socket appears to be completely missing—and JFK's face was intact in death. (See also Crenshaw, Charles)
SOURCES: WR 66–7 • WCH VI, 51 • HT 43, 451, 460 • RTJ 52, 54, 58 • BISHOP 156 • HOS 182 • ME 35, 53

K

KAACK, MILTON R., Oswald witness; FBI agent. According to the WR, Kaack ran the first FBI background check on Oswald after Oswald's return from the USSR. Kaack gave his gathered information to Dallas agent James P. Hosty, who was in charge of Oswald's case and had interviewed Oswald since his return to the United States. In this manner, Hosty learned that Oswald had lied to him on a number of points: his wife's maiden name was not Prossa, and he and Marina had not been married in Fort Worth, Texas.

Kaack's report also revealed that Oswald had lied when he told his arresting officers in New Orleans that he had been born in Cuba.

Nina Gardner, Oswald's landlady in New Orleans, says she was questioned about Oswald by Kaack less than three weeks after Oswald's arrival in New Orleans. According to author Anthony Summers, Kaack "did indeed investigate Oswald," but refuses to discuss his investigation. FBI Director J. Edgar Hoover told the WC that he had submitted an affidavit from every FBI agent who had contacted Oswald—yet there was none from Kaack. (See also Hosty, James P.)
SOURCES: WR 412 • HSCA Report 191 • SUMMERS 281

KAIL, SAMUEL, colonel, U.S. Army Intelligence. Kail, a Texan, worked closely with George DeMohrenschildt after DeMohrenschildt left Dallas and moved to Haiti. According to author Anthony Summers, "Kail specialized in Cuban intelligence operations involving Army intelligence and the CIA." Kail says that he met DeMohrenschildt at an Army intelligence meeting. (See also DeMohrenschildt, George)
SOURCES: SUMMERS 219, 505–6

KAISER, FRANKIE, TSBD employee. Kaiser found Oswald's work clipboard on December 2, 1963, on the sixth floor of the TSBD in the corner near the stairs, not far from where a rifle had been discovered ten days earlier. How thorough could the initial search of the sixth floor have been? Perhaps the clipboard had been placed there sometime after the assassination to further incriminate Oswald.

SOURCES: WR 133 • WCH VI, 341 • BELIN 56–7

KALUGIN, OLEG DANILOVICH, former Russian major general. Kalugin headed the KGB's foreign counterintelligence service. In 1990, Kalugin denounced the KGB, where he had been employed for 32 years. He told the *New York Times* (January 20, 1992) that Oswald was not recruited by the KGB in the USSR because he was viewed as a CIA plant.

KAMINSKY, EILEEN, Ruby witness; his sister. Ruby called Kaminsky in Chicago about 90 minutes after the assassination. She said that Ruby was "completely unnerved and crying about President Kennedy's death."

SOURCES: WR 315 • WCH XV, 275 • COA 152 • GERTZ, many • PWW 40 • BLAKEY 282–3

KANTOR, SETH, a.w.; Parkland witness; Ruby witness. Kantor rode in motorcade as a reporter for the Scripps-Howard newspapers and told the WC that he saw and *spoke to* Ruby at Parkland Hospital around 1:28 P.M., just before JFK's death was announced. The WC chose to believe that Kantor was mistaken. It is unlikely that he was, since he had known Ruby for a long time and engaged him in conversation. If Ruby was in Parkland Hospital at that time, he could have planted the pristine bullet (WCE 399) on a stretcher, thus linking the assassination with the "Oswald" rifle.

Kantor is the author of *Who Was Jack Ruby?* (Everest House, 1978), reissued as *The Ruby Cover-Up* (Zebra, 1992). He died at 67, on August 17, 1993, of cardiac arrest in a Washington hospital, one week before hundreds of thousands of pages of long-sealed JFK assassination files were released to the National Archives. (See also Tice, Wilma)

SOURCES: WR 313–4 • WCH XV, 71 • HSCA Report 158–9 • EVICA 162 • ME 24 • RTJ 263–5, 267–70, 384 • COA 100, 125–6, 234, 256 • GERTZ 527 • BISHOP 33, 80–1, 205, 311–2, 370 • CF 206–7, 366–7 • PWW 265 • SUMMERS 104–5, 455, 466, 470 • FMG I, 22–3, 25, 30, 67, 74 • BLAKEY 291, 293, 297, 308, 315, 318 • DAVIS 222, 297–9 • NORTH 406, 496

KAPLAN, JOHN, coauthor with Jon R. Waltz of *The Trial of Jack Ruby* (Macmillan, 1965).

SOURCE: GERTZ 42, 251–61, 343

KARAMESSINES, TOM, CIA agent. Karamessines was Richard Helms's assistant and alleged author of a 1966 internal CIA memo to Helms stating that E. Howard Hunt had been in Dallas on November 22, 1963, while working on CIA business. The memo expressed concern that this fact

would be discovered. (See also Helms, Richard; Helperan, Sammy; Hunt, E. Howard)
SOURCE: HT 345

KARNEI, ROBERT, Bethesda witness; U.S. Navy pathologist. Karnei was stationed at the door to the autopsy room and determined who was allowed in and out. Karnei says the autopsy was limited by orders from representatives of the Kennedy family.
SOURCES: HT2 120, 140–1, 156, 199, 234, 300, 334, 581

KATZENBACH, NICHOLAS deB., deputy attorney general. On November 25, 1963, Katzenbach wrote a memo to LBJ press secretary Bill Moyers, which stated:

It is important that all of the facts surrounding President Kennedy's assassination be made public in a way which will satisfy people in the United States and abroad that all of the facts have been told and that a statement to this effect be made now, 1) The public must be satisfied that Oswald was the assassin; that he did not have confederates who are still at large; and that the evidence was such that he would have been convicted at trial. 2) Speculation about Oswald's motivation ought to be cut off, and we should have some basis for rebutting thought that this was a Communist conspiracy or (as the Iron Curtain press is saying) a right-wing conspiracy to blame it on the communists. Unfortunately, the facts on Oswald seem too pat—too obvious (Marxist, Cuba, Russian wife, etc.) The Dallas police have put out statements on the Communist conspiracy theory, and it was they who were in charge when he was shot and thus silenced. 3) The matter has been handled thus far with neither dignity nor conviction. Facts have been mixed with rumor and speculation. We can scarcely let the world see us totally in the image of the Dallas police when our President is murdered...I think this objective may be satisfied by making public as soon as possible a complete and thorough FBI report on Oswald and the assassination. This may run into the difficulty of pointing to inconsistencies between the report and statements by Dallas police officials. But the reputation of the Bureau is such that it may do the whole job.

SOURCES: HSCA Report 238 • OGLESBY 11–2 • ME 12, 232 • HT 257 • COA 19–20, 209–10, 221, 433 • DOP, many • DAVIS 266, 268, 274–6, 283, 305, 308–10, 317, 319, 334 • NORTH, many • PD 41, 51–2

KAUFMAN, STANLEY M., Ruby witness; attorney who handled Ruby's frequent civil cases. Kaufman told the WC that he had a client named

Willie Mitchell who had been an inmate in the Dallas County Jail at the time of the assassination, with a cell that overlooked Dealey Plaza and into the TSBD. Kaufman said that Mitchell had not seen anything revealing. (There were many prisoners who saw the assassination, but the WC failed to question any of them.)

Kaufman testified at Ruby's murder trial that Ruby had called him on the day following the assassination in a "state of alarm." But Ruby says he called Kaufman at 6:00 P.M. on the day of the assassination to ask what time temple services were to be that night.

SOURCES: WR 324 • WCH XV, 513 • GERTZ 35, 61, 112, 126, 182–3 • BISHOP 358 • FMG III, 5 • OTT 94

KAY, KATHY (See OLSEN, KAY HELEN)

KEETON, STANLEY, assassination researcher. In *The Continuing Inquiry* (February 1978), Keeton wrote: "One can look in vain through the Warren Report and Exhibits and never find...the death certificate of President Kennedy. Until 1975, it had been suppressed from public examination. The death certificate was drafted on November 23, 1963, by Dr. George Burkley. According to Dr. Burkley, the non-fatal posterior wound was located in the back, at about the third thoracic vertebra." The WC did not want this information to appear in the WR because they needed to move the entrance wound high enough in JFK's back to correspond with the throat wound, and preserve the single-bullet theory. In the same article, Keeton wrote: "The truth is that the alleged autopsy photographs and X-rays have never been and cannot be authenticated. They are totally at variance with the autopsy report itself, and with all the other evidence... it is apparent that some of the autopsy materials have been fabricated." (See also Burkley, George)

SOURCE: HT 26, 76, 111–3

KELLERMAN, ROY, a.w.; Parkland witness; Bethesda witness; SS agent. Kellerman rode in the front passenger seat of the presidential limousine. He quoted JFK as saying, "My God, I am hit." No one else heard the president say anything at all after he was first wounded. (According to Howard Donahue's shooting-sequence scenario, JFK would have been able to say those words. Assassination researcher Bonar Menninger believes that the first shot did not strike JFK in the throat but rather struck Elm Street behind JFK's limo and hit the back of JFK's head with a bullet fragment.)

Kellerman attended JFK's autopsy. He told the WC: "A Colonel [Pierre A.] Finck—during the examination of the President, from the hole that was

WHO'S WHO IN THE JFK ASSASSINATION

in his shoulder, and with a probe, and we are standing right alongside of him, he is probing inside the shoulder with this instrument and I said, 'Colonel, where did it go?' He said, 'There are no lanes for an outlet of this entry in this man's shoulder.'" This does not sound like the same autopsy that determined that the bullet had not entered JFK's shoulder, but rather his neck, and that the bullet was not without outlet, but rather exited through his throat. (See also Donahue, Howard; Finck, Pierre; Greer, William)

SOURCES: WR, many • WCH II, 61 • HSCA Report 40 • EVICA 77, 92 • ME 32, 41–3, 69, 105, 110–1, 163, 218, 220, 249 • HT 55–6, 93, 148 • BELIN 4, 15–6, 27 • BISHOP, many • DOP, many • CF 12 • OTT 244 • SUMMERS 19, 21–2, 539 • BLAKEY 11 • NORTH 351, 379, 385, 406

KELLEY, THOMAS J. (also shown as Kelly), Oswald witness; SS inspector. Kelley was involved in the interrogation of Oswald following his arrest and recalls that Oswald said that the photos of him holding weapons were faked and that the Dallas police were probably responsible. Kelley was also the SS inspector in charge of evaluating SS effectiveness in Dallas, particularly in regard to reports that many SS agents had been out drinking for much of the night before the assassination in a sleazy Fort Worth nightclub. Kelley concluded, "No agent violated any [SS] rule." (See also Kirkwood, Pat)

SOURCES: WCH V, 129, 175; VII, 403, 590 • HSCA Report 233, 235, 237 • RTJ 361 • GERTZ 81, 84 • BISHOP 281, 352, 425–7, 462, 496, 528 • DOP 524 • PWW 34, 114, 127, 142, 163, 263–4 • FMG 1, 151 • EVICA 45, 149, 153

KELLY, EDWARD, 21-year-old porter at Dallas City Hall. Kelly told the WC that he was asked to leave the basement area of the DPD station before the transfer of Oswald, and he did so. He neither saw nor heard Ruby or Oswald.

SOURCE: WCH XIII, 146

KELLY, HERBERT CHARLES, Ruby witness; kitchen and food service manager at Ruby's Sovereign Club; Kelly said that he found it difficult to reconcile Ruby's stinginess (sometimes even refusing to pay his employees) with his generosity toward the DPD.

SOURCE: RTJ 235

KENNEDY, EDWARD MOORE, Democratic senator, Massachusetts; youngest brother of JFK. In a 1992 interview with WGMC-TV in Worcester, Massachusetts, Kennedy said that, although he did not plan to see Oliver Stone's movie *JFK*, he did support the film's plea that all records on the assassination be released. Kennedy said, "We're for all of the—any items that are out of our control, clearly—and other items, obviously, ought to be made public." According to a *New York Post* article (January 11, 1992), by items "out of our control" Kennedy was referring to "all records except autopsy photos and the slain president's blood-stained clothing—items that the Kennedy family has requested be made available only to forensic scholars."

Kennedy said during the WGMC interview, "I think you'll find out over any period of time that the [WC's conclusion] was clearly the most responsible result. But I respect other people's conclusions." His use of "responsible" rather than "correct" is interesting. (See also Kopechne, Mary Jo)

SOURCES: BLAKEY 18, 95, 379 • DAVIS 386, 402, 485, 505, 580–2 • PD 202

KENNEDY, JACQUELINE BOUVIER, a.w.; First Lady. Mrs. Kennedy sat to the left of JFK in the presidential limousine and said, immediately following the shooting, "No, no, they've killed Jack, I'm holding his brains in my hand." After the shooting, Mrs. Kennedy crawled onto the back of the limo to retrieve a portion of her husband's head. She had no recollection of doing this. She refused to change her clothes following the shooting and appeared in public bloodstained, saying, "I want the world to see what they did to Jack." Mrs. Kennedy's brave manner following the assassination, at the various ceremonies and the funeral, helped heal a torn nation. She told the WC:

> Well, I remember... Mrs. Connally said, "We will soon be there." We could see a tunnel in front of us. Everything was really slow then. And I remember thinking it would be so cool under that tunnel... You know, there is always noise in a motorcade and there are always motorcycles beside us, a lot of them backfiring. So I was looking to the left, I guess there was a noise, but it didn't seem like any different noise, motorcycles and things. But then Governor Connally was yelling, "Oh, no, no, no."... I was looking... to the left, and I heard these terrible noises. You know. And my husband never made a sound. So I turned to the right. And all I remember is seeing my husband, he had this sort of quizzical look on his face, and his hand was up, it must have been his left hand. And just as I turned and looked at him, I could see a piece of his skull and I remember it was flesh colored. I remember thinking he just looked as if he had a slight headache. I just remember seeing that. No blood or anything... And then I just remember falling on him and saying... "Oh my God, they have shot my husband," and "I love you, Jack." I remember I was shouting. And just being down in the car with his head in my

lap... There must have been two [shots] because the one that made me turn around was Governor Connally yelling. And it used to confuse me because first I remembered there were three and I used to think my husband didn't make any sound when he was shot. And Governor Connally screamed. And then I read the other day that it was the same shot that hit them both... But I used to think if I only had been looking to the right, I would have seen the first shot hit him, then I could have pulled him down, and then the second shot would not have hit him. But I heard Governor Connally yelling and that made me turn around, and as I turned around, my husband was doing this [holds hand to neck]. He was receiving a bullet. And those are the only two I remember.

(See also DeMohrenschildt, George; Dugger, Robert; Greer, William; Hill, Clint)

SOURCES: WR, many • WCH V, 178 • HSCA Report 38, 40 • ME 19, 55–6, 82, 110, 116, 230 • FLAMMONDE 154, 164, 195–7 • EVICA 67, 104 • OGLESBY 11, 13 • HT 18–9, 40–1, 97, 230, 448 • BELIN 2, 4, 16, 27, 35–6, 39, 41, 43 • RTJ 38, 41, 46, 49, 57, 62, 67, 72, 383–4 • COA 21, 128, 162, 166 • GERTZ 81, 185, 188, 413 • BISHOP, many • DOP, many • CF 11–15 • PWW 70, 100, 158–60, 162, 164, 202–4, 227, 230–1, 280, 284 • SUMMERS 3–4, 13–4, 18–9, 22 • FMG I, 11, 18, 28, 40, 65, 87, 150, 153, 185; III, 94, 103 • BLAKEY, many • HOS 177, 182, 190 • FOX 119–22 • DAVIS 96, 195, 308, 325, 328–9, 450 • PD 30, 51

KENNEDY, JAMES, FBI agent. With Will Griffin, Kennedy interviewed Oswald's housekeeper, Earlene Roberts. She told them, "About 1:00 P.M. on November 22, 1963, I looked out the front window and saw police car No. 207." (See also Alexander, William; Hill, Gerald L.; Roberts, Earlene; Valentine, James)

SOURCE: FMG I, 173

KENNEDY, JOHN FITZGERALD, 35th president of the United States; assassination victim. JFK managed to make a lot of enemies by the time he traveled to Dallas in November 1963. He had assigned his brother, Attorney General Robert F. Kennedy, to take on organized crime. He slept with women who also slept with mobsters. He considered dumping LBJ as his vice-presidential candidate in 1964. JFK wanted to eliminate the oil-depletion allowance, increasing federal revenues by cutting oil profits. Anti-Castro Cubans blamed him for botching the Bay of Pigs. He threatened to dismantle the CIA and alienated other right-wing factions by stating that the Vietnam War was "South Vietnam's to win or lose" and that U.S. presence there was temporary. He also made plans to retire FBI Director J. Edgar Hoover against Hoover's wishes. (See also Greer, William)

SOURCES: All texts

KENNEDY, REGIS, FBI agent. Kennedy was identified by Beverly Oliver, "The Babushka Lady," as one of two men who took from her the film she had taken of the assassination. Kennedy worked on the New Orleans part of the assassination investigation and reportedly told FBI Director J. Edgar Hoover that assassination suspect Carlos Marcello was nothing more than a "tomato salesman," Marcello's legitimate business. Kennedy is described in *High Treason* as being "deeply involved in this case." He refused to testify before the New Orleans grand jury investigating the assassination, citing "executive privilege"—i.e., LBJ gave him permission not to testify. Penn Jones Jr. wrote at the time: "It is inconceivable to us that every Federal cop in the country can refuse to talk to a secret grand jury on grounds that he works for the President; therefore can remain silent." Kennedy died in 1978, not long after testifying for the HSCA. (See also Carlson, Alex; Oliver, Beverly)
    SOURCES: HT 121, 145, 420 • COA 40 • FMG III 4, 61–3 • SUMMERS 496–7 • BLAKEY 257, 344 • FLAMMONDE 26, 59, 294 • DAVIS 84, 129–30, 152, 217–8, 235, 251, 260, 357 • NORTH, many

KENNEDY, ROBERT FRANCIS, brother of JFK; U.S. Attorney General. RFK later ran for president and was also assassinated (1968). At the time of his brother's death, RFK was on a tireless campaign to wipe out organized crime. (See also Braden, Tom; Brading, Eugene Hale; Hepburn, James; Marcello, Carlos; Hoffa, Jimmy; Partin, Edward; Sirhan, Sirhan)
    SOURCES: WR 72–3, 350 • HSCA Report 30–1, 33–4, 36, 238, • OGLESBY 4, 6 • FLAMMONDE, many • EVICA, many • ME, many • BELIN 36, 50, 114–5, 118–9, 124–6, 130, 132, 159 • RTJ 46 • BISHOP, many • DOP, many • CF 171–9, 383 • FMG III 23–4, 28, 57, 67–8, 70, 104 • PWW 9 • SUMMERS, many • FMG I, 132, 187 • BLAKEY, many • HOS 190, 193 • DAVIS, many • NORTH, many

KENNEY, EDWARD, Bethesda witness; admiral and surgeon general, U.S. Navy.
    SOURCES: BE 298, 417–8, 480, 483, 550, 608, 613, 633 • HOS 197

KERSTA, LAWRENCE, WC acoustics expert; physicist; employee, Bell Telephone Acoustics and Speech Laboratory. Kersta analyzed the DPD Dictabelt recording of the assassination 14 years before the HSCA used analyses of the same tape to conclude that there must have been a shot fired from the grassy knoll, and therefore a second gunman in Dealey Plaza. Kersta's report for the WC said: "The spectrograms indicated that there were six non-voiced noises [on the tape]." Perhaps because of this conclusion the WR made no mention of these tests.

SOURCE: HSCA Report 65–6

KERTZ, CHARLIE, Oswald witness; founder of the New Orleans Charlie's Saints Marching Band. Kertz was the deputy constable who, in 1963, evicted Oswald from his apartment at 4907 Magazine Street. "I'll never forget it," Kertz said to New Orleans *Times-Picayune* columnist Angus Lind in 1991. "It was a Friday afternoon, and it was very unusual to evict someone on a Friday afternoon." According to Lind, "Kertz said he confronted Oswald with the order to evict, showed him his credentials and told him to get his personal belongings out of the furnished apartment; otherwise they would be placed on the sidewalk, routine eviction procedure."

"The guy was so weird," said Kertz. "He didn't say a word. There was a woman with him who had a child. He came down the steps, took a right, and headed toward Audubon Park." After that, Kertz never saw him again. According to Lind, "[Kertz] and another constable went in, put a baby bed and some clothes on the sidewalk, then opened a closet and found three rifles. They unloaded them and put them out on the sidewalk. They then removed about 30 paperbacks from the closet... and underneath them were two handguns, which they unloaded and put under the mattress of the baby bed. Kertz said he figured Oswald was 'some kind of hunter.'" Neighbors of Oswald's when he lived at the Magazine Street apartment in New Orleans remember him as an odd duck. There are reports that Oswald was often seen walking backwards.

KHRUSHCHEV, NIKITA SERGEEVICH, Soviet premier. Soon after the assassination, Texas right-wing oil billionaire H. L. Hunt financed the publication of a book by Michael Eddowes titled *Khrushchev Killed Kennedy,* which has since been retitled *The Oswald File.* (See also Eddowes, Michael)

SOURCES: WR 238 • HSCA Report 25–6, 106, 132, 213 • BELIN 162 • COA 186, 193 • BISHOP 19, 52, 63, 412 • DOP 113, 366, 447, 574, 611, 653–4 • KKK, many • SUMMERS 396 • FMG I, 42 • BLAKEY 4, 109–11, 135, 139, 378 • HOS 209, 231 • FLAMMONDE 249–51, 259 • EVICA 213 • OGLESBY 6, 76–8 • PD 98, 108

KIKER, DOUGLAS, a.w.; *New York Herald Tribune* reporter. Kiker rode in the motorcade; he joined NBC in 1966 and covered the Watergate scandal for NBC. In 1970, he won a Peabody Award for his reporting on the war in Jordan. Kiker spent the last 18 years of his life covering Washington politics. He died in his sleep on August 14, 1991, in Cape Cod, Massachusetts, of an apparent heart attack at the age of 61.

SOURCE: DOP 119, 174

KILDUFF, MALCOLM "MAC," a.w.; White House assistant press secretary. Kilduff rode in the motorcade, in the front seat of the White House press-pool car. Sitting to Kilduff's left was Merriman Smith of UPI. Kilduff was the first to announce JFK's death to reporters at Parkland Hospital at 1:30 P.M. (See also Smith, Merriman)
SOURCES: WR 70, 313 • RTJ 264 • *Four Days* 32 • BISHOP, many • DOP, many • BLAKEY 17, 315 • DAVIS 222

KILGALLEN, DOROTHY, Ruby witness; suspicious death; *New York Journal American* columnist and game-show panelist on *What's My Line?* After meeting with Ruby in prison, Kilgallen said she was going to "break open the Kennedy case." Soon thereafter (November 8, 1965), before she could write an exposé, Kilgallen died in her New York home of a drug overdose. She was 52. It took eight days to officially determine the cause of death as "ingestion of alcohol and barbiturates." Her good friend and confidante, Mrs. Earl T. Smith, died only two days later, cause of death officially unknown. (See also Smith, Mrs. Earl T.)
SOURCES: HT 129, 138 • COA 32–3, 414 • GERTZ 141, 146 • FMG I, 22, 24 • FLAMMONDE 260 • OGLESBY 72

KILLAM, THOMAS HENRY "HANK," suspicious death; possible Ruby/Oswald connection. Killam worked as a house painter with John Carter, who lived in the rooming house at 1026 North Beckley in the Oak Cliff section of Dallas at the same time as Oswald. He was married to Wanda Joyce Killam, who was a longtime friend and ex-employee of Ruby. Killam was found dead on March 17, 1964, of a cut throat, surrounded by the shattered glass of a department-store window in Pensacola, Florida. According to the coroner, Killam was the only man ever, to his knowledge, to successfully commit suicide by throwing himself through a plate-glass window. According to Penn Jones Jr., Killam was "'hounded' by Federal Agents" before his death. (See also Carter, John; Killam, Wanda [below])
SOURCES: HSCA Report 148 • HT 129, 137–8 • COA 33 • FMG I, 8, 10, 24; III, 7

KILLAM, WANDA JOYCE, Ruby witness; wife of Thomas Henry "Hank" Killam (above). According to the WR, "[Wanda] had known Jack Ruby since shortly after he moved to Dallas in 1947 and worked for him from July 1963 to early November 1963.
SOURCES: WR 339–40 • FMG I, 7–8; III, 7 • COA 33 • HT 129, 137–8

KILLION, CHARLES L., FBI firearms identification expert. Killion examined the four cartridges reportedly found at the scene of the Tippit killing and determined that they came from the revolver reportedly found on Oswald at the time of his Dallas arrest.

SOURCES: WCH VII, 591 • BISHOP 493

KIMBLE, JULES RICCO (also shown as Jules Ron Kimble, Jules Rocco Kimble), right-wing fanatic; pilot; admitted member of the Ku Klux Klan. Kimble told Jim Garrison in 1963 that he had been introduced to Clay Shaw by David Ferrie in 1960 or 1961. According to author Paris Flammonde, Kimble "claimed that he drove a KKK official, Jack Helm, to [assassination suspect David] Ferrie's apartment on the day after [Ferrie's] death, and observed Helm remove a valise full of papers to a bank deposit box."

Kimble's name is particularly interesting to assassination conspiracy theorists because it has also been connected with the 1968 killing of Martin Luther King, Jr. According to researchers John Edgington and John Sergeant in their article "The Murder of Martin Luther King Jr." (*Covert Action Information Bulletin #34*, Summer 1990), Kimble—who is currently a convicted murderer serving a life sentence in the El Reno Federal Penitentiary in El Reno, Oklahoma—has admitted being involved in a widespread conspiracy that resulted in King's death:

> Kimble, a shadowy figure with ties to the U.S. intelligence community and organized crime... alleges that [convicted King assassin James Earl] Ray, though involved in the plot, did not shoot King and was in fact set up to take the fall for the assassination... Kimble, in implicating the mob and the CIA in the assassination, claims to have introduced Ray to a CIA identities specialist in Montreal, Canada, from whom Ray gained four principle [sic] aliases... Kimble cannot be dismissed out-of-hand. For a start he has a long record of mob activity and violence, often with political overtones... He has proven links to the Louisiana mob empire of Carlos Marcello... and admits to having done mob related work in New Orleans, Montreal and Memphis during the late sixties... Investigative records from the period confirm Kimble to have been involved with the underworld and the KKK, to have been in Montreal in the summer of 1967, and to have been called in for questioning in connection with the Kennedy assassination by then-New Orleans District Attorney Jim Garrison. During this questioning, Kimble admitted being linked to the local FBI and CIA and Garrison accepted this admission as true... Kimble had been living in Crescent City, California during the early 1960s and was associating with gangsters, segregationists, the FBI and, he forcefully asserts, the CIA. He is known to have been in contact with David Ferrie, the dead CIA flier who has been repeatedly implicated in the assassination of John Kennedy.

***

During the summer of 1963, Kimble maintained a New Orleans post-office box in the same building as Oswald, assassination suspect David Ferrie, and suspected Oswald impersonator Kerry W. Thornley. (See also Ferrie, David; Garrison, Jim; Marcello, Carlos; Shaw, Clay; Thornley, Kerry)
SOURCES: AO 118 • FLAMMONDE 206–7

KING, GLEN D., DPD captain in charge of press relations. King reported directly to DPD Chief Jesse Curry. He testified at Ruby's murder trial that Ruby had said shortly after killing Oswald, "You didn't think I was going to let him get away with it, did you?" King said that when Ruby was searched he had $2,015.33 on him in cash and another $60 in traveler's checks. (See also Harrison, William)
SOURCES: WR 206, 208, 210, 214, 221, 223 • WCH XV, 51 • GERTZ 49, 88, 91, 415 • BISHOP 88–9, 226, 256, 280–1, 419, 450–2, 465, 528 • EVICA 24

KINNEY, SAMUEL, a.w.; SS agent. Kinney drove the SS backup car immediately behind JFK's limo.
SOURCES: BISHOP 58–9, 102, 377, 423 • ME 60, 101, 116, 222–3, 252–3

KINSLEY, EDDIE, t.k.w. (aftermath). Kinsley was the assistant to ambulance driver Clayton Butler, who picked up Officer J. D. Tippit's body in Oak Cliff.
SOURCE: RTJ 194

KIRKWOOD, JAMES, author of *American Grotesque: An Account of the Clay Shaw–Jim Garrison Affair in New Orleans* (Simon & Schuster, 1970).

KIRKWOOD, PAT, soldier of fortune; licensed pilot. Kirkwood owned a twin-engine plane and flew to Mexico hours after JFK's death. He was also owner of the Fort Worth nightclub called "The Cellar," where some SS men partied until 3:00 A.M. (one until 5:00 A.M.) on the eve of the assassination. The Cellar was a "beatnik" establishment with a sign on the wall that read, "Evil Spelled Backwards is Live." Kirkwood was quoted in the *Fort Worth Star Telegram* as saying:

> After midnight the night before, some reporters called me from the Press Club, which didn't have a license to sell drinks after midnight. Said they had about 17 members of the Secret Service and asked if they could bring them to my place. I said sure. About 3:30 in the morning, these Secret Service men were sitting around giggling about how the firemen were guarding the President over at the Hotel Texas. That night got The Cellar mentioned in the Warren Report. But we

were involved in the Kennedy thing in other ways. Jack Ruby used to come over on Friday nights and steal my girls. Lee Harvey Oswald washed glasses for two nights at the San Antonio Cellar... We didn't say anything, but those [SS] guys were bombed. They were drinking pure Everclear [alcohol].

According to Dallas reporter Jim Marrs, Kirkwood was the sort of nightclub owner who had friends in powerful places. Among his acquaintances were organized crime figures (Meyer Lansky, Dino Cellini), big-money oilmen (H. L. Hunt, Clint Murchison) and politicians (LBJ, John Connally). (See also McWillie, Lewis)

SOURCES: HT 15, 150 • CF 15, 246–51 • CRENSHAW 26

KIVETT, JERRY D., a.w.; SS agent. Kivett rode in the Dallas motorcade in the SS vice-presidential follow-up car, three cars behind JFK's limo. Kivett sat on the far right of the front seat, immediately next to LBJ aide Clifton C. Carter. In a November 29, 1963, affidavit, Kivett wrote: "I heard a loud noise... It sounded more like an extremely large firecracker, in that it did not seem to have the sharp report of a rifle. As I was looking in the direction of the noise, which was to my right rear, I heard another report— then there was no doubt in my mind what was happening."

SOURCES: FMG III, 17 • ME 308

KLAUSE, ROBERT G., printer of the "Wanted for Treason" handbill attacking JFK that was distributed in the streets of Dallas for two days before JFK's arrival. Klause did the job "on the side" for 38-year-old printing salesman Robert A. Surrey, who was a business partner of Major General Edwin A. Walker. Klause charged Surrey $60 for the job. Klause and Surrey were former coworkers at the Johnson Printing Company. (See also Surrey, Robert; Walker, Edwin A.)

SOURCE: WCH V, 535

KLEIN, FRANK, chief assistant district attorney in New Orleans during Jim Garrison's assassination investigation and Clay Shaw's trial. Garrison wrote that among those involved in his assassination investigation, Klein had the "best mind."

SOURCE: OTT, many

KLEINLERER, ALEXANDER, Oswald witness; acquaintance of the Oswalds in Dallas. He was the Polish-born foreign representative of Loma Industries (plastics). He came to Texas in May, 1956, and became a U.S. citizen in May, 1963. He was the boyfriend of dental technician Elena Hall, who had helped Marina Oswald with dental problems. He met the Oswalds

through Hall and visited the Oswalds twice with her. He strongly disliked Lee and pitied Marina.
SOURCE: WCH XI, 118

KLEINMAN, ABRAHAM, Ruby witness; Dallas public accountant. Kleinman did accounting work for Ruby and tried to do Ruby's taxes for him, but never finished the job because he wasn't supplied with sufficient documentation. He last saw Ruby on November 23, 1963, in Sol's Turf Bar, where he agrees with other witnesses at that bar that Ruby was ranting about the anti-JFK ad that had run in the previous day's *Dallas Morning News* and the IMPEACH EARL WARREN road sign he had photographed the previous night.
SOURCE: WCH XV, 383

KLINE, WILLIAM, United States customs agent. Kline gave the WC an affidavit stating that he had no knowledge of any check made on Oswald by the U.S. Public Health Service upon either his entry into or his exit from Mexico in September 1963.
SOURCE: WCH XV, 640

KNAPP, DAVID, Oswald witness. Knapp was the 18-year-old member of the police lineup at which cabdriver William Whaley identified Oswald as the man he had driven from the Greyhound bus station in downtown Dallas to the Oak Cliff section of Dallas minutes after the assassination. (See also Whaley, William)
SOURCE: WR 152

KNIGHT, FRANCES G., director of the Passport Office, U.S. State Department. Knight told the WC that, when Oswald applied for a passport in December 1961, from the USSR, there was nothing in his file indicating he shouldn't receive a passport. She said there was no "lookout card" (notification of Communist activities or criminal record) in Oswald's file and she said, "I do know that the FBI was reviewing his file at regular intervals, and I think the file shows that."
SOURCE: WCH V, 371

KNIGHT, RUSSELL (See MOORE, RUSSELL LEE)

KOETHE, JAMES F., suspicious death; staff writer, *Dallas Times Herald.* Along with two other reporters, Koethe attended a meeting in Ruby's apartment with Ruby roommate George Senator during the evening of November 24. All three of the journalists died soon after the meeting. Koethe was murdered in his Dallas apartment on September 21, 1964, reportedly just as he had stepped out of the shower. According to A. L. Goodhart in the *Law Quarterly Review* (January 1967), "... Koethe was a beer-drinking bully who liked to hang out with thugs; he had been strangled, not 'karate chopped,' (as some reports have said) and police suggested that homosexuality may have been a motive." (See also Howard, Thomas; Hunter, William; Senator, George)

SOURCES: HT 129, 137 • RTJ 284 • COA 32, 133 • FMG I, 5–7, 22, 24

KOHLMAN, HERMAN, one of New Orleans District Attorney Jim Garrison's assistant district attorneys during the investigation and trial of Clay Shaw. When Jack Martin decided to report his suspicions that Oswald and David Ferrie had conspired to kill JFK, he first told his story to Kohlman. (See also Garrison, Jim; Martin, Jack)

SOURCES: HSCA Report 143 • OTT 7, 29 • FLAMMONDE 39

KOHLY, MARIO, assassination suspect; leader in the Cuban resistance movement (considered president-in-exile of a free Cuba). Kohly was, according to the ex-CIA agent and author Robert Morrow, a major player in the plot to kill JFK. (See also Barnes, Tracy; Diggs, Marshall)

SOURCE: MORROW, many

KOPECHNE, MARY JO, suspicious death; secretary who died in Senator Edward Kennedy's car in 1969 at Chappaquidick. According to Penn Jones Jr., she had once been roommates with Nancy Carole Tyler, the secretary of right-winger and Nixon crony Senator George Smathers. Tyler is reported to have leaked to LBJ's friend Bobby Baker that Johnson was going to be dumped from the Kennedy ticket for the 1964 election. Tyler, like Kopechne, died mysteriously in an accident involving water. The plane in which she was riding was lost over the Atlantic. (See also Baker, Bobby; Tyler, Nancy Carole)

SOURCES: HT 321, 325 • FMG III, 83

KORTH, FRED, secretary of the navy; friend of LBJ. Korth was appointed at LBJ's insistence and was about to be dumped, according to author Seth Kantor, because he had been using his position to "further some of his Fort Worth banking investments." According to author Craig I. Zirbel, "Korth knew the Oswald family since several years before; as a lawyer in private practice, he represented Oswald's mother in her divorce."

SOURCES: TEX 232 • KANTOR 51

KOSTIKOV, VALERI VLADIMIROVICH. According to author Michael H. B. Eddowes in his book *Khrushchev Killed Kennedy*, this man—along with Russian Premier Nikita Khrushchev—was part of the plot to assassinate JFK. Eddowes writes: "Clandestine KGB officer stationed at the Soviet Embassy in Mexico City, Mexico." Kostikov was believed to be a member of Department 13, the sabotage and assassination squad of the KGB during

September and October 1963. According to the CIA, Oswald met or attempted to meet with Kostikov in September 1963. If this meeting never occurred, it is an indication that the "dirty little secret" that perhaps caused the WC whitewash was wholly false. Kostikov is believed by the WC to be the "Comrade Kostin" mentioned by Oswald as the man he met in Mexico City in a letter Oswald, according to Ruth Paine, wrote to the Soviet embassy in Washington, D.C., on November 9, 1963. Eddowes says that Kostin and Kostikov are separate individuals. (See also Eddowes, Michael; Kostin, Valeri [below])
    SOURCES: KKK, iii • WR 286 • BLAKEY 110, 133 • DAVIS 163, 239, 270–2, 438–9, 441 • PD 47, 53–4, 60, 63, 78

KOSTIN, VALERI DMITREVICH, clandestine KGB officer theorized to have been stationed at the Soviet embassy in Havana during September and October 1963. According to author Michael H. B. Eddowes, Kostin was part of the plot to assassinate JFK. (See also Eddowes, Michael; Kostikov, Valeri [above])
    SOURCE: KKK, iii

KOUNAS, DOLORES A., a.w. Kounas stood near the southwest corner of Elm and Houston Streets. Although directly across the street from the TSBD, she thought "the shots came from a westerly direction in the vicinity of the viaduct [triple underpass]."
    SOURCES: RTJ 112 • CF 33

KRAMER, MONICA, Oswald witness; British tourist. Kramer traveled through the USSR during the summer of 1961 with her friend Rita Naman, and, for a time, with Marie Hyde, an elderly American tourist who claimed to have gotten separated from her tour group and was seeking companionship. Before meeting Hyde, Kramer and Naman encountered an American while leaving the site of the Moscow Film Festival. They discussed nothing of importance with the stranger and were soon urged to move on by their tour guide, who seemed agitated by the man's presence. Soon thereafter, Kramer and Naman hooked up with Hyde, and together they went to Minsk where, ten days after the first encounter, they again ran into the same American man. They again spoke with him briefly and this time, at Hyde's urging, took a photo of the man—who turned out to be Oswald. At the time of the assassination, this photograph was in the possession of the CIA, which reportedly made a "routine" copy, as it often did with the film of American tourists returning from the Soviet Union. The CIA claims that it didn't even know the photo was of Oswald until after the assassination. When discussing the photographing of Oswald in Minsk, the WR leaves out

the presence of Hyde, whose story doesn't ring true to those familiar with restrictions upon U.S. tourists in the USSR at the time. (See also Hyde, Marie)
SOURCES: WR 268 • WCH XI, 212; XX, 474 • HSCA Report 206 • SUMMERS 181–3

KRAVITZ, HERBERT B., Ruby witness; 26-year-old self-employed publisher (20th Century Publishers, Inc.). Kravitz met Ruby four to six months before the assassination in a Chinese restaurant. He accepted Ruby's invitation to visit the Carousel Club; and told the WC he last saw Ruby about a week before JFK's death. He remembered nothing unusual about Ruby's behavior.
SOURCE: WCH XV, 231

KRISS, HARRY M., o.k.w.; DPD reserve force. Kriss did not see Ruby enter the basement.
SOURCE: WCH XII, 266

KRYSTINIK, RAYMOND FRANKLIN, Oswald witness; research engineer at Bell Helicopter Research Laboratory; coworker of Oswald associate Michael R. Paine. Krystinik met Oswald once at an ACLU meeting in October 1963. He said that Paine cried when he heard of JFK's death and told the WC that, when the radio announcer said Oswald had been arrested with a gun, Paine said, "He is not even supposed to have a gun." (See also Paine, Michael)
SOURCE: WCH IX, 461

KULLAWAY, KURT (See VAGANOV, IGOR)

KUNSTLER, WILLIAM, Ruby witness; trial attorney who joined Ruby's appeals team following his conviction for murder with malice.
SOURCE: GERTZ, many

KUPCINET, KARYN, suspicious death; 22-year-old daughter of *Chicago Sun-Times* columnist Irv Kupcinet, who, according to Penn Jones Jr., was one of Ruby's childhood friends. She reportedly had foreknowledge of the assassination and was overheard talking about it by a telephone operator. She died on November 28, 1963, only six days after JFK died, and was found dead on the evening of November 30, on the living-room couch in her home. According to the *New York Times* (December 1, 1992):

> Her body was found on its side, with flecks of blood on her face and a pillow. There were no notes or any indications of suicide, officers said...She had apparently been dead two or three days, sheriff's investigators said. Friends discovered her body when they came to her apartment...When her body was found, the apartment door was

unlocked and the television set was on but turned down, according to the friends, Mark Goddard, actor, and his wife, Marcia. A bowl of cigarettes and a coffeepot had been knocked to the floor and a lamp turned over, they said.

On December 2, 1963, the *New York Times* reported that the cause of death was strangulation. There was no evidence of sexual assault. Karyn was a screen, stage, and television actress, best known for her appearance in the 1961 film *The Ladies' Man.*
SOURCE: HT 141

KUTNER, LUIS, staff attorney for the 1950 Kefauver Senate Committee investigating organized crime. Kutner later said that his staff had learned that Ruby was a "syndicate lieutenant" sent to Dallas as "a liaison for Chicago mobsters."
SOURCE: SUMMERS 434

L

LAMARR, HERVÉ (See HEPBURN, JAMES)

LANCELOT, JACQUELINE, informant. According to the HSCA, Lancelot told Palm Beach stockbroker Joseph Dwyer, that George DeMohrenschildt deposited $200,000 to 250,000 in his Port-au-Prince account soon after the assassination. According to HT, "The money in the account was subsequently paid out, although she did not know to whom, and DeMohrenschildt left Haiti soon thereafter." Lancelot's source was "the person who handed out funds at the bank." She also told Dwyer that DeMohrenschildt was good friends with Haitian President "Papa Doc" Duvalier and that Duvalier had said, in a speech before the JFK assassination, that "the big man in the White House wasn't going to be there much longer." (See also DeMohrenschildt, George)

SOURCES: HSCA App. XII, 60–1 • HT 300, 302

LANDIS, PAUL E., JR., a.w.; SS agent. Landis, standing on the right running board of the SS presidential follow-up car immediately behind JFK's limo, later said: "I heard what sounded like a report of a high-powered rifle from behind me...[I drew my gun and] I heard a second report and saw the President's head split open and pieces of flesh and blood flying through the air. My reaction at that time was that the shot came from somewhere toward the front...and [I] looked along the right side of the road." In his written report, Landis said that his initial impression was that "the [head] shot came from somewhere toward the front, right-hand side of the road."

SOURCES: WCH XVIII, 758 • HSCA Report 89 • RTJ 42 • BISHOP 97, 102, 124, 317, 320, 373, 516 • DOP 61, 347, 388, 391 • CF 14 • SUMMERS 23–4 • ME 60, 80, 101, 180, 218 • OGLESBY 35 • ME 294

LANDRIGAN, STEVE, Parkland witness; Parkland press relations man.

245

Landrigan escorted Father Huber into Trauma Room #1 so that the priest could give JFK the last rites of the Catholic church. Later, he helped SS agent Clint Hill arrange for the purchase of a casket.

SOURCE: BISHOP 172, 179, 189, 218

LANE, DOYLE E., Ruby witness; Western Union telegraph office clerk. Lane told the WC that Ruby sent a telegram from his Western Union office located 350 feet from the top of the Main Street ramp that led down into the DPD station basement. The telegram was sent at 11:17 A.M., on November 24, only three minutes before Ruby arrived in the basement to shoot Oswald.

SOURCES: WCH XII, 221 • RTJ 226 • GERTZ 45–6, 493–4

LANE, MARK R., attorney and author; dean of WC critics. Lane was retained by Marguerite Oswald soon after her son's death to defend his memory. The result was the book *Rush to Judgment* (Holt, Rinehart, Winston, 1966). If the WR is the case for the prosecution against Oswald, then *RTJ* is the case for the defense. Lane gathered evidence that Oswald was framed. Lane is still working on the JFK case. In 1985, Lane successfully defended the Washington tabloid the *Spotlight*, published by the ultra-right-wing Liberty Lobby, against a $1 million lawsuit brought by assassination suspect E. Howard Hunt for defamation over an article published in the *Spotlight* by former CIA agent Victor Marchetti. It claimed that E. Howard Hunt played a substantial role in the JFK assassination. Lane wrote a book about the case, *Plausible Denial* (Thunder's Mouth Press, 1991), which claims to "definitely prove" that the CIA killed JFK— Hunt was Lane's principal suspect. The most spectacular new evidence in the new book involves the statements of Marita Lorenz, who claims she saw E. Howard Hunt in Dallas the day before the assassination, meeting with a group of people, including her ex-lover, CIA contact agent Frank Sturgis— who subsequently told her that he was involved in the JFK killing.

Lane's role in the uncovering of a JFK assassination conspiracy is made more intriguing by the fact that Lane was a lawyer for Jim Jones's People's Temple in Jonestown, Guyana, and managed to escape the bizarre community just before the massacre. According to researcher John Judge (*Critique*, Spring/Summer 1986), Jonestown was not a religious community at all, but rather a part of the CIA mind-control program known as MK/ULTRA.

Lane is among those who have successfully used the Freedom of Information Act. He brought a suit by the ACLU seeking assassination records under control of the SS and the Treasury Department. Some records were released. (*Lane v. United States Secret Service*, 76-0227 [D.D.C.] • See also D'Antonio, Emile; Farrington, Fenella; Lorenz, Marita; Hunt, E. Howard; Sturgis, Frank; Thornley, Kerry; Waldo, Thayer; Walter, William)

SOURCES: WR 276–7, 344 • WCH II, 32; IV, 546 • HT 364–5 • BELIN 20–2, 30–2, 42, 183, 200, 221, 223, 226 • GERTZ, many • FMG I, 74–7; III, 42, 59 • OTT 66, 195, 197, 219–20, 244, 250–1, 324 • BLAKEY 41, 52, 64, 96 • KANTOR 90 • DAVIS 272, 286, 364, 422, 435 • NORTH 407, 458, 488, 502, 507 • PD, many

LANSKY, MEYER, "Godfather of Godfathers." Lansky was the Mafia financial wizard who, according to HT, had an empire that overlapped that of Texas oil billionaire Clint Murchison. (See also McWillie, Lewis)

SOURCES: HSCA Report 151 • EVICA, many • HT 151, 282, 318 • COA, many • CF 168–71 • SUMMERS 236–7 • BLAKEY, many • KANTOR 13–4, 24, 28, 130, 134–5 • DAVIS, many • NORTH, many

LANZ, PEDRO DIAZ, assassination suspect; Cuban exile leader; former major and chief of the Cuban Air Force under Castro. Lanz fled to Miami because of "Communist influence in the armed forces and government." Marita Lorenz, a former undercover CIA and FBI operative, told the *New York Daily News* that, a few days before the assassination, she rode in a car from Miami to Dallas. With her in the car, she claims, were Pedro Diaz Lanz and Orlando Bosch (both Cuban exile leaders), CIA contact agent Frank Sturgis, Lee Harvey Oswald, ONI operative Gerry Hemming and two Cuban brothers named Novis. Lorenz claimed that her companions on the trip were members of a secret CIA guerilla group known as Operation 40, first formed by the CIA in 1960 as part of plans for the Bay of Pigs invasion. (See also Bosch, Orlando; Hemming, Gerry; Hunt, E. Howard; Lorenz, Marita; Sturgis, Frank)

SOURCES: HT 347–8 • BLAKEY 158, 175 • PD 300

LARDNER, GEORGE, JR., journalist; son of famous writer Ring Lardner. Lardner covered the HSCA hearings for the *Washington Post*. He was with David Ferrie on February 22, 1967, the day Ferrie died. It was determined that Ferrie died of "natural causes," a "brain hemorrhage" to be precise. Jim Garrison, however, claims that two typed suicide notes were found in Ferrie's apartment.

Lardner told the *New Orleans States-Item* that he interviewed Ferrie from midnight to 4:00 A.M. on February 22. New Orleans District Attorney Jim Garrison told the *New York Post* that the estimated time of Ferrie's death, based on the rigor mortis of Ferrie's body, was 3:00 A.M.—information based on the conclusions of medical examiner Nicholas Chetta who also died mysteriously. Ferrie's body was found at noon that same day, naked, with a sheet pulled over its head. (See also Chetta, Nicholas; Ferrie, David; Garrison, Jim)

SOURCES: HT 136, 362, 364, 366–7, 391 • BELIN 98–9 • COA 39 • FLAMMONDE 34, 36, 124, 261 • PD 31, 325–7

LARKIN, ROBERT, Ruby witness. Larkin was mentioned briefly in the WR's chronology of Ruby's movements between the JFK assassination and the time he shot Oswald. Larkin said he "saw [Ruby] downtown at about 6:00 P.M." on November 23. Others have said that Ruby was in the Carousel Club between 6:00 and 7:00 P.M. on Saturday—yet Ruby's sister, Eva Grant, says that Ruby was at her home from 4:00 to 8:00 P.M. (See also Grant, Eva)

SOURCE:WR 324

LATONA, SEBASTIAN FRANCIS, supervisor of the latent fingerprint section of the indentification division of the FBI. Latona examined the alleged assassination rifle on November 23, 1963, for fingerprints and found none—including the "Oswald palm print" supposedly later found by the DPD. (See also Wittmus, Ronald G.)

SOURCES: WR 117, 127, 130, 231–2 • WCH IV, 1 • RTJ 153–7

LATTIMER, JOHN K., New York urologist; ballistics expert; World War II combat surgeon; author of *Kennedy and Lincoln: Medical and Ballistic Comparisons of Their Assassinations* (Harcourt Brace Jovanovich, 1980). Lattimer explained that the wound at the front of JFK's throat was so small, despite being officially an exit wound, because it was beneath JFK's tightly buttoned collar and necktie. Lattimer theorizes that the hole was so small because the bullet penetrated before the skin could stretch outward. He concluded that JFK might have died even if he had never been struck in the head, that the bullet to his neck had cracked a vertebra, causing a "probably fatal" spinal injury.

SOURCE: ME 34–5, 68, 198–202

LAULICHT, MURRAY J., WC staff member. Laulicht was a 24-year-old law clerk, assigned by WC General Counsel J. Lee Rankin to assist in the writing of the chapter on Oswald's death and the actions of Ruby.

LAWRENCE, JACK, employee of Downtown Lincoln-Mercury, the same Dallas car dealership where, several weeks before, a man claiming to be Oswald had come in to wildly test-drive a car. Lawrence called the FBI to report that incident, against the wishes of his coworkers. According to author Gary J. Shaw, Lawrence borrowed a car from the dealership on the eve of the assassination and then did not show up for work that Friday morning. The next his fellow employees saw him was when "30 minutes after the assassination, Lawrence, muddy and sweating profusely, came running into the dealership and was overcome by nausea. His abandoned vehicle was later found parked behind the wooden fence on the Grassy Knoll...[After his coworkers called the police] Jack Lawrence was arrested later that afternoon and held in jail for 24 hours. Judging from his peculiar behavior on November 22, one cannot help but garner the idea that he was somehow involved in the assassination." Lawrence's story is that he was late for work because of a hangover and parked his car where he did because of the traffic jam caused by the assassination.

Lawrence quit his job the next day. It was later learned that he had used a phony story to get his job in the first place. According to Beverly Oliver ("The Babushka Lady"), Lawrence was a regular at Ruby's Carousel Club and was close friends with George Senator, Ruby's roommate. According to Shaw, Lawrence was an "ardent Right-Wing speaker" and had moved to Dallas from Los Angeles. Records show that during his stint in the military, Lawrence had been an expert marksman. (See also Bogard, Albert; Oliver, Beverly; Pizzo, Frank; Senator, George; Willis, Phillip; Wilson, Eugene)

SOURCES: WCE 2970, 3080, 3093 • HT 133–4 • CF 339–40 • OGLESBY 50 • SHAW 90, 110

LAWRENCE, JOHN STEVENS RUTTER, a.w. Lawrence corroborates the statements of Philip B. Hathaway, the coworker with whom he watched the motorcade. (See also Hathaway, Philip B.)

SOURCES: WCE 2003, p. 214; 5323, p. 482 • CF 17–8

LAWRENCE, LINCOLN, pen name of the author of *Were We Controlled?* (University Books, 1967). Lawrence makes the point that there is evidence of foreknowledge of the assassination among Wall Street insiders, who made an estimated $600 million by selling short before the drop in stock prices caused by JFK's death.

SOURCE: FMG III, 8

LAWRENCE, PERDUE W., DPD captain. Lawrence's original plan for motorcade motorcycle security was changed (and made less effective) by the SS.

SOURCES: WR 424–5 • WCH VII, 577 • BISHOP 40–1, 75, 103–4, 129, 202 • PWW 167–9

LAWSON, WINSTON G., a.w.; DPD officer. With SS agent Forrest Sorrells, Lawson selected the motorcade route and was in charge of protecting the motorcade. He rode in the front passenger seat in the

motorcade's lead car, an enclosed sedan driven by Dallas Police Chief Jesse Curry, directly in front of JFK's limo. According to HSCA testimony, "[Captain Perdue] Lawrence said there would be four motorcycles on either side of the motorcade immediately to the rear of the President's vehicle. Mr. Lawson stated that this was too many, that he thought two motorcycles on either side would be sufficient, about even with the rear fender of the President's car. Lawrence was instructed to disperse the other two along each side of the motorcade to the rear." In a five-page, typed statement dated December 1, 1963, Lawson said: "As the Lead Car was passing under the bridge I heard the first loud, sharp report and in more rapid succession two more sounds like gunfire. I could see persons to the left of the motorcade vehicles running away. I noticed Agent [George] Hickey standing up in the [presidential] follow-up car and first thought that he might have fired at someone." This statement is used by author Bonar Menninger to support his theory that JFK was killed accidentally by SS agent Hickey. (See also Curry, Jesse; Grant, David B.; Hickey, George; Sorrells, Forrest)
SOURCES: WR, many • WCH IV, 317; XVII, 632 • HSCA XI, 527–30 • BELIN 2 • HT 151–3, 155, 157 • BISHOP, many • DOP, many • CF 11, 13–4 • FMG I, 152 • EVICA 45 • ME 104, 106, 220–1, 233, 253, 271 • DAVIS 190 • NORTH 343, 351, 357–9, 376

LEAVELLE, JAMES R., o.k.w.; DPD detective. Leavelle was handcuffed to Oswald, immediately to Oswald's right, when Ruby shot him. (See also Brown, Charles)
SOURCES: WR, 200–1, 213 • WCH VII, 260; VIII, 14 • BELIN 62–3 • RTJ 189, 209–12, 214–5 • GERTZ 14, 46, 59, 71, 97–101, 415, 512–3 • BISHOP 122, 290–1, 355, 399 • DOP 520, 523 • FLAMMONDE 208 • DAVIS 227

LeBLANC, CHARLES JOSEPH, Oswald witness; Oswald coworker and maintenance man at the William B. Reily Company. LeBlanc trained Oswald and told the WC that Oswald was lazy. He said, "I tell you, he was a boy of very few words."
SOURCES: WCH X, 213

LEDBETTER, LAYTON, Bethesda witness. Ledbetter spoke of a decoy coffin being used when transporting JFK's body into Bethesda for autopsy.
SOURCES: SUMMERS 483 • BE 419, 589, 592, 635

LEE, IVAN D., FBI agent. Lee photographed the rear of Major General Edwin A. Walker's home, to compare with the similar photos found among Oswald's belongings. He conducted the postassassination interview with mob figure Joseph Francis Civello, assassination suspect Carlos Marcello's number-one lieutenant in Dallas, which showed up in the WCH devoid of references to organized crime and with Civello's name spelled incorrectly

(Cirello). (See also Civello, Joseph; Walker, Edwin A.)
SOURCES: WCH XI, 481

LEE, O. H. (See OSWALD, LEE HARVEY)

LEE, VINCENT THEODORE, FPCC national director. The New Orleans chapter of his organization had one member, Oswald.
SOURCES: WR 270, 382–5 • WCH X, 86; XI, 208 • HSCA Report 140 • BELIN 210 • BLAKEY 161, 291, 358 • NORTH 473

LEEK, SYBIL, coauthor, with Bert R. Sugar, of *The Assassination Chain* (Corwin Books, 1976).

LEEMANS, FRED. Leemans appeared on a June 1967, NBC-TV special called "The Case of Jim Garrison," saying that the New Orleans district attorney had offered him $2,500 to say he had seen accused conspirator Clay Shaw and Oswald together in a Turkish bath he operated. Garrison claims he had never heard of Leemans until the program aired. (See also Garrison, Jim; Shaw, Clay)
SOURCES: OTT 169–70 • FLAMMONDE 303–4, 308–9

LEHRER, JAMES, reporter for the *Dallas Times Herald*; currently coanchor with a.w. Robert MacNeil of PBS TV's *MacNeil-Lehrer NewsHour.* On November 28, 1963, Lehrer witnessed fellow reporter Hunter Schmidt Jr. attempting to verify a report from possible Oswald witness Dial Ryder that Oswald had gotten his rifle sight fixed in a gunshop in Irving, Texas. Later, Ryder denied ever having spoken with Schmidt.
SOURCES: WCH XI, 464 • GERTZ 162 • FLAMMONDE 229 • KANTOR 153

LEVINE, ISAAC DON. According to researcher Peter Dale Scott, Levine is a former CIA agent who coached Marina Oswald before she gave her WC testimony. Levine allegedly spent an "intensive week with Marina before she first testified on February 3, 1964, and as a representative of Time-Life, Inc., helped to arrange for Marina to receive a $25,000 advance for a book that was never written. (See also Oswald, Marina)
SOURCES: HT 158–9, 284 • EVICA 166

LEWALLEN, JAMES, former apartment mate of assassination suspect David Ferrie in Kenner, a New Orleans suburb. When the men moved into New Orleans proper, they lived next door to each other on Dauphine Street, in the same building as Dante Marachini, one of four of Lee Harvey Oswald's coworkers at the William Reily Coffee Company who all quit soon after Oswald left the company and later went on to work for NASA. (See also Ferrie, David; Marachini, Dante)
SOURCES: OTT 115–6 • FLAMMONDE 60, 78, 180–1

LEWIS, AUBREY LEE, possible Oswald witness; 26-year-old Western

Union Telegraph Company branch manager. Lewis told the WC that Oswald had once come into his Western Union office to cash a money order and Lewis asked for I.D., and that Oswald showed a Navy I.D. card. He says that Oswald was with a Latino companion. He couldn't identify Oswald for the WC from a photograph.
  SOURCES: WCH IX, 318 • NORTH 320

LEWIS, CLINT L. "LUMMIE," a.w. (aftermath); suspicious death; Dallas deputy sheriff. Lewis arrested "Jim Braden" (aka Eugene Hale Brading) in Dealey Plaza after the assassination. Lewis died in 1978 "of natural causes" before he could testify to the HSCA. Found among Ruby's possessions following his arrest on November 24, 1963, was Lewis's signed permanent pass to the Carousel Club. (See also Brading, Eugene Hale)
  SOURCES: COA 111 • FMG I, 31 • EVICA 164

LEWIS, DAVID L. (also shown as David F.). According to HT, Lewis "...saw...Oswald with [assassination suspect David] Ferrie and Carlos Quiroga, a friend of Archacha Smith, with [Guy] Banister."

  New Orleans States-Item reporters Rosemary James and Jack Windlaw wrote in their book *Plot or Politics?* (Pelican, 1967), "the Lewis story is that late in 1962, he was drinking coffee with Banister's secretary, Delphine Roberts, in Mancuso's Restaurant, when Carlos Quiroga, a Cuban exile, came in with a fellow he introduced as *Leon* Oswald...Lewis was working for Banister at the time. Then, a few days later, Lewis entered Banister's office and there was a meeting in progress of Banister, Quiroga, Ferrie, Leon Oswald, and another person. Lewis was asked to leave." Lewis told the *New York World Journal Tribune* (February 22, 1967) that the New Orleans conspiracy investigation was "not a hoax on anyone's part. There was a plot. I know about it and I know the people involved." When Lewis was asked by the *New York Post* (February 20, 1967) why he was telling Garrison things that he hadn't told the FBI, he replied, "The FBI didn't ask me about it." (See also Banister, Guy; Ferrie, David; Quiroga, Carlos)
  SOURCES: HT 289 • FLAMMONDE 23–4, 179–80 • SUMMERS 324–5

LEWIS, ERWIN DONALD, Oswald witness; USMC acquaintance. Lewis told the WC: "I knew [Oswald] casually as a working acquaintance...[He] was very quiet, kept to himself and did not appear to have any close friends...It was a matter of common knowledge among squadron members that he could read, write and speak Russian..."
  SOURCES: WCH VIII, 323 • AO 96

LEWIS, L. J., t.k.w. Lewis was employed at the Reynolds Motor Company one block away from the Tippit slaying on East Jefferson Boulevard. He told the FBI that he saw a man fleeing the scene several minutes after he heard the shots and that the man was trying to conceal "an automatic pistol or a revolver" in his belt. He could not identify the man as Oswald. Lewis's time reference does not agree with any of the other witnesses, who agree that Tippit's murderer fled immediately.

SOURCES: WCH XV, 703 • RTJ 276–8 • GERTZ 528

LEWIS, R. D., DPD detective. Lewis administered a polygraph examination to Oswald witness Buell Wesley Frazier on the evening of November 22, 1963. The procedure lasted approximately 50 minutes, and, although Frazier seemed anxious, the examination seemed to indicate that he was telling the truth when he said Oswald brought "curtain rods" with him to work that morning. (See also Frazier, Buell Wesley)

SOURCE: BISHOP 447, 471–2, 492

LEWIS, RICHARD WARREN, coauthor, with Lawrence Schiller, of *The Scavengers and Critics of the Warren Report* (Dell, 1967).

LIDDY, G. GORDON, Watergate conspirator. On August 10, 1973, Dan Rather asked Liddy on CBS radio, "Lee Harvey Oswald—the man who shot President Kennedy—did he ever know or have contact with E. Howard Hunt or Gordon Liddy or any of the others in that mysterious and dangerous crew convicted in the Watergate crime?"

According to assassination researcher Bernard Fensterwald, "[Liddy] has been reliably linked to two separate alleged murder plans during his work for Nixon's top aides." Liddy was also allegedly involved in one successful murder plot during his previous FBI career. (See also Nixon, Richard M.)

SOURCES: HT 324, 327, 418, 420 • EVICA 283, 312, 316 • PD 50, 174–5, 187–8, 199–205

LIEBELER, WESLEY J., WC counsel; assisted Albert E. Jenner in investigating Oswald's domestic activities. Liebeler was a supporter of David Lifton during Lifton's writing of *Best Evidence* (see below). According to Bernard Fensterwald, Liebeler found evidence in 1964 supporting Sylvia Odio's story that she had been visited before the assassination by a "Leon Oswald." This angered WC chief counsel J. Lee Rankin, who said reportedly, "At this stage we are supposed to be closing doors, not opening them." (See also Jenner, Albert E.; Lifton, David; Odio, Sylvia)

SOURCES: HSCA Report 138, 193 • ME 72–3 • EVICA 125 • OGLESBY 61, 68 • HT 328 • BELIN 46 • BE, many • COA 213 • CF 27–8 • FMG III, 71 • PWW 15–6, 18, 20–1, 27–8, 53, 63, 65, 202–4 • SUMMERS 356 • BLAKEY 42–3, 81, 164 • FLAMMONDE 21, 26–7, 44–50, 60, 113, 121, 125 • HOS 19 • KANTOR 84

LIFTON, DAVID, author of *Best Evidence* (Macmillan, 1981; Carroll & Graf, 1988). Troubled by the gross discrepancy between the descriptions of JFK's wounds at Parkland and Bethesda (in Dallas, Kennedy appeared to have been shot from the front, in Maryland the president appeared to have been shot from the rear), Lifton obtained frightening evidence that JFK's body was tampered with somewhere between Parkland and Bethesda. Lifton's best theory maintains that between 2:18 and 2:32 P.M., fourteen minutes during which "it appeared, from the public record, that the coffin was... unattended," JFK's body was removed from its coffin and hidden until Air Force One landed at Andrews Air Force Base in Washington. At that time, Lifton alleges—while the nation watched an empty coffin being removed, accompanied by Jacqueline and Robert Kennedy—JFK's body was deplaned through a right-front door and loaded onto a helicopter. The body was flown to Walter Reed Hospital and, while there, it was altered to appear as if it had been shot only from the rear.

According to HT, "Mandatory to this hypothesis is the necessity for the coffin to have been left unattended... Dave Powers, a longtime friend and close aide of President Kennedy, told... Harrison Livingstone on June 23, 1987, that 'the coffin was never left unattended... I never had my hands or eyes off of it during that period [Lifton] says it was unattended...'" (See also Liebeler, Wesley; Powers, David; Sibert, James)
   SOURCES: HT 39–41 • BELIN 28–9, 223, 226 • CF 69, 373–8 • PWW 145 • SUMMERS 477–86 • FLAMMONDE 26–7 • ME 53 • OGLESBY 42

LIGHT, FREDERICK W., JR., physician; U.S. Army wound ballistics expert. Light reported, with Dr. Joseph Dolce, in April 1964, that Governor Connally was struck by two bullets—the main reason for this conclusion was that the "'magic bullet' [WCE 399] couldn't have caused Connally's wrist wound yet remained pristine." The WR takes a different slant on Light's testimony, claiming that, "Based on the other circumstances, such as the relative positions of the President and the Governor in the automobile, Dr. Light concluded that it was probable that the same bullet" caused all of the nonfatal wounds. (See also Dolce, Joseph)
   SOURCES: WR 106 • WCH V, 94

LIMBAUGH, CLYDE, Ruby witness. On March 7, 1967, Limbaugh told New Orleans District Attorney Jim Garrison that he had worked at Ruby's Carousel Club from 1961 to 1963, and knew of Ruby's involvement in a plot to kill JFK. Garrison's aide William Gurvich told the *New Orleans States-Item* (March 9, 1967) that Limbaugh was "totally unreliable," adding, "this sort of thing makes a mockery of our investigation."

SOURCE: FLAMMONDE 181–2

LINCOLN, EVELYN, a.w. (aftermath); JFK's private secretary. Lincoln rode in the VIP bus at the rear of the motorcade.
SOURCES: DOP, many • BISHOP, many

LINDENBERG, RICHARD, member HSCA medical panel; director of neuropathology for the Maryland Department of Public Health. Lindenberg examined the JFK autopsy photos and X rays. The panel concluded that JFK was shot exclusively from the rear.
SOURCE: BELIN 181

LITCHFIELD, WILBYRN WALDON "ROBERT" II, Ruby witness. Litchfield told the WC that, during a visit to the Carousel Club in late October or early November 1963, he saw a man who resembled Oswald enter Ruby's office. Litchfield said that the man who resembled Oswald had pockmarks on the right side of his chin. (See also Frazier, Buell Wesley)
SOURCES: WCH XIV, 95 • NORTH 345

LIVINGSTONE, HARRISON EDWARD, coauthor, with Robert J. Groden, of *High Treason* (Berkley Books, 1990) and author of *High Treason 2* (Carroll & Graf, 1992).
SOURCES: ME 53–4 • SUMMERS 484

LOCKE, EUGENE, Dallas attorney; 1968 candidate for governor of Texas. According to Penn Jones Jr., the decision to swing the Dallas motorcade past the TSBD was made in Locke's office. Locke also served as the deputy ambassador to Vietnam under LBJ. He was Governor John Connally's first campaign manager and, when Locke ran for governor, Connally's brother was Locke's campaign manager. According to the WC, Locke was also Mrs. J. D. (Marie) Tippit's attorney before the assassination. (See also Connally, John; Tippit, Marie)
SOURCES: FMG III, 14, 80 • WCH XX, 426

LOCURTO, JOE (See BONDS, JOE)

LOGAN, DAVID, a "young friend" of David Ferrie, who says he met Clay Shaw several times while in Bourbon Street bars with Ferrie. (See also Ferrie, David; Shaw, Clay)
SOURCE: OTT 119

LONG, RUSSELL, Louisiana senator; son of Huey Long. Long reportedly talked New Orleans District Attorney Jim Garrison into opening the Kennedy investigation. He reputedly had ties with Carlos Marcello. (See also Garrison, Jim; Marcello, Carlos)
SOURCES: OTT 13 • DAVIS 112, 343–4, 368, 373, 398, 419 • NORTH 65, 95, 414)

LOPEZ, EDWIN JUAN, HSCA attorney. Lopez investigated Oswald's alleged trip to Mexico in September 1963, and concluded that an impostor had made the visits to the Soviet and Cuban embassies in Mexico City, posing as Oswald. He based this conclusion on CIA photos of "Oswald" in Mexico taken at three different sites, which show a man who is obviously not Oswald. In 1989, Lopez wrote to author Anthony Summers saying, "It was very obvious, from dealing with people at the CIA for approximately ten years, that the CIA was covering something up. We weren't sure if it had to do with some element of the CIA having assassinated the President, but we knew at the very least they were covering up something they knew about the assassination. I came away feeling that we could not trust our government, that what we had been told all along was a sham. And I thought the American people deserved better."

SOURCES: HT 182–3 • OTT 65, 305–6 • SUMMERS 535 • OGLESBY 66 • DAVIS 165–6, 602 • PD 146

LOPEZ, GILBERTO POLICARPO, assassination suspect. According to the HSCA:

> ... in early December 1963, CIA headquarters received a classified message stating that a source had requested "urgent traces on U.S. citizen Gilberto P. Lopez."... Lopez had arrived in Mexico in November 1963 and had disappeared with no record of his trip to Havana. The message added that Lopez had obtained tourist card No. 24553 in Tampa on November 20, that he had left Mexico for Havana November 27 on Cubana Airlines, and that his U.S. passport number was 310162... [On the same day] the FBI had been advised that Lopez entered Mexico on November 27 at Nuevo Laredo... Two days later these details were added: Lopez had crossed the border at Laredo, Texas, on November 23; registered at the Roosevelt Hotel in Mexico City on November 25; and departed Mexico on November 27 on a Cubana flight for Havana. Another dispatch noted that Lopez was the only passenger on Cubana flight 465 on November 27 to Havana. It said he used a U.S. passport and Cuban courtesy visa.

It was determined that the Lopez in question was born on January 26, 1940, and that he was a different person from the Gilberto Lopez in Los Angeles who was active in pro-Castro groups.

In March 1964, CIA headquarters received a message from a source who stated that a U.S. citizen named Gilberto Lopes [sic] "had been involved in the Kennedy assassination." According to the HSCA, the message stated "that Lopes had entered Mexico on foot from Laredo, Texas, on November

23, carrying U.S. passport 319962, which had been issued July 13, 1960; that he had been issued Mexican travel form B24553 in Nuevo Laredo; that Lopes had proceeded by bus to Mexico City 'where he entered the Cuban Embassy'; and that he left the Cuban Embassy on November 27 and was the only passenger on flight 465 for Cuba." The CIA disregarded the March 1964 message because of the discrepancies in details between it and the December 1963 information, a move that prompted the HSCA to ask "why the CIA had not taken more aggressive investigative steps to determine whether there had been a connection between Lopez and the assassination."

The FBI filed a report on August 26, 1964, which contained an interview with Lopez's cousin, Guillermo Serpa Rodriguez, conducted in Key West, Florida. Rodriguez said that Lopez had come to the United States after Castro took over in Cuba, had returned to Cuba after about a year because he was homesick, then returned to the United States in 1960 or 1961 to avoid the Cuban draft.

Lopez had told Rodriguez of his plans to return to Cuba in November 1963, saying that he was afraid of getting drafted into the U.S. military—which could be construed as his using the same excuse once too often. Rodriguez said that Lopez was passionately pro-Castro but was not politically active, although Rodriguez revealed that Lopez had once gotten into a fistfight because of his pro-Castro beliefs.

The August 26, 1964, FBI report also contained an interview with Lopez's wife, also conducted in Key West. She listed for the FBI the places where Lopez had been employed. The HSCA points out that the list included "a construction firm in Tampa." The woman also said her husband was hospitalized at Jackson Memorial Hospital in early 1963 in Miami because he had begun to suffer from epileptic attacks. He had also been treated for the condition by doctors in Key West and Coral Gables. In the opinion of Lopez's wife, his seizures were brought on by worry for his family in Cuba. She said that Lopez had written her since his return to Cuba, telling her that his trip had been made with financial assistance from "an organization in Tampa." The woman verified that Lopez would not have been able to afford the trip on his own. According to the FBI, Lopez attended an FPCC meeting in Tampa on November 20, 1963. The FBI later (March 1964) changed the date of that meeting to November 7, 1963. The HSCA reported that, at that meeting, "Lopez had said he had not been granted permission to return to Cuba but that he was awaiting a phone call about his return to his homeland." The March 1964 FBI report stated that a Tampa FPCC member claimed that she had called a friend in Cuba on December 8, 1963, and was assured of Lopez's safe arrival. She said that Lopez had made the trip via Mexico because he lacked a passport and that he had been given $190 by the FPCC for the trip.

But Lopez *did* have a passport. It was #310162 and had been issued in January 1960. The FBI reportedly verified that Lopez's Mexican tourist card was #M8-24553, issued November 20, 1963, in Tampa; that he entered Mexico by automobile on November 23 at Laredo, Texas; and that he had flown to Havana November 27 as the plane's lone passenger.

The HSCA said, in summary, "Lopez' association with the [FPCC]... coupled with... the dates of his travel to Mexico [indicate] that Lopez' activities were 'suspicious,'... a troublesome circumstance that the committee was unable to resolve with confidence."

SOURCE: HSCA Report, many

LOQUVAM, GEORGE S. HSCA forensic expert; member of the nine-doctor panel that concluded JFK had been shot exclusively from behind. During HSCA questioning of JFK autopsist James Humes, during which Humes said that the JFK "autopsy photos" did not correspond to his recollection of the wounds, Loquvam said, "I don't think this discussion belongs on the record... We have no business recording this." (See also Humes, James)

SOURCE: HT 57

LORD, BILLY JOE, Oswald witness; passenger with Oswald on the SS *Marion Lykes.* Lord had just graduated from high school and was on his way to France to continue his education. He and Oswald were two of four passengers aboard the ship.

SOURCES: WCH XI, 117 • DUFFY 30

LORENZ, MARITA, CIA and FBI undercover operative; Lorenz is the former mistress of Fidel Castro; claims to have had Castro's child; under CIA orders she once attempted to assassinate Castro with a poison pill. Lorenz was also the former mistress of CIA contact agent and assassination suspect Frank Sturgis. According to the *New York Daily News* (November 3, 1977), Lorenz was:

> a former spy [who] says that she accompanied... Oswald and an "assassin squad" to Dallas a few days before President Kennedy was murdered there... [Lorenz] told the *News* that her companions on the car trip from Miami to Dallas were Oswald, CIA contact agent Frank

Sturgis, Cuban exile leaders Orlando Bosch and Pedro Diaz Lanz, and two Cuban brothers whose names she did not know.

She said that they were members of Operation 40, a secret guerilla group originally formed by the CIA in 1960 in preparation for the Bay of Pigs invasion...

Ms. Lorenz described Operation 40 as an "assassination squad" consisting of about 30 anti-Castro Cubans and their American advisors. She claimed the group conspired to kill Cuban Premier Fidel Castro and President Kennedy, whom it blamed for the Bay of Pigs fiasco...

She said Oswald... visited an Operation 40 training camp in the Florida Everglades. The next time she saw him, Ms. Lorenz said, was... in the Miami home of Orlando Bosch, who is now in a Venezuelan prison on murder charges in connection with the explosion and crash of a Cuban jetliner that killed 73 persons last year [1976. Bosch was later acquitted].

Ms. Lorenz claimed that this meeting was attended by Sturgis, Oswald, Bosch and Diaz Lanz, former Chief of the Cuban Air Force. She said the men spread Dallas street maps on a table and studied them...

She said they left for Dallas in two cars soon after the meeting. They took turns driving, she said, and the 1,300-mile trip took about two days. She added that they carried weapons—"rifles and scopes"—in the cars...

Sturgis reportedly recruited Ms. Lorenz for the CIA in 1959 while she was living with Castro in Havana. She later fled Cuba but returned on two secret missions. The first was to steal papers from Castro's suite in the Havana Hilton; the second mission was to kill him with a poison capsule, but it dissolved while concealed in a jar of cold cream.

Informed of her story, Sturgis told the *News* yesterday: "To the best of my knowledge, I never met Oswald."

According to HT, "A few days after this story came out, Sturgis was arrested in Lorenz's apartment, where he had gone to discuss matters with her."

Lorenz later testified for the HSCA, where she named Frank Sturgis as one of the men who had fired upon JFK. The HSCA dismissed her testimony, since they "found no evidence" to support it.

In January 1985, testifying for the defendent in the case *E. Howard Hunt* v. *Liberty Lobby*, Lorenz repeated her story. Her memory had improved. She now recalled that the two Cuban brothers were surnamed Novis.

In January 1985, Lorenz gave a deposition to attorney Mark Lane, defending Liberty Lobby in a defamation suit filed by accused assassination conspirator E. Howard Hunt, with cross-examination by Hunt's attorney Kevin A Dunne. She basically repeated her story, but included the following new information: 1) while staying a a Dallas motel on November 21, 1963, the group was visited by Hunt and Ruby. Hunt delivered a package of money. 2) Among those at Bosch's home while assassination plans were discussed was CIA-employee Alexander Rorke Jr., now deceased.

Lorenz told Dunne that, soon after the assassination, she had divulged everything she knew, including the names she had just named, to the FBI. She said, "They didn't want to go into it. They were CIA activities, not FBI."

She told Dunne that, after the assassination, Sturgis had said to her, "[You missed] the really big one [in Dallas]. We killed the president that day. You could have been part of it—you know, part of history. You should have stayed. It was safe. Everything was covered in advance. No arrests, no real newspaper investigation. It was all covered, very professional."

Sturgis and Hunt deny there is any truth to Lorenz's statements. Obviously, the real Oswald couldn't have ridden in the caravan since he was steadily employed at the TSBD at the time. (See also Bosch, Orlando; Castro, Fidel; Hemming, Gerry; Hunt, E. Howard; Lane, Mark; Lanz, Pedro Diaz; Rorke, Alexander; Sturgis, Frank)
    SOURCES: HSCA X, 93 • HT 327, 347–9 • SPOT, many • PD, many • BLAKEY 175 • EVICA 201, 203–4, 210, 246, 248, 259, 317–20

LORENZO, AURELIA, a.w.; *Dallas Morning News* employee. Lorenzo stood on the north side of Elm Street, "in the grassy knoll area," with three of her coworkers: Mary Woodward, Maggie Brown, and Ann Donaldson. All four said that the shots came from behind them and to their right, i.e., from the direction of the wooden picket fence atop the grassy knoll.
    SOURCE: SUMMERS 27

LOVELADY, BILLY NOLAN, a.w.; TSBD employee; Oswald look-alike. The famous AP photo taken by J. W. Altgens at the precise moment JFK was first shot shows a man standing in the doorway of the TSBD who looks remarkably like Oswald. The WC said that this could not have been Oswald because Oswald was on the sixth floor at the time, and that this was actually Billy Lovelady. The photo seems to show the man wearing Oswald's clothes as well. The man in the picture is wearing a light T-shirt with a dark heavy-textured shirt over it, unbuttoned halfway to the waist. This is what Oswald was wearing at the time of his arrest. Lovelady said that he was wearing "a red and white vertical striped shirt" that day. Also, witnesses near the doorway said that Lovelady was sitting at the time of the shooting. He could have stood up at the last second, of course. And no one stepped forward to say they saw Oswald in the doorway. Photos of Lovelady proved hard to obtain, and when one was finally made available, researchers learned that Lovelady did resemble the accused assassin. Lovelady died in January of 1979 during the HSCA hearings from complications following a heart attack.

Lovelady told the WC: "The shots came from right there around that concrete little deal on that knoll."

Lovelady said that the last time he saw Oswald was at 11:45 A.M. on the day on the assassination. As Lovelady rode down from the sixth floor on the elevator with coworker, a.w. Bonnie Ray Williams, they heard Oswald call down for him to send the elevator back up when they were done with it. (See also Shelley, William)

SOURCES: WR 137, 143–4 • WCH VI, 336 • WCE 1058, 1381, 1407, 1980, 2003 • HSCA Report 58 • RTJ 354–6 • BISHOP 47, 100, 121, 127 • CF 45–6, 53 • PWW, many • OTT 17

LOWERY, ROY LEE, o.k.w.; 32-year-old DPD detective (Juvenile Bureau). Lowery stood within four feet of Oswald when the latter was shot. He didn't see Ruby until the moment of the shooting.

SOURCE: WCH XII, 271

LUJAN, DANIEL GUTIERREZ, Oswald witness. Lujan appeared in the police lineup at which cabdriver William Whaley identified Oswald as the man he had driven from the Greyhound bus station in downtown Dallas to the Oak Cliff section of Dallas, moments after the assassination. Lujan was 26 years old at the time. He was #4 in the lineup. Oswald was #3.

SOURCE: WCH VII, 243

LUMPKIN, GEORGE L., a.w. (prelude); Dallas assistant police chief. Lumpkin told the SS during the planning stages of the motorcade route that the Elm Street to Stemmons Freeway route was preferable to a Main Street to Industrial Boulevard route because the Industrial course was "filled with winos and broken pavement." He rode in the presidential motorcade's "pilot car," which preceded the president by 1/4-mile.

SOURCES: HT 151 • BISHOP, many • CF 9 • FMG I, 45 • BLAKEY 16

LUMPKIN, W. G., a.w.; DPD motorcycle patrolman. Lumpkin was one of five motorcycle patrolmen who rode a half-block ahead of JFK's limo. His number that day was 152.

SOURCE: FMG III, 54

LUTZ, MONTY C., member, HSCA ballistics panel; Wisconsin Regional Crime Laboratory firearms examiner. The panel concluded that JFK was shot twice, both times from above and to the rear.
SOURCE: ME 229

LUX, J. PHILLIP, H. L. Green Company store manager. Lux told the WC that the store stocked 6.5mm Mannlicher-Carcano rifles in 1963, but records show that none had the serial number C2766, as did the TSBD rifle.
SOURCE: WCH XI, 206

M

McBRIDE, G. C., a.w.; member DPD. According to Penn Jones Jr., McBride was among the motorcycle policemen who rode in front of JFK's limo.
SOURCES: WCH XX, 489 • HT 22 • FMG III, 54

McBRIDE, PALMER, Oswald witness; New Orleans acquaintance when Oswald was a teenager. According to the WR, McBride stated, "Oswald said he would like to kill President Eisenhower because he was exploiting the working class. Oswald praised Khrushchev and suggested that he and McBride join the Communist Party 'to take advantage of the social functions.'" Soon thereafter, Oswald joined the USMC.
SOURCE: WR 360

McCABE, J. A., Irving (Texas) police detective. McCabe arrested Buell Wesley Frazier at the Irving Professional Center, where Frazier had been visiting his father on the evening of November 22, 1963. Frazier was sought by the DPD as a material witness because he was a neighbor of Marina Oswald and had given Oswald a ride to work that morning. The DPD wanted Frazier brought in for questioning, but did not intend to have him arrested. Frazier was arrested nonetheless because of a failure in communication. Frazier, who told police that Oswald had, that morning, carried a long thin package purportedly containing curtain rods into the TSBD, was released by the DPD after passing a polygraph examination. (See also Frazier, Buell Wesley)
SOURCE: BISHOP 335, 342, 367

McCAMY, CALVIN, HSCA ballistics expert. McCamy was one of a panel of 22 experts who analyzed the path and number of bullets fired in Dealey Plaza. Speaking for the panel, McCamy testified that the Zapruder film

"might show" JFK and Governor Connally reacting to a single shot.
  SOURCES: *Congressional Record*, February 16, 1977 • HT 376

MacCANNON, JIM, Texas Theatre witness. MacCannon photographed Oswald being apprehended and taken out of the Texas Theatre. His photos were introduced into evidence to the WC as "Hill Exhibits A and B." What was MacCannon doing there with a camera? How many guys who get caught sneaking into a movie theater have their picture taken during their apprehension?
  SOURCE: PWW 207

McCARTHY, ELIZABETH, handwriting expert; prosecution witness at the New Orleans conspiracy trial of Clay Shaw. McCarthy said that a signature reading "Clay Bertrand" on a guest register at the VIP Room of the New Orleans International Airport was in the handwriting of Clay Shaw. Showing that Shaw and Bertrand were the same person was key to District Attorney Jim Garrison's case because Bertrand was the name Shaw used when seen with Oswald and David Ferrie.
  SOURCE: OTT 241–2

McCLELLAND, ROBERT N., Parkland witness; attending physician to JFK. McClelland told a reporter that he and the other Dallas doctors were puzzled by the reconstruction of the crime by the authorities (that JFK had been shot exclusively from behind) and said that he and his colleagues saw bullet wounds every day and there was no doubt in their minds that the wound to JFK's throat was an entrance wound. He wrote that JFK died as a result of a gunshot to the "left temple"—he probably meant the right temple—and has repeatedly told researchers and members of the press that he recalls a gaping hole in the back of JFK's head, which does not appear in the autopsy photos. McClelland says in a British TV documentary: "[There was] a jagged wound that involved the right side of the back of the head. My initial impression was that it was probably an exit wound. So it was a very large wound. Twenty to twenty-five percent of the entire brain was missing. My most vivid impression of the entire agitated scene was that his head had almost been destroyed. His face was intact but very swollen. It was obvious he had a massive wound to the head. A fifth to a quarter of the right back part of the head had been blasted out along with most of the brain tissue in that area." (See also Patman, Ralph)
  SOURCES: WR 66–7, 70 • WCH VI, 30; XVII, 11–2 • RTJ 51–2, 58–9 • HT 37, 42–5, 68, 451, 453, 456–7 • BISHOP 156, 219, 271 • DOP 524 • MOORE 104–5 • BE, many • SUMMERS 479–80, 484–6 • OTT 91–2 • SUMMERS 479–80, 484–6 • FLAMMONDE 268 • ME 53 • OGLESBY 39 • NORTH 407 • PD 355–6

McCLOY, JOHN JAY, member of the WC; former president of the World Bank; former assistant secretary of defense; former U.S. High Commissioner for Germany. According to Kai Bird in the book *The Chairman: John Jay McCloy* (S & S Trade, 1992), McCloy described his agenda on the WC as showing that America was not "a banana republic, where a government can be changed by conspiracy."
  SOURCES: HSCA Report 257 • EVICA 18 • ME 12 • OGLESBY 12 • DAVIS 296, 412 • BELIN 13, 115–6, 126–7, 162, 217, 221–2 • RTJ 7, 23, 73, 92–3, 367, 371–2 • FMG III, 32, 66 • HT 67, 86, 263, 330 • MOORE 17 • BE 73, 85, 106, 129, 283, 298, 424, 697 • BLAKEY 24, 28, 71, 266 • HOS 85 • *Village Voice*, March 31, 1992

McCONE, JOHN ALEX, CIA director. McCone told the WC that "no one connected with the CIA had ever interviewed Oswald or communicated with him in any way." Jack Anderson wrote in a 1976 column that McCone briefed LBJ only a few days after the assassination regarding a cable from the U.S. embassy in Mexico City that said "the Cubans may have been behind the assassination."
  SOURCES: WCH V, 120 • HSCA Report 33, 136, 196–7 • FLAMMONDE 160–1 • EVICA 257 • DAVIS 270, 275, 302 • NORTH 108, 133, 239, 437, 446, 481 • PD 98, 108 • RTJ 371 • DOP 140, 253, 256–7, 260, 346, 454, 533, 543, 573, 575 • HT 312, 354, 356 • SUMMERS 131, 140, 506, 512, 531 • OTT 290 • BLAKEY 18–9, 25, 30, 55–6, 59–61, 77

McCULLOUGH, JOHN G., o.k.w.; Ruby witness; *Philadelphia Bulletin* reporter. McCullough saw Ruby on the evening of November 22 in the DPD station. He said that Ruby was carrying a 8" to 12" square box with the word ALPACUNA written on it. On Sunday morning he saw Ruby shoot Oswald. Perhaps the box contained a "twist board," an exercise gimmick that Ruby was trying to market.
  SOURCE: WCH XV, 373

McCURDY, DANNY PATRICK, Ruby witness; KLIF radio employee. McCurdy spoke to Ruby at 1:00 A.M. on November 23, 1963, in the station's studios. He said that Ruby bragged about closing his nightclubs for the weekend, even though it might cost him as much as $1,500. Ruby said he would chalk the loss up as a show of respect for the fallen president.
  SOURCES: WR 319 • WCH XV, 529 • BISHOP 502

MacDONALD, BETTY M. (See MOONEY, NANCY J.)

McDONALD, HUGH C., author of *Appointment in Dallas* (Zebra Books, 1975) and *LBJ and the JFK Conspiracy* (Condor, 1978); former chief of detectives, Los Angeles County Sheriff's Department; graduate of the FBI Academy; author of three instructional books about police work, which are standard texts in many police academies. According to McDonald, while he was assigned to Barry Goldwater's 1964 presidential campaign security team, a CIA agent told him that (1) JFK had been assassinated by a professional assassin shooting from a second-story window in the Dallas County Records building on the southeast corner of Houston and Elm; (2) The real assassin had been photographed by the CIA in late September 1963 in Mexico City while exiting the Russian or Cuban embassy; (3) These photos had been furnished to the FBI by the CIA on the *morning* of November 22, 1963; and (4) These photos had been mistakenly labeled Lee Harvey Oswald. (The photos appear in the WCH [WCE 237].) For reasons that he does not state, McDonald began to call the assassin "Saul."

Using a network of international intelligence operatives, McDonald claims to have searched for Saul for years—and finally found him in London, England, in 1972. During a confessional meeting in London's Westbury Hotel, Saul reportedly told McDonald that he had been hired to kill JFK while in Haiti by a man whose name he did not know, although they had worked together previously in Guatemala preparing for the Bay of Pigs invasion. He claims to have been paid $50,000, half in advance. The man told Saul that he had a "friend" who would be the patsy—obviously Oswald—who had been told to shoot at JFK and miss, thus scaring the president into realizing how much he needed the SS and better security. The SS were expected to return Oswald's fire, at which time Saul would shoot Oswald and escape. The SS would get credit for killing Oswald, the assumed assassin. Saul reportedly told McDonald that he had been in Mexico City to view Oswald so that it would easier for him to recognize his second target.

Saul reportedly said that he walked to Dealey Plaza from his hotel on the morning of the assassination with his preloaded semiautomatic European rifle (mounted with a German-built scope) strapped to his upper body under his right armpit and down his pant leg. He appeared to be a man with a limp, carrying nothing at all. He said he used high-velocity disintegrating ammunition, and that five shots were fired in all: three by Oswald and two by him. Their first shots practically coincided—Oswald missed, and Saul fired the shot that caused all of the nonfatal wounds, the bullet disintegrating when it hit Governor Connally's rib. (WCE 399, the "magic bullet," was a plant to link Oswald's weapon with the crime, Saul reportedly assumes.) Saul's second shot, he reportedly said, killed JFK. Oswald's last two shots also missed. Saul reportedly said that he failed to kill Oswald because the SS never returned fire. He hid his weapon once again inside his clothes, and was out of the country two hours later. (See also White, Roscoe)

McDONALD, M. N. "NICK," Texas Theatre witness; DPD patrolman who arrested Oswald. McDonald was described by author Jim Bishop as a "moon-faced man with dark skin and a high forehead." He said that Oswald, upon learning he was under arrest, tried to hit him and then pulled a gun and tried to shoot him. During the ensuing struggle, Oswald received bruises to his face. (See also Hawkins, Ray)

SOURCES: WR 26, 164–7 • WCH III, 295 • BELIN 24–7 • BISHOP 200–1, 203, 213–5 • DOP 513 • MOORE 65–7 • SUMMERS 53–4 • PD 348

McFARLAND, JOHN BRYAN and MERYL, possible Oswald witnesses. Dr. and Mrs. McFarland were British passengers on the bus to Mexico City with "Oswald" in September 1963. They told the WC that they saw Oswald riding alone on their bus from Houston to Laredo, Texas, when they awoke on that bus at 6:00 A.M. on September 26, 1963.

SOURCES: WR 300 • WCH XI, 214 • SUMMERS 343

McGANN, GEORGE, Dallas mobster. Soon after JFK's death, McGann married Beverly Oliver, who later claimed to be "The Babushka Lady," the woman wearing the triangular kerchief who filmed the assassination from the south side of Elm Street. Oliver worked at the Colony Club at the time of the assassination, which was next door to Ruby's Carousel Club. She claims that Ruby once introduced her to "Lee Oswald of the CIA," and that David Ferrie visited the Carousel Club with such frequency that she mistook him for the manager. Oliver claims that she and McGann visited for two hours with Richard M. Nixon in a Miami hotel during the 1968 presidential campaign. McGann, was gunned down gangland-style in 1970 in West Texas. (See also Nixon, Richard M.; Oliver, Beverly)

SOURCES: CF 36 • HT 122, 142

McGEE, FRANK, NBC-TV news anchor. McGee gave the message to NBC viewers that JFK was dead. McGee relayed the message by telephone from Robert MacNeil, NBC's correspondent in Dallas.

SOURCE: FMG I, 123, 125, 127–8

McGEHEE, EDWIN, Oswald witness; Clinton, Louisiana, town barber. McGehee testified at Clay Shaw's trial that in September 1963, during a town registration drive for blacks, Oswald came in for a haircut, showed his USMC discharge card and told him that he was interested in getting a job at the hospital in nearby Jackson. Oswald appeared shocked when McGehee informed him that this was a mental hospital, but continued to express interest in the job. (See also Morgan, Reeves)

SOURCES: OTT 107 • HOS 241

McGUIRE, DENNIS, a.w. (prelude); Parkland witness. McGuire was the attendant in the ambulance that picked up Jerry B. Belknap in front of the TSBD and took him to Parkland Hospital moments before the assassination. Belknap was having an apparent epileptic seizure. It has long been suspected that Belknap's seizure was planned and designed as a diversion, in spite of the fact that Belknap claims to have had problems with seizures since childhood.

With Aubrey Rike, McGuire wrapped JFK's body in a plastic sheet before closing the coffin at Parkland Hospital. This is significant because there is considerable eyewitness evidence that JFK's body was in a military-type body bag when it arrived at Bethesda for autopsy. (See also Belknap, Jerry; Rike, Aubrey)

SOURCES: HT 449 • BE 674

McHUGH, GODFREY, a.w. (rode in motorcade); general, U.S. Army; Bethesda witness; JFK aide. McHugh helped carry JFK's coffin from the ambulance into Air Force One at Love Field in Dallas. He told author David Lifton, on November 19, 1967, that he had participated in the photography of JFK's body at Bethesda. "I was holding his body several times when they were turning it and photographing it," he said. "... people keep on saying that his [JFK's] face was demolished and all; he was in absolute perfect shape, except the back of the head, top back of the head, had an explosive bullet in it and was badly damaged... and that had blown part of his forehead, which was recuperated [sic] and put intact, back in place... so his face was exactly as it had been alive... I think they took photographs before, during and after [the autopsy]; they kept on taking photographs. They took photographs from the time they got the body out until it was put into the new casket..."

Author Harrison Edward Livingstone (*High Treason 2*, Carroll & Graf, 1992) writes that McHugh and Jackie Kennedy had been romantically involved "back in her Paris days." Livingstone writes that McHugh "just happened to be connected to the Texas oilmen, and connected to General Charles Cabell," who was the brother of the mayor of Dallas. His name appeared in *Who's Who in the CIA*. Author Penn Jones Jr. wrote, "we now feel that General McHugh was a high-ranking traitor for the military inside the Kennedy camp." (See also Clifton, Chester V.; Lifton, David)

SOURCES: BE, many • FMG IV, 29–30 • HT 41 • HT2 76, 81, 128, 567–71

MACK, GARY, assassination researcher and author of useful articles published in the JFK-assassination periodical the *Continuing Inquiry*.

Mack was one of the researchers (with Jack White) who extensively studied the Polaroid photograph of the assassination taken by Mary Moorman. (See also Moorman, Mary; White, Jack)
SOURCES: HT 44, 75, 77, 241, 246–7, 254, 256, 259 • MOORE 143 • ME 111 • DAVIS 328

McKENZIE, WILLIAM, attorney. McKenzie accompanied Marina Oswald during her testimony to the WC, McKenzie was the office mate of Pete White, whose name was in Ruby's notebook. (See also Oswald, Marina)
SOURCES: RTJ 314–5, 350 • HT 283

McKEOWN, ROBERT RAY, Ruby witness; convicted smuggler of arms to Cuba (1958, arrested with former Cuban president Carlos Prio Socarras). According to an FBI report, in January 1959, about one week after Castro took over leadership of Cuba, McKeown received a frantic phone call from a man in Dallas who identified himself as "Rubenstein." This man offered McKeown $15,000 if he could get three individuals who were being held by Castro out of Cuba. Evidence indicates that one of these prisoners was Miami mob boss and assassination suspect Santos Trafficante. Rubenstein said that a person in Las Vegas, Nevada, would put up the money. The price eventually went up to $25,000, and McKeown met with Ruby (positively identifying him later) in person to discuss the matter. McKeown lived in Baycliff, Texas, at the time of JFK's death. He claimed to be close to Texas oil billionaire Clint Murchison. (See also McWillie, Lewis; Murchison, Clint; Prio Socarras, Carlos; Trafficante, Santos)
SOURCES: HSCA Report 152 • HSCA IX, 589 • RTJ 298–300 • COA 199–200, 202, 431 • GERTZ 529–30 • SUMMERS 437 • BLAKEY 294–5 • FLAMMONDE 168–9 • EVICA 171, 306–7

McKINNEY, STEWART B., HSCA member (R-Connecticut).

McKINNON, CHERYL, a.w. McKinnon later became a *San Diego Star News* reporter. She wrote in 1983: "On November 22, 1963, I stood... on the Grassy Knoll in Dealey Plaza... Suddenly three shots in rapid succession rang out. Myself [sic] and dozens of others standing nearby turned in horror toward the back of the Grassy Knoll where it seemed the shots had originated. Puffs of white smoke still hung in the air in small patches. But no one was visible."
SOURCE: CF 71

McKINZIE, LOUIS, 54-year-old Dallas City Hall porter. McKinzie told the WC that the fire-escape doors on the first floor of the Municipal Building (DPD station/City Hall) are never locked and that Ruby theoretically could have entered the building that way. He said he was ordered

on the morning of Oswald's transfer to "stop the elevators," which he did. He did not see Ruby enter building.
    SOURCE: WCH XIII, 147

McLAIN, H. B., a.w.; DPD officer. McLain rode his motorcycle approximately 150 feet behind JFK's limo. It is suspected that it was McLain's radio mike that was jammed in the open position, thus causing the Dictabelt recording the HSCA used to determine that there was a second gunman in Dealey Plaza. McLain says that it couldn't have been his mike because he turned his siren on immediately following the shooting, and there is no siren audible on the Dictabelt recording. Acoustical analysis indicated that the microphone was 154 feet behind the presidential limo at the time of the third shot.
    SOURCES: HSCA Report 75, 487, 492–3 • BELIN 191–2 • HT 249 • MOORE 141, 143 • SUMMERS 15–6 • BLAKEY 16, 103–6, 267

McLANE, ALFRED, Ruby witness; a friend of Ruby's; suspicious death; mob lawyer. According to Peter Dale Scott: "McLane... represented the oil-gas interests of the Murchisons, Wofford Cain of the Del Charro set and Lyndon Johnson's business representative Frank Denius." Ruby brought up McLane's name during his testimony to Chief Justice Earl Warren, and Warren, with unexpected knowledge, stated, "Alfred was killed in a taxi in New York." McLane died on March 16, 1960, in a two-car, hit-and-run accident in which he was the only one injured.
    SOURCES: Peter, Dale Scott, *Crime and Cover-up,* p. 45 • HT 282, 298 • WCH V, 206 • BLAKEY 297 • KANTOR 12–3, 130, 134

McLENDON, GORDON, Ruby witness; Dallas journalist; operator of KLIF radio in Dallas. Ruby said he tried to call McLendon around midnight, November 23, but couldn't get through. During his testimony to Chief Justice Earl Warren, Ruby asked, out of the blue, whether Warren had heard of McLendon. Warren replied that he had not.
    SOURCES: HT 298 • GERTZ 106, 108, 111–2, 184

McMAINES, LILLIE MAE (See MOFFETT, SANDRA)

McMEEKIN, ROBERT R., lieutenant colonel, U.S. Army, Armed Forces Institute of Pathology aerospace pathologist; member HSCA medical panel. McMeekin examined the JFK autopsy photos and X rays. The panel concluded that the shots were fired exclusively from the rear.
    SOURCE: BELIN 181

McMILLAN, PRISCILLA (See JOHNSON, PRISCILLA)

McMILLON, THOMAS DONALD, o.k.w.; member DPD. McMillon was walking a few steps behind Oswald when he was shot and helped subdue

Ruby at the scene. Testifying at Ruby's murder trial, McMillon quoted Ruby as saying, as he pulled the trigger, "You rat sonofabitch, you shot the president." He said Ruby told him he had intended to shoot Oswald three times, but the Dallas police had been too quick and had stopped him. He also quoted Ruby as saying, soon after he was subdued, "Don't you know who I am? Don't you know who I am? I'm Jack Ruby! I'm Jack Ruby!"

SOURCES: WR 198 • WCH XIII, 37 • RTJ 210 • GERTZ 47–8, 57, 71, 76, 86–92, 415

McNALLY, JOSEPH P., document expert; member of the American Society of Questioned Document Examiners. McNally was called upon by the HSCA, along with Charles C. Scott and David J. Purtell, to assess the authenticity of the "Historic Diary" Oswald supposedly kept in the USSR. They determined that the diary was written by Oswald, but in one or two sittings, rather than daily.

SOURCE: DUFFY 48–50

MacNEIL, ROBERT, a.w.; Oswald witness; NBC television news correspondent; currently cohost of PBS's *The MacNeil-Lehrer NewsHour*. Mac-Neil rode in the motorcade. When he heard the shots and saw the commotion in Dealey Plaza, he jumped out of his car and ran toward the TSBD's front entrance. At the door he asked a man where he could find a phone, and the man pointed inside. It was only later that MacNeil realized that the man was Oswald. (Interestingly, Oswald, too, remembered the encounter, but slightly differently. According to the DPD, Oswald said that, as he was leaving the TSBD, he encountered a man asking for a telephone. The man, Oswald claimed, produced SS identification.) Later, at Parkland, it was MacNeil who, while talking on the telephone to NBC news anchor Frank McGee, broke the news of the president's death to NBC viewers.

SOURCES: BISHOP 143, 204 • DOP 279 • SUMMERS 82 • NORTH 389

McVEY, O. S., a.w. McVey was standing atop the triple underpass. The only record of McVey's presence on the underpass comes from a Dallas sheriff's department report. That department apparently never interviewed McVey.

SOURCE: WCE [Decker] 5323, p. 517

McVICKAR, JOHN A., Oswald witness; foreign service officer and vice consul stationed at the American embassy in the Soviet Union from 1959 to 1961. McVickar spoke to Oswald soon after his arrival in the USSR and said that Oswald wanted to renounce his U.S. citizenship and "threatened to reveal the military secrets he had." Later he said that Oswald appeared to be "following a pattern of behavior in which he had been tutored by person or persons unknown..." McVickar's statement that Oswald threatened to divulge U.S. military secrets is strong evidence that Oswald was working in some capacity for the U.S. government. If he were not a U.S. agent, he would have been arrested for treason upon his return to the United States.

SOURCES: WCH V, 299, 318 • HSCA Report 213 • HT 163 • SUMMERS 120–1, 155 • FLAMMONDE 141

McWATTERS, CECIL J., Oswald witness; Dallas bus driver. According to the WC, immediately after the assassination, Oswald left the TSBD and walked a few blocks east. He then boarded a westbound bus driven by McWatters at the corner of Elm and Murphy streets. He asked for a transfer. The bus became caught in traffic, and Oswald got off the bus two blocks or so after getting on. McWatters was taken to a lineup the night after the assassination and said that the #2 man (Oswald) "resembled" the man on his bus. The man, he remembered, had grinned when hearing that the president had been shot. The following day, Milton Jones got on McWatters's bus, and the bus driver realized that it was this man—and not Oswald—who had gotten on and grinned inappropriately. McWatters attempted to rescind his earlier statement, but was ignored. The balance of the evidence still indicates that Oswald was on this bus. A passenger, Mary Bledsoe, also identified him, and he was found with the appropriate transfer when he was arrested. (See also Bledsoe, Mary; Jones, Milton)

SOURCES: WR 147–8, 234 • WCH II, 262 • BELIN 72 • RTJ 91, 159–63, 387 • BISHOP 161–3, 351–4 • MOORE 60

McWILLIE, LEWIS J., Ruby witness; prominent gambler in Havana, Dallas, and Las Vegas. Ruby traveled to Havana at McWillie's invitation in 1959. McWillie said that Ruby had once "mailed me a pistol." Ruby had said to friends that McWillie was his idol. McWillie was a close friend of Fort Worth nightclub owner Pat Kirkwood, who entertained the SS the night before the assassination in his beatnik nightclub, The Cellar. McWillie was a business associate of Santos Trafficante and Meyer Lansky, both organized crime bigwigs. He ran the Tropicana Casino in Havana before Castro's takeover and was arrested by Castro after the revolution. (See also Kirkwood, Pat; Lansky, Meyer; Trafficante, Santos)

SOURCES: WR 346 • HSCA Report 151, 173 • HSCA XIV, 459 • RTJ 301 • COA, many • GERTZ 184, 488, 494, 529–30 • CF 393–401 • HT 150, 283, 319 • SUMMERS 423, 437–41, 445–6 • BLAKEY 38, 82–3, 143, 293–302, 304, 308, 314, 336 • FLAM-MONDE 168–9 • EVICA, many • NORTH, many • KANTOR 4, 11, 13, 24, 31, 123, 129–32, 138, 211

MAHEU, ROBERT, intermediary between CIA Security Director Sheffield Edwards and crime boss Sam Giancana to discuss "several clandestine efforts" in Cuba during the early 1960s. According to HT, Maheu worked closely with Oswald associate Guy Banister and "figured prominently" in the Watergate scandal. Maheu was a top aide to Howard Hughes and he worked with mobster Johnny Roselli and General Charles Cabell on murder plots against Fidel Castro. (See also Banister, Guy; Cabell, Charles; Edwards, Sheffield; Hughes, Howard; Giancana, Sam; Roselli, John)

SOURCES: HSCA Report 114, 173 • EVICA, many • DAVIS 98, 405 • NORTH 64, 598 • BELIN 100, 104, 106–10, 113 • HT 154, 312, 314–5, 378–9, 413 • COA 193 • SUMMERS 238, 496, 594 • BLAKEY 53–5, 58–9, 381, 385 • KANTOR 25

MALLEY, JAMES R., FBI inspector; in charge of all FBI agents assigned to the assassination case in Dallas as of 6:00 P.M., November 22, 1963. At that time, the FBI had no legitimate jurisdiction because JFK's murder was not a federal crime. Malley told the WC that the CIA would not release the photo purportedly of Oswald leaving the Cuban embassy in Mexico City in September 1963, unless all background detail was trimmed away. What remained was a silhouetted photo of a man (decidedly not Oswald) that could have been taken by anybody, anywhere, at any time.

SOURCES: WCH XI, 468 • RTJ 352 • BISHOP 361 • BE 116, 304 • BLAKEY 77–8

MALLORY, KATHERINE, Oswald witness; tourist in Minsk, USSR. Mallory told the WC that, during the second week in March 1961, she was in Minsk touring the Soviet Union with the University of Michigan Symphonic Band. She found herself encircled at one point by curious Russians whose questions she did not understand. A young man, she says, who told her he was an ex-Marine and a Texan, stepped out of the crowd and offered to be her interpreter. She gladly accepted his offer, and he translated for her for the next 15 or 20 minutes. She and the young man continued to speak even after the small crowd's curiosity had been appeased. He told her he despised the United States and that he wanted to stay in Minsk for the rest of his life. She stated that she couldn't swear that the man was Oswald, but that she was "personally convinced."

SOURCES: WCH XI, 210 • DUFFY 42

MAMANTOV, ILYA A., member of the Dallas Russian-speaking community. On the evening of November 22, 1963, Mamantov served as Marina Oswald's interpreter during her interrogation by Dallas police. Ruth Paine, who had accompanied Marina to the police station, was not allowed to act as Marina's interpreter because she, too, was a witness in the case. (See also Oswald, Marina)

SOURCES: WR 261 • WCH IX, 102 • BISHOP 379–81

MANCHESTER, JOHN, Oswald witness; Clinton, Louisiana, town marshall. Manchester testified at Clay Shaw's trial that he had seen Shaw, David Ferrie, and Oswald together two months before the assassination attending a voter-registration drive for blacks (at which Oswald attempted to register). The men arrived in a "big black car" and the driver identified himself to Manchester as "a representative of the International Trade Mart in New Orleans." (See also Ferrie, David; Shaw, Clay)
SOURCE: OTT 232

MANCHESTER, WILLIAM, author of *The Death of a President* (Harper & Row, 1967).
SOURCES: HT 419, 463–4 • PWW 21, 124 • BE, many • MOORE, many • BLAKEY 22 • FLAMMONDE 262 • ME 100–1, 110–1 • PD 71

MANCUSO, MARLENE, former beauty queen, former wife of suspected Oswald impersonator Gordon Novel. On May 5, 1967, Mancuso gave a statement to New Orleans District Attorney Jim Garrison's office, through Garrison's chief investigator Louis Ivon, that appears to reveal a plot by NBC-TV to discredit Garrison's case against Clay Shaw. She said:

> Richard Townley told me that he had been trying to contact me for a couple of weeks. He said that he worked for NBC and the reason he wanted to talk to me was so that he could tape an interview with me. I told him that I was not a star witness [at the Shaw trial]. He said that his intuition told him that I would be involved in a part of it eventually... He said Mr. Garrison was going to be destroyed and that it was all a fraud. He said they were not going to merely discredit the probe—he said Garrison would get a jail sentence. He said he figured that I was going to be Mr. Garrison's star witness, and that Mr. Garrison was going to use me to discredit Gordon [Novel] and make him appear as a second Oswald. He kept going back that he wanted a taped interview that would show me in a good light. He said that otherwise I would probably be subpoenaed and there would be a lots [sic] of newspapermen around me and a state of confusion and I would look very bad... Jerry Monday [a friend of Townley's who also worked at NBC] said that for the past two weeks he has been working on this Garrison thing and that I should realize that in the next two weeks that Mr. Garrison is going to be destroyed.

(See also Novel, Gordon)
SOURCES: OTT 166–7 • FLAMMONDE 103, 312–4

MANDEL, GEORGE (aka Mantello, Giorgio), founder of the Swiss corporation Permindex, suspected by assassination investigator William Torbitt of being the "master cylinder" behind the JFK assassination. In 1959, Mandel (whose name was Italianized to Giorgio Mantello when he worked in Italy) created the *Società Italo-Americana*, the purpose of which was announced as industry and commerce. The Italian newspaper *Paesa Sera* reported (March 4, 1967) that on November 14, 1959, Mandel inaugurated his "most important creation," the Italo-American Hotel Corporation. The object of the corporation was the building of the Exposition Universale Roma's Hotel du Lac. Three foreign credit groups were the corporation's largest shareholders. They were "represented in Italy by the *Banca Nazionale del Lavoro*, the *DeFamaco Astalde Vaduz* (Swiss), the *Miami Astalde Vaduz* (American), and the Seligman Bank of Basel. The DeFamaco and Seligman institutions were among the most powerful stockholders of the [CMC]." CMC counted Clay Shaw as a member of its board of directors.

Researcher Paris Flammonde writes that Mandel was "a Hungarian refugee, Austrian citizen, functioning in Italy, Switzerland, and elsewhere with financial transactions reaching throughout Europe, Africa, and America, who has, according to *Paesa Sera*, been condemned for his 'criminal activities' in Switzerland." Allegations of Mandel's "criminal activities" were first reported in the August 19, 1961, issue of *A-Z*, a Basel newspaper. Mandel filed a defamation suit against *A-Z* but then withdrew it. *A-Z* commented, "Too bad; we would have heard some great things at the trial."

Mario Ceravolo, a Christian Democrat and member of CMC's board of directors, wrote *Paesa Sera* a letter, which appeared in the paper's March 11–12, 1967, issue. It said, in part. "To avoid misunderstandings and false interpretations, I ask that you please publish the fact that I left the administrative board of the CMC on 25 July 1962 because it was no longer possible to understand the sources of great sums of money obtained abroad by Mr. Giovanni [Giorgio] Mantello, and the real destination of the money."

On March 6, 1967, *Paesa Sera* said:

It is certain that Clay Shaw, who was arrested in New Orleans... (and therefore, whether on true grounds or not, is a person who is certainly not limited to the quiet pursuit of his profession as a director of industry, but who must therefore have his finger in the pies of it is not clear what political activities) had a position on the board of the CMC in Rome... It is certain that the CMC (taking advantage of the good faith of... Italians who were involved in that disastrous enterprise) has not fulfilled any of the activities for which it was originally projected. It is certain that an important shareholder in the CMC was an ex-official of the American service... Concerning the CMC and the organizations formed by Mandel, it is not clear on whose account many Hungarian refugees who were implicated in espionage activities were working, nor through what agencies large financial dealings in European political movements have been taking place.

SOURCE: FLAMMONDE 214–6, 218, 220, 222–3

MANDELLA, ARTHUR, New York City Police Department fingerprint expert. At the request of the WC, Mandella "conducted an independent examination [of the Mannlicher-Carcano rifle found after the assassination on the sixth floor of the TSBD] and also determined that this was the right palm-print of Oswald." The portion of the palm that had left the print on the rifle was the right heel on the little-finger side. Mandella also independently verified Oswald's fingerprints as those found on boxes on the TSBD sixth floor and concluded that the prints were "probably made within a day or a day-and-a-half of the examination on November 22," which is not startling since Oswald worked in that building and on that floor.

SOURCES: WR 118, 127, 132 • WCH IV, 48

MANTELLO, GIORGIO (See MANDEL, GEORGE)

MARACHINI, DANTE, Oswald witness; one of four men (with Alfred Claude, John Branyon, and Emmett Barbee) who began work at the Reily Coffee Company in New Orleans at approximately the same time as Oswald—in Marachini's case, the same day—then quit soon after Oswald left. All four went on to work for NASA.

As of March 3, 1967, when he was first subpoenaed by New Orleans District Attorney Jim Garrison, Marachini's address was 4951 Music, New Orleans. Soon thereafter, the 42-year-old parts scheduler for the Chrysler Corporation's Michoud Assembly Facility was questioned. He told the DA's office that he had gone to work for the Standard Coffee Company—a subsidiary of the William B. Reily Company. He said that the company had two locations—at 725 and 640 Magazine Street—and that, during this same period, Oswald and he were coworkers at the 640 Magazine site. (Marachini's statement gives us our only indication that the "Reily Coffee Company" was somewhat more than a "mom-and-pop" store where they grind beans.) Paris Flammonde writes: "Subsequently, the press noted that he was reputedly a friend and neighbor of Clay Shaw." (See also Barbee,

Emmett; Branyon, John; Claude, Alfred; Lewallen, James)
SOURCES: OTT 115–6 • FLAMMONDE 78, 180–1

MARCADES, MELBA CHRISTINE (See CHERAMIE, ROSE)

MARCELLO, CARLOS (né Minacero, Calogero), boss of America's oldest Mafia family, based in New Orleans, during the 1950s, 1960s, and 1970s. Marcello, whose power spread westward across the south to encompass Dallas, sought revenge upon the Kennedys after Attorney General Robert Kennedy had him deported in April 1961, about the time of the Bay of Pigs invasion. Marcello was "kidnapped" and flown to Guatemala without being allowed to call anyone or pick up a toothbrush. While in Latin America, Marcello had a hellish experience, spending several days in the jungle at one point with a broken rib. He was flown back into the country four months later, according to the U.S. Border Patrol, by CIA pilot (and assassination suspect) David Ferrie. Upon his return, Marcello is reported to have said of the Kennedys: "Take the stone out of my shoe."

At the time of the assassination, Ferrie was working for Marcello's lawyer, G. Wray Gill, on Marcello's defense against immigration fraud charges. (Marcello was acquitted of these charges on the day of the assassination.)

FBI reports regarding Ferrie—which fell into the hands of author David Lifton through WC staffer Wesley Liebeler—indicated that Ferrie flew to Guatamala aboard Delta Airlines twice during the fall of 1963, evidence that Ferrie's detective work for G. Wray Gill was directly related to his defense of Carlos Marcello's immigration-fraud charges.

Between February 1979 and February 1980, the FBI made 1,350 tapes of Marcello's conversations, as part of an FBI sting called BRILAB. The tapes were made by agents Mike Wacks and Larry Montague, along with a man named Joe Hauser, who is described by *New York Post* columnist Jack Newfield as a "sleazy swindler." The tapes were sealed by Judge Morey Sear at the start of Marcello's bribery and conspiracy trial in 1981. The judge ordered them permanantly sealed, ruling that they would prejudice the jury against Marcello. According to former HSCA Chief Counsel Robert Blakey, Marcello "implicated himself in the assassination on three of those tapes... On one tape, Marcello asked the other person to leave the room and resume the conversation in the secrecy of his car when the assassination came up. Marcello said something like. 'We don't talk about that in here.'" Author John H. Davis has described the tapes based on interviews with the two FBI agents and the "swindler" who taped them. He says that the tapes amount to a veiled "admission of complicity" by Marcello and his brother Joe. Davis filed a 1988 Freedom of Information Act suit for the release of the tapes. In May 1991, Federal Judge Thomas Penfield Jackson ruled in Davis's favor and ordered the tapes released. The FBI, however, appealed the decision, and the tapes remain sealed at this time.

Las Vegas private investigator Ed Becker says that in September 1962, Marcello told him about a plan to assassinate JFK, which included using a "nut" to deflect blame from the mob. Becker says he told the FBI about the plot a year before the assassination. In 1978, Becker repeated the story to the HSCA, which found him credible.

Some researchers feel that the assassination, as executed, was beyond the scope of mobsters. According to HT: "There is no way Carlos Marcello [and other mobsters]... could have done all this alone or covered any of it up. Neither these Mafia bosses nor the men who work for them had this kind of access to the evidence."

Recently new evidence has surfaced implicating Marcello in the assassination. For 27 years Frank Ragano was the lawyer for Florida mob boss Santos Trafficante, and for 15 years he represented Teamster president Jimmy Hoffa. In the January 14, 1992, edition of the *New York Post*, Ragano revealed knowledge of a plot involving Hoffa, Trafficante, and New Orleans mob boss Carlos Marcello to assassinate the president. Hoffa, Marcello, and Trafficante are now dead. Ragano, who at the time was 68 years old, told Jack Newfield of the *Post* that he became an "unwitting intermediary" to the plot when he met with Hoffa at Teamster headquarters in Washington, D.C. in January or February 1963. Ragano, who was about to fly to New Orleans for a meeting with Trafficante and Marcello, says Hoffa told him, "Tell Marcello and Trafficante they have to kill the president."

Ragano continued, "Hoffa said to me, 'This has to be done.' Jimmy was ranting and raving for a long time. I didn't take it seriously because I knew Jimmy was a hothead with a short attention span. Marcello and Trafficante never met Hoffa. I had lawyer-client privilege with Hoffa and Trafficante, so I was designated intermediary. Marcello and Trafficante were extremely cautious. They always wanted to be able to truthfully tell a grand jury they never met Hoffa." A few days later, Ragano claims he met with Trafficante and Marcello at the Royal Orleans Hotel. Ragano continued, "I told them, 'You won't believe what Hoffa wants me to tell you. Jimmy wants you to kill the president.' They didn't laugh. They were dead serious. They looked at each other in a way that made me uncomfortable. Their looks scared me. It made me think they already had such a thought in mind."

When Ragano returned to Washington, Hoffa asked him if he had delivered the message. Ragano said he had. Hoffa reportedly replied, "It is going to be done."

On the day of the assassination, Hoffa called Ragano three or four minutes after the first news bulletins. "Have you heard the good news?" Hoffa asked. "They killed the SOB. This means Bobby is out as Attorney General."

Marcello gave immunized testimony to the HSCA on January 11, 1978. During that testimony, "Marcello expressed 'a deep dislike' for Robert Kennedy... claiming that he had been 'illegally kidnapped' by Government agents during [his] deportation." He told the committee that, yes, Ferrie worked for his lawyer G. Wray Gill, but denied that Ferrie worked directly for him or that he had a close relationship with Ferrie.

The HSCA concluded that

> Marcello had the motive, means and opportunity to have President John F. Kennedy assassinated, though [the HSCA] was unable to establish direct evidence of Marcello's complicity... In its investigation of Marcello, the committee identified the presence of one critical evidentiary element that was lacking with the other organized crime figures examined by the committee: credible associations relating both Lee Harvey Oswald and Jack Ruby to figures having a relationship, albeit tenuous, with Marcello's crime family or organization.

Oswald's uncle, Dutz Murret, worked for Marcello. Oswald's mother had dated men who worked for Marcello. Both Guy Banister and Ferrie had done work for Marcello. As a mob leader whose turf was "based in New Orleans but extend[ed] throughout Louisiana and Texas, Marcello was one of the prime targets of Justice Department efforts during the Kennedy administration."

The HSCA established also "associations between Jack Ruby and several individuals affiliated with the underworld activities of Carlos Marcello. Ruby was a personal acquaintance of Joseph Civello, the Marcello associate who allegedly headed organized crime activities in Dallas... [and] a New Orleans nightclub figure, Harold Tannenbaum with whom Ruby was considering going into partnership in the fall of 1963."

A primary criticism of the assassination investigation of New Orleans District Attorney Jim Garrison was that it didn't include the possibility of Marcello's involvement. When questioned, Garrison has always said that he has seen no evidence that Marcello is a member of organized crime. An explanation for Garrison's blind spot is offered by *Life* magazine (September 8, 1967), which noted that Garrison knew Marcello aide Mario Marino and that Marino "picked up a couple of hotel bills" for Garrison on visits to Las Vegas.

Marcello died at age 83 in his suburban New Orleans home on March 2, 1993. (See also Becker, Edward; Bruneau, Emile; Civello, Joseph; Davis, John H.; Dolan, James; Ferrie, David; Gill, C. Wray; Hoffa, James; Kennedy, Regis; Kimble, Jules; Long, Richard; Marino, Mario; Moore, Bobby Gene; Murret, Charles; Partin, Edward; Scheim, David; Traffi- cante, Santos; Tregle, Bernard)

SOURCES: HSCA Report 143–5, 147, 154–6, 169–72, 179, 246 • HSCA X, 112 • EVICA 163, 166, 171, 182, 221, 223, 235–6, 265 • ME 213 • OGLESBY 24, 27, 79 • DAVIS, many • NORTH, many • COA, many • HT 119, 288, 319, 326, 378–9, 412, 421 • DUFFY 163–72 • CF 164–7 • MOORE 145 • SUMMERS, many • OTT 288, 300–2, 304–5 • BLAKEY, many • FLAMMONDE 27–8, 327 • KANTOR 28, 83, 136, 212

MARCHETTI, VICTOR, former CIA agent and assistant to CIA Director Richard Helms; cowrote, with John Marks, *The CIA and the Cult of Intelligence* (Alfred A. Knopf, 1974). Marchetti confirmed New Orleans District Attorney Jim Garrison's allegations that Clay Shaw was "intimately connected" to the CIA and wrote that CIA Director Richard Helms was concerned that Garrison would blow Shaw's cover. Marchetti contends that Richard M. Nixon, General Charles Cabell, Bernard Barker, Frank Sturgis, E. Howard Hunt, David Ferrie, and Clay Shaw all worked together during the planning stages of the CIA's Bay of Pigs operation. He says that the public should not get too excited about the possible release of secret government files, as any documentation of U.S. government complicity in the assassination has surely been destroyed. He wrote an article for the *Spotlight*, a Washington, D.C., right-wing magazine, which claimed that E. Howard Hunt was in Dallas on the day of the assassination (a claim Hunt denies) and that a CIA memo reveals that Hunt had a "substantial" role in the JFK killing. Hunt sued the *Spotlight* for $1 million for defamation. Attorney and assassination researcher Mark Lane successfully defended the *Spotlight* in the jury trial. Not only did Hunt not get his $1 million, but he was ordered to pay the magazine $25,000 in court costs. (See also

Barker, Bernard; Cabell, Charles; Ferrie, David; Helms, Richard; Hunt, E. Howard; Nixon, Richard M.; Shaw, Clay; Sturgis, Frank)
   SOURCES: HT 144, 186, 289, 292, 346, 411 • SUMMERS 143–6, 300–1 • OTT 234–5, 251, 276, 324 • EVICA 131 • OGLESBY 83 • PD, many

MARCUS, RAYMOND, author of *The Bastard Bullet: A Search for Legitimacy for Commission Exhibit 399* (Randall Publications, 1966).

MARINO, MARIO, aide to New Orleans crime boss Carlos Marcello. Marino paid hotel bills for New Orleans District Attorney Jim Garrison on several occasions when Garrison visited Las Vegas—before Garrison arrested Clay Shaw for conspiracy to assassinate JFK. A primary criticism of Garrison's investigation has been that it stubbornly refused to admit the possibility of Marcello's involvement. (See also Marcello, Carlos)
   SOURCES: FLAMMONDE 327 • *Life*, September 8, 1967

MARKHAM, HELEN LOUISE, t.k.w.; waitress in downtown Dallas. Markham told the WC that she was waiting for traffic to pass at the northwest corner of Tenth Street and Patton Avenue in the Oak Cliff section of Dallas at approximately 1:15 P.M. on the day of the assassination, so that she could cross Tenth, when she spotted a man at the opposite (southeast) corner of the intersection just about to step up onto the curb. At that point she was approximately 50 feet away from the man, who proceeded away from her slowly along Tenth.

According to the WR. "Mrs. Markham saw a police car slowly approach the man from the rear and stop alongside of him. She saw the man come to the right window of the police car. As he talked he leaned on the ledge of the right window with his arms. The man appeared to step back as the policeman 'calmly opened the car door' and very slowly got out and walked toward the front of the car. The man pulled a gun. Mrs. Markham heard three shots and saw the policeman fall to the ground near the left front wheel." She saw the man "fooling with" the gun (probably ejecting the shells) and then heading "in kind of a little trot" down Patton toward Jefferson Boulevard, which was a block away. Markham says she immediately ran to the policeman's side, where he was lying in a pool of blood and trying to talk to her as she attempted to comfort him.

Her testimony to the WC was used to "convict Oswald of the shooting of Officer Tippit." But a transcript of her testimony casts serious doubts on what she saw and didn't see that afternoon. She was near-hysterical after the Tippit shooting all the way through the time she was taken to the police station to view Oswald in a lineup. Here is one exchange that took place during her WC testimony:

Q: Now when you went into the room you looked these people over, these four men?

Markham: Yes, sir.

Q: Did you recognize anyone in the lineup?

Markham: No, sir.

Q: You did not? Did you see anybody—I asked you that question before—did you recognize anybody from their face?

Markham: From their face, no.

Q: Did you identify anybody in these four people?

Markham: I didn't know nobody.

Q: I know you didn't know anybody, but did anyone in that lineup look like anybody you had seen before?

Markham: No. I had never seen none of them, none of these men...

Q: Was there a number two man in there?

Markham: Number two is the one I picked.

Q: I thought you just told me that you hadn't—

Markham: I thought you wanted me to describe their clothing.

Q: You recognized him from his appearance?

Markham: I asked—I looked at him. When I saw this man I wasn't sure, but I had cold chills run all over me.

This is what the WC called a "positive identification." Markham claimed that she was "the only" witness to the shooting and that she remained for 20 minutes with the dying officer, talking with him ("he tried to talk to me," she said), before anyone else arrived. Every other witness to the shooting said that the officer was killed immediately and that a crowd of people gathered "quickly" around the crime scene. Markham's credibility is further strained by her statement that the gunman spoke to Tippit through the right window of the police car, since photos of the car taken at the crime scene show that the window of police car #10 was rolled shut. (See also Ables, Don; Austin, Emory; Barnes, Willie; Brown, Charles; Callaway, Ted; Clark, Richard; Leavelle, J. R.; Perry, W. E.; Tatum, Jack)

SOURCES: WR 25, 156, 159, 162–3 • WCH III, 305; VII, 499 • BELIN 19–20, 28, 32 • RTJ 177–93, 201, 208, 269, 280–2, 330, 346, 384 • BISHOP 199–200, 257, 290, 298, 324, 356 • CF 340–2, 345–6 • MOORE 64, 68 • BE 100 • SUMMERS 86–7, 92–4 • OTT 195–6 • HOS 67–9 • OGLESBY 60–1 • PD 365–6

MARKS, JOHN, coauthor, with Victor Marchetti, of *The CIA and the Cult of Intelligence.* (Alfred A. Knopf, 1974). (See also Marchetti, Victor)

SOURCE: HT 439

MARMOR, ARTHUR, WC staff member, attorney. Marmor assisted in the writing of the WR's Appendix VII, entitled, "A Brief History of Presidential Protection."

MARRS, JIM, Dallas reporter and author of *Crossfire* (Carroll & Graf, 1989).
SOURCE: MOORE 189, 192, 216–8

MARTELLO, FRANCIS L., Oswald witness; New Orleans police lieutenant. When Oswald was arrested in New Orleans during the summer of 1963, he told Martello that he did not speak English when around Marina and June because "he did not want them to become Americanized." Martello said that, following his arrest, Oswald was "a very cool speaker... He displayed little emotion and was completely aloof. He seemed to have them set up to create an incident. When the incident occurred, he seemed peaceful and gentle..."
SOURCES: WR 392–3 • WCH XI, 471 • SUMMERS 100, 272, 414 • FLAMMONDE 122

MARTENS, LAYTON, associate of David Ferrie. Martens was arrested in New Orleans along with fellow Ferrie associate Alvin Beauboeuf on November 25, 1963. According to the *New Orleans States-Item* (April 25, 1967), suspected Oswald impersonator Gordon Novel said that Martens, Ferrie, and Sergio Arcacha Smith were part of a CIA team working to supply munitions for the Bay of Pigs invasion.

In 1967, Martens was an accomplished cellist and a 24-year-old senior at the University of Southwestern Louisiana at Lafayette.

According to author Paris Flammonde:

Garrison subpoenaed Layton Martens on March 23, 1967, to appear before the grand jury [for the Clay Shaw case] during the following week. The district attorney's office would offer no explanation, but an assistant district attorney said that... the new figure in the probe was the man who traveled to Houston with David Ferrie on November 22, 1963... [information which turned out to be wrong. Melvin Coffey was the man who had made the trip]. Three days later, on November 25, Martens was arrested, with Ferrie and Alvin Beauboeuf, by the district attorney's office, which said that it was holding the middle-aged pilot and the two young men (Martens was 20, Beaubouef was 19) for the FBI and Secret Service. At the time, Martens, who shared quarters with the older man for a while, gave his address as 3330 Louisiana Avenue Parkway—Ferrie's address.

***

On April 5, 1967, Martens was indicted by the Orleans Parish grand jury for perjury relating to the testimony he had given Clay Shaw's grand jury the week before, specifically that he had lied about his knowledge of Gordon Novel, Sergio Arcacha Smith, and other reported CIA agents involved in a 1961 munitions burglary to supply weapons for the anti-Castro cause. (See also Beauboeuf, Alvin; Ferrie, David)

SOURCES: HSCA Report 144 • DAVIS 213–4, 276, 336 • NORTH 431, 437, 444 • OTT, many • COA 41 • BLAKEY 50 • FLAMMONDE 81, 102, 118, 183–5

MARTIN, B. J., a.w.; DPD motorcycle patrolman. Martin rode behind and to the left of the presidential limo and testified that, after the fatal shot, his motorcycle windshield, his helmet, and the shoulder of his uniform were covered with blood, particles of flesh and other matter. This would indicate that the shot came from in front and to the right of the car, from the direction of the knoll.

SOURCES: WCH VI, 289 • RTJ 57 • HT 231 • BISHOP 104, 141 • CF 15 • BE 44 • OGLESBY 35 • NORTH 385

MARTIN, FRANK M, suspicious death; DPD captain. Martin told the WC that he "had better not talk." According to researcher J. Gary Shaw, Martin got sick in May 1966, and died of "apparent" cancer less than a month later.

SOURCES: WCH XII, 277 • SHAW 20–21

MARTIN, JACK S., Oswald witness; occasional New Orleans private detective who frequented the offices of Guy Banister Associates during the summer of 1963. Martin told the WC that Oswald was taught to shoot a rifle by assassination suspect David Ferrie in 1956; Ferrie had been Oswald's Civil Air Patrol leader before Oswald joined the USMC. Once in the marines, Martin says, Oswald was sent to Naval Intelligence School at the Memphis Naval Base from June through August 1957. According to author Paris Flammonde, "Ferrie was originally linked to the Kennedy assassination by... Martin, who told the district attorney's office, soon after the assassination, that Ferrie and Oswald had served in the Civil Air Patrol together, that Ferrie had instructed Oswald in the use of a telescope sight, and that the pair had discussed murdering the president."

Guy Banister had an occasional drink but was not known to drink to excess (according to Jim Garrison anyway—other sources have described Banister as an alcoholic). He certainly drank to excess, however, on November 22, 1963. When Banister got the word that JFK had been assassinated, he "made a noble effort to polish off all of the liquor in the

Katzenjammer Bar on the 500 block of Camp Street." With Banister on the binge was Martin. After leaving the bar, the pair returned to Banister's office, where they got into a heated argument. The row ended with Banister's pistol-whipping Martin so severely that Martin had to be hospitalized. (New Orleans Police Department report number K-12634-63, November 22, 1963.) Soon thereafter, Martin began to tell his friends that he suspected that David Ferrie, another frequenter of Banister's office, had "driven to Dallas on the day of the assassination to serve as the getaway pilot for the men involved in the assassination." (See also Banister, Guy; Ferrie, David)

SOURCES: WCH XXIII, 455 • OTT 5, 7, 29–32, 37–9, 273 • FLAMMONDE 24, 301 • COA 32, 133 • HT 186 • BLAKEY 46–7, 166–7 • DAVIS 205–6, 214, 216–9, 276, 290, 309, 311, 572, 584

MARTIN, JAMES HERBERT, Marina Oswald's post assassination business manager. Martin told the WC that advances for her stories from publishers totaled $132,350. In January 1964, Marina Oswald and Martin told Lee Harvey Oswald's brother Robert that Lee had once threatened to shoot Richard M. Nixon—but Marina failed to mention this when she testified before the WC February 3–6, 1964. The WC first learned of the alleged Nixon threat when Robert Oswald told FBI agents the story on February 21, 1963. (See also Oswald, Marina; Oswald, Robert)

SOURCES: WR 175 • WCH I, 469; II, 1 • HSCA Report 143–4 • EVICA 153, 166–7 • NORTH 494 • RTJ 307, 360 • HT 283–4 • BLAKEY 75

MARTIN, WILFRED JAMES "JIM," Ruby witness; defense attorney. Martin represented Ruby after his arrest for killing Oswald. As soon as George Senator, Ruby's roommate, heard that Oswald had been shot, he called Martin—even before he knew Ruby had done it. Then, when he learned that Ruby was Oswald's murderer, Senator drove to Martin's house. According to the WR, "Martin recalled that Senator's concern was for his friend Ruby and not for himself. Martin and Senator drove to the [DPD] where Senator voluntarily submitted himself to police questioning..." (See also Senator, George)

SOURCES: WR 348 • RTJ 282–4 • FMG I, 2–5, 9–10 • COA 32, 133)

MARTINO, JOHN, organized crime figure; worked in Havana's casinos before Castro's revolution; admitted CIA contact agent. Martino reportedly told Texas businessman Fred Claasen in 1975: "The anti-Castro people put Oswald together. Oswald didn't know who he was working for—he was ignorant of who was really putting him together. Oswald was to meet his contact at the Texas Theatre... There was no way we could get to him. They

had Ruby kill him." (See also Claasen, Fred)
SOURCES: HT 145–6 • SUMMERS 451

MASEN, JOHN THOMAS, Dallas gun-shop owner; alleged Oswald look-alike. Wally Weston, Ruby's former Carousel Club emcee, told the *New York Daily News* (July 18, 1976) that, in September or October of 1963, Oswald—or a man who looked like Oswald—came into the Carousel. Weston and Oswald got into a verbal altercation, during which "Oswald" called Weston a Communist and Weston hit "Oswald." At that point Ruby interjected and bounced "Oswald" from the premises, saying, "I told you never to come in here again." According to author George Michael Evica, Masen is the Oswald look-alike who was ejected from the Carousel that night.

Frank Ellsworth—a Treasury agent who was present, with another Treasury agent, on the sixth floor of the TSBD at the time the rifle was found and who was allegedly involved in Oswald's interrogation—told author Dick Russell in 1976 that he had knowledge of an "Oswald double" who had been associating with the right-wing Dallas Minutemen in 1963. Ellsworth told Russell that the Oswald double was still alive and resided in Dallas. Ellsworth said that this man (whom he did not name) was the man mistaken for Oswald repeatedly in and around Dallas during the weeks and months before the assassination. Ellsworth said that this "twin" was a frequent traveler to Mexico, had associations with the family of oil billionaire H. L. Hunt, and had been convicted of a federal arms violation. (According to a WC memo, the member of the Minutemen whom Ellsworth had been investigating was a "local gun shop owner.") Ellsworth said that the "twin" associated with anti-Castro Cuban exiles, was associated with the anti-Castro group known as Alpha 66 and had admitted to supplying arms to a terrorist Cuban organization. Among the look-alike's other associates was Major General Edwin A. Walker. Ellsworth told Russell that he had gone undercover, posing as a criminal involved in Mexican smuggling, to track the Oswald twin—and had eventually gotten the twin convicted on a gun violation.

Masen told Ellsworth that he had once sold guns to Alpha 66 bigwig Manuel Orcarberro Rodriguez, and that Alpha 66 had developed a large cache of arms in Dallas. According to former CIA agent Robert D. Morrow, this group had their Dallas headquarters in the home of Jorge Salazar at 3126 Harlendale Avenue. In 1976, author Dick Russell met Masen in the North Dallas gunshop where Masen worked. Referring to Masen's reputa-

tion as an Oswald look-alike, Russell wrote "you could still see the resemblance." (See also Ellsworth, Frank; Salazar, Jorge; Walker, Edwin A.; Weston, Wally)
SOURCES: WCE 2694 · EVICA 101–2, 104, 106–9, 111, 144, 315 · RUSSELL 35, 541–44, 546, 711

MASFERRER, ROLANDO, assassination suspect; suspicious death; anti-Castro Cuban exile. Masferrer, according to author Robert D. Morrow, put together teams of assassins to kill Fidel Castro for Florida mobster Santos Trafficante. Morrow writes that Masferrer, along with Eladio del Valle and Mario Kohly, "assist[ed] in the implementation of the JFK assassination scheme."

Masferrer was killed in Miami, Florida, on October 31, 1975, by a dynamite bomb in his car. (See also del Valle, Eladio; Kohly, Mario; Trafficante, Santos)
SOURCES: MORROW, many · RUSSELL, many

MASH, ESTHER ANN, Ruby witness; waitress at Ruby's Carousel Club. Mash told Jack Anderson on the nationally syndicated TV show *Who Murdered JFK* in 1988, "One night Jack [Ruby] had a meeting with several other men, there were seven men at the table with Oswald being the seventh and they were there [in the Carousel] until about 1:00 A.M."

MATHER, CARL, close friend of J. D. Tippit. Mather lived in Garland, Texas, and owned a blue four-door 1957 Plymouth with the Texas license plate # PP 4537. On December 4, 1963, the FBI received a report from Wes Wise, a reporter for KRLD-TV in Dallas (who was later elected mayor of Dallas) that at 2:00 P.M. on the day of the assassination a mechanic named T. F. White had spotted a man who "looked like Lee Harvey Oswald" sitting in a *red* 1957 Plymouth with the Texas license plate # PP 4537 in the parking lot of the El Chico Restaurant, not far from the site of the Tippit slaying. (At that time the real Oswald was already under arrest.) White wrote down the license plate number and told his boss, who told Wise.

According to Mather's wife, Mather was working until 2:00 P.M. that day, at which time he returned home so he could take his family to the Tippit home to pay their condolences. Mather's wife later denied owning any type of red car. The FBI interviewed Mrs. Mather twice but never spoke to Carl. Wes Wise had dinner with the Mathers and said that, although Carl was too nervous to eat, his wife was "cool, very cool." At the time of the assassination, Mathers worked in Richardson, Texas, for the Collins Radio Company, where he had been employed for 21 years. He had once worked for that company at Andrews Air Force Base in Washington, D.C., where he had been assigned to do electronic repairs on Vice President Lyndon B. Johnson's Air Force II. According to HT, "From this evidence, it would appear that someone borrowed the license plates from Mather's Plymouth then returned them." (See also Benavides, Domingo; White, T. F.)

SOURCES: HSCA XII, 36–42 • HT 278

MATHEWS, JIM, author of *Four Dark Days in History* (Special Publications, 1963).

MATHEWS, RUSSELL D., Ruby witness and friend; "idol" of assassination suspect Charles Harrelson. Mathews was the best man at the wedding of "Babushka Lady" Beverly Oliver and George McCann, who was later murdered.

The WC found that the only substantiated rumor of Ruby's being involved in pro- or anti-Castro activities involved his January 1959 "preliminary inquiries, as a middle-man [sic], concerning the possible sale to Cuba of some surplus jeeps located in Shreveport, Louisiana, and [he] asked about the possible release of prisoners from a Cuban prison." One of these prisoners is alleged to have been assassination suspect Santos Trafficante.

Regarding Mathews, the WR says:

> During the period of the "jeep sale," R. D. Mathews, a gambler and a "passing acquaintance" of Ruby, returned to Dallas from Havana where he had been living. In mid-1959, he returned to Cuba until mid-1960. On October 3, 1963, a telephone call was made from the Carousel Club to Mathews's former wife in Shreveport. No evidence has been uncovered that Mathews was associated with the sale of jeeps or the release of prisoners or that he knew of Oswald prior to the assassination. Mathews's ex-wife did not recall the phone call in October of 1963, and she asserted that she did not know Jack Ruby or anyone working for him.

(See also Harrelson, Charles; Oliver, Beverly)

SOURCES: WR 345 • HT 142 • CF 36–7, 335 • BLAKEY 314 • NORTH 320, 357, 631

MAXEY, BILLY JOE, o.k.w.; DPD sergeant; passenger in the "lead car" designed to escort the car carrying Oswald from the DPD to the county jail, accompanied by Sgt. James A. Putnam and the driver, Lt. Rio S. Pierce. Maxey sat in the backseat. The car was standing at the top of the Main Street ramp when Ruby shot Oswald.

SOURCES: WR 200 • WCH XII, 285

MAYFIELD, DOUGLAS, Bethesda witness; member U.S. Army. With six others, Mayfield attended JFK's body from the time it arrived in Washington, D.C., until it was buried. He served as a security guard at Bethesda Naval Hospital during the autopsy.
SOURCES: BE 398 • *Dallas Morning News*, November 26, 1963, p. 15

MAYO, JOHN B., author of *Bulletin from Dallas: The President Is Dead* (Exposition Press, 1967).

MAYO, LOGAN W., o.k.w.; 56-year-old DPD reservist. Mayo guarded the Commerce Street ramp during Oswald's aborted transfer. He didn't see Ruby enter and told the WC that a tall man in a suit who said he was a minister and that Oswald needed him was denied entry before the transfer. He also turned away a man who claimed to be Ruby's roommate, who arrived 10 minutes after the shooting. According to Mayo, the man said that "Ruby had quite a sum of money on his person and he wanted to go down and see if he wanted him to handle it for him."
SOURCE: WCH XII, 291

MAZZEI, IRVIN C., Ruby witness and acquaintance; western regional director of AGVA. Mazzei told the FBI that Ruby had once told him he had "squashed a complaint against him for beating one of his dancers" with the assistance of "his friends in the [DPD]."
SOURCES: RTJ 237 • COA 80, 245–7, 254, 424

MEAGHER, SYLVIA, author of *Accessories After the Fact* (Bobbs Merrill, 1967), one of the first books to expose the inner workings of the WC and its deaf ear toward all evidence that did not support its predetermined conclusion. Meagher also did assassination researchers a great favor by publishing a comprehensive index of the WR and the 26 volumes of WC testimony and exhibits (*Subject Index to the Warren Report and Hearings and Exhibits*, Scarecrow Press, 1966). Meagher put the spook-laden puzzle of Oswald into a nutshell when she wrote in *Accesories After the Fact*:

> Decision after decision, the [State] Department removed every obstacle before Oswald...on his path from Minsk to Dallas. The State Department's extraordinary and unorthodox decisions and the decisions taken by other U.S. official agencies in regard to Oswald fall into several general categories: (1) repeated failure to prepare a 'lookout card' to check Oswald's movement outside the U.S.; (2) grant and renewal of Oswald's passport despite cause for negative action; (3) apparent inaction and indifference to Oswald's possible disclosure of classified military data; and (4) pressure exerted and exceptional

measures taken on behalf of Marina Oswald's entry into the U.S.

SOURCES: BELIN 26 • COA 163 • CF 489–90 • HT 76 • FMG III, 93 • MOORE, many • BE 13, 109, 116, 155, 226, 265 • OTT 15 • BLAKEY 41, 44–5 • HOS 237–9 • FLAMMONDE 114–5, 141, 148–50, 173, 329–31 • EVICA 7, 22, 31–2, 168 • DAVIS 295, 364, 422

MELLER, TEOFIL and ANNA N., Oswald witnesses; two of the first members of Dallas's Russian-speaking community to meet Lee and Marina. Anna was introduced to the Oswalds by consulting petroleum engineer Peter Paul Gregory soon after Lee and Marina arrived in the Dallas–Fort Worth area, after returning from the USSR. The Mellers, being staunch anti-Communists like their friends, became concerned about the Oswalds when Anna visited them at their apartment and spotted a copy of Karl Marx's *Das Kapital* on a table. Teofil became so concerned about this that he called the FBI, who informed the Mellers that Lee was "all right." (See also Gregory, Peter)
SOURCES: WR 260 • WCH VIII, 379 • OTT 54 • BLAKEY 351 • FLAMMONDE 154, 160 • NORTH 176

MENDOZA, CHARLES (aka Mendez, Charles); physician. According to Jim Marrs, Oswald's friend and CIA informant George DeMohrenschildt did not begin having the mental problems that eventually led to his institutionalization—and, theoretically, to his death—until after he commenced "treatments" from a "shadowy" doctor named Charles Mendoza. According to DeMohrenschildt's wife, Jeanne, "George underwent two or three hours of 'therapy' at a time with Dr. Mendoza, which involved intravenous injections. George did not know exactly what the injections were." (See also DeMohrenschildt, George)
SOURCE: HT 304–5

MENNINGER, BONAR, author of *Mortal Error* (St. Martin's Press, 1992), based on 25 years of research by Maryland ballistics expert Howard Donahue. The book claims that JFK was killed accidentally by SS agent George Hickey, who rode in the presidential follow-up car. When Oswald began to shoot at JFK from the TSBD, Hickey turned, reached for his rifle and slipped off the safety. As he tried to stand up on the backseat of the car, he lost his balance and accidentally pulled the trigger to his AR-15 (now called an M-16). The theory states that Oswald fired only twice, missing the first shot and delivering all of the nonfatal wounds with the second shot. The third and fatal shot, it says, was fired by Hickey. (See also Hickey, George; Donahue, Howard

MERCER, JULIA ANN, a.w. (prelude). Before 11:00 A.M. on November

22, 1963, Mercer was driving west on Elm Street past the grassy knoll when she was forced to stop temporarily by a truck parked on the right side of the road. It was a green Ford pickup with a Texas license plate and the words "AIR CONDITIONING" painted on the side. A heavyset middle-aged man was sitting behind the wheel. Another man, who appeared in his late 20s and was wearing a plaid shirt, was outside the truck pulling a gun case from over the tailgate. As she last saw the second man, he was carrying the gun case up the grassy slope. In the early morning of November 23, Mercer was shown a series of photographs and was asked whether any of them looked like either of the men she had seen. She picked out two photos of men who appeared similar to the man behind the wheel. She turned over one of the photos and read the name "Jack Ruby." That means that authorities considered Ruby a suspect in the assassination one day before he shot Oswald. Mercer claims that her story, as printed by the WC, was altered before it was made public. (See also Bowers, Lee; Murphy, Joe)

SOURCES: WCH XIX, 483–4 • FMG I, 25–7 • OTT 15–6, 206, 216–9, 229, 275, 281 • RTJ 29–31, 33, 36–7 • CF 18–9, 324–5 • HT 135 • HOS 43, 170–4, 178 • FLAMMONDE 167, 268 • DAVIS 195

MERTZ, JOHN MICHAEL, assassination suspect. According to author Robert D. Morrow, Mertz was a CIA assassin and a member of the JFK hit squad.

SOURCE: MORROW 188, 191

MERTZ, MICHAEL VICTOR, named by assassination researcher J. Gary Shaw as the real "Maurice Bishop" (aka QJ/WIN), CIA executive action executioner. Author Henry Hurt says that Mertz was actually a benevolent character who had once infiltrated a French terrorist organization and was "credited with once saving the life of President de Gaulle during an OAS terrorist attack." (See also Phillips, David Atlee)

SOURCE: HT 515

MERTZ, MICHAEL (See SOUETRE, JEAN)

MEYER, MARY PINCHOT, suspicious death; mistress of JFK; murdered in Washington, D.C., in 1964; described as a "stunning 43-year-old bohemian aristocrat." According to author Leo Damore, JFK had planned on dumping Jackie and marrying Mary, who had turned him on to pot and LSD in 1962. Mary's husband, Cord Meyer, had worked for the CIA. According to Damore, who was quoted in the *New York Post* in 1991, "She had access to the highest levels. She was involved in illegal drug activity. What do you think it would do to the beatification of Kennedy if this woman

said, 'It wasn't Camelot, it was Caligula's court'?" After Meyer was murdered, her diary and letters were obtained by CIA counterintelligence chief James Angleton. Angleton claimed that he burned them, but Damore is convinced that they still exist. (See also Crump, Raymond, Jr.)
SOURCE: OGLESBY 71

MEYERS, LAWRENCE V., Ruby witness; Chicago sporting-goods salesman. Meyers checked into the Teamster-financed Cubana Hotel in Dallas on November 21, 1963, the same day that assassination suspect Eugene Hale Brading checked into the same hotel. That night, the eve of the assassination, Meyers was seen in Dallas's Egyptian Lounge during a meeting with Ruby and Dallas mobster Joseph Campisi. The WR says that Meyers and Ruby "conversed for about an hour" in the Carousel Club during the early evening of November 21, 1963. Ruby called Meyers on the evening of November 23 as well. According to Meyers's WC testimony, "during their telephone conversation, Ruby asked him what he thought of this 'terrible thing.' Ruby then began to criticize his competitors, Abe and Barney Weinstein, for failing to close their clubs on Saturday night. In the course of his conversation about the Weinsteins and the assassination, Ruby said, 'I've got to do something about this.' Meyers initially understood that remark to refer to the Weinsteins. Upon reflection after Oswald was shot, Meyers was uncertain whether Ruby was referring to his competitors, or to the assassination... " The pair ended their conversation, according to Meyers, by agreeing to have dinner together the following evening. By that time, Ruby would be in jail.

According to author Paris Flammonde, "David Ferrie's telephone records included a call to WH4–4970 in Chicago; the same number was called from Kansas City on November 20, 1963 by... Meyers, who arrived in Dallas that same evening." The phone number belonged to Jean Aase, who was Meyers's reportedly fun-loving travel companion during his suspicious trip to Dallas before the assassination. (See also Aase, Jean; Brading, Eugene; Campisi, Joseph)
SOURCES: WR 312–3, 325, 333 • WCH XV, 620 • WCE 2266–8 • COA 90, 263, 442 • CF 338 • HT 319 • OTT 111–3 • BLAKEY 37, 288, 313 • FLAMMONDE 208 • EVICA 148, 162–4, 166 • NORTH 192, 313, 373 • KANTOR 37

MICHAELIS, HEINZ W., manager of gun dealership Seaport Traders, Inc. According to the WR, Michaelis was

office manager of both George Rose & Co., Inc., and Seaport Traders, Inc., which showed that a ".38 S and W Special two-inch

Commando, serial number V510210" was shipped on March 20, 1963, to A. J. Hidell, Post Office Box 2915, Dallas, Tex. The invoice was prepared on March 13, 1963; the revolver was actually shipped on March 20 by Railway Express. The balance due on the purchase was $19.95. Michaelis furnished the shipping copy of the invoice [to the WC], plus $1.27 shipping charge, had been collected by the consignee, Hidell.

The order form had a space for a witness to attest to the fact that the person ordering the gun was a U.S. citizen and was not a convicted felon. The name written in this space was D. F. Drittal. WC handwriting experts said the Drittal name was written in Oswald's handwriting.
SOURCES: WR 161 • WCH VII, 372

MIDGETT, BILL, Parkland witness; second-year ob-gyn resident. Midgett was the first doctor to see JFK outside the emergency room and helped roll JFK into Trauma Room #1. He also delivered Marina Oswald's baby, Rachel, on October 20, 1963.
SOURCE: CRENSHAW 74

MILLER, AUSTIN L, a.w. Miller, who watched from the triple underpass, stated in a November 22, 1963, affidavit. "One shot apparently hit the street past the car... I saw something, which I thought was smoke or steam coming from a group of trees north of Elm off the railroad tracks." He said he thought shots came from "right there in the car." (See also Hickey, George)
SOURCES: WR 82 • WCH VI, 223; XIX, 485 • WCE 2003 • RTJ 40 • COA 22 • CF 59 • MOORE 31 • ME 107

MILLER, DAVE L., Ruby witness; 55 years old; owner and operator of Enquire Shine & Press on Commerce Street, three doors from the Carousel Club. Miller told the WC that Ruby brought his clothes in two or three times a week to have them cleaned and pressed and said he allowed Ruby to place handbills for his club in the front window of his shop. He saw Ruby on the afternoon of the assassination, and Ruby asked him not to display the handbills, because the club was going to be closed. Miller said that Ruby also stopped into his shop on November 23, just to say hello.
SOURCES: WCH XV, 450 • COA 74, 329

MILLER, LOUIS D., o.k.w.; 34-year-old DPD detective (Juvenile Bureau). By far, Miller was the most uncooperative and disagreeable witness called before the WC. He was openly hostile to all questions and said that he dragged Ruby back into the DPD station after Ruby shot

Oswald. With William Harrison, Miller is suspected by author Seth Kantor of informing Ruby of the precise time of Oswald's transfer. (See also Harrison, William)

SOURCE: WCH XII, 297

MILLER, TOM, author of *The Assassination Please Almanac* (Henry Regnery Co., 1977).

MILLICAN, A. J., a.w. Millican, standing on the north side of Elm midway between Houston and the triple underpass, told sheriff's deputies that he saw "a truck from 'Honest Joe's Pawn Shop' park close to the TSBD, then drive off five to ten minutes before the assassination." Millican stated: "Just after the President's car passed, I heard three shots from up toward Elm right by the Book Depository Building, and then immediately I heard two more shots come from the arcade between the Book Store [TSBD] and the Underpass, then three more shots came from the same direction only sounded further back. It sounded approximately like a .45 automatic, or a high-powered rifle." (See also Goldstein, Joe; Hill, Jean)

SOURCES: WCH XIX, 486 • CF 28

MILTEER, JOSEPH ADAMS, assassination suspect; possible a.w.; suspicious death. Milteer was a wealthy, politically active racist from Georgia. On November 9, 1963, in the downtown Miami apartment of Miami police informant Willie Somersett, Milteer was taped as he said that it was "in the working" that JFK was going to be killed. He said that the hit was going to take place from an office building with a high-powered rifle, and that someone was going to be arrested within an hour of the shooting, just to throw off the public.

Since JFK was scheduled to be in a motorcade on November 18 in Miami, that motorcade was canceled and JFK instead traveled to and from his speaking engagement by helicopter.

Milteer was interviewed by the FBI after they received the tape, and released. He died on February 9, 1974. According to HT: "A Coleman stove blew up in his Quitman, Georgia, mansion and Milteer was sent to the hospital. His condition improved steadily for two weeks, but then he died suddenly. The mortician preparing the body examined the wounds from the explosion and felt that the damage was not severe enough to have caused Milteer's death."

According to author Carl Oglesby, "Milteer is suspected of a role in the September 1963, bombing of a church in Birmingham, Alabama, in which four black children were killed."

According to HT, Milteer was "photographed in Dealey Plaza," as a spectator, on November 22, 1963. (See also Somersett, Willie)

SOURCES: HSCA Report 91, 232–4, 637 • NORTH 352–3, 375, 379 • CF 265–7 • HT 13–4, 414, 474–7 • FMG III, 91 • BLAKEY 8–9 • OGLESBY 49, 73

MINACORE, CALOGERO (See MARCELLO, CARLOS)

MITCHELL, MARY ANN, a.w.; deputy district clerk for Dallas County. Mitchell was standing with coworker James N. Crawford at the southeast corner of Elm and Houston streets. After the shooting was over, Crawford pointed to the TSBD and told Mitchell, "Those shots came from that building." (See also Crawford, James N.)

SOURCES: WR 78 • WCH VI, 175

MITCHELL, WILLIE, a.w.; inmate at the Dallas County Jail on the east side of Houston Street, whose window overlooked Dealey Plaza. Mitchell said he "glanced" at the sniper's nest TSBD window, but didn't see anyone in it. Many inmates watched the assassination, but none were asked questions by law-enforcement officials about what they saw. (See also Kaufman, Stanley)

SOURCE: OTT 94

MODEL, PETER, coauthor, with Robert Groden, of *JFK: The Case for Conspiracy* (Manor Books, 1976).

SOURCES: BELIN 188 • HT 208 • MOORE, many

MOFFETT, SANDRA (aka McMaines, Lillie Mae), former girlfriend of Perry Raymond Russo. During the summer of 1963, she briefly attended a party with Russo at David Ferrie's apartment in New Orleans. At the party were Clay Shaw, a man calling himself "Leon Oswald" and a smattering of anti-Castro Cubans. According to Russo, plans to assassinate JFK were discussed at the party.

Moffett was in Nebraska at the time of the Clay Shaw trial, and attempts by New Orleans District Attorney Jim Garrison to extradite her were unsuccessful. (See also Russo, Perry)

SOURCES: OTT 152, 181, 228 • FLAMMONDE 62, 82, 109, 186–91, 200, 226, 238–9, 303

MOLINA, JOE R., a.w.; TSBD credit manager. Molina was standing on the front steps of the TSBD and told the FBI that he thought the shots came from the west of the building. He was treated as a suspect by the DPD during the first 24 hours following the shooting. Molina was a Dallas-born navy veteran who had worked at the TSBD since 1947. According to the WR, he became a suspect because of his employment—and because he was a member of a veterans' group called the American G.I. Forum, which the DPD considered "possibly subversive." The WR says:

> Dallas policemen searched Molina's home with his permission, at about 1:30 A.M., Saturday, November 23. During the day Molina was intermittently interrogated at police headquarters for six or seven hours...He was never arrested, charged or held in custody...According to Molina, he had never spoken to Oswald...Molina lost his job in December. He felt that he was being discharged because of the unfavorable publicity he had received, but officials at the Depository claimed that automation was the reason.

Molina told the WC that he had had difficulty securing a new job and had finally settled for a position at lower pay than he had earned at the TSBD.
SOURCES: WR 219–21 • WCH VI, 368 • RTJ 112 • CF 54

MONROE, MARILYN, suspicious death; JFK mistress; world-famous movie star. According to Charles and Sam Giancana in their book *Double Cross*, Monroe was murdered on August 4, 1962, with a drug-laden suppository by employees of assassination suspect Sam Giancana (the author's uncle). The autopsy revealed a bruised colon; her death was listed officially as a suicide. (See also Giancana, Momo "Sam")

MONTGOMERY, LESLIE D., o.k.w.; DPD detective. Montgomery stood just behind Oswald at the time he was shot. He testified that Oswald had to slow up, making him an easier target, because the car that was supposed to receive him had not yet backed into place.
SOURCES: WR 201 • WCH VII, 96; XIII, 21 • RTJ 214–5 • COA 123

MOON, MARILYN MAGYAR (See MOONEY, NANCY JANE)

MOONEY, LUKE, a.w. (aftermath); Dallas deputy sheriff. Mooney was involved in the search of the sixth floor of the TSBD immediately following the assassination. He was one of the first to see the alleged murder weapon, which was thought at the time to be a 7.65 German Mauser.
SOURCES: WR 27, 84 • WCH III, 281 • HSCA Report 50 • RTJ 114, 120 • BISHOP 196 • DOP 282 • MOORE 41, 47 • EVICA 17–9, 22, 50 • OGLESBY 17

MOONEY, NANCY JANE (aka MacDonald, Betty; Moon, Marilyn Magyar; Walle, Marilyn April), Ruby witness; t.k.w.; former Carousel Club stripper; suspicious death. Warren Reynolds was shot in the head before he had a chance to testify that he didn't think the fleeing assailant was Oswald. He survived the attack, miraculously, and later made a positive identification of Oswald. The man accused of shooting Reynolds was

Darrell Wayne Garner, who had bragged of the shooting while drunk. Garner was eventually released by Dallas police because he received an alibi from Nancy Jane Mooney, who said she was with him elsewhere at the time of the Reynolds shooting. Eight days after Garner's release, Mooney was arrested for "disturbing the peace" and died in jail. According to Dallas police, she hanged herself in her cell with her own toreador pants.

According to HT, Nancy Jane Mooney and Marilyn Walle were separate individuals, but both were former Ruby strippers. According to Groden and Livingstone, Walle planned to write a book about the assassination and was murdered on September 1, 1966, by her husband of 24 days. (See also Garner, Darrell; Moore, Patsy; Tippit, J. D.; Reynolds, Warren)

SOURCES: RTJ 278–80 • HT 138, 143 • COA 35–6 • GERTZ 528 • PWW 127 • PD 366

MOONEYHAM, LILLIAN, a.w.; 95th District court clerk. Mooneyham viewed assassination from windows in the Dallas Criminal Courts Building on the east side of Houston Street. She heard three shots and thought the first was a firecracker. She said the second and third shots came close together. According to a January 10, 1964, FBI report:

> Mrs. Mooneyham estimated that it was about four and a half to five minutes following the shots... that she looked up towards the sixth floor of the Texas School Book Depository building and observed the figure of a man standing in the sixth floor window behind some cardboard boxes. The man appeared to Mrs. Mooneyham to be looking out the window; however, the man was not close up to the window but was standing slightly back from it, so that Mrs. Mooneyham could not make out his features.

By this time, Oswald had already been seen on the second floor of the TSBD and, by most accounts, had already left the building.

SOURCES: WCH XXIV, 531 • CF 52–3

MOORE, BOBBY GENE, Ruby witness. Moore worked in the 1950s as a pianist in Ruby's Vegas Club. Moore lived in Oakland, California in 1963 and reported to the FBI on November 27, 1963, that Ruby had "gangster connections" including Carlos Marcello's Dallas lieutenant, Joseph Civello.

SOURCES: DAVIS 157, 277, 285, 289, 309, 311–3, 457

MOORE, HENRY M., member DPD. With officers Richard S. Stovall and Guy F. Rose, Moore obtained a search warrant and searched the home of Michael and Ruth Paine in Irving, Texas, where Marina Oswald was living at the time of the assassination. In the Paine garage, the officers found, among other things, the rolled-up blanket that, according to Marina, had held Oswald's rifle and reportedly phony photographs (which Marina claims she took) of Oswald holding a rifle, wearing a handgun in a holster, and holding Communist literature. (See also Paine, Michael; Paine, Ruth; Rose, Guy; Stovall, Richard)

SOURCES: WR 168 • WCH VII, 212

MOORE, J. WALTON, Dallas's top CIA man in 1963; close friend of Oswald's mentor, George DeMohrenschildt. In his WC testimony, DeMohrenschildt said that he had discussed Oswald with Moore. Moore denies that such a conversation ever took place. (See also DeMohrenschildt, George)

SOURCES: HSCA Report 217–8 • HT 130, 301–2

MOORE, PATSY SWOPE, Nancy Jane Mooney's roommate. Moore told the FBI that she "specifically recalled" that Mooney had worked for Ruby. When Mooney was arrested for disturbing the peace, the charges were that she had fought with Moore. (See also Mooney, Nancy Jane)

SOURCES: WCH XXV, 872 • RTJ 278

MOORE, RUSSELL LEE (aka Russell Lee Knight, "The Weird Beard"), Ruby witness; disc jockey on KLIF in Dallas. At 1:45 A.M. on November 23, 1963, Jack Ruby visited KLIF. He stayed for 45 minutes and left with Moore. While standing outside the station, according to Moore, Ruby handed him a radio script titled "Heroism," from a conservative radio program funded by oil billionaire H. L. Hunt called "Life Line." According to the WR, the script "extolled the virtues of those who embark on risky ventures and stand firmly for causes they believe to be correct." Ruby asked Moore's opinion on the script and then warned the DJ that there was a group of "radicals" in Dallas who may have been responsible for JFK's death. Because of the nature of the script and Ruby's possible misuse of the word "radical," the disc jockey was unclear whether Ruby was referring to a group of left- or right-wingers. At the end of their conversation outside KLIF, Ruby got in his car and left alone. Moore next heard from Ruby in the early evening of November 23, when Jack called him at the radio station and, according to Moore, asked him who Earl Warren was.

Moore is the DJ's real name. In Dallas, however, he was known almost exclusively by his on-air monicker: Russ Knight, the Weird Beard.

SOURCES: WR 319–20, 325 • WCH XV, 251 • COA 127, 424 • GERTZ 61, 105–8, 112 • BISHOP 433, 489, 495–6, 501

MOORMAN, MARY ANN, a.w. Moorman took Polaroid photos of the presidential motorcade as it passed. She watched the motorcade with her friend Jean Hill on the south side of Elm Street, directly across from the grassy knoll. One of her photos has become famous because it shows a clear view of the grassy knoll at the time of the shooting and appears to show a man on the other side of the wooden picket fence firing a rifle. Another shot that Moorman took with her Polaroid isn't so famous. It clearly shows the TSBD in the background, including the "Oswald" window. It was confiscated at the scene by Chief Criminal Deputy Sheriff Allan Sweatt, who turned it over to SS Agent William Patterson. It was declared to be of no value and hasn't been seen since.

Moorman testified for the prosecution at Clay Shaw's conspiracy trial. (See also Arnold, Gordon; Hill, Jean; Mack, Gary; Sarti, Lucien; White, Jack)

SOURCES: WCE 1426, 2003, 2582 • HSCA Report 84–5 • RTJ 344–8 • BISHOP 128, 137 • CF 37–8, 79–82, 324 • HT 123 • PWW, many • MOORE 30, 96, 119–22, 125 • BE 8, 18 • OTT 238 • ME 55 • OGLESBY 51 • NORTH 481

MOREN, RELMAN, author of *Assassination: The Death of President Kennedy* (New American Library, 1968).

MORGAN, EDWARD P., Washington, D.C., attorney. Morgan told the FBI on March 21, 1967, that he was representing clients (nameless) with information regarding JFK's assassination. His clients, he claimed, said that Castro was behind the assassination, in retaliation for bungled CIA assassination plots against him.

SOURCES: HSCA Report 114 • EVICA 121, 213–4, 217, 228–30, 234–5, 293 • DUFFY 132–5 • BLAKEY 152–3, 385

MORGAN, REEVES, Oswald witness; state representative for Clinton, Louisiana. In September 1963, when eyewitnesses in Clinton say that assassination suspects Clay Shaw, David Ferrie, and Oswald attended a voter-registration drive for blacks, Oswald reportedly stopped and got a haircut from barber Edwin McGehee and expressed interest in securing a job at the mental hospital in nearby Jackson. McGehee referred Oswald to Morgan. Oswald visited Morgan at his home, and Morgan told him he would have a better chance of getting the job if he were a registered voter in the parish.

Morgan testified for the prosecution at the Clay Shaw trial, telling the jury that he called the FBI after the assassination and the FBI told him that they already knew about Oswald's visit to Clinton. (See also Ferrie, David; McGehee, Edwin; Shaw, Clay)

SOURCES: HSCA Report 142 • NORTH 306, 411 • OTT 107–8, 232

MORGAN, RUSSELL, pathology expert; member of 1968 Justice Department pathology panel. Morgan was allowed access to JFK's autopsy photos and X rays. (See also Fisher, Russell)
SOURCE: ME 63–4

MORRISON, DeLESSEPS CHEP, suspicious death; mayor of New Orleans; died in a plane crash May 23, 1965, in Mexico. Piloting the plane was Hugh Ward, business partner of Oswald associate Guy Banister, who died within ten days of Morrison. According to Penn Jones Jr., before the assassination Morrison's secretary had made several inquiring phone calls seeking to rent an apartment for Guy Banister's "business use."

According to author Paris Flammonde, Morrison introduced Clay Shaw to JFK on a plane flight in 1963. (See also Banister, Guy; Shaw, Clay; Ward, Hugh)
SOURCES: HT 144 • FMG III, 46–7 • BLAKEY 181, 186 • FLAMMONDE 8, 115 • DAVIS 70, 72, 80–1

MORROW, HUBERT, possible Oswald witness; manager, Allright Parking Systems, Dallas. Morrow says that on November 10, 1963, when Oswald was in Irving, Texas, a man identifying himself as Oswald applied for a job as a parking attendant and asked if the Southland Hotel, adjacent to the parking lot, provided a good view of downtown Dallas.
SOURCE: DAVIS 169

MORROW, ROBERT D., former CIA operative; author of *Betrayal* (Henry Regnery Co., 1976), a detailed, seemingly privy assassination scenario, involving Ruby as a shooter of JFK, Oswald look-alikes, and a motive that involved JFK's failure to fully back the Bay of Pigs invasion.

Here is Morrow's own short-take on his uncorroborated scenario:

> Oswald, who went to Russia for the CIA and was an FBI informant by the summer of 1963, was brought into an assassination plot led by CIA consultant Clay Shaw, using right-wing CIA operatives and anti-Castro Cubans headed by Jack Ruby in Dallas and Guy Banister in New Orleans. This group, operating outside Agency control, manipulated events to insure Oswald being named as the assassin. They also used an Oswald lookalike to incriminate the ex-Marine by firing shots from the Texas School Book Depository. Dallas policeman J. D. Tippit was killed by this Oswald substitute when he failed to go along with the group's scheme to have Tippit kill the real Oswald in the Texas Theatre. With the capture of Oswald, Ruby was compelled to stalk and finally kill the accused assassin.

***

An August 3, 1976, UPI dispatch announced that Representative Thomas Downing was distributing a 79-page booklet by Morrow titled *Motivation Behind the Assassination of John F. Kennedy.* According to UPI:

> The material... alleged that Vice President Richard Nixon was the "CIA action man in the White House in earlier stages of planning for the Bay of Pigs attack..." Morrow alleged that a recognized right-wing leader of Cuban exiles, Mario Garcia Kohly Sr., told him a year ago [1975] he had an understanding with the CIA that top left-wing Cuban exiles "would be eliminated after a successful invasion of the Bay of Pigs"... Nixon, while a lawyer in the 1960s, served Kohly, apparently without fee... Downing would not vouch for [the booklet's] authenticity, but he said that the material "does raise a number of questions which I believe need to be answered. I would like to know what was behind the intense interest shown by President Nixon and his staff in the Bay of Pigs [as revealed in the Watergate White House tapes]."

In 1992, Morrow released a new book (*First Hand Knowledge*, S.p.i. Books) in which he discussed his own reported involvement in a CIA-Mafia plot to kill JFK. (See also Banister, Guy; Barnes, Tracy; Diggs, Marshall; Kohly, Mario; Masferrer, Rolando; Mertz, John Michael; Nixon, Richard M.; Shaw, Clay; Rodriguez, Manuel; Tippit, J. D.)
SOURCES: HT 320, 343–4 • CF 201 • MOORE 216 • EVICA 59–60, 100, 104–5, 109, 245–6, 310 • NORTH 308, 597

MORTIZ, ALAN, pathology expert; member of 1968 Justice Department pathology panel that concluded that JFK was shot exclusively from behind. Mortiz was allowed access to JFK's autopsy photos and X rays. (See also Fisher, Russell)
SOURCE: ME 63–4

MOSBY, ALINE, Oswald witness; newspaper correspondent. Mosby spoke to Oswald soon after he arrived in Moscow in 1959. Oswald told Mosby that he had financed his trip with $1,500 he had saved out of his USMC salary.
SOURCE: WR 238, 242, 247

MOSK, RICHARD M., WC staff member; California attorney. When assassination researcher David Lifton called Mosk with questions about the WR, Mosk is said to have commented sarcastically, "Oh, you're one of those buffs. What's the matter? Are you worried we didn't catch all the assassins?"

SOURCE: BE 27

MOYERS, BILL, LBJ aide; current PBS-TV host. Moyers told the *Village Voice* on March 31, 1992, "Back then [1963], what government said *was* the news... In the 1950s and early '60s, the official view of reality was the Washington press corps... I think it is quite revealing that it's Oliver Stone that's forcing Congress to open up the files and not the *Washington Post*, the *New York Times*, or CBS." (See also Katzenbach, Nicholas)
   SOURCES: HT 152, 257 • FMG III, 18 • BLAKEY 23 • EVICA 255 • DAVIS 275–7 • NORTH 437–8, 524, 641 • PD 51

MUCHMORE, MARIA, a.w. Muchmore filmed the assassination sequence from the center of the grassy triangle on the south side of Elm Street. Her film shows the fatal shot, Jackie Kennedy's crawl onto the back of the limo, and the motorcade's disappearance into the tunnel. (See also Bond, Wilma)
   SOURCES: WR 100, 106 • MOORE 120 • CF 35 • PWW 16, 42, 45–6, 123, 176, 281

MUDD, F. LEE, a.w. Mudd was standing on the "north curb of Elm," 75 to 100 feet west of the TSBD and told author Josiah Thompson that "one or more of the shots came from the direction of the Dal-Tex Building." Mudd fell prone when he heard the shots, his eyes looking toward the corner of Elm and Houston. Earlier he told the Sheriff's Department that he had heard two shots, thought they came from the TSBD, and that the shots were "less than a second apart." (See also Brading, Eugene)
   SOURCE: WCE 2108

MULKEY, CHARLES, a.w. (aftermath); *Dallas Morning News* employee (advertising department); was with coworkers in Dealey Plaza "soon" after the assassination when he saw a mysterious pool of blood, more than a pint, on a concrete sidewalk near the pergola. According to UTM, to verify that it was blood, Mulkey stuck a finger in it and tasted it. Later claims he was told by the FBI not to mention the blood. (See also Couch, Malcolm; Coley, Jerry; Hood, Jim)

MUMFORD, PAMELA, possible Oswald witness; originally from Australia. Mumford was a passenger, with her friend Patricia Winston, on the bus to Mexico City with "Oswald" in September 1963. She says that her friend and Oswald were the only two English-speaking people on the bus, except for a young English couple and an older English gentleman in his 60s who sat with Oswald. She told the WC that Oswald chatted with her and her girlfriend throughout the trip, described Russia, showed them his passport and recommended the Hotel Cuba in Mexico City to them. (See also Osborne, Albert)

SOURCE: WCH XI, 215

MURCHISON, CLINT SR., Texas oil billionaire. According to author Penn Jones Jr., Murchison held a party at his home on November 21, 1963. In attendance were Richard Nixon and J. Edgar Hoover. Right after the assassination, Sylvia Odio, whose story contradicts the official facts, was hidden in the home of Ralph Rogers, president of Murchison's company, Texas Industries.

Immediately following Oswald's death, Marina Oswald was placed in seclusion in a motel owned by Murchison business partner Bobby Winn and kept there as she was prepared for her appearance before the WC, writes Peter Dale Scott in *Crime & Cover-up* (Westworks, 1977).

According to Pete Brewton's book *The Mafia, CIA & George Bush* (S.p.i. Books, 1992, p. 99, 193), "[In the 1950s,] both Clint [Murchison] Sr. and his son were close to New Orleans Mafia boss Carlos Marcello and the CIA. The father had business interests in Haiti, and one of the employers who looked after these interests was CIA asset George DeMohrenschildt... DeMohrenschildt was... keeping an eye on Clint Murchinson's meat-packing business and cattle ranches there." (See also DeMohrenschildt, George; Hoover, J. Edgar; Jones, Penn; Kirkwood, Pat; Lansky, Meyer; McLane, Alfred; Nixon, Richard M.; Odio, Sylvia; Raigorodsky, Paul; Sirhan, Sirhan)

SOURCES: HT 14, 151, 237, 281–2, 285, 291, 305 • EVICA 9–10, 163, 166 • DAVIS 347, 474–5, 483 • NORTH, many • FMG III, 85 • FMG IV, 114 • TEX 247 • Scott, Peter Dale, *Crime and Cover-up*, p. 35

MURPHY, JOE E., a.w. (prelude); member DPD. At approximately 11:00 A.M. on the morning of the assassination, Murphy radioed in from Dealey Plaza, "Could you send a city wrecker to the triple underpass, just west of the underpass on Elm, to clear a stalled truck from the route of the escort?" A few minutes later, Murphy again went on the air, saying, "Disregard the wrecker at the triple underpass. We got a truck to push him out of here." This incident takes place at approximately the location and time of suspicious activities reported by witness Julia A. Mercer. At the time of the assassination, Murphy was stationed atop the Stemmons Freeway overpass, west of the triple underpass, and farther from the TSBD. (See also Mercer, Julia)

SOURCES: WR 80–1 • WCH VI, 256 • BISHOP 88

MURPHY, PAUL EDWARD, Oswald witness; USMC acquaintance. Murphy told the WC:

***

...I was stationed at Atsugi, Japan, and thereafter at Santa Ana, California with Lee Harvey Oswald...the unit which was stationed at Atsugi spent four to six weeks in Okinawa late in 1957...another trip took it to Corregidor...Oswald was self-contained and withdrawn...I am of the opinion that he was generally in sympathy with Castro...One night in the barracks in Japan, I heard a shot in the adjoining cubicle. I rushed to the cubicle to find Oswald sitting on a foot locker looking at a wound in his arm. When I asked what happened, Oswald very unemotionally replied, "I believe I shot myself." Oswald was at that time in possession of a small caliber pistol which he was not authorized to possess....While at Santa Ana, Oswald had a subscription to a newspaper printed in English which I believe was titled either "The Worker" or "The Socialist Worker."...I do not recall Oswald receiving other literature of a Socialist nature. I remember that Oswald could speak a little Russian, even when he was overseas...[He was] proficient at his assigned job, but was below average in...discipline and military courtesy. He was, however, personally quite neat...His temperament was such that he would push companions to the verge of fighting him, but seldom, if ever, actually took the step of engaging in a fight...While overseas, however, Oswald had an active social life...Oswald seldom left his post in Santa Ana...

SOURCES: WCH VIII, 319 • AO 90–2

MURPHY, THOMAS J., a.w.; mail foreman at the Union Terminal Company. Murphy was standing on top of the triple underpass. He told author Mark Lane that he saw smoke coming from the trees on the knoll after the assassination and told the WC that he "heard two shots [that] came from a spot just west of the Depository."
SOURCES: WR 82 • RTJ 40 • CF 58–9 • BE 16

MURRAY, DAVID CHRISTIE, JR., Oswald witness; USMC acquaintance; stationed with Oswald at Santa Ana, California. Murray told the WC:

Oswald did not associate with his fellow Marines...I personally stayed away from Oswald because I heard a rumor to the effect that he was a homosexual...[He] was never satisfied with any event or situation. He was quietly sarcastic...was not a show-off; he did not want to be the center of attention. I regarded Oswald as quite intelligent...[and] was of the opinion that he had received a college education...[He] was studying Russian. He often made remarks in

Russian; the less intelligent members of the unit admired him for
this... He played chess a good deal...

SOURCE: WCH VIII, 319

MURRAY, JIM, a.w. (aftermath); photographer for the Black Star Photo
Service. Murray took photos of Dealey Plaza minutes after the assassination. A series of these photos show Dallas Deputy Sheriff Buddy Walthers
and an unidentified and neatly dressed blond man with a plastic radio
receiver clipped to his ear looking at something in the grass on the south
side of Elm Street. The blond man picks up the object and puts it in his
pocket in the series of photos. There has been speculation that the object
was a bullet. (See also Walthers, Buddy)
SOURCE: OTT 209

MURRAY, NORBERT, author of *Legacy of an Assassination* (Pro-People
Press, 1964).

MURRET, CHARLES "DUTZ," Oswald witness and 63-year-old uncle.
Murret had strong organized crime ties and reportedly was a father figure
to his nephew. He was alleged to have been a bookmaker in New Orleans,
working for the Carlos Marcello crime family. Murret testified before the
WC, which never asked him what he did for a living. He told the WC that
Oswald used to raise his voice when he spoke to his mother, but that was
about all he could remember. The HSCA determined that Murret was:

> a minor underworld gambling figure... who served as a surrogate
> father of sorts throughout much of Oswald's life in New Orleans, was
> in the 1940s and 1950s and possibly until his death in 1964 an
> associate of significant organized crime figures affiliated with the
> Marcello organization. The committee established that Oswald was
> familiar with his uncle's underworld activities and had discussed
> them with his wife, Marina, in 1963.

(See also Marcello, Carlos)
SOURCES: WCH VIII, 180 • HSCA Report 140, 142, 170 • OGLESBY 24 • DAVIS, many •
NORTH 262, 268–9, 296–7 • COA 4, 42–3, 57, 167, 231 • OTT 304 • BLAKEY 161,
341–5, 347, 357–9, 364

MURRET, JOHN MARTIAL "BOOGIE," Oswald witness and 29-
year-old cousin; son of "Dutz" and Lillian. Murret told the WC that he once
tried to teach Oswald to drive, with no success.
SOURCE: WCH VIII, 188

MURRET, LILLIAN, Oswald witness and aunt; 64-year-old sister of

Marguerite Oswald, wife of "Dutz." Murret told WC that Lee was a loner and uncomfortable with his peers. Oswald stayed with the Murrets for a few weeks during the summer of 1963, just before he got his job at the Reily Coffee Company.

SOURCES: WR 289, 354, 359 • WCH VIII, 91; XI, 472 • BLAKEY 161, 341–3, 346, 357–8, 364 • DAVIS 135–6

MURRET, MARILYN DOROTHEA, Oswald witness and cousin; daughter of "Dutz" and Lillian, sister of "Boogie." According to *Houston Post* reporter Lonnie Hudkins, Murret was a CIA agent assigned to Japan—and it was she who set up Oswald's contacts when he traveled to the USSR. An FBI memo (WCD 942) states that Murret "was linked in some manner with the apparatus of Professor Harold Isaacs—an MIT research associate who himself was suspected of being an intelligence agent. Murret told the WC that Oswald witness Ed Voebel was the friend who convinced Oswald to join the Civil Air Patrol when he was a teenager. She said that Carlos Marcello associate Emile Bruneau was the person who got Oswald out of jail after he was arrested in New Orleans for disturbing the peace and told the WC, "He was just a darling child." (See also Hudkins, Lonnie; Isaacs, Harold)

SOURCES: WCH VIII, 154 • WCD 942 • RUSSELL 28, 38, 119–20, 122, 123, 133

N

NAGELL, RICHARD CASE, (aka Nolan, Robert C.) possible Oswald witness; possible FOI agent. Nagel told New Orleans District Attorney Jim Garrison that he had been a "federal intelligence agent" who, in mid-1963, had discovered a plot to kill JFK. WCD 197, regarding Nagell, says in its entirety: "For the record he would like to say that his association with Oswald was purely social and that he had met him in Mexico City and in Texas."

At an outdoor clandestine meeting with Garrison during Garrison's Clay Shaw investigation, Nagell reportedly said that in 1963 he had been working for a federal agency (he refused to identify which one). He claimed to have been assigned to find out about "a project" involving Oswald and others. During his investigation, he learned that a "large operation" was under way to kill JFK, but he did not know where or when. At this time, Nagell's direct contact was moved to another part of the country, so Nagell wrote a letter reporting what he knew to J. Edgar Hoover. When he received no reply, he feared he was being suckered into a trap. Nagell figured that his best bet was to be in prison whenever the hit took place, so that he could not possibly be charged with the crime. Pursuing a criminal-mischief charge, he entered an El Paso bank, fired two shots into the ceiling, and then went outside and sat on the curb. However, Nagell was not charged with mischief, but rather with armed robbery. He was convicted and served three years of a ten-year sentence. He told Garrison that the other men who were working with Oswald were "Guy Banister, Clay Shaw, and David Ferrie." Although Nagell was willing to testify at Shaw's trial, Garrison chose not to put him on the stand, feeling that he would have been "eaten alive" during cross-examination because of his deliberate vagueness.

Nagell is the subject of Dick Russell's *The Man Who Knew Too Much* (Carroll & Graf, 1992). (See also Banister, William Guy; Ferrie, David; Garrison, Jim; Hoover, J. Edgar; Russell, Dick; Shaw, Clay)
SOURCES: OTT 182–6, 226, 229 • FLAMMONDE 207–8 • RUSSELL, many

NAGY, FERENC, exiled former Hungarian premier; formerly the leader of the principal Hungarian anti-Communist party; president of Permindex, an international covert operation and money-laundering corporation based in Switzerland. According to researcher William Torbitt, Nagy met with assassination suspect Albert Osborne in Laredo, Texas, a short time before the assassination.

Along with Clay Shaw and L. M. Bloomfield, Nagy was on the board of directors of CMC, Permindex's "first cousin," and was, according to reports in the Italian press, a heavy contributor to Fascist causes. The Canadian newspaper *Le Devoir* (March 16, 1967), reported: "Nagy... maintains close ties with the CIA which link him with the Miami Cuban colony." According to Jim Garrison, "Nagy subsequently emigrated to the United States, making himself at home in Dallas." (See also Bloomfield, L. M.; Shaw, Clay; Osborne, Albert)
SOURCE: OTT 88–9

NAMAN, RITA, Oswald witness. Naman was a tourist in Minsk in 1961. (See also Hyde, Marie; Kramer, Monica)
SOURCES: WCH XI, 213 • SUMMERS 181–3

NAVARRO, HORACIO DURAN, Oswald witness; husband of Silvia Tirado de Duran, an employee of the Mexico City Cuban embassy's visa section who met with someone calling himself Lee Harvey Oswald in September 1963, in the embassy and was later held and heavily interrogated by the Mexican police at the orders of the CIA. About the couple, the WR stated: "Although Senora Duran denies being a member of the Communist Party or otherwise connected with it, both Durans have been active in far left political affairs in Mexico, believe in Marxist ideology, and sympathize with the government of Fidel Castro, and Senor Duran [Navarro] has written articles for *El Dia*, a pro-Communist newspaper in Mexico City." (See also Duran, Silvia)
SOURCE: WR 281

NECHIPORENKO, OLEG MAXIMOVICH, possible Oswald witness. Nechiporenko was a retired KGB agent who, on January 9, 1992, called a press conference in Moscow, claimed that he had "new data" concerning JFK's death and urged "the creation of a joint Russian–U.S. investigatory commission." He said that his "historical information" would cast new light on the events of November 22, 1963, but refused to give details; made it clear that he intended to be paid for the information, and added, "If I gave it out now, it would be unfair to the other people who took part and it would be premature."

According to AP, Nechiporenko was a senior KGB agent before his retirement and had been kicked out of Mexico in 1971 for purportedly scheming to topple its government. The AP wrote:

Nechiporenko said he and two other agents met Oswald on Sept. 27–28, 1963, at the Soviet Embassy in Mexico City, where Oswald was trying to get a visa to re-enter the Soviet Union... There was no immediate way to verify Nechiporenko's claim to have met Oswald in Mexico City. The KGB and Russian Foreign Ministry could not be reached for comment... But Nechiporenko is known to have been a spy in Mexico in this period. He said he was twice posted at the Soviet Embassy in Mexico City, from 1961 to 1965 and from 1967 until 1971. He later was sent to Vietnam... He said his name never came up in connection with the assassination because Oswald never used it during bugged telephone conversations. Oswald spent days in Mexico City trying to get visas from Cuban or Soviet diplomats, who reportedly were under orders to refuse. Oswald eventually gave up and returned to the United States.

Nechiporenko is the author of *Passport to Assassination* (Birch Lane Press, 1993).

NELSON, DORIS MAE, Parkland witness; supervising nurse. She was asked to remove Mrs. Kennedy from the overcrowded Trauma Room #1 during JFK's emergency treatment. Mrs. Kennedy left only temporarily, however, and reentered the room moments later, despite Nelson's protests. After the president was pronounced dead, Nelson asked Mrs. Kennedy whether she wanted to wash up and she declined, as she would to others who made the same suggestion during the course of the day. Moments later, Nelson asked the SS agents what arrangements would be made for the body and was informed that the undertaker and casket were en route. When hospital staffers were having trouble with JFK's body—his massive head wound was still oozing and had already soaked through four sheets, and they didn't want to stain the white satin interior of the casket—it was Nelson who suggested, "Go up to Central Supply and get one of those plastic mattress covers."
SOURCES: WCH VI, 143 • BISHOP 148, 157, 168, 175, 189, 208, 228 • DOP 181–3, 185–6, 189, 236, 290, 294, 304 • HT 43–4, 454 • BE 193, 289, 599

NELSON, SHARON, a.w.; 20-year-old TSBD employee. Nelson was standing on the north side of Elm Street midway between the TSBD and the triple underpass. She said that she never returned to work following the assassination. The WC claimed that Oswald was the only TSBD employee missing at a roll call held after the assassination. Nelson stated that she did not see Oswald at the time of the shooting and that she encountered no strangers in the TSBD that morning at work.

SOURCES: WCH XX, 665 • RTJ 109

NEWCOMB, FRED, Los Angeles assassination researcher. Newcomb was among the first to discover that one photo, taken by Philip Willis just after the assassination, had been retouched—presumably by the FBI, which had the photograph in its possession for five weeks after it was processed by Kodak.

The November 24, 1967, edition of *Life* showed two photos of Dealey Plaza taken within seconds of one another. In the Willis photo (shown on p. 93), no boxcar is visible behind the pergola atop the grassy knoll. In a photo taken by Wilma Bond, a boxcar is clearly shown. Penn Jones Jr. writes: "We think the boxcar was eliminated from the picture to try to erase all traces of the three men who were arrested in a boxcar behind the pagoda [i.e., pergola] just after the shooting." (See also Willis, Phillip)

SOURCES: FMG III, 59–60 • BE 681

NEWMAN, ALBERT, researcher and author of *The Assassination of President Kennedy—The Reasons Why* (Clarkson N. Potter, 1970).

SOURCE: MOORE 193–5, 216

NEWMAN, JEAN, a.w.; 21-year-old manufacturing company employee. Newman stood on the north curb of Elm between the TSBD and the Stemmons Freeway sign. She said she thought the shots came from her right, i.e., from the direction of the grassy knoll and the triple underpass.

SOURCES: CF 29 • NORTH 379–80, 385

NEWMAN, WILLIAM J. and GAYLE, a.w. William, a young design engineer, was standing with his wife, Gayle, and their two children on the north side of Elm Street just west of the Stemmons Freeway sign. Newman apparently gave a name to a very important piece of real estate when, during a TV interview just after the assassination, he was asked where he thought the shots had come from. "Back up on the, uh, knoll," Newman said.

The Newmans were standing directly in front of a.w. Abraham Zapruder during the assassination, and at first they thought Zapruder had fired the shots, since they seemed to have come from behind them.

Newman told Dallas reporter Jim Marrs:

***

We hadn't been there five minutes when the President turned onto Elm Street. As he was coming toward us there was a boom, boom, real close together. I thought someone was throwing firecrackers. He got this bewildered look on his face . . . Then he got nearer to us and, bam, a shot took the right side of his head off. His ear flew off. I heard Mrs. Kennedy say, "Oh my God, no, they shot Jack!" He was knocked violently back against the seat, almost as if he had been hit by a baseball bat. At the time I was looking right at the President and I thought the shots were coming from directly behind us. I said, "That's it! Get on the ground!" The car momentarily stopped and the driver seemed to have a radio or phone up to his ear and he seemed to be waiting on some word. Some Secret Service men reached into their car and came up with some sort of machine gun. Then the cars roared off. Very soon after this a man asked us what happened and we told him and he took us to Channel 8 (WFAA-TV) studios . . . I was a little disappointed that I didn't get to testify to the Warren Commission. Someone told me that the reason I wasn't asked to testify was that I was talking about shots from someplace other than the Depository Building . . . it's hard for me to believe that it was the act of one lone individual.

Newman's impression that JFK's ear flew off may seem bizarre until the Zapruder film is examined closely. The fatal shot formed a flap of scalp and skull bone that fell downward, covering JFK's ear, creating the impression to eyewitnesses that his ear had been shot off.

William Newman was a prosecution witness at the conspiracy trial of Clay Shaw in New Orleans. (See also Shaw, Clay; Zapruder, Abraham)
    SOURCES: WCH XII, 314 • HSCA Report 88–9, 606 • OGLESBY 36 • NORTH 380, 385 • CF 70 • GERTZ 519 • MOORE 121 • BE 18, 43, 330 • BLAKEY 88–9, 267

NEWNAM, JOHN, Ruby witness; member of the *Dallas Morning News* advertising staff. As of 12:20 P.M. on the day of the assassination, ten minutes before the shooting, Ruby was sitting across from Newnam's desk, submitting his weekend ads for the Carousel Club. The *Dallas Morning News* building is only a couple of blocks from Dealey Plaza. Newnam left Ruby alone to finish his copy and returned ten minutes after the assassination. Ruby was sitting right where he had been. At that point, according to Newnam, neither man knew that the assassination had occurred. When the news that JFK had been shot came in, Newnam says that Ruby seemed stunned, but no more so than anyone else. Ruby reportedly said, "John, I will have to leave Dallas."

Newman testified at Ruby's murder trial that, just before the assassination, Ruby had been complaining bitterly about the full-page ad in that day's *Morning News* accusing JFK of treason. Ruby was very interested in who Bernard Weissman was, since his name, with a post-office box, appeared in the ad, and sounded Jewish.

SOURCES: WR 312–4 • WCH XV, 534 • RTJ 261–2 • GERTZ 43–4, 104, 526

NIKOLAYEVNA, MARINA (See OSWALD, MARINA)

NICHOLS, ALICE REAVES, Ruby witness; former girlfriend. Nichols testified at Ruby's murder trial that she had known Jack since 1949 and the two had discussed marriage. She said that Ruby had visited her at her office on the day of the assassination and that he seemed very upset. She told the court that, although Ruby was quick-tempered and very emotional, she did not think he was insane. Nichols provides us with our only glimpse of Ruby's "normal" sexuality—a facet of Ruby's life which is otherwise represented by the fact that he called his favorite dog (Sheba) his "wife," his infrequent boasts that he had a sexual relationship with each and every woman who worked for him and the statements of stripper Jada saying that Ruby had once asked her to live with him platonically so that people would stop thinking he was a homosexual.

SOURCES: WR 315–6 • WCH XIV, 110 • GERTZ 62, 104 • BISHOP 328 • BLAKEY 297, 316

NICHOLS, H. LOUIS, Oswald witness; former president of the Dallas Bar Association. Nichols visited Oswald at the DPD station on Saturday afternoon, November 23, 1963. Oswald told Nichols that he was interested in being represented by either New York attorney John Abt or someone from the ACLU. According to Jim Bishop, "Nichols did not know Abt or a lawyer from ACLU. The interview was friendly and useless."

SOURCES: WR 189 • WCH VII, 325 • BISHOP 491

NICHOLS, JOHN, pathology and forensic pathology expert; prosecution witness at the Clay Shaw trial. After watching the Zapruder film with the rest of the courtroom, Nichols testified, "Having viewed...the Zapruder film, I find that it is compatible with the gunshot having been delivered from the front." (See also Shaw, Clay)

SOURCES: OTT 239–41, 247 • ME 200–1

NICHOLSON, JOHN (See VAGANOV, IGOR)

NICOL, JOSEPH D., firearms identification expert for the Bureau of Criminal Identification and Investigation, Illinois Department of Public Safety. Nicol positively identified for the WC, "the nearly whole bullet from the stretcher and the two larger bullet fragments found in the presidential limousine as having been fired in the C2766 Mannlicher-Carcano rifle found in the Depository to the exclusion of all other weapons." Nicol also "examined the four cartridge cases found near the site of the [Tippit] homicide and compared them with the test cartridge cases fired from the Smith & Wesson revolver taken from Oswald." He also examined the bullet that had been fired at Major General Edwin A. Walker—it being the WC's conclusion that Oswald fired that shot—but Nicol was less certain in his identification than he had been in the case of the assassination and Tippit evidence; he said the bullet "could have come, and even perhaps a little stronger, . . . probably came from this [rifle], without going so far as to say to the exclusion of all other guns. This I could not do." (See also Walker, Edwin A.)

SOURCES: WR 86–7, 160, 174 • WCH III, 496 • RTJ 197, 199 • MOORE 68 • EVICA 94

NICOLETTI, CHARLES, possible witness; suspicious death. Nicoletti was scheduled to testify before the HSCA about possible connections between JFK's assassination and CIA/Mafia plots against Castro, but he died first, on March 29, 1977. He was shot three times in the back of the head and his car was fire-bombed. Nicoletti died on the same day as Oswald mentor and CIA informant George DeMohrenschildt, who was also scheduled to testify before the HSCA. (See also White, Geneva)

SOURCES: HT 369 • EVICA 188, 226, 300–1, 303–4, 316–7 • OGLESBY 74

NICOLI, MICHEL, French mobster turned U.S. government informant. Nicoli corroborates the statements of gangster Christian David that three Corsican assassins, one of whom was Lucien Sarti, killed JFK. Nicoli, who has been given a new identity by the U.S. government, made his statements on the 1988 television documentary *The Men Who Killed Kennedy,* produced by Nigel Turner. According to Nicoli, Sarti had wanted to shoot from the triple underpass but found it guarded on the morning of the assassination and so, instead, moved behind the wooden fence atop the grassy knoll. Nicoli says that Sarti fired the fatal shot using a frangible bullet. Nicoli and David agree that the assassins were paid in heroin. Nicoli converted the heroin into cash in his Buenos Aires apartment, not knowing what the payment was for. He says that the assassination was Mafia-sponsored and that, when the Corsican Mafia was thrown out of Cuba by Castro, they moved to Montreal where they established a heroin-smuggling ring. (See also David, Christian; Rivele, Steve; Sarti, Lucien)

NIELL, JAMES, Dallas attorney who represented DPD Officer Roy

Vaughn. Niell was hired by Vaughn because Vaughn felt he was being made into a scapegoat by the DPD and the WC. Vaughn was the officer standing guard at the Main Street ramp of the DPD building on the morning of November 24, 1963, when Ruby reportedly entered the building through that entrance to shoot Oswald. Niell claims that Ruby did not enter through the ramp, as per the official scenario, but was, rather, escorted in by Assistant Chief of Police Charles Batchelor. (See also Batchelor, Charles)
SOURCE: HT 236

NIX, ORVILLE O., a.w.; air-conditioning repairman for the General Service Administration in the Dallas SS building. Nix took a motion picture of the assassination, facing the grassy knoll. It graphically shows a piece of Kennedy's head flying off and landing on the back of the limo. It is this skull fragment that Mrs. Kennedy was trying to retrieve when she made her famous crawl onto the back of the car.

The film shows what Dallas reporter Jim Marrs refers to as "suspicious flashes of light" on the grassy knoll. The film also shows clearly that the limo's brake lights are on after shots have been fired and that the limo slows to a near stop before the fatal shot. Some researchers have claimed that there is a visible gunman on the grassy knoll in the film. In 1966, the CIA-linked Itek Corporation—at the request of UPI—studied the film and determined that the gunman was really shadows from a tree branch.

Nix sold the film to UPI in 1963 for $5,000. He died in 1988. Recently, Nix's granddaughter, Gayle Nix Jackson, has been fighting to get the film back in her family's possession. She told the *Village Voice* (March 31, 1992) that the film brought her grandfather nothing but heartache. She says: "The FBI had issued a dictum to all of Dallas's film labs that any assassination photos had to be turned over to the FBI. The lab called my granddad first and, like the good American he was, he rushed it to the FBI. They [the FBI] took the camera [as well] for five months. They returned it in pieces."

In 1967, Nix participated in a CBS News re-creation of the assassination. Each time he told the interviewer that he thought the shots came from the grassy knoll, the director shouted, "Cut!" Finally, according to Ms. Jackson, the producer informed Orville that the WC had determined the shots came from the TSBD, and that was what they wanted to hear—so that was what Nix told them.
SOURCES: WR 100, 106 • WCE 2109–10 • HSCA Report 84–6 • NORTH 398, 504, 511–2, 517 • MOORE 105, 120 • CF 35 • RTJ 57 • HT 224 • PWW 16, 123–4, 277, 280

NIXON, RICHARD M., lost to JFK in the 1960 presidential election; ran the CIA as vice-president under Eisenhower; later became the 37th

President of the United States and resigned from office in disgrace after the Watergate scandal. Among the Watergate conspirators were assassination suspects Frank Sturgis and E. Howard Hunt. A 1947 FBI memo states: "It is my sworn statement that one Jack Rubenstein of Chicago, noted as a potential witness for hearings of the House Committee on Un-American Activities, is performing information functions for the staff of Congressman Richard Nixon, Republican of California. It is requested Rubenstein not be called for open testimony in the aforementioned hearings." That same year Rubenstein changed his name to Ruby and moved to Dallas. Nixon was in Dallas on November 20–22, 1963, for a soft-drink bottlers' convention (he was counsel for Pepsico) and left Dallas only three hours before the assassination. According to former CIC agent Russell Bintliff (and reported by the *Washington Star* on December 5, 1976), Pepsi set up a bottling plant in the 1960s in Vientiane, Laos, that didn't produce any soft drinks. Instead, it manufactured heroin. (See also Barker, Bernard; Bintliff, Russell; Bremer, Arthur; Cohen, Mickey; Colson, Charles; Cooper, Marrion; Cushman, Major General; Dalitz, Moe; Haldeman, H. R.; Hoover, J. Edgar; Hunt, E. Howard; Hunt, H. L.; Jenner, Albert; Liddy, G. Gordon; McGann, George; Marchetti, Victor; Morrow, Robert; Murchison, Clint; Oliver, Beverly)

SOURCES: WR 175–6 • HSCA Report 34, 104 • EVICA, many • ME 127, 216 • OGLESBY 5 • DAVIS, many • NORTH 56 • PD 25, 107–10, 179, 202, 206, 217, 256, 260 • BLAKEY 3, 10, 64, 136, 138, 203 • BELIN 85, 121, 140, 146–7, 152–3 • RTJ 308, 311 • COA, many • BISHOP 11, 19, 21, 53, 178 • DOP, many • CF 267–74 • HT, many • FMG III, 24, 85 • PWW 228 • KANTOR 105, 200–1, 218

NORMAN, HAROLD, a.w. Norman was one of three men who watched the assassination from the fifth floor of the TSBD, one floor below the "sniper's nest." He told the WC that he heard the action of a rifle bolt and the sound of shells hitting the floor coming from above. (See also Jarman, James; Williams, Bonnie Ray)

SOURCES: WR 78, 80, 134–5, 143, 232 • WCH III, 186 • BELIN 11, 60, 73, 220 • RTJ 89–90, 100–102, 104–8, 113 • BISHOP 121, 134, 141, 150 • CF 47–9 • PWW 132 • MOORE 62

NORTON, ROBERT L., Ruby witness; manager of the Pago Club in Dallas. Ruby visited the Pago Club around midnight on Saturday, November 23. He sat down at a central table and ordered a Coke. Norton joined Ruby a few minutes later. According to the WR:

[Norton] expressed to Ruby his concern as to whether or not it was proper to operate the Pago Club that evening. Ruby indicated that the

Carousel Club was closed but did not criticize Norton for remaining open. Norton raised the topic of President Kennedy's death and said, "[W]e couldn't do enough to that person that [did] this sort of thing." Norton added, however, that "Nobody has the right to take the life of another one." Ruby expressed no strong opinion, and closed the conversation by saying he was going home because he was tired.

SOURCES: WR 329 · WCH XV, 546

NORTON, TERESA (See CARLIN, KAREN BENNETT)

NOSENKO, YURI, KGB officer stationed at the KGB Center in Moscow, from 1959 to 1964. According to author Michael H. B. Eddowes in his book *Khrushchev Killed Kennedy*, Nosenko—along with Russian Premier Nikita Khrushchev—was part of the plot to assassinate JFK. Two months after the assassination, Nosenko was a 36-year-old KGB officer attending Geneva disarmament talks when he sent a coded message to CIA headquarters in Virginia, stating that he wished to defect. He was a member of the senior rank of the KGB's counterintelligence department within the USSR, with a background in postwar naval intelligence. He was suspected of specializing in the recruitment and blackmailing of foreigners—especially British and American. Even before his coded message, he had sold information to the CIA for small sums of money.

When the CIA first received Nosenko's coded message it tried to discourage him from defecting; it would have meant leaving his wife and children behind. They told him that he would be a far greater asset to the U.S. as an informant in Moscow. Nosenko insisted, saying that he had reason to believe Soviet officials already knew he wanted to defect. A return to Moscow would be fatal. (Nosenko later admitted that this claim of detection was false, a story invented to make sure that the U.S. accepted him.) The CIA removed Nosenko from Switzerland, by this time aware of the potentially frightening importance of his information.

Nosenko claimed to have been in charge of Oswald's file during the time Oswald lived in the USSR. He claimed that the KGB had never heard of Oswald until the ex-marine requested to become a permanent Soviet resident. At that point, Nosenko claimed, the KGB did not know about Oswald's USMC background, secret status, and U-2 knowledge—and, astoundingly, Nosenko claimed that they would *not* have been interested in Oswald even if they *had* known. Nosenko said that the KGB, when it did investigate Oswald, found him unintelligent and unstable. He was never debriefed on his military background and the KGB never considered his usefulness as an agent. Nosenko said, "...the interest of KGB headquarters in Oswald was practically nil."

The KGB, Nosenko continued, was not even concerned when Oswald married a Russian girl and returned to the U.S. with her. They had done a quick check on Marina and had discovered that she wasn't terribly bright, either. After the assassination, the KGB conducted an "urgent" investigation into Oswald's Soviet activities. Nosenko remained in charge of the case. The large report sent to Premier Khrushchev stated that Soviet Intelligence was innocent of any malevolent connections to Oswald or the assassination.

The question of whether or not to believe Nosenko's angelic tale created a rift in the CIA that was to have an effect on the company's functioning for more than a decade. For the following four years, Nosenko was held in solitary confinement by the CIA and subjected to "hostile interrogation." The CIA built a special vault-like building to hold his single-room cell. Although Nosenko became increasingly uncertain of the details of his past during the interrogation, his story never changed. When Nosenko was finally released he was given a new identity and an annual salary for the rest of his life—as a reward for his services. (See also Angleton, James Jesus; Paisley, John Arthur)

SOURCES: WCD 434, 451, released in 1975 • HSCA Report 101–2, 255–6, 490, 509–10 • HSCA XII, 475 • DUFFY 52–8 • HT 189, 329, 376 • KKK, iii • BLAKEY 113, 115–34, 153 • CF 130–4 • OGLESBY 77 • PD 154, 311–6

NOVEL, GORDON, CIA employee in New Orleans in 1963. According to researcher William Torbitt, Novel was seen by a Dallas attorney having meetings with Ruby and William Seymour in Ruby's Carousel Club during October and November 1963. As of 1986, Novel was working for John Z. DeLorean.

According to author Paris Flammonde, Novel was questioned by the FBI on five separate occasions following JFK's assassination. Flammonde writes: "Novel was a buddy of [assassination suspect David] Ferrie's who had been working with the CIA since 1959...[Novel] worked through the Double-Chek Corporation and the Evergreen Advertising Agency and he had carried out several missions in the Caribbean, was involved with arms purchases, and knew both Ruby and Oswald."

Novel was subpoenaed by New Orleans District Attorney Jim Garrison in 1967, but Novel fled to Ohio, where Garrison failed to obtain his extradition. According to Garrison, "we...learned from...Novel...that David Ferrie, one of the leaders of the local [New Orleans] Cuban

Revolutionary Front, and a handful of others from [Guy] Banister's office drove one night to the blimp air base at Houma, a town deep in southern Louisiana. They entered one of the Schlumberger Corporation's explosive bunkers and removed the land mines, hand grenades, and rifle grenades stored there."

While Garrison was attempting to extradite Novel from Ohio in April 1967, principally to testify about the Schlumberger affair, Novel let it be known that the bunker robbery had been a CIA job.

As reported in an April 25, 1967, *New Orleans States-Item* article titled "Evidence Links CIA to DA Probe," Novel had been telling friends that he was a CIA agent and would be cleared of all charges, that the robbery was actually a CIA "war matériel pickup" for the Bay of Pigs attack. Novel said that all of the men involved in the "pickup" were Company men and they included Ferrie and Sergio Acacha Smith.

Later, Garrison found a letter written by Novel, confirmed authentic by a handwriting expert and Novel's lawyer, written in January 1967 to Novel's CIA contact, "Mr. Weiss." The letter stated that because several men involved in the Schlumberger affair were also suspected by Garrison of being assassination conspirators, the Company should take "counteraction" against Garrison. Novel even suggested that, as Garrison had ready-reserve status in the Louisiana Army National Guard, it might be a good idea to call the D.A. into active duty. (See also Carlson, Alex; DeMenil, Jean; Mancuso, Marlene)

SOURCES: OTT 40, 166, 179–80, 228, 301 • FMG III, 40 • FLAMMONDE, many • DAVIS 362

NOYES, PETER, CBS newsman and author of *Legacy of Doubt* (Pinnacle, 1973).

SOURCES: CF 337–8 • HT 319 • MOORE 216 • BLAKEY 396 • EVICA 164, 264 • DAVIS 208, 221, 421–2 • NORTH 440

O

O'BRIEN, JOHN J., WC staff member; Internal Revenue Service agent; with Edward A. Conroy and Phillip Barson, analysed Oswald's finances in Appendix XIV of the WR.

O'BRIEN, LAWRENCE F., a.w.; Parkland witness; Bethesda witness; assistant to JFK. O'Brien rode in motorcade and returned to Washington aboard Air Force One. He later became Democratic Party chief and commissioner of the National Basketball Association.

SOURCES: WR 72 • WCH VII, 457 • BISHOP, many • DOP, many • BE 390, 395, 577–8, 677–8 • ME 111 • DAVIS 402

O'CONNOR, PAUL K., Bethesda witness; laboratory technician. O'Connor was one of the major witnesses supporting David Lifton's theory that JFK's body was altered somewhere between Parkland and Bethesda and made to appear as if it had been shot only from the rear, while all evidence to the contrary was removed. Lifton speculates that JFK's body was taken off Air Force One and placed on a helicopter, which took it to another hospital—most likely Walter Reed—where the alterations were made. It was then delivered by helicopter to Bethesda for the autopsy. The casket that a worldwide television audience saw unloaded from Air Force One was actually empty.

O'Connor says that he heard helicopters (perhaps two of them) outside of Bethesda, landing on the helicopter pad, and several moments later saw six to eight men carrying a casket into the hospital. He says that the body was in a military body bag when it arrived at Bethesda, which is odd, because it had been wrapped in a clear plastic mattress cover when it left Parkland.

According to author Harrison Edward Livingstone, O'Connor misperceived these happenings due to stress, perhaps confusing JFK's casket with that of a naval major that arrived around the same time. Livingstone believes that the autopsy photos and X rays were forged and JFK's body was unaltered.

O'Connor says that JFK's brain had already been removed by the time the body got to Bethesda, and that there was only "half of a handful" of brain matter left inside the skull, which would mean that the autopsists were lying when they said the brain was removed, weighed and preserved, and yielded bullet fragments.

O'Connor said to Nigel Turner, producer and director of the 1988 British television documentary *The Men Who Killed Kennedy*:

> There were mysterious men in civilian clothes at the autopsy. They seemed to command a lot of respect and attention—sinister looking people. They would come up and look over my shoulder or over Dr. [J. Thornton] Boswell's shoulder, then they'd go back and have a little conference in the corner. Then one of them would say, "Stop what you're doing and go on to another procedure." We jumped back and forth, back and forth. There was no smooth flow of procedure at all.

(See also Rike, Aubrey)
SOURCES: BE, many • HT 448, 450, 453, 465 • OGLESBY 41

ODIO, ANNIE LAURIE, possible Oswald witness; sister of Sylvia Odio (see below). Her statements corroborate those made by her sister. Annie had been with her sister when she received her visit from the three men, and it was Annie who answered the door when they knocked.
SOURCES: RTJ 341 • COA 44 • BLAKEY 44, 163, 165 • FLAMMONDE 113 • DAVIS 162

ODIO, SYLVIA, possible Oswald witness; Cuban exile living in Dallas. Odio's parents were imprisoned by the Castro government for purchasing anti-Castro arms. While the "real" Oswald was supposedly en route to Mexico during the last week of September, 1963, Odio received a visit from two Latin men and a white man introduced as "Leon Oswald." Later, one of the Latin men called Odio on the phone and said that Oswald thought "the Cubans had no guts and should shoot the President." This is yet another indication that there was more than one "Oswald" functioning in 1963.

According to Penn Jones Jr., "Right after the assassination Mrs. Odio was hidden in the home of Jack Rogers of Dallas, whose father, Ralph Rogers, is president of Texas Industries, one of the many firms controlled by the Murchison people." (See also Hall, Loran; Howard, Lawrence; Seymour, William; Liebeler, Wesley; Murchison, Clint)

SOURCES: WR 298–301 • WCH XI, 367 • HSCA Report 128, 137–9, 615 • RTJ 336–42, 386 • COA 44 • HT 191, 328, 399–400 • FMG III, 85 • MOORE 95 • OTT 67 • BLAKEY 35, 43–4, 81, 147, 162–5, 174–5, 177, 364, 387 • FLAMMONDE 112–5, 201–2, 206 • EVICA 120, 123–4, 126, 129, 136, 142, 280, 308, 314–5 • DAVIS 162–3 • NORTH 313–5

ODOM, LEE, possible conspiratorial link; in Clay Shaw's address book, the following notation was written: "LEE ODOM, P.O. BOX 19106, Dallas, Texas." The citation "19106" was also found in Oswald's notebook.

In 1967 the *New Orleans States-Item* discovered that there really was a Lee Odom living in Irving, Texas. Odom was interviewed and said that he had been in touch with Shaw repeatedly regarding the possibility of promoting a bullfight in New Orleans. New Orleans District Attorney Jim Garrison, who was then prosecuting Shaw for conspiracy to kill JFK, responded, "That is not the point. The point is that Clay Shaw and Lee Oswald have the same post-office box number in their address books and this is, in coded form, the unpublished phone number of Jack Ruby in 1963."

SOURCE: OTT 146

O'DONNELL, P. KENNETH "KEN," a.w.; special assistant to JFK; coordinator of the Texas swing of the president's trip. O'Donnell urged a motorcade through the heart of Dallas, so that JFK and Jackie could be seen by as many people as possible. According to a CIA liaison man's 1975 statement to congressional investigators, O'Donnell originally thought the shots came from elsewhere than the TSBD, but altered his statements to conform to the official version of the facts following a "warning" from FBI Director J. Edgar Hoover. He told Tip O'Neill, "I testified the way they wanted me to. I just didn't want to stir up any more pain and trouble for the family." (See also Hoover, J. Edgar)

SOURCES: WR 20, 50, 57–9, 61, 70–2 • WCH VII, 440 • HSCA Report 177, 228 • BELIN 1–4 • DOP, many • CF 436 • HT 41, 423 • BE 389–90, 400, 577–8, 677–8 • OTT 178 • BLAKEY 7, 10–1, 18–9, 57 • HOS 228–9 • ME 60, 101, 111, 234–5, 252 • PD 27–8, 102–3

O'DONNELL, WILLIAM, Ruby witness and friend of 16 years. O'Donnell said that Ruby knew at least 700 of the 1,200 men on the Dallas police force and that he was not at all surprised that Ruby had been allowed into the basement of police headquarters to view the transfer of Oswald.

SOURCE: RTJ 233, 235

ODUM, BARDWELL D., FBI agent; assassination investigator. Odum interviewed many of the witnesses to the JFK and Tippit murders. Marguerite Oswald says she was interrogated by Agent Odum on November

23, 1963, the day before Ruby shot her son. At that time, she claimed, Odum showed her a photo and asked her if the man looked familiar. She later came to believe that it was a photo of Ruby. (Julia Ann Mercer also claimed she was shown Ruby's photo by law enforcement officials before Ruby shot Oswald.)

According to the WR, "In the course of Marguerite's testimony, the Commission asked the FBI for a copy of the photograph displayed by Odum to her. When Marguerite viewed the photograph provided the Commission, she stated that the picture was different from the one she saw in November, in part because the 'top two corners' were cut differently and because the man depicted was not Jack Ruby." The WR then explains Mrs. Oswald's confusion this way: "On November 22 the CIA had provided the FBI with a photograph of a man who, it was thought at the time, might have been associated with Oswald. To prevent the viewer from determining precisely where the picture had been taken, FBI Agent Odum had trimmed the background... by making a series of straight cuts which reduced the picture to an irregular hexagonal shape." According to the FBI, this was the same photo as supplied to the WC, except that the WC's version had been trimmed of all background so that only a silhouette image of the man remained. The WR concluded, "Neither picture was of Jack Ruby. The original photograph had been taken by the CIA outside of the United States sometime between July 1, 1963 and November 22, 1963, during all of which time Ruby was within the country."

The WR seems to be referring to a photo taken in September 1963, in Mexico City of a man (referred to by author Hugh C. McDonald as "Saul") whom the CIA allegedly at the time believed to be Oswald, exiting the Russian or Cuban embassy there. The man did not look like Ruby or Oswald. (See also McDonald, Hugh C.)

SOURCES: WR 340–1 • WCH XI, 468 • RTJ 117, 198, 351–2 • BISHOP 369–70 • EVICA 25, 43, 51, 58, 125, 136 • PD 61

OFSTEIN, DENNIS HYMAN, Oswald witness. Ofstein was an employee of Jaggars-Chiles-Stovall in Dallas during the time Oswald worked there.

SOURCE: WCH X, 194

OGLESBY, CARL, author of *Who Killed JFK?* (Odonian Press, 1992) and *JFK Assassination: The Facts and the Theories* (Signet, 1992). Oglesby is one of the founders and leaders of the Washington-based Assassination Information Bureau.

O'GRADY, THOMAS J., Ruby witness; former DPD officer. Grady once

worked for Ruby as a bouncer. According to the WR, Ruby called O'Grady at 8:30 P.M. on November 23 and "criticized his competitors for remaining open and complained about the 'Impeach Earl Warren' sign."
SOURCE: WR 325

O'HARA, MALCOLM, New Orleans judge. With Judges Bernard Bagert and Matthew Braniff, O'Hara was part of a three-judge panel at Clay Shaw's preliminary hearing. They ruled, on March 17, 1967, that Jim Garrison's prosecution had presented sufficient evidence for Shaw to be held over for trial. (See also Garrison, Jim; Shaw, Clay)
SOURCES: OTT 156 • FLAMMONDE 6, 11–2, 79, 90, 95, 325–6

OKUI, YAEKO, Oswald witness. George and Jeanne DeMohrenschildt invited Lee and Marina Oswald to a party celebrating Russian Christmas 1962 at the home of Declan and Katherine Ford. The party was attended by members of Dallas's Russian-speaking community. Lev Aronson, first cellist for the Dallas Symphony Orchestra, brought to the party a Japanese woman named Yaeko Okui, with whom Lee spoke at length in Russian. Lee had been stationed in Japan in the USMC. Okui told federal investigators that, after that party, she never saw the Oswalds again.

This may not be so, however. Marina later told journalist Priscilla Johnson McMillan that she thought Okui might be a spy. Marina said she feared Lee and Okui were having an affair, and that she and Lee had fought over the matter.
SOURCES: WR 643 • RUSSELL, 28, 161–2, 169, 174, 276

OLDS, GREGORY LEE, president of the Dallas ACLU. Olds called DPD Captain Will Fritz around 11:00 P.M., November 22, 1963, to make sure that Oswald's civil rights were being protected. Fritz told him that the prisoner had been informed of his rights and, despite his public protests that he was being held without legal representation, Oswald was not tenaciously seeking a lawyer. Justifiably dissatisfied, Olds sent two ACLU men to speak to Justice of the Peace David Johnston, who erroneously assured the men that Oswald had "declined counsel." Olds gave up, and Oswald remained without a lawyer until his death. (See also Fritz, Will)
SOURCES: WCH VII, 322 • BISHOP 463–6, 483 • FMG III, 82 • NORTH 499

OLIVER, BEVERLY (aka "The Babushka Lady"), a.w.; Ruby witness; possible Oswald witness; 19 years old. Oliver claims she was standing on the south side of Elm Street with a triangular kerchief on her head. For years, despite a "thorough" search, her identity was unknown. She was sought not just because she was one of the closest witnesses to the shot that killed JFK, but also because photographic evidence (the Zapruder film, the

Muchmore film, et al.) showed that she was filming the motorcade. Because of her position, it was suspected that her film showed both the TSBD and the grassy knoll at the time of the shots.

Oliver came forward in the mid–1970s, when she told her story to author J. Gary Shaw. It was a story so wild that it boggles the imagination. On November 22, 1963, she was a stripper at the Colony Club, immediately next door to Ruby's Carousel Club. She knew Ruby and many of the women who worked for him. Oliver says that on or about November 8, 1963, she met a man in the Carousel Club whom Ruby introduced as "Lee Oswald of the CIA;" she recognized Oswald later when she saw him on TV. Oliver says that assassination suspect David Ferrie was such a frequent visitor to the Carousel Club that she mistook him for the manager. Why did she keep quiet? A friend of hers who knew of Ruby and Oswald's relationship had disappeared, she says.

In 1970, Oliver married George McGann, a Dallas mobster. The best man at the wedding was Russell D. Mathews, a close friend of Ruby. In 1968, during the presidential campaign, Oliver and McGann met for two hours in a Miami hotel with Richard M. Nixon. In 1970, McGann was murdered gangland-style in West Texas. Oliver claims that she never saw the film she took of JFK's death with a Super-8 Yashica movie camera. On November 25, 1963, she says, she was approached by two men near the Colony Club. The men did not identify themselves, but she believed them to be U.S. government agents—FBI, CIA, or SS. They told her they knew about the film and needed it for evidence. She handed it over and never saw it again. There is no mention of Oliver or her film in the WR. She was later shown many photos and identified FBI agent Regis Kennedy as one of the two men who had taken her film. Regis worked on the New Orleans part of the investigation and reportedly told FBI Director J. Edgar Hoover that Carlos Marcello was no more than a "tomato salesman," Marcello's legitimate business. (See also Conforto, Janet; Kennedy, Regis; Lawrence, Jack; McGann, George; Mathews, Russell)
    SOURCES: CF 35–9, 189 • HT 121–2, 133, 292, 419–20, 461 • MOORE 121

OLIVER, REVILO PENDLETON, John Birch Society council member. Oliver was one of the most bizarre witnesses to testify before the WC. Although he had nothing relevant to say about the assassination, he managed to fill over 150 pages (all published) with neo-Nazi ravings. He was dismayed that some people mourned JFK's death but nobody mourned Hitler's death and believed the assassination was part of a Communist conspiracy. (They killed JFK, he said, because they were afraid he was about to "turn American.") The WC gave Oliver more room in its report than it did to Jackie Kennedy, Governor Connally, and Nellie Connally combined.

SOURCES: WCH XV, 709 • RTJ 383

OLIVIER, ALFRED G., ballistics expert; veterinarian who had spent seven years in wounds ballistics research for the U.S. Army. In 1964 the WC assigned Olivier to conduct tests designed to prove that the "magic bullet" could have done the damage it allegedly did to JFK and Governor Connally while emerging from the experience pristine. The tests were held at the U.S. army's Edgewood Arsenal in Maryland. Olivier shot bullets through blocks of gelatin and goat cadavers, but failed to come up with a single undeformed bullet. Olivier also used the goat cadavers to determine the size of an exit wound from a Mannlicher-Carcano bullet. According to author Bonar Menninger, "While Olivier's entrance holes were the same size as the one in Kennedy's back, he found the smallest exit hole to be 10 millimeters in diameter, more than twice as large as the wound in the front of the President's throat."

While biophysics director at the Aberdeen Proving Grounds, Olivier served on the HSCA medical panel. He examined the JFK autopsy photos and X rays and concluded that JFK was shot only from behind.

SOURCES: WR 89, 105 • WCH V, 74 • BELIN 181 • RTJ 70, 77–8 • ME 35, 37–8, 83–5, 152, 206, 228

OLSEN, HARRY N., Ruby witness and "acquaintance"; member DPD; on restricted duty because of a broken kneecap he had suffered earlier in the year. Olsen dated (and later married) Ruby stripper Kay Helen Coleman, who worked under the name Kathy Kay. Olsen told the WC that on the day of the assassination he spent the entire day working as a security guard at an estate in Oak Cliff whose owner and address he could not remember. As can best be pinpointed from his vague testimony, he was on Eighth Street someplace, about five or six blocks from the Thornton Expressway. According to Penn Jones Jr. this location would put him in an elevated section of Oak Cliff, possibly in a position to monitor the movements of Tippit and Tippit's assailant below. (Tippit last radioed in his location as Eighth Street and Lancaster.) He would also have been only a few blocks away from Ruby's apartment. Given that everyone who was alive remembers where he or she was at the time of the assassination, the vagueness of his testimony should have raised a few eyebrows.

DPD Chief Jesse Curry wrote that Olsen had a reputation for being "unstable" and was known to carry an illegal gun and brass knuckles. Officially, Olsen was in the Carousel Club, visiting Kay at 11:00 P.M. on the evening of the assassination. Although Olsen was single and married Kay within a month, Ruby assumed that he was already married and was meeting the stripper on the sly. At that time, according to Olsen, Ruby bragged about having seen Oswald at the DPD station. When Olsen asked Ruby what he thought of the prisoner, Ruby replied, "He looked just like a little rat. He was sneaky looking, like a weasel." (See also Cheek, Bertha; Olsen, Kay [below])

SOURCES: WR 319–20, 327 • WCH XIV, 624 • COA 130–2, 148, 268 • BISHOP 509–11, 520 • FMG I, 78–80, 82–5, 87, 90–2, 96, 98 • NORTH 413–4, 490 • KANTOR 7–8, 48–50, 215

OLSEN, KAY HELEN (née Coleman; aka Kay, Kathy), Ruby witness; Carousel Club stripper. The British-born Olsen lived on Ewing Street in Oak Cliff, only a few blocks from Ruby's residence. According to the WR, Olsen (then single but attached to DPD member Harry Olsen—the only member of the DPD who couldn't remember precisely where he was at the time of the assassination) saw Ruby on the night of the assassination for one hour outside a parking garage at Jackson and Field streets in Dallas. Kay says she told Ruby, regarding Oswald, "In England they would drag him through the streets and would have hung [sic] him." Kay, again accompanied by Harry Olsen, saw Ruby outside the Carousel Club on Saturday evening as well, but, according to the WR, only to exchange greetings. The Olsens were married in either December 1963 or January 1964 and soon thereafter moved to California. (See also Olsen, Harry [above])

SOURCES: WR 320, 327 • WCH XIV, 640 • BISHOP 509–11 • FMG I, 79–80, 83–4, 86–90

O'NEILL, FRANCIS X., Bethesda witness; FBI agent. O'Neill, with agent James W. Sibert, attended JFK's autopsy. (See also Bouck, Robert; Sibert, James W.; Stover, J. H.)

SOURCES: BISHOP 348–9, 362, 367, 385, 431, 449, 493 • BE, many • HT 94, 112, 235

ORCARBERRO, MANUEL RODRIGUEZ (See RODRIGUEZ, MANUEL ORCARBERRO)

ORR, MAURICE, a.w. Orr stood on the north side of Elm Street between the TSBD and the steps to the pergola and was one of the closest eyewitnesses to the president at the time of the fatal head shot. According to author Anthony Summers, Orr was interviewed a few minutes after the shooting by a "Dallas researcher" and said he heard five shots but was never interviewed about what he had seen and heard by any official entity.

SOURCE: SUMMERS 20, 23

ORTIZ, AUTULIO RAMIREZ, informant. According to the HSCA:

> Ortiz... hijacked an aircraft to Cuba in 1961 [and] claimed that while
> being held by the Cuban Government, he worked in an intelligence
> facility where he found a dossier on Oswald. It was labeled the
> "Osvaldo-Kennedy" file and contained a photograph of "Kennedy's
> future assassin." In the Spanish-language manuscript of a book he
> wrote, Ramirez [Ortiz] claimed the Oswald file read in part, "... The
> KGB has recommended this individual... He is a North American,
> married to an agent of the Soviet organism who has orders to go and
> reside in the United States. Oswald is an adventurer. Our Embassy in
> Mexico has orders to get in contact with him. Be very careful."

The Cubans returned Ortiz to the U.S., where he was imprisoned for
hijacking. He told the HSCA on April 11, 1978, that—among other
things—he could not describe the photo of Oswald he had seen and that the
file was written in Russian, which he cannot read. However, all of his other
statements that could be corroborated independently, including the names
and positions of Cuban officials, proved accurate. The HSCA concluded:
"While some details of his story could be corroborated, the essential
aspects of his allegation were incredible."

SOURCE: HSCA Report, many

OSBORNE, P. DAVID, Bethesda witness; captain (later admiral), U.S.
Navy; Bethesda chief of surgery. Osborne originally said he had seen an
"intact bullet... not deformed in any way" fall from JFK's wrappings onto
the autopsy table; later told the HSCA that he was "not sure" he had seen
this.

SOURCES: HSCA VII, 15–6 • HT 235, 455 • OGLESBY 55

OSBORNE, MACK, Oswald witness; USMC acquaintance. Osborne told
WC that Oswald:

> spent a great deal of his free time reading papers printed in
> Russian... with the aid of a Russian-English dictionary... [He] did
> not go out in the evening... he was saving his money, making some
> statement to the effect that one day he would do something that would
> make him famous, it was my belief—although he said nothing to this
> effect—that he had his trip to Russia in mind... [F]ellow Marines
> sometimes accused him of being a Russian spy. In my opinion, he
> took such accusations in fun. Although I did not regard Oswald as

particularly intelligent, I got the idea that he thought he was intelligent and tried verbally to suggest to others that he was... Although he would discuss religion with others, he was non-committal as to his own opinions. Oswald seldom if ever went out with women. I suspect that this was part of his program for saving money... I do not recall any remarks on his part concerning Communism, Russia or Cuba.

SOURCES: WCH VIII, 321 • AO 96–7 • OTT 46

OSBORNE, WILLIAM, Parkland witness; surgeon; with Dr. John Parker, assisted the chief of orthopedic surgery, Charles F. Gregory, in operating on the wounds in Governor Connally's right wrist between 4:00 and 4:50 P.M. on November 22, 1963. According to the WR, "The wound on the back of the wrist was left partially open for draining, and the wound on the palm side was enlarged, cleansed and closed. The fracture was set, and a cast was applied with some traction utilized."
SOURCE: WR 69

OSBOURNE, ALBERT (perhaps aka Bowen, John), possible Oswald witness; fervent Nazi supporter; member of the American Council of Christian Churches. Osbourne reportedly ran an anti-Communist missionary school for orphans in Puebla, Mexico. The school allegedly served as a cover for training marksmen. Osbourne accompanied "Oswald" by bus from New Orleans to Mexico City on September 26, 1963. On the bus, Oswald was heard to say he was "going to Havana." Osbourne later denied to the WC that it was Oswald next to him on the bus, saying that man was "Mexican or Puerto Rican." The WC, citing Osbourne's shady past, refused to believe him. According to researcher William Torbitt, Osborne and ten of his professional killers were living at 3126 Harlendale in the Oak Cliff section of Dallas on November 22, 1963. (See also Bloomfield, Louis; Grossi, John; Nagy, Ferenc; Seymour, William; Torbitt, William)
SOURCES: WR 283 • RTJ 390–2 • BLAKEY 34

OSER, ALVIN, New Orleans assistant district attorney at the time Clay Shaw was tried for conspiracy to assassinate JFK. Oser often questioned witnesses in Jim Garrison's stead, as Garrison kept a low profile during the trial, reportedly due to the repeated attempts to discredit him. (See also Garrison, Jim; Shaw, Clay)
SOURCES: FMG III, 53, 65 • OTT 151–2, 231, 239–40, 246–9, 275

O'SULLIVAN, FREDERICK S., Oswald witness; acquaintance of Oswald at Beauregard Junior High School in New Orleans. O'Sullivan recruited Oswald into the Civil Air Patrol in 1955, when assassination suspect David Ferrie was the squadron commander.

SOURCES: WCH VIII, 27 • BLAKEY 347

OSWALD, JUNE LEE, daughter of the alleged assassin; born February 15, 1961.

OSWALD, LEE HARVEY (aka Lee, O. H; Hidell, Alek J.; Osbourne, Lee), historically recognized as the murderer of JFK and Officer J. D. Tippit. Oswald was born in New Orleans on October 18, 1939, two months after his father's death and was named Lee after his father and Harvey after his paternal grandmother's maiden name. He had one older brother, Robert, born in 1934, and a half-brother from his mother's previous marriage, John Edward Pic, born in 1931. When Lee was born, Oswald's mother, Marguerite, and her boys lived in a rough section of New Orleans's French Quarter called Exchange Alley, which was rife with vice-ridden bars and gambling under the auspices of organized crime.

Lee's mother, once divorced and once widowed, was both a clinging and a chilly parent, whose lack of true nurturing instincts were the cause of familial dysfunction. All three of her sons fled the nest and joined the military at the first opportunity. She lived a nomadic, carefree life, moving from man to man and from place to place, only vaguely cognizant of the responsibilities of motherhood. In May 1945 Marguerite married Edwin A. Ekdahl, a man in whom Lee found a father figure. However, Marguerite's third marriage was stormy and ended in divorce in June 1948. At that point, Marguerite bought a small house in Benbook, Texas, a suburb of Fort Worth, where John and Robert slept on the porch and Lee and his mother slept together—a sleeping arrangement the family maintained until Lee was almost 11 years old.

By August 1952, both of Lee's older brothers were in the military: John in the U.S. Coast Guard and Robert in the U.S. Marines. Lee and Marguerite now lived in New York City because John was stationed there. At first they lived with John and his wife, but Marguerite and her daughter-in-law did not get along. By September, Lee and his mother were in their own apartment in the Bronx.

When school started, Lee developed a truancy problem (instead of going to school, he often went to the Bronx Zoo) and was remanded to Youth House, where he was evaluated from April 16 to May 7. The psychiatric examinations showed a boy with no neurological impairment or psychotic changes, but rather one with "personality pattern disturbance with schizoid features and passive-aggressive tendencies." The evaluation continued: "Lee has to be seen as an emotionally quite disturbed youngster who suffers the impact of really existing emotional deprivation, lack of affection, absences of family life and rejection by a self-involved and conflicted mother."

Lee was given an I.Q. examination at this time and scored 118 on the Wechsler Intelligence Scale for Children, putting him in the "upper range of bright normal intelligence." He also scored above average on reading and arithmetic exams. He was released on probation from Youth House. Defying court orders and psychologist's advice, on January 10, 1954, Marguerite moved with her son to New Orleans, before Lee's probation had expired.

Oswald was probably dyslexic. His writing shows difficulties out of sync with his intelligence. This learning disability would explain Oswald's trouble in school and, later, in maintaining steady employment.

In New Orleans, the Oswalds moved in with Marguerite's sister Lillian and her husband, Charles "Dutz" Murret. Murret, Lee's new father figure, promoted prizefighters in New Orleans and was known as a gambler with ties to the Carlos Marcello gambling syndicate. (Marguerite also had ties to Marcello. She had once dated Clem Sehrt, Marcello's attorney, and she was also friends with Sam Termine, a Louisiana crime figure and former Marcello bodyguard.)

Oswald's life changed in the early summer of 1955 when he was between the ninth and tenth grades: He began attending meetings of the student aviation organization, the Civil Air Patrol, which met twice a week at the Lakefront Airport. His commander was David Ferrie a freakish individual who, along with being a pedophilic homosexual, was a crack pilot and fervent anti-Communist. Ferrie claimed to have no body hair because of *alopecia praecox*, a rare disease. He painted on his eyebrows and wore a crude reddish wig, which he kept held to his head with a glop of purplish glue.

Born in Cleveland in 1918, Ferrie loved to recruit young boys into his strange world. He had a Svengali-like presence and was known to practice hypnosis. Ferrie was expelled from the Civil Air Patrol in late 1955, after it came to light that he had been holding wild, nude drinking parties with his boys.

In October of that year, just after Oswald turned 16, he attempted to enlist in the marines, but failed because he was too young. According to his mother, Lee spent the entire following year waiting until he turned 17 so that he could be a marine. Oswald enlisted on October 24, 1956, six days after his 17th birthday. That same year, Oswald began to brag about his prolific reading of Communist literature. It is suspected that, even at this early age, Oswald was already preparing himself for a life in the world of counterintelligence. His mother confirmed that Lee's favorite television series at that time was *I Led Three Lives*, about an FBI agent who had infiltrated the Communist Party. Two weeks before Oswald enlisted, he wrote a letter to the Young People's Socialist League of the Socialist Party of America, seeking information.

Oswald was treated uniquely by the USMC. Although his scores on the rifle range were below average, indicating less-than-gifted hand-eye coordination, and his mathematics and pattern analysis were well below average, he was assigned to the Marine Air Control Squadron at Atsugi Air Force Base in Japan, 20 miles west of Tokyo, as a radar operator. During this time, Oswald continued to brag about his obsession with Communist literature. In spite of his communist leanings, Oswald was granted a "confidential" clearance, a necessity for his job, since Atsugi was home base for the U-2 spy plane that was regularly flying over the Soviet Union. During his entire stint in the marines, Oswald would spend large portions of his free time away from his fellow marines, during which none of them knew where he went or what he did. It is suspected by W. R. Morris and R. B. Cutler, authors of *alias Oswald*—as well as by Michael Eddowes, author of *Khrushchev Killed Kennedy*—that, during one of these times "away," Oswald was replaced by a man named Alek James Hidell, who lived out the rest of Oswald's life for him as an agent [a U.S. agent according to Cutler and Morris; a KGB agent according to Eddowes]. This, they say, would explain why Oswald was 5'11" tall when entered the USMC, but only 5'9" when he was discharged. (Sloppy paperwork would be another explanation.) None has a theory about what happened to the real Oswald after the switch was made.

At Atsugi, Oswald's fellow marines began calling him "Oswaldskovich," because of his interest in everything Soviet. He read Russian-language newspapers and claimed to be teaching himself the language, yet still did not lose his security clearance. Atsugi was reportedly more than just the base from which the U-2 spy plane took off and landed. It was also alleged to be the home of a CIA mind-control program code-named MK/ULTRA, which was said to have used LSD and other drugs to turn men into robots, fogging their ability to question authority and tell right from wrong. Allegations that Oswald was not the run-of-the-mill marine are supported by the fact that on September 16, 1958, while in Japan, he was treated for a venereal disease, which originated, according to his medical records, "in the line of duty, not due to his own misconduct." It was believed by Oswald's fellow marines that he was teaching himself Russian, but this was probably not the case. Records show that the marines tested him in his Russian proficiency on February 25, 1959—and it is unlikely that they would have done this if they had not been teaching him the language as well.

Twice in 1957 Oswald was court-martialed: once for possession of an unauthorized weapon (a .22 pistol, with which Oswald accidentally shot himself in the arm) and once for pouring a drink on a noncommissioned officer (a sergeant). His combined punishment for these offenses was 48 days in confinement and a fine of $105. These incidents created more time when his fellow marines had no contact with him.

Although Oswald was obliged to serve in the USMC until December 7, 1959, two years from the date of his induction plus his time of confinement, Oswald managed to have himself honorably discharged early because—or so he claimed—his mother was ill and needed him. (Oswald's family hardship discharge was not changed to "undesirable" until after he "defected" to the Soviet Union.) Marguerite was not ill. She had been in an accident early in the year, which laid her up for a time, but she was fully recovered by the time Oswald applied for his early discharge. Besides, according to Lee's brothers, it was doubtful that he would have gone out of his way to help his mother, regardless of the circumstances.

Seven days before he was discharged, on September 4, 1959, Oswald applied for a U.S. passport so that, as stated on his application, he could attend the Albert Schweitzer College and the University of Turku in Finland—as well as to travel to Cuba, the Dominican Republic, England, France, Germany, and the Soviet Union. This is hardly a plan that jibes with a family-hardship early-discharge from the marines. The passport was issued on September 10, and he was discharged from the marines the following day. On September 14, he arrived in Fort Worth, Texas, where his mother was living, and gave her $100. On September 17, he left for New Orleans, the first step in his "attempted" defection to Russia.

The trouble with tracing Oswald's movements in the Soviet Union comes from the fact that none of the sources of information regarding his movements overseas can be corroborated.

For years, the principal source of information for Oswald in Russia was his own "Historic Diary." Unfortunately, the authenticity of that diary is now officially in doubt. While some experts feel that Oswald did not write the diary at all, others believe that Oswald did write the diary but that it was written in one or two sittings rather than in daily, contemporaneous with the events it depicts.

Other sources include Marina Oswald, the woman Lee would meet and marry while in the USSR, and Yuri Nosenko, a former KGB agent who defected to the U.S. and frantically attempted to convince American intelligence agents that the KGB had never had an interest in Oswald and hadn't even bothered to interrogate him about his knowledge of the U.S.'s most sophisticated spy plane. So this, as best as can be pieced together, is what happened to Oswald after he left the marines and planned to defect to the USSR:

After making travel arrangements through a New Orleans travel agency and filling out the appropriate "Passenger Immigration Questionaire" (upon which he listed as his occupation "shipping export agent"), and paying $220.75 for his ticket, on September 19, 1959, Oswald embarked aboard the SS *Marion Lykes* from New Orleans to Le Havre, France. He was one of four passengers aboard the freighter. The ship arrived in France on October 8 and Oswald was in Russia a week later, following a roundabout but well-conceived route through Great Britain and Finland.

There are several physical impossibilities and bureaucratic improbabilities in the official version of Oswald's movements. He took flights when no flights were scheduled and received his visa at the Russian consulate in Helsinki in 48 hours—when a full work week was considered the minimum. Red tape was cut to make things easier for Oswald, perhaps in this case by the Soviet consul in Helsinki, Gregory Golub, who has been suspected by U.S. intelligence of being a KGB agent. It has been suggested that the only way to get into the Soviet Union as quickly as Oswald managed to do was through Golub, which supports the theory that something—or someone—was steering Oswald in the proper direction.

Oswald was met at the Moscow railroad station on October 16 by a Russian tourist agent and driven to the Hotel Berlin. He identified himself as a student. Soon thereafter, he wrote a letter to the Supreme Soviet requesting Soviet citizenship. However, according to Oswald's diary, this is where his knack for "getting permission" came to a halt. Instead of getting a positive response to his request for citizenship, he received a message from the Soviet Passport and Visa Department that his visa had expired and he had two hours to get out of the country. The diary says he returned to his room and slashed his left wrist, trying to end it all because of the despair and disappointment he was suffering. He was taken to Botkinskaya Hospital for three days in the psychiatric ward and four days in the "somatic" ward before being released. The suicide attempt successfully delayed his expulsion from the country. Living illegally in the country—at least technically—after his release from the hospital, Oswald checked out of his room at the Hotel Berlin and checked into the Metropole Hotel. He obviously wasn't on the run, or he wasn't fooling anyone if he was, because later that day on October 28, Oswald was contacted by the Pass and Registration Office, which wanted to know whether he was still interested in becoming a Soviet citizen. He said that he was. They told him they would have a decision for him in three days or more.

Exactly three days later, on October 31, Oswald apparently became impatient and took a taxi to the American embassy in Moscow, tossed his passport on a staffer's desk and demanded to "dissolve his American citizenship." He then did a peculiar thing. Knowing that Section 349 of the United States Immigration and Nationality Act provided several easy ways of casting off U.S. citizenship without a lot of hassle, he told Richard E. Snyder, the second secretary and senior consular official at the embassy, that he was an ex-marine with secrets the Russians might be interested in. Seeking to stall the overzealous ex-marine, Snyder told Oswald that he couldn't dissolve his U.S. citizenship until the following Monday. This angered Oswald—but he had no choice but to wait. Over the next few days, he granted interviews to the Soviet-based correspondents for both major wire services (AP and UPI) and several other reporters. He talked about his love of Communism and how he did not want to end up in "poverty" as his mother had. Back home, his story made the papers, and Marguerite Oswald learned for the first time of her son's whereabouts. She became convinced that Lee was working as an undercover U.S. agent.

Snyder's stalling technique worked. Oswald never did follow through on his extreme request to dissolve his U.S. citizenship. Oswald therefore was left a "window of escape" when it came time for him to return.

The integrity of Oswald's diary is damaged (at least in the sense that it was not written contemporaneously with the events it depicts) by the fact that, in a letter to his brother Robert and in interviews with a UPI correspondent on November 8 and 13, Oswald stated that he had been told by Soviet officials that he had been given permission to stay. In his diary, however, Oswald says that he did not learn until later—perhaps as late as November 16—that he had been given temporary permission to stay in the USSR.

On January 4, 1960, Oswald was called to the Soviet Passport Office, where he was informed that he was being sent to Minsk, being given a rent-free apartment and a well-paying job at the Belorussian Radio and Television Factory. (Oswald made about as much as the factory's foreman.) He lived "big" for a year and dated many women. Recently released KGB files indicate that all of his dates were government agents or informants. Because Lee's Russian friends thought his first name sounded Chinese, they called him "Alik."

In January 1961, the Soviet Passport Office summoned him again and asked whether he still wanted to be a Soviet citizen. He said no, but he wouldn't mind staying for another year under the same cushy conditions. On February 13, 1961, the American embassy received a letter from Oswald postmarked in Minsk on February 5, saying that he wanted to return to the United States. Snyder wrote back, stating that Oswald would have to appear in person at the American embassy. On March 5 Oswald wrote again, explaining that he was not allowed to leave Minsk without permission, but the letter did not arrive at its Moscow destination until March 20. According to the WC, the Soviets must have intercepted the second letter, because soon thereafter Oswald's Red Cross aid ceased. It was at this time that Oswald found Marina, the woman who would sell him out posthumously only two-and-a-half years later.

On March 17, 1961, Oswald met 19-year-old Marina Nikolayevna Prusakova at a dance at the Palace of Culture for Professional Workers in Minsk. She, like Lee, had never known her father. Her mother had died in 1957. She had lived for a time with her step-father but they had quarreled. When she met Lee, she was living with her uncle and aunt, Mr. and Mrs. Ilya Vasilyevich Prusakov. According to Marina, her uncle was a top official in the Minsk MVD. (It has often been alleged that Marina's uncle was a KGB agent, and this may be true; but Marina strongly denies it, insisting that his title would translate as Minister of Domestic Affairs, or the Russian equivalent of an FBI agent.)

Oswald asked Marina to marry him sometime before April 11, 1961. By April 20, they filed their intent-to-marry notice with the registrar and had received all necessary permission for a Russian woman to marry a foreigner. Marina told the WC that, when she married Lee, she had no idea that he planned to—or even that he was able to—leave the USSR and return to the United States. Nonetheless, by the end of May 1961, the Oswalds were making plans to come to the U.S. (Oswald's diary says that he didn't tell Marina that they were going to the U.S. until "the last days of June," but the American embassy in Moscow received a letter from Oswald on May 25, asking for assurances that he would not be prosecuted upon his return.) Making the arrangements to return proved problematic, with most of the delays stemming from Marina's difficulties getting a visa and the fact that she was pregnant with their first child. June Oswald was born to Lee and Marina on February 15, 1962, and on June 1 the Oswalds boarded a train bound for the Netherlands. They left Holland via the SS *Maasdam* on June 4 and arrived in Hoboken, New Jersey, on June 13. They were put up overnight in a Times Square hotel by a representative of the New York State Department of Welfare, who also lent them money. On June 14, the same representative put them on a commercial flight bound for Fort Worth, Texas. (This is hardly the treatment one would expect for a man who defected to a Communist country and, while there, offered to divulge the military secrets he knew.)

The biggest problem we have in gauging the quality of information regarding Oswald's movements after his return to the United States stems from evidence that several men impersonated Oswald and laid down false trails for reasons unknown. There is evidence that Oswald was being impersonated as early as 1961. There were certainly Oswald impersonators working in Dallas during the weeks leading up to the assassination.

Lee and Marina went to Fort Worth because Lee's brother Robert lived there, and Robert had sent Lee a letter in the Soviet Union inviting Lee's family to come stay with him. Those who think the Oswald who came back from Russia was a different man from the one who enlisted in the Marine Corps are quick to point out the radical change in Lee's appearance, a change that members of his family couldn't help noticing. Robert noticed immediately that Lee had lost a great deal of hair and that he was thinner. There is also evidence that Lee was two inches shorter upon returning to the U.S. than he had been when he left. (At the time of Oswald's arrest, he was 5'9". His Defense Department identification card, found in his wallet following his arrest, lists his height as 5'11".)

On June 26, 1962, the FBI interviewed Oswald for the first time.

Although the FBI said Oswald was "arrogant" during the interview, Oswald later said that he thought the interview went "just fine." As the interrogations by the FBI became a regular event and the FBI attempted to question Marina when Lee was not around, Oswald became increasingly hostile toward the feds.

Lee, Marina, and June Oswald lived with Robert for about a month. During this time, Lee's mother moved to Fort Worth, so the Oswalds moved into her apartment at 1501 West 7th Street sometime in July. Lee and his mother did not get along, however, and "around the middle of August" the Oswalds moved to their own one-bedroom apartment at 2703 Mercedes Street. The apartment was described by visitors as "poorly furnished" and "decrepit."

During the third week of July 1962, Oswald got a job as a sheet-metal worker at the Leslie Welding Company. He worked there until October, when he quit. His coworkers described him as a loner.

Through Lee's efforts to publish an article about his Soviet experiences, the Oswalds became acquainted with the Dallas–Fort Worth Russian-speaking community—a small but tight-knit group with language in common.

Most of these people—a disproportionate number of whom were geologists or had degrees in geology—liked Marina, disliked Lee and feared that Lee was abusing his wife. When Marina sported a black eye, most likely because Lee had hit her, some of her friends tried to convince her that it would be in her best interests to get away from Lee for a while. This was a very difficult decision for Marina to make. Lee was all she had. Without him she was halfway around the world from home without much hope of ever getting back.

One of the Texas Russians who did take a liking to Lee was George S. DeMohrenschildt, a White Russian count with a background in intelligence. The Oswalds were still living in Fort Worth when they were first visited by DeMohrenschildt on October 7, 1962. He convinced them that, because most of their Russian-speaking friends lived in Dallas, they should move there—and the Oswalds did. While in Dallas, DeMohrenschildt urged Lee to mingle with the Soviet émigré community, many of whom were right-wing "Solidarists" who had sided with the Nazis against the Communists during World War II. (There is evidence that DeMohrenschildt worked for the Nazis during World War II, as well.)

After Oswald's arrest, DeMohrenschildt spoke out in Lee's defense.

According to DeMohrenschildt, Oswald spoke nearly flawless Russian and owned a Beretta handgun unlike the one reportedly found on him at the time of his arrest. DeMohrenschildt's background makes one wonder about his real relationship to Oswald.

On August 16, 1962, the FBI interviewed Oswald again, this time in the backseat of a car parked in front of his home on Mercedes Street. The questions covered the same ground as the first interview. No, Oswald had not tried to become a Russian citizen; no, he had never talked to anyone from the KGB. Oswald acted livid toward the interviewers, seemingly unable to understand why they couldn't leave him alone.

In October, Marina agreed to move with the baby into the Fort Worth home of Mrs. Elena Hall, a woman of Russian heritage who was born in Iran. It was agreed that Marina and the baby would be more comfortable there until Lee could get another job.

Officially, Lee was then recommended through an employment agency for a job at Jaggars-Chiles-Stovall, which the WR refers to as "a graphic arts company." The company also did photographic work, much of it highly secret, for the United States government. This would seem like the last place Oswald would be hired, considering his background, Marxist leanings and questionable allegiance. Nonetheless, Lee got a job there as a photoprint trainee on October 11.

No one knows for certain where Lee lived during October 1962. He lived in a YMCA from October 15 to 19 and rented an apartment at 605 Elsbeth Street in Dallas on November 3. For two weeks, it is not known where Oswald spent his nights. After securing a job and renting an apartment, Lee and Marina were reunited, but the couple got along no better than before. Marina and the baby stayed on Elsbeth Street for only a few days when they again moved out and went to live with various Russian-speaking friends. Within a few weeks—after Oswald, according to Marina, cried and begged—Marina and the baby moved back in with him.

On Thanksgiving, 1962, Robert Oswald invited his half-brother, John Pic, and Lee, along with their families, to his house for dinner. This would be the last Lee would see of his brothers until after the assassination almost a year later.

Oswald continued to lay out paperwork that would indicate him to be a Communist activist. He subscribed to Communist literature and wrote to the American Communist Party, asking if, considering his background, it was a good idea for him to "continue the fight" for the cause of

Communism.

According to the WC, Oswald mail-ordered a Wesson .38 revolver from Los Angeles on January 27, 1963, using the name A. J. Hidell. On March 12, 1963, again according to the WC, Oswald ordered a Mannlicher-Carcano bolt-action rifle from Klein's Sporting Goods in Chicago, this time using the name A. Hidell. (A Texan who mail-orders weapons from out of state is akin to an Alaskan sending to California for ice cubes.) Despite the difference in the ordering dates for the revolver and the rifle, mail records show that both weapons arrived in Dallas at Oswald's post-office box on the same day, March 20.

In interrogation after his arrest, Oswald is reported to have admitted owning the handgun (which was reportedly taken away from him in the Texas Theatre), while steadfastly denying that he had ever owned a rifle.

Oswald lost his job at Jaggars-Chiles-Stovall on April 6, 1963. His employer said that "he could not do the work." Later, Stovall refused to give Oswald a recommendation for employment, making note of Lee's "communistic tendencies."

On March 3, 1963, the Oswalds moved from their Elsbeth Street apartment to an upstairs apartment only a few blocks away at 214 West Neely Street. (It was in the backyard of this apartment that Marina claims to have taken the incriminating photos of Lee holding his weapons and Communist literature. The photos, however, appear to be phonies.) Around this time, Lee and Marina learned that they were expecting their second child.

On April 10, 1963, at about 9:00 P.M., someone took a shot at the celebrated right-wing Texan, Major General Edwin A. Walker, a man who had been forced to retire from the U.S. Army in 1961 because of the ultra-right-wing films he had been showing to the troops under his command. The assailant had apparently leaned a rifle against the top of a fence behind the Walker home and fired through a window, "barely missing" Walker.

At the time of the attack, police believed that the shooting was the work of several men. Eyewitnesses reported a small group of men behaving suspiciously around the Walker home before the shot was fired. But, until after Lee's death, when Marina said her husband had been the gunman, there were no suspects. Marina further incriminated her husband after his death by stating that he had also contemplated shooting Richard M. Nixon. There, in a nutshell, is all of the existing evidence showing that Oswald had a capacity for violence.

According to the WC, there is other evidence that Oswald was involved in the attempt on Walker's life (if indeed that was what the shooting was). The WC says that there was a "firearm identification" of the bullet found in the Walker home with the Mannlicher-Carcano rifle that Oswald theoretically owned.

Among Oswald's belongings, after his arrest, was "found" a photo of the Walker home taken from the alley behind the house, showing a car parked in the driveway. By the time the photo was made public by the FBI, however, someone had cut a hole in it so that one couldn't read the license plate number on the car. Also found was a note to Marina telling her what to do in case he was caught. The note does not specify what he might be caught doing. Experts have testified that the note was written in Lee's handwriting. By the time the WR was published, the suspicious activities of groups of men around the Walker home before and during the evening of the shooting had been forgotten, and the shooting, like the assassination, was said to have been the effort of a "lone nut."

Since Marina was in a precarious position after Lee's arrest in Dallas, assassination researchers suspect that she was used. Theoretically, she could have been threatened with deportation if she didn't tell law-enforcement officials precisely what they wanted to hear. None of the testimony of Marina Oswald before the WC would have been allowed before a court of law, and without that testimony the case against Oswald for the assassination is vitiated considerably.

On April 24, 1963, Oswald reportedly decided that there was no chance of getting any work in Dallas. Marina suggested that he look for work in New Orleans, where he had relatives. Marina later told interrogators that she actually wanted him to get out of Dallas because of the Walker incident. Oswald took a bus to New Orleans, and Marina moved in with Ruth Paine, her dear friend and member of the Dallas Russian-speaking community in Irving for the first time.

When Oswald arrived at the New Orleans bus station he called his aunt, Lillian Murret, and asked if he could stay with her and Uncle Dutz for a while. Lillian had been unaware that he was back from Russia—and had no idea that he was married and had a baby. But, since he was alone and had not shown up with his entire family, she agreed.

On May 9, 1963, according to the WR, Oswald, in response to a newspaper ad, was hired by the William B. Reily Coffee Company. (On his job application, he listed as one of his references Sgt. Robert Hidell.) The firm was located at 640 Magazine Street in New Orleans.

There is evidence that this was not a real job, but rather a cover for other activities. One eyewitness has said that Oswald never seemed to do any work for the coffee company. Also there is the unsettling fact that four of his coworkers at Reily (Emmet Barbee, John Branyon, Alfred Claude, and Dante Marachini) quit within weeks of his leaving, and all four went to work for NASA.

On the same day that he started at Reily, Oswald rented an apartment at 4905 Magazine Street with the help of Myrtle Evans, a woman who had known him as a child. He called Marina and asked her to rejoin him, and she agreed quickly. "Daddy loves us," Ruth Paine says Marina sang to the baby after getting off the phone.

Oswald moved into the Magazine Street apartment on May 10, and Marina and June, driven by Mrs. Paine, arrived the following day. Ruth toured the city for a few days and returned to Irving on May 14. Lee was once again employed and had his family with him. That lasted until July 19, when Lee was fired from his job at the coffee company for laziness. Around this time, according to Marina, Lee began to talk about going to Cuba.

In May and June 1963, Oswald became involved in a New York pro-Castro organization known as the Fair Play for Cuba Committee (FPCC). Oswald opened up his own chapter in New Orleans; he was the only member. The only other name associated with the New Orleans chapter of the FPCC was A. J. Hidell, who was listed as another officer of the organization separate from Oswald. He ordered a batch of printed circulars using the alias Lee Osborne.

Oswald listed the address for his "Committee" as 544 Camp Street, which also happened to be the address of intelligence agent Guy Banister, who in turn was working with David Ferrie, the strange, hairless man who had been Oswald's supervisor in the Civil Air Patrol. Ferrie is suspected of recruiting Oswald into the world of espionage in the first place. At that time he was a CIA pilot and private investigator for New Orleans's crime boss Carlos Marcello.

Oswald was seen meeting with Banister and Ferrie during the summer of 1963. He used the Camp Street address only on his first batch of FPCC pamphlets. After that he listed the address of the organization only by a post office box number 30016, an unfortunate error on his part since the post office box he had actually rented (under his name, his wife's name, and the Hidell alias) was 30061. He inverted the last two numbers on the pamphlets, as well as when he wrote down the number in his notebook. It is doubtful whether he ever received any recruits because of this error.

Oswald had actually known a man called "Hidell" in the USMC. Rene Heindel, whose nickname was Hidell, was reportedly living in New Orleans during the summer of 1963. If one believes that Oswald was framed, then the post-office box and the Hidell alias were used to connect Oswald with the murder weapons of JFK and Officer J. D. Tippit.

On August 5, 1963, Oswald went to a New Orleans store managed by the fiercely anti-Castro Cuban exile Carlos Bringuier. According to the WR, Oswald and Bringuier chatted about the struggle against Castro. The WC would have us believe that this was an act on Oswald's part, but it may be a brief glimpse of the real Lee. Certainly there is evidence that Oswald and Bringuier were in collusion about something. On August 9, Oswald stood on a street corner in New Orleans and handed out his FPCC leaflets. Carlos Bringuier happened by. The two got into an argument (which some spectators later said appeared to be staged) and Bringuier finally struck Oswald. According to one eyewitness, Oswald said, "Go ahead and hit me" just before Bringuier struck him. The police came and Oswald was arrested.

He spent only one night in jail before getting bailed out by a representative of Carlos Marcello, but while he was there he did something very strange. He asked to be visited by an FBI agent and his request was granted. What was this about? If we are to believe the official scenario, the FBI would be the last people Oswald would want to see. On August 16, Oswald was back out on the New Orleans streets handing out his FPCC leaflets, which were headlined "HANDS OFF CUBA!" This time he worked in front of the International Trade Mart in New Orleans (whose director was Clay Shaw, the man who four years later would be indicted, tried, and acquitted of conspiracy to assassinate the president by New Orleans District Attorney Jim Garrison). Someone notified the media this time as well, and that night on the television news everyone in town got to see the ex-Soviet defector handing out his Commie literature. The publicity did nothing for Oswald's ability to find a job. For the second session of leaflet distribution, Oswald even went so far as to get help from a casual labor pool—a peculiar move for a man who theoretically was broke.

Near the end of September, with Lee again out of work and Marina very pregnant, it was decided that Marina and June would again move in with Ruth Paine, at least until the baby was born. According to Marina's later testimony, Lee had been talking about going to Cuba via Mexico for much of the summer and, according to the WC, Marina and Ruth left New Orleans for Irving on September 23. The next day, according to the WC, Oswald was on his way to Mexico. Again, as is the case with the Walker shooting, we have little evidence that Oswald planned to go to Mexico beyond his wife's testimony. The truth is that we don't know where Oswald went, but there is strong evidence that an impostor (or several)—and not Oswald himself—went to Mexico.

The question of whether the real Oswald went to Mexico from September 26 to October 3, 1963, is one of ultimate importance. While in Mexico City, "Oswald" is reported to have visited both the Cuban and Soviet embassies, where his brash manner and outrageous requests made him memorable to all he encountered. He showed acceptable I.D. and announced that he was seeking a visa to Cuba in transit to the USSR— behavior that leaves the impression that Oswald was a bitter, desperate man, always living in a place where he felt he didn't belong, a man who felt that his greatness and divine mission in life were going universally and frustratingly unrecognized. His requests were denied, and he returned to the U.S. as he had departed, by bus.

The problem with this scenario is that there is much evidence that it is fake. Photographs, claimed by the CIA to be taken of Oswald in Mexico City, show an entirely different man (see McDonald, Hugh). Sound recordings, now reportedly destroyed, of "Oswald" speaking with a Soviet official are of a man with a rudimentary knowledge of Russian; the real Oswald was fluent. Witnesses in Mexico City who saw Oswald have described a different man from the one who was arrested in Dallas less than two months later (see Azcue, Eusebio; Duran, Silvia). At the same time, we find persistently positive identifications of Oswald in the U.S., when officially he is said to have been in Mexico (see Odio, Sylvia). If Oswald did not go to Mexico—and he denied doing so after his arrest— someone or some group tried to make it appear as if he did. If the story is fake, it adds immeasurable credence to Oswald's claim that he was a patsy and casts considerable doubt on the remainder of the official story. For those who believe that members of organized crime were solely responsible for JFK's death, this possibility presents a problem. Impersonators who work scams on foreign officials for the purpose of creating a false background for an individual don't work exclusively for mobsters. This behavior has all of the earmarks of a covert intelligence operation.

According to the WR, Oswald returned to Dallas on the afternoon of October 3 and spent the night at the YMCA. The next day he applied for a job at Padgett Printing Company but was rejected when his job superintendent at Jaggars-Chiles-Stovall refused to recommend him, saying that he had "communistic tendencies." He visited Marina at the Paine home on October 4 and returned to Dallas on October 7. He rented a room at 621 Marsalis Street from Mrs. Mary Bledsoe, who later would become an eyewitness to Oswald's alleged "getaway" from the TSBD. Oswald lived at that address for only one week. Bledsoe refused to rent the room to him for another week because she did not like him. After spending a weekend at the Paines's, Oswald took a room on October 14 at 1026 North Beckley, where he registered under the name O. H. Lee. This was to be his last address. That same day, Ruth mentioned to her neighbor, Linnie Mae Randle, that Lee was looking for work. Randle said that her younger brother, Buell Wesley Frazier, with whom she lived, had recently gotten a job at the TSBD. Maybe Lee should try there. Ruth called TSBD Superintendant Roy S. Truly, told him of Lee and Truly said Lee should come by in person for an interview. Oswald made a favorable impression and began work as an order filler on Wednesday, October 16.

Lee continued to spend weekends at the Paines', now getting rides to and from Irving with his coworker Frazier. On October 20, Marina gave birth to her second daughter, named Rachel. On November 1, Oswald rented Dallas P.O. Box #6225 at the Terminal Annex, across Dealey Plaza from the TSBD. He noted on his application that the box would be used to receive mail for the FPCC and the ACLU. On Thursday, November 21, Oswald asked Frazier to take him to Irving, the first time he had made such a request on any day other than a Friday—and the first time without calling Marina first. Frazier asked about this. Oswald reportedly told him that he had to go out to the Paines to pick up some curtain rods he needed for his room. That night, Lee and Marina fought—she had learned that he was living in Dallas under an assumed name—and he retired early. In the morning, he left Marina some money (which was normal) and put his wedding ring in a cup in her room (which wasn't normal) and went to Randle's house to meet Frazier.

Both Randle and Frazier saw Oswald carrying a "long and bulky package" which they said he slipped onto the backseat of Frazier's car.

Oswald denied carrying such a package after his arrest, saying he had brought only his lunch to work with him that morning. Frazier says that Oswald told him the package contained the curtain rods he had told him about the previous day. Both Frazier and Randle made it clear in their statements that they thought the package was too short to have contained a rifle—even one that was broken down. No one else saw Oswald carrying a package of any kind.

By most accounts, Oswald left the TSBD approximately three minutes after the assassination through the front entrance and walked seven blocks east. (The most notable dissenting eyewitness is Deputy Sheriff Roger Craig, who says that Oswald left the building a full 15 minutes after the assassination and entered a Nash station wagon on Elm Street.)

Oswald boarded a southbound Marsalis bus at the corner of Elm and Murphy which was headed west, back in the direction of the TSBD. Author Michael H. B. Eddowes theorizes that, since Oswald took the Marsalis Street bus, which came within only seven blocks of his rooming house at 1026 North Beckley, instead of the Beckley bus, which would have dropped him off right outside his home, he must have been heading somewhere other than his home, perhaps to Ruby's apartment. This theory is bolstered by the fact that Oswald reportedly purchased a 23-cent ticket when boarding the bus, a ticket that, according to Eddowes, "would have deposited him two short blocks west of [Ruby's] apartment." However, it is reasonable to assume that Oswald was in a hurry—if not yet panicky—and may have gotten on the first bus to come along that headed toward the Oak Cliff section of Dallas.

On the bus was Mary Bledsoe, his former landlady with whom he had not gotten along. The bus driver, Cecil McWatters, gave Oswald a Lakewood-Marsalis transfer dated November 22, 1963. This transfer was found in his shirt pocket well after his arrest.

The bus quickly became entangled in traffic around Dealey Plaza caused by the assassination. He stayed on the bus for only two blocks before getting off at the corner of Elm and Lamar—another indication that he was in a hurry. It might have been the traffic that caused him to get off, or it might have been the presence of Mrs. Bledsoe. (Both Bledsoe and McWatters positively identified Oswald at a police lineup later in the day, although McWatters admitted that, because Oswald had facial injuries and was the only one wearing just a T-shirt, the lineup was conducted in an unfair manner.) Oswald was on the bus for approximately four minutes.

From Elm and Lamar, Oswald theoretically walked two blocks south to the Greyhound bus station at Commerce and Lamar (still only two blocks from Dealey Plaza), where he got into the front passenger seat of a taxicab driven by William Whaley. According to all evidence, this is the only time in his life that he had ever ridden in an American taxicab.

Oswald did not appear nervous, nor particularly in a hurry. According to Whaley, he even offered to give up the cab to a woman, who declined his offer and asked Whaley to call the dispatcher for a cab for her.

Mark Lane points out that Whaley listed this cab ride as beginning at 12:30, which was the time of the assassination, but Whaley later said that he often rounded off the times in his log book to the nearest quarter-hour.

Whaley drove Oswald to the Oak Cliff section of Dallas. According to the WR, "He directed the driver of the car to a point 20 feet north of the northwest corner of the intersection of Beckley and Neely...on the 700 block of Beckley."

According to his housekeeper, Earlene Roberts, Oswald entered his rooming house at about 1:00 P.M. and seemed in an unusual hurry. He went directly to his room and emerged after three or four minutes zipping up a jacket. While Oswald was in his room, she said, a DPD car pulled up in front of the house containing two uniformed officers. It honked twice and then drove off. Her first statement was that this was car #207. She later expressed doubt as to the number. Oswald left the house at about 1:04 and was last seen by Roberts standing at a bus stop. About 11 minutes later, Officer J. D. Tippit was shot and killed near the corner of Tenth Street and Patton Avenue, only three tenths of a mile from Ruby's apartment. If Oswald had gotten on the bus that Roberts says she saw him waiting for, it would not have taken him in the direction of the Tippit murder. The only eyewitness who identified Oswald as the man who shot Tippit was Helen Markham, and her identification was extremely shaky. Other witnesses who identified Oswald identified him merely as a man they had seen fleeing the scene.

According to the WR, after shooting Tippit, Oswald reloaded his gun, throwing the empty shells into some bushes at the corner of Tenth and Patton. He then ran south on Patton one block to Jefferson Blvd. and turned right. Heading west, he stopped briefly in a parking lot behind a gas station where he allegedly threw away his jacket. He then continued west on Jefferson to the Texas Theatre, where he was arrested. Officially, Oswald entered the theater at 1:45. By 1:51 he was under arrest and on his way to the DPD station.

No explanation has been given for the time difficulties presented by this scenario. Oswald is said to have covered the 10 blocks between his rooming-house and the scene of the Tippit murder in 11 minutes, yet it supposedly took him (in a fast walk or trot) 30 minutes to get from the shooting site to the theater, a seven-block distance.

Between his arrest on November 22 and his death on November 24, Oswald was interrogated for approximately 12 hours. Captain Fritz of the DPD (Homicide & Robbery) did most of the questioning. According to the WR, Fritz "kept no notes" of the interrogation. There were no stenographic or tape recordings made. All reports on what Oswald said come from the memories of those law-enforcement officials who were present. A paraffin test was administered on the evening of November 22 to determine whether Oswald had fired a gun during the previous 24 hours. Officially, the results were positive for Oswald's hands, but negative for his right cheek. Therefore, Oswald had not fired a rifle. The WR said the test was "unreliable."

By all accounts, Oswald denied ever shooting anyone. He denied owning a rifle or keeping one in the Paines' garage. He said he had seen Roy Truly showing some TSBD coworkers a rifle a few days before. He admitted to owning a pistol, but said that he had bought it in Fort Worth. On November 23 (and again on November 24), Oswald was shown photographs of himself holding a rifle and wearing a handgun in a holster. The WR says, "Oswald sneered, saying that they were fake photographs, that he had been photographed a number of times the day before by the police" and that the photos were composites. He refused to comment in any way on the "Alek Hidell" identification found in his wallet. Referring to the I.D. card, Oswald reportedly told Fritz, "You know as much about it as I do." (Fritz disagrees with this quote, saying that Oswald told him he had picked up the Hidell name while working for the FPCC in New Orleans that summer.)

Oswald admitted renting P.O. Box 2915 in Dallas—where the weapons were allegedly sent—but denied that A. J. Hidell ever received a package through that box. When asked about P.O. Box 30061 in New Orleans, which he also reportedly rented under both names, Oswald said, "I don't know anything about that." He said that he never allowed anyone—except for perhaps his wife—to use his post-office boxes. He was asked why he had rented his room under the name O. H. Lee. He said that the landlady had simply made a mistake. He said he never told Frazier anything about curtain rods and that the only bag he took to work with him on Friday morning contained his lunch. He said that when JFK was shot, he was eating lunch in the TSBD's first-floor lunchroom. He admitted to the encounter with Roy Truly and Officer Marrion Baker about 90 seconds after the shooting on the second floor, saying he had gone there to get a Coke. He said that he then walked out the front door of the building and talked to coworker Bill Shelley for 5 to 10 minutes. Shelley told him that there probably wasn't going to be any more work that day, so he went home. (Shelley denied seeing Oswald at any time after noon, although he admitted to being out in front of the building at the appropriate time.) Oswald reportedly confirmed that he had taken a bus and a cab to his rooming house. He said he went directly from his home to the movies.

When asked about his views of JFK, Oswald said, "My wife and I like the president's family. They are interesting people. I have my own views on the president's national policy. I have a right to express my views but because of the charges I do not think I should comment further. I am not a malcontent; nothing irritated me about the president."

Reportedly, Oswald remained calm throughout the interrogation sessions, except when FBI agent James P. Hosty entered the room, at which point Oswald flared up and accused Hosty of accosting his wife.

Oswald said that he wanted attorney John J. Abt of New York City, a lawyer known for handling political conspiracy cases. He was allowed to call Abt, but Abt was away for the weekend. No attorney ever stepped forward to assist Oswald, and he died without legal representation.

Oswald was arraigned for the Tippit murder at 7:10 P.M., November 22, and for JFK's murder at 1:35 A.M., November 23—both before Judge David Johnston.

While Oswald was being held prisoner there, the DPD station was a madhouse, jam-packed with reporters who shouted questions at Oswald each time the prisoner was moved from one place to another. Oswald told the press that he hadn't shot anybody, that he was a patsy—and he asked for someone to step forward and give him legal assistance. No one did. Lurking in that madhouse throughout the weekend was Ruby, with a gun in his pocket.

At 11:21 A.M. on November 24, 1963, Oswald was being transferred from the DPD station to the county jail, and was being led from the station through the basement parking lot when Ruby stepped out from behind a plainclothes police officer and fired a single bullet into Oswald's abdomen.

Oswald was rushed by ambulance to Parkland Hospital—the same hospital where JFK and Governor Connally had been taken—and there he died at 1:13 P.M. (See also all Oswald witnesses, all o.k.w.s, all t.k.w.s, and all Texas Theatre witnesses)

SOURCES: All texts

OSWALD, MARGUERITE CLAVERIE, Oswald witness; mother of the alleged assassin. Marguerite Oswald claimed from the start that her son was a patsy and had been working as an agent for the U.S. government. She died of cancer in January 1982. After the HSCA's 1979 conclusion that JFK was "probably assassinated as a result of a conspiracy," Oswald's mother commented to reporters, "The committee members have made a first step in the right direction... I hope and know the future will vindicate my son entirely. It took us 15 years to come this far. It may take another 15 years or longer... but the world will know that Lee Harvey Oswald was innocent of the charges against him."

Her opinion of the WC is clearly expressed in this letter she wrote to several congressmen in 1973: "Because I was critical of the commission, I was asked, 'Mrs. Oswald, are you implying that the Chief Justice would whitewash evidence or hide information so that the American people, as well as the whole world, would never learn the truth?' I answered yes, in the name of security, men of integrity... who have the welfare of the country at heart, would be most likely to do what the White House wanted and thought necessary."

Grinning, as if pleased by all of the attention she was getting, she said during a filmed interview in the 1960s, "The only thing I know for sure is that I did not kill the president—and there's another thing I am sure of, I did not raise my sons to kill."

The HSCA reported that Marguerite "was acquainted with several men associated with lieutenants in the [assassination suspect Carlos] Marcello organization. One such acquaintance, who was an associate of [Marguerite's brother-in-law] Dutz Murret, reportedly served as a personal aide or driver to Marcello at one time."

According to the WC testimony of Oswald witness Peter Paul Gregory, a member of Dallas's Russian-speaking community, Marguerite signed up for and attended his Russian-language classes before the assassination, presumably so that she would better be able to communicate with her daughter-in-law Marina.

Following the assassination, Marguerite retained attorney Mark Lane to defend the memory of her son. Lane has never given up. (See also Carro, John, Gregory, Peter; Lane, Mark; Odum, Bardwell; Pic, Edward; Pic, John; Siegel, Evelyn)

SOURCES: WR, many • HSCA Report 100, 140, 170, 221, 249, 255 • MOORE 80, 202 • FMG I, many; III, 77 • OTT 304 • BLAKEY 36, 38, 161, 340–6, 349–50 • CF 91–9 • WCH I, 126 • BELIN 206–7 • RTJ 9, 255, 317–22, 351–2, 367, 375 • COA 43–4, 442 • GERTZ 340, 369, 444, 508 • BISHOP, many • DOP, many • CF 91–9 • HT 164 • FLAMMONDE 20, 53, 135–6, 152, 156–7 • EVICA 299 • PD 21–2, 62–3, 73, 344, 351 • NORTH 151, 153, 418, 454–5, 468–9, 498, 502 • KANTOR 19–20, 80, 87, 177

OSWALD, MARINA (née Marina Nikolayevna Prusakova, later Marina Porter), Oswald witness; wife of the alleged assassin; Russian woman whom Oswald met while living in the Soviet Union. The pair returned together, but were estranged at the time of the assassination. Marina's testimony to the WC damned Lee, but was shaky and full of contradictions. It would not have been allowed in a court of law.

Among her uncorroborated claims used against her husband were that she took the photos of Oswald holding the alleged murder weapons, that Oswald had confessed to her that he had taken a shot at right-winger Major General Edwin A. Walker, that Oswald had planned to shoot Richard M. Nixon, and that Oswald owned a rifle, which he kept wrapped in a blanket in Ruth Paine's garage.

WC critics claim that Marina was threatened with deportation by U.S. government officials and, out of fear, told them what they wanted to hear. Without Marina's testimony, the WC had no evidence demonstrating Oswald's capacity for violence.

Although it has been widely rumored that Marina's uncle in the Soviet Union was a KGB agent, Marina denies this. She told journalist Jack Anderson that her uncle was a Minister of Internal Affairs, the Russian equivalent of an FBI agent.

Although Marina still insists that she took the photographs of Lee holding weapons, she now believes that there *were* people impersonating her and her husband in the weeks and months leading up to the assassination. Marina told Jack Anderson in 1988, regarding eyewitness reports that she and her husband had been seen in a rifle-repair shop/furniture store seeking to have a scope for a gun repaired, "I thought at first that maybe I just didn't recall being there, that maybe I was losing my mind. The FBI took me there and I knew I had never been there before in my life."

On February 22, 1963, George and Jeanne DeMohrenschildt invited Marina to a dinner party and it was there that she met Mrs. Ruth Paine, with whom she was living at the time of the assassination. Mrs. Paine, who had a "difficult to define" separation from her husband Michael, found everything about the Soviet Union fascinating, and was a housewife with children who were trying to learn Russian. (See also Adamcik, John P.; Andrews, Dean; Aronson, Lev; Bouhe, George A.; Clark, Max E.; Coulter, Harris; Davison, Alex; Dymitruk, Lydia; Ford, Declan P. and Katherine N.; Frazier, Buell Wesley; George, M. Waldo; Gerasimov, Vitaliy; Gopadze, Leon I.; Gravitis, Dorothy; Greener, Charles W.; Gregory, Peter Paul; Hall, John Raymond and Elena A.; Holmes, Harry D.; James, Virginia H.; Joesten, Joachim; Johnson, Priscilla; Levine, Isaac Don; McKenzie, William; Mamantor, Ilya A.; Martello, Francis L.; Martin, James Herbert; Meller, Teofil and Anna N.; Midgett, Bill; Okui, Yaeko; Paine, Ruth; Prusakova, Ilya; Raigorodsky, Paul M.; Ray, Valentina A.; Redlich, Norman; Sawyer, Forrest; Taylor, Gary E.; Walker, Edwin A.; Webster, Robert; Whitworth, Edith)

SOURCES: WR, many • WCH I, 1; V, 387, 410, 588; XI, 275 • HSCA Report, many • FLAMMONDE, many • EVICA, many • ME 14, 16, 18, 115, 130 • OGLESBY 54, 58, 63, 78 • NORTH, many • PD 21, 48, 62, 65–71, 343–4, 350, 353–4 • BELIN 2, 10, 37, 58, 60, 210–1 • RTJ, many • COA 41, 43, 213 • GERTZ 145, 444–5 • BISHOP, many • DOP, many • DUFFY, many • CF 40–1, 124–34 • HT, many • PWW 30, 84, 146, 234 • MOORE 20, 59, 69, 87, 127, 201–2, 210 • FMG I, 157; III, 106 • OTT 54, 62 • BE 99 • BLAKEY 30, 32–3, 75, 124, 147, 161, 341–2, 345, 348–65 • HOS 41, 93, 133–4

OSWALD, RACHEL, daughter of alleged assassin; born October 20, 1963.

OSWALD, ROBERT EDWARD LEE, SR., Marguerite Oswald's second husband and father of the accused assassin.

OSWALD, ROBERT EDWARD LEE, JR., Oswald witness; brother of the accused assassin. Robert visited his brother in the Dallas jail, and Lee told him not to pay any attention to the "so-called evidence."

Robert told the WC, "I still do not know why or how, but Mr. and Mrs. [Michael and Ruth] Paine are somehow involved in this affair."

Regarding Lee's early relationship with assassination suspect David Ferrie, Robert recalled in the October 17, 1967, issue of *Look*:

Mother and Lee returned to New Orleans in January 1954. A few months later, a schoolmate, Frederick O'Sullivan, spoke to Lee and another student named Edward Voebel about joining the Civil Air Patrol [CAP]...The boys went out to the airport in New Orleans together to see what the CAP unit was doing. At the time, the leader of the unit may have been an Eastern Airlines pilot named David Ferrie.

O'Sullivan remembered the leader as "Captain Ferrie." Voebel said he *thought* Captain Ferrie was in charge. Lee bought a CAP uniform and attended several meetings, then lost interest... According to Lee's own later statements, 1954 was the year when he first became interested in communism. It is only a guess, but in view of the later developments involving David Ferrie in 1967, and his dramatic death, I can't help wondering whether it might have been Ferrie who introduced Lee to Communist ideas.

Robert is the author of *Lee: A Portrait of Lee Harvey Oswald* (Coward-McCann, 1967). (See also Martin, James; Paine, Michael)
SOURCES: WR, many • WCH I, 264 • BELIN 206 • RTJ 320 • GERTZ 462, 468 • BISHOP 12, 286–8, 382–3, 390–2, 406, 437, 448–9 • DOP 49, 92, 447, 457, 528–9, 555, 568 • CF 96–9 • HT 292 • FMG III, 77–8 • MOORE 20, 216 • BE 352 • BLAKEY 341, 349–50, 363 • FLAMMONDE 20–1, 135, 152, 156 • EVICA 166, 299 • NORTH 154

O'TOOLE, GEORGE, former CIA agent; author of *The Assassination Tapes* (Penthouse Press, 1975). In his book, O'Toole uses an instrument called a Psychological Stress Evaluator (PSE) to determine, from the sound of their voice on tape recordings, whether people are telling the truth. Generally, O'Toole concludes that everybody except Oswald was lying.
SOURCES: BELIN 25, 29–30, 223, 226 • HT 177, 184, 235, 290, 349 • MOORE 216 • EVICA 21, 133, 135, 140, 142, 299 • PD 25

OWENS, CALVIN BUD, Texas Theatre witness; DPD sergeant; helped remove Oswald from the theater. Owens was Officer J. D. Tippit's immediate boss. He described Tippit as a reliable cop, but one who would never advance in rank because he lacked formal education and did not do well on written examinations.
SOURCES: WCH VII, 78 • BISHOP 117, 215

OXFORD, J. L., a.w.; Dallas deputy sheriff. Oxford heard the shots and ran across Dealey Plaza toward the grassy knoll. He said, "When we got there, everyone was looking over into the railroad yards." Later in the day, Oxford was among those who searched the home of Ruth Paine in Irving, Texas, where Marina Oswald had been living. It was during this search that the blanket that Marina said held Lee's rifle was found empty in the garage. Found the next day, in the same garage, were the damaging (and reportedly phony) photographs of Lee holding weapons and Communist literature, which Marina later said she took.
SOURCES: RTJ 42 • COA 23 • BISHOP 277 • BE 19

P

PAINE, MICHAEL R., Oswald witness; husband of Ruth Paine (see below). Paine had worked for defense contractor Bell Helicopter in Fort Worth since 1958, under the supervision of former Nazi general Walter Dornberger. Paine was a member of the ACLU. Paine moved out of his home in Irving just in time for his wife to take in Marina Oswald and her two children. According to Jim Bishop, the separation of the Paines was a "friendly estrangement, difficult to define." Paine says that, at the time of the assassination, he was having lunch with a coworker, Dave Noel, and that they were discussing "the character of assassins" *before* they heard the news. Michael arrived at the Paine home in Irving around 3:00 P.M. on the day of the assassination while it was being searched by police. He said, "As soon as I found out about it, I hurried over to see if I could help." The Paines then watched in dismay as the Dallas police tore up their house in search of evidence. According to author Charles Crenshaw, Paine was overheard on November 23, 1963, talking to his wife on the phone. He said that he was sure Oswald had killed JFK but didn't think he was responsible. "We both know who is responsible," he reportedly added. Robert Oswald, Lee's brother, told the WC, "I still do not know how or why, but Mr. and Mrs. Paine are somehow involved in this affair." (See also Dornberger, Walter; Gregory, Peter; Krystinik, Raymond; Oswald, Marina; Oswald, Robert; Torbitt, William)

SOURCES: WR 122, 263, 265–6, 272 • WCH II, 384; IX, 434; XI, 398 • BISHOP 279, 299–301, 335, 378–9, 381–2, 412–3 • DOP 95–6, 98–100, 148–9, 207 • HT 169 • FMG III, 78 • MOORE 10–1, 45, 59, 102, 210 • OTT 62–3, 315 • BLAKEY 33, 349, 353–4, 360–1 • HOS 93, 133 • NORTH 329, 479 • EVICA 11–2, 299 • CRENSHAW 125

PAINE, RUTH HYDE, Oswald witness; wife of Michael (above); housemate of Marina Oswald. Paine, a member of Dallas's Russian-speaking community, was responsible for getting Oswald his job at the TSBD. She owned a station wagon, much like the one repeatedly spotted in Dealey Plaza following the assassination, once picking up a passenger who looked like Oswald. When asked about the car, Oswald reportedly said that it belonged to Mrs. Paine and to "leave her out of this. She didn't have anything to do with it."

Ruth was fascinated with all things Russian and learned Russian at the Berlitz School. Before meeting Marina, she had had a Russian pen pal named Ella in the USSR. (Coincidentally, Lee had been in love with a woman named Ella in the USSR before meeting Marina.)

Ruth was enamored with Marina. They both had young children—and husbands who were not around—and each could help the other with her second language. They comforted one another.

Both Ruth and Michael Paine have been suspected of complicity in the assassination by many researchers. The reasons for the suspicion stem from (1) Michael's connection with the military-industrial complex, a suspected sponsor of the coup—he worked for Bell Helicopter under the supervision of Walter Dornberger; (2) Ruth's convenient situation with her husband that allowed Marina to live indefinitely in their home in Irving, Texas; (3) the fact that Ruth was responsible for Oswald's employment at the TSBD, which overlooked the presidential motorcade route; (4) the fact that much of the damaging evidence against Oswald was found in the Paine home (including the reportedly phony backyard photos of Oswald holding his weapons and the blanket that supposedly held Oswald's rifle), and (5) reports that Ruth owned a station wagon (although DOP says it was a Chevy) with a luggage rack on top.

Michael told the WC that it was decided in New Orleans around September 20, 1963, that Marina, pregnant with the Oswalds' second child, would stay at Ruth's house so that there would be better care for her and the expected baby. Ruth spent the weekend with the Oswalds in New Orleans and, on September 23, Marina, Ruth, and their children left for Irving, leaving Lee alone. Before they left, Lee told them that he was going to go to Houston, or possibly Philadelphia, to look for work. He mentioned that he had a friend in Houston. Ruth and Marina had no contact with Lee between September 23 and October 4. (Officially, during this time, Oswald is said to have traveled to Mexico City, but was spotted elsewhere, including in the home of Sylvia Odio.) On October 4, Lee hitchhiked from Dallas to Irving to visit, and from then until the assassination, visited regularly on weekends.

Ruth told the WC that one weekend in October, Lee asked to use her husband's drill press to drill a hole in a coin. Later, a peso turned into a necklace was found, and this, along with other souvenirs, was used as evidence that Lee had actually been in Mexico. Lee never mentioned his trip to Mexico to Ruth.

Ruth claims that Lee left a typed letter on her desk, which she read two weeks before the assassination. It mentioned his trip to Mexico, that while there he had had an interview with a "Comrade Kostine," and that "the FBI is not now interested in my activities." She said that she wanted to show the letter to the FBI immediately, but never got around to it—so nobody else saw it until after JFK's death.

Ruth told the WC that she recalled seeing the blanket that allegedly held the Mannlicher-Carcano rifle on the floor of her garage, but remembered it appearing flatter than it would have been if a rifle were inside it.

When asked about arranging the job at the TSBD for Oswald, Ruth said that she had called Roy Truly on October 14 or 15, since her neighbor Buell Wesley Frazier worked there. Lee applied for the job on October 15 and started work the next day.

On the evening of November 21, 1963, the only weekday night that Lee ever spent at the Paines, Ruth says she did not see Lee in the garage, where the rifle was allegedly kept—although she says she did notice that the garage light had been left on and had assumed that it was Lee who had forgotten to turn it off. (See also Adamcik, John P.; Craig, Roger; DeMohrenschildt, George; Dornberger, Walter; Frazier, Buell Wesley; Gregory, Peter; Hyde, William; Oswald, Marina; Oswald, Robert; Oxford, J.L.; Paine, Michael; Randle, Linnie Mae; Weatherford, Harry)

SOURCES: WR, many • WCH II, 384; III, 1; IX, 331; XI, 153, 389 • HSCA Report 52–3, 187, 189, 194 • DAVIS 161, 168, 190 • NORTH, many • FLAMMONDE 27, 146, 151, 205, 230 • EVICA 8, 11, 98, 299, 326–7 • PD 244–55, 257 • BELIN 58, 64, 66–7, 206, 209–10 • RTJ 174, 308–9, 333, 335 • BISHOP, many • DOP 95–105, 148, 205, 248, 283, 285, 526, 555, 636 • CF 40–1 • HT 125, 169, 187, 291, 300 • FMG III, 29, 31, 78, 106 • PWW 57, 146 • MOORE 10–1, 45, 59, 102, 210 • FMG I, 30, 157, 186 • OTT 62–3, 70, 74, 95, 275, 315 • BLAKEY 31, 33, 35–6, 349, 353–4, 357–62, 364 • HOS 41, 93, 133–4 • KANTOR 19

PAISLEY, JOHN ARTHUR, suspicious death (murder); CIA agent; friend of KGB "defector" Yuri Nosenko (and therefore suspected by some of being a Soviet agent); next-door neighbor of attorney/assassination researcher Bernard Fensterwald (who once represented convicted Martin Luther King assassin James Earl Ray). According to former CIA agent and

author Victor Marchetti, Paisley knew a great deal about the assassination and was murdered during the HSCA investigation because he was "about to blow the whistle." Paisley's body was found floating in Chesapeake Bay in September of 1978. The cause of death was officially a suicide. Because of circumstantial evidence, author Dick Russell theorizes that Paisley may have been closely monitoring the CIA defection program that sent Oswald to the USSR. (See also Marchetti, Victor; Nosenko, Yuri)
    SOURCES: HT 189, 329–30 • RUSSELL, many

PALMER, THOMAS STEWART, Ruby witness; occasional fill-in comedian and magician at the Carousel Club; Dallas branch manager of AGVA. Palmer told the WC that Ruby violated several AGVA rules, including the use of strippers as B-girls (both Janet "Jada" Conforto and Karen "Little Lynn" Carlin submitted affidavits to AGVA on this point), and the physical abuse of employees. He told the WC that Ruby had a high employee turnover and that he wouldn't permit racial or religious jokes "of an obviously dirty nature." (However, Ruby did allow entertainers to work in blackface). Palmer said that Carlin was living with a DPD officer at least six months before the assassination. (See also Carlin, Karen; Conforto, Janet)
    SOURCE: WCH XV, 206

PANZECA, SALVADORE. Panzeca was Clay Shaw's attorney at the time of Shaw's arrest on March 1, 1967.
    SOURCES: OTT 145, 148 • FLAMMONDE 79, 240–1

PAPPAS, ICARUS M. "IKE," o.k.w.; Ruby witness; New York City radio reporter (WNEW-AM). Pappas was the reporter closest to Oswald when Ruby shot him. He had just asked Oswald, "Do you have anything to say in your defense?" when Ruby pulled the trigger. Pappas had seen Ruby previously that weekend in the DPD station.
    SOURCES: WR 318 • WCH XV, 360 • COA 129–30, 424 • GERTZ 53 • BISHOP 488–9 • BLAKEY 331 • KANTOR 48, 65–6, 68

PARKER, MRS. JESSE, prosecution witness at the Clay Shaw trial. Parker testified that, while working as a hostess at the New Orleans International Airport's VIP room, she had seen Clay Shaw in December of 1966 sign the guest register "Clay Bertrand." Establishing that "Bertrand" was an alias used by Shaw was a key to the prosecution's case, since this was the name he went by when seen in the company of David Ferrie and Oswald.
    SOURCE: OTT 241

PARKER, JOHN, Parkland witness; surgeon. Parker assisted in the

operation on Governor Connally's wrist. (See also Osborne, William)
SOURCE: WR 69

PARTIN, EDWARD GRADY, Teamster lieutenant under Jimmy Hoffa. According to the HSCA:

> Hoffa and...Partin...did, in fact, discuss the planning of an assassination conspiracy against President Kennedy's brother, Attorney General Robert F. Kennedy, in July or August 1962...In an interview with the Committee, Partin...stated that Hoffa had believed that having the Attorney General murdered would be the most effective way of ending the Federal Government's intense [sic] investigation of the Teamsters and organized crime...Hoffa... approached him about the assassination proposal because Hoffa believed him to be close to various figures in Carlos Marcello's syndicate organization.

Partin passed a polygraph examination authorized by FBI Director J. Edgar Hoover in 1962, soon after Partin first told the FBI about his discussion with Hoffa.

According to the HSCA, Partin was a "Baton Rouge Teamsters official with a criminal record, [who] was then a leading Teamsters Union official in Louisiana. Partin was also a key Federal witness against Hoffa in the 1964 trial that led to Hoffa's eventual imprisonment."

According to Partin's HSCA testimony, Hoffa discussed "the possible use of a lone gunman equipped with a rifle with a telescopic sight, the advisability of having the assassination committed somewhere in the South, as well as the potential desirability of having Robert Kennedy shot while riding in a convertible." Partin said that Hoffa believed "that by having Kennedy shot as he rode in a convertible, the origin of the fatal shot or shots would be obscured." Hoffa said this could be done only "upon the recruitment of an assassin without any identifiable connection to the Teamsters organization or Hoffa himself." (See also Hoffa, James Riddle)
SOURCES: HSCA Report 176–8 • DUFFY 160 • BLAKEY 202 • EVICA 236 • DAVIS, many • NORTH 56, 151, 191, 203

PASCILLIO, LORENZO (See HALL, LORAN)

PATERNOSTRO, SAM, a.w.; Dallas County assistant district attorney. Paternostro watched from the second floor of the Dallas County Criminal Courts Building on the east side of Houston Street. He was with court clerk Ruth Thornton and heard three shots, with a long pause between the first

two shots. He told the FBI that he heard "a shot [come] from the depository or the Criminal Courts Building or the triple overpass [sic]."
    SOURCE: WCE 1998, 2106–7

PATMAN, RALPH DON, Parkland witness. Patman, with Drs. Robert McClelland and Charles Baxter, assisted Dr. George T. Shires in operating on the bullet wound in Governor John Connally's thigh between 4:00 and 6:00 P.M. on November 22, 1963. According to the WR, "This puncture missile wound, about two-fifths of an inch in diameter (one centimeter) and located approximately 5 inches above the left knee, was cleansed and closed with sutures; but a small metallic fragment remained in the Governor's leg." This metallic fragment is significant because of the pristine nature of WCE 399, the bullet that—according to the WC—caused Connally's thigh wound, along with all other nonfatal wounds suffered in JFK's limo.
    SOURCE: WR 70

PATRICK, JERRY (See HEMMING, GERRY PATRICK)

PATTERSON, B. M. "PAT," t.k.w. Patterson was one of four men employed at the Reynolds Motor Company on East Jefferson Boulevard who saw a man running with a gun in his hand south on Patton Avenue toward Jefferson. The FBI claimed that Patterson identified Oswald from a photo shown to him, but he later claimed that he saw no such photo. (See also Reynolds, Warren)
    SOURCES: WR 159, 162 • WCH XV, 744 • RTJ 276–8 • GERTZ 528

PATTERSON, BOBBY G., o.k.w.; 33-year-old DPD patrolman. Patterson guarded the Commerce Street ramp to the DPD station basement on November 22 from 9:30 A.M. until the shooting. He says that he did not see Ruby enter.
    SOURCE: WCH XII, 334

PATTERSON, ROBERT CARL, Ruby witness; 20-year-old guitarist and singer. Patterson worked during the summer of 1963 at Ruby's Vegas Club. He told the WC that Ruby was going to get him a recording contract with Reprise Records and that Ruby bragged about having a connection there. He last talked with Ruby in Ruby's apartment two weeks before JFK's death and said that Ruby wanted him to work nightly at the Vegas Club, but that he declined.
    SOURCE: WCH XIV, 126

PATTERSON, ROBERT K., Ruby witness; Dallas electronics salesman. According to the WR, Patterson claimed that, on November 1, 1963 (a date he established using sales records), Ruby and a man who greatly

resembled Oswald came into his store. The WC points out that Patterson never positively identified the man he had seen as Oswald and that other employees who saw the interaction (Ruby purchased some "equipment") could not identify the man they had seen as Oswald. The WR suggests that Ruby's actual companion that day was Larry Crafard, his employee, who lived at the Carousel Club from mid-October 1963 until the day after the assassination (and the day before Ruby shot Oswald), at which time Crafard fled Dallas. Oswald's TSBD worksheet for November 1, 1963, shows that he put in a full day.
SOURCE: WR 335

PAUL, RALPH, Ruby witness and Dallas restaurant owner and business associate. Paul spoke with Ruby by phone the night before Ruby shot Oswald. He did not testify as to what was said, but was overheard by a waitress saying to Ruby, "Are you crazy? A gun?" Paul's girlfriend was Carousel stripper Nancy Powell (aka Tammy True).
SOURCES: WR 312–6, 327, 329, 333–4, 341, 349 • WCH XIV, 126; XV, 664 • RTJ 271 • COA 85, 134–5, 143, 263, 441 • GERTZ 2, 104, 112, 487, 493, 527 • BISHOP 404 • HT 279 • FMG I, 19, 111 • BLAKEY 37–8, 291, 303, 313, 316, 324 • KANTOR 24, 107–8, 189

PECORA, NOFIA, Ruby witness; lieutenant to New Orleans mob boss Carlos Marcello. According to phone records, Pecora received a phone call from Ruby on October 30, 1963. (See also Davis, John H.; Marcello, Carlos)
SOURCES: NORTH 56, 231, 264, 283, 293, 296–7, 321, 335 • DAVIS, many

PEÑA, OREST, Oswald witness; owner of the Habana Bar in New Orleans. Peña told the FBI that Oswald came into his bar in August 1963, accompanied by a man who appeared Latin American and who spoke Spanish. He said that Oswald ordered a lemonade, immediately vomited it back up onto his table and then left. (See also Easterling, Robert)
SOURCES: WR 302 • WCH XI, 346 • HSCA Report 191–3 • NORTH 294 • PD 55 • RTJ 339

PEÑA, RUPERTO, possible Oswald witness; brother of Orest (above) and coworker at the Habana Bar. Peña was a friend of Oswald's alleged political foe, Carlos Bringiuer. Peña said he had an argument in the bar with several pro-Castro people, one of whom he was told was Oswald, but could not identify Oswald from a photo.
SOURCE: WCH XI, 364

PENN, MRS. LOVELL, possible Oswald witness. In early October 1963, Penn kicked three men off her property just outside Dallas, where they had been firing a rifle. She said one of the men resembled Oswald. She found a

6.5mm Mannlicher-Carcano cartridge on her land and turned it over to the
FBI, which determined that it had not been fired by the alleged
assassination weapon.
    SOURCES: SUMMERS 381 • NORTH 320

PERRIN, ROBERT, Ruby witness; suspicious death. Perrin once ran
guns by boat into Spain for Franco during the Spanish Civil War. At a
meeting in Dallas, in 1962, Perrin was offered $10,000 to use a boat to pick
up Cuban refugees in Cuba and deliver them to Miami. The man carrying
the cash at that meeting was Ruby. Perrin eventually declined the offer
because there were too many "police types" involved.
    Perrin who had married Nancy Rich, a Carousel Club bartender, died on
August 28, 1962, of arsenic poisoning. His death was ruled a suicide by
the New Orleans coroner's office. It has been theorized—by Penn Jones Jr.
and others—that Perrin faked his own death and that the real victim was a
man named Starr, with whom Perrin switched places. (See also Chetta,
Nicholas; Rich, Nancy)
    SOURCES: RTJ 287–8, 290, 293 • COA 203 • HT 136 • FMG I, 102–3, 107, 112–3, 118;
    III, 40–7, 57

PERRY, MALCOLM O. "MAC," Parkland witness; surgeon. Perry
attended JFK. He performed a tracheotomy on JFK over the small wound in
JFK's throat, thus inadvertently destroying the evidence that this was an
entry wound. Still, every medical professional who saw JFK in Parkland
described the throat wound as an entry wound.
    SOURCES: WR 66–7, 91–4 • WCH III, 366; VI, 7 • RTJ 47, 51–4 • BISHOP 148–9, 156,
    180, 219–20, 338 • DOP 184–8, 215–6, 218, 221–2, 432–3, 524 • MOORE 151, 156–7 •
    BE, many • ME 31, 33, 35 • OGLESBY 39 • PD 355

PERRY, W. E., Oswald witness; member DPD. Perry participated in the
police lineup in which Helen Markham identified Oswald as the man she
saw shoot Officer J. D. Tippit. Perry was #1 in the lineup, Oswald #2.
(See also Markham, Helen)
    SOURCES: WCH VII, 232 • BISHOP 290–1

PETERMAN, VIOLA, Oswald witness; neighbor of Marguerite Oswald
and her sons in New Orleans when Lee was a child. Peterman told the WC,
"Lee was a good little child, and Marguerite took good care of him."
    SOURCE: WCH VIII, 38

PETERS, PAUL C., Parkland witness. Peterman was one of many
physicians in Dallas who testified that there was a large exit wound in the
back of JFK's head. When asked whether there was a smaller entrance
wound in the back of JFK's head (as appears on the autopsy photographs

supposedly taken later that day in Bethesda), he replied no.

SOURCES: WR 66–7 • WCH VI, 68 • RTJ 59 • BISHOP 156 • BE, many • ME 53

PETERSON, ARNOLD, national secretary and treasurer of the American Socialist Party in 1963. Peterson told the WC that "a search of the records of the national headquarters reveals no record pertaining to Oswald. He explained that letters requesting literature are "routinely destroyed."

SOURCE: WR 269

PETERSON, JOSEPH ALEXANDER, Ruby witness; assistant to Ruby associate Breck Wall. Peterson was once punched by Ruby after Wall withdrew from a business deal when Ruby would not sign a contract. Peterson was described by James Henry Dolan, a longtime associate of assassination suspect Eugene Hale Brading, as a "little fairy." Dolan said that Ruby had been "a bully" when he hit Peterson. According to Ruby's written account of his activities between the assassination and his shooting of Oswald, he called Peterson on the morning of November 23, 1963, at the Adolphus Hotel and was told that Peterson had left town for three days. Someone at the hotel gave Ruby a number where Peterson could be reached in Galveston, Texas, which Ruby called and talked to either Peterson or Wall. Ruby told one of them that he had closed the Carousel Club for three days, and the man at the other end of the line said that "they also wanted to get away." (See also Dolan, James; Wall, Breck)

SOURCES: WCH XIV, 615 • GERTZ 112 • BLAKEY 306

PHENIX, GEORGE R., o.k.w.; Dallas television cameraman. Phenix filmed Ruby's shooting Oswald, on 16mm black-and-white film for TV-station KRLD.

SOURCES: WCH XIII, 123 • PWW 123, 281

PHILLIPS, DAVID ATLEE, possible Oswald witness; former CIA station chief in Mexico City. Phillips alleged before the HSCA that the CIA had reports of a meeting between Oswald and Cuban agents. HT calls Phillips a "propaganda specialist." He once worked with assassination suspect E. Howard Hunt in Havana. It has been suspected—by the HSCA, researcher Anthony Summers and others—that Phillips's code name was "Maurice Bishop" and that he was "deeply involved" with Alpha 66, the Cuban exile/CIA assassination team plotting to kill Fidel Castro. Phillips told the HSCA that Oswald had offered information to the Russians while in Mexico City in September 1963 and had requested free passage to the USSR. (See also Veciana, Antonio; Hunt, E. Howard)

SOURCES: HSCA Report 135–7 • HT 182–3, 193–5, 286–7, 350, 356 • EVICA 131–41,

144, 246–8, 258, 300, 305, 313 • PD, many • SUMMERS 358–60, 363–6, 504–19

PIC, EDWARD JOHN. Marguerite Oswald's first husband. They were married from 1929 to 1930.
SOURCES: WCH VIII, 196; XI, 82 • BELIN 206 • BLAKEY 340, 344

PIC, JOHN EDWARD, JR. Oswald witness; Lee's half-brother. Those who believe that the Oswald who came back from the Soviet Union was a different man than the one who entered the Marine Corps will note that Pic, the Thanksgiving before the assassination, was struck by the fact that Lee referred to him as his "half-brother." Until that time, Lee had simply called John his "brother." Pic also noted a drastic change in Lee's appearance following his return from the USSR: "His hair was much thinner. He didn't have as much hair... his face features were somewhat different... when he went in the Marines [he had] a bull neck... I looked for this, I didn't notice this at all... "

In 1978, the U.S. Defense Department acknowledged that it had once carried out an investigation of Pic, but did not say why. (See also Huff, Larry)
SOURCES: WR 28–9, 353–5, 358, 360 • WCH XIII, 1 • BISHOP 282, 286, 383, 390 • CF 97 • HT 274 • HSCA XI, 542 • BLAKEY 341, 343

PIERCE, EDWARD E., 45-year-old Dallas City Hall maintenance employee. Pierce told the WC that the doorway from an alley to the Municipal Building (DPD station/City Hall) was locked all day on November 24, 1963. Therefore Ruby could not have entered that way to shoot Oswald.
SOURCE: WCH XIII, 156

PIERCE, RIO S., o.k.w.; DPD lieutenant. Pierce drove his squad car up the ramp onto Main Street from the DPD station just as Ruby was supposed to have gone down the ramp on his way to shoot Oswald. He says he didn't see Ruby. Because of the aftermath of this situation, it is not unusual that no one will admit seeing Ruby enter the building.
SOURCES: WR 199–204, 206 • WCH VII, 76; XII, 337 • RTJ 225 • DOP 522 • PWW 269 • KANTOR 61–2, 72, 74–6, 145–6, 180

PIKE, MIKE (See RYAN, MIKE)

PIKE, ROY (See RYAN, MIKE)

PINKSTON, NAT A., FBI agent. Pinkston testified before the WC regarding the clipboard found many days after the assassination on the sixth floor of the TSBD. Theoretically, this was Oswald's work clipboard, with the orders he had filled on it, which Oswald allegedly had left on the sixth floor. Since the clipboard was not found immediately when that floor

was searched, either the search was not thorough, or the clipboard was planted later to further incriminate Oswald.
SOURCE: WCH VI, 334

PIPER, EDDIE, Oswald witness; TSBD janitor. Piper last saw Oswald at noon on the first floor. According to the WR, Piper was a "confused witness" without "exact memory of the events of that afternoon."
SOURCES: WR 143 • WCH VI, 334; VII, 388

PITTS, ELNORA, Ruby witness and cleaning lady. Pitts testified that she called Ruby at 8:30 A.M. on November 24, 1963, about three hours before Ruby shot Oswald. She says that a man who claimed to be Ruby answered the phone, but he didn't sound like Ruby and didn't seem to know who she was. "He never did sound like hisself [sic]," Pitts said. Was someone providing an alibi for Ruby?

Pitts was a defense witness at Ruby's murder trial. The defense used her to show that Ruby was disoriented following the assassination, and also— since "Ruby" had told her that he would call her back on Sunday afternoon—to show that Ruby murdered without malice.
SOURCES: WR 330–1 • WCH XIII, 228 • COA 146, 148 • GERTZ 59 • KANTOR 59–60, 65

PITZER, WILLIAM BRUCE, Bethesda witness; lieutenant commander, U.S. Navy; suspicious death. Pitzer reportedly attended JFK's autopsy (although his name does not appear on the official list of those present) and, according to several accounts, filmed the Bethesda autopsy. On October 29, 1966, Pitzer was found dead in his office in Bethesda of a .45 caliber pistol wound. According to HT, Pitzer was murdered as a warning to all autopsy witnesses not to talk about what they had seen.

Pitzer was found dead just before he was scheduled for retirement after 28 years in the military. Just before his death, Pitzer had been offered a job working for a "network television station" for $45,000 a year. HT says, "His family was told that his death was a suicide, and no one in his family believes it. The government refuses to give up a copy of the autopsy report... His widow stated... that Pitzer left ... notes for the smallest thing and would have left a suicide note... His widow said that his left hand was so mangled that they could not remove his wedding ring to give it to her, but he was right-handed. The question is, if he shot himself in his office with his right hand, how could his left hand be mangled?" According to the Waukegan, Illinois, *News-Sun* on May 1, 1975, Pitzer had taken the JFK autopsy photos and had been threatened repeatedly because of what he had seen. According to Dennis David, a medical corpsman who officially attended the autopsy, "Pitzer filmed in detail the Kennedy autopsy." (See also David, Dennis)

SOURCES: HT 57–60, 95–6, 106, 143 • FMG III, 95–6 • BE, many)

PIZZO, FRANK, Oswald witness; employee of the Downtown Lincoln-Mercury agency in Dallas. Pizzo's statements corroborate those of Albert G. Bogard; that Oswald came in and recklessly test-drove a Mercury Comet about two weeks before the assassination. This is odd because Oswald did not drive.

Pizzo and Bogard were coworkers at the car dealership at the time of the assassination, along with the suspicious Jack Lawrence. (See also Bogard, Albert; Lawrence, Jack; Wilson, Eugene)

SOURCES: WR 298 • WCH X, 340 • RTJ 331–3 • OTT 68–9

POE, J. M., t.k.w. (aftermath); DPD officer. At the scene of the Tippit killing, Poe was handed two shells by witness Domingo Benavides. Poe was instructed by Sergeant Gerald Hill to "mark them for evidence"; that is, to initial them so they could be identified later. Poe later said that he couldn't swear to initialing the shells because when he was shown the shells supposedly found at the scene of the Tippit killing on June 12, 1964; those that ballistically matched the "Oswald" gun did not bear his initials. Did Poe forget to initial the shells, or were the shells switched? (See also Barnes, Willie E.; Hill, Gerald)

SOURCES: WR 156, 162 • WCH VII, 66 • RTJ 197–8 • CF 343 • OTT 201)

POLLAK, STUART, WC staff member. Pollak, a Justice Department attorney, was assistant to WC General Counsel J. Lee Rankin. Pollak assisted in the writing of the WR chapter about Oswald's movements abroad.

SOURCE: WCH XV, 373; XXVI, 582

POPKIN, RICHARD, former chairman of the philosophy department at the University of California at San Diego; author of *The Second Oswald* (Avon, 1966).

SOURCES: MOORE 75, 79, 94–5, 112, 216 • BE 109, 245, 306 • FLAMMONDE 331

PORTER, MARINA (See OSWALD, MARINA)

POSTAL, JULIA, Texas Theatre witness; theater cashier. When shoe-store manager Johnny Calvin Brewer saw a suspicious man enter the Texas Theatre without buying a ticket, he informed Postal. She called the police between 1:40 and 1:45 P.M. In minutes, the theater was surrounded by police and Oswald was arrested inside. Postal claimed that she had seen the man as he "ducked into" the theater, but she did not react until Brewer told her that the man appeared to be trying to evade the police. There has

never been an official explanation for why it took Oswald between 24 and 29 minutes to take the short walk from the scene of Tippit's murder to the theater. (See also Brewer, Johnny Calvin)
SOURCES: WR 26, 164 • WCH VII, 8 • BISHOP 211–3 • MOORE 65)

POTTER, NOLAN H., a.w. Potter stood on top of the triple underpass. Like many of the other triple-underpass witnesses, Potter saw smoke coming from the bushes atop the grassy knoll after the shooting sequence.
SOURCE: CF 58

POTTS, WALTER EUGENE, Oswald witness; member DPD (Homicide). Potts participated in one police lineup with Oswald. He told the WC that Oswald complained bitterly during the lineup and that he was in a T-shirt while the other "suspects" were all dressed nicely. With E. L. Cunningham, Bill Senkel, and F. M. Turner, Potts searched Oswald's Beckley Street room, where nothing incriminating was found.
SOURCE: WCH VII, 195

POWELL, JAMES, W., a.w.; military intelligence agent. Powell took a photo "minutes after the shooting," which appears to show a man in the "sniper's-nest" window. When the Dal-Tex Building on Houston Street was sealed off immediately following the assassination, Powell was trapped inside. Assassination suspect Eugene Hale Brading (who was using the name Jim Braden) was arrested in this same building. (See also Dillard, Thomas)
SOURCES: HSCA Report 86 • CF 53 • HT 185

POWELL, JOHN, a.w. Powell was on the sixth floor of the Dallas County Jail on Houston Street, where he was incarcerated at the time. He says he and other inmates saw two men in the "sniper's-nest" window before the shooting, that one of them appeared to be Latin, and that the men appeared to be adjusting the scope on a rifle.
SOURCES: HT 228 • SUMMERS 74–5 • OTT 94

POWELL, NANCY MONNELL (aka Tammy True); Ruby witness; Carousel Club stripper; "girlfriend" of Ruby business associate Ralph Paul. Powell had many unnamed houseguests from out of town during the assassination weekend. Immediately following the shooting, she drove from her Fort Worth home to Parkland, as did Ruby.

During the evening of November 23, 1963, Powell drove coworker Karen Carlin ("Little Lynn") and her husband from Fort Worth to Dallas. The threesome went to the Colony Club, one of the Carousel's competitors (where a.w. Beverly Oliver reportedly worked), and from there Karen Carlin called Ruby to ask for money. This fact is significant because the wiring of money to Carlin the following morning would be part of Ruby's alibi that he murdered without malice. (See also Paul, Ralph)

SOURCES: WR 325 • WCH XV, 404 • COA 115, 138, 140–3, 255, 265 • KANTOR 169, 196

POWERS, DANIEL PATRICK, Oswald witness; USMC acquaintance. Powers told the WC that Oswald was "an individual you could brainwash, and quite easy [sic]... [but] I think once he believed in something... he stood in his beliefs... [he was] somewhat the frail, little puppy in the litter... [Oswald] would take the easy way out to avoid a conflict... a lot of his mannerisms were closely related to other homosexuals I had seen... "

SOURCES: WR 361–2 • WCH VIII, 266 • AO 92

POWERS, DAVID, a.w.; presidential assistant. Powers rode with the SS in the presidential follow-up car, directly behind JFK's limo. He told the WC:

> ... the first shot went off and it sounded to me as if it were a firecracker. I noticed then that the President moved quite far to his left after the shot, from the extreme right-hand side where he had been sitting. There was a second shot and Governor Connally disappeared from sight and then there was a third shot, which took off the top of the president's head and had the sickening sound of a grapefruit splattering against the side of a wall. The total time between the first and third shots was about five or six seconds. My first impression was that the shots came from the right and overhead but I also had a fleeting impression that the noise appeared to come from the front in the area of the triple underpass. This may have resulted from my feeling, when I looked forward toward the overpass, that we might have ridden into an ambush.

Others in that car were George W. Hickey, Paul E. Landis, Glen A. Bennett, John D. Ready, William T. McIntyre, Clinton J. Hill, Emory P. Roberts, Samuel Kinney, and Kenneth O'Donnell.

Powers accompanied JFK's casket on Air Force One from Dallas to Andrews Air Force Base and refutes David Lifton's theory that the body was moved during the trip so that it could be taken off the jet secretly and altered before it arrived at Bethesda for the autopsy. Powers says that the casket was never left unattended, so there was no opportunity for the body to have been moved or altered. (See also Lifton, David)

SOURCES: WR 56, 59, 61, 64, 72 • WCH VII, 473 • CF 15–6, 436 • MOORE 97 • BE 284, 389, 400, 577–8 • OTT 46 • ME 60, 101, 106, 217, 223, 234–5, 251–2 • OGLESBY 35

PREYER, RICHARDSON, member of HSCA (D-North Carolina); former federal judge; former FBI agent. Preyer attempted to reconcile the autopsy report with the autopsy photos.
SOURCES: HSCA Report 495 • HT 360, 369–70, 374–5, 389, 393–6 • MOORE 137–8 • BE 549, 555

PRICE, CHARLES JACK, Parkland witness; hospital administrator. Price helped clear the way as JFK's casket was removed from the hospital through the emergency-room entrance.
SOURCES: WCH VI, 148 • BISHOP 152, 179, 189, 228, 312 • BE 673

PRICE, JESSE C., a.w. Price stood on the roof of the Terminal Annex Building. (Dealey Plaza is symmetrical. The Terminal Annex Building is the southern counterpart to the TSBD, at the southwest corner of Houston and Commerce.) He told the Dallas sheriff's office 30 minutes after the shooting that he heard a "volley of shots" and then saw a man running from behind the wooden fence on the grassy knoll toward the railroad cars. He said the man was about 5'6" or 5'7", 145 lbs. with long, dark hair and that he had something in his hand. He was about 25 years old and wore a white dress shirt and khaki trousers. (This last statement is consistent with testimony offered by witnesses Lee Bowers and Julia Mercer.) On March 27, 1966, Price told author Mark Lane, "He was bare-headed, and he was running very fast, which gave me the suspicion that he was doing the shooting, but I could have been mistaken." Lane asked Price to explain more specifically where he had seen the man run. Price said, "Over behind that wooden fence past the cars and over behind the Texas Depository Building." Price added that he was carrying something "in his right hand" that "might have been a gun." (See also Bowers, Lee; Mercer, Julia; Vaganov, Igor)
SOURCES: WCE 2003, p. 222 • RTJ 32–3, 36–7 • COA 24 • CF 39 • MOORE 28–9, 35 • OTT 16 • NORTH 386

PRICE, MALCOLM H., JR., possible Oswald witness. Price was among those who saw a man resembling Oswald practicing at the Sports Drome Rifle Range in Dallas on several occasions between late September and early November 1963. Price got a good look at the individual, as he helped "Oswald" adjust the scope on his rifle, and was confident that the man he had seen was Oswald. The WC concluded that the man could not be Oswald because one of the sightings took place while the "real" Oswald was in Mexico City.
SOURCES: WR 295–6 • WCH X, 369 • RTJ 334–5

PRIDDY, HAL, JR., 25-year-old relief dispatcher at the Oneal funeral

parlor in Dallas. Priddy received the call from the police that Oswald had been shot and sent ambulance #605 to the scene. It arrived in near-record time.
SOURCE: WCH XIII, 239

PRIO SOCARRAS, CARLOS, former president of Cuba; head of the anti-Castro organization called the Free Cuba Committee; suspicious death. Prio Socarras was being sought by the HSCA in April 1977, because of his supposed knowledge of alleged ties between anti-Castro Cubans and Ruby, when he died of a pistol shot—official cause of death: suicide. He died seven days after George DeMohrenschildt, who was also sought by the HSCA for questioning. (See also Bloomfield, Louis; DeMohrenschildt, George; McKeown, Robert; Torbitt, William; Wade, Henry)
SOURCES: HT 145 • BLAKEY 172, 229 • OGLESBY 74

PROEBER, RICHARD W., Ruby witness; part-time Ruby employee. Proeber told the FBI that he had heard rumors that Ruby was "paying off" the Dallas police in return for "special favors."
SOURCE: RTJ 234–5

PROUTY, L. FLETCHER, Chief of Special Operations for the Joint Chiefs of Staff; author, *JFK: The CIA, Vietnam and the Plot to Assassinate John F. Kennedy* (Birch Lane Press, 1992). Prouty was in New Zealand at the time of the assassination and bought a newspaper later in the day. *Christchurch* (New Zealand) *Star* named Oswald as the assassin and included a photo of Oswald dressed in a suit and tie. Later, Prouty was reportedly horrified to discover that Oswald's biography (defection to Russia, pro-Castro, Russian wife, etc.) and photo (looking sharp) went out over the international news wire before Oswald was arrested by the Dallas police. (Author Harrison Edward Livingstone checked this claim and found that the information had actually gone over the wire two hours *after* Oswald's arrest.)

Prouty was consultant to the film *JFK*. The character "X," played by Donald Sutherland, was based on Prouty.
SOURCES: HT, many • HT2 481–2, 494, 531 • PD 96–8, 102–3, 331

PRUSAKOV, ILYA, Oswald witness. Prusakov was Marina Oswald's uncle and an alleged MVD agent. (See also Oswald, Marina)
SOURCE: HT 163

PRUSAKOVA, MARINA (See OSWALD, MARINA)

PRYOR, ROY A., Ruby witness; printer at the *Dallas Times Herald*. Pryor once worked for Ruby at one of his nightclubs. He was a defense witness at Ruby's murder trial, where he established Ruby's emotional nature with an anecdote: Jack's taking presents to a Catholic orphanage—a ploy by the defense team not only to tug juror heartstrings, but also, perhaps, to defuse any anti-Semitism present on the Dallas jury.

Pryor then established Ruby's deteriorating mental state following the assassination by describing how he had run into Ruby at 4:00 A.M. on November 23. Ruby had discussed the great loss to the nation and the Kennedy family. Ruby bragged that he had "scooped" other Dallas nightclub proprietors by changing his newspaper ad into a "memorial" to JFK. Ruby expressed his pleasure at having overheard Dallas District Attorney Henry Wade talking on the phone and the way he had corrected one of Wade's factual errors.

(This incident actually occurred while Wade was speaking to reporters in the Dallas police station. Wade had erroneously stated that Oswald was a member of the "Free Cuba Committee." Ruby corrected him, saying that Oswald actually belonged to the "Fair Play For Cuba Committee." This incident is made more interesting by the fact that there really is a Free Cuba Committee, but it is not a pro-Castro organization such as the one Oswald supposedly belonged to. It was, rather, right wing and anti-Castro, and reportedly not above suspicion in the assassination.)

Pryor testified, "Jack was happy about being able to feel like he could assist the district attorney in making that correction, and he told me, he said that he knew Mr. Wade and that he knew influential people."

On cross-examination, Pryor told the prosecution that Ruby thought it was a rare privilege to see Oswald in person at the midnight press conference and that Ruby described Oswald as "a little weasel of a guy." (See also Prio Socarras, Carlos)
SOURCES: WR 320)(WCH XV, 554 • GERTZ 52–3

PUGH, ORAN, U.S. Customs agent-in-charge. Pugh's WC testimony corroborates the affidavit of William Kline that no check was made on Oswald by the U.S. Public Health Service upon his entry into or exit from Mexico in September 1963.
SOURCE: WCH XV, 640

PULLMAN, MRS. EDWARD J., Ruby witness; Carousel Club hostess. Pullman told the WC that DPD members were always served on the house; added that, although DPD members frequented the club, they never drank alcoholic beverages while on duty.
SOURCES: WCH XV, 222 • RTJ 233, 235 • GERTZ 522

PURTELL, DAVID J., HSCA handwriting expert; member of the American Society of Questioned Document Examiners. Purtell was called

upon by the HSCA, along with Joseph P. McNally and Charles C. Scott, to assess the authenticity of the "Historic Diary" that Lee Harvey Oswald supposedly kept in the USSR. They determined that, though the diary was written by Oswald, it was written in one or two sittings, rather than daily.
    SOURCE: DUFFY 48-50

PUTNAM, JAMES A., Parkland witness; DPD inspector. Putnam was one of three drivers who drove LBJ, Lady Bird, and their party from Parkland Hospital to Love Field in unmarked police cars following JFK's death.
    SOURCES: WR 200 • WCH VII, 74; XII, 341 • BISHOP 202

Q

QUIGLEY, JOHN LESTER, Oswald witness; FBI agent. On August 9, 1963, when Oswald was arrested on Canal Street and jailed for disturbing the peace by the New Orleans police, he requested a meeting with an FBI agent. Quigley was sent to interview him. According to the WR, the police had not given the FBI Oswald's name when they summoned Quigley on August 10. Therefore, Quigley had not had an opportunity to do a background check on Oswald—and did not know that Oswald had attempted to defect to the USSR and had already been interviewed by the FBI since his return to the United States.

Quigley testified that Oswald was cooperative when answering questions about his general background—but was not so cooperative when asked about the FPCC:

> When I began asking him specific details with respect to his activities in the [FPCC] in New Orleans as to where meetings were held, who was involved, what occurred, he was reticent to furnish information, reluctant and actually as far as I was concerned, was completely evasive on them... [Oswald] was probably making a self-serving statement in attempting to explain to me why he was distributing this literature, and for no other reason, and when I got to questioning him further than he felt that his purpose had been served, he wouldn't say anything further.

A background check revealed that among the lies Oswald told Quigley at that interview were that Marina's maiden name was Prossa and that they had been married in Fort Worth. Quigley burned the notes he took during the Oswald interview.

371

SOURCES: WR 304, 411–3, 415 • WCH IV, 431 • WCE 825–6, 1141 • HSCA Report 185, 191 • NORTH 296, 301 • OTT 25–6, 224, 312 • HOS 140–1

QUINN, ROSALEEN, Oswald witness; the aunt of Oswald's fellow marine in MACS-9, Henry J. Roussel Jr. Quinn once dated Oswald while he was in the USMC. According to researcher Edward Jay Epstein:

> ...one Marine asked [Oswald] to have dinner with his aunt...an extremely attractive airline stewardess from New Orleans, because she was studying Russian for the State Department's foreign-language examination. She met Oswald in a cafeteria in Santa Ana [California] and they spoke Russian for about two hours. Although she had been studying Russian with a Berlitz tutor for more than a year, she found that Oswald had a more confident command of the language than she did and could string entire sentences together without much hesitation. She asked how he had learned Russian, and he shrugged and said that he had "taught himself" by listening to Radio Moscow...Just before she left Santa Ana, Oswald took her to see the film *South Pacific*, and afterward they had a drink at a neighborhood bar. Again they practiced their Russian and spoke of traveling. This time Oswald told her that he had plans to go to Europe, but he did not mention what they were...

After the assassination, the FBI interviewed Quinn and reported, "[She] recalled that Oswald was a quiet individual and that it was difficult to converse with him...The evening date...did not prove to be a very interesting one...she concluded by stating that she has never seen nor heard from Oswald since." (See also Roussel, Henry J.)
SOURCES: WCH XXIV, 430 • WCE 2015 • AO 97–8 • LEGEND 87

QUIROGA, CARLOS, possible Oswald witness; anti-Castro activist. According to author Anthony Summers, witness David Lewis saw Quiroga in the company of Oswald, assassination suspect David Ferrie, and Guy Banister.

Quiroga was a friend of Carlos Bringuier, the man who got into a public scuffle with Oswald in New Orleans and later debated Oswald on the radio. When Bringuier was uncertain what Oswald was up to (acting anti-Castro one day and pro-Castro the next), he sent Quiroga to Oswald's house to see what he could find out. (See also Bringuier, Carlos; Lewis, David)
SOURCES: HSCA Report 141 • HT 289 • SUMMERS 324–5 • BLAKEY 162, 169 • FLAMMONDE 23–4, 121, 226

R

RACHEL, JOHN R., Oswald witness; Louisiana department of labor employee in New Orleans. Rachel first interviewed Oswald on April 26, 1963. He referred Oswald to the George Reppel Studio for a photographic job, but Oswald never showed up for the interview. After Oswald appeared on New Orleans TV as a pro-Castro activist, Rachel consulted his supervisor and they agreed to stay away from Oswald.
SOURCE: WCH XI, 474

RACKLEY, GEORGE W., SR., a.w.; employee of the Coordinated Railroad Company; told WC he was two blocks north of Dealey Plaza at the corner of Ross and Market streets; didn't see motorcade, heard no shots; told WC, "...there was something like 100 pigeons flew up like you shot into them."
SOURCE: WCH VI, 273

RAGANO, FRANK. For 27 years Frank Ragano was the lawyer for Florida mob boss Santos Trafficante and for 15 years he represented Teamster president Jimmy Hoffa. In the January 14, 1992, edition of the *New York Post*, Ragano revealed knowledge of a plot involving Hoffa, Trafficante, and New Orleans mob boss Carlos Marcello to assassinate the president. Hoffa disappeared and is presumed dead. Trafficante is dead. When Ragano sang, Marcello was in jail and claiming to suffer from Alzheimer's disease. Marcello has since died. Details of Ragano's story are included in the entry for Marcello. (See also Hoffa, James; Marcello, Carlos; Trafficante, Santos

RAIGORODSKY, PAUL M., Oswald witness; leading member of Dallas's Russian-speaking community, which called him "The Czar." Raigorodsky was an acquaintance of Lee and Marina Oswald, and a leading Dallas

373

socialite who often appeared in the papers in tails and top hat attending select gatherings. In 1968, Raigorodsky cohosted a party given in Dallas by Mrs. Clint Murchison, Jr.

SOURCES: WCH IX, 1 • FMG III, 14, 79, 84 • EVICA 296

RAIKIN, SPAS T., Oswald witness. Raikin met the Oswalds in June 1962 at the New York City pier upon their arrival from the Soviet Union. The WC says that Raikin was working for the Traveler's Aid Society and had been asked by the State Department to meet the Oswalds. According to New Orleans District Attorney Jim Garrison, Raikin was also at the time the secretary-general of the "American Friends of the Anti-Bolshevik Nations, Inc., a private anti-communist operation with extensive intelligence connections."

SOURCES: WCH XXVI, WCE 2655 • WR 713 • OTT 51 • SUMMERS 217

RAMSEY, NORMAN F., Justice Department acoustics expert; Higgins professor of physics at Harvard University and chairman of the 1982 Committee on Ballistic Acoustics of the National Research Council. The committee reported: "The [Dictabelt] acoustic analyses do not demonstrate that there was a grassy knoll shot."

SOURCES: BELIN 198 • HT 247, 249, 252

RAND, MICHAEL, author of *The Assassination of President Kennedy* (Jonathan Cape, 1967).

RANDLE, LINNIE MAE, Oswald witness; sister of Buell Wesley Frazier and neighbor of Ruth Paine. With Frazier, Randle is the only witness who saw Oswald carrying a package in a brown paper bag on the morning of the assassination, the bag the WC claims contained his rifle. Like her brother, she told the WC that the package Oswald carried that morning was too short to have contained a rifle, even one that had been broken down. She said that Frazier had informed her the night before the assassination that Oswald had come to Irving to pick up curtain rods. (See also Frazier, Buell Wesley; Paine, Ruth)

SOURCES: WR 123–7, 168, 229, 397 • WCH II, 245 • BELIN 58, 60, 64, 68 • RTJ 142–3, 146–7, 384 • BISHOP 26–7, 278, 334–5, 356, 368, 419, 492 • CF 40–1 • HT 291 • MOORE 69 • NORTH 325, 374

RANKIN, J. LEE, general counsel to the WC. Rankin, a former U.S. solicitor general, did more work for the WC than any other commissioner or staff member. He organized the investigation and served as its executive director, as well as counsel. Later, he superintended the writing of the WR.

SOURCES: HSCA Report 137–8, 168, 211–2, 245, 257–8 • FLAMMONDE 71, 157–9,

287 • EVICA, many • ME 123 • DAVIS 287, 291, 310–1, 317–8, 411–2, 610–1 • NORTH, many • PD 22, 24, 44, 55–8, 63, 65–6, 367 • BELIN 13, 46–8, 66 • RTJ, many • COA 160, 211 • GERTZ 138–9, 530 • HT 86, 111–2, 158, 170, 327–8 • PWW, many • MOORE 18–20 • FMG I, 47, 71, 149 • BE, many • OTT 97 • BLAKEY, many

RATHER, DAN, a.w. (aftermath). In 1993, Rather was a *CBS Evening News* anchorman. In 1963, Rather was bureau chief for the CBS affiliate in Dallas. He was in charge of setting up CBS's coverage of JFK's visit to Dallas. He claims he was on the west side of the triple underpass at the time of the assassination, waiting to pick up a reel of film shot during the motorcade, but photographic evidence suggests that he was not there. Rather was the first man to approach Abraham Zapruder following the assassination to acquire his film of the shooting. According to WC Counsel David W. Belin, "[Rather] took the film and was able to have the processing of the film expedited." Rather viewed the film and later misrepresented it to the American public, saying that JFK's head snaps forward instead of backward from the impact of the fatal shot. He was the first to report the name and background of the accused assassin.

From that point on, Rather's rise to the top was rapid. In recent years, his career has been marred by controversy, including an incident in which he was mugged by a man who kept repeating the phrase, "What's the frequency, Kenneth?" When former CIA director George Bush wanted to rid himself of his "wimp" image during his campaign for president, he chose to confront Dan Rather on live TV to accomplish this.

In a February 6, 1992, AP interview, Rather said he was "at the end of the motorcade route outside the plaza, waiting for the final 'film drop' for the motorcade's camera crew...The motorcade never passed me. Here comes the limousine, but it seems to be going awful fast and it sort of streaks by in a blur. And I sensed that something was wrong. I had no idea. I had heard no shots." Rather ran into Dealey Plaza—he didn't say whether he went under or over the triple underpass—and "Now I had in front of me the grassy knoll, the School Book Depository. God, the chaos and confusion! People were on the ground, screaming. Police were running around. It was clear then...something was wrong." The AP reports that Rather "sprinted the few blocks back to the CBS affiliate, and heard the first radio bulletins that shots had been fired in Dealey Plaza...Rather called [Parkland] and confirmed the death with emergency room witnesses, breaking the story 17 minutes before the official report that the president was dead."

"It was the longest 17 minutes of my professional career," Rather said.

(See also Jackson, C. D.; Tilson, Tom)
    SOURCES: WCE 1937, 2983, 3101 • BELIN 182–3 • CF 68 • HT 89, 117–8, 327, 418 •
    FMG III, 91, 96–7 • BE 319, 429

RAY, ELLEN, documentary filmmaker. In 1967 Ray went to New Orleans
to film the Jim Garrison story. In 1991, she told journalist Steven Hager,
"People were getting killed left and right. Garrison would subpeona a
witness and two days later the witness would be killed by a parked car. I
thought Garrison was the great American patriot. But things got a little too
heavy when I started getting strange phone calls from men with Cuban
accents." Ray did not complete her documentary. After several death
threats, she fled the country. In 1993, Ray was director of the Institute for
Media Analysis.

RAY, THOMAS M. and NATALIE, Oswald witnesses; Dallas acquaintances. Natalie was a member of the Dallas Russian-speaking community.
She was born in Stalingrad and sent to Germany by the Nazis in 1943. She
is a writer. She said she met Lee and Marina at a party, commented that
Lee spoke excellent Russian and later wondered whether he were a Soviet
agent. Thomas was a commission salesman for Gulf Oil of Paris, Texas, at
the time of JFK's death. He basically corroborated his wife's testimony;
regarding Oswald, he said, "Well, frankly, I just didn't pay much attention
to the guy."
    SOURCE: WCH IX, 27, 38

RAY, VALENTINA A., Oswald witness; member of the Dallas Russian-
speaking community. Ray was originally from the Ukraine. She met Lee
and Marina Oswald in November 1962. She told the WC that Marina told
her that Lee was mean to her and hit her. Ray said Oswald was "rather
arrogant."
    SOURCE: WCH VIII, 415

REA, BILLY A., Ruby witness; 40-year-old member of the advertising
staff of the *Dallas Morning News.* Rea saw Ruby at 1:00 P.M. in the
pressroom. He believed that Ruby had been in the pressroom all afternoon,
but couldn't be sure. Rea said that Ruby was sitting at fellow employee Don
Campbell's desk all alone. He said, "This guy had an ashen, pale look that,
you know, like he was in a state of shock."
    SOURCE: WCH XV, 571

READY, JOHN D., a.w.; SS special agent. Ready rode on the right front
running board of the SS's presidential follow-up car. According to the WR,
"Ready... heard noises that sounded like firecrackers and ran toward the
Presidential limousine. But he was immediately called back by Special

Agent Emory P. Roberts, in charge of the followup car, who did not believe he could reach the president's car at the speed it was traveling." At that point, the president's car was traveling at approximately 11 miles per hour and was slowing down. (See also Roberts, Emory)

SOURCES: WR 60, 64 • ME 60, 101, 218, 226, 234

REDLICH, NORMAN, WC counsel. In a February 28, 1964, memo, Redlich wrote: "Marina [Oswald] has repeatedly lied . . . on matters which are of vital concern." (See also Oswald, Marina)

SOURCES: HT 159 • FMG III, 71 • PWW, many • MOORE 84 • BE 25, 28, 71, 86, 98–9, 108, 157, 162 • BLAKEY 42, 72, 74–5, 79 • EVICA 89 • ME 226 • NORTH 399, 526–7, 645 • PD 44, 62

REEVES, HUEY, Ruby witness; garage attendant at Nichols garage, adjacent to Ruby's Carousel Club. Reeves has been suspected by some researchers of being used to provide an alibi for Ruby. Reeves told the WC that he spoke to Ruby around 9:00 P.M. on November 23, the night before Ruby shot Oswald. They discussed making arrangements to give a $5 loan to Carousel Club stripper Karen Bennett Carlin. The amount of the loan, the time of the meeting and other details, however, vary depending on which of Ruby's cronies told the story. The loan to Carlin is crucial because this was Ruby's excuse for being in the vicinity of the DPD station at the time Oswald was to be transferred. Ruby claimed to be at the Western Union office (less than a block from the murder site) to lend money to Carlin. (See also Carlin, Karen)

SOURCES: WR 325, 327 • WCH XIII, 243 • COA 140–3

REID, BARBARA, Oswald witness; longtime New Orleans French Quarter resident. Reid told New Orleans District Attorney Jim Garrison that Oswald's old marine buddy, Kerry Thornley, lived in New Orleans during the summer of 1963. She said she knew Thornley and Oswald and had seen them together on several occasions. (See also Thornley, Kerry W.)

SOURCE: OTT 71

REID, ELIZABETH (shown in some places as Mrs. Robert Reid; Elizabeth Reed), a.w.; Oswald witness. Reid was employed on the second floor of the TSBD and saw Oswald on the second floor two minutes after the shooting. He was heading for the front stairway, presumably to leave the building. Reid was the last person to see Oswald inside the TSBD. (See also Baker, Marrion)

SOURCES: WR 144–5, 234 • WCH III, 270 • BELIN 57, 72 • CF 27, 51–2 • PWW 29, 49, 92

REILLY, FRANK E., a.w.; electrician at Union Terminal. Reed was

standing atop the triple underpass. He told the WC that the shots came from the trees "on the north side of Elm Street at the corner up there."
SOURCES: WR 82 • WCH VI, 227 • MOORE 31 • BE 16 • NORTH 268, 290

REILY, WILLIAM, Oswald witness; owner of the Reily Coffee Company, where Oswald was employed during the summer of 1963. According to New Orleans District Attorney Jim Garrison, Reily had "actively supported the anti-Castro movement for years." (See also Branyon, John; Claude, Alfred; Marachini, Dante; Barbee, Emmett)
SOURCE: OTT 27

REVILL, JACK, DPD lieutenant in charge of intelligence. At 2:50 P.M., November 22, Revill met with FBI agent James Hosty and for the first time learned that Oswald had been known by the feds to be a Communist living in Dallas. Revill immediately wrote a memo to Captain W. P. Gannaway to that effect, in which he indicated Oswald's address as 605 Elsbeth Street, an address at which Oswald had never lived. It had been eight months since Oswald had lived on Elsbeth Street, and when he did, he lived at 602. When the WC asked Revill his source for that piece of information, he failed to answer.

Revill was a defense witness at Ruby's murder trial—he was used to identify photos of the Oswald shooting that showed various prosecution witnesses looking at neither Oswald nor Ruby when the shot was fired. (See also Hosty, James; Gannaway, W. P.; Robertson, Mary Jane; Patterson, B. M.)
SOURCES: WCH V, 33; XII, 73 • COA 145, 426 • GERTZ 59 • BISHOP 74, 227, 232, 248–9, 306, 342, 363 • HT 123, 183, 185

REYNOLDS, HAROLD, Abilene photographer. On June 6, 1979, Reynolds told the *Dallas Morning News* that on November 17, 1963, his longtime friend, Pedro Valeriano Gonzales—president of the anti-Castro group, the Cuban Liberation Committee—had received a note slipped under his door, which said, "Call me immediately. Urgent. [signed] Lee Oswald." Reynolds says that Gonzales became very nervous when he received the note and went to the street to make a phone call from a pay phone, despite having a telephone in his apartment. (See also Gonzales, Pedro)
SOURCES: CF 152 • NORTH 366, 432

REYNOLDS, WARREN ALLEN, t.k.w. Reynolds observed a man fleeing the site of the Tippit killing. Initially he refused to identify the man as Oswald. Later, Reynolds was shot in the head in the basement of his used-car dealership. Recovering miraculously from the wound, he later testified that the man he had seen was Oswald. (See also Garner, Darrell Wayne; Mooney, Nancy Jane)

SOURCES: WR 159, 162 • WCH XI, 434 • RTJ 201, 276, 278–80 • COA 35–6 • GERTZ 528 • CF 342 • HT 138, 142–3 • PWW 127 • OTT 195 • HOS 70 • OGLESBY 61 • PD 366

RHEINSTEIN, FREDERIC, Ruby witness; NBC producer-director. Rheinstein told the WC that he saw a man whom he was "reasonably certain" was Ruby in the DPD station around 5:00 P.M. on November 23, 1963.

SOURCES: WCH XV, 354 • COA 127 • BLAKEY 319 • NORTH 418

RHODES, JAMES H., Ruby witness; Carousel Club bartender. Rhodes told the FBI that Ruby had once held a private party for 30 or 40 police officers at the Carousel, and that "the chief" was there. Ruby had picked up the tab.

SOURCES: RTJ 234–5 • COA 112, 392 • BE 433

RICH, JOE HENRY, a.w. Rich was the driver of the vice-presidential SS follow-up car.

SOURCES: FMG III, 17 • NORTH 380

RICH, NANCY PERRIN (aka Zeigman, Nancy; Cody, Julie Ann), Ruby witness; Carousel Club bartender. Rich told the WC that her husband, Robert Perrin, who had once run guns for Franco during the Spanish Civil War, had been offered $10,000 by a group of men that included Ruby to smuggle Cuban refugees out of Cuba and into Miami by boat. Perrin declined the job on the grounds that too many "police types" were involved.

Rich's background shows that she had created a small business for herself by informing for the police. She once volunteered her services to and obtained evidence for the DPD that led to the conviction of an abortionist. In Oakland, California, she had unsuccessfully attempted to help police by obtaining a nightclub job and informing on the owner. A polygraph examination given to Rich regarding Ruby on December 5, 1963, was inconclusive, due to her heavy drug use. (See also Perrin, Robert)

SOURCES: WCH XIV, 330 • RTJ 230–2, 287–98, 384 • COA 107, 112–3, 115, 202–4 • GERTZ 520–2 • HT 136, 303, 308 • FMG I, 99–100, 104; III, 40–6, 51 • FLAMMONDE 126–7, 172 • EVICA 167, 181, 317 • PD 366 • KANTOR 138

RICHEY, MARJORIE R., Ruby witness; 20-year-old Carousel Club waitress from June 1963 until the assassination. Richey said that stripper Kay Olsen ("Kathy Kay") lived with a policeman (probably Harry Olsen). She also said that Ruby would not tolerate stripper Janet "Jada" Conforto "popping her G-string" in her act, a move that violated Texas obscenity

laws. (See also Conforto, Janet; Olsen, Harry; Olsen, Kay)
SOURCE: WCH XV, 192

RICHEY, WARREN E., Ruby witness; Fort Worth television engineer. Richey was standing on top of a TV truck parked outside the DPD station on the morning of November 24, 1963. He told the WC that he saw Ruby in front of the building at 8:00 A.M. and then again at 10:00 A.M. This contradicts Ruby's claim that he wasn't in the vicinity until just a few minutes before Oswald was to be transferred. (See also Smith, John)
SOURCES: WR 329–30 • WCH XIII, 255 • COA 144–5, 426

RIEBE, FLOYD, Bethesda witness; photographic technician. Riebe photographed JFK's autopsy. According to HT, Riebe said JFK had "a big gaping hole in the back of the head...like somebody put a piece of dynamite in a can and lit it off." Shown the published JFK autopsy photos, Riebe said, "[It's] not what I saw that night...It's being phonied someplace. It's make-believe."
SOURCE: HT 449–50

RIGGS, ALFREADIA, 35-year-old Dallas City Hall porter. The WC called Riggs to help determine how Ruby got into the DPD station basement to shoot Oswald. Riggs told the WC that the service gate between the police station and the Municipal Building was locked on the day of Oswald's aborted transfer, but that the fire escape was never locked.
SOURCES: WCH XIII, 166

RIGGS, CHESTER ALLEN, JR., Oswald witness; landlord of the Oswalds when they lived at 2703 Mercedes in Fort Worth from June to October 1962. Riggs testified via affidavit. He said that his impression of Oswald was that he was a man who did a lot of reading.
SOURCE: WCH X, 229

RIKE, AUBREY "AL," a.w. (prelude); Parkland witness. Rike drove the ambulance that took Jerry B. Belknap, who apparently had a seizure in front of the TSBD moments before the presidential motorcade passed (an event long suspected of functioning as a diversion), to Parkland Hospital. Coincidentally, Rike also drove the ambulance that took JFK's body from Parkland to Love Field.

On the 1988 British television documentary, *The Men Who Killed Kennedy*, Rike described "pushing and shoving" between the SS and Parkland officials as the SS attempted—and eventually succeeded—in illegally removing the body from the hospital so they could fly it back to Washington. Rike said that he had to hold onto the cross on the casket to keep it from falling off because of the way the casket was being pushed and pulled back and forth. He insisted that when JFK's body left Parkland it was wrapped in a clear plastic sheet, like those used to cover mattresses. This is odd, because when the body arrived at Bethesda for autopsy, it was wrapped in a military-type dark body bag.

By Texas laws, all homicides must be autopsied locally. Though plotting to assassinate the president was a federal crime, actually shooting a president was not in 1963. Since the Dallas authorities lost the chain of evidence for JFK's body at Love Field, there should have been no discussion of the Bethesda autopsy in front of a jury at Oswald's trial. When the DPD turned their hard evidence over to the FBI, they lost any chance to convict Oswald of murder in a Texas court. (See also Belknap, Jerry; McGuire, Dennis; O'Connor, Paul)
SOURCES: CF 42–3 • HT 449 • BE 600, 674 • OGLESBY 40–1

RITCHIE, JAMES L., State Department passport officer. According to author Paris Flammonde, "On October 23, 1963, in the wake of Oswald's trip to Mexico City to apply unsuccessfully for visas to Cuba and the USSR... Ritchie... received a wire dated October 22, 1963, from the CIA informing him of Oswald's visit to the Cuban and Russian Embassies." Ritchie told the WC that, at that point, he had gone over Oswald's entire file and "Made a judgment that there was no passport action to be taken, and marked the file to be filed."
SOURCES: WCH XI, 191 • FLAMMONDE 151

RIVELE, STEVE, assassination researcher. Rivele first revealed the assassination's supposed Corsican connection, involving assassination suspects Lucien Sarti and Christian David. Rivele's material gained public attention when it was included in the 1988 British television documentary, *The Men Who Killed Kennedy*. Rivele is currently living in hiding. (See also David, Christian; Sarti, Lucien

RIVERA, GERALDO, TV personality/journalist. It was on Rivera's show, *Goodnight America* (ABC-TV, March 6, 1975), that the Zapruder film made its national television debut. More than any other single factor, this broadcast was responsible for the formation of the HSCA.
SOURCES: HT 340 • MOORE 92, 101

ROBERTS, CARSON A., lieutenant general, USMC. Former marine navigator Larry Huff alleged that Roberts was in charge of a military investigation into JFK's assassination run out of Camp Smith, Hawaii. The Defense Department denies that any such investigation took place. (See also Huff, Larry)
SOURCES: HSCA XI, 541–49 • HT 273

ROBERTS, CHARLES, a.w. *Newsweek* reporter. Roberts rode in the motorcade in the press bus 100 yards behind JFK's limo. He is the author of *The Truth About the Assassination* (Grosset & Dunlap, 1967), which wholeheartedly supports the WC's conclusions.
SOURCE: FLAMMONDE 288

ROBERTS, DELPHINE, Oswald witness; secretary to Guy Banister. Roberts's statements corroborate other eyewitness evidence that Oswald was a regular visitor to Guy Banister Associates in New Orleans during the summer of 1963. (See also Banister, William Guy)
SOURCES: HSCA Report 145–6 • DAVIS 205 • NORTH 265–6, 276, 412 • HT 289 • OTT 43 • BLAKEY 166–7 • FLAMMONDE 23

ROBERTS, EARLENE, Oswald witness; Oswald's landlady at 1026 North Beckley Street. Roberts told the WC that at about 1:00 P.M. on November 22, 1963, about one-half hour after the assassination, Oswald entered her rooming house in an unusual hurry. He came into the house in his shirtsleeves and left zipping up a jacket. He stayed only a few minutes. During the time Oswald was in the house, she said, a DPD squad car parked in front of the house. In the car were two uniformed policemen. The car honked its horn twice ("tit-tit" was how she described it), then drove off. After Oswald left the house, Roberts saw him standing at the bus stop on the east side of the street. The next time she looked out the window, he was gone.

Officer J. D. Tippit was shot to death 8–12 minutes later, about a mile away. The bus Oswald was supposedly waiting for would not have taken him in the direction of the Tippit murder. Mrs. Roberts first said she thought the police car's number was 207. Car 207 was supposedly at the TSBD at that time. (The last known people in that car were Sergeant Gerald Hill and Officer Jim Valentine of the DPD, and reporter Jim Ewell of the *Dallas Morning News*, all of whom arrived at the assassination scene in it.) After receiving an argument from interrogators, she later listed other squad-car numbers as possibilities as well. The DPD said that no police car was in that vicinity at the time. The WC said that Oswald went from his room to the scene of the Tippit killing on foot, which would require moving at quite a clip. Some have speculated that Oswald got a ride from Officer Tippit, who was driving Car 10. If so, who was the other man in the car?

Roberts's sister, Bertha Cheek, once considered buying a portion of Ruby's Carousel Club and had, on one occasion a few days before the assassination, visited the Carousel. (See also Cheek, Bertha; Johnson, Mr. and Mrs. Arthur; Tatum, Jack)

SOURCES: WR 25, 154, 163, 234, 339 • WCH VI, 434; VII, 439 • HSCA Report 148 •
OGLESBY 68 • DAVIS 210 • RTJ 168–71, 173–4 • BISHOP 181–3, 241, 356, 426, 452 •
DOP 638 • MOORE 61, 87 • FMG I, 92, 97–8, 171, 174, 183; III, 79 • OTT 194 •
BLAKEY 38

ROBERTS, EMORY P., a.w.; SS special agent in charge of the presidential follow-up car. When SS Special Agent John D. Ready hopped off the follow-up car's right front running board at the first sounds of gunfire, Roberts immediately called him back because he didn't think Ready would be able to reach the presidential limousine at the speed it was then traveling (11 m.p.h.). (See also Ready, John D.)
SOURCES: WR 64 • ME 60, 101, 222–3, 253

ROBERTS, RAY, a.w.; (D–Texas). Rode in the same car in the Dallas motorcade as Elizabeth Cabell. The car was on Houston Street during the shooting sequence. Roberts says he smelled gunpowder as he traveled through Dealey Plaza, evidence that at least one of the shots was fired from ground level. (See also Cabell, Elizabeth; Yarborough, Ralph W.)
SOURCES: WR 77 • CF 16

ROBERTSON, MARY JANE, DPD clerk/typist. Robertson told WC that she took a letter on the day of the assassination from Lieutenant Jack Revill—most likely the letter stating that the FBI had known Oswald to be a "Communist" living in Dallas. (See also Revill, Jack)
SOURCE: WCH VII, 404

ROBERTSON, VICTOR F., JR., Ruby witness; Dallas reporter for WFAA radio and television. Robertson told the WC that on November 22, 1963, during the early evening, he saw Ruby in the DPD building trying to open the door to Captain Will Fritz's office, where Oswald was being interrogated, and then heard a voice say, "You can't go in there, Jack." Ruby claims that his shooting of Oswald two days later was spontaneous. (See also Fritz, Will; Rutledge, John)
SOURCES: WCH XV, 347 • COA 126–7 • DAVIS 223

ROBINSON, MARVIN C., a.w. According to an FBI agent's report dated November 23, 1963, "... Robinson advised me that between 12:30 and 1 P.M. ... he crossed the intersection of Elm and Houston streets ... after he crossed Houston Street and was in front of the Texas School Book Depository, a light-colored Nash station wagon suddenly appeared before him. He stated this vehicle stopped and a white male came down the grass-covered incline between the building and the street and entered the station wagon, after which it drove off in the direction of the Oak Cliff section of Dallas." This statement corroborates the observations of Roger Craig and

Richard Randolph Carr, both of whom found their lives made miserable by what they saw. (See also Carr, Richard; Craig, Roger; Paine, Ruth)
SOURCES: WCD 5, p.70 • HSCA App. XIII, 18 • HURT 119–20

ROCCO, EDDIE, Ruby witness; free-lance photographer. Nightclub emcee William D. Crowe Jr., who sometimes worked at Ruby's Carousel Club, claimed to have seen Oswald in the Carousel. The WR explains this apparent contradiction to the official version of the facts this way:

> A possible explanation for Crowe's belief that Oswald's face seemed familiar was supplied by a freelance photographer, Eddie Rocco, who had taken pictures of the Carousel Club for Ruby at about the time Crowe worked there. Rocco produced one of these photographs which depicted a man who might have been mistaken for Oswald by persons having no reason to remember the man at the time they saw him. When shown the Rocco photograph, Crowe said there was as strong a possibility that the man he recalled seeing was the man in the photograph as there was that he was Oswald.

The WR offers no hints as to who the man in the photograph is, but the best guess is that it was Carousel employee Larry Crafard, whose theoretic resemblance to Oswald was used elsewhere by the WC to explain sightings of Ruby and Oswald together. (See also Crafard, Curtis; Crowe, William; Masen, John Thomas; Thornley, Kerry Wendell)
SOURCE: WR 336

RODRIGUEZ, EVARISTO, Oswald witness; bartender at the Habana Bar in New Orleans. Rodriguez's statements corroborate those of Orest Peña, owner of the Habana, that Oswald came into the bar in August 1963 with a man who appeared to be Latin American and who spoke Spanish. (See also Easterling, Robert; Peña, Orest)
SOURCES: WR 301 • WCH XI, 339 • RTJ 339 • BLAKEY 45, 81

RODRIGUEZ, MANUEL ORCARBERRO (aka Orcarberro, Manuel Rodriguez), violent anti-Castro Cuban. Rodriguez was investigated by the Protective Research Division of the SS following the assassination because of the anti-JFK remarks he had made after the Bay of Pigs defeat.

According to author George Michael Evica, whose source is an unnamed FBI informant, Rodriguez was president of Alpha 66. Evica writes: "Rodriguez worked for the Coca-Cola Bottling Company in Cuba until 1958 when he joined Castro. Rodriguez may have been involved in clandestine anti-Castro activity while seemingly cooperating with the revolutionary leader. After Castro came to power, Rodriguez returned to Coca-Cola, probably plotting against the Cuban premier, but soon took refuge in the Brazilian Embassy in Havana, escaping to the United States in November 1960. Rodgriguez obtained a job as a dishwasher in a Miami Beach hotel, staying there until September 1963... In September 1963... Rodriguez registered as an alien in Dallas, Texas, and headed the Alpha 66 anti-Castro operation which met at 3126 Harlendale Avenue"—a home belonging to Jorge Salazar. This address is alleged to have been "the headquarters for the assassination teams in the JFK assassination plot," according to former CIA agent Robert D. Morrow. Morrow testified to the HSCA that Rodriguez "was known to have worked closely with [Mario] Kohly's Free Cuba Committee, [Guy] Banister's Citizens for a Free Cuba Committee, and Loran Hall's funder, the Committee to Free Cuba, etc. . . . " (See also Banister, William Guy; Hall, Loran; Morrow, Robert; Salazar, Jorge)

SOURCES: EVICA 101–4, 109, 120, 123, 144, 318

ROFFMAN, HOWARD, author of *Presumed Guilty* (Fairleigh Dickinson Press, 1975).

SOURCES: HT 78–80 • MOORE 77, 216 • EVICA 10, 87, 93

ROGERS, CHARLES FREDERICK (aka Montoya, Richard; Rojas, Richard), assassination suspect; also the sole suspect in the double homicide of his own mother and father on Father's Day, June 23, 1965, in Houston, Texas. Rogers has been positively identified by Houston police forensic artist Lois Gibson as "Frenchy," the shortest of the three tramps apprehended in Dealey Plaza moments after the assassination, hiding in a railroad car behind the grassy knoll.

According to private detective John R. Craig, Rogers has worked for the CIA since 1956. He is a physicist with graduate training in nuclear physics, a linguist, and was a close personal friend of assassination suspect David Ferrie. He was born in 1921. He graduated from the University of Houston with a degree in physics and was a member of Sigma Phi Sigma fraternity. He was a member of the Civil Air Patrol in the mid-1950s. He was a seismologist for Shell Oil for nine years after World War II.

Officially, Rogers disappeared in 1965 and hasn't been seen since. It is Craig's theory, however, that Rogers is alive and active as a secret agent.

On November 17, 1991, at the JFK Assassination Symposium in Dallas, Texas, Craig said, "He [Rogers] has been active with the CIA since he murdered his parents. The last place we have [placed] him is in 1986 in

Guatemala where he was still working in the Iran-Contra program. He is a pilot and flew for Air America."

Police were alerted to the house of Rogers's parents in June 1965 after a cousin became concerned about Fred and Edwina Rogers' whereabouts. According to Craig:

> When Officer Bullock first opened the refrigerator, he thought that what he had seen was a butchered hog. When Officer Bullock, who was a young patrolman at the time, bent down to look in the crisper, he discovered the severed head of Edwina Rogers. Their [sic] viscera had been removed, diced up, and flushed down the commode. The father's head and hands had been placed in a sack and he was in the process of attempting to dispose of them. The couple was killed on Father's Day. The mother had confronted the son because of her deep concern over phone calls. Charles Rogers had disappeared for several months after the incident in Dallas; he had left the country in a CIA plane to South America. . . . In the house they found a very sophisticated short-wave radio set up and a wire that led up into the attic where there was a half-wave antenna for broadcasting. The radio found upstairs was not a usual short wave but an unusual piece of equipment developed for government use. . . During World War II, Rogers served with the Organization of Naval Intelligence. When the Navy tested him at the start of the war he scored at genius level on an I.Q. test. He spent 30 months in the South Pacific on two ships upon which he was the chief cryptographer. He had been trained in cryptography by Naval Intelligence. He even did work for Shell Oil in that field.

In 1975, Rogers was declared legally dead so that his estate could be probated. Craig continued, "Fred Rogers was also brilliant. He was one of the first men in the country to receive a degree in electrical engineering, which he did at Texas A&M. There were no jobs in that field, however, so he became a salesman and later worked from 1954 to 1963 as a bookie in Galveston under the auspices of [New Orleans mobster] Carlos Marcello."

ROGERS, ERIC, Oswald witness; neighbor of the Oswalds at 4907 Magazine Street in New Orleans. Rogers told the WC that he never actually met Oswald, but did see the Oswalds move out. He said that once a Latino man came looking for Oswald when he wasn't home.
SOURCE: WCH XI, 460

ROGERS, PHILLIP A., researcher who—with forensic artist Lois

Gibson and private detective John R. Craig—positively identified the "three tramps" as Charles Frederick Rogers, Chauncy Marvin Holt, and Charles Voyd Harrelson. The identification was made public at the Kennedy Assassination Symposium in Dallas on November 17, 1992. (See also Craig, John R.; Gibson, Lois; Harrelson, Charles; Holt, Chauncy; Rogers, Charles)

ROJAS, RICHARD (See ROGERS, CHARLES FREDERICK)

ROMACK, JAMES E., a.w.; 39 years old; employee of Coordinated Railroad. Romack was standing near the intersection of Houston and Ross streets, 125 yards north of the TSBD. He heard three shots from near the top of the TSBD. Later he "guarded" the TSBD's back door at the request of "the police." He saw no one exit, no one running away.
SOURCES: WCH VI, 277

RORKE, ALEXANDER, JR., suspect. While under oath, Marita Lorenz named Rorke who, according to her, is now dead, as an assassination conspirator. Officially, Rorke died on September 30, 1963. He was flying in a private plane off Mexico's Yucatan Peninsula when the plane disappeared. If this is true, of course, his participation in the assassination would be impossible. (See also Lorenz, Marita)
SOURCES: Hinckle, Warren, and Turner, William, *Deadly Secrets*, Thunder's Mouth Press, 1993, pp. 227–229 • PD 301

ROSE, EARL, Parkland witness; Dallas medical examiner. When the SS announced that it intended to return JFK's body to Washington immediately—thus breaking a Dallas law requiring an immediate, locally performed autopsy in all cases of homicide—Dr. Rose physically attempted to stop the body from being removed. This started a vulgar shouting and shoving match (which took place in front of Jackie Kennedy) that Dr. Rose lost.

Dr. Rose also served on the HSCA's panel of medical experts, whose conclusions about JFK's wounds and the shots that caused them basically agreed with the WC.
SOURCES: WCE 22–78 • OGLESBY 40 • ME 110–1, 163, 228

ROSE, GUY F., DPD detective; partner of Detective Richard Stovall. Rose was one of the first policemen to interrogate Oswald at the police station following his arrest. He says that when he asked the prisoner his name, he replied, "Alex Hidell." Later, when Rose and Stovall went to the Paine home in Irving, where Marina Oswald had been living, at about 3:00 P.M. November 22, they found the rolled-up blanket in the garage that

Marina told them held her husband's rifle. (See also Moore, Henry; Paine, Michael; Paine, Ruth; Stovall, Richard)
SOURCES: WR 124, 167 • WCH VII, 227; XXV, 222 • BISHOP 224, 275–9, 334–5, 342, 367–8, 378, 419, 446–7

ROSELLI, JOHNNY, Ruby witness; suspicious death; organized crime figure; assassination informant. After agreeing to testify to the Senate and speaking to columnist Jack Anderson, Roselli was found garroted, stabbed, and dismembered, floating in an oil drum off the coast of Florida in July 1976. Roselli had said that Ruby was "one of our boys" and that Ruby had killed Oswald to silence him. According to William Scott Malone in *New Times*, (January 23, 1978) Roselli met twice with Ruby in Miami in the autumn of 1963. Roselli may have known Ruby as early as 1933, when both had dealings with Santa Anita Racetrack in Los Angeles. (See also Edwards, Sheffield; Maheu, Robert; Thornley, Kerry)
SOURCES: HSCA Report 114–6, 173, 246 • BELIN 104, 107, 114 • COA, many • HT, many • OTT 76–7, 287, 301, 316 • BLAKEY, many • EVICA, many • ME 132, 185 • OGLESBY 73 • DAVIS, many • NORTH 116–7, 131, 171–2 • KANTOR 32–3, 111, 131, 135–6, 211–2

ROSS, BARNEY (né Rasofsky, Barney), Ruby witness and childhood friend in Chicago. WWII hero and former welterweight boxing champion; Ross was a defense witness at Ruby's murder trial. He testified that, when young, Ruby frequently had tantrums and was very easily aroused. Ross said that Ruby's childhood was spent in a grim environment and that, despite the squalor, Ruby was considered honest and reputable. After Ruby's conviction, Ross worked with a group to raise funds for Ruby's substantial legal bills.
SOURCES: WCE 1244, 1261, 1288, 1322 • GERTZ 51, 116–7, 145 • BISHOP 445 • DOP 7, 33, 207, 249, 369, 390, 413, 505, 531, 592 • BLAKEY 283 • KANTOR 92, 98

ROSS, HENRIETTA M., Parkland witness; operating-room technician. Ross guarded the hallway. She told WC that the last she saw of Connally's stretcher, it was being pushed up toward room 3, which would leave it in the appropriate position to have the "magic bullet" found on it.
SOURCE: WCH VI, 123

ROSSI, JOSEPH, Ruby witness and friend. Rossi is originally from Chicago, but claims not to have known Jack back "in the old days." He last saw Ruby on November 20, 1963, when Jack asked him his opinion of the "twist board" he was attempting to sell. Rossi told the WC, "Ruby was well known by the police. He was a friend to them."
SOURCE: WCH XV, 235

ROUSSEL, HENRY J., JR., Oswald witness; USMC acquaintance.

Roussel was stationed for "three or four months" with Oswald in MACS-9. He told the WC, "I recall no serious political remarks on the part of Oswald. On occasion, however, Oswald when addressing other Marines, would refer to them as 'Comrade.' It seemed to me . . . that Oswald used this term in fun . . . [He] complained about the orders he was given, but no more than did the average Marine . . . [I thought he was] quite intelligent . . . I do not recall Oswald's having any dates other than the one I arranged for him with my aunt . . . " Roussel's aunt was Rosaleen Quinn, an attractive New Orleans stewardess who was studying Russian with a Berlitz tutor for the State Department's foreign-language exam. (See also Quinn, Rosaleen)
SOURCES: WCH VIII, 320 • AO 97 • LEGEND 87

ROUX, MICHEL (See SOUETRE, JEAN)

ROWLAND, ARNOLD LOUIS and BARBARA, a.w. The Rowlands were standing at the west entrance of the Dallas County Records Building on Houston Street, about 150 feet from the sixth floor of the TSBD. Rowland told FBI agents that at 12:15 P.M., 15 minutes before the assassination, he saw a man with a "high-powered rifle" standing about five feet from the southwest corner window, on the other side of the building from the "sniper's nest." Rowland, who had better than $^{20}/_{20}$ vision, described the man as 140 to 150 lbs., light-complected, with short-cropped dark hair. He was wearing an unbuttoned light-colored shirt over a T-shirt and dark slacks. In the "sniper's-nest" window, Rowland saw a second man, black, about 55 years old, practically bald and very thin. That man was there until five minutes before the assassination. Rowland assumed the men were SS agents. When the shots were fired, he ran in the direction of the grassy knoll with everyone else. Rowland's wife, Barbara, could not corroborate what her husband had seen. She is nearsighted and was not wearing her glasses. (Why would someone go to a presidential motorcade without glasses? • See also Arnold, Carolyn; Henderson, Ruby; Walther, Carolyn)
SOURCES: WR 232–5 • WCH II, 165; VI, 177 • RTJ 94–8, 102, 232, 384, 395–7 • BISHOP 128 • CF 20, 50, 329 • HT 140, 175, 228 • FMG III, 64 • OTT 92, 94 • DAVIS 195–6, 209, 459 • NORTH 377–8

ROWLEY, JAMES J., chief, SS. Rowley was in Washington, D.C., at the time of the assassination. (See also Hepburn, James)
SOURCES: WR 350, 426–8, 439, 443 • BE, many • BLAKEY 71, 152 • WCH V, 449 • BISHOP, many • DOP 61, 141, 155, 362, 384, 390, 411, 545, 572 • HT 148 • ME 60, 219–20, 234, 252–3 • DAVIS 271, 286, 360, 441 • NORTH 102, 458, 596

RUBENSTEIN, FANNIE, mother of Jack Ruby. She reportedly suffered

from mental illness and had a near-lifelong delusion that a fishbone was caught in her throat. She died in a mental hospital.
  SOURCE: GERTZ 117, 409–10

RUBENSTEIN, HYMAN, elder brother of Jack Ruby. After Ruby killed Oswald, Hyman, speaking for the family, said, "Our brother did this for only one reason—he's a good patriotic American, and he got carried away."
  SOURCES: WR 317, 342 • WCH XV, 1 • COA 75, 77–8, 89, 240 • GERTZ 117–8, 124, 145, 147, 523 • BISHOP 404 • BLAKEY 282, 284–5, 287, 305, 317–8 • FLAMMONDE 164

RUBY, EARL, younger brother of Jack. Earl lived in Detroit, Michigan, at the time of the assassination. After Jack killed Oswald, Earl said that Jack was always quick-tempered and overemotional and that he killed Oswald because he was "almost aggressively patriotic." In 1991, Earl Ruby sold the gun that had killed Lee Harvey Oswald at an auction to an unnamed New Jersey collector for $220,000. In New York City, on February 13, 1992, Ruby sold the same collector Jack's size 7 gray Cavanaugh hat for $12,100 and Ruby's black wingtip Florsheim shoes for $1,320.
  SOURCES: WR 341, 346 • WCH V, 181; XIV, 504 • HSCA Report 159 • EVICA 225 • GERTZ, many • MOORE 87 • BLAKEY 282–5, 287, 303–4, 325–7, 338

RUBY, JACK LEON (né Rubenstein, Jack "Sparky"); Oswald's killer; suspicious death; assassination suspect. Ruby was born on March 25, 1911, in Chicago and grew up in Chicago around mobsters, making money as a youngster running numbers for Al Capone through Frank Nitti. At the time of the assassination, Ruby was living with George Senator at 323 South Ewing Street in the Oak Cliff section of Dallas. Ruby was convicted of Oswald's murder and sentenced to death. Just before his appeal began (January 1967), Ruby died of cancer. He told family members that he had been "injected with cancer cells."

When Ruby's lawyers were preparing his initial defense on charges of murder with malice, they asked Jack to write down his experiences during the period November 22–24, 1963. Here, verbatim (with some explanatory notes in brackets), is what Jack wrote:

I. 11/22/63
  11:00 A.M. FRI. Went to Tony Zoppi office to pick up Weimar brochure.
  11:10 Talked to salesman about the owner of the Castaway Club.
  12:00 Saw John Newman [Newnam] at the [*Dallas Morning*] news talked to him for few minutes, and then saw different people running

back and forth, and went to watch the television set, and then heard the tragic news.

Called Eva [his sister] at home and she was hysterical John was standing nearby and knew Eva was crying so put the receiver to John's ear. Phone was ringing constantly and people were complaining about [the anti-JFK] ad in paper—Then John Newman comment to someone that they shouldn't have taken the ad, and he said that were his superiors and their was nothing he could do about it, and he said to someone standing nearby "that you saw the fellow when he paid for part of the ad.—called Chicago spoke to [his other sister] Eileen [Kaminsky].

II. Then I called Andy [Armstrong] at the club and told him I would be there in a little while. Left the news and drove back to the club, told Andy to call everyone that we wouldn't be open tonite. Larry [Crafard] was their [sic] also.

Called Alice [Nichols] at her office, and left RI2-6189 for her to call back.

Phoned Ralph Paul.

Called Al Druber in Calif. and apologized for not sending dog, and started to cry and had to hang up.

Delivery boy from Gibson's came by and I paid for some records and gave him some cards to take back with him.

2:30 P.M. Went to Rita delicattessen and bought quite a few (groceries) to take to Eve [Eva],

Arrived at Eves house and received a call from Andy to call Don Saf[f]ran, I called Don and he asked me if we were going to close, that the Cabena & Century Rooms were closing, and that he asked the other two clubs and didn't know yet, and I answered that I've made up my mind to close, and I didn't have to ask if anyone else was closing. That I already had decided to close by around 1:30 P.M. and then he asked me about Sat. and I said I didn't know yet, he said he would be there for another 45 min. that I could phone him back, and I hung up, and I said to her that were going to close, and I called Don back immediately and told him we were going to close Fri. & Sat. & Sun. and that it didn't take me long to make up my mind to decide. Then I called back again and spoke to Mr. Porter and to told him to tell Don that I wish we wouldn't tell the other clubs what I was going to do, that let them decide for themselves whether or not they should close.

I called the Morning news and the composing room, and [told] them to change my ad.

I called Dr. Jacobson about going to Synogaugue and asked what time service would be, also I called the synogaugue to inquire the time of the services.

7:30 Then had gone home to dress and go to the services. Stayed for services and said greetings to Rabbi and talked about Eve.

9:30 P.M. Then went into reception room and had some refreshments and said hello Joe Colman, and Elaine.

11:15 From their went to Phils Delecatteson told counter man to make up sandwiches—called Sims of homicide, if he wanted sandwiches, and he said they were winding everything up and was going to tell the boys about my thoughts for them.

11:30 Then wanted to find phone number for K.L.I.F., because I wanted to bring sandwiches there.

Looked through my clothing and every place I could think of but couldn't find Russ' *number*.

Tried to look for Russ Knight's number but couldn't find it, then called information, but somehow couldn't remember Russ's real name. However, I dialed information and tried anyway, and mentioned that his name was Roberts and that he lived on Northwest Highway, but she couldn't help me.

Then I decided to call the Gordon McLendon home, and asked a young lady if anyone else was at home, and told her my name, but she said there wasn't anyone else at home, and I asked her name, and I think she said Christine, and told her I wanted to bring sandwiches to the station and could she get me the number, and she said her mother already had brought some food, then she left and gave me a Riverside number which was discontinued. I had made so many calls that the woman behind the counter asked if I would like to use the business phone, but I told her I was through.

The counter man helped me with the sandwiches, and thanked him for making such wonderful sandwiches for a good cause, and told him if he ever wanted to come down to the club he was welcome.

Drove down to the station to look for Joe Long to try to find the number so I could get into the radio station, parked car with dog on corner of Harvard & Commerce, and thought I would run up for a minute just to get number.

12:00 MID. Taken the elevator to 2nd or 3rd fl. and asked policemen if he knew Joe Long from K.L.I.F., and he let me go by.

Ran into some officers I knew, and even had asked a police-officer if he could help me, and he called out loudly throught the hall, but no answer to the page.

At different intervals I would spot check and ask someone if they were Joe Long.

Then as I was standing in the hallway they brought the prisoner

[Oswald] out, that was the first time I had ever seen him, I don't recall if he was with Capt. Fritz or Chief Curry or both.

Then the reporters shouted if there was a better place they could gather so as to have room for all the reporters.

The authorities said they would go down to the assembly room in the basement, and that is where I had gone too.

They brought the prisoner out and he mumbled something unintelligable and it wasn't [long] before they had taken him back again.

Then Henry Wade started to answer many questions whether or not he was the man.

Then everyone left the room, and two fellows walked by as I was walking out of the room, one I had recognized who had worked at a service station across from the Vegas Club., but I asked the other fellow if he was Joe Long, and he asked why, and I said I had some sandwiches to bring to K.L.I.F. and I couldn't get in, unless I had the right phone number and he said we are from K.B.O.X. what about them, and I said next time, and he did give me the number, and I spoke to the other fellow for a minute and was surprised he was working for radio, I believe his name was Sam.

I went around the desk and dialed the number, and spoke to some disk jockey by name of Ken, and I told him I had sandwiches for the boys, and he was very [pleased] about it, but then I suddenly said you would like to talk to Henry Wade and to have his tape ready, and he became very excited and said definitely yes. Wade was on the phone talking to New York I believe, to another radio station I surely though[t] he wouldn't object to talking to this other disk-jockey, and I shouted to Mr. Wade just as he was about to hang up the receiver, or perhaps they were waiting for someone to come to the phone, and I did get him to leave and he did talk to this fellow, when they had finished I got on the phone again and he was thrilled and didn't know how to thank me enough, and said if I would leave immediately they would leave the door open for me.

As I was leaving and walked up one flight of stairs, I saw Russ Knight talking to someone and he seemed to be asking for information. What he was asking was where the assembly room was, and then he saw me, and I immediately told him that I got an interview with Henry Wade for his station and replied that is what he come for, and I said follow me, and taken him to Henry Wade and shouted here is Russ Knight Henry and he answered Oh! The Wierd Beard!!!

Then I left and drove over to K.L.I.F. but the door was closed, because I had taken too much time getting there. Waited for Rus[s] for about 15 minutes and we both had gone up, he was so happy for what I had done that he definitely was going to tell Gordon McLendon what I had accomplished.

They started to work in splicing the tape in bringing both interviews together somehow. They called the New York and told them they had a story for them.

We all started in on the sandwiches and soft drinks, and they certainly enjoyed them.

We talked about a number of things, and I mentioned how much respect I had for Gordon, that he was the only one who came out with an editorial after the incident with Adlai Stevenson. Russ Knight had agreed with me. Mentioned that the prisoner resembled a very popular movie actor [Paul Newman]. Also that he had a scratch on his forehead and a little discoloring around his eye.

2:00 Russ had made the 2:00 A.M. news bulletin and put the Henry Wade interview on the air.

Russ and I had left and we spoke on the way to my car, and I mentioned that I had some literature I picked up at the H. L. Hunt's exhibit at the Texas States Invention at Market Hall. Told him he could have some, that I was certain I had copy for myself. Also mentioned the way Hunt was told he could pull out of the New York's World Fair.

Said good nite to Russ and drove on...

Went to the Times Herald to bring a twist board I had promised to Pat Godosh for some time. Went to composing room and demonstrated board, a few of printers gathered around and they enjoyed my agile way of doing it.

2:30 Then the subject came with a woman who works in a little anteroom about the big ad the news had taken, and I remarked don't worry, the phones were ringing off the desks, and people were cancelling subscriptions, and ads from all over the United States.

Told Pat to put my ad in that I was closing.

I had taken the elevator down and spoke to the nite watchman at the door for a few minutes, and got in my car and drove home, and then awakened George [Senator], and he said he had seen my ads in the newspaper that I was closing for three days, and we talked about the tragedy, and he was heartbroken too!

3:30 A.M. I made him [Senator] get out of bed and told him I wanted him to go with me, and called Larry [Crafard] at the club got him out of bed and asked him if he knew how to work a polaroid camera, and he said yes, I told him to be down in the garage in ten minutes with the camera and bring plenty of film and bulbs. George and I got to the garage and he wasn't there, and I became impatient thinking that he may have gone back to bed again, and had nite man call him, and he said he would be right down.

4:00 A.M. We drove to E. Ross and Expressway and took photos of a billboard that read

IMPEACH EARL WARREN
WRITE TO BELTHAM
BOX 1757 MASS.

The above sign was above another sign that read POTTER'S WROUGHT IRON, Located somewhere on Expressway.

We had taken three snapshots of same, then stopped at post-office asked man how does it happen that they have given a box to person placing an ad of that sort in the newspaper. He said he didn't have a thing to do with it. He went and checked again and said their was a person and that is all he could answer me. I went to look at the amount of mail that Box 1792, and tried to make certain I would remember if the contents would be removed the next time I'd stop by. George was with me, and Larry was sitting in the car.

From there we had gone to Habb's Coffee Shop in the Southland Hotel, they had some coffee and I had some juice. I spoke to the owner for about a minute. I don't recall what I had said to him, perhaps about hunting?

However, when I got back to the apartment I decided I would go to bed.

It wasn't long before I got a phone call, and it was Larry, and I asked him what did he want very angrily, and he wanted to know what kind of dog food he should buy, then I asked what time it was, and when [he] said 8:30 A.M. I bawled the heck out of him for getting me up at this early hour forgetting that I had mentioned that I wasn't going to bed, and then hung up on him. 8:30 A.M. SAT.

11:00 A.M. That same morning I phoned Andy or he may have called me and he said that Larry had left, that he had given the key to Mac at the garage and to tell me thanks for everything, and later Andy said that he took seven dollars from the cash register, and I felt quite sad and guilty because [he] was a wonderful person.

That same morning I think George also had stayed in the apartment and watched television, and we watched all of the dignitaries pull up in their limousines to go and pay their last respects, and my heart was just broke, because of all these wonderful people. And how they grieved for their friend and beloved president.

Then I watched on television a memorial given by some synogaugue and a Rabbi Saligman [Seligman] of New York for Sabbath services in honor of the late President Kennedy, and it just tore me apart when he said to think that our president had untold courage to combat anything and everywhere and then to be struck down by some enemy from behind.

I really don't know what time I left the apartment, and Andy said that he phoned me or I phoned him.

I drove towards town and either had gone to the club first or had gone to look at the wreaths?

I pulled my car north on Houston St. past Elm St. to park my car, their [there] was a policeman on that corner guiding the heavy traffic, and I walked down Elm St. toward the underpass and saw officer Chaney their [there], I've known him for many years, and had asked him which one of the windows was used and he pointed or described it to me. We talked for a few minutes and then I couldn't talk anymore and had to walk off because I was choking and holding my tears back.

Walked up on the north bank of Elm to look at the wreaths and started to cry when I read the car[d] on one that read "We Grieve For You."

Then I said to myself that I was going to send flowers.

Walked a little further down Elm closer to the underpass and started to make it across the other side where the Plaza is located so as to see the rest of the wreaths, but the traffic was bearing down to[o] fast and [I] had to wait a minute. However, I was determined to get across regardless of what would happen to me, and I finally dashed across recklessly, and people driving must have thought I was crazy, because the cars were speeding very fast at that point.

Saw the wreaths on the Plaza and started to cry again. Crossed over to the other side of Houston St., and walked north to cross over Elm.

As a [I] reached the other side of Elm and about 50 ft. from the corner, I ran into Wes Wise parked in a K.R.L.D. News car, and stopped to talk and he mentioned that I get a scoop for K.L.I.F. and I said it was just a little something that happened, and didn't talk more about it.

3:00 P.M.? Got into my car and must have circled back either to the club first or had gone to Sol's Turf Lounge, I had gone their [there] to look up my accountant Abe Kleinman went in and heard a lot of comment about the big ad in the news, and they were complaining why a newspaper would take such an ad. Mr. Kleinman was their [there] and jewelry designer by name of Be[l]loc[c]hio. It became quite a discussion, and heard Belochio say that he is leaving Dallas and was very emphatic about it, that his mind was made. I jumped all over him telling him that Dallas was good enough for him when he was making his living here, and now he wants to quit and run. I kept repeating don't say that because you will start something we won't be able to stop.

Then I had taken out my three photos of impeach Earl Warren, and he could not believe that it could happen here, and he became very beligerent that he wanted one and I practically had to fight him off from taking one from me. I said I've got a special purpose for these. I'm going to give them to Gordon McLendon so he can run an editorial on soon. He insisted that I show the picture to a fellow sitting at the bar, because he knew the Potter's and surely they wouldn't allow something like that. Abe Kleinman was witness to all this. SAT. 3:30 P.M.

From there we went to sister Val's [Eva?] apartment, and told her I wanted to send some flowers to the Plaza, but she said not to have the same place when I ordered for her when she was at Caston Hosp. The nurse told her one of plants or flowers were stale.

Then I told Eve I was tired after watching television for awhile and took the phone with me to her bedroom and called Russ Knight and told him I had more pictures and he said that was swell to hold them for awhile, that this wasn't the time for it. That he would tell Gordon about it. Their [there] was also something about Leonard Woods and Eve and I spoke about my visiting Chicago 3 days.

Then I must have called Stanley Kaufman and also told him about the photos, and he thought that was wonderful as to what I was going to do with them. I believe he told me that some persons checked about the person that placed the ad. Didn't have any residence in Dallas that their [there] wasn't any such person in this area. I told him how I checked the box number etc.

SAT. Then I think I had taken a nap, and awakened and then had gone down to the club, and Andy was cleaning, and he thought he was going to get off early, and I insisted that he will have to stay until 9:00 P.M. and gave him an ultimatum that it would have to be that way. I may have called Ralph Paul and told him we were closing.

I called the Adolphus Hotel and asked for Joe Petersen, they said he left town for three days, they gave me the phone number in Galveston and I called and talked to Joe or Breck [Wall]? and told them that I had closed for three days and they said they also wanted to get away.

SAT. 8:00 P.M. Had gone back to my apartment and showered and shaved. Phoned Andy and told him about the new girl and to go over and catch the show over at the Colony Club, and to see about the audition show and I would give them their money back.

10:20 SAT. Phoned Eve and asked her if she was watching

television.

10:30 P.M. Drove to town and drove out to Bob Horton at the Pogo Club, and a girl came over and asked me what I would like and I ordered a coke but didn't feel like drinking it, I sat for about 15 or 20 minutes, and didn't want anyone to recognize me, because I didn't want to explain to anyone why, if I didn't want to dance or to have a drink. I sort of sat in a shell and didn't want to be recognized. Bob Horton came over and apologized saying he didn't know I was there or he would have been there sooner. 11:00 P.M.

We talked and he started to explain why he remained open etc. I stopped him and didn't want to hear any of it. That was his business.

Told him that my type of entertainment was different than his, my [mine] was burlesque, and I wouldn't want the performers to put on our type of show at a time like this. Anyway, I liked Bob too much as a friend to make him feel uneasy in my presence. SAT.

He gave me $25.00 and I asked him for what, and he explained and I refused to take it but he insisted. Said good-nite and drove downtown and pulled into the garage asked the attendant something and then drove to my apartment. SAT.

12:40 A.M. Phoned Eve and told her something asked why she didn't go to bed. SUN.

SUN. 10:00 A.M. Received call from Lynn [Karen "Little Lynn" Bennett Carlin], said she had to have some money, told her that I don't have to let her draw money, that all I'm obligated to do was to pay her salary, but she said she had to pay her rent, and then it dawned on me that we are going to be closed tonite, and thought she may desperately need some money and then I said how can I get the money to you, and I think she said she will come to my apartment but I certainly didn't want that because of her supposed to be husband, and that is all I would need for them to know where I live. I took time to ask her how to send it, because all I know her by was Little Lynn, I think I wrote her name out and spelled it Karren Bennet, and asked her if she knew where the Western Union was in Ft. Worth. By the way she said she was broke, and didn't have a penny, and I asked her if she get it somewhere else, and she could return it the next day, and then I think I asked her where husband was and I thought he would let her have the money but I think she said he was out of town.—Anyway I told her it would be in care of Will Call Western ($25.00) George Senator was there during all this. SUN. A.M.

Then left the apartment and spoke to a neighbor for a minute— Curtiss?—about some fences I promised him then left to go to Western Union to send money to Lynn. 10:45 A.M.

Was always in the habit of taking the freeway straight down Commerce St., but since the tragedy have been going by to see the wreaths, and remember their [there] would be more traffic on Main St., because it is where their [there] is more activity going on than Commerce St., and if I was in a hurry to get anywhere I certainly would have stayed on Commerce, especially Sunday, the street is dead. 10:45 A.M.

Anyway I passed the intersection where I was to turn left and then right on Industrial, so I could pass where the wreaths were and at the same time drive towards the Western Union. I backed up in reverse, so as to make correct turn.

10:50 Did pass where all the wreaths were and then passed the County Jail on the left and saw the largest crowd I had ever seen there, and thought to myself that they already have transferred the prisoner, and continued to drive on the Western Union, and pulled in to a parking lot on the left. Waited my turn, because the clerk was waiting on someone else, and I filled out a form to send money. When I passed by the station, I looked down the ramp to my right and saw a lot of people down in the basement so when I finished with the Western, I had walked west and down the ramp just out of curiosity. When I walked by to go down the ramp I saw this officer guide a car out of the upper portions of the ramp, and thought the officer was there only to guide the cars coming out.

I continued *walking* down the ramp and just hit the *bottom* part of the ramp. That is all I remember...

In June 1964, Chief Justice Earl Warren and Congressman Gerald Ford personally traveled to Dallas to question Ruby in the county jail. Throughout the interrogation, the questioners behaved like men afraid that they would hear too much, while Ruby acted desperate to talk, but afraid for his life. Ruby told them:

Is there any way to get me to Washington? [Warren says no.] I don't think I will get a fair representation with my counsel, Joe Tonahill, I don't think so. I would like to request that I go to Washington and you take all the [polygraph?] tests that I have to take. It is very important... Gentlemen, unless you get me to Washington, you can't get a fair shake out of me. If you understand my way of talking, you have to bring me to Washington to get the tests... I want to tell the truth, and I can't tell it here. I can't tell it here. Does that make sense to you?... Gentlemen, my life is in danger here. Not with my guilty plea of execution... Do I sound sober enough to you as I say this?... I will tell you gentlemen, my whole family is in jeopardy. My sisters, as to their lives... There is a certain organization here, Chief Justice Warren, if it takes my life at this moment to say it, and [Dallas County Sheriff] Bill Decker said be a man and say it, there is a John Birch Society right now in activity, and [Major General] Edwin Walker is one of the top men of this organization—take it for what it is worth, Chief Justice Warren... Unfortunately for me, for me giving the people the opportunity to get in power, because of the act I committed, has put a lot of people in jeopardy with their lives. Don't register with you, does it? [Warren says, "No, I don't understand that."] Would you rather I just delete what I said and just pretend that nothing is going on?... Well, I said my life, I won't be living long now. I know that my family's lives will be gone... You can get more out of me. Let's not break up too soon... Mr. Bill Decker said be a man and speak up. I am making a statement now that I may not live the next hour when I walk out of this room.

According to author Seth Kantor, these are the ten facts that need to be investigated further in order to obtain a full understanding of Ruby's role during the assassination weekend:

1. Leading up to the assassination, Ruby was in debt and seeking money. 2. On the afternoon of Kennedy's assassination, Dallas bank officer Bill Cox saw Ruby with several thousand dollars in hand at the bank, but Ruby moved none of it into or out of his account. 3. Ruby's best sources of money were in organized crime and he met privately with syndicate paymaster Paul Rowland Jones... only hours before President Kennedy reached Texas. 4. Organized crime had a known history of control inside the [DPD]. 5. When Ruby sprang at... Oswald, he came from behind a policeman... [W.J.] Blackie Harrison. 6. Harrison had been in position at two different times that Sunday morning to let Ruby know by telephone precisely what the plans were for moving the prisoner Oswald. 7. Ruby left his apartment on the route which led to the silencing of Oswald, after Harrison was in position to make the second and final telephone call to the apartment. 8. Harrison and his partner, detective L. D. Miller, became strangely reluctant witnesses. Miller acted more like a suspect than a witness, refusing at first to become a sworn witness—when all he had done was to have coffee with Harrison on the morning of Oswald's murder. 9. The evidence shows Ruby lied about his entry to the [DPD]

basement. 10. Ruby then tried to conceal his private meeting with police officer Harry N. Olsen soon after Oswald was arraigned as a cop killer.

From prison, Ruby told a reporter that he had taken 30 Dexedrine and antibiotic tablets before shooting Oswald. "They stimulate you," he said.

According to Penn Jones Jr., "Ruby had $2,000 on his person [at the time of his arrest] and the authorities found $10,000 in their search of his apartment. The statement by the authorities concerning money in Ruby's car was: 'The trunk was full of money.'... In a storeroom reserved for Jack Ruby at his apartment house, the police found a case of hand grenades, several M16 rifles, a Browning automatic rifle, and several thousand rounds of ammunition."

Among Ruby's close friends was John M. Crawford, who died in a mysterious plane crash near Huntsville, Texas, on Tuesday, April 15, 1969. One of Crawford's lifelong friends was Buell Wesley Frazier, Oswald's coworker at the TSBD who gave Oswald a ride to work on the morning of the assassination. Again, according to Jones, "several high ranking telephone people in Dallas hurried to the police shortly after Jack Ruby killed Lee Harvey Oswald, with phone company records proving that Ruby and Oswald knew each other... At Dallas police headquarters, the men were told to go home and forget it. All the phone company men were hastily transferred out of Dallas."

On February 27, 1964, FBI Director J. Edgar Hoover wrote a memo to WC General Counsel J. Lee Rankin, saying, "Ruby had been contacted nine times by the FBI in 1959, from March 11 to October 2, 'to furnish information.'" Hoover asked that the WC keep this secret, and they agreed to do so.

In letters smuggled out of jail, Ruby said LBJ was the mastermind behind the assassination. Ruby wrote:

First you must realize that the people here want everyone to think I am crazy...isn't it strange that Oswald...should be fortunate enough to get a job at the [TSBD] two weeks before...Only one person could have had that information, and that man was Johnson...because he is the one who was going to arrange the trip...The only one who gained by the shooting...They also planned the killing, by they I mean Johnson and the others...you may learn quite a bit about Johnson and how he has fooled everyone...

(See also all Ruby witnesses; all o.k.w.; Johnson, Lyndon B.)
SOURCES: All texts

RUBY, SAMUEL DAVID, brother of Jack, washing machine repairman; lived in Dallas; told the WC that he hadn't seen Jack for four weeks when Jack shot Oswald. Sam said he was not in business with Jack and only spoke to him on the phone regarding family matters.
SOURCES: WCH XIV, 488 • GERTZ 17, 117, 166, 523 • BISHOP 434

RUDNICKI, JAN GAIL "NICK," Bethesda witness; assistant to autopsist J. Thornton Boswell. Rudnicki recalls no entrance wound in the back of JFK's head.
SOURCE: HT2 203-8

RUSK, DEAN, secretary of state. Rusk told the WC: "I have seen no evidence that would indicate to me that the Soviet Union considered that it had an interest in the removal of President Kennedy or that it was in any way involved in the removal of President Kennedy."
SOURCES: WR 237–9, 286, 350, 432 • WCH V, 363 • HSCA Report, many • FLAMMONDE 263 • NORTH 241 • BE 37 • OTT 293 • BLAKEY 18–9, 30, 61, 112, 133, 136–7, 139

RUSSELL, DICK, author, *The Man Who Knew Too Much* (Carroll & Graf, 1992). Book focuses on intelligence agent Richard Case Nagell and his knowledge of the JFK assassination. (See also Masen, John Thomas; Nagell, Richard Case

RUSSELL, HAROLD, t.k.w.; suspicious death; employee of Reynolds Motor Company on East Jefferson Boulevard. With his coworkers, Russell saw a man fleeing south on Patton Avenue toward Jefferson with a handgun in his hand moments after hearing shots. He could not identify the man. According to author Penn Jones Jr., Russell died in police custody in February 1967, after going berserk at a party screaming that he was going to be killed. According to the *Spotlight*, "Russell . . . was beaten to death by a policeman wielding a revolver on July 23, 1965, in Sulphur, Oklahoma."
SOURCES: WR 159 • WCH VII, 594 • RTJ 266-7 • GERTZ 528 • HT 129, 139 • FMG II, 4, 6-7, 35

RUSSELL, RICHARD B., member of the WC (D–Georgia); senator; chairman of the Senate Armed Services Committee. Senator Russell was a no-show commissioner, and was present to hear only 6 percent of the testimony. Among the seven members of the WC, Russell had the highest absentee rate. Russell strongly disapproved of the "single-bullet" theory and threatened not to sign the report if the theory was included.

SOURCES: HSCA Report 256 • EVICA, many • ME 12 • OGLESBY 12, 27 • NORTH 398, 436, 447, 473, 503, 517 • PD 48, 56, 66–7 • BELIN 13, 48 • RTJ 7, 23, 312–4, 367, 370–1 • COA 211 • DOP 572 • HT 67, 181, 310 • MOORE 17 • BE 136, 453 • OTT 14 • BLAKEY 24, 27–8, 73–4, 266

RUSSO, PERRY RAYMOND, Oswald witness; longtime friend of assassination suspect David Ferrie; 21 years old at the time of the assassination. Russo became a key witness in Jim Garrison's prosecution of Clay Shaw for conspiracy to assassinate JFK in 1967 when he positively identified a photo of Clay Shaw as "Clay Bertrand," a man he had overheard discussing plans to assassinate JFK. During the Shaw investigation, Russo was working as an insurance agent for Equitable.

According to Garrison, "Russo overheard Shaw and Ferrie engaging in a discussion of the prospective murder of John Kennedy." Under close medical supervision, Garrison had Russo hypnotized and given sodium pentothal (a truth serum), both of which revealed that Russo was telling the truth. The meeting, Russo said, took place "somewhere around the middle of September 1963" in David Ferrie's New Orleans apartment. Also at the meeting initially were several anti-Castro Cubans and a man who was introduced to him as "Leon Oswald." According to Garrison, "The talk turned to the possibility of assassinating Fidel Castro. This conversation was speculative and strongly anti-Kennedy... [After the Cubans left, leaving Bertrand, Ferrie, Russo, and "Oswald" alone] Ferrie, Russo said, was pacing back and forth, saying that they could get rid of Kennedy and blame it on Castro. Then there could be an excuse to invade Cuba... All they had to do was get Kennedy out in the open... Ferrie emphasized that 'triangulation of crossfire' was the way to do it."

At the Clay Shaw trial, Russo's testimony was—apparently successfully—discredited by the defense attorneys with claims that Garrison had hypnotized and drugged Russo to get him to say what he did. During cross-examination at the Clay Shaw trial, Russo said:

Dave Ferrie talked about so many things. When he would talk to me, he would give me advice or make statements and he would refer to certain books—certain pages—and advise that I read them... there was some talk of the assassination last summer, but we talked about many things. He talked about a cure for cancer. You name it, he talked about it. I learned not to argue with him. I knew that he knew everything. I believed him. People say to me about Ferrie, "What was he like?" To me, he was a walking encyclopedia... he knew it all... all the answers... why should I question him? That was the way it was. . . . later, after being around David for some time, you didn't question him; he gave you all the answers before a question was necessary. You got out of the habit of asking questions.

Earlier, during direct examination, Russo described the meeting he had attended in September 1963, in Ferrie's apartment. Present were Russo, Ferrie, Shaw (using the name Clay Bertrand), and a man who was introduced as "Leon Oswald":

> . . . Ferrie took the initiative in the conversation, pacing back and forth as he talked. . . [He said] an assassination attempt would have to involve diversionary tactics. . . there would have to be a minimum of three people involved. Two of the persons would shoot diversionary shots and the third. . . would shoot the 'good shot.'. . . [You would have to create] a triangulation of crossfire. . . If there were three people, one of them would have to be sacrificed.

On June 19, 1967, New Orleans ADA Andrew J. Sciambra delivered to Garrison a "memorandum of information" supplied by Russo, which stated that Walter Sheridan and Richard Townley of NBC and magazine writer James Phelan had made attempts to get Russo to desert Garrison and help them "destroy" Garrison and his case. (See also Fatter, Esmond; Ferrie, David; Garrison, Jim; Moffett, Sandra; Shaw, Clay)
 SOURCES: OTT 151–6, 162, 181, 237–8, 275 • FLAMMONDE, many • BLAKEY 48–9, 169 • HOS 240

RUTLEDGE, JOHN, Ruby witness; *Dallas Morning News* reporter. Rutledge saw Ruby in DPD headquarters. According to the WR, Ruby arrived on the third floor of the DPD headquarters near the homicide bureau by about 11:30 P.M. on the evening of the assassination. Ruby was mingling with the many reporters who had congregated in the area, and it was here that he was seen by Rutledge, who gave the following statement:

> I saw Jack and two out-of-state reporters, whom I did not know, leave the elevator door and proceed toward those television cameras, to go around the corner where Captain Fritz's office was. Jack walked between them. These two out-of-state reporters had big press cards pinned on their coats, great big red ones. I think they said "President Kennedy's Visit to Dallas—Press" or something like that. And Jack didn't have one, but the man on either side of him did. And they walked pretty rapidly from the elevator area past the policeman, and

Jack was bent over like this—writing on a piece of paper, and talking to one of the reporters, and pointing to something on the piece of paper, he was kind of hunched over.

(See also Robertson, Victor F.)
SOURCES: WR 317 • NORTH 412

RYAN, MIKE "MICKEY" (aka Pike, Roy William; Pike, Mike), Ruby witness; Ruby's bookkeeper; bartender at the North Park Inn in Dallas. Ryan, husband of Tuesday Ryan (aka Wagner, Ramona), a Carousel stripper; left Dallas on November 30, 1963. Carousel employee Andrew Armstrong told the WC that Ryan had visited Ruby at the Carousel on the night before the assassination. However, Ryan told the WC that he had not seen Ruby for two weeks before JFK's death. (See also Armstrong, Andrew)
SOURCES: WCE 1229, 2322 • COA 80, 115, 260, 422

RYDER, DIAL D., possible Oswald witness; employee of the Irving Sports Shop. Ryder says that two or three weeks before the assassination, a man who identified himself as "Oswald" came into the shop with a rifle that he wanted drilled and tapped so that a telescopic sight could be mounted. The WC might have believed Ryder, especially since the transaction slip still existed with the word "Oswald" written on it, but Ryder said that he had never worked on an Italian rifle like the one Oswald supposedly owned. This meant that either (1) the transaction never occurred; (2) someone posed as Oswald; (3) Oswald owned two guns or (4) Ryder was mistaken about never having worked on an Italian rifle. (See also Greener, Charles)
SOURCES: WR 291–2 • WCH XI, 224 • RTJ 325 • NORTH 344, 427, 445

S

SAFFRAN, DON, Ruby witness; columnist for the *Dallas Times-Herald*. Ruby said he called Saffran from his sister's home, sometime between 5:30 and 7:30 P.M., on November 22, 1963. They discussed whether Ruby should close his nightclubs because of the "tragedy." Ruby hung up and had a brief conversation with his sister, during which he decided he should close his clubs. Ruby then called Saffran back and told him of his decision.
SOURCE: WR 315–6

SAHAKIAN, JUANITA SLUSHER DALE PHILLIPS (aka Barr, Candy), Ruby witness; former stripper; "girlfriend" of mobster and sex blackmailer Mickey Cohen. Between April 1963 and JFK's death, Sahakian received more than five calls from Ruby at her home in Edna, Texas, despite the fact that her parole conditions prohibited her from stripping. (See also Cohen, Mickey)
SOURCE: KANTOR 54

SALAZAR, JORGE, reputed owner of the home at 3126 Harlendale Avenue in Dallas, which was reportedly a hotbed of activity by the Cuban exile anti-Castro organization Alpha 66. (See also Masen, John Thomas; Rodriguez, Manuel)
SOURCE: EVICA 102

SALISBURY, HARRISON E., assistant managing editor, *New York Times*. Salisbury wrote the introduction to the WR, in which he said, because "we had a role in a society which... gave birth to a young man who... became distorted into an assassin... there remains in each of us some communal share of guilt..." For this reason, he believes, the WR will not be seen as "the final word."
SOURCE: WR xv–xxix

SALYER, KENNETH EVERETT, Parkland witness; first-year resident in surgery; 27 years old. Salyer set up the intravenous tube for JFK. He saw a "sucking wound" in JFK's neck and described his head wound as being in the "right temporal region."
SOURCES: WCH VI, 80 • BISHOP 156

SANDERS, DAVID, Parkland witness; orderly. Sanders assisted in the preparation of JFK's body for the coffin.
SOURCES: HT 454 • BE 193, 599

SARTI, LUCIEN, assassination suspect; professional Corsican assassin. A 1988 British television documentary produced by Nigel Turner, *The Men Who Killed Kennedy,* which was nominated for awards but was not aired in the United States until September–October 1991 on the Arts & Entertainment cable television network, named Sarti as the man visible and apparently firing a rifle ("badge man") from behind the wooden fence atop the grassy knoll in computer-enhanced enlargements of a Polaroid photo taken at the moment of the fatal shot by assassination witness Mary Moorman. The documentary based its claims on the statements of two French gangsters, Michel Nicoli and Christian David, who originally gave their story to assassination researcher Steve Rivele. Rivele is currently in hiding.

Sarti was reportedly a reckless killer who was despised even by his colleagues because of the chances he took, and a master of disguise. He reportedly wore a uniform while firing the fatal shot, which would concur with the photographic evidence that the rifleman was wearing a policeman's uniform. (See also David, Christian; Moorman, Mary; Nicoli, Michel; Rivele, Steve)
SOURCE: SUMMERS 523–7

SAUL, alleged code-name of JFK's killer. (See also McDonald, Hugh; White, Roscoe)

SAUNDERS, RICHARD L., a.w.; Ruby witness. Saunders, on the advertising staff of the *Dallas Morning News,* was 100 yards west of the triple underpass outside Dealey Plaza during the shooting. He heard no shots; returned to his office and found Ruby near his desk. Saunders said, "He was virtually speechless, which is quite unusual for Jack Ruby."
SOURCE: WCH XV, 577

SAUVAGE, LEO, French author of *The Oswald Affair* (World Publishing Co., 1966).
SOURCES: MOORE 75, 96, 216 • BE 109, 306 • PD 72

SAWYER, FORREST, ABC-TV news reporter. Sawyer spent two-and-a-half months in Moscow, in a "sterile" room with an interpreter and a notepad, and was allowed the first U.S. access to the many 12-inch-thick volumes of files the KGB has kept on Oswald. According to Sawyer, who presented his report in the ABC-TV show *Nightline,* on November 22, 1991, "Looking at those files, holding Oswald's signed entry and exit visas in my hand... The whole process was a surreal experience. Privately, several ranking KGB officials have reached the conclusion that he [Oswald] could not have acted alone. That he was incapable. And that is based on an incredibly intensive, exhaustive profile based on constant surveillance over 2½ years."

Sawyer's report goes on to say that *all* of Oswald's female companions during his stay in the Soviet Union were KGB agents or informers, that the Soviets allowed Oswald to buy a gun and to join a hunting club so that they could monitor his ability to shoot, and that the apartment he shared in Minsk with his wife Marina was bugged. The Soviets, he said, felt that Oswald was "too badly messed up, clearly not together enough in the head," to have been the lone JFK assassin. (See also Oswald, Marina)

SAWYER, HAROLD, HSCA member; congressman (R-Michigan). Sawyer dissented from the HSCA conclusion that a fourth shot was fired from the grassy knoll because of the absence of sirens on the Dictabelt recording. (See also McLain, H. B.)
SOURCE: BELIN 194–5

SAWYER, J. HERBERT, DPD inspector. According to the transcript of the DPD radio log, it was Sawyer who first broadcast a description of the assailant on November 22, at 12:44 P.M., 14 minutes after the JFK shooting: "The wanted person in this is a slender white male about thirty, five feet ten, one sixty-five, carrying what looked to be a 30–30 or some type of Winchester." Dispatch then asked Sawyer whether there was a description of the suspect's clothing. "Current witness can't remember that," Sawyer replied.

Later, Sawyer couldn't remember who the witness was who gave him the description. He didn't get the man's name, didn't remember what he looked like, what he was wearing or how old he was. "He was a white man... and he was there... That is [sic] the only two things I can remember about him," Sawyer said. The WC claims that the initial description of the suspect came from witness Howard Brennan.

It is unlikely that Brennan gave the description to Sawyer however, since

Brennan was a construction worker wearing a hardhat at the time, and it is unlikely that Sawyer could have taken a statement from him without remembering what he was wearing.

At 1:11 P.M., 41 minutes after the assassination, Sawyer went on the air with misinformation, stating to the dispatcher, that empty rifle shells had been found on the third floor of the TSBD. (See also Brennan, Howard; Harkness, D. V.)
    SOURCES: WR 27, 82, 145, 235 • WCH VI, 315 • RTJ 87–8, 108 • BISHOP 160–1, 197 • DOP 151, 177, 280 • PWW 32–3 • BE 368

SAWYER, MILDRED, Oswald witness. Sawyer was a neighbor and acquaintance of Oswald in New Orleans when he was 14. She was impressed by Lee's politeness.
    SOURCE: WCH VIII, 31

SCHEIM, DAVID E., author of *Contract on America: The Mafia Murder of President John F. Kennedy* (Shapolsky Publishers, 1988). In 1989, Scheim was asked by researcher Blaine Taylor who he thought had ordered JFK's assassination. Scheim replied:

> The three people are Carlos Marcello, the Mafia boss of New Orleans... The second figure is Santos Trafficante, who was the Mafia boss at Tampa, Florida. The third is Jimmy Hoffa, the Teamsters' boss who was killed... Like Carlos Marcello, each of the other two had spoken openly of assassination plots against the Kennedys, and this all occurred in the summer months of 1962. All three of them were very close friends, and, when we look at Jack Ruby's telephone records, we find an astonishing peak in the number of out-of-state calls in the months before the assassination—it's actually 25-fold greater than in the month of the previous January. Most of those calls are to organized crime figures, in particular to top associates of Marcello, Trafficante, and Hoffa.

Scheim went on to say that he believes one of the actual gunmen in the assassination was Oswald and that there were two others, whose identities he does not know—one behind the stockade fence atop the grassy knoll and the other shooting from a window in the Dal-Tex building on the east side of Houston Street. (See also Hoffa, James; Marcello, Carlos; Trafficante, Santos)
    SOURCES: BELIN 30–1, 42, 202 • CF 513 • MOORE 77, 216 • OTT 302 • NORTH 184

SCHILLER, LAWRENCE, coauthor, with Richard Warren Lewis, of *The Scavengers and Critics of the Warren Report* (Dell, 1967).

SCHMIDT, HUNTER, JR., city editor, *Dallas Times Herald*. Schmidt reported on a gun shop in Irving, Texas, where Oswald allegedly had his rifle sight repaired. Schmidt claimed to have talked to Dial Ryder at the shop, but Ryder later denied ever speaking with him. (See also Lehrer, James)

SOURCE: WCH XI, 240

SCHMIDT, LARRIE H., right-wing activist. With Bernard W. Weissman, William B. Burley, and Joseph P. Grinnan, Schmidt wrote and placed the full-page, black-bordered anti-JFK ad that ran in the *Dallas Morning News* on the day of the assassination. Weissman, Burley, and Schmidt were right-wing activists who had served together in the U.S. army in Munich in 1962. (Grinnan was an independent Dallas oil operator and local John Birch Society coordinator.) According to the WR, "Schmidt was the first [of the three] to leave the service; settling in Dallas in October 1962, he became a life insurance salesman and quickly engaged in numerous [right-wing] political activities." Larrie's brother Bob worked as General Edwin Walker's driver and Walker told author Dick Russell that he had received information that the Schmidt brothers might have been involved in the shooting attempt on his life, April 10, 1963, along with Oswald. (See also Burley, William; Grinnan, Joseph; Weissman, Bernard)

SOURCES: WR 273–6 • FMG I, 121–5, 127–8, 130, 132–5, 139–45, 147 • RUSSELL 37, 320–27, 329, 684, 707

SCHMIDT, VOLKMAR, Oswald witness; Schmidt hosted the party at which the Oswalds met Ruth Paine. According to Dick Russell in *The Man Who Knew Too Much* (Carroll & Graf, 1992), Schmidt once told researcher Edward Jay Epstein that he was "fascinated with techniques of hypnosis." Schmidt admits to "studying and living with Dr. Wilhelm Kuetemeyer, a professor of psychosomatic medicine" who was involved in a 1944 "plot to assassinate Hitler." Schmidt was introduced to the Oswalds by George DeMohrenschildt. (See also DeMohrenschildt, George; Paine, Ruth)

SOURCE: RUSSELL 29, 310

SCHRAND, MARTIN, Oswald witness; suspicious death; USMC private; Schrand served in the marines with Oswald in Biloxi, Mississippi, Santa Ana, California, and Cubi Point in the Philippines; at Cubi Point the marines were reportedly used to guard the hangar where the U-2 spy plane was kept. Officially, on January 5, 1958, Schrand shot himself fatally in the armpit with his own weapon while on guard duty. How he managed to shoot himself in the armpit is a mystery. Interestingly, the Office of Naval Intelligence investigated Oswald in connection with Schrand's death, and according to Marine Donald Camarata, there was a "rumor [at the time] that Oswald had been in some way responsible for the death." (See also Wilcott, James B.)

SOURCES: WCH VIII, 316; XXV, 862, 865 • HSPA App. XI, 542 • RUSSELL 155–7, 174

SCIAMBRA, ANDREW, New Orleans native. Sciambra became a member of New Orleans District Attorney Jim Garrison's assassination-investigation team.

SOURCES: OTT, many • FLAMMONDE 60, 67, 187, 225, 243, 289–90, 306, 309 • HOS 7 • PD 138

SCIBOR, MITCHELL J., employee of Klein's Sporting Goods, from which Oswald allegedly mail-ordered the Mannlicher-Carcano.

SOURCE: WCH VII, 370

SCOBEY, ALFREDDA, WC staff member; Scobey later published "A Lawyer's Notes on the Warren Commission's Report" (*American Bar Association Journal*, January 1965, Volume 51, pp. 39–43).

SOURCES: RTJ 14 • KANTOR 80

SCOGGINS, WILLIAM W., t.k.w.; Dallas taxicab driver. Scoggins was parked on the east side of Patton Avenue facing north, a few feet from the corner of Tenth Street. He did not see the shooting itself because there was shrubbery in the way. He told the WC: "I saw him coming kind of toward me...I could see his face, his features, and everything plain...kind of loping, trotting...He had a pistol in his left hand...I heard him mutter something like 'poor damn cop,' or 'poor dumb cop.' He said that over twice." After the shooting, Scoggins got out of his cab, then hid behind it when he saw the assailant approaching. The man cut across a lawn, ran into some bushes and then passed within 12 feet of his cab. The man proceded south on Patton Avenue. Scoggins later identified the man as Oswald. Scoggins's testimony also included the statement that the assailant had been walking west when he first encountered Tippit's car, which was heading east on Tenth Street and had just passed directly in front of Scoggins's cab. The WC insists that Oswald had to have been walking east on Tenth at the time he encountered Tippit, since he didn't have time to make it from his rooming house to the scene of the shooting in eight minutes on foot taking any other route. (See also Davis, Virginia)

SOURCES: WR 26, 154–6, 159, 163 • WCH III, 322 • BELIN 18–21, 27–8, 31–2 • RTJ 177, 191, 201 • BISHOP 199–200, 356 • CF 341 • MOORE 68, 82

SCOTT, CHARLES C., HSCA questioned-document expert; member of the American Society of Questioned Document Examiners. Scott was called upon by the HSCA, along with Joseph P. McNally and David J.

Purtell, to assess the authenticity of the "Historic Diary" Oswald supposedly kept in the USSR. They determined that, though the diary was written by Oswald, it was written in one or two sittings rather than daily.
   SOURCE: DUFFY 48–50

SCOTT, PETER DALE, author of *Crime and Cover-Up: The CIA, the Mafia, and the Dallas-Watergate Connection* (Westworks, 1977) and coauthor, with Paul Hoch and Russell Statler, of *The Assassinations: Dallas and Beyond* (Random House, 1976).
   SOURCES: HT 281, 291, 346–7 • FMG III 101 • MOORE 216 • BE 15 • HOS 238 • EVICA, many

SEARCY, B. D., t.k.w. Searcy was Ted Callaway's assistant at the used-car lot at Jefferson Boulevard and Patton Avenue, only a block from the scene of the Tippit killing. Searcy and Callaway watched the gunman approach them on Patton, then turn right on Jefferson Boulevard. Searcy said he could not identify the man. (See also Callaway, Ted)
   SOURCE: BISHOP 200

SEELEY, CARROLL HAMILTON, JR., assistant chief, Legal Division, Passport Office, State Department. On October 22, 1963, exactly one month before the assassination, Seeley received a wire from the CIA informing him of Oswald's visits to the Cuban and Russian embassies in Mexico City in September 1963, during which Oswald (according to the wire) unsuccessfully sought visas to travel to Cuba and the Soviet Union.
   Seeley told the WC that he had read Oswald's entire file—he was aware that Oswald had attempted to defect to the USSR in 1959, had lived in Russia for three years, and had offered the USSR military secrets—yet saw no reason to revoke Oswald's passport. Author Paris Flammonde comments: "Even the Commission's mild interrogation made Seeley squirm but he never, of course, was asked the key question: What was it in Oswald's file that reassured you that no further action was required? Perhaps a certificate of employment from the Central Intelligence Agency?"
   SOURCES: WCH XI, 193 • FLAMMONDE 151–2

SELIGMAN, RABBI, On Saturday morning, November 23, 1963, Rabbi Seligman's eulogy for JFK was telecast from New York City. Among those watching the telecast was Ruby, who was deeply moved. According to Ruby, it was the rabbi's words that inspired him to kill.
   SOURCES: BELIN 35 • GERTZ 110 • DOP 523

SELZER, ROBERT, member of the HSCA photoanalysis panel. Selzer examined the film taken in Dealey Plaza by a.w. Robert Hughes and reported that there was "probably" movement visible in several TSBD

sixth-floor windows, and that it was "probably" human.
SOURCES: HSCA App. VI, 108–38 • HT 229)

SEMINGSEN, W. W., Western Union Telegraph Company vice-president, Gulf division. Semingsen gave the WC the record of Ruby's money order to Carousel Club stripper Karen "Little Lynn" Carlin, used by Ruby to show that he killed Oswald without malice. Semingsen also told the WC that he had no record of Oswald's receiving a money order.
SOURCE: WCH X, 405

SENATOR, GEORGE, Ruby witness and roommate. On the evening of November 24, 1963, the night after Ruby shot Oswald, Senator held a meeting in the apartment he shared with Ruby. Attending the meeting were Ruby's lawyer, Tom Howard, and two members of the press, James F. Koethe and Bill Hunter. What was discussed at the meeting is unknown, but all three men who met with Senator died shortly thereafter. Howard was the last to die, on March 27, 1965. (See also Crafard, Curtis; Downey, William; Howard, Thomas; Hunter, William; Koethe, James; Oliver, Beverly; Osborne, Albert; Slaughter, Malcolm)
SOURCES: WR 320, 322–3, 329–31, 347–8 • WCH XIV, 164 • RTJ 270, 282–4 • COA, many • GERTZ 17, 51–2, 60, 109–10, 114, 118, 522, 529 • HT 133, 137 • FMG I, 2, 5–6, 9–11, 18–20, 24, 38, 41 • BLAKEY 319–20 • EVICA 10 • DAVIS 158, 226 • NORTH 490 • KANTOR 50–3, 58–9, 62–5, 169–71, 183, 217

SENSENEY, CHARLES, CIA weapons specialist. According to author Jim Marrs, Senseney "developed weaponry for the CIA" and "described a dart-firing weapon he developed as looking like an umbrella. He said the dart gun was silent to operate; it fired through the webbing when the umbrella was open. Senseney said the CIA had ordered about fifty such dart weapons and that they were operational in 1963." This is pertinent because one a.w. mysteriously opened and pumped an umbrella during the assassination. (See also Witt, Louis)
SOURCE: CF 30

SEYMOUR, WILLIAM, suspected Oswald lookalike. The WC concluded that Seymour was one of the three men who visited Cuban exile Sylvia Odio (one of whom identified himself as Leon Oswald) on either September 25 or 26, 1963 when—according to the official version of the facts—the real Oswald was on his way by bus to Mexico City.

HSCA member and author G. Robert Blakey writes that he interviewed Loran Hall, Lawrence Howard, and William Seymour and has "determined they could not have been the three visitors [to Sylvia Odio]." All three of these anti-Castro activists were members of INTERPEN (International

Penetration Force), a soldier-of-fortune group used for information by the Miami office of the FBI.

However, according to author Paris Flammonde, Seymour "claimed— with some proof—to have been in Miami at the time [of JFK's death]." (See also Del Valle, Eladio; Hall, Loran; Howard, Lawrence; Novel, Gordon; Osborne, Albert; Odio, Sylvia)

SOURCES: WR 301 • HSCA Report 138–9 • EVICA 314 • FLAMMONDE 115, 202–3 • RTJ 339–42 • BLAKEY 164, 174–5

SHAFFER, CHARLES N., JR., WC staff member. Shaffer was a Justice Department lawyer who served the WC as administrative aide; he had been recommended for the position by RFK. In 1973, Shaffer represented John Dean during the Watergate scandal.

SOURCES: HSCA Report 177 • HT 328

SHANEYFELT, LYNDAL L., FBI photography expert. Shaneyfelt told the WC that, after examining the photos of Oswald holding the alleged murder weapons (supposedly taken by Marina Oswald), he could not determine whether the rifle in the photo was the same as the one found on the sixth floor of the TSBD. Despite Shaneyfelt's testimony, the WC stated unequivocally that the rifle in the photo was the alleged murder weapon. Shaneyfelt also examined the Zapruder film and determined that the "rifleman" supposedly visible at frame 413 couldn't be a man because the tree the man seems to be hiding behind was only six feet tall and was only five feet from Zapruder. Shaneyfelt also verified Oswald's handwriting in the Oswald diary and the mail-order forms used to order the "murder weapons." (See also Oswald, Marina)

SOURCES: WR 101, 119–20 • WCH IV, 279; V, 138, 176; VII, 410; X, 309 • BELIN 179 • RTJ 356–9, 361–2 • FMG III, 59 • PWW 17–8, 20, 22–4, 61–2, 72, 96, 142, 144–5, 150, 207 • BE 48, 121 • EVICA 65, 89–90 • ME 221

SHANKLIN, J. GORDON, FBI agent in charge of the Dallas office. Shanklin told the WC in a signed affidavit that Oswald was not a paid FBI informant. After the assassination, he ordered FBI agent James P. Hosty to destroy a note he had received from Oswald before the assassination. (See also Hosty, James P.)

SOURCES: WR 416 • HSCA Report 194–6, 222, 250 • EVICA 58, 76, 79, 140, 320 • ME 130 • NORTH 392, 395, 406, 409, 421, 425–9, 459 • PD 56 • FMG I, 46 • BE 591 • OTT 224 • BLAKEY 20, 22 • RTJ 103, 148–52, 372–4, 384 • HT 125

SHARP, WILLIAM, a.w.; Sharp was apprehended after the assassination because, according to J. R. Leavelle of the DPD, "he had been in the building across the street from the [TSBD] without a good excuse."

SOURCE: WCE 2003, p. 310

SHASTEEN, CLIFTON M., Oswald witness; 39-year-old owner of barber shop in Irving, Texas. Shasteen said that Oswald came in to get his hair cut every two weeks, and that he cut his hair three or four times. He told the WC there was a 14-year-old boy who used to come in with Oswald sometimes. Once the boy came in by himself and began to spout Marxist ideology from the barber's chair, shocking the adults in the shop. Nobody could identify the boy.
SOURCE: WCH X, 309

SHAW, CLAY (aka Bertrand, Clay), Oswald witness; suspicious death; former member, OSS; CIA asset. Shaw was tried and acquitted for conspiracy to assassinate the president. He died in August 1974, possibly of cancer—no autopsy was performed. On December 1, 1962, Shaw told *Who's Who in the South and Southwest* that he was a director for the Swiss corporation Permindex, a company suspected of being a CIA-front involved in the assassination attempts on French Prime Minister Charles de Gaulle in 1961 and 1962. According to evidence in the WC hearings, Permindex was suspected of funding political assassinations and laundering money for organized crime. Shaw was also on the board of directors of Permindex's sister corporation, *Centro Mondiale Commercial* (CMC). According to author Flammonde, CMC was "composed of channels through which money flowed back and forth, with no one knowing the sources or the destination of these liquid assets." According to Garrison, CMC is "representative of the paramilitary right in Europe, including Italian fascists, American CIA, and other interests." (See also Andrews, Dean; Bethell, Tom; Bloomfield, Louis; Brading, Eugene; Broshears, Raymond; Bundy, Vernon; Carr, Richard; DeBrueys, Warren; Del Valle, Eladio; DiSpadaforo, Gutierrez; Dymond, F. Irvin; Fatter, Esmond; Frazier, Robert; Haggerty, Judge; Johnson, Clyde; Johnson, Guy; Kimble, Jules; Klein, Frank; Kohlman, Herman; Leemans, Fred; Logan, David; Long, Richard; McCarthy, Elizabeth; McGehee, Edwin; Manchester, John; Marchetti, Victor; Moffett, Sandra; Moorman, Mary; Morgan, Reeves; Morrow, Robert; Nagell, Richard; Nagy, Ferenc; Newman, William J.; Nichols, John; Odom, Lee; Oser, Alvin; Panzeca, Salvadore; Parker, Mrs. Jesse; Russo, Perry; Spencer, John; Spiesel, Charles; Tadin, Nicolas; Thornley, Kerry; Torbitt, William; Torres, Miguel; Ward, Hugh; Whalen, Edward; Willis, Phillip; Zigiotti, Giuseppi)
SOURCES: HSCA Report 142–3, 145 • OGLESBY 73, 82–3 • DAVIS 524–5, 616–7 • FLAMMONDE, many • EVICA 59, 87, 91, 94, 163, 263 • ME 62, 89 • COA 48 • CF 68, 498–515 • OTT, many • HT 144–5, 186, 288–9, 292 • FMG III, many • BE 80, 89, 278,

282, 439 • BLAKEY 48–9, 169–70 • HOS 235–6, 243

SHAW, J. GARY, independent researcher; codirector, with Larry N. Howard, of the JFK Assassination Information Center in Dallas; coauthor, with Larry R. Harris, of the self-published *Cover-up: The Governmental Conspiracy to Conceal the Facts About the Public Execution of John Kennedy*, 1976; coauthor, with Dr. Charles Crenshaw and Jen Hansen of *JFK: Conspiracy of Silence* (Signet, 1992). On October 24, 1979, J. Gary Shaw made a formal request to the FBI under the Freedom of Information Act for copies of photographs of participants in an event called the Quebec-Washington-Guantanamo Walk for Peace. The photographs are attached to an FBI memorandum dealing with allegations that Oswald was in Montreal during the summer of 1963. The FBI denied his request, stating that it did not have to release material that had been gathered for law-enforcement purposes (*J. Gary Shaw* v. *Federal Bureau of Investigation*, Apellant. No. 84-5084. United States Court of Appeals, District of Columbia Circuit). Oswald's presence in Montreal is relevant because the North American headquarters of Permindex was in Montreal. (See also Bloomfield, Louis; Shaw, Clay; Torbitt, William)
    SOURCES: CF 31, 37, 449 • HT 67, 132, 234, 236, 420 • MOORE 77, 187–8, 216 • BLAKEY 92 • DAVIS 524–5, 616–7 • PD 25, 138, 220–4, 240

SHAW, ROBERT ROEDER, Parkland witness; surgeon. Shaw treated Governor Connally's wounds. He told the WC that the "magic bullet" could not have caused Connally's wounds because there would have been "more in the way of loss of substance to the bullet or deformation of the bullet." (See also Connally, John)
    SOURCES: WR 69, 95-6 • WCH IV, 101; VI, 83 • RTJ 55, 74–5, 77, 79 • COA 213 • BISHOP 156, 187–8, 270 • HT 64–5 • BE 58, 73, 90 • EVICA 77 • OGLESBY 28–9

SHELLEY, WILLIAM H., a.w.; TSBD manager; Oswald's immediate supervisor; Shelley stood just outside the main entrance to the TSBD. He told the FBI that a.w. Billy Lovelady was seated on the steps in front of him at the time of the shooting; he thought the shots came from "west of the Depository." (See also Lovelady, Billy)
    SOURCES: WR 137, 143–4, 170 • WCH VI, 327; VII, 390 • RTJ 110–1, 355 • BISHOP 46, 99, 121, 176 • CF 46, 49, 53 • PWW 67, 191 • MOORE 69–70

SHERIDAN, WALTER, RFK's investigator with both the Justice Department and, in the 1950s, with the anti-crime McClellan Committee. In June 1967, Sheridan produced an hour-long special for NBC–TV that helped destroy the Garrison investigation in New Orleans. He didn't work for NBC before or after that. In 1986, Sheridan was an aide-de-camp for Ted

Kennedy. (See also Garrison, Jim)
SOURCES: COA 48, 165, 286, 300 • OTT 165–8, 179 • BLAKEY 51, 201–3 • FLAMMONDE, many • EVICA 222 • DAVIS 307, 365, 368, 373, 383, 399 • NORTH 69, 169, 203, 376

SHERIN, LEO, Ruby witness and friend; Sherin told the FBI that Ruby often fixed up members of the DPD with strippers from his club, using the phrase "she will play."
SOURCES: RTJ 234–5 • FLAMMONDE 172

SHERMAN, MARY STULTS, suspicious death; physician "connected" to David Ferrie. According to researcher Penn Jones, Dr. Sherman was "shot in bed and set on fire." According to author Paris Flammonde, Dr. Sherman was a "respected physician, affiliated with the Ochsner Hospital...[who] had been one of those associated with Ferrie in his cancer research. Hacked to death with a chef's knife from her own kitchen, her corpse was discovered by Juan Valdes, a playwright friend of Clay Shaw's, who was employed at the Trade Mart." (See also Chetta, Nicolas; Ferrie, David)
SOURCES: HT 136 • FMG III, 57 • FLAMMONDE 32, 177–8 • DAVIS 372

SHIRES, GEORGE, Parkland witness; surgeon. Shires treated Governor Connally's wounds; he told the WC that he did not think JFK and Connally were struck by the same bullet. (See Connally, John)
SOURCES: WR 56 • WCH VI, 104 • HT 64

SHIRAKOVA, RIMA, Oswald witness. Shirakova was the young Russian woman assigned by Intourist in October 1959 to be Oswald's guide during his (initially believed to be brief) visit to the USSR. Upon their meeting, Oswald told her that he was leaving the U.S. forever and was planning to become a Soviet citizen. (See also Sawyer, Forrest)
SOURCES: WR 242 • DUFFY 35

SHITOV, ALEXANDR I. (aka Alekseev, Alexandr I.). Shitov was the veteran clandestine KGB officer stationed (as Alekseev) at the Soviet embassy in Havana, Cuba, from 1959 to 1962. Under his alias, Shitov was ambassador to Cuba from 1962 to 1968. According to author Michael H. B. Eddowes, this man—along with Soviet Premier Nikita Khrushchev—was part of the plot to assassinate JFK. Eddowes never mentions the fact that, if you were named Shitov and had to deal with English-speaking people, you would change your name, too.
SOURCE: KKK, iii

SIBERT, JAMES W., Bethesda witness; FBI agent. Sibert and FBI agent Francis X. O'Neill reported in a memo that a "missle" [sic] had been

removed from JFK's body at the autopsy—a bullet otherwise unreported—
that led researchers to believe that the autopsy report covered up ballistic
evidence. O'Neill's and Sibert's official report, stating that JFK appeared to
have had "surgery of the head" before reaching the autopsy table, led David
Lifton, author of *Best Evidence* (Macmillan, 1981; Carroll & Graf, 1988) on
the trail toward his belief that JFK's body was altered somewhere between
Parkland and Bethesda to appear that he had been shot only from the rear.
(See also Bouck, Robert; Lifton, David; Stover, J. H.)
    SOURCES: BE, many • OTT 244 • BISHOP 348–9, 362, 367, 385, 431, 449, 493 • HT 94,
    112, 235

SIEGEL, EVELYN GRACE STRICKMAN, Oswald witness; New York
City social worker. Siegel interviewed both Lee Oswald and his mother
Marguerite while Lee was detained in Youth House from April 16 to May
17, 1953, in the Bronx because of chronic truancy. In her report, she wrote
that Lee "confided that the worst thing about Youth House was the fact that
he had to be with other boys all the time, was disturbed about disrobing in
front of them, taking showers with them, etc." She also noted that Lee was a
"seriously detached, withdrawn youngster... a rather pleasant quality
about this emotionally starved, affectionless youngster [appears] which
grows as one speaks to him." She felt that he was detached because

> no one in [his life] ever met any of his needs for love... [he] withdrew
> into a completely solitary existence where he did as he wanted and he
> didn't have to live by any rules or come into contact with peo-
> ple... [He] just felt that his mother never gave a damn for him. He
> always felt like a burden that she simply just had to toler-
> ate... Despite his withdrawal, he gives the impression that he is not
> so difficult to reach as he appears and patient, prolonged effort in a
> sustained relationship with one therapist might bring results. There
> are indications that he has suffered serious personality damage but if
> he can receive help quickly this might be repaired to some extent.

In describing Marguerite, Mrs. Siegel wrote that she was "a smartly
dressed, gray-haired woman, very self-possessed and alert and super-
ficially affable, [yet essentially] a defensive, rigid, self-involved person
who had real difficulty in accepting and relating to people." Siegel noted
that Lee's mother had "little understanding" of "the protective shell he has
drawn around himself." (See also Oswald, Marguerite)
    SOURCES: WR 355–8 • WCH VIII, 224

SILVERMAN, HILLEL, Ruby witness; Ruby's rabbi. Silverman spoke

to Ruby on November 25, 1963, in jail. Ruby told him that, if he had wanted to, he could have killed Oswald at the Friday-night press conference at which Oswald was being interviewed. "...had I intended to kill him," Silverman reported Ruby as saying, "I could have pulled my trigger on the spot, because the gun was in my pocket."
SOURCES: WR 317 • MOORE 145 • BLAKEY 318, 337 • BELIN 34–9, 196, 215 • GERTZ 30, 60 • BISHOP 434–5

SIMILAS, NORMAN, a.w.; Ruby witness; Canadian advertising man and amateur photographer. Similas was standing on the south side of Elm Street about ten feet from JFK's limo at the time of the first shot. He claims to have taken a photo that showed a rifle protruding from the "sniper's nest" window, with two men hovering over it. According to Liberty magazine, Similas submitted the developed negatives to a daily newspaper in Toronto, where the key negative was "lost." Interestingly, Similas spent one hour on the eve of the assassination at Ruby's Carousel Club and spoke with Ruby. Earlier, on November 21, 1963, Similas photographed and spoke to LBJ. Similas was quoted in the November 23, 1963, New York Times as saying, "I could see a hole in the President's left temple and his head and hair were bathed in blood."
SOURCES: CF 22–3 • PWW 81–94, 97, 212, 214–22, 224–35, 237–40 • HT 230 • BE 46

SIMMONS, JAMES L., a.w. Simmons stood on the triple underpass. Like others who witnessed the events from that vantage point, he saw a puff of smoke coming from the trees on the grassy knoll. In the 1966 film Rush to Judgment, he said "[The shot] sounded like it came from...toward the wooden fence. And there was a puff of smoke that came from underneath the trees on the embankment directly in front of the wooden fence." Simmons ran behind the wooden fence atop the grassy knoll after the shots were fired. He saw footprints behind the fence as well as on the fences two-by-four railing; and said there were also muddy footprints "on a car bumper there, as if someone had stood up there looking over the fence." Simmons was a prosecution witness at the Clay Shaw trial. Many have wondered why JFK's limo slowed down during the shooting sequence in Dealey Plaza. Simmons's testimony may provide an answer:

Q: Did the car speed up?
A: No, in fact the car stopped, or almost stopped.
Q: Then did the car speed up?
A: Yes, after they got the motorcycle policeman out of the way.

***

According to Penn Jones Jr., Simmons later said that he believed it was the "cop at the left front of the automobile who got in the way."
SOURCES: RTJ 34, 40 • COA 22, 24 • CF 58–9 • HT 22 • FMG III, 53–4 • MOORE 31 • BE 16 • OTT 238

SIMMONS, RONALD, weapons evaluation expert; chief of the Infantry Weapons Evaluation Branch of the Ballistics Research Laboratory of the Department of the Army. Simmons reported to the WC the somewhat artificial results of an experiment in which three military marksmen attempted to duplicate Oswald's alleged shooting feat. He told the WC that before the Mannlicher-Carcano rifle could be fired using its scope, two shims had to be put under it.
SOURCES: WR 177, 181 • WCH III, 441 • RTJ 126–9 • FMG III, 65–6

SIMMONS, WILLIAM F., Ruby witness; piano player; Carousel Club employee from September 17 to November 21, 1963. In its attempt to locate links between Oswald and Ruby, the WC investigated Simmons, who lived at 2539 West 5th Street in Irving, Texas. This address was considered significant because at that time Ruth Paine and Marina Oswald lived at 2115 West 5th Street in Irving. Simmons said he did not know Ruth, Marina, or Lee—and that his only relationship with Ruby was as an employee.
SOURCE: WR 340

SIMPSON, RALPH, possible a.w.; resident of Victoria, British Columbia. Simpson called Officer P. T. Dean (DPD) collect during the WC hearings. He said he had undeveloped film of the assassination and would send it to the DPD. The last we heard, it still hadn't arrived.
SOURCES: WCH V, 256; XII, 443–6

SIMS, RICHARD M., Ruby witness; DPD homicide detective. Sims told the WC that sometime after 10:00 P.M., on November 22, 1963, Jack Ruby called the station and offered to bring up sandwiches. Sims informed Ruby that sandwiches were not needed. Soon thereafter, Ruby showed up at the police station anyway, claiming to be a translator for the Israeli press.
SOURCES: WCH VII, 158 • BISHOP 73, 225, 233, 290–1, 354, 443, 473, 481 • BLAKEY 318

SINKLE, BILLY, a.w. (prelude); member DPD; Sinkle rode in the presidential motorcade "pilot car," which preceded the motorcade by ¼ mile.
SOURCE: BISHOP 101

SIRHAN, SIRHAN, alleged RFK assassin. Sirhan worked as an exercise

boy for several racetracks, including the Del Mar Race Track in Las Vegas, where he incurred serious debts resulting from compulsive gambling. The Del Mar was owned by Clint Murchison and was frequented by J. Edgar Hoover.
SOURCE: COA 219–20

SITZMAN, MARILYN, a.w.; Abraham Zapruder's secretary. Sitzman held his legs to steady him while he shot the most important piece of film in history. (See also Zapruder, Abraham)
SOURCES: MOORE 118, 120 • BE 44, 330 • CF 65 • NORTH 385

SKELTON, ROYCE G., a.w.; rail worker. Skelton stood on top of the triple underpass. In a November 22, 1963, affidavit, he wrote: "I saw something hit the pavement to the left rear of the [presidential limo]... and I heard two more shots... then heard another shot and saw a bullet hit the pavement. The concrete was knocked to the south away from the car. It hit the pavement in the left or center lane." Skelton said he thought the shots came from "around the President's car." (See also Baker, Mrs. Donald; Hickey, George)
SOURCES: WR 76, 111 • WCH VI, 236 • BISHOP 134 • CF 59 • MOORE 198, 200, 204

SLACK, GARLAND GLENWILL, possible Oswald witness. Slack was one of many witnesses who saw a man resembling Oswald practicing at the Sports Drome Rifle Range in Dallas. He took special note of the man, becoming irritated with him at one point because "Oswald" was shooting at Slack's target rather than his own. Slack said that the man had received a ride to the rifle range from a man named "Frazier" from Irving, Texas. (Buell Wesley Frazier denies having done so.) Slack died in September 1978 during the HSCA hearings. (See also Frazier, Buell Wesley)
SOURCES: WR 295–7 • WCH X, 378 • RTJ 334–5

SLACK, WILLIE B., Oswald witness; DPD patrolman. Slack worked in the jail office and booked Oswald out on the morning of his aborted transfer.
SOURCE: WCH XII, 347

SLAWSON, W. DAVID, WC counsel; Denver attorney. Slawson assisted William T. Coleman in the WC investigation of the possibility that JFK died as a result of a foreign conspiracy. He found no such evidence.
SOURCES: HSCA Report 130, 134, 254 • BELIN 46–7 • BE 306, 433 • BLAKEY 72, 78–80, 115–6, 131, 140, 161, 364

SLOAN, BILL, author of *JFK: The Last Dissenting Witness* (Pelican, 1992), a book about the experiences of a.w. Jean Hill. (See also Hill, Jean

SMART, VERNON S., o.k.w.; DPD lieutenant (Auto Theft Division).

Smart arrived at the DPD station basement around 11:00 A.M. on November 24, 1963. He helped with the armored truck, which was to be used as a decoy during the transfer but was too tall to make it down the ramp into the basement. After the shooting, Smart searched Ruby's car and found Ruby's dog and wallet; in the car's trunk he found bags of money, Carousel Club "girlie pictures," and newspapers.
SOURCES: RTJ 210 • WCH XIII, 266

SMITH, MRS. EARL T., suspicious death; friend and confidante of newspaper columnist and game-show panelist Dorothy Kilgallen. Kilgallen claimed, after interviewing Ruby in jail, that she was going to break the Kennedy case wide open. She never got an opportunity—she was found dead of a drug overdose on November 8, 1965, in her New York home. Mrs. Smith died two days later. The medical examiner was never able to determine the cause of her death. (See also Kilgallen, Dorothy)
SOURCES: COA 33 • HT 138

SMITH, EDGAR LEON, JR., a.w.; DPD member. Smith stood on Houston Street across from the TSBD; he was assigned to crowd control. Smith heard three shots, which he thought came from the pergola. He ran there and searched the area but found nothing. Later, he says, he became unsure of where the shots had come from.
SOURCE: WCH VII, 565

SMITH, GLENN EMMETT, possible Oswald witness; 53-year-old Irving, Texas, service station attendant. Smith corroborates the testimony of Robert Taylor, about an Oswald look-alike selling a rifle. (See also Taylor, Robert)
SOURCE: WCH X, 399

SMITH, HILDA L., Oswald witness; employee of the Louisiana Department of Labor in New Orleans. Smith interviewed Oswald regarding his interstate unemployment claim.
SOURCE: WCH XI, 474

SMITH, JOE (separate individual from Joe Marshall Smith, below), a.w. (aftermath); *Fort Worth Star* news photographer. Smith was one of three photographers who took photographs of the three "tramps" as they were led from a railcar near Dealey Plaza to the Dallas County sheriff's office, presumably to be questioned. The other photographers who took "tramp" photos were Jack Beers of the *Dallas Morning News*, and William Allen of the *Dallas Times Herald*.
SOURCES: OTT 207–8 • NORTH 386, 482

SMITH, JOE MARSHALL, a.w.; DPD patrolman. Smith was standing at the corner of Elm and Houston, in front of the TSBD. He thought the shots came from "the bushes of the overpass" and ran in that direction. When he got behind the wooden fence on top of the grassy knoll, he says he smelled gunpowder. In his December 9, 1963, report to the FBI, Smith said he ran into a man in the parking lot behind the stockade fence: "I pulled my pistol from my holster, and I thought, this is silly, I don't know who I am looking for, and I put it back. Just as I did he showed me he was a Secret Service agent." However, all real Secret Service agents had followed the motorcade to Parkland Hospital.

SOURCES: WCH VII, 531 • HSCA Report 184 • RTJ 43–4 • COA 22, 24 • CF 74–5, 319–20 • PWW 168–9 • MOORE 30 • BE 19, 369 • OTT 20–1, 97

SMITH, JOHN ALLISON, Ruby witness; Fort Worth television technician. Smith was sitting in a TV truck parked outside the DPD station on November 24, the morning that Oswald was shot. He corroborates Warren Richey's testimony that Ruby appeared outside the building twice that morning, at 8:00 and 10:00 A.M. (See also Richey, Warren)

SOURCES: WR 329–30 • WCH XIII, 277 • COA 145, 426

SMITH, L. C., a.w.; Dallas deputy sheriff. Smith was standing in front of the sheriff's office on Main Street at the time of the shooting. Later Smith wrote in his official report: "I heard a woman unknown to me say... the shots came from the fence on the north side of Elm." The best guess is that the woman was Jean Hill. (See also Hill, Jean)

SOURCES: OTT 18 • COA 23 • CF 19

SMITH, MERRIMAN, a.w., UPI White House reporter. Smith filed this report on Saturday, November 23, 1963:

I was riding in the so-called White House press "pool" car, a telephone company vehicle equipped with a mobile radio-telephone. I was in the front seat between a driver from the telephone company and Malcolm Kilduff, acting White House press secretary for the President's Texas tour. Three other pool reporters were wedged in the back seat... Suddenly we heard three loud, almost painfully loud cracks. The first sounded as if it might be a large firecracker. But the second and third blasts were unmistakable. Gunfire... the President's car, possibly as much as 150 or 200 yards ahead, seemed to falter briefly. We saw a flurry of activity in the Secret Service follow-up car... Our car stood still for probably only a few seconds, but it seemed like a lifetime... [then] we saw the big bubble-top [JFK's limo] and a motorcycle escort roar away at high speed.

***

Smith won a Pulitzer Prize for his assassination reporting. Years later, he committed suicide. (See also Kilduff, Malcolm)
SOURCES: BE 45 • BLAKEY 18 • *Four Days* 32 • BISHOP, many • DOP, many • HT 20 • FMG IV, 94

SMITH, ROBERT, assassination researcher. Smith and Dr. Cyril Wecht are members of the private research group, "Committee to Investigate Assassinations." (See also Wecht, Cyril)
SOURCES: HT 124 • BE 504, 513, 520

SMITH, SERGIO ARCACHA, former leader of the anti-Castro Cuban exile group, the Cuban Revolutionary Front. Smith had his office at 544 Camp Street, home of Guy Banister Associates in New Orleans. He fled from New Orleans to Dallas during New Orleans District Attorney Jim Garrison's prosecution of Clay Shaw. While in Dallas, Smith was protected from extradition by Assistant District Attorney Bill Alexander and Governor John Connally. (See also Alexander, William; Banister, Guy; Connally, John; Shaw, Clay)
SOURCES: HSCA Report 141, 144–5 • DAVIS 97, 146, 174–5, 336, 405, 407, 410, 575 • NORTH 56, 92, 104, 127, 432 • HT 289 • FMG III, 5, 40 • OTT 180, 305 • SUMMERS 297–9, 302, 338 • FLAMMONDE, many • BLAKEY 46, 165–6, 168–9, 177

SMITH, WILLIAM ARTHUR, t.k.w. According to the WR, Smith "was about a block east of Tenth and Patton when he heard shots. He looked west on Tenth and saw a man running to the west and a policemen falling to the ground. Smith failed to make himself known to police on November 22. Several days later, he reported what he had seen and was questioned by FBI agents. Smith subsequently told a WC staff member that he saw Oswald on TV the night of the murder and thought that Oswald was the man he had seen running away from the shooting."
SOURCES: WR 158, 163 • WCH VII, 82

SNOW, CLYDE, forensic pathologist. Those who believe that the JFK autopsy X rays are forgeries have to deal with the statements of Dr. Snow, who says that he has verified the authenticity of those X rays by comparing them with premortem X rays of JFK's "sinus print"—the ridge of bone at the rear of the nose.
SOURCE: MOORE 216

SNYDER, RICHARD EDWARD, Oswald witness; Foreign Service officer stationed in the United States embassy in the Soviet Union, from 1959 to 1961. Snyder was the consul to whom Oswald spoke initially on October 31, 1959. Oswald told Snyder that he wanted to renounce his U.S.

citizenship. Snyder refused to accept his renunciation and told Oswald that he would have to return "to complete the necessary papers." Before he left, Oswald gave Snyder his passport and a handwritten statement requesting that his U.S. citizenship be revoked. During that first 40-minute conversation, Oswald told Snyder that he had been a USMC radar operator and intimated that he might know things that were of value to the USSR. However, Oswald never did file a formal renunciation.

Oswald met with Snyder again almost two years later, on Monday, July 10, 1961, this time in connection with leaving the Soviet Union and returning to the U.S. Because Oswald had not officially expatriated himself, his passport was given back to him. According to the WR, Snyder testified that he could

recall nothing that indicated Oswald was being guided or assisted by a third party when he appeared in the Embassy in July 1961. On the contrary, the arrogant and presumptuous attitude which Oswald displayed in his correspondance [sic] with the Embassy from early 1961 until June 1962, when he finally departed from Russia, undoubtedly hindered his attempts to return to the United States. Snyder... testified that although he made a sincere effort to treat Oswald's application objectively, Oswald's attitude made this very difficult.

SOURCES: HSCA Report 209–10, 214–5 • PD 69 • FLAMMONDE 141 • WR 245–6, 255–7, 369 • WCH V, 260

SOCARRAS, CARLOS PRIO (See PRIO SOCARRAS, CARLOS)

SOKOLOW, IRVING, Oswald witness; psychologist at Youth House where Oswald was detained in the Bronx from April 16 to May 7, 1953, because of chronic truancy. During one examination of Oswald, Sokolow administered a human figure-drawing test, and later reported:

The Human Figure Drawings are empty, poor characterizations of persons approximately the same age as the subject. They reflect a considerable amount of impoverishment in the social and emotional areas. He appears to be a somewhat insecure youngster exhibiting much inclination for warm and satisfying relationships to others. There is some indication that he may relate to men more easily than women in view of the more mature conceptualisation [sic]. He appears slightly withdrawn and in view of the lack of detail within the drawings that may assume a more significant characteristic. He exhibits some difficulty in relationship to the maternal figure suggesting more anxiety in this area than in any other.

SOURCE: WR 357

SOLOMON, JAMES MAURICE, DPD captain; DPD reservist coordinator. Solomon testified regarding the claims of DPD reservist Harold B. Holly that Ruby had been allowed into the DPD station basement to shoot Oswald by a reservist. He told the WC: "Holly was confused."
SOURCES: WCH XII, 87

SOLON, JOHN, a.w. Solon watched from the Main Street entrance to the Old Courthouse, looking north toward the county jail. He heard three shots, but couldn't tell where the shots came from. He heard a pause between the first and second shots and said that the second and third shots came close together.
SOURCE: WCE 2105

SOMERSETT, WILLIE, union organizer with extensive right-wing political ties; Miami police informant. On November 9, 1963, Somersett participated in a taped coversation in his seedy downtown Miami apartment with right-wing leader Joseph Milteer, during which Milteer said that it was "in the works" for JFK to be shot from an office building with a high-powered rifle, and that someone would be arrested soon after the shooting to mislead the public. (See also Milteer, Joseph)
SOURCES: CF 265–7 • NORTH 352–3, 375

SORRELS, FORREST V., a.w.; SS agent. With Winston G. Lawson, Sorrels selected the motorcade route. He was in charge of protecting the motorcade on the day of the assassination and sat in the backseat of the motorcade's lead car, which was an enclosed sedan. The SS was criticized after the assassination for not making any attempt to secure the buildings or overpasses along the motorcade route. Although SS regulations prohibit turns sharper than 90 degrees in a presidential motorcade, JFK's limo made a 120-degree turn onto Elm Street just before the shots rang out. The turn forced the car to slow to a snail's pace to make the turn, thus creating a much easier target. (See also Behn, Gerald; Curry, Jesse; Lawson, Winston)
SOURCES: WR 29, 31–2, 39, 43, 52, 146, 191–3, 422, 424, 428 • WCH VII, 332, 592 • BELIN 2 • RTJ 42, 86–7, 89, 92, 97–8, 108, 163 • GERTZ 49, 71–86, 92–3, 101, 433–4, 452 • BISHOP, many • DOP, many • CF 14, 35, 321 • HT 148, 151, 155, 157 • PWW 15, 34–5, 61–3, 114, 138, 163, 178, 180, 182, 264 • MOORE 9 • FMG I, 71, 152 • OTT 17 • BLAKEY 9, 11, 22, 321, 324, 331 • HOS 180 • FLAMMONDE 127 • ME 221 • OGLESBY 34–5 • DAVIS 190 • NORTH 343, 358–9 • KANTOR 2, 72, 75–6

SOUETRE, JEAN RENE, (aka Mertz, Michel; Roux, Michel) assassination suspect; French Secret Army Organization (OAS) terrorist. According to CIA document #632-796, obtained in 1977 by independent researcher Mary Ferrell through the Freedom of Information Act, dated April 1, 1964, the French Intelligence claimed that Souetre was in Fort Worth, Texas, during the morning of November 22, 1963, and in Dallas that afternoon. According to French Intelligence, Souetre was picked up by U.S. authorities in Texas within 48 hours of JFK's death and was immediately expelled from the country. Some assassination researchers theorize that Souetre's code name was QJ/WIN, and that he was a foreign national with Mafia connections recruited by the CIA to be part of its "assassination unit." Today, according to author Henry Hurt, Souetre is public relations director for an elegant and reportedly Mafia-run French gambling casino. (See also Davis, Thomas Eli)
SOURCE: HURT 414-9

SPARROW, JOHN, author of *After the Assassination: A Positive Appraisal of the Warren Report* (Chilmark Press, 1968).

SPEAKER, SANDY, a.w.; job foreman to WC star witness Howard Brennan. Speaker told Dallas reporter Jim Marrs, "They took [Brennan] off for about three weeks. I don't know if they were Secret Service or FBI, but they were Federal people. He came back a nervous wreck and within a year his hair had turned snow white... He was scared to death. They made him say what they wanted him to say." Speaker was less than half a block from Dealey Plaza at the time of the shooting and told Marrs, "I heard at least five shots and they came from different locations. I was a combat Marine... in World War II... and I know what I am talking about." (See also Brennan, Howard)
SOURCE: CF 26, 28-9

SPECTER, ARLEN, WC counsel; Philadephia lawyer; 33 years old when appointed; so-called "Author of the Single-Bullet Theory." Specter has earned a reputation for bullying witnesses—a reputation reinforced in 1991 by his rough questioning of Anita Hill during the Clarence Thomas confirmation hearings. (See also Adams, Francis)
SOURCES: BELIN 40, 52 • HT 2, 64-5, 85, 263, 281, 331, 363, 365 • PWW 32, 72, 112, 260 • FMG I, 12-4, 20, 82 • BE, many • EVICA 16, 75, 86 • ME 41-2, 221, 226 • DAVIS 412 • PD 324 • KANTOR 4, 62-3, 81, 84, 155, 178-9, 182

SPENCER, JOHN, friend of Clay Shaw and, at the time of the assassination, landlord to Oswald-doppelganger Kerry W. Thornley.
SOURCE: OTT 75-6

SPIESEL, CHARLES, New York City accountant. Just before the start of the Clay Shaw trial, Spiesel approached New Orleans District Attorney Jim Garrison and said that he had met David Ferrie and Clay Shaw while visiting New Orleans and had heard them plotting to kill JFK. On the witness stand, however, Spiesel began to sound either mad or like a plant to discredit the prosecution. He said that he was constantly afraid that people were attempting to hypnotize him, and that he fingerprinted his daughter when she left and returned from school to make sure she had not been replaced by a duplicate. Spiesel's testimony tended to make Garrison's other witnesses, who were an eccentric lot, seem much less credible.

SOURCE: OTT 230, 236–7, 241

SPITZ, WERNER U., medical expert; Chief Medical Examiner of Wayne County, Michigan, and a member of a panel of medical experts assembled by the HSCA to examine JFK's autopsy photos and X rays. The panel concluded that JFK was shot exclusively from the rear. However, the validity of those photos and X rays has been questioned.

SOURCES: BELIN 180–1 • BE 669

SPRAGUE, RICHARD A., first chief counsel of the HSCA, later "forced out" and replaced by G. Robert Blakey. The HSCA was formed in September 1976, with Sprague as its chief counsel. However, Sprague's intended use of lie detectors and stress evaluators caused a rift with then-chairman Henry B. Gonzalez (D–Texas). Gonzalez tried and failed to fire Sprague but the move was quashed by the full committee. When the investigation finally began in 1977, Gonzalez and Sprague were both gone, replaced respectively by Louis Stokes (D–Ohio) and G. Robert Blakey.

SOURCES: HSCA Report 494 • DAVIS 423, 427–8, 457 • FLAMMONDE 331 • EVICA 161 • ME 133–7 • PD 29–35, 79, 82, 84 • BELIN 188–9 • HT 342, 360–71 • FMG III, 59 • PWW 28, 98, 105–7 • MOORE 137 • OTT 207–8, 318 • BLAKEY 64–5, 67–8 • HOS 235 • KANTOR 136, 210–4

STAFFORD, JEAN, author of *A Mother in History* (Farrar, Straus, Giroux, 1965), a look at three days in the life of Marguerite Oswald.

STANDIFER, ROY E., Ruby witness; member DPD. Standifer told the WC that he spoke to Ruby in the third-floor hallway of the DPD station at 7:30 P.M. on the evening of the assassination.

SOURCES: WCH XV, 614 • COA 126

STANDRIDGE, RUTH JEANNETTE, Parkland witness; head nurse of operating rooms. When word arrived that the presidential motorcade was on its way to Parkland, Standridge quickly reported that Trauma Room #1, where the president would be treated, was already set up.

SOURCES: WCH VI, 115 • BISHOP 148

STANTON, SARAH, a.w.; TSBD clerk; Stanton stood on the front steps of the TSBD. She was among those who verified that Billy Lovelady also watched from that position. (See also Altgens, James; Lovelady, Billy)
SOURCE: CF 46

STAPLES, ALBERT F., dentist at Baylor University College of Dentistry. Dr. Staples found and delivered Marina Oswald's dental records to the WC. His affidavit testimony never touches upon the relevance of Marina's teeth.
SOURCE: WCH XI, 210

STAPLES, LOU, suspicious death; Dallas radio personality. Staples announced that he was going to break the JFK case, but didn't get the chance. He died in May 1977 of a gunshot wound to the head. His death was officially ruled a suicide.
SOURCE: CF 565

STATMAN, IRVING, assistant district director of the Dallas District, Texas Employment Commission. Statman interpreted Oswald's intrastate work-credit claim for the WC.
SOURCE: WCH X, 149

STEELE, CHARLES HALL, JR., Oswald witness. Steele was a 20-year-old resident of New Orleans who was hired by Oswald out of a casual labor pool and assisted Oswald in the distribution of FPCC handbills for which he earned $2. Much to his chagrin, he was filmed passing out the handbills.
SOURCE: WCH X, 62

STEELE, CHARLES HALL, SR., father of Charles, Jr.; New Orleans deputy sheriff. Steele told the WC that he believed his son (above) was telling the truth.
SOURCE: WCH X, 71

STEELE, DON FRANCIS, 32-year-old DPD sergeant (Patrol Division). On November 24, 1963, Steele searched buildings surrounding the DPD station in preparation for Oswald's transfer. He was in the county jail when Oswald was shot.
SOURCE: WCH XII, 353

STERN, SAMUEL A., WC counsel; Washington, D.C., attorney. Once a law clerk for Chief Justice Earl Warren; Stern's duties included analyzing JFK's SS protection.
SOURCES: BELIN 62 • BE 116

STEVENSON, ADLAI E., U.S. ambassador to the United Nations;

Democratic presidential candidate (1952, 1956). One of the reasons that the Kennedy camp was nervous about traveling to Dallas was that Stevenson had visited there earlier in the year and had been attacked by thrown objects. One woman had hit him over the head with her protest sign. With this in mind, SS and Dallas police were theoretically preoccupied with hecklers in the crowd who might throw things, rather than with gunmen.

SOURCES: WR 49, 55, 271, 273, 390–2 • HSCA Report 36, 182 • GERTZ 108 • BISHOP 9, 92, 115, 218, 264, 445, 495, 501 • DOP, many • HT 15, 428 • MOORE 9 • FMG I, 122–3, 183 • BLAKEY 5 • FLAMMONDE 211, 256–7 • NORTH 332

STEVENSON, M. W., Oswald witness; Ruby witness; DPD deputy chief. At the time of the assassination, Stevenson was stationed at the Dallas Trade Mart, where JFK had been scheduled to speak. He was present at Oswald's arraignment for the murder with malice of JFK (Case #F154, *State of Texas* v. *Lee Harvey Oswald*). The arraignment, which took place at 1:35 A.M., on November 23, 1963, was held not in a courtroom, but rather in a small room without outside witnesses on the fourth floor of the DPD station. Stevenson said that Oswald screamed for a lawyer as he was arraigned.

Stevenson witnessed Ruby's interrogation by SS Agent Forrest V. Sorrels. Here is a portion of Stevenson's written report regarding that interrogation, dated February 18, 1964, nearly three months after the event took place:

> Sorrels asked Ruby if he had thought or planned to kill Oswald and Ruby stated he first thought of killing him when he observed Oswald in the showup room two nights prior. He stated the thought came to him when he observed the sarcastic sneer on Oswald's face when he was on the showup stage. He stated that when he saw Oswald on that night he thought it would be ridiculous to have a trial for him when he knew the results would be the death penalty, since Oswald had killed the President and Officer Tippit... Ruby also stated that he and his sister were very emotional people and that his sister had just gotten out of the hospital and she was also taking this hard, and that with the facts of the incident already known to him was the motivation for his shooting Oswald. Ruby then stated some words to the effect, "I also want the world to know that Jews do have guts."

This interview was conducted in the outside corridor of the jail cells on the fifth-floor city jail five to ten minutes after Ruby's shooting of Oswald. (See also Sorrels, Forrest)

SOURCES: WR 193–5, 199 • WCH XII, 91; XV, 133 • GERTZ 78 • BISHOP 8, 74, 121–3,

159, 504 • PWW 264 • OGLESBY 9

STOKES, LOUIS, congressman (D–Ohio) and third chairman (after Thomas Downing and Henry Gonzales) of the HSCA. Since the release of the film *JFK* in 1991, Stokes has called for the HSCA's sealed files to be opened, to remove any doubt that there had been a governmental cover-up of assassination facts. (See also Downing, Thomas; Gonzalez, Henry)
SOURCES: HSCA Report 490, 492, 494 • BELIN 188–9 • HT, many • MOORE 137 • BE 550, 553, 596 • BLAKEY 67, 94–6, 99, 141–2, 274 • EVICA 282–3 • ME 136, 155, 226 • DAVIS 423, 570 • KANTOR 214

STOLLEY, RICHARD B., Los Angeles bureau chief for *Life* magazine at the time of the assassination; in 1993, the editorial director of Time Inc. Magazines. Stolley was instrumental in *Life's* initial purchase of the Zapruder film. In the January 17, 1992, edition of *Entertainment Weekly* magazine, Stolley told how *Life* came to purchase the film.

At about 6:00 P.M. on November 22, the day of the assassination, Stolley received a phone call from one of *Life's* part-time reporters, Patsy Swank, who was at Dallas police headquarters speaking in a whisper. She told him that Oswald was being interrogated in an office nearby and that the corridors in the building were a mob scene of police and reporters. She had received a tip that the assassination had been filmed by a local garment manufacturer named Zapruder. Stolley looked up Zapruder's phone number in a phone book and called him every 15 minutes until he received an answer at 11:00 P.M. that night. Stolley writes:

> It was Zapruder himself. He had been driving around trying to calm his nerves. After photographing the shooting, he had literally stumbled back to his office nearby, muttering, "They killed him, they killed him." ... Incredibly, nobody in authority was much interested in [the film]. Zapruder had contacted the Dallas police, but by mid-afternoon they had Oswald in custody and the film seemed of marginal importance. Both the Secret Service and the FBI said it was his property to dispose of as he saw fit but that they would like copies. Zapruder took his 8 mm film to a Kodak lab, and by evening had the original and three copies in hand.

Stolley viewed the film for the first time the following day. He purchased the original and a copy for $50,000 and agreed, according to Zapruder's wishes, that the film would never be used to ghoulishly exploit the president's death.

Stolley defends charges that *Life* had covered up evidence by holding the film without allowing it to be seen:

> *Life* did not bury the Zapruder film for 12 years as [film director
> Oliver] Stone charges. All the relevant images were printed imme-
> diately except for frame 313. We felt publishing that grisly picture
> would constitute an unnecessary affront to the Kennedy family and to
> the President's memory. Today, that may seem a strange, even foolish,
> decision. But this was 1963, a few years before Vietnam brought
> carnage into American living rooms...*Life* decided not to sell the
> Zapruder film for TV or movie showing for reasons of both taste and
> competition...There have been charges that *Life* tampered with the
> film, removed or reversed frames, diddled with it to confound the
> truth. Nothing like that ever happened. I have inspected the film
> many times, as have others; the frames are all there, in proper order.

Stolley's story of the early history of the Zapruder film does not jibe with
David Belin's. (See also Belin, David; Rather, Dan; Zapruder, Abraham)

STOMBAUGH, PAUL MORGAN, FBI hair and fiber expert. Stombaugh
was among those who examined "Oswald's" Mannlicher-Carcano rifle at the
FBI laboratories. According to the WR:

> In a crevice between the butt plate of the rifle and the wooden stock
> [of the Mannlicher-Carcano rifle] was a tuft of several cotton fibers of
> dark blue, gray-black and orange-yellow shades. On November 23,
> 1963, these fibers were examined by...Stombaugh...[who] com-
> pared them with the fibers found in the shirt Oswald was wearing
> when arrested in the Texas Theatre. This shirt was also composed of
> dark blue, gray-black and orange-yellow cotton fibers. Stombaugh
> testified that the colors, shades, and twist of the fibers found in the
> tuft on the rifle matched those in Oswald's shirt.

SOURCES: WR 118–20, 122, 129 • WCH IV, 56; XV, 702 • FMG III, 65

STONE, OLIVER, director and coscreenwriter of the film *JFK*. After the
release of his movie, Stone was an active lobbyist for the release of U.S.
government files on the assassination.

STOREY, ROBERT G., Ruby witness; special counsel to the attorney
general of Texas. Storey was present during the WC's interrogation of Ruby
by Chief Justice Earl Warren in the Dallas county jail.
SOURCES: RTJ 243 • FMG I, 50

STOUT, ZACK, Oswald witness; USMC acquaintance. Stout told re-

searcher Edward Jay Epstein, "Oswald was honest and blunt...that's usually what got him into trouble...His diction was good...he used his hands when he talked...he seemed to think about what he was going to say...He was absolutely truthful, the kind of guy I'd trust completely."
SOURCES: AO 93 • LEGEND 68–71

STOVALL, RICHARD S., DPD detective. Stovall was involved in the search of the Paine home in Irving, Texas where Marina Oswald lived, on November 22, the afternoon of the assassination. During the search, a blanket was found in the garage; Marina said it formerly had held her husband's rifle. (See also Moore, Henry; Paine, Michael; Paine, Ruth; Rose, Guy)
SOURCES: WR 167 • WCH VII, 186 • BISHOP 224, 232, 275–6, 278, 343, 419, 446, 492

STOVALL, ROBERT L., Oswald witness; Oswald's boss and president of the firm of Jaggars-Chiles-Stovall, for which Oswald had done photographic work from October 1962 to April 1963. The firm was a defense contractor. (One has to wonder how a man who had recently attempted to defect to USSR could get a job doing photographic work for the U.S. Defense Department.) Oswald listed Stovall as a reference for future employment but, on at least one occasion, Stovall failed to recommend Oswald. When Oswald applied for a job at the Padgett Printing Company, on the back of his job application form was written: "Bob Stovall does not recommend this man. He was released because of his record as a troublemaker—has Communistic tendencies." (See Bowen, Jack)
SOURCES: WR 228 • WCH X, 167 • BELIN 63 • BLAKEY 360

STOVER, JOHN H., JR., Bethesda witness; captain, U.S. Navy; commanding officer of the U.S. Naval Medical School, National Naval Medical Center, Bethesda, Maryland. On November 22, 1963, Stover received a memo from JFK autopsy attendees FBI agents Francis X. O'Neill Jr. and James W. Sibert, reading: "We hereby acknowledge receipt of a missle [sic] removed by Commander James J. Humes, MC, USN on this date." Officially, no bullet was removed from JFK's body at the autopsy or at any other time. The memo was released in 1976 to author Mark Lane under the Freedom of Information Act. (See also O'Neill, Francis; Sibert, James W.)
SOURCES: OTT 244 • BE, many

STRINGER, H. H., DPD sergeant. Stringer was in the DPD station at the time of the assassination. He was among those who first examined the jacket Oswald purportedly threw away after shooting Officer J. D. Tippit.

From the scene, Stringer radioed in: "The jacket the suspect was wearing over here on Jefferson bears a laundry tag with the letter B 9738. See if there is any way you can check this laundry tag." The WC was unable to locate the laundry that issued this tag, and Marina Oswald said she didn't remember her husband ever using professional laundry services.

SOURCES: RTJ 202 • BISHOP 147

STROUD, MARTHA JO, assistant U.S. attorney in Dallas. Stroud's official notification to the WC on June 9, 1964, of the mark on the curb caused by the bullet that indirectly wounded a.w. Tague, forced the WC to recognize that one shot missed. This missed shot created the necessity for the "magic bullet" theory.

SOURCES: PWW 102, 104–6, 251–3

STUBBLEFIELD, MR. and MRS. WILLIAM H., a.w. The Stubblefields are the parents of a.w. Marilyn Willis. Marilyn and her parents watched the motorcade from the north side of Elm Street, directly in front of the pergola. Marilyn's husband Phillip and their daughters were on the other side of the street. (See also Willis, Marilyn; Willis, Phillip)

SOURCE: PWW 179, 181

STUCKEY, WILLIAM KIRK, Oswald witness. Stuckey was New Orleans radio-program director ("Carte Blanche") who arranged for a radio debate on WDSU on August 21, 1963, between pro-Castro activist Lee Harvey Oswald and anti-Castro activist Carlos Bringuier. Stuckey told the WC:

> ...I was a columnist with the *New Orleans States-Item* with an interest in Latin America...I had been looking for representatives of the Fair Play for Cuba Committee [in New Orleans]...There haven't been any. Most of the organizations that I had contact with were refugee organizations, very violently anti-Castro groups...I was in the bank and I ran across a refugee friend...Carlos Bringuier...he said that a representative of the [FPCC] had appeared in New Orleans and that he had had an encounter with him...[Oswald] said somehow he knew Bringuier was connected with the Revolutionary Student Directorate, how I don't know. But at any rate...he offered his services...Bringuier told me...he ran into this young man again...distributing literature, handbills... "Join the Fair Play for Cuba Committee in New Orleans, Charter Member Branch"... Bringuier, who was rather an excitable fellow,...got into a shouting match...on the street corner, and I think some blows were exchanged, I'm not sure...[Bringuier told me] the police arrived on the

scene and took everybody down to the jail...I was interested in locating the fellow and...Bringuier gave me his name...and he lived on Magazine Street, somewhere in the 4000 block...It was [Saturday] August 17 when I went by [Oswald's] house...So we had a few cursory remarks about the organization. [He showed me his card which] identified him as the secretary of the New Orleans chapter...and it was signed A. J. Hidell, president...I never thought of the name again until after the assassination when Mr. Henry Wade [Dallas district attorney], on Dallas television on Sunday [November 24, 1963] I believe, mentioned that Oswald purchased a rifle from a Chicago mail order house and had used the name A. Hidell in purchasing the rifle...As I recall, [Oswald] insisted he was...the [FPCC] secretary and this other gentleman, Hidell, was the president...He appeared to be a very logical, intelligent fellow, and the only strange thing about him was his organization...he did not seem the type at all...I was arrested by his cleancutness [sic]. I expected a folk-singer type...a beard and sandals...instead I found this fellow who was neat and clean...I asked him to meet me at the radio station...and he agreed...[There] was to be a recorded interview prior to a broadcast...instead of just interviewing him for five minutes, I would just let him talk...this was a 37-minute rambling interview between Oswald and myself...we played it back...He was satisfied...and I think he had scored quite a coup. Then I went back over it in his presence...we had a couple of his comments...and the rest was largely my summarizing...and [four-and-a-half minutes of it] was broadcast on schedule that night...next Monday I called the News Director...and he said...there would be more public interest if we did not run this tape at all, but instead arrange a...debate panel show with some local anti-communists on... "Conversation Carte Blanche"...a 25-minute public affairs progam that runs daily...I picked Mr. Edward S. Butler...Executive Director...of an anti-Communist propaganda organization...a friend of mine. I knew him as a columnist...[F]or the other panelist I asked Mr. Bringuier...During that day, Wednesday, August 21, one of my news sources called me up and said, "I hear you are going to have Oswald on Carte Blanche...We have some information on Mr. Oswald, the fact that he lived in Russia for three years." [Oswald] had omitted reference to this in the 37-minute previous interview and in all of our conversations...[In the 37-minute interview Oswald lied:] "I entered the United States Marine Corps in 1956. I spent three years in the United States Marine Corps working my way up through the ranks to the position of buck sergeant, and I served honorably having been discharged. Then I went back to work in Texas and have recently arrived in New Orleans with my family.". . . [When he arrived at the station he] was unaware [we knew he had lived in Russia.] During that day Mr. Butler called and said he too had found out the same thing. . . his source was the House Un-American Activities Committee or something like that. At any rate, we thought this was very interesting and we agreed together to produce this information on the program that night. . . so it was a somewhat touchy exchange there between Bringuier and Oswald. Bringuier started. . . "You know I thought you were a very nice boy. You really made a good impression on me when I first met you. . . I cannot understand how you have allowed yourself to become entangled with this group. . . I don't think you know what you are doing." Oswald said something to the effect that, "I don't think *you* know what *you* are doing." And back and forth. . . Bringuier said, "Anytime you want to get out of your organization and join mine there is a place for you." And again Oswald says, "I hope you see the light.". . . I left. . . to get Bill Slatter. . . the official moderator of the program, and we came back and picked up our participants and went into the broadcast room.

At this point in Stuckey's testimony, WC interrogator Assistant Counsel Albert E. Jenner offered Stuckey a copy of the transcript of the WDSU debate to refer to before he continued.

Stuckey continued, "I would like to say this about the transcript. I think it is very unfair. These people have put in all of Oswald's hesitations, his 'er's' and that sort of thing. . . They were apparently trying to make him look stupid. Everyone else was using 'er's', but they didn't put those in. . . I think it's an unfair thing." Stuckey then returned his comments to the debate itself:

> . . . the principal thing that came out. . . aside from the Russian residence. . . was his admission that he was a Marxist. We asked him if he was a Communist—we were always doing this—he was very clever about avoiding the question. He would usually say, "As I said before, I belong to no organization other than the Fair Play for Cuba Committee.". . . and I asked, "Are you a Marxist?", and he said, "Yes.". . . The program largely consisted of speeches by Bringuier, and Butler, and Oswald did not have a chance to ramble much or talk much as he had, and most of the answers are rather short. . . It was my impression that he had done a lot of reading. . . it was difficult to appraise the full measure of his learning because of his oblique way

of answering and dodging questions whenever he did not want to speak about a particular point....[He seemed] confident, self-assured, logical... very well qualified to handle questions , articulate... if he could use a six-syllable word instead of a two-syllable word he would do so... his manner was sort of quasi-legal... as if he were a young attorney.

Jenner asked Stuckey whether the debate had become heated. Stuckey replied:

Yes, it did. Mr. Butler in particular... took the offensive and tried to trip him up... and Mr. Oswald handled himself very well, as usual. I think we finished him on that program. I think that after that program the Fair Play for Cuba Committee, if there ever was one in New Orleans, had no future there, because we had publicly linked the Fair Play for Cuba Committee with a fellow who had lived in Russia for three years and who was an admitted Marxist... Oswald seemed like such a nice, bright boy and was extremely believable before this. We thought the fellow could probably get quite a few members if he was really indeed serious about getting members. We figured after this broadcast of August 21, why, that was no longer possible. After all, you have to recognize that Oswald—they were ganging up on him... There were three people who disagreed with him, and he was only one man, and the fact that he kept his composure with this type of environment indicates discipline...

(See also Bringuier, Carlos; Butler, Edward)
SOURCES: WR 366, 384, 413 • WCH XI, 156 • HSCA Report 141 • FLAMMONDE 9 • NORTH 300–1, 303 • DUFFY 184 • AO 122–6

STUDEBAKER, ROBERT LEE, a.w. (aftermath); member DPD; police photographer. Studebaker took photos of the sixth floor of the TSBD soon after the assassination. According to Harold Weisberg, "In taking a picture of the rifle [the alleged assassination weapon] in place... Studebaker got a better picture of his own knee."
SOURCES: WCH VII, 137 • PWW 121

STURGIS, FRANK (aka Fiorino, Frank), assassination suspect; CIA contract agent. According to the sworn statements of former Castro mistress and CIA asset Marita Lorenz, Sturgis was one of the men who conspired to kill JFK. Sturgis and Lorenz have also been linked romantically—and were lovers at the time that Sturgis sent her into Cuba with a

438 WHO'S WHO IN THE JFK ASSASSINATION

poison capsule to attempt to assassinate Fidel Castro. Later, Sturgis became well known after his arrest in connection with the Watergate break-in. Sturgis was identified in *Coup d'État in America* by Michael Canfield and Alan J. Weberman, along with fellow CIA agent E. Howard Hunt, as one of the three suspicious "tramps" apprehended behind the grassy knoll soon after the assassination. The weight of the evidence, however, indicates that Sturgis and Hunt probably were not tramps.

Sturgis has said alternately that he was in Miami and Washington, D.C., at the time of the assassination. In both versions of his alibi, he was watching TV at the time. He says the FBI questioned him about JFK's death "right after" it happened because, they said, "Frank, if there's anybody capable of killing the President of the United States, you're the guy who can do it." (See also Barker, Bernard; Bosch, Orlando; Hemming, Gerry; Hunt, E. Howard; Lanz, Pedro Diaz; Lorenz, Marita; Marchetti, Victor; Torbitt, William)

SOURCES: HSCA Report 91 • COA 189, 192 • HT, many • BLAKEY 175 • CANFIELD 198, 226 • EVICA, many • OGLESBY 47 • DAVIS 4012-2, 405, 410 • PD, many

STYLES, SANDRA, a.w.; TSBD employee. Styles watched the motorcade from a fourth-floor window in the TSBD. She could not tell from which direction the shots came. She ran down the TSBD stairs immediately following the shooting and did not hear anyone else using them. Officially, Oswald ran down those same stairs immediately following the shooting so that he could get from the sixth floor to the second floor in 90 seconds. He must have done so silently. If this scenario is correct, we know that Oswald must have used the stairs because both of the TSBD elevators were still at the top of the building when police first entered the building. (See also Adams, Victoria; Dorman, Elsie; Garner, Dorothy)

SOURCES: CF 44 • PWW 51

SUGAR, BERT R., With Sybil Leek, Sugar is coauthor of *The Assassination Chain* (Corwin Books, 1976).

SULLIVAN, WILLIAM, suspicious death; head of the FBI's Division 5 (counterespionage and domestic intelligence); former #3 man in the bureau; Sullivan was in Washington, D.C., at the time of the assassination. According to Jim Bishop, by 6:00 P.M. that day, Sullivan was "in charge of the internal security aspects—and background—of...Oswald." In November 1977, Sullivan died just prior to the HSCA investigation in a "hunting accident." The man who shot him said, "I thought he was a deer." (See also Angleton, James; Haldeman, H. R.; Hosty, James; Torbitt, William)

SOURCES: COA 209, 218, 220 • BISHOP 361–2 • DOP 367 • CF 217, 564 • HT 145, 333, 384–5 • BLAKEY 26, 76–7, 363–5 • NORTH, many • EVICA 172, 324–8 • DAVIS 259, 270, 279, 297, 310, 381 • KANTOR 87, 89

SUMMERS, ANTHONY, author of *Conspiracy* (Paragon House, 1980, 1991). Summers claims that in 1981 and 1982, he became privy to some notes and CIA documents upon which the 300-page HSCA classified report regarding Oswald's supposed visit to Mexico City was based. He learned that 12 CIA photos had been taken of "Oswald," 11 of which were of the unknown man who appears in the WCH, and one of the real Oswald. The latter was destroyed. (See also McDonald, Hugh)

SOURCES: BELIN 28 • HT 8, 234, 287 • MOORE 29, 37, 77, 129, 131–2, 217 • OTT 64 • OGLESBY 32, 45 • DAVIS 166–7, 215, 262–3, 265–6, 444 • NORTH 386)

SUMMERS, H. W., t.k.w. (aftermath); DPD patrolman. Summers was involved in the immediate search for the murderer of Officer J. D. Tippit and rode in patrol car #221. Soon after the killing was reported, Summers radioed in from Oak Cliff that he had "an eyeball witness to the getaway man." The assailant was described as having black, wavy hair and wearing dark trousers, a white shirt, and a light-colored Eisenhower jacket. Summers reported that the suspect was "apparently armed with a .32, dark finish automatic pistol." Moments later, Sergeant Gerald Hill of the DPD, went on the air stating, "The shell at the scene indicates that the suspect is armed with an automatic .38 rather than a pistol." (See Hill, Gerald Lynn)
SOURCE: OTT 198

SUMMERS, MALCOLM, a.w.; Summers was standing on the south side of Elm Street across from the grassy knoll at the time of the shooting. Summers, who was born and raised in Dallas, owned a direct-mail business and had just been to the Terminal Annex Building at Houston and Commerce streets when he went to Dealey Plaza to see JFK. In 1991 Summers addressed an assassination symposium in Dallas, Texas:

I'm a Republican but he [JFK] was one Democrat I voted for, so I wanted to get close. I was sick for two weeks after it happened. I couldn't believe it happened in Dallas. I was right next to the car when Jackie crawled on the back and helped pull the FBI guy [actually SS]. I heard three shots. The first shot came right after the car turned the corner [from Houston onto Elm]—and I thought it was more like the sound of a firecracker than anything else. And I thought it was a firecracker and I thought, "Well, that's a cheap trick." And I saw the FBI guys [again, he means SS] looking around on the ground like that was what they thought too . . . Then came the second and third shot and they came so close together that I thought they were coming from different directions. I didn't know where they were coming from initially—but I certainly did think there was more than one [person] shooting. A motorcycle cop came by me and he was looking in my direction so I hit the ground because I thought there might be someone shooting from behind me and I didn't want to get caught in the crossfire there. After the motorcade got by, I ran across the grassy knoll because there was some people beginning to run toward the railroad tracks. I was stopped by a guy, a well-dressed person—he had a topcoat on his shoulder—he said, "Y'all better not come up here or else you could get shot." He had a gun under that raincoat. All I could see was the barrel of it and I couldn't tell you what kind of gun it was. I didn't argue with the man because there wasn't any reason to argue with him. He seemed in authority and he was stopping people there—so I went back to the postal annex so I could call my wife and tell her what happened. After a couple of days, I reported this to the Sheriff's office. One of the main reasons that I came forward was because when I went back to the postal annex, there were three men, what I call Mexicans, getting in a car and driving off toward Oak Cliff at a high rate of speed. I never did know where the shots came from but I do know that the second and third shots came so close together that there's no way one man could be doing it.

SOURCE: OTT 18

SUMNER, GENE, possible Oswald witness; FBI informant. On November 27, 1963, Sumner told the FBI that a man resembling Oswald received a large cash payment from New Orleans mob boss Carlos Marcello's brother, Joseph, during the spring of 1963, at the Town & Country Motel, headquarters for the Marcello organization. (See also Marcello, Carlos)
SOURCE: DAVIS, many

SURREY, ROBERT ALAN, suspicious death; publisher of the handbill attacking JFK. Surrey was an aide to Major General Edwin A. Walker, the man at whom Oswald allegedly took a shot on the evening of April 10, 1963. On the night of the shooting, Surrey told police that four days earlier, at about 9:00 P.M., he saw two men sitting in a dark purple or brown 1963 Ford behind Walker's house. He said the two men got out of the car and walked around the house. Suspicious, Surrey followed the car for awhile before losing it and, in the process, noticed that the car had no license plates. Surrey was being sought by the HSCA in April 1977 because of his supposed knowledge of alleged ties between anti-Castro Cubans and Ruby, when he died of a pistol shot. Official cause of death: suicide. (See Hosty, James; Klause, Robert; Walker, Edwin A.)

SOURCES: WR 277–9 • WCH V, 420 • HSCA Report 98 • NORTH 253, 469, 479 • COA 188 • DUFFY 180–1 • HT 185, 307–8 • FMG I, 156 • BLAKEY 356

SWEATT, ALLAN, Dallas County Chief Criminal Deputy Sheriff. Mary Ann Moorman, whose photo of the assassination has become famous, took more than one photo with her Polaroid camera that day. One photo, which supposedly shows the sixth-floor windows of the TSBD in the background, was confiscated at the scene by Deputy Sheriff Sweatt and handed over to the SS.

Originally responsible for obtaining information indicating that Oswald was a paid informant for the FBI, Sweatt gave his evidence to Texas Attorney General Waggoner Carr who, in turn, contacted the WC. Following an emergency meeting on January 27, 1964, the commission disregarded the information. (See Moorman, Mary)

SOURCES: RTJ 344–5, 348 • HT 185, 307–8 • PWW 32, 45 • FLAMMONDE 157 • EVICA 99 • NORTH 512 • KANTOR 36

SWINDAL, JAMES, colonel, USAF; pilot of Air Force One. Swindal flew JFK's body from Love Field in Dallas to Andrews Air Force Base.

SOURCES: DOP, many • BE 642, 677

T

TADIN, NICOLAS and MATHILDA, musicians' union chief and his wife. The Tadins told New Orleans District Attorney Jim Garrison that they met Clay Shaw in a Bourbon Street bar through David Ferrie while arranging to have Ferrie give their son flying lessons. (See also Ferrie, David; Garrison, Jim; Shaw, Clay)
SOURCES: OTT 119

TAGUE, JAMES T., a.w. Tague was the third man wounded in the assassination. He was standing near the entrance to the triple underpass at the time of the shooting. One bullet struck a curb and kicked up a piece of concrete that cut Tague on the chin. The bullet obviously missed JFK's limo. This is important because it forced the WC to admit that at least one shot missed, thus creating the necessity for the "magic-bullet" theory. If Tague had not been wounded, the WC might have been able to claim that one shot hit Kennedy in the back, another hit him in the head, and the third wounded Connally. This would have relieved the WC of the uncomfortable argument that one bullet caused all of the nonfatal wounds. Tague told the WC that the shots came from "behind the concrete monument" between the TSBD and the knoll. (If one believes eyewitness evidence that the first shot missed, striking Elm Street behind JFK's limo, then Tague's testimony would seem to indicate a second missed shot. • See Walthers, Eddy)
SOURCES: WR 111 • WCH VII, 552 • RTJ 69 • BISHOP 129, 133–5, 149, 386, 529 • CF 60–4, 485 • HT 3, 17, 214, 222, 225–6, 241 • FMG III, 98 • MOORE 198 • BE 20 • EVICA 69, 71, 83, 88, 95 • ME 15, 75 • OGLESBY 15

TALBERT, CECIL E., captain, DPD; in charge of building security while Oswald was held prisoner. According to the WR:

[Talbert], who was in charge of the patrol division for the city of Dallas

442

on the morning of November 24, retained a small number of policemen in the building when he took charge that morning and later ordered other patrolmen from several districts to report to the basement... With the patrolmen and the reserve policemen available to him, Captain Talbert, on his own initiative, undertook to secure the basement of the police department building. He placed policemen outside the building at the top of the Commerce Street ramp to keep all spectators on the opposite side of Commerce Street. Later, Talbert directed that patrolmen be assigned to all street intersections the transfer vehicle would cross along the route to the county jail. His most significant security precautions, however, were steps designed to exclude unauthorized persons from the basement... Shortly after 9 o'clock Sunday morning, policemen cleared the basement of all but police personnel. Guards were stationed at the top of the Main and Commerce Street auto ramps leading down into the garage, and at the double doors leading to the public hallway adjacent to the jail office.

The WR, now critical of the seemingly stringent—yet obviously penetrable—basement security, concludes: "Talbert undertook to secure the basement, with only minimal coordination with those responsible for and familiar with the route Oswald would take through the basement."
    SOURCES: WR 195–9, 212 • WCH XII, 108; XV, 182 • RTJ 206 • BISHOP 254, 342, 387 • BLAKEY 320

TANNENBAUM, ROBERT, HSCA attorney who interviewed FBI informant Jose Aleman. (See also Aleman, Jose)
    SOURCES: CF 37 • BLAKEY 303 • ME 137 • DAVIS 240, 243 • PD 31–2, 34–5

TASKER, HARRY T., Dallas cabdriver. Tasker was parked outside the DPD station (near the Main Street ramp) when Oswald was shot. He didn't see Ruby enter the building.
    SOURCE: WCH XV, 679

TATUM, JACK RAY, t.k.w. Tatum told researchers that Helen Markham, the WC's star witness to the Tippit killing, was anxious to leave the scene of the crime because she did not want to miss the 1:12 bus that would take her to work. If this is true, and Markham wasn't confused about how late it was, then Tippit was shot too early for Oswald to have gotten from his rooming house to the scene on foot. According to the HSCA:

Tatum... saw a young white male walking on the sidewalk near the squad car. Both the young male and the squad car were heading east on Tenth Street. As Tatum approached the squad car, he saw the young male leaning over the passenger side of the police car, with both hands in his zipped jacket. Tatum said that as he drove through the intersection of Tenth and Patton he heard three shots in quick succession... At that point he saw the police officer lying on the ground near the front of the police car, with the young male standing near him. Tatum said the man ran toward the back of the police car with a gun in his hand. The man then stepped back into the street and shot the police officer as he was lying on the ground. The man then started to run in Tatum's direction. Tatum said he then sped off in his car and last saw the man running south on Patton toward Jefferson.

(See Roberts, Earlene; Markham, Helen)
SOURCES: HSCA Report 59–60 • HSCA Appendix XII, 41–2 • CF 348 • HT 278–9

TAYLOR, GARY E., Oswald witness; 23-year-old acquaintance of the Oswalds in Texas; husband, at the time of Alexandra DeMohrenschildt; son-in-law of Oswald's friend George DeMohrenschildt. Marina and June Oswald lived with the Taylors for three days (October 8 to October 10, 1962) while Lee looked for work. This was the first of many times that Lee and Marina Oswald would live apart during their marriage. Taylor told the WC of DeMohrenschildt's tremendous influence over Oswald, adding, "If there was any assistance or plotters in the assassination... it was, in my opinion, most probably the DeMohrenschildts." He said that DeMohrenschildt was in Guatemala while the Bay of Pigs troops were being trained there. (See also DeMohrenschildt, George; Gibson, Mrs. Donald)
SOURCES: WCH IX, 73; XI, 470 • BLAKEY 350

TAYLOR, GEORGE (See EASTERLING, ROBERT)

TAYLOR, ROBERT ADRIAN, possible Oswald witness; service-station mechanic in Irving, Texas. In December 1963, about three weeks after JFK's death, Taylor reported to the FBI that Oswald may have been a passenger in a car that had stopped at his station for repairs back in March or April 1963. According to Taylor, no one in the car had enough money to pay for the repairs so the man believed to be Oswald sold Taylor a rifle. The WR says, "However, a second employee at the service station, who recalled the incident, believed that, despite a slight resemblance, the passenger was not Oswald." (See also Smith, Glenn)
SOURCE: WR 295

TAYLOR, WARREN W., a.w.; SS agent. Taylor rode in the backseat, on the left-hand side, of the vice-presidential follow-up car in the Dallas motorcade, three cars behind JFK's limo. In the famous AP photo of the

assassination taken by James W. Altgens, it is shown that a fraction of a second after the first shot was fired, Taylor already had his door open in response. None of the SS agents in charge of guarding JFK had yet made a move. Several had not reacted at all to the first report. Taylor wrote in a November 29, 1963, affidavit: "I heard a bang which sounded to me like a possible firecracker—the sound coming from my right rear. Out of the corner of my eye and off slightly to the right rear of our car, I noticed what now seems to me might have been a short piece of streamer flying in the air close to the ground, but due to the confusion of the moment, I thought that it was a firecracker going off." (See also Altgens, James)
SOURCES: FMG III, 17 • ME 73, 311

TERRY, L. R., a.w.; unknown whether Terry is a man or a woman. Terry spoke only to Dallas reporter Jim Marrs. Terry stood on the south side of Elm Street across from the TSBD to view the motorcade and saw a rifle sticking out of an upper-floor window, but could see only the shooter's hand. Terry added, "There was a man with him." (See also Brennan, Howard)
SOURCE: CF 26–7

THOMPSON, GEORGE, author of *The Quest for Truth* (1964), which sets forth the theory that the assassination was committed by the man in the black hat and cape ("Cape Man") visible in some frames of the Zapruder film on the south side of Elm Street by the reflecting pool near the corner of Houston Street, very close to the position of a.w. Phillip Willis.
SOURCE: Cutler, R. B., *The Umbrella Man*, 19, 70–1

THOMPSON, JOSIAH, author of *Six Seconds in Dallas* (Bernard Geis Associates, 1967), an early and successful matching of the evidence to a triangulation of gunfire.
SOURCES: HT 109, 119 • FMG III, 101 • MOORE, many • BE 43, 334, 348, 381, 438, 447 • HOS 236 • FLAMMONDE 265, 331 • ME 25–7, 39–40, 43, 50, 62, 201, 240 • NORTH 379–87, 407

THOMPSON, LLEWELLYN E., Oswald witness; former U.S. ambassador to the Soviet Union. Thompson interviewed Oswald repeatedly in October and November of 1959 in the U.S. consulate in Moscow regarding Oswald's desire to renounce his U.S. citizenship. He later became under secretary of state, the position he held at the time of JFK's death.
SOURCES: WCH V, 567 • DOP 30, 141, 207, 260–1, 481, 527, 574, 612

THONE, CHARLES, HSCA member; (R-Nebraska).

THORNBERRY, HOMER, Parkland witness; federal judge; friend of LBJ. Thornberry was a member of the presidential party in Dallas. He aided in the protection of LBJ during the first chaotic minutes after the assassination and rode from Parkland to Love Field for the return to Washington in a car with LBJ, driven by DPD Chief Jesse Curry.

SOURCE: WR 70–1

THORNLEY, KERRY WENDELL, Oswald witness; Thornley was the only man to write a book—albeit a novel—about Oswald before JFK's assassination; was in the marines at the USMC's El Toro Annex in California in 1959 when he met Oswald. In 1962, he wrote the novel *The Idle Warriors*, about a disgruntled marine who defects to the USSR. He called his hero Private Johnny Shellburn. The book was not published until 1991, although Thornley shopped it around a great deal. After meeting Oswald, the strange marine became an obsession with Thornley, and from that point on their lives formed an interesting parallel. Thornley was stationed in Atsugi, Japan. So was Oswald (although not at the same time). Atsugi was rumored to be the home of a military LSD/mind control program known as MK/ULTRA. Because of the manuscript Thornley was trying to sell, Thornley was interviewed by FBI agents two days after JFK's assassination. He testified for the WC and a copy of his manuscript was placed in the National Archives.

Thornley told the WC that he was a "close acquaintance" but not a "good friend" of Oswald in the Marines; he quoted Oswald as saying that "the Marxist morality was the most rational morality," and that Communism was "the best system in the world"; he said that during the spring of 1959, Oswald's assignments were primarily janitorial, because he had lost his clearance. Oswald's interest included "philosophy, politics, [and] religion." Since neither Oswald nor Thornley believed in God, they once got into a conversation about atheism, during which Oswald asked, "What do you think about Communism?"

"I replied I didn't think too much of Communism," Thornley testified.

> ...and he said, "Well, I think the best religion is Communism." And I got the impression at the time...he was playing the galleries...he said it very gently. He didn't seem to be a glassy-eyed fanatic by any means...I did know at the time he was learning the Russian language. I knew he was subscribing to Pravda...All of this I took to be a sign of his interest in the subject, and not as a sign of any active commitment to the Communist ends...I didn't feel there was any rabid devotion...His shoes were always unshined...He walked around with the bill of his cap down over his eyes...so he wouldn't

have to look at anything around him...to blot out the military...It was well-known in the outfit that...Oswald had Communist sympathies...Master Sergeant Spar, our section chief, jumped up on a fender one day and said, "All right, everybody gather around," and Oswald said in a very thick Russian accent, "Ah ha, collective farm lecture," in a very delighted tone. This brought him laughs at the time...

Thornley testified that he believed Oswald understood the distinctions between Marxism, communism, and democracy "as well as most reasonably educated people do," and that he was "extremely unpredictable" when it came to personal relationships.

"He and I stopped speaking before I finally left the outfit," Thornley testified, then described the incident that led to the tension between them:

It was a Saturday morning...Every now and then we had to give up our Saturday morning liberty to go march in one of those parades...[and] to look forward to a morning of standing out in the hot sun and marching around, was irritable. So, we were involved at the moment in a "hurry up and wait" routine...waiting at the moment...sitting. Oswald and I happened to be sitting next to each other on a log...he turned to me and said something about the stupidity of the parade...and I said, I believe my words were, "Well, come the revolution you will change all that." At which time he looked at me like a betrayed Caesar and screamed, screamed definitely, "Not you too, Thornley." And I remember his voice cracked as he put his hands in his pockets, pulled his hat down over his eyes and walked away...and sat down someplace else alone...and I never said anything to him again and he never said anything to me again. This happened with many people, this reaction of Oswald's and therefore he had few friends...He seemed to guard against developing real close frienships...

In a segment of Thornley's WC testimony that deserves scrutiny, he states, "...there was someone else in the outfit who spoke Russian, don't ask me who, they used to exchange a few comments in the morning at muster and say hello to each other..."

Don Hudson of the *New Orleans States-Item* quoted Thornley (November 27, 1963) as saying that Oswald "was very resentful of the military; he was very much the type of man who would 'play' the role of assassin. But I'm still not sure he committed the assassination. He never showed any tendency toward violence, he was more of a talker."

Thornley's own book, *Oswald* (New Classics, 1965), states:

> When news of Oswald first began to appear, I wondered how any man could have changed so thoroughly in a few short years. A national news magazine called him a psychopath, a schizoid, a paranoid, and probable homesexual—all in the same single column of print. Suddenly I was reading that he was constantly fighting with his fellow Marines and that in the service he displayed a conspicuous yen for physical violence. I observed no such traits. That an appendix of the Warren Report had to be devoted to speculation and rumors is in my mind argument enough that a good deal of fabrication and exaggeration was involved somewhere along the line. While Oswald had his psychological problems, I doubt that he would have been found legally insane had he lived to face a jury...

After being discharged from the marines, Thornley moved to New Orleans, as had Oswald. Oswald and Thornley lived in New Orleans at the same time, although Thornley claims he never ran into Oswald there. Jim Garrison didn't believe this was true. Garrison claimed that there was at least one eyewitness (Barbara Reid) who placed Thornley and Oswald together in a New Orleans restaurant just weeks before the assassination. Garrison called Thornley as a witness at the Clay Shaw trial and later charged Thornley with perjury. Garrison's claims against Thornley were 1) Thornley and Oswald were involved together in covert CIA operations. 2) Thornley impersonated Oswald as early as 1961. 3) Thornley's writings about Oswald were actually CIA disinformation. Garrison eventually dropped the perjury charge, although his second claim is worth considering, in light of the fact that Thornley made a short visit to Mexico City in September 1963, just as Oswald is supposed to have done. While living in New Orleans, Thornley became an admitted acquaintance of Guy Banister and David Ferrie. After living in New Orleans, Thornley moved to Los Angeles where he got a job as a doorman at the building where Johnny Roselli lived. Then he moved to Atlanta where he told authorities that, back in New Orleans before the assassination, he had been told by a man named Gary Kirstein that JFK and Martin Luther King Jr. would be murdered. Thornley now suspected that Kirstein was actually E. Howard Hunt. After telling this story, Thornley was pistol-whipped by ski-masked intruders at a friend's birthday party. The only thing the intruders stole was Thornley's identification.

According to the *New York Press* (June 19–25, 1991), Thornley's odd life has gotten to him. Thornley now believes "he and Lee Harvey Oswald were products of genetic tests carried out by a secret proto-Nazi sect of eugenicists, the Vril Society... that a bugging device was implanted in his body at birth, and that both he and Oswald were secretly watched and manipulated from childhood by shadowy, powerful Vril overlords."

Regarding his and Oswald's proximity in New Orleans during the summer of 1963, Thornley wrote that Oswald "was even reputedly stopping in now and then at a bar where I hung out. We may have passed each other on the street but, if so, we didn't recognize each other. Only after the assassination did I realize that Oswald had been right under my nose for over two weeks..."

On September 28, 1967, Thornley gave a sworn affidavit in Los Angeles that read:

> ...The famous "U-2 incident" occured when I was stationed with MABS-11, which was then on maneuvers in the Philippines from the "home" base at Atsugi, Japan. While at Atsugi, before going on maneuvers, my fellow Marines and I frequently observed what later turned out to be the U-2 taking off and landing at Atsugi. At the same time I was there, this was referred to, among the noncoms as the "blackbird" or the "mystery plane," because it had no markings on it and was black in color... It was kept in a hangar which, rumor had it, was guarded by civilians. At one time, when I was in the vicinity of this hangar, I was asked politely to leave the area by such a civilian. Most of us assumed, myself included, that this black airplane was some kind of experimimental aircraft. We did not realize its true function until the story broke in the newspapers and hence that information was declassified.

On the February 24, 1992, edition of the television program *A Current Affair* Thornley said that he was part of a conspiracy to assassinate JFK and that his co-conspirators were men he called "Brother-in-law" and "Slim."

Thornley stated that he was offended by Jim Garrison's claims that he had set up his former friend Oswald. " I would gladly have killed Kennedy, but I would never have betrayed Oswald," Thornley said. "I wanted him dead. I would have shot him myself. Two weeks before the assassination, Brother-in-law had it all planned out. The only question, as far as Brother-in-law was concerned, was who to frame it on. Brother-in-law said, 'We'll pin it on some jailbird.' I said, 'Why don't you frame some Communist?' and smirked." (See also Banister, Guy; Donovan, James; Farrington, Fenella; Ferrie, David; Hunt, E. Howard; Kimble, Jules; Reid, Barbara; Roselli, John; Shaw, Clay; Spencer, John)

SOURCES: WR 361-2, 364-5 • OTT 47, 66-7, 70-8, 80, 119, 274-5 • WCH XI, 82; XXI, 669 • DUFFY 22 • CF 108-10 • FLAMMONDE 138-9, 208-9

THORNTON, RUTH, a.w. Thornton watched from the second floor of the Dallas County Criminal Courts Building, with Assistant District Attorney Sam Paternostro. She heard three shots but couldn't determine their source.

SOURCE: WCE 2106-7

TICE, WILMA MAY, Ruby witness; Parkland witness. Tice told the WC that she had seen Ruby at Parkland Hospital at the time JFK's death was announced; she said, "If it wasn't him, it was his twin brother." This corroborates reporter Seth Kantor's testimony. (See also Kantor, Seth)

SOURCES: WCH XV, 388 • RTJ 265-70, 273-4, 384 • COA 126 • GERTZ 527-8 • DAVIS 298 • KANTOR 192-3

TILSON, TOM G., JR., a.w.; member DPD. Tilson had the day off on November 22. His usual beat was covered by Officer J. D. Tippit, who did not survive the day. Just after the assassination, Tilson was involved in a strange car chase. At 12:30, Tilson and his daughter were driving downtown and had just turned east on Commerce Street from Industrial Boulevard (just west of the triple underpass) when he heard reports of the shooting on his police radio. Tilson told the *Dallas Morning News* on August 20, 1978:

... I saw all these people running to the scene of the shooting. By that time I had come across under Stemmons. Everybody was jumping out of their cars and pulling up on the median strip. My daughter Judy noticed [JFK's] limousine come under the underpass. They took a right turn onto Stemmons toward Parkland Hospital. Well, the limousine just sped past [this] car parked on the grass on the north side of Elm Street near the west side of the underpass. Here's one guy coming from the railroad tracks. He came down that grassy slope on the west side of the triple underpass, on the Elm Street side. He had (this) car parked there, a black car. And, he threw something in the back seat and went around the front hurriedly and got in the car and took off. I was on Commerce Street right there across from [the car], fixing to go under the triple underpass going into town. I saw all this and I said, "That doesn't make sense, everybody running to the scene and one person running from it. That's suspicious as hell." So, I speeded up and went through the triple underpass up to Houston... made a left... [came] back on Main... and caught up with him because he got caught on a light. He made a left turn, going south on Industrial. I told my daughter to get a pencil and some paper and write down what I tell you. By this time, we had gotten to the toll road [then the Dallas-Fort Worth Turnpike, now Interstate 30] going toward Fort Worth. I got the license number and description of the car and I saw what the man looked like. He was stocky, about five-foot-nine, weighing 185 to 195 pounds and wearing a dark suit... If that wasn't Jack Ruby, it was someone who was his twin brother...

Tilson later called in the information. According to Jim Marrs, "Tilson's story is corroborated by his daughter, now Mrs. Judy Ladner, although photos taken west of the triple underpass at the time do not show a black car... Also, Dallas police logs for the day do not indicate any alert for such a car as described by Tilson." Interestingly, if Tilson and Dan Rather are both telling the truth, then Ruby (holding a rifle case) and Rather must have crossed paths on the west side of the triple underpass, on the north side of Elm Street. (See also Rather, Dan; Tippit, J. D.)
SOURCES: CF 325–7 • OTT 206–7

TIPPIT, GAYLE M., DPD detective. (No relation to J. D. Tippit.) Some assassination researchers who want to refute evidence that Ruby knew Officer Tippit say that he actually knew this man, and not the officer who was killed. This Tippit, however, admits only to being an "acquaintance" of Ruby's.
SOURCES: RTJ 253 • BLAKEY 326

TIPPIT, JEFFERSON DAVIS "J. D.," DPD officer; murder victim; possible friend of Ruby; allegedly killed by Oswald; Tippit was found dead lying in front of his police car on Tenth Street between Denver Street and Patton Avenue in the Oak Cliff section of Dallas 40–46 minutes after the assassination. He had been shot four times and was killed immediately. Tippit was one of very few policemen in Dallas that day who had not been called to Dealey Plaza to help investigate the assassination. He was the so-called "officer-at-large," in charge of covering whatever came up. According to the WC, Tippit called Oswald over to his car at 1:15 P.M., 45 minutes after the assassination, for questioning (supposedly because Oswald resembled the description of the assassin that had been broadcast on police radio). Tippit got out of the car and walked around the front toward Oswald, who was standing on the passenger side. When Tippit got in front of his car, Oswald (according to the WC) shot him dead.

Tippit's death may be the least-investigated homicide of a police officer in history. It was just assumed that Oswald shot him, and no one questioned the matter until critics of the WR began to see the Tippit killing as a possibly penetrable crack in the suspected assassination conspiracy.

There are witnesses who saw Tippit and Ruby together in the weeks and months before the assassination who claim that they were close friends. Tippit was killed only a few blocks from Ruby's apartment. Some witnesses claim that two men fled the scene after Tippit was shot and that one of them was a short, heavy, middle-aged man.

UPI reported in 1964, "(Tippit's widow) stands to collect $225 a month in pension money, half to her and half to the three children. A grateful world has so far given the Tippit widow and children more than $50,000." (See also Benavides, Domingo; Clemons, Acquila; Dowling, Ada; Grant, Eva; Hardee, Jack; Hill, Gerald; Hulse, Clifford; Jackson, Murray; Kinsley, Eddie; Markham, Helen; Mather, Carl; Morrow, Robert; Owens, Calvin; Tilson, Tom; Tippit, Gayle; Tippit, Marie; Vaganov, Igor; Waldo, Thayer; White, Roscoe; White, T. F.; Williams, Harold; Wright, Frank)

SOURCES: WR, many • *Four Days* 61 • BELIN, many • RTJ, many • COA 19, 35–6, 213, 268–9 • GERTZ 77, 119, 145, 524–5, 528–9 • BISHOP, many • DOP 262, 274, 276, 279, 283, 286, 414, 425–6, 567 • CF 340–50 • HT, many • MOORE, many • FMG I, many; III, 77, 87 • BE 100 • OTT 193–203 • BLAKEY 19, 29, 92, 108, 316 • KANTOR, many

TIPPIT, MRS. J. D. (MARIE), widow of the DPD officer slain on November 22, 1963. Before the death of her husband, Mrs. Tippit was legally represented by Eugene Locke, who later became campaign manager for Governor John Connally, deputy ambassador to Vietnam and a candidate himself for governor of Texas. Mrs. Tippit was also a bridesmaid at the wedding of Mr. and Mrs. Roscoe White. (See also Connally, John; Locke, Eugene; White, Geneva; White, Roscoe)

SOURCES: DOP 435, 635 • WCH XX, 426 • FMG III, 80

TOBIAS, MR. and MRS. MAHLON F., SR., Oswald witnesses. The Tobiases were managers of the apartment house at 602 Elsbeth Street, where the Oswalds lived in Dallas. In March 1963, FBI Agent James P. Hosty Jr. visited Mrs. Tobias. She told Hosty that, during the time the Oswalds had lived in the building, other tenants had complained "because Oswald was drinking to excess and beating his wife." The weight of the

evidence indicates that she was probably wrong about the drinking. (See also Hosty, James)
SOURCES: WR 410 • WCH X, 231, 251

TOMLINSON, DARRELL C., Parkland witness; senior engineer. Tomlinson discovered the "magic bullet" jammed into a corner of a stretcher in the hallway in the emergency area of the hospital on November 22. To this day, he claims that the bullet was found on a stretcher that had been used by neither Governor Connally nor JFK. The WC concluded that Tomlinson must have been mistaken. (See also Beavers, William Robert; Connally, John)
SOURCES: WR 85 • WCH VI, 128 • RTJ 79–80, 386 • HT 66, 119, 456 • BE 90, 198, 289, 360, 591, 650 • ME 22 • OGLESBY 18, 55

TONAHILL, JOE, Ruby witness. Tonahill was one of Ruby's defense lawyers at his murder trial. By the time Ruby was administered his WC lie-detector test, he had—for reasons unknown—lost all trust in Tonahill.
SOURCES: HSCA Report 158 • RTJ 227, 241–2, 247 • COA 128, 152–3 • GERTZ, many • HT 297 • FMG I, 14, 17, 178–80 • BLAKEY 327–8, 333–6 • FLAMMONDE 288 • NORTH 498, 506 • KANTOR, many

TORBITT, WILLIAM, pseudonymous author of *Nomenclature of an Assassination Cabal*, (independently published, 1970) commonly referred to as "The Torbitt Document." Torbitt's book outlines in detail how the Swiss corporation Permindex engineered the assassination of JFK. Permindex is also suspected of involvement in assassination attempts on French premier Charles de Gaulle in 1961 and 1962, as well as the 1968 assassination of Martin Luther King Jr. According to Torbitt, Permindex was comprised of five wings:

(1) The Solidarists, a Czarist, Russian, Eastern European, and Middle East exile organization;

(2) A section of the ACCC headed by H. L. Hunt of Dallas, Texas;

(3) A Cuban exile group called the Free Cuba Committee, headed by Carlos Prio Socarras, Cuban ex-president, who is reported to have worked closely with Jack Ruby and Frank Sturgis;

(4) An American organization known as The Syndicate, headed by Clifford Jones, ex-lieutenant governor of Nevada and Bobby Baker, close friend of LBJ. This group worked closely with Mafia leader Joseph Bonnano.

(5) The Security Division of NASA headed by Wernher von Braun, head of the German Nazi rocket program from 1932 to 1945. Torbitt's assassination scenario includes 40 names, all of whom were recruited from one of

Permindex's five wings.

According to the short biography provided at the back of the document:

> The author is a lawyer in the southwestern part of the United States. For two years, he served as a prosecuting attorney in criminal cases during 1949, 1950, and part of 1951. He has engaged in both civil and criminal practices and is licensed in all state and federal courts in his areas and the court of tax appeals... The author has participated in cases in the southwest where professional Mexican assassins have been used to commit political murder... Close relatives of the gambling syndicate members have used the legal services of Torbitt in complicated cases involving tracing financial dealings of organized crime in Texas and their foreign connecting links... Except for five years foreign service in the U.S. Navy during World War II, Torbitt is a life-long resident of Texas. He holds a law degree from the University of Texas at Austin... The author says, "The Fascist cabal who assassinated John Kennedy planned to lay the blame on honest right-wing conservatives, if their first ploy, to lay the blame on Oswald and the Communists, was not bought."

(See also Baker, Bobby; Bloomfield, L.M.; Ferrie, David; Gatlin, Maurice; Hunt, H. L.; Prio, Carlos Socarras; Sullivan, William; Sturgis, Frank; Vaganov, Igor; von Braun, Wernher; Voshinen, Igor)
    SOURCE: *Critique*, #21/22, p. 82

TORMEY, JAMES J., executive secretary of the Hall-Davis Defense Commission. Tormey told the WC that Oswald was not a member of his organization. (See also Davis, Benjamin; Hall, Gus)
    SOURCES: WR 268 • WCH X, 107

TORRES, MIGUEL, convicted burglar serving time at the Louisiana State Penitentiary at Angola at the time of New Orleans District Attorney Jim Garrison's Clay Shaw investigation. NBC-TV interviewed Torres for a special titled "The Case of Jim Garrison," which was broadcast in June 1967. Torres told NBC that Garrison's office had tried to get him to falsely testify that (a) Clay Shaw had made a sexual pass at him, and (b) Clay Shaw and Clay Bertrand were the same man. The inmate claimed that, in return for this testimony, he had been promised a vacation in Florida and a large quantity of heroin. (See also Garrison, Jim; Shaw, Clay)
    SOURCES: OTT 166, 169–70 • FLAMMONDE 226, 301, 305–6, 308

TOWNER, JIM, a.w. Towner took a photo after the shooting that shows the "umbrella man" and his Latin companion sitting on the north curb of

Elm Street. The Latin man appears to be speaking into a walkie-talkie. (See also Witt, Louis)

SOURCE: CF 31

TRAFFICANTE, SANTOS, assassination suspect; Ruby witness; Florida Mafia boss, based in Tampa. During a 30-year span, including the time of the assassination, Trafficante controlled mob operations in Cuba before Castro's revolution and maintained close ties to the paramilitary Cuban exiles. He died in 1987.

On January 14, 1992, Jack Newfield of the *New York Post* quoted Frank Ragano, Trafficante's lawyer of 27 years, as saying that Jimmy Hoffa had sent him to New Orleans to instruct Trafficante and New Orleans mob boss Carlos Marcello to kill the president. The HSCA reported that:

Trafficante, like [assassination suspect Carlos] Marcello, had the motive, means and opportunity to assassinate President Kennedy... Trafficante was a key subject of the Justice Department crackdown on organized crime during the Kennedy administration, with his name being added to a list of the top 10 syndicate leaders targeted for investigation. [RFK's] strong interest in having Trafficante prosecuted occurred during the same period in which CIA officials, unbeknown to the Attorney General, were using Trafficante's services in assassination plots against... Fidel Castro.

The committee found that... Trafficante's stature in the national syndicate of organized crime, notably the violent narcotics trade, and his role as the mob's chief liaison to criminal figures within the Cuban exile community, provided him with the capability of formulating an assassination conspiracy against President Kennedy. Trafficante had recruited Cuban nationals to help plan and execute the CIA's assignment to assassinate Castro. (The CIA gave the assignment to former FBI agent Robert Maheu, who passed the contract along to Mafia figures Sam Giancana and John Roselli. They, in turn, enlisted Trafficante to have the intended assassination carried out.)

Trafficante admitted to his role in the plot to kill Castro during his HSCA testimony. However, in his September 28, 1978, HSCA testimony, he "categorically denied ever having discussed any plans to assassinate President Kennedy."

Regarding Trafficante's association with Jack Ruby, the HSCA reports; "Ruby may have met with Trafficante at Trescornia prison in Cuba during one of his visits to Havana in 1959, as the CIA had learned but had discounted in 1964. While the committee was not able to determine the purpose of the meeting, there was considerable evidence that it did take place."

On November 28, 1963, the CIA sent a copy of a memo to LBJ aide McGeorge Bundy, stating that, in 1959, Trafficante had been visited by Ruby in jail in Cuba. A July 21, 1961, Treasury Department memo made public in 1976 stated that there were "unconfirmed rumors in the Cuban refugee population in Miami that when Fidel Castro ran the American racketeers out of Cuba and seized the casinos, he kept...Trafficante...in jail to make it appear he had a personal dislike for Trafficante, when in fact Trafficante is an agent of Castro. Trafficante is allegedly Castro's outlet for illegal contraband in this country."

According to author Anthony Summers, Ruby arrived in Havana on August 8, 1959, having told his doctor that he was going to make some money gambling at the (Havana) Tropicana, where he was subsequently seen by many witnesses in the company of Lewis McWillie, who was managing the Tropicana for Trafficante. CIA agent Gerry Hemming has said that Ruby met with an American close to Castro to help secure Trafficante's release. One of Trafficante's fellow inmates, English journalist John Wilson Hudson, remembers seeing Ruby bring food to Santos.

Trafficante died following triple-bypass surgery in 1987 in Houston, Texas. On his deathbed, he told his lawyer, Frank Ragano, "Carlos [Marcello] fucked up. We should not have killed Giovanni [JFK]. We should have killed Bobby." (See Aleman, Jose; Barker, Bernard; Dolan, James; Hoffa, James; McWillie, Lewis; Davis, John; Marcello, Carlos; Ragano, Frank; Scheim, David)

SOURCES: HSCA Report 151–4, 156, 169, 172–5, 179 • HSCA App. V, 357 • COA, many • CF 37, 168–71, 391, 395–401 • HT 119, 151, 319–20, 377–9, 412, 421 • OTT 287, 300 • BLAKEY, many • EVICA, many • ME 185 • DAVIS, many • NORTH, many • OGLESBY 70 • KANTOR 136, 211–4

TRAMMEL, CONNIE, Ruby witness. On Thursday, November 21, 1963, Trammel, with Jack Ruby, under the guise of "job-hunting," visited the office of Lamar Hunt, son of Texas oil billionaire H. L. Hunt. (See also Hunt, Lamar)

SOURCES: WR 344 • RTJ 261 • COA 259–60, 424 • GERTZ 526

TREGLE, BERNARD "BEN," business associate of assassination suspect Carlos Marcello; New Orleans bar owner. Tregle was overheard by one of his employees (ex-marine Eugene DeLaparra) in April 1963, having

a suspicious discussion with friends. Tregle was looking at an ad in a detective magazine for a $12.95 foreign rifle. Tregle said to everyone there, including DeLaparra, "This would be a nice rifle to buy to get the President. There is a price on the President's head, and other members of the Kennedy family. Somebody will kill Kennedy when he comes down south." (See also DeLaparra, Eugene; Marcello, Carlos)
SOURCE: DAVIS, many

TRUE, TAMMY (See POWELL, NANCY)

TRULY, ROY SANSOM, a.w.; Oswald witness; TSBD superintendent; Truly, who had hired Oswald, watched the assassination from the north curb of Elm Street, in front of the TSBD. He told the WC that he thought the shots came from the direction of the concrete monument adjacent to the wooden fence atop the grassy knoll. Truly was the first known person to see Oswald after the assassination. At the time (about 90 seconds after the shooting) Oswald was on the second floor of the building, calmly drinking a Coke.

According to Oswald, a few days before the assassination, Truly was seen showing off a rifle inside the TSBD. (See Baker, Marrion; Wade, Henry)
SOURCES: WR 23–4, 28, 139–47, 229–30, 234 • WCH III, 212; VII, 380, 591 • HSCA Report 57–8 • OGLESBY 16, 53 • DAVIS 207 • NORTH 326–7, 331, 338–9, 387–9 • PD 353 • BELIN 57, 64–5 • RTJ 86, 111–2 • BISHOP, many • DOP, many • CF 14, 27, 41, 51 • HT 175 • PWW 189 • MOORE 11, 45, 51–4, 82 • BE 350 • HOS 52, 134 • KANTOR 208–9

TSCHEPPE-WEIDENBACH, ADOLF (See WILLOUGHBY, CHARLES)

TURNER, F. M., a.w. (prelude); member DPD. Turner rode in the presidential motorcade's "pilot car," which preceded the motorcade by a quarter mile.
SOURCES: WR 204 • WCH VII, 217 • BISHOP 101

TURNER, JIMMY, Ruby witness; Fort Worth television director. Turner saw Ruby's entrance into the DPD station via the Main Street ramp moments before Ruby shot Oswald. Here is a key passage in Turner's testimony to WC attorney Leon Hubert:

Q: Did he have to go through any great mass of people?
A: No.
Q: Did he have to push or shoulder his way up there?
A: No.
Q: He could just walk up and get into position?
A: That's right.

SOURCES: WCH XIII, 130 • GERTZ 511, 519

TURNER, NIGEL, filmmaker who, after five years of research, made the 1988 TV documentary *The Men Who Killed Kennedy* for Central Independent Television in Birmingham, England. The documentary was first shown in the United States in 1991 (Arts & Entertainment cable-television network).

TWIFORD, HORACE ELROY and ESTELLE, Oswald witnesses. Twiford was the national committeeman at large for the Socialist Labor Party in Fort Worth. He was informed by the party's New York headquarters in July 1963 that Oswald had written, requesting literature. On September 11, 1963, Twiford complied with the request and mailed the materials to Oswald's post-office box in Dallas. According to the WR, "On his way to Mexico City in September 1963, Oswald attempted to contact Twiford at his home in Houston; Oswald spoke briefly with Twiford's wife, identifying himself as a member of the [FPCC], but since Twiford was out of town at the time, Oswald was unable to speak with him."

SOURCES: WR 268 • WCH XI, 179

TYLER, NANCY CAROLE "CAROLE," suspicious death; secretary to scandalized LBJ associate Bobby Baker at the time of the assassination, and roommates with a coworker of Mary Jo Kopechne, then secretary to Florida Senator George Smathers. Kopechne later died in the Chappaquidick incident. According to Penn Jones Jr., Baker learned through Tyler and Kopechne that LBJ was to be dumped from the Kennedy ticket for the 1964 presidential election and replaced by Smathers. Tyler died at age 26 in a mysterious plane crash on May 10, 1965, over the Atlantic Ocean near Ocean City, Maryland. Her body was recovered the following day. (See also Baker, Bobby; Kopechne, Mary Jo)

SOURCES: FMG III, 83 • NORTH 332, 497, 519

U

UGARTE, GILBERTO ALVARADO (See ALVARADO, GILBERTO UGARTE)

UNDERHILL, GARY, suspicious death; former OSS agent; was occasionally used for operations by the CIA; former military affairs editor for *Life*. On November 28, 1963, six days after JFK's death, Underhill told friends in New Jersey that he knew who had ordered the assassination, claiming it was "a Far Eastern group in the CIA." Underhill died soon thereafter (on May 8, 1964) in his Washington, D.C., apartment with a bullet in his brain. The death was ruled a suicide in spite of the fact that the bullet entered the right-handed Underhill's head behind the left ear.
SOURCES: HT 143–4 • FMG III, 9 • OGLESBY 71

UNDERWOOD, JAMES R., a.w. (aftermath); assistant news director at KRLD-TV in Dallas. Underwood was on the scene in Dealey Plaza moments after the assassination and spoke to 15-year-old a.w. Amos L. Euins. Euins told him that he had seen a man with a rifle in the TSBD and that the man was black. By the time Euins testified to the WC, the color of the gunman had become impossible to determine. (See also Euins, Amos)
SOURCES: WR 76–7 • WCH VI, 167 • RTJ 281 • MOORE 62

V

VAGANOV, IGOR "TURK" (aka NICHOLSON, JOHN; KULLAWAY, KURT; CARSON, VINCE; BAGAVOV, IGOR), possible t.k.w.; once considered a suspect in the Tippit killing. Vaganov, in his early twenties, was a Latvian émigré who lived in Philadelphia but who suspiciously moved to Dallas two weeks before Tippit's death. One t.k.w., Domingo Benavides, testified that he had seen a red 1961 Ford with a man sitting in it, parked about six cars away from Tippit's car at the scene of the murder. Vaganov was driving a red Ford Thunderbird that day, lived near the site of the crime, was dressed the same that day as a man placed at the scene by t.k.w. Acquilla Clemons and cannot adequately account for his whereabouts at 1:15 P.M., November 22, 1963. Writer John Berendt described Vaganov in the August 1967 issue of *Esquire*: "He was tall and thin, and his green eyes were set beneath a high forehead in a perpetual squint. The corners of his mouth were habitually turned down... A hitch in the Navy had left him with just enough polish, just enough superficial cool, to get by on... Born in Latvia, he had lived in Germany during [World War II] and had come to America when he was about nine. He spoke four languages."

In late September 1963, about the time the White House announced there would be motorcades during JFK's Texas trip, Vaganov was working as a credit manager in a branch of General Electric Credit Corporation in a suburb of Philadelphia. Without warning, he requested a transfer to Dallas. The company turned him down. In October he asked again—and again was denied. In the first week of October, Turk met 18-year-old Anne Dulin, a soda jerk at Doc Ornsteen's drugstore in Village Green, where Turk hung out because he shared an interest in citizen band (CB) radios with Doc. Anne and Turk quickly became an item. In his red Thunderbird

460

convertible, Turk had a CB radio worth $225 with enough power to exceed FCC regulations, strong enough to broadcast 5–8 miles in a city with tall buildings. Acquaintances say Turk was a crack shot with a rifle and owned a "250–3000"—only .006 of an inch smaller in caliber than the Mannlicher-Carcano rifle reportedly owned by Oswald. According to Turk's first wife, from whom he was already divorced by 1963, his other hobbies included torturing dogs and cats.

On November 5, he made his third request to be transferred to Dallas. When he was again turned down, he quit his job and made plans to go to Dallas anyway. John Berendt picks up the story:

> Going straight to his apartment at 1116 Seventh Ave. in Swarthmore, Vaganov spent the next day and a half selling his furniture and packing his clothes... Anne could go with him if she liked, and she did, so the two of them left town on November 7 in his Thunderbird... With him also went his two-way radio, the rifle in the trunk and $800 in his pocket... In addition Vaganov carried a .38 caliber pistol. Loading one bullet into it, he placed it between himself and Anne on the front seat, "Just in case we see any deer." Anne was frightened, she admitted later, but she didn't let on... They were married in South Carolina and, stopping briefly in Georgia and Alabama to visit two of Vaganov's friends, they arrived in Dallas on the tenth or eleventh of November. On the twelfth, they took an apartment at Sunset Manor in the Oak Cliff section of town.

Each day in Dallas, Turk put on a suit and tie and left the apartment at 7:30 A.M., not returning until 5:00 P.M. He never told anyone precisely what he did. He told his wife he was looking for a job and his landlady that he had been transferred from Philadelphia. Still, he paid the bills and even opened a bank account. Anne's sister met Turk for the first time during this period and was disturbed by his attitudes. He hated "niggers and Jews" and "was proud to be a member of the master race." On Tuesday, November 19, a short, stocky man came to the Vaganov home while Turk was out. Turk later would not discuss who the man was. (According to Anne, Turk told her in 1965 that the man was "Mike from the CIA.") On the night before the assassination, Anne called her sister, who lived in Conroe, Texas, and screamed hysterically, "Turk is going to do something horrible tomorrow!" She didn't elaborate.

On Friday morning, November 22, Turk broke his daily pattern and slept in, not getting up until noon. According to his landlady, he wore khaki pants and "possibly a white shirt or jacket." According to all accounts, Turk didn't leave the apartment until 12:45, fifteen minutes after the assassination. While he was coming down the stairs, his landlord told him that JFK had been shot. Turk was "elated" and ran back upstairs. He watched TV for several minutes with his wife, then, at 12:50 P.M., he left suddenly, telling his wife that he had to go to the bank. Bank records show that he never arrived. Less than a half hour later, Tippit was murdered with a .38 pistol. Domingo Benavides said he saw a red car at the scene. Acquila Clemons said she saw two men flee the murder: one a "heavy . . . short guy," the other a tall thin man in a white shirt and khaki pants. Berendt notes, "The first description fitted Vaganov's mysterious caller; the second fitted Vaganov."

At about 2:20, Turk returned home. Anne says that when she told Turk a cop had been shot nearby, "he seemed to know it." Later in the afternoon, the couple got in the car and toured the sites of both murders. At 4:30 P.M., the Vaganovs were visited by two FBI agents; the FBI had been alerted by Anne's sister because of Anne's hysterical phone call the night before. The FBI interviewed the Vaganovs, checked Turk's rifle and pistol, determined that they had not been fired, seemed satisfied, and left. During the early evening, Turk told his wife that he had to return immediately to Philadelphia to "take care of a few things with General Electric." Anne, near-hysterical again, called her sister, who immediately came to pick her up and take her home with her. By the next morning, Turk was out of Dallas, on his way to Philadelphia. He stayed in Philadelphia for only a few days, then moved back in with his first wife in Atlanta. Six months after the assassination, the FBI discovered "a bundle of Vaganov's clothes" in a Dallas phone booth. In 1967, *Esquire* gave Vaganov an opportunity to explain his strange movements and he took it:

Vaganov says he wanted to go to Dallas because he believed his first wife was living in Garland, Texas, with her grandmother. He says that once he got there with a new wife, he felt obligated to her and did not go to visit the first. . . During the week he was in Dallas, Vaganov said he worked at two places. Half a day at Art Grindle Motors. Grindle has since sold his business and moved, so it was impossible to check. Vaganov says that at Art Grindle's there were too many salesmen on the line, and that's why he left. Then he worked a day and a half at the Texas Consumer Finance Corporation. Vaganov says he left that job on the second day (the day before the assassination), when a report from G.E. in Philadelphia reached his new employer, telling them about the items he had stolen back East. General Electric insisted that they could not give him a favorable recommendation unless he returned and straightened out matters with them. Discouraged, Vaganov slept late the next day (the day of the assassination) and went back to Philadelphia that night.

Checking the story, *Esquire* discovered that the Texas Consumer Finance Corporation could find no record of having hired Vaganov. They said, however, that, because Vaganov's job had lasted for less than two shifts, the records may have been destroyed routinely. (Vaganov applied for that job in an office at 1310 Commerce Street, Dallas—which was only a few doors away from Ruby's Carousel Club.) Vaganov denied torturing animals and being a crack shot. He said he didn't know the short and heavy man who came to see him in Dallas, and that "Mike" was actually an ex-cop he'd met in Los Angeles well after JFK's death. He said the hysterical phone call his wife had made to her sister concerned a domestic fight—Anne had been afraid that he was going to hurt her or himself—and didn't have anything to do with the assassination.

Vaganov offered *Esquire* his explanation of where he had been at the time of the Tippit murder: "According to him, he left the apartment just before one o'clock, [about] twenty minutes before Tippit was killed. He did intend to go to the bank, but first he went downstairs and took his car around the corner to have two front tires replaced for the return to Philadelphia. He got back to his apartment an hour or an hour and a half later, at which time the FBI arrived." Turk's landlady says he returned to the apartment a full two hours later than he said he did. *Esquire* talked to the gas station attendant who could have provided Turk with an alibi—his name was Jack Griffis—and he said that, though he remembered that he changed the tires on a car at about the time of the assassination, he could remember neither the make of the car nor the appearance of the driver.

For a time it was suspected that the discarded jacket found near the Tippit murder, which officially belonged to Oswald, might actually have been Vaganov's. This theory, however, was discarded when it was learned that Vaganov wore 36-inch sleeves, while the jacket in the National Archives had 32½-inch sleeves. Vaganov had no explanation for why a bundle of his clothes might have been found in a Dallas phone booth six months after he left town. *Esquire* concluded:

***

True, Vaganov tells a tall tale once in a while, he has acute fuzz paranoia [fear of police] and there are coincidences which lend sinister implications to his visit to Dallas. But his lies are usually the self-aggrandizing type, his fear of cops stems from his bad-check days and his coincidental movements are no fault of his own. Vaganov's willingness to be questioned, to have his picture published in a national magazine [such a photo accompanies the *Esquire* article], to go to Dallas and face the Tippit eyewitnesses [for a fee] would by themselves tend to rule him out. Furthermore, there is not one shred of evidence linking him with either killing that day or with any of the principals involved. If indeed he was involved in something shady in Dallas, it was something other than the assassination.

(See also Ballen, Samuel; Clemons, Acquilla; Price, Jesse C.)
SOURCE: FLAMMONDE 191–2

VALENTINE, JIM M., a.w. (aftermath); member DPD. Valentine rode from the DPD station to Dealey Plaza upon hearing of the assassination in car #207. Accompanying him were Sergeant Gerald Hill (DPD) and *Dallas Morning News* reporter Jim E. Well. (Car #207 is the car seen by Earlene Roberts outside of Oswald's rooming house approximately 30 minutes following the assassination. Officially, that car was still parked outside the TSBD at that time. • See also Hill, Gerald)
SOURCE: WCH XXV, 171

VALLEE, THOMAS ARTHUR, lithographer. Vallee was arrested November 2, 1963, in Chicago, the day JFK was to ride through Chicago in a motorcade, for carrying a concealed weapon (an M-1 rifle) and ammunition; drove car with NY state license plate #311-ORF. The FBI has restricted all information regarding that number—although Chicago legal researcher Sherman Skolnick claims the number was registered to a man calling himself "Lee Harvey Oswald." Vallee's arrest, at the corner of Wilson and Damen Streets, was witnessed by SS agent Abraham Bolden. (See Bolden, Abraham)
SOURCES: WCD 149 • FMG IV, 7–8

VAUGHN, ROY EUGENE, o.k.w. (prelude); DPD oficer. Vaughn was sole guard of the Main Street ramp at DPD headquarters on the morning Oswald was shot. According to the WC, Ruby gained entrance to that building via the Main Street ramp, yet Vaughn denies seeing him pass. Others have testified that a man did walk by Vaughn unquestioned two or three minutes before the shooting and that the man could have been Ruby. Vaughn said on the 1988 British television documentary, *The Men Who Killed Kennedy* (produced by Nigel Turner), "Jack Ruby did not come down that ramp. I'll go to my grave saying that man did not come down that ramp." (See also Daniels, Napoleon; Hall, C. Ray)

SOURCES: WR 200, 204–5 • WCH XII, 357 • RTJ 220–6 • GERTZ 518–9 • DOP 521–2 • HT 236–7 • FMG I, 71 • BLAKEY 321 • KANTOR 68–9, 74–5, 150

VECIANA, ANTONIO (aka Blanch, Antonio Veciana), possible Oswald witness; former Cuban bank accountant; founder of the militant anti-Castro Cuban group known as Alpha 66, a group that received heavy CIA support. Veciana told the HSCA that his contact with the CIA was an agent named "Maurice Bishop," with whom he met more than 100 times to discuss anti-Castro activities, including the attempted assassination of the Cuban premier. He claims that, during a visit to Dallas in August or September 1963, he saw "Bishop" talking to a man he later recognized to be Oswald and claims that, after the assassination, Bishop told him he should offer one of his relatives in Mexico "a large sum of money" to say that this relative had met Oswald during Oswald's trip to Mexico City in September 1963. Soon after testifying, Veciana was shot in the head but survived the attack—and now refuses to comment further on the subject.

Veciana is suspected by author George Michael Evica of being one of the men who visited Sylvia Odio. (See also Odio, Sylvia; Phillips, David Atlee)

SOURCES: HSCA Report 135, 237 • EVICA, many • DAVIS 439, 442 • CF 149–54 • HT 144, 192–3, 286–90 • BLAKEY 346–7

VOEBEL, EDWARD, Oswald witness; acquaintance at Beauregard Junior High School in New Orleans. Once, in the ninth grade, Oswald was punched by an older high-school student and received a bloody lip and a loosened tooth. After this incident, Voebel took Oswald back to school to tend to his wounds. The pair developed a "mild friendship" because of this incident. Voebel told the WC that Oswald had once had a plan to cut the glass out of a store window and steal a pistol, although this was probably normal adolescent fantasy. He said Oswald "wouldn't start any fights, but if you wanted to start one with him, he was going to make sure that he ended it, or you were really going to have one, because he wasn't going to take anything from anybody."

SOURCES: WR 359 • WCH VIII, 1 • FLAMMONDE 20–1 • DAVIS 217

VOLPERT, ANN, Ruby witness and Ruby's sister. Volpert received a call from Ruby at her Chicago home, shortly after 9:00 P.M., on November 22,

1963. He was distressed and mentioned leaving Dallas and returning to Chicago.
SOURCE: WR 316

von BRAUN, WERNHER, former Nazi rocket scientist; NASA official. According to author Carl Oglesby, "The most extreme [conspiracy] theory traces the assassination to a group in the Defense Department that emerged around...von Braun and the Nazi rocket scientists the U.S. military imported into the country, illegally and against specific orders, and installed at Huntsville, Alabama at the end of WW II—the famous Operation Paperclip." (See also Torbitt, William)
SOURCE: OGLESBY 82–3

VOSHININ, IGOR VLADIMIR and NATASHA, Oswald witnesses; members of Dallas's Russian-speaking community; friends of Oswald associate George DeMohrenschildt. Voshinin was an influential White Russian working in petrochemicals. According to *Haagse Post* (September 30, 1967), "The only one of the Russian community who seems to have been *au courant* with the whole affair was a certain Igor Voshinin."

Natasha was 45-years-old at the time of JFK's death. Born in Labinsk, Russia; she became a naturalized American in 1955 and held a degree in geology. She described for the WC a feud within the Dallas Russian community over church liturgy (whether services should be in Old Church Slavonic or in English) and said they were no longer on speaking terms with George Bouhe because of this. She was first employed in the United States by geologist George DeMohrenschildt as a secretary. She told the WC that DeMohrenschilt was very politically provocative and could switch from the left to the right, depending on the situation. She said she never met the Oswalds because she believed Lee was a Soviet agent, a notion she got from Marguerite Oswald. She told the WC she felt that DeMohrenschildt was visiting some "politically unsavory" character during his frequent trips to Houston.

Igor was 58 years old and was employed by Mullen & Powell as a structural engineer. He was born in Russia before the revolution and told the WC that George DeMohrenschildt was friends with a rich oilman in Mexico named Tito Harper, and that DeMohrenschildt also befriended Anastas Mikoyan (a top Communist and "Butcher of the Stalin times," later head of the Presidium) in Mexico. Like his wife, he never met the Oswalds. (See also DeMohrenschildt, George; Torbitt, William)
SOURCES: WCH VIII, 425, 448 • FLAMMONDE 195 • EVICA 297–8

W

WADE, HENRY MENASCO, Oswald witness; Ruby witness; Dallas district attorney; formerly Governor John Connally's college roommate. WR critics have long wondered why the DPD made a beeline for Oswald after the assassination. This mistatement made by D.A. Henry Wade on November 24, 1963, has added to the confusion: "A police officer, immediately after the assassination, ran in the building and saw this man [Oswald] in a corner and started to arrest him, but the manager of the building [Roy Truly] said that he was an employee and was all right. Every other employee was located but this defendant, of the company. A description and name of him went out by police to look for him." A careful study of the facts finds several things wrong with this statement. Oswald was not in a "corner" when first approached by police, was not a suspect "by name" until after he was arrested, and was not the only employee of the TSBD missing from the building after the assassination.

Wade was also the D.A. in charge of prosecuting Ruby in the years preceding the assassination for various vice and assault charges, a task Wade performed without tenacity, never achieving a conviction. (See also del Valle, Eladio; Dowe, Kenneth; Duncan, William)

SOURCES: WR 189, 193, 215–9, 319–9, 323–4, 417 • WCH V, 213 • RTJ, many • COA 114, 126–7 • GERTZ, many • BISHOP, many • DOP 287, 302, 304, 331, 333, 458–9, 568 • MOORE 20 • FMG I, many • BE 356, 693 • OTT 98 • BLAKEY 37, 318, 328–30, 332–3 • FLAMMONDE 132, 158–9, 231 • HOS 162, 187, 204 • EVICA 15, 22–4, 162 • DAVIS 223–4 • NORTH, many • PD 15–6, 18, 337–48 • KANTOR, many

WALDMAN, WILLIAM J., possible Oswald witness; vice president of Klein's Sporting Goods Company in Chicago at the time Oswald mail-ordered the purported murder weapons from that company. Waldman told the WC that his company sent a Mannlicher-Carcano rifle to "A. Hidell,

PO Box 2915, Dallas" and that accompanying the mail-order coupon was a postal money order purchased on March 12, 1963.
    SOURCES: WR 114 • WCH VII, 360 • BISHOP 521

WALDO, THAYER, staff reporter, *Fort Worth Star-Telegram*. Waldo told author Mark Lane that on the evening of November 14, 1963, he knew of a two-hour meeting that took place at the Carousel Club. At the meeting were Jack Ruby, Officer J. D. Tippit, and Bernard Weissman, a Dallas right-winger who signed a full-page anti-JFK ad that ran in the *Dallas Morning News* on November 22. Lane refused to give the WC his source concerning the information on the November 14 meeting. The WC failed to ask Waldo where he had gotten the information. (See also Tippit, J. D.; Weissman, Bernard)
    SOURCES: WCH XV, 585 • RTJ 249 • COA 127 • BISHOP 453 • FMG I, 161, 163, 167, 171 • NORTH 418 • KANTOR 55, 66-7

WALKER, C.T., Texas Theatre witness; member DPD. Walker pursued Officer Tippit's killer in the Oak Cliff section of Dallas and was in on the arrest of Oswald in the Texas Theatre. With Patrolmen T. A. Hutson, Ray Hawkins and M. N. "Nick" McDonald, he entered the theater through the rear entrance. (See also Hawkins, Ray; Hutson, T. A.; McDonald, M. N.)
    SOURCES: WR 164 • WCH VII, 34 • BISHOP 203-4, 213-4

WALKER, EDWIN A., major general, U.S. Army; right-wing activist. Marina Oswald told the WC her husband took a shot at Walker on April 10, 1963, from outside Walker's home. (A shooting really happened; the bullet missed Walker completely.) Among the effects found in Oswald's possession after his arrest was a photograph of Walker's home. By the time that photograph was released by the FBI, a hole had been cut into it, obliterating the license plate on a car that is parked in the driveway. Other than Marina's testimony, there is nothing to connect Oswald with the attempted shooting of Walker. Walker's right-wing beliefs were so extreme that he was forced to retire from the U.S. Army in 1961, not long after it was discovered he had been showing right-wing films to the troops under his command. The balance of the evidence indicates that Oswald probably had nothing to do with the Walker incident, and that perhaps the incident had been staged to make Walker appear a "martyr" to his supporters. (See also Coleman, Walter; Duff, William; Ellsworth, Frank; Hosty, James; Johnson, Arnold; Klause, Robert; Nicol, Joseph D.; Surrey, Robert)
    SOURCES: WR, many • WCH XI, 404 • HSCA Report 35, 63, 195 • BELIN 204-6 • RTJ 248, 308, 349-50, 384 • COA 155, 188 • BISHOP 11, 115, 126, 250, 380, 416, 529 • CF 255-65, 403 • HT 167, 179, 211-2, 296, 307-9, 437-8 • MOORE 193 • FMG I, 123-5, 142, 156 • BLAKEY 5, 29, 108, 353-6, 363-4 • FLAMMONDE 125-7, 133, 176, 195 •

EVICA 7, 58–9, 75–6, 80, 95, 101, 109 • ME 16, 115 • OGLESBY 57–60 • DAVIS 135, 231 • NORTH, many • PD 344, 351

WALKER, IRA N., JR., Ruby witness; WBAP-TV broadcast technician in Fort Worth. Walker was sitting in a truck parked outside the DPD station on the morning of November 24, 1963. He told the WC he spoke to Ruby twice after 10:30 that morning, and Ruby had asked him, "Has he [Oswald] been brought down yet?" This is further corroboration that Ruby was lying when he said that the shooting of Oswald was spontaneous and that he was in the vicinity of the DPD station only a few minutes before the shooting.
SOURCES: WR 329–30 • WCH XIII, 289 • COA 144–5 • GERTZ 56–7 • BLAKEY 320

WALL, BRECK (aka WILSON, BILLY RAY), Ruby witness; president of the Dallas council of AGVA. Wall was responsible for reviewing complaints by performers against nightclub operators. Ruby called Wall four times during November 1963. Later, Wall couldn't remember what the calls were about. He told the FBI in 1963 that, back in 1960, he had almost worked a deal for a "nightclub review" he produced to appear at Ruby's Carousel Club, which was then called the Sovereign Club. Also in on the deal was James Henry Dolan, an AGVA/Mafia man from Denver. When Ruby refused to put the deal on paper, Wall backed out. This upset Ruby so much that he punched Wall's assistant, Joseph Peterson—a man whom Dolan described as "a little fairy."

Wall appears in the exploitation film *Naughty Dallas*, much of which was filmed in Ruby's Carousel Club. (See also Dolan, James; Peterson, Joseph)
SOURCES: WR 327, 329, 333–4 • WCH XIV, 599 • COA 111, 250 • FMG I, 19 • BLAKEY 37–8, 306 • HOS 117 • DAVIS 213, 225 • NORTH 420

WALLE, MARILYN APRIL (See MOONEY, NANCY JANE)

WALTER, WILLIAM S., FBI employee; night clerk at the FBI's New Orleans office. On November 17, 1963, Walter received a memo via telex warning of a plot to kill JFK; he told five agents of the memo and considered his job done. Walter's story was authenticated in 1976, when assassination researcher Mark Lane successfully invoked the Freedom of Information Act to obtain a copy of the telex. It read:

URGENT: 1:45 AM EST 11-17-63 HLF 1 PAGE
TO: ALL SACS
FROM: DIRECTOR
    THREAT TO ASSASSINATE PRESIDENT KENNEDY IN DALLAS
TEXAS NOVEMBER 22 DASH THREE NINETEEN SIXTY THREE.
MISC INFORMATION CONCERNING. INFORMATION HAS BEEN

RECEIVED BY THE BUREAS [sic] BUREAU HAS DETERMINED THAT A MILITANT REVOLUTIONARY GROUP MAY ATTEMPT TO ASSASSINATE PRESIDENT KENNEDY ON HIS PROPOSED TRIP TO DALLAS TEXAS NOVEMBER TWENTY TWO DASH TWENTY THREE NINETEEN SIXTY THREE. ALL RECEIVING OFFICES SHOULD IMMEDIATELY CONTACT ALL CIS, PCIS LOGICAL RACE AND HATE GROUP INFORMANTS AND DETERMINE IF ANY BASIS FOR THREAT. BUREAU SHOULD BE KEPT ADVISED OF ALL DEVELOPMENTS BY TELETYPE. OTHER OFFICES HAVE BEEN ADVISED. END AND ACK PLS.
SOURCES: HSCA Report 191–2 • FLAMMONDE 274 • OTT 220–1

WALTHER, CAROLYN, a.w. Walter told author Josiah Thompson that she saw two men in an upper-floor TSBD window moments before the assassination and that one of them had a rifle. She did not think the men were as high as the sixth floor. Walter was not asked to testify or submit an affidavit for the WC. She said the man with the gun "was wearing a white shirt and had blond or light brown hair" and that the other was "a man in a brown suit coat." Witnesses James Worrell and Richard Randolph Carr also saw the man in the brown coat. (See also Carr, Richard; Henderson, Ruby; Worrell, James)
SOURCES: WCE 2086 • RTJ 396 • BISHOP 129 • CF 20–1 • HT 140, 175, 228 • FMG III, 64 • OTT 92–3 • ME 23 • DAVIS 196, 209, 459

WALTHERS, EDDY RAYMOND "BUDDY," a.w.; Ruby witness; suspicious death; Dallas County deputy sheriff; Walthers was the first law enforcement official to speak to James T. Tague, who was cut by a flying object during the assassination. He searched the area near the mouth of the triple underpass, where Tague had been standing, and found a bullet mark "on the top edge of the curb on Main Street near the underpass." Walthers appears in photographs taken on the south side of Elm Street, across the street from the pergola, exactly ten minutes after the shooting. In the photos are Walthers and two men in business suits, assumed to be federal agents of some sort. In the sequence of photos, one of the suited men reaches down and picks something up out of the grass, clutches it firmly in his palm, and then slips it into his pocket. Walthers originally reported that a bullet had been found and then, for reasons unknown, withdrew this statement, saying that it actually was a piece of JFK's head that had been found. Officially, the object doesn't exist.

After Ruby was arrested for shooting Oswald, his possessions were searched and among them was Walthers's signed permanant pass to the

Carousel Club. Walthers died on January 10, 1969. Officially, he was shot through the heart by an escaped prisoner. However, according to HT, "it was admitted that he 'could' have been shot by a fellow officer."
SOURCES: WR 111, 165 • WCH VII, 544 • RTJ 69 • COA 111 • CF 61, 313 • HT 131, 214 • FMG I, 33; III, 71–2 • OTT 95, 209, 323 • FLAMMONDE 127

WALTZ, JON R., coauthor, with John Kaplan, of *The Trial of Jack Ruby* (Macmillan, 1965).
SOURCES: GERTZ 42, 251–61, 343 • BLAKEY 325–6, 328, 330, 332

WARD, HUGH, suspicious death; business partner of Oswald associate Guy Banister. Banister and Ward died within ten days of one another—Ward on May 23, 1965, in a plane crash in Mexico—just before the WC concluded its hearings. Ward was the pilot of the plane. A passenger on the same flight was New Orleans Mayor DeLesseps Chep Morrison, who once introduced Clay Shaw to JFK. (See also Banister, William Guy; Morrison, DeLesseps)
SOURCES: FMG III, 47 • FLAMMONDE 115–7

WARNER, ROGER C., SS agent. On November 24, 1963, the day Ruby killed Oswald, Warner interviewed Ruby stripper Karen Carlin. In his report on the interview, Warner wrote, "Mrs. Carlin was highly agitated and was reluctant to make any statement to me. She stated to me that she was under the impression that... Oswald,... Ruby and other individuals unknown to her were involved in a plot to assassinate [JFK] and that she would be killed if she gave any information to the authorities." Carlin was reportedly murdered soon thereafter. (See also Carlin, Karen)
SOURCES: WCH XV, 619 • COA 137–8 • BISHOP 52

WARREN, EARL, Ruby witness; head of the WC; chief justice, U.S. Supreme Court. Warren's chief contribution to the WC's investigation was his light-handed and uninquisitive interrogation of Ruby in the Dallas County Jail. (See also McLane, Alfred)
SOURCES: HSCA Report, many • EVICA 212–3, 217 • FLAMMONDE, many • ME 11, 19, 109, 145 • OGLESBY 12, 69, 77–8 • DAVIS, many • NORTH, many • PD, many • BELIN 12–3, 37–40, 44–7, 217–8, 227 • RTJ, many • COA, many • GERTZ, many • BISHOP 113, 315, 319 • DOP, many • CF 461–72 • HT 263, 294–8 • FMG I, 16, 160, 185; III, 48, 52, 77 • BE 85, 99, 141, 173, 225, 358, 424, 509 • OTT 160, 273, 282 • BLAKEY, many • HOS 19, 81, 85, 130, 204, 206 • KANTOR, many

WARREN, EDWARD (See HUNT, E. HOWARD)

WATHERWAX, ARTHUR WILLIAM, Ruby witness; *Dallas Times-Herald* printer. Watherwax was one of the newspaper employees who spoke to Ruby in the newspaper building at approximately 4:00 A.M. on November 23, 1963, while Ruby visited there. According to the WR, Ruby "sought Watherwax's views on his decision to close his clubs and indicated he was going to attempt to persuade other club-owners to do likewise. Watherwax described Ruby as 'pretty shaken up' about the assassination and at the same time 'excited' that he had attended Oswald's Friday night press conference."

SOURCES: WR 320, 322 • WCH XV, 564

WATSON, JAMES C., o.k.w.; 43-year-old DPD detective (Auto Theft Bureau) stationed at the Trade Mart during the assassination. Watson was in the DPD station basement when Oswald was shot, but didn't see Ruby until the shooting.

SOURCE: WCH XII, 372

WEATHERFORD, HARRY, a.w.; Dallas County deputy sheriff. Weatherford filed this statement for his office on November 23: "I heard a loud report which I thought was a railroad torpedo, as it sounded like it came from the railroad yard. I recognized the following reports as rifle shots and ran toward the railroad yards to investigate." At 3:00 P.M. on the day of the assassination, Weatherford was involved in the search and seizure of evidence at the Paine home in Irving, Texas, where Marina Oswald had been living. It was here that police found the photographs of Oswald holding a rifle that Marina later claimed she took. The photos have been suspected by photographic experts of being phonies. Also found was a rolled-up blanket in the garage, which Marina claimed had held Oswald's rifle. Oswald claimed that he owned no rifle.

According to researcher Penn Jones Jr., Weatherford was a "crackshot" and was on top of the Dallas County Jail building at the time of the assassination. A researcher had once asked him if he had shot JFK. Weatherford replied, "You little son of a bitch, I shoot lots of people." Jones also wrote that a custom-made silencer for a rifle had been delivered to Weatherford "a few weeks" before the assassination.

Interestingly, when Dallas County Sheriff Bill Decker lay dying in 1970, Weatherford was at his death bed. (See also Decker, J. E.; Oswald, Marina; Paine, Ruth)

SOURCES: RTJ 42 • BISHOP 277 • HT 188 • FMG III, 35–6, 100; IV, 445

WEBERMAN, A. J., coauthor, with Michael Canfield, of *Coup d'État in America* (Third Press, 1975), which concludes that assassination suspects E. Howard Hunt and Frank Sturgis—both of whom would later become public figures due to the Watergate scandal—were two of the "three tramps" arrested near Dealey Plaza just after the assassination. (See also Canfield, Michael; Hunt, E. Howard; Sturgis, Frank)

SOURCE: HT 345

WEBSTER, ROBERT E., possible Oswald double. Webster was an American who told officials he planned to defect to the USSR, less than two weeks before Oswald did the same. He was a former navy man; ex-employee of the CIA-connected Rand Corporation; a young plastics expert who went to Moscow to work at an American trade exhibition and did not return with his colleagues. While in the Soviet Union, Webster (who was already married in the U.S.) lived with a Soviet woman and with her had a child. Like Oswald, he became "disenchanted" with Soviet life and returned to the U.S. "about the same time" as Oswald. According to CF, "Years later in America, Marina [Oswald] told an acquaintance that her husband had defected after working at an American exhibition in Moscow. This, of course, reflects Webster's story, not Oswald's. After the assassination, when American Intelligence was looking into Marina's background, they discovered an address in her address book matching that of Webster's Leningrad apartment." (See also Oswald, Marina)
SOURCES: CF 116–21 • SUMMERS 176

WECHT, CYRIL, pathology expert. Wecht was a member of the HSCA's nine-man forensic pathology panel, which frequently voted 8-1 on matters regarding the numbers and direction of the bullets fired in Dealey Plaza, with Wecht being the lone dissenter. He is one of the world's most vocal critics of the "single-bullet theory."
SOURCES: HSCA Report 43 • DAVIS 436–7 • FLAMMONDE 37 • ME 88, 129, 152, 231 • HT, many • MOORE 107, 178, 182 • BE, many • OTT 244–5

WEGMANN, EDWARD F. and WILLIAM, brothers; with Irvin Dymond, members of the legal team defending Clay Shaw at his assassination conspiracy trial. (See also Dymond, Irvin)
SOURCES: OTT 146–7, 157, 233 • FLAMMONDE 71, 79, 91, 93, 212–3, 225, 238, 244–5, 290

WEIGMAN, DAVE, a.w.; NBC cameraman. Weigman was riding in the seventh car of the motorcade. He kept his camera rolling; jumped out of the press-pool station wagon, and ran up onto the grassy knoll. Before the public got to see the Zapruder film, Weigman's herky-jerky motion picture of the assassination scene was the most famous film, since it was shown repeatedly on NBC during the days following the assassination. It is claimed that, when Weigman's film is examined frame by frame, there is one shot—just as the presidential limo disappears into the tunnel—that shows puffs of smoke coming from the bushes atop the grassy knoll. (See also Holland, Sam M.)

SOURCE: CF 58

WEINREB, LLOYD L., WC staff member. Weinreb was a Justice Department lawyer who wrote the WR's 72-page appendix regarding Oswald's biography.

WEINSTEIN, ABE and BARNEY, Ruby witnesses; brothers. The Weinsteins were nightclub-owning competitors of Ruby whom Ruby criticized repeatedly after the assassination for not closing their clubs the way he had his.
SOURCES: WR 325, 327, 329, 333–4

WEISBERG, HAROLD, former senate investigator; independent assassination researcher and author of *Oswald in New Orleans* (Canyon, 1967) as well as many self-published books.
SOURCES: HT 67, 74, 98, 104–5, 109, 234–5, 332, 390–1 • FMG III, 17, 39, 43 • MOORE, many • OTT 54 • BE 117, 306, 435, 508, 648 • EVICA 16, 48, 160, • FLAMMONDE, many • ME 21, 25–6, 123, 213–5 • DAVIS 269, 326, 364, 411, 422, 435, 463 • NORTH 458

WEISS, MARK, HSCA acoustics expert. With Ernest Ashkensky, said they were "95% sure" that the police Dictabelt recording indicated a fourth shot from the grassy knoll.
SOURCES: HSCA Report 69, 486, 495, 507 • OGLESBY 44 • ME 182 • BELIN 191 • COA 26–8, 34 • HT 249, 261–2 • MOORE 141 • BE 563 • BLAKEY 95, 101–2, 104, 266

WEISSMAN, BERNARD, Dallas right-winger; signer of the black-bordered anti-JFK ad that ran in the *Dallas Morning News* on the morning of the assassination. Information obtained by reporter Thayer Waldo says that Weissman was involved in a two-hour, three-man meeting at the Carousel Club on November 14, 1963. According to that information, the other two men at the meeting were Ruby and Officer J. D. Tippit. (See also Tippit, J. D.; Waldo, Thayer)
SOURCES: WR 272–8, 313, 320, 324, 332, 344–5 • WCH V, 487; XI, 428 • RTJ 248–51, 254–9 • GERTZ 19, 119, 267, 524 • BISHOP 19, 77, 94, 118, 495 • DOP 204, 286 • FMG I, 75–7, 88, 120, 125, 128, 134, 136

WEITZMAN, SEYMOUR, a.w.; Dallas County deputy constable. Weitzman ran toward the wooden fence atop the grassy knoll following the shooting and encountered, as did others in that area, a man carrying SS identification. (Weitzman later identified this man as CIA freelancer and Watergate burglar Bernard Barker.) While there, a railroad worker told him that he had seen a man behind the fence throw something into a bush. The railroad worker was never identified and, as far as we know, nothing of note was ever found in the bushes. Behind the wooden fence, Weitzman saw "numerous kinds of footprints that did not make sense because they were going in different directions." Weitzman witnessed the discovery of a portion of JFK's skull on the south side of Elm Street. After that discovery, he moved to the TSBD, where he was involved in the discovery of the rifle on the sixth floor, and he signed an affidavit to the effect that the rifle found in the TSBD was a 7.65 Mauser (rather than a Mannlicher-Carcano, as is officially claimed). Weitzman should know the difference because he once owned a gun shop. (See also Barker, Bernard; Boone, Eugene; Harper, Billy)

SOURCES: WR 85–6 • WCH VII, 105 • RTJ 35–7, 56, 114–5, 118–20, 383–4 • COA 23–4 • BISHOP 142, 161 • CF 74, 321 • HT 144, 229–33 • MOORE 30, 47 • OTT 98, 100 • BE 19 • CANFIELD 226 • EVICA 16–23, 25, 47–50, 52, 54–5, 58, 60

WELL, JIM E. (aka Ewell, Jim), reporter for the *Dallas Morning News* and witness to much of the pertinent DPD activity on the day of the assassination. (See Hill, Gerald Lynn)

SOURCE: WCH VII, 43

WEST, JEAN (See AASE, JEAN)

WEST, LOUIS JOLYAN, Ruby witness; psychiatrist; CIA mind-control expert (MK-ULTRA program); Dr. West "treated" Ruby in jail and concluded that Ruby was in a "paranoid state, manifested by delusions, visual and auditory hallucinations and suicidal impulses." Ruby's #1 delusion was his belief that Dallas had been transformed by Nazis into a giant concentration camp where Jews were being systematically extermi- nated. West prescribed medication.

According to authors Martin A. Lee and Bruce Shlain in *Acid Dreams* (Grove Press, 1985), West experimented in the 1950s with a combination of hypnosis and LSD upon human guinea pigs. Sadly, West once killed an elephant with an overdose of LSD and other drugs. (See also Fowler, Clayton

WEST, ROBERT H., a.w.; Dallas County surveyor. West stood on Houston Street near Main Street; he said that the first shot sounded like a "motorcycle backfire" followed by three reports that sounded like rifle shots. According to author Jim Marrs, West said that the shots sounded as if they were coming from the "northwest quadrant of Dealey Plaza."

SOURCE: CF 20

WEST, TROY EUGENE, a.w.; Oswald witness; West, a TSBD employee who had been a TSBD mail-wrapper for 16 years, told the WC that he was eating lunch on the first floor of the TSBD during the assassination and heard no shots. WC questioner David Belin asked West if Oswald had ever borrowed wrapping paper—presumably so he could wrap his rifle for

transportation on the morning of the assassination. West said no.
SOURCES: WCH VI, 356 • BELIN 15 • BISHOP 44–5

WESTBROOK, KAREN, a.w.; TSBD employee. Westbrook was standing next to a.w. John Chism and Gloria Calvery near the "Stemmons
Freeway" sign on the north side of Elm Street. She was never questioned
officially.
SOURCES: CF 28 • NORTH 379 • SSID 61–3

WESTBROOK, W. R., t.k.w. (aftermath); DPD captain. Westbrook was
in the DPD station at the time of the assassination. Later, according to the
WC, Westbrook discovered a jacket near the scene of the Tippit killing that
supposedly belonged to Oswald. According to author Mark Lane, Westbrook denies that he discovered the jacket, which casts doubt on the
jacket's origins.

The WR states, "At 1:24 P.M. [November 22, 1963], the police radio
reported, 'The suspect last seen running west on Jefferson from 400 East
Jefferson.'... Westbrook and several other officers concentrated their
search along Jefferson Boulevard. Westbrook walked through the parking
lot behind the gas station and found a light-colored jacket lying under the
rear of one of the cars. Westbrook identified Commission Exhibit No. 162
as the...jacket."
SOURCES: WR 163 • WCH VII, 109 • RTJ 202–3 • BISHOP 146–7

WESTER, JANE CAROLYN, Parkland witness; registered nurse.
Wester was present for 10 to 15 minutes while JFK was being treated and
then was sent to help with Governor Connally. She says she did not get a
close look at JFK's wounds.
SOURCE: WCH VI, 120

WESTON, JAMES, pathologist; member, HSCA Forensic Pathology
Panel that was allowed to see the JFK autopsy material. Panel concluded
JFK was shot exclusively from the rear.
SOURCES: HSCA I, 145, 204, 376; VII 5, 75–7, 199, 202–3 • ME 231

WESTON, WALLY, Ruby witness; possible Oswald witness; former
Carousel Club emcee. In 1976, Weston told the *New York Daily News* (July
18, 1976) that, in September or October of 1963, Oswald (or an Oswald
look-alike) came into the Carousel. Weston and Oswald got into an
argument, during which "Oswald" called Weston a Communist and Weston
hit "Oswald." At that point, Ruby broke in and bounced "Oswald" from the
premises, saying, "I told you never to come in here again." (See also
Masen, John)
SOURCE: EVICA 97, 100, 111

WHALEN, EDWARD, professional criminal from Philadelphia, Pennsylvania. Whalen told New Orleans District Attorney Jim Garrison in 1967 that he had been offered $25,000 by assassination suspects David Ferrie and Clay Shaw (who was using his alias "Clay Bertrand") during a 1967 meeting in a Bourbon Street bar to "hit" Garrison. Whalen refused the offer. (See also Andrews, Dean; Ferrie, David; Garrison, Jim; Shaw, Clay)
SOURCE: OTT 122–4

WHALEY, WILLIAM WAYNE, Oswald witness; suspicious death; Dallas cabdriver. According to the WC, Whaley was instrumental in Oswald's flight from the assassination scene. According to Whaley's logbook, he took a passenger from the Greyhound bus station near Dealey Plaza to 500 North Beckley from 12:30 to 12:45 P.M., on November 22. This would have meant that Oswald was dropped off 4/10 of a mile from his rooming house, and that he would have boarded the cab at just about the time the president was being shot. Whaley later said that the man was relaxed and not in a hurry, even at one point offering to give up the cab to an older woman.

Whaley was killed in an accident in his cab in December 1965. He was the first Dallas cabbie to die on duty since 1937. (See Click, Darryl; Knapp, David; Lujan, Daniel)
SOURCES: WR 150–3, 234 • WCH II, 253, 292; VI, 428 • RTJ 164–8, 193, 333, 384 • COA 37 • DOP 457, 638 • HT 129, 139 • MOORE 60–1 • FMG I, 174 • BE 351 • PD 346, 367

WHEELES, JAMES E., possible Oswald witness. Wheeles was among the witnesses who saw a man resembling Oswald firing a rifle at the Sports Drome Rifle Range in Dallas in the weeks preceding the assassination. (See also Davis, Floyd; Price, Malcolm)
SOURCE: RTJ 334

WHITE, GENEVA, Ruby witness; wife of assassination suspect Roscoe White. White was a former Carousel Club B-girl (she worked there briefly just before assassination). She was interviewed by journalist Ron Laytner in August 1990, in the presence of author Harrison Edward Livingstone, several months before her death from lung cancer. She said she had overheard Roscoe and Ruby plotting to kill JFK. When they caught her eavesdropping, Ruby wanted to kill her, but Roscoe talked him out of it, saying they should just give her electroshock treatments until she forgot what she had heard. White said she once went to a rifle range with Roscoe and Oswald and that Oswald was a "real bad shot." She said that, after the assassination, she went to New Orleans without Roscoe and, while there, was threatened by mobster Charles Nicoletti, who said that her children would be tortured and killed if she ever talked. White said, "We at first thought the assassination was more Mob [but later realized] it was more CIA." She said she and Roscoe knew the Tippits well and that the conspirators "took care" of Tippit's wife and kids after Tippit's death. (See also Nicoletti, Charles; White, Roscoe)

SOURCE: HT2 463–9

WHITE, JACK, assassination researcher. With Gary Mack, White has extensively studied the Polaroid photograph of JFK at the moment of the fatal shot taken by a.w. Mary Moorman. According to White and Mack, the photo shows a man dressed in a policeman's uniform firing at JFK from behind the wooden fence atop the grassy knoll. Standing in front of the fence and to one side of the man in the uniform is a man in a serviceman's uniform who appears to be filming the assassination. This figure is suspected of being Gordon Arnold, who says this was where he stood and that shots whistled past his left ear. Standing next to the rifleman is a man wearing a hardhat, who appears to be looking in the direction of the TSBD.

White has also extensively studied the Zapruder film and says that there is evidence of retouching on some frames. Suspicion is that the back of JFK's head was darkened artificially on the frames following the fatal shot, covering up the gaping exit wound. (See also Moorman, Mary)

SOURCES: CF 69 • BE 557 • HT 203–4, 207, 209–10, 215, 257 • OGLESBY 52 • DAVIS 524, 579

WHITE, J.C., a.w.; member DPD. White was standing on the west side of the triple underpass. He told the WC that he saw and heard nothing because a train was moving between him and Dealey Plaza. However, film of the assassination shows no trains moving.

SOURCES: WR 80 • WCH VI, 253 • CF 56

WHITE, ROSCOE (ROCK), DPD officer; assassination suspect; suspicious death. On August 6, 1990, Roscoe White's son, unemployed oil-equipment salesman Ricky White, claimed that his father had killed JFK. White said that a detailed description of the assassination plot was in Roscoe's diary, which disappeared after it was inspected by the FBI. Ricky White said that he had no intention of telling what he knew until the FBI began to question him persistently in May 1988. Ricky claimed that Roscoe, who had joined the DPD two months before the assassination, shot twice at the president, including the bullet that killed him, and that it was his dad who had killed J. D. Tippit. (White left the DPD soon thereafter. Today a portion of the DPD's file on White appears to be missing.) Ricky said Oswald was involved in the plot but did not fire any shots. Ricky claimed to have a rifle which had belonged to his dad and which used ammunition similar to that used in the Mannlicher-Carcano long assumed to be the assassination weapon. Ricky further pointed out that Oswald and his father had served in the marines together—even traveling to Japan on the same boat—and that he had in his possession three faded messages which he believes were sent by a U.S. intelligence official to his father ordering the assassination.

Ricky claimed that the diary detailed the plot, which included a three-man shooting team. The other two gunmen were referred to in the diary only by their code names "Lebanon" and "Saul." Those two men fired their shots, Ricky said, from the TSBD and the County Records Building, both to JFK's rear at the time of the shooting. Ricky said that his father fired from behind the wooden fence atop the grassy knoll, and that Roscoe's code name in the operation was "Mandarin." The CIA denied that White was ever an employee or associated in any way with the agency, and the story died after a couple of days of making newspaper headlines. Roscoe White died in an explosive fire in 1971.

Those who have studied the famous backyard photos of Oswald holding a rifle have noticed a lump on Oswald's right wrist. Photographic evidence indicates that, while Oswald did not have such a lump on his wrist, White did. According to author Anthony Summers:

> In 1976, when the Senate Intelligence Committee was probing the role of the intelligence agencies in investigating the assassination, it found [a previously unknown] pose in the same series of [Oswald backyard] pictures. This was in the possession of a Dallas police-man's widow, the former Mrs. Roscoe White. She said her husband told her it would be very valuable one day. [As the HSCA later wrote], policeman White had "acquired" the picture in the course of his duties after the assassination. A fellow officer has mentioned "numerous" copies of the Oswald pictures for his colleagues... Why was there no copy of [this print] in the evidence assembled for [the WC]?

Summers points out that, at one time, police must have known about the pose because they used that pose in their photo reenactments. No other copy of this photo has turned up.

Roscoe was overheard by his wife, Geneva—a Carousel Club B-girl—

plotting JFK's death with Ruby. According to Reverend Jack Shaw, who was with White as he lay dying of burns, White confessed to being a professional "hit man" who had committed many murders.

According to Harrison Edward Livingstone, based on a deathbed interview with White's widow, this is how the Tippit killing happened:

> ... White asked Tippit to drive Oswald to Redbird Airport... Tippit balked, suspecting they were involved in the assassination he had just heard about, and White had to shoot him right then. Oswald ran away. There is a report that an extra police shirt was found in the backseat of Tippit's car, and we surmise that this belonged to Roscoe, who changed his clothes there. It is also thought that Tippit's car was the one that stopped at Oswald's house and beeped, and then picked him up down the street.

Mrs. J. D. Tippit was a bridesmaid at White's wedding. (See also January, Wayne; Lewis, Ron; McDonald, Hugh; Roberts, Earlene; Tippit, J. D.; White, Geneva)

SOURCES: HSCA App. II, 321; VI, 141, 153 • SUMMERS 66–7 • HT2 77, 463–9

WHITE, STEPHEN, author of *Should We Now Believe the Warren Report?* (Macmillan, 1968).

WHITE, T. F., auto mechanic. White says that, at 2:00 P.M. on November 22, 1963, he saw a man who looked a great deal like Oswald in a red four-door 1957 Plymouth in the parking lot of the El Chico restaurant. He wrote down the license-plate number (because of the description of the assassin coming in over the radio): TEXAS PP 4537. This number was traced to a blue '57 Plymouth belonging to Carl Mather, a close friend of Officer J. D. Tippit. (See also Benavides, Domingo; Mather, Carl)

SOURCES: HT 277

WHITMEYER, GEORGE, a.w. (prelude); lieutenant colonel, U.S. Army; commander of Dallas's Army Intelligence unit. Whitmeyer rode in the presidential motorcade "pilot car," which preceded the president by 1/4-mile.

SOURCES: CF 9 • HT 185

WHITWORTH, EDITH, possible Oswald witness; operator of the Furniture Mart in Irving, Texas. Whitworth told the WC that, in early November 1963, a man she later came to believe was Oswald came into her store with his wife and two small children to inquire about having his rifle fixed. Marina denied that she ever went to this place with her husband and

children. Whitworth later positively identified Marina as the woman she had seen with Oswald. The WC chose to believe Marina.
SOURCES: WR 292 • WCH XI, 262 • RTJ 327–30

WIGGINS, WOODROW, o.k.w.; DPD lieutenant; involved in the aborted Oswald transfer. Citing incidents of poor communication within the DPD, the WR notes, "Several officers recalled that... Wiggins was directed to clear the basement jail office, but Wiggins testified that he received no such assignment."
SOURCES: WR 212 • RTJ 211 • WCH XII, 388

WILCOTT, JAMES B., Oswald witness; CIA finance officer. Wilcott told the HSCA that Oswald had been recruited from the USMC while stationed in Atsugi, Japan, by the CIA "with the express purpose of a double-agent assignment in the USSR." He testified that he had personally handled the funding for Oswald's assignment. According to Jim Garrison, "Predictably, a chorus line of other agency witnesses, whose names Wilcott had mentioned, denied all knowledge of such a project. The committee did not pursue the lead." (See also Paisley, John Arthur; Schrand, Martin)
SOURCES: HSCA Report 198–200 • OTT 49 • RUSSELL 155

WILCOX, LAURANCE R., district manager of the Western Union Telegraph Company in Dallas, Texas. Wilcox searched his office records and could find no record of any transaction of any kind with a Lee Harvey Oswald or Alek Hidell.
SOURCE: WCH X, 414

WILKINS, GEORGE, Oswald witness; USMC acquaintance. Wilkins told researcher Edward Jay Epstein, "Ozzie [Oswald] reacted to most of that crap [from superiors] by looking at you with that half grin on his face... Hell, we all thought we were smarter and better than any of the officers, and Ozzie was just like the rest of us... "
SOURCE: AO 93 • LEGEND 68–71

WILLIAMS, BONNIE RAY, a.w.; TSBD employee. Williams watched from the fifth floor of the TSBD with coworkers James Jarman and Harold Norman, directly below the "sniper's nest." He ate his lunch on the sixth floor that day, leaving at 12:20, only ten minutes before the shots were fired. The remains of this lunch (a brown paper bag once containing chicken, bread, and a bag of potato chips) were found near the sniper's nest. As of 12:20, there was no sign of Oswald on the sixth floor. Williams originally told the FBI (November 22, 1963) that he heard two shots, but later changed his story to three. (See also Jarman, James; Norman, Harold)
SOURCES: WR 78–80, 143, 232 • WCH III, 161 • BELIN 11, 60, 65, 73, 220 • RTJ

89–90, 100–7, 113 • BISHOP 45, 98–100, 120–1, 141 • CF 47–9 • MOORE 62 • ME 23, 115 • DAVIS 432 • NORTH 331

WILLIAMS, D'ALTON, attorney; member of Jim Garrison's assassination investigation team. Williams was not a trial lawyer. His specialty was administrative supervision. (See also Garrison, Jim)
SOURCE: OTT 108, 113, 137–40, 275

WILLIAMS, HAROLD RICHARD, Ruby witness; chef at the after-hours Mikado Club in Dallas, a competitor of Ruby's clubs. Williams was arrested and roughed up during a vice raid at the Mikado during the early part of November 1963. He claims that when he was placed in a police car, Officer J. D. Tippit was driving and Ruby was riding shotgun. The driver referred to the passenger as "Rube," Williams claims. This would imply that Ruby was working with Tippit in a scheme to harass his competition. After the assassination, DPD members threatened Williams, telling him that he would be charged with a serious crime that "they would make stick" if he didn't stop talking about seeing Tippit and Ruby together. Williams never made his statements under oath.
SOURCE: RTJ 253–4, 285–6

WILLIAMS, OTIS N., a.w. Williams stood on the front steps of the TSBD. He told FBI agents, "I thought these... shots came from the direction of the viaduct [triple underpass] which crosses Elm Street." In *Look* (December 2, 1967), Josiah Thompson quotes Williams as making this contradictory statement: "[I] thought those loud blasts came from the location of the courthouse."
SOURCES: WCH XXII, 683 • RTJ 111

WILLIE, DONNA, Parkland witness; nurse; told the *Jenkintown* (Pa.) *Times-Chronicle*, regarding JFK's throat wound, "I know he was shot from the front."

WILLENS, HOWARD P., WC counsel. Willens worked as a liaison between the WC and the Department of Justice.
SOURCES: WR 2 • MOORE 19

WILLIS, BILLY JOE, Ruby witness; former Ruby employee. Willis said that he had seen a man who resembled Oswald in the Carousel Club but, according to the WR, "did not think the man was Oswald."
SOURCE: WR 336

WILLIS, LINDA KAY, a.w.; daughter of Phillip and Marilyn; sister of Rosemary; 14 years old. Willis was with her father on the south side of Elm Street. She told author Jim Marrs in 1978, "[the] shots came from somewhere other than the Depository. And where we were standing, we had a good view."

SOURCES: WCH VII, 498 • COA 28–9 • CF 25 • HT 454

WILLIS, MARILYN, a.w.; wife of Phillip; mother of Rosemary and Linda. Willis watched with her parents, Mr. and Mrs. William H. Stubblefield, from the north side of Elm Street directly in front of the pergola.

SOURCES: PWW 179, 181 • OTT 238

WILLIS, PHILLIP L., a.w.; possible Ruby witness; retired air force major who took 12 pictures around Dealey Plaza before, during, and after the assassination, all of which were published in the WR's 26 volumes of testimony and exhibits. Willis himself designated slide #8 as one of significance since it shows a man who greatly resembles Ruby at the assassination scene minutes after the shots were fired. In the WC's 26 volumes, that photo is cropped right through the face of that man. Willis commented on the photo to an investigator for the Citizens' Committee of Inquiry, "It looks so much like him [Ruby], it's pitiful."

A number of odd coincidences have crossed Willis's life. There are those who say that there are two dates in the twentieth century during which people remember precisely where they were. Those dates are November 22, 1963 (JFK's assassination) and December 7, 1941 (the Japanese attack on Pearl Harbor). Willis was in Dealey Plaza on November 22, 1963, and he was in Pearl Harbor, serving with the navy on December 7, 1941.

Willis was a prosecution witness at the New Orleans conspiracy trial of Clay Shaw. (See also Newcomb, Fred; Shaw, Clay; Thompson, George; Wilson, Eugene)

SOURCES: WR 109 • WCH VII, 492 • RTJ 348–9 • CF 24–5, 73 • HT 217, 254 • FMG III, 59–60 • MOORE 87, 118, 121, 123 • BE 10, 366, 510

WILLIS, ROSEMARY, a.w.; daughter of Phillip and Marilyn; sister of Linda Kay. Stood on the north side of Elm, across the street from the TSBD. She is visible in the Zapruder film in her white sweatshirt running alongside JFK's limo.

SOURCE: MOORE 118

WILLOUGHBY, CHARLES (aka Tscheppe-Weidenbach, Adolf), CIC agent; U.S. Army major general; General Douglas MacArthur's chief of intelligence during the Korean War. After the war Willoughby worked out of a Washington, D.C., headquarters. Author Russell writes "[his] domestic associations extended from the Cuban exile community to the H. L. Hunt family." MacArthur reportedly referred to Willoughby as "my little Fascist." Willoughby formed the ultra-secret intelligence agency known as

FOI, which theoretically specialized in rooting out Communist spies. In the 1950s Willoughby worked with "Japanese Warlords," "German Nazis," and CIA Director Allen Dulles in an attempt to establish a "global anti-Communist alliance." Russell writes, "The case for Willoughby's involvement in the Kennedy conspiracy can be no more than circumstantial. But Willoughby was a master of intrigue who... was assuredly in a position to make the right connections from his Washington domain." (See also Bishop, William; Dulles, Allen; Hunt, H. L.)
SOURCE: RUSSELL, many

WILLS, GARY, coauthor, with Ovid Demaris, of *Jack Ruby* (New American Library, 1968).

WILSON, BILLY RAY (See WALL, BRECK)

WILLMON, JIM, a.w.; *Dallas Morning News* ad salesman. Willmon was standing on Houston between Main and Elm streets. According to Dallas reporter Jim Marrs, Willmon thought the first shot was a backfire. "People ran toward the grassy knoll," Willmon added.
SOURCE: CF 44

WILSON, EUGENE M., possible Oswald witness; salesman at Downtown Lincoln-Mercury in Dallas. Wilson's statements corroborate those of Albert G. Bogard, who says that a man greatly resembling Oswald test-drove a car on the afternoon of November 9, 1963. The real Oswald did not know how to drive a car. Wilson added to speculation that the man who test drove the car was not the real Oswald by telling the WC that the man he saw was "only about five feet tall." (See also Bogard, Albert; Lawrence, Jack; Pizzo, Frank)
SOURCES: OTT 68–9 • RTJ 331–3

WILSON, STEVEN F., a.w. Wilson watched the motorcade from a third-floor window of the TSBD. On March 25, 1964, he told an FBI agent that "the shots came from the west end of the building or from the colonnade [pergola] located on Elm Street across from the west end of our building. The shots really did not sound like they came from above me." After making this statement, Wilson was visited repeatedly by the FBI. "I couldn't get any work done. They were always there," he said. He refused to change his statement and was not called as a WC witness. No TSBD employees who thought the shots came from elsewhere other than the building itself were called as WC witnesses.
SOURCES: RTJ 112–3 • CF 44 • BE 16)

WINBORN, WALTER L., a.w. Winborn watched the motorcade from

atop the triple underpass and saw smoke atop the grassy knoll following the shooting.
SOURCES: RTJ 40 • COA 22 • CF 58 • BE 16 • OGLESBY 36

WINSTON, PATRICIA, possible Oswald witness. Winston and Pamela Mumford were passengers with a man calling himself Oswald aboard a bus to Mexico City in September 1963. (See also Mumford, Pamela)
SOURCE: WCH XI, 215

WISE, DAN, coauthor, with Marietta Maxfield, of *The Day Kennedy Died* (Naylor, 1964).

WISE, WESLEY, Ruby witness; KRLD reporter in Dallas; later mayor of Dallas. Wise reported seeing Ruby near the TSBD moments after the assassination. He testified at Ruby's murder trial for the prosecution that at 3:00 P.M. on November 23, 1963, Ruby had tapped on the glass of Wise's mobile TV unit near the TSBD and had suggested that he photograph the two DPD officers who had been assigned to the assassination investigation. (See also Couch, Malcolm; Mather, Carl)
SOURCES: RTJ 263 • GERTZ 45, 111 • CF 325 • HT 277–8 • KANTOR 54, 192

WISEMAN, JOHN, a.w. (aftermath); Dallas County deputy sheriff. Wiseman confiscated a.w. Mary Ann Moorman's Polaroid camera photograph taken moments before the assassination that shows the "Oswald" window; turned the photo over to his superior (Chief Criminal Deputy Sheriff Allan Sweatt), who then turned it over to the SS. (See also Hester, Charles; Hill, Jean; Moorman, Mary)
SOURCES: RTJ 345 • HT 123

WITT, LOUIS STEVEN, a.w.; claims to be the "umbrella man." At the time of the assassination, two of the most unusual characters were men standing on the north curb of Elm Street very close to the Stemmons Freeway sign. One man, who appeared Hispanic, raised his fist in the air as the president passed. The other opened an umbrella and pumped it up and down over his head. The umbrella might have been the last thing that JFK ever saw.

Many think these men were signaling to the assassins, as they were positioned to be visible from both the buildings to the rear of the president and from the grassy knoll in front. Others think that the pumping of the umbrella was a symbolic gesture, since JFK had failed to provide the umbrella coverage at the Bay of Pigs that might have avoided the disaster. Certainly, no one else had an umbrella in Dealey Plaza, because it was a bright, sunny day. The umbrella was open only during the shooting sequence. It was closed before the motorcade arrived, and the man closed it again as soon as the shooting was over.

After the shooting, while everyone else was running around and chaos reigned, these two men sat calmly on the curb. The Latin man appears at one point, according to photographic evidence, to be speaking into a walkie-talkie. After a while, the two men left the scene, walking slowly in opposite directions.

Some assassination researchers have suggested that the umbrella might have been a weapon that shot paralyzing darts. This would explain why the entrance wound seen in JFK's throat when he was first brought to Parkland Hospital was almost too small to be a bullet wound and why so many witnesses describe the sound of the first shot as being different from the others. Witt told the HSCA that he was the umbrella man. He says that he did not actually see the shooting because he had the umbrella open in front of his face, testimony which contradicts the photographic evidence. (See also Senseney, Charles; Towner, Jim)
    SOURCES: CF 32 • ME 159

WITTMUS, RONALD G., FBI fingerprint expert. Wittmus confirmed the findings of Sebastian F. Latona—that the palm print found on the Mannlicher-Carcano rifle was Oswald's—for the WC. (See also Latona, Sebastian)
    SOURCES: WR 118, 127, 132 • WCH VII, 590

WOOD, HOMER and STERLING C., possible Oswald witnesses. The Woods corroborated evidence that Oswald or an Oswald look-alike practiced with a rifle at the Sports Drome Rifle Range in Dallas in early November 1963.
    SOURCES: WR 296–7 • WCH X, 385, 390, 398 • RTJ 334

WOOD, WILLIAM C. (aka Boxley, Bill), member of Jim Garrison's investigative team; Woods was a reformed alcoholic who said that he had worked for the CIA until he was fired because of his drinking. He worked for Garrison as a volunteer. Garrison wrote:

> Because of the curiosity of the news media about our activity, we decided that it would be best if we kept it quiet that we had a former Agency man aboard. So we used the name "Boxley" instead of Wood. Bill Boxley became a familiar figure in and out of the office. He always carried a loaded .45 automatic pistol, which he kept in a holster under his armpit. This indicated to me that his original intelligence service had been in the U.S. Army, because all of the

other American intelligence services used the .38 caliber revolver. He also always carried with him a large rectangular black briefcase. He was an indefatigable worker, and it was apparent that he was dedicated to our effort.

Later Garrison learned that there was nothing dedicated whatsoever about Wood's work for the effort, and there was nothing ex- about his relationship with the federal government. A Philadelphia attorney named Vincent Salabria told Garrison that Wood was working for the feds, reporting on the investigation, and conspiring to discredit Garrison. When Wood eventually disappeared, he took many of Garrison's files with him. (See also Garrison, Jim)

SOURCES: OTT 174–5, 187–92, 228 · FMG III, 38–45, 47

WOODWARD, MARY ELIZABETH, a.w.; *Dallas Morning News* employee. Woodward watched from in front of and just to the left of the wooden fence atop the grassy knoll. She was the journalist closest to the president at the moment of the fatal shot and wrote that "suddenly there was a horrible, ear-shattering noise from behind us and a little to the right." She had completed writing her story before JFK's death was announced.

SOURCES: WCE 2084 · RTJ 41 · CF 28 · ME 107

WORLEY, GANO E., o.k.w.; 38-year-old member of the DPD reserve force. Worley told the WC that the reason the armored truck didn't make it down the ramp was that it was too tall to fit. He said he saw one man jump the guard railing to get into the area where Oswald was to be transferred, but that the man was ejected and was not Ruby.

SOURCE: WCH XII, 378

WORRELL, JAMES RICHARD "DICKIE," JR., a.w.; suspicious death. Worrell was walking along Houston Street after the shooting when he saw a man running from the back of the TSBD wearing a brown sport or suit coat. The man headed south on Houston. Worrell's observations of the man in the brown coat are corroborated by witnesses Carolyn Walther and Richard Randolph Carr. Worrell died on November 9, 1966, at the age of 23 in a car-motorcycle accident. (See also Carr, Richard; Walther, Carolyn)

SOURCES: WR 235 · WCH II, 190 · WCE 363, 2003 · BISHOP 134, 141 · HT 129, 139 · FMG III, 64 · NORTH 387

WRIGHT, FRANK and MARY, t.k.w.; residents of 501 East Tenth Street in the Oak Cliff section of Dallas in 1963. It was Mrs. Wright who put in the call for an ambulance just after Officer Tippit was shot. Neither were interviewed by the FBI or asked by the WC to testify. According to Jim

Garrison: "Mr. Wright, who had been inside the house, came out in time to see Officer Tippit roll over on the ground, probably the last move[ment] of his life. Wright observed another man looking down on the fallen officer. Then the man circled around the police car and got into an old gray car on the other side of it. He drove off rapidly."

SOURCES: OTT 197–8 • RTJ 194 • FLAMMONDE 183

WRIGHT, NORMAN EARL, Ruby witness. Wright worked as an emcee and comic in the Carousel Club during the autumn of 1963. He told the WC that Ruby was sensitive about Jewish jokes, his receding hairline, and his slight lisp—and that Ruby was afraid people would think he was a homosexual. Wright was out of town on the day of the assassination. He told WC regarding the shooting of Oswald: "In my opinion, the police department is just as much to blame as Jack in a roundabout way, because there was no reason in the world, with all the police they had, for Jack to walk directly straight through that many people and... shoot him. I personally believe that they shared at least fifty percent of the blame."

SOURCE: WCH XV, 244

WULF, WILLIAM E., Oswald witness; acquaintance of Oswald in his youth. In 1954, when Oswald was living in New Orleans, he became interested in the New Orleans Amateur Astronomy Association, an organization of high-school students. Wulf was the association's president at the time and later recalled that Oswald "started expounding the Communist doctrine and saying that he was highly interested in communism, that communism was the only way of life for the worker, etc." This occurred at Wulf's home. Oswald and Wulf got into an argument. Wulf testified, "... my father came into the room, heard what we were arguing on communism, and that this boy was loud-mouthed, boisterous, and my father asked him to leave the house, and that is the last I have seen or spoken with Oswald."

SOURCES: WR 360 • WCH VIII, 15

Y

YARAS, DAVE, Ruby witness. Yaras was a Teamster hit man with "strong ties" to Ruby. (See also Hoffa, James R.)
SOURCES: HSCA Report 150–1, 178 • HT 295 • BLAKEY 188, 287–8, 304–5 • EVICA 148, 154–5, 167, 199 • DAVIS 21 • NORTH 56, 294 • KANTOR 31–2, 37

YARBOROUGH, RALPH W., a.w.; Texas senator. Yarborough rode in the vice-presidential limo; he said he smelled gunpowder as his limo approached the triple underpass. He was not the only one to smell gunpowder, indicating that at least one shot came from ground level rather than from a sixth-floor window. On November 21, 1963, there was a fight between JFK and LBJ regarding the seating in the next day's motorcade. According to author Craig I. Zirbel, LBJ "wanted Connally out of JFK's car and [LBJ's] enemy... Yarborough to sit in Connally's seat." (See also Arnold, Gordon; Johnson, Lyndon B.)
SOURCES: WR 20, 57, 59, 65 • WCH VII, 439 • HSCA Report 38 • ME 14, 77, 102, 106, 220 • OGLESBY 9 • NORTH 370 • RTJ 44 • COA 22 • BISHOP, many • DOP, many • CF 6, 8, 16, 79 • HT 16–7, 148–9, 461 • FMG III, 89 • PWW 73 • BLAKEY 4, 10 • KANTOR 19, 40 • TEX 254

YATSKOV, PAUL ANTONOVICH, clandestine KGB officer stationed at the Soviet embassy in Mexico City from September to October 1963. According to author Michael H. B. Eddowes, Yatskov—along with Russian Premier Nikita Khrushchev—was part of the plot to assassinate JFK. (See Eddowes, Michael)
SOURCE: KKK, iii

YEARGAN, ALBERT C., JR., employee of H. C. Green in Dallas. Yeargan corroborates the testimony of Philip J. Lux that, though their store carried 6.5mm Mannlicher-Carcano rifles, they did not at any time possess one with the serial number C2766 (the TSBD rifle).
SOURCE: WCH XI, 207

YOUNG, ARTHUR and RUTH FORBES, stepfather and mother of Michael Paine. (See Paine, Michael)
SOURCE: WR 264

YOUNGBLOOD, RUFUS WAYNE, a.w.; SS agent. Youngblood rode in the vice-presidential limo, two cars behind JFK's. He covered LBJ during the gunfire.
SOURCES: WR 21, 59, 61, 64–5, 70–1, 429 • WCH II, 144 • COA 267 • BISHOP, many • DOP, many • CF 9 • FMG III, 17, 89 • BE 678 • BLAKEY 17 • ME 104, 220, 252

Z

ZAHM, JAMES A., major sergeant, USMC; USMC expert on marksmanship; noncommissioned officer in charge of the Marksmanship Training Unit in the Weapons Training Battalion of the USMC School at Quantico, Virginia. Zahm told the WC that a rifle with a four-power telescope was "the ideal type of weapon for moving targets" and described shooting JFK from the TSBD's "sniper's nest" as "very easy."
SOURCES: WR 177–9, 181–2 • WCH XI, 306

ZANGRETTI, JACK, suspicious death; motel manager in Altus, Oklahoma. According to Penn Jones Jr., Zangretti had remarked on November 23, 1963, that three men, not Oswald, had killed JFK and that Oswald would be shot the next day "by a man named Ruby." Zangretti added that soon thereafter a member of the Frank Sinatra family would be kidnapped to "take some of the attention away from the assasssination." Two weeks later, Zangretti was found, shot twice in the chest and dumped in Lake Lugert, Texas.
SOURCE: FMG IV, 108–9

ZAPRUDER, ABRAHAM, a.w., Zapruder was standing on a pedestal at the western-most section of the pergola at the time of the shooting and took the most famous film of the assassination. The WC would have had a much easier time selling the American public its version of the facts had the Zapruder film not existed. The Zapruder film is, by far, the most important eyewitness to the events in Dealey Plaza. Zapruder told the FBI he thought the shots had come from directly behind him. Zapruder died in Dallas in 1970 at the age of 65. (See also Jackson, C. D.; Newman, William J.; Rather, Dan; Rivera, Geraldo; Sitzman, Marilyn; White, Jack; Willis, Rosemary)
(WR 62, 75, 100–2, 105–7, 109–10, 429 • WCH VII, 569 • HSCA Report, many •

491

OGLESBY 15, 26, 37–9 • DAVIS 374 • NORTH, many • BELIN 50, 178, 182–3 • RTJ 41, 64, 66, 70, 73, 380 • COA 29 • BISHOP 127, 136, 529 • DOP, many • CF 24, 26, 30, 64–72 • HT 16, 214, 220 • FMG III 52–3, 63, 82, 96 • PWW, many • MOORE, many • BE 4, 18, 21, 23, 43, 70 • BLAKEY 29, 42–3, 62, 98, 105–7, 267 • EVICA 65 • FLAMMONDE 242, 266 • ME, many)

ZEIGMAN, NANCY (See RICH, NANCY PERRIN)

ZIGIOTTI, GIUSEPPI. With Clay Shaw and L. M. Bloomfield, Zigiotti was on the board of directors of the mysterious CMC—Permindex's sister corporation. Zigiotti was president of the Fascist National Association for Militia Arms. (See also Bloomfield, Louis; Shaw, Clay)
SOURCE: OTT 88

ZIRBEL, CRAIG I, author of *The Texas Connection: The Assassination of John F. Kennedy* (The Texas Connection Co., 1991). Attorney Zirbel argues that LBJ was behind the assassination. Here are the major points of evidence Zirbel uses: (1) Before the shooting, Johnson confided to his longtime mistress, Madeleine Brown, that Kennedy would be killed in Dallas; (2) Johnson was head of the team that planned the president's route—which took him past the TSBD, where gunman Oswald was waiting; (3) LBJ desperately tried to get his pal, Texas Governor John Connally, out of the Kennedy limousine—and put in his place a political enemy (Senator Ralph Yarborough) who would be directly in the line of fire; (4) After Oswald was killed, Ruby smuggled a letter out of prison in which he named Johnson as the brains behind the assassination. Ruby wrote, "They alone planned the killing. By they I mean Johnson and the others." (See also Connally, John; Johnson, Lyndon B.

ZOPPI, TONY, Ruby witness; *Dallas Morning News* columnist; Ruby visited Zoppi a little more than one hour before the assassination. During that visit, Ruby said, he "obtained a brochure on his new master of ceremonies that he wanted to use in preparing copy for his advertisements."
SOURCE: WR 312

BIBLIOGRAPHY

Abrams, Malcolm. "I'm Being Framed as JFK's Killer." *Midnight/Globe*, November 29, 1977. Story about Frank Sturgis.

Alleged Assassination Plots Involving Foreign Leaders. Interim Report of the Select Committee to Study Governmental Operations, with Respect to Intelligence Activities. U.S. Senate, Washington D.C.: U.S. Government Printing Office, 1975.

"Alleged Oswald Letter Checked for Its Authenticity by FBI Agents," *Dallas Morning News*, February 6, 1977.

"A Matter of Reasonable Doubt," *Life*, November 24, 1966.

"And Finally, as to John F. Kennedy," *Texas Observer*, June 11, 1965.

"A New Theory: 3 French Gangsters Killed JFK," *Dallas Morning News*, October 26, 1988.

Anson, Robert Sam. "JFK The Movie: Oliver Stone Reshoots History." *Esquire*, November 1991.

Anson, Robert Sam. *"They've Killed the President!"* New York: Bantam, 1975.

"Any Oswald-Rubenstein Tie in Dallas Sought by Police." *Dallas Morning News*, November 26, 1963.

Appendix to the Report of the House Select Committee on Assassinations (JFK section: 12 volumes; Martin Luther King Jr. section: 13 volumes)

"Area Woman to Testify in JFK Slaying Probe." *Lubbock Avalanche-Journal*, April 10, 1977.

"Assassination Inquiry Stumbling—Is Fensterwald a CIA Plant?" *Washington Star*, October 4, 1976.

"The Assassination of President John F. Kennedy—How the CIA Set Up Oswald." *Hustler*, October 1978, p. 50.

"Assassination: The Trail to a Verdict." *Life*, October 2, 1964.

"Author Not the First to Ask Exhumation." *Fort Worth Star-Telegram*, January 11, 1979. Battle over whether it was really Oswald buried in Oswald's grave.

"Autopsy on the Warren Commission." *Time*, September 16, 1966.

"Autopsy Studied Again." *New York Times*, April 26, 1975, p. 12.

Banta, Thomas J. "The Kennedy Assassination: Early Thoughts and Emotions." *Public Opinion Quarterly*, Summer 1964.

Belin, David W. "The Case Against Conspiracy." *New York Times Magazine*, July 15, 1979, p. 40.

———. *Final Disclosure*. New York: Charles Scribner's Sons, 1988. Staunch defense of the WR by former WC counsel.

———. *November 22, 1963: You Are the Jury*. New York: Quadrangle Books, 1973.

Belli, Melvin, M. (with Carroll, Maurice C.). *Dallas Justice: The Real Story of Jack Ruby and His Trial*, New York: David, 1964.

Berendt, John. "'If They've Found Another Assassin, Let Them Name Names and Produce Their Evidence.'—Allen Dulles, July 1966; Name: Igor 'Turk' Vaganov. Evidence: See Below." *Esquire*, August 1967.

Bickel, Alexander M. "The Failure of the Warren Report." *Commentary*, October 1966.

Bishop, Jim. *The Day Kennedy Was Shot*. New York: Funk & Wagnalls, 1968.

Blakey, G. Robert and Billings, Richard N. *Fatal Hour*. New York: Berkley, 1992.

Blakey, G. Robert and Billings, Richard N. *The Plot to Kill the President*. New York: New York Times Books, 1981.

Bloomgarden, Henry S. *The Gun*. New York: Bantam Books, 1976.

Blum, Andrew. "JFK Conundrum." *National Law Journal*, Vol. 14, No. 16, December 23, 1991.

Blumenthal, Sid and Yazijian, Harvey, eds. *Government by Gunplay*, New York: New American Library, Signet, 1976.

Blythe, Myrna and Farrell, Jane. "Marina Oswald—Twenty-five Years Later," *Ladies Home Journal*, November 1988.

"Body of JFK Assassin Is Under Guard in FW," *Fort Worth Press*, November 25, 1963.

Boyles, Peter. "Fear and Loathing on the Assassination Trail." *Denver Magazine*, November 1980.

Brancato, Paul. *Coup D'État*. Forrestville, Cal.: Eclipse Enterprises, 1991.

Brashler, William. *The Don: The Life and Death of Sam Giancana*. New York: Harper & Row, 1977.

Brener, Milton E. *The Garrison Case: A Study in the Abuse of Power*. New York: Clarkson N. Potter, 1969.

Brennan, Howard, with Cherryholmes, J. Edward. *Eyewitness to History*. Waco, Tex.: Texian Press, 1987.

Breslin, Jimmy. "A Death in Emergency Room No. One." *Saturday Evening Post*, December 14, 1963.

Bringuier, Carlos. *Red Friday: November 22, 1963*. Chicago: C. Hallberg, 1969.

Buchanan, Thomas G. *Who Killed Kennedy?* London: Secker & Warburg, 1964.

Burney, Peggy. "I Saw Him Die, Woman Cries," *Dallas Times-Herald*, November 22, 1963.

Burnham, David. "Assassination Panel Facing Budget Trim." *New York Times*, January 25, 1977, p. 17.

————. "Assassination Panel Is Warned on Its Techniques." *New York Times*, January 6, 1977, p. 15.

————. "Assassination Panel's Fate in Doubt as Sprague Faces New Allegations." *New York Times*, February 12, 1977, p. 11.

————. "Assassination Study Requests $13 Million." *New York Times*, December 10, 1976, p. 19.

————. "Gonzalez, Assailing His Committee, Quits as Assassination Inquiry Head." *New York Times*, March 3, 1977, p. 1.

————. "House Gives Assassination Panel Authority to Continue Temporarily." *New York Times*, February 3, 1977, p. 21.

————. "New Assassination Panel Is Blocked." *New York Times*, January 12, 1977.

————. "Sprague Ouster Is Upset by Panel on Assassination." *New York Times*, February 10, 1977, p. 1.

Campbell, Alex. "What Did Happen in Dallas?" *New Republic*, June 25, 1966.

Canfield, Michael, with Weberman, Alan J. *Coup d'Etat in America: The CIA and the Assassination of John F. Kennedy*. New York: Third Press, 1975.

"Capture: It's All Over Now." *New York Herald Tribune*, November 23, 1963.

Carter, Bill. "ABC Finds K.G.B. Fickle on Oswald." *New York Times*, November 21, 1991.

"Chagra Says Harrelson Told Him He Also Killed JFK." *Fort Worth Star-Telegram*, November 2, 1982.

Chariton, Wallace O. *Unsolved Texas Mysteries*. Plano, Texas: Worldware Publishing, 1991.

"CIA Involvement Is Alleged in Plots to Kill 3 Dictators." *New York Times*, March 10, 1975, p. 49.

Cohen, Jacob. "The Warren Commission Report and Its Critics." *Frontier*, November 1966.

————. "What the Warren Report Omits: Vital Documents." *Nation*, July 11, 1966.

————. "Conspiracy Fever." *Commentary*, October 1975.

Columbia Journalism Review, Winter 1964. Entire issue dedicated to analysis of media coverage of the assassination.

Connally, John. "Why Kennedy Went to Texas." *Life*, November 24, 1967.

Corliss, Richard. "Who Killed J.F.K.?" *Time*, December 23, 1991.

Cowan, Edward. "New Study Urged in Kennedy Death." *New York Times*, July 21, 1975, p. 27.

Crawford, Kenneth. "The Warren Impeachers." *Newsweek*, October 19, 1964.

Crenshaw, Charles A., M.D., with Hansen, Jens, and Shaw, J. Gary. *JFK: Conspiracy of Silence*. New York: Signet, 1992.

Crewdson, John M. "Rockefeller Unit Said to Check Report of CIA Link to Kennedy Assassination." *New York Times*, March 8, 1975, p. 11.

"Cuban's Friend Believes Oswald Contacted Exile Leader." *Dallas Morning News*, June 10, 1979.

Curry, Jesse. *JFK Assassination File*. American Poster and Publishing Co., 1969.

Cutler, Robert B. *The Flight of CE-399: Evidence of Conspiracy*. Beverly, Mass.: Cutler Designs, 1970.

_____. *The Umbrella Man: Evidence of Conspiracy*. Danvers, Mass.: Bett's and Mirror Press, 1975.

"Dallas After All." *Texas Observer*, March 6, 1964.

"Dallas Ex-Police Chief Alleges an FBI Cover-Up on Oswald." *New York Times*, September 2, 1975, p. 12.

"Dallas Man Claims FBI Had Oswald Film." *Fort Worth Star-Telegram*, September 20, 1978.

Dallas, Tita, and Ratcliffe, Jeanira. *The Kennedy Case*. New York: Popular Library, 1973.

Dallos, Robert E. "New Witness Alleges That He Was Offered Money to Aid Garrison in Investigation of Assassination." *New York Times*, June 19, 1967, p. 27.

Davis, John H. *Mafia Kingfish: Carlos Marcello and the Assassination of John F. Kennedy*. New York: McGraw-Hill, 1988.

Davison, Jean. *Oswald's Game*. New York: W. W. Norton & Co., 1983.

"The Deadly Kennedy Probe: Execution for the Witnesses." *Rolling Stone*, June 2, 1977.

Demaris, Ovid, and Wills, Gary. *Jack Ruby*. New York: New American Library, 1968.

Denson, R. B., ed., *Destiny in Dallas*. Dallas, Tex.: Denco Corporation, 1964.

Devlin, Lord. "Death of a President: The Established Facts," *Atlantic*, March 1965.

Diamond, John. "Kennedy: Open Secret JFK Files." *New Orleans Times-Picayune*, January 11, 1992.

DiGiacomo, Frank, and Molloy, Joanna, "Down Memory Lane to Dallas." *New York Post*, July 1, 1991, p. 6.

_____. "He Says Feds Offed JFK's Mary." *New York Post*, July 15, 1991, p. 6.

DiMaio, Vincent J. M. "The Exhumation and Identification of Lee Harvey Oswald." *Journal of Forensic Sciences*, vol. 29, no. 1, January 1984.

"Dispute on JFK Assassination Evidence Persists." *Boston Sunday Globe*, June 21, 1981.

"District Attorneys Pay for Dinner, Garrison Cancels It." *New York Times*, March 17, 1968, p. 78.

"Docs in Dispute on JFK Wounds." *New York Daily News*, April 3, 1992.

Donnelly, Judy. *Who Shot the President?* New York: Random House, 1988.

Donovan, Robert J. *The Assassins*. New York: Harper Bros., 1964.

Duffy, James R. *Who Killed JFK?* New York: Shapolsky Publishers, 1988.

Dugger, Ronnie. "The Last Voyage of Mr. Kennedy." *Texas Observer*, November 29, 1963.

Eddowes, Michael H. B. *Khrushchev Killed Kennedy*. Dallas: self-published, 1975.

————. *November 22: How They Killed Kennedy*. London: Neville Spearman Ltd., 1976.

————. *The Oswald File*. New York: Clarkson N. Potter, 1977.

Edginton, John, and Sergeant, John. "The Murder of Martin Luther King, Jr." *Covert Action Information Bulletin*, no. 34, Summer 1990.

Ellis, David. "Did JFK Really Commit Suicide?" *Time*, April 13, 1992, p. 64.

Epstein, Edward Jay. *The Assassination Chronicles*. New York: Carroll & Graf, 1992.

————. *Counterplot*. New York: Viking, 1969.

————. *Inquest*. New York: Viking, 1966.

————. *Legend: The Secret World of Lee Harvey Oswald*. New York: Reader's Digest Press, 1978.

Evica, George Michael. *And We Are All Mortal: New Evidence and Analysis in the Assassination of John F. Kennedy*. West Hartford, Conn.: University of Hartford Press, 1978.

————. "The White Baron (Parts I–IV)." *Assassination Journal*, April 13, April 20, April 27, and May 4, 1977.

"Ex-Agent Sixth to Die in Six-Month Span." *Fort Worth Star-Telegram*, November 10, 1977.

"Ex-Castro Aide Talks on JFK." *Hartford Courant*, October 6, 1977.

Exner, Judith. "Forget Camelot's Mystique." *New York Daily News*, October 8, 1991.

"Ex-Officer Suspects He Chased '2nd Gun.'" *Dallas Morning News*, August 20, 1978.

Farolino, Audrey. "JFK: New Furor." *New York Post*, December 19, 1991.

"FBI Data Seen Spiking Reports of Conspiracy." *Dallas Morning News*, December 4, 1963.

"FBI Eyes on Ruby Strippers in JFK Case." *Dallas Times Herald*, May 22, 1975.

Fein, Arnold L. "JFK in Dallas: The Warren Report and Its Critics." *Saturday Review*, October 22, 1966.

Feldman, Harold. "Fifty-two Witnesses: The Grassy Knoll." *Minority of One*, March 1965.

Fensterwald, Bernard, Jr., and Ewing, Michael. *Coincidence or Conspiracy*. New York: Kensington Publishing Corp., 1977.

"52% Believe 'Group' Tied to JFK Slaying." *Dallas Morning News*, December 6, 1963.

Flammonde, Paris. *The Kennedy Conspiracy*. Meredith Press, 1969.

Fonzi, Gaeton. "The Last Investigation." *Third Decade*, November 1984.

498   WHO'S WHO IN THE JFK ASSASSINATION

_____. "The Warren Commission, Arlen Specter, and the Truth." *Greater Philadelphia Magazine*, August 1966.

_____. "Who Killed JFK?" *Washingtonian*, November 1980.

"Food for the Suspicious." *Time*, January 1, 1979.

Ford, Gerald. "Piecing Together the Evidence." *Life*, October 2, 1964.

Ford, Gerald, with Stiles, John R. *Portrait of the Assassin*. New York: Simon & Schuster, 1965.

"Four Days That Stopped America," *Life*, November 1983.

Four Days: The Historical Record of the Death of President Kennedy. American Heritage Publishing Company, Inc., 1964. Photos and essays compiled by United Press International and American Heritage Magazine.

Fox, Sylvan. *The Unanswered Questions About President Kennedy's Assassination.* New York: Award Books, 1965.

Franklin, Ben A. "Assassination Panel Names Top Counsel." *New York Times*, October 5, 1976, p. 17.

_____. "Sprague Urges Carter to Set Up Inquiry Into Murders of Kennedy and Dr. King." *New York Times*, April 12, 1977, p. 18.

Freund, Charles Paul. "Who Killed JFK?" *McCall's*, January 1992.

Gage, Nicolas. "Roselli Called a Victim of Mafia Because of His Senate Testimony." *Los Angeles Times*, February 25, 1977.

Gandolfo, Ted. *The House Select Committee on Assassinations Coverup* [sic]. Self-published, 1987.

"Garrison Arrests an Ex-Major in Conspiracy to Kill Kennedy." *New York Times*, March 2, 1967, p. 24. Re: The arrest of Clay Shaw.

Garrison, Jim. *A Heritage of Stone*. New York: G. P. Putnam's Sons, 1970.

_____. *On the Trail of the Assassins*. New York: Sheridan Square Press, 1988.

"Garrison Record Shows Disability." *New York Times*, December 30, 1967, p. 28.

"Garrison Says Assassin Killed Kennedy From Sewer Manhole." *New York Times*, December 11, 1967, p. 28.

"Garrison Says Kennedy Was Killed in Crossfire." *New York Times*, May 24, 1967, p. 50.

"Garrison Says Some Policemen in Dallas Aided Kennedy Plot." *New York Times*, September 22, 1967, p. 28.

"Garrison Seeks High Court Help." *Fort Worth Star-Telegram*, February 20, 1969.

Gershman, Bennett L. "Will the Real Jim Garrison Please Stand Up?" *New York Law Journal*, January 27, 1992.

Gertz, Elmer. *Moment of Madness: The People vs. Jack Ruby*. Chicago: Follett Publishing Company, 1968.

Giancana, Charles, and Giancana, Sam. *Double Cross: The Explosive History of the Mobster Who Controlled America*. New York: Warner Books, 1992.

Goldberg, Alfred. *Conspiracy Interpretations of the Assassination of President Kennedy: International and Domestic*. Los Angeles: University of California Press, 1968.

Goldberg, Jeff, and Yazijian, Harvey. "The Death of 'Crazy Billy' Sullivan." *New Times*, July 24, 1978.

Goldberg, Jeff. "Waiting for Justice." *The Continuing Inquiry*, March 1980.

Golz, Earl. "Confidential: The FBI's Files on JFK." *Gallery*, November 1982.

Goodhart, A. L. "The Mysteries of the Kennedy Assassination and the English Press." *Law Quarterly Review*, London, January 1967.

Graham, Fred. "Mystery Cloaks Fate of Brain of Kennedy." *New York Times*, August 27, 1972, p.1.

Greenberg, Bradley J. "Diffusion of News of the Kennedy Assassination." *Public Opinion Quarterly*, Summer 1964.

Groden, Robert and Model, Peter. *J.F.K.: The Case for Conspiracy*. New York: Manor Books, 1976.

Groden, Robert J., and Livingstone, Harrison Edward. *High Treason*. New York: Berkley Books, 1990.

Grunwald, Lisa. "Why We Still Care." *Life*, December 1991.

Gun, Nerin. *Red Roses from Texas*. London: Frederick Muller, 1964.

Guth, DeLloyd J., and Wrone, David R. *The Assassination of John F. Kennedy: A Comprehensive Historical and Legal Bibliography 1963–1979*. Westport, Conn.: Greenwood Press, 1980.

Habighorst, Elsie T. "Policeman Was Telling the Truth." *New Orleans Times-Picayune*, January 3, 1992.

Hager, Steven. "Heritage of Stone." *High Times*, September 1991.

Hamill, Pete. "Mob Had Lots of Reasons to Want JFK Dead." *New York Post*, January 16, 1992.

Hanson, William. *The Shooting of John F. Kennedy*. San Antonio: Naylor, 1969.

Hargis, D. W. "Dallas Policeman Recounts Instant Assassin Struck." *Dallas Times-Herald*, November 22, 1963.

Hartogs, Renatus, and Freeman, Lucy. *The Two Assassins*. New York: Thomas Y. Crowell Co., 1965.

Hazlitt, Bill, and Nelson, Jack. "The White House, the Teamsters and the Mafia." *Los Angeles Times, Miami Herald*, June 3, 1973.

Healey, Robert. "Time to Reopen the Dallas Files." *Boston Globe*, April 25, 1975.

Hearings Before the President's Commission on the Assassination of President Kennedy, Volumes 1–26, Washington, D.C.: U.S. Government Printing Office, 1964.

Hennelly, Robert, and Policoff, Jerry. "JFK: How the Media Assassinated the Real Story." *Village Voice*, March 31, 1992, p. 33.

Hepburn, James. *Farewell America*. Vaduz, Liechtenstein: Frontiers Publishing Company, 1968.

"Hill Unit Open Hearings on JFK." *Washington Post*, September 6, 1978, p. A6.

"Hint JFK Witness Was in CIA." *New York Daily News*, March 31, 1977. Story about George DeMohrenschildt.

Hoberman, Jo. "The President's Brain Is Missing." *Village Voice*, December 31, 1991.

Hoch, Paul. "The Final Investigation?" *Third Decade*, July 1985, p. 2.

────── and Marshall, Jonathan. "JFK: The Unsolved Murder." *Inquiry*, December 25, 1978.

Hockberg, Sandy, with Valliere, James T. *The Conspirators*, New York: special edition of *Win* magazine, February 1, 1969.

"Hoover Called Oswald 'A Nut' FBI Files Show." *Fort Worth Star-Telegram*, December 7, 1977.

"Hoover's Vendetta Targeted Dallas Police, Memos Reveal." *Dallas Morning News*, December 30, 1980.

Horrock, Nicholas M. "Ford Would Sift Data in Kennedy, King Slayings." *New York Times*, November 27, 1975, p. 1.

──────. "Panel Studies FBI Links to Oswald and Ruby in '63." *New York Times*, October 14, 1975, p. 1.

──────. "Warren Panel Aide Calls for 2nd Inquiry Into Kennedy Killing." *New York Times*, November 23, 1975, p. 1.

Hougan, Jim. *Secret Agenda*. New York: Ballantine Books, 1984. An examination of the ongoing mystery of Watergate.

──────. *Spooks*. New York: William Morrow & Company, 1978.

"House Inquiry Into Killing of Kennedys and King Due." *New York Times*, September 15, 1976, p. 24.

"House Panel Claims Plots Likely in JFK, King Slayings." *Fort Worth Star-Telegram*, December 31, 1978.

"How the CIA Tried to Break Defector in Oswald Case." *Washington Star*, September 16, 1978.

Huber, Oscar L. "President Kennedy's Final Hours," *Denver Register*, December 8, 1963.

Hunter, Diana with Anderson, Alice. *Jack Ruby's Girls*, Atlanta, Ga.: Hallux, Inc., 1970.

Hurt, Henry. *Reasonable Doubt. An Investigation into the Asssassination of John F. Kennedy*. New York: Holt, Rinehart, 1986

Illson, Murray. "Johnson in '69 Suspected Foreign Ties with Oswald." *New York Times*, April 26, 1975, p. 12.

Investigation of the Assassination of President John F. Kennedy. Book V, Final Report of the Select Committee to Study Governmental Operations, with Respect to Intelligence Activities. U.S. Senate, 1976.

"Is Kennedy Assassin Sitting in Texas Jail?" *Forth Worth News Tribune*, June 11, 1982. Article about Charles V. Harrelson.

"Jack Ruby's Gun on the Block." *New York Post*, October 22, 1991.

"Jack Ruby's Gunrunning to Castro Claimed." *Dallas Morning News*, August 18, 1978.

Jackson, Bob. "Lensman Heard Shots, Saw Gun." *Dallas Times-Herald*, November 22, 1963.

James, Rosemary, and Wardlaw, Jack. *Plot or Politics?* New Orleans: Pelican Publishing Company, 1967.

Janos, Leo. "The Last Days of the President." *Atlantic*, July 1973.

Janson, Donald. "Oswald, While Idle, Led a Frugal Life." *New York Times*, December 1, 1963.

"JFK Assassination Film No One Wanted to See." *Midnight*, March 1, 1977, pp. 21-2.

"JFK Film May Reveal Two Gunmen." *Dallas Morning News*, December 19, 1978.

"The JFK Hearings." *Clandestine America*, vol. 2, no. 4.

"JFK Killing Witness Not Surprised Tests Indicated 2nd Gunman." *Fort Worth Star-Telegram*, December 22, 1978.

"JFK-King Panel Seeks Seclusion." *Fort Worth Star-Telegram*, June 21, 1977.

"JFK Murder Hatched in Ruby's Club—Oswald Was There." *Midnight*, November 15, 1976.

"JFK Panel Photo Expert Alleges Cover-Up." *Fort Worth Star-Telegram*, May 16, 1979.

"JFK: Settling Some Doubts." *Newsweek*, September 18, 1978.

J.F.K.: The Mystery Unraveled (Reprinted from *Spotlight*), Liberty Lobby, Inc. 1986.

Joesten, Joachim. *The Garrison Enquiry*. London, Peter Dawnay Ltd., 1967.

———. *Marina Oswald*. London: Peter Dawnay Ltd., 1967.

———. *Oswald: Assassin or Fall Guy?* New York: Marzani & Munsell, 1964.

———. *Oswald: The Truth*. London: Peter Dawnay Ltd., 1967.

"John F. Kennedy Memorial Edition." *Life*, Winter 1988.

Jones, Penn, Jr., *Forgive My Grief* (Volumes I–IV), Midlothian, Tex.: *Midlothian Mirror*, 1966, 1967, 1969 (revised 1976), 1978.

———. "Disappearing Witnesses." *Rebel*, January 1984, p. 42.

Jovich, John B. *Reflections on JFK's Assassination*. Miami, Fla.: Woodbine House, 1988.

"Judge Restrains Shaw Prosecutor." *New York Times*, May 29, 1968, p. 28.

Juffe, Mel. "Open and Shut! Feds Now Say JFK Files Should Be Kept Secret." *New York Post*, April 29, 1992.

———. "Oswald & Ruby Tied to Mafia Boss in JFK 'Hit.'" *New York Post*, January 22, 1992.

———. "Ted Wants JFK Slay File Opened." *New York Post*, January 11, 1992.

———. "Was Oswald a CIA Agent? Rep Plans to Ask KGB." *New York Post*, February 6, 1992.

"Jury Acquits DA Garrison in Bribe Case." *Fort Worth Star-Telegram*, September 28, 1973.

Kantor, Seth. *Who Was Jack Ruby?* New York: Everest House, 1978.

Kaplan, John. "The Assassins." *Stanford Law Review*, May 1967.

——— and Waltz, Jon R. *The Trial of Jack Ruby*. New York: Macmillan, 1965.

Karmin, Jacob. *Myth, Fantasy, or Fact? The Story of Lee Harvey Oswald*. New York: Vantage Press, 1977.

Katz, Joseph. "President Kennedy's Assassination." *Psychoanalytic Review*, Winter 1964–65.

Keeton, Stanley. "The Autopsy Photographs and X-Rays of President Kennedy: A Question of Authenticity." *Continuing Inquiry*, December 1977, January 1978, February 1978.

"KGB Agent in 'JFK Part 2.'" *Newsday*, January 10, 1992. Story about Oleg M. Nechiporenko.

"King's Widow Thinks U.S. Plotted Death." Associated Press, November 28, 1975.

Kirkwood, James. *American Grotesque: An Account of the Clay Shaw–Jim Garrison Affair in New Orleans.* New York: Simon & Schuster, 1970.

Kirschner, David. "The Death of a President." *Behavioral Science*, January 1965.

Knebel, Fletcher. "A New Wave of Doubt." *Look*, July 12, 1966.

Kohn, Howard. "Execution for the Witnesses." *Rolling Stone*, June 2, 1977.

————. "Strange Bedfellows: The Hughes–Nixon–Lansky Connection—The Secret Alliances of the CIA From World War II to Watergate." *Rolling Stone*, May 20, 1976.

Krauss, Clifford. "28 Years After Kennedy's Assassination, Conspiracy Theories Refuse to Die." *New York Times*, January 5, 1992.

Kurtz, Michael. *Crime of the Century.* Knoxville, Tenn.: University of Tennessee Press, 1982.

Lambert, Patricia. "The Secret Service at Dealey Plaza." *Third Decade*, March, 1985.

Lane, Mark. *A Citizen's Dissent.* New York: Dell, 1975.

————. "CIA Conspired to Kill Kennedy." *L.A. Free Press*, #1, 1978.

————. "The Mysterious Death of a Key JFK Witness." *Gallery*, November 1977. Story about George DeMohrenschildt.

————. *Plausible Denial.* New York: Thunder's Mouth Press, 1991.

————. *Rush to Judgment. A Critique of the Warren Commission's Inquiry into the Murders of President John F. Kennedy, Officer J. D. Tippit and Lee Harvey Oswald.* New York: Holt, Rinehart & Winston, 1966.

Lardner, George, Jr. "Connallys Tell of 'Terrible Ride.'" *Washington Post*, September 7, 1978, p. A1.

————. "Experts Track Mystery JFK Bullet." *Washington Post*, December 22, 1978, p. A1.

————. "50-50 Chance of a 4th Shot in Dallas, JFK Panel Is Told." *Washington Post*, September 12, 1978, p. A2.

————. "JFK Panel Gets Evidence of Conspiracy." *Washington Post*, December 21, 1978, p. A1.

————. "New Tests to Match Fragments in Kennedy, Connally." *Washington Post*, September 9, 1978, p. A3.

————. "Second JFK Gunman, Experts Say." *Washington Post*, December 31, 1978, p. A1.

————. "Warren Commission Backed." *Washington Post*, September 8, 1978, p. A1.

"Last Seconds of the Motorcade." *Life*, November 24, 1967.

Lattimer, John K. *Kennedy and Lincoln—Medical and Ballistic Comparisons of Their Assassinations*. New York: Harcourt Brace Jovanovich, 1980.

_____. "The Kennedy-Connally Single-Bullet Theory." *International Surgery*, December 1968.

_____. "Observations Based on a Review of the Autopsy, Photographs, X-rays, and Related Materials of the Late President John F. Kennedy." *Resident and Staff Physician*, May 1972.

Lawrence, Lincoln. *Were We Controlled?* New Hyde Park, N.Y.: University Books, 1967.

Leek, Sybil, and Sugar, Burt R. *The Assassination Chain*. New York: Corwin Books, 1976.

Lehrer, Jim. "Warren Panel Prober's Tactics Trigger Removal." *Dallas Times-Herald*, April 5, 1964.

Leslie, Warren. *Dallas City Limit*. New York: Grossman Publishers, 1964.

"Letters Reveal CIA Opened Mail to Oswald." *Fort Worth Star Telegram*, September 12, 1978.

Lewis, Richard Warren, and Schiller, Lawrence. *The Scavengers and Critics of the Warren Report*. New York: Dell, 1967.

Lifton, David. *Best Evidence: Disguise and Deception in the Assassination of John F. Kennedy*. New York: Macmillan, 1981, Carroll & Graf, 1988.

_____ and Welsh, David. "The Case for Three Assassins." *Ramparts*, January 1967.

Lippman, Thomas W. "Court Denies JFK Photos to Garrison." *Washington Post*, January 18, 1969, p. 1.

Livingstone, Harrison E. "Parkland Doctors' Testimony Shows Autopsy Photos Forged." *Baltimore Chronicle*, July 30, 1979.

Livingstone, Harrison Edward. *High Treason 2*. New York: Carroll & Graf, 1992.

"Louisiana Trial of Shaw Assured." *New York Times*, December 10, 1968, p. 42.

McDarrah, Timothy. "KGB: Oswald Couldn't Have Done It Alone." *New York Post*, November 21, 1991.

McDonald, Hugh C. (as told to Bocca, Geoffrey). *Appointment in Dallas: The Final Solution to the Assassination of JFK*. New York: Zebra Books, 1975, 1992.

McDonald, Hugh (with Moore, Robin). *LBJ and the JFK Conspiracy*. Westport, Conn.: Condor, 1978.

Mack, Gary. "J. D. Tippit: The 'Missing' Broadcasts." *Coverups*, September 1984.

McKinley, James. *Assassination in America*. New York: Harper & Row, 1977.

McMillan, Priscilla J. *Marina and Lee*. New York: Harper & Row, 1977.

Madden, Richard L. "House Votes to Keep Assassination Panel After Sprague Quits." *New York Times*, March 31, 1977, p. 1.

"Magician Says Oswald Was Patron in Ruby Night Club." *Dallas Morning News*, November 25, 1963.

Magruder, Jeb Stuart. *An American Life*. New York: Athenicum, 1974.

Malone, William Scott. "The Secret Life of Jack Ruby." *New Times*, January 23, 1978, pp. 46-51.

"Man Believes He Saw Ruby at Scene of Oswald's Arrest." *Dallas Morning News*, March 11, 1979.

"Man Claims He Found Live Bullet Buried Under Top of Grassy Knoll." *Dallas Morning News*, December 23, 1978.

Manchester, William. *The Death of a President*. New York: Harper & Row, 1967.

Marchetti, Victor, and Marks, John. *The CIA and the Cult of Intelligence*. New York: Alfred A. Knopf, 1974; Dell, 1975.

Marcus, Raymond. *The Bastard Bullet: A Search for Legitimacy for Commission Exhibit 399*. Los Angeles: Randall Publications, 1966.

"Marguerite Oswald Not Bitter After 10-Year Infamy." *Fort Worth Star-Telegram*, November 18, 1973.

Matthews, James P. *Four Dark Days in History*. Carmel, Cal.: Special Publications, Inc., 1963.

Mayo, John B. *Bulletin from Dallas: The President Is Dead*. New York: Exposition Press, 1967.

Meagher, Sylvia. *Accessories After the Fact*. Indianapolis: Bobbs-Merrill, 1967.

―――. *Subject Index to the Warren Report and Hearings and Exhibits*. New York: Scarecrow Press, 1966.

Melanson, Philip H. "High-Tech Mysterious Deaths." *Critique*, vol. 4, no. 3, 4, Fall/Winter, 1984–5.

―――. *Spy Saga: Lee Harvey Oswald and U.S. Intelligence*. New York: Praeger, 1990.

Menninger, Bonar. *Mortal Error*. New York: St. Martin's Press, 1992.

Miller, Tom. *The Assassination Please Almanac*. Chicago: Henry Regnery Co., 1977.

Morin, Relman. *Assassination: The Death of President John F. Kennedy*. New York: New American Library, 1968.

Morris, W. R., and Cutler, R. B. *Alek James Hidell, Alias Oswald, Who Died in a Heroic Attempt to Save His President's Life*. Manchester, Mass.: GKG Partners, 1985.

Morris, W. R. *The Men Behind the Guns*. Lexington, Tenn.: Angel Lea Books, 1975.

Morrow, Robert D. *Betrayal: Reconstruction of Certain Clandestine Events from the Bay of Pigs to the Assassination of John F. Kennedy*. Chicago: Henry Regnery Co., 1976.

―――. *First Hand Knowledge: How I Participated in the CIA-Mafia Murder of President Kennedy*. New York: S.P.I. Books, 1992.

"Mother of Oswald Blames Officers." *Fort Worth Star-Telegram*, December 2, 1963.

Murray, Norbert. *Legacy of an Assassination*. New York: Pro-People Press, 1964.

Nash, George, and Nash, Patricia. "The Other Witnesses." *New Leader*, October 12, 1964.

"National Archives—Security Classification Problems Involving Warren Commission Files and Other Records." *Hearings Before the House Subcommittee on Governmental Information*, 1976.

Navasky, Victor. *Kennedy Justice*. New York: Atheneum, 1971.

"New Evidence on Slaying: JFK Second Rifle." *National Examiner*, July 12, 1977.

"New Hurdle on JFK File." *New York Daily News*, April 29, 1992.

"New Oswald Clue Reportedly Found." *New York Times*, February 19, 1967, p. 43.

Newfield, Jack. "Hoffa Had the Mob Murder JFK." *New York Post*, January 14, 1992.

_____. "Secret Tapes May Hold Key to JFK Plot." *New York Post*, January 28, 1992.

_____ and Juffe, Mel. "Top JFK Prober Backs Hoffa Story." *New York Post*, January 15, 1992.

Newman, Albert H. *The Assassination of John F. Kennedy: The Reasons Why*. New York: Clarkson N. Potter, 1970.

Nichols, John, M.D. "The Wounding of Governor John Connally of Texas." *Maryland State Medical Journal*. October 1977.

"1968 Panel (Ramsey Clark) Review of Photographs, X-Ray Films, Documents and Other Evidence Pertaining to the Fatal Wounding of President John F. Kennedy." *Maryland State Medical Journal*, March 1977, pp. 69–77.

North, Mark. *Act of Treason: The Role of J. Edgar Hoover in the Assassination of President Kennedy*. New York: Carroll & Graf, 1991.

Norton, Linda E., M.D., et al. "The Exhumation and Identification of Lee Harvey Oswald." *Journal of Forensic Sciences*, January 1984.

"'Not Sure' on Oswald, Author Curry Indicates." *Dallas Morning News*, November 6, 1969.

Noyes, Peter. *Legacy of Doubt*, New York: Pinnacle, 1973.

O'Byrne, James. "The Garrison Probe." *New Orleans Times-Picayune*, December 15, 1991.

"Officer Recalls Oswald Capture." *Dallas Morning News*, November 24, 1963.

"Officer Says JFK Tape Not His." *Fort Worth Star-Telegram*, January 5, 1979.

Oglesby, Carl. "The Conspiracy That Won't Go Away." *Playboy*, February 1992, p. 74.

_____. *The JFK Assassination—The Facts and the Theories*. New York: Signet, 1992.

_____. *Who Killed JFK?* Berkeley, Cal.: Odonian Press, 1992.

_____. *The Yankee and Cowboy War*. Mission, Kan.: Sheed, Andrews and McMeel, 1976.

Oglesby, Carl, and Goldberg, Jeff. "Did the Mob Kill Kennedy?" *Washington Post*, February 25, 1979, pp. B1–B4.

"Open JFK Murder Files." *New Orleans Times-Picayune*, January 15, 1992.

"Oswald Called It My 'Historic Diary'—And It Is." *Life*, July 10, 1964.

"Oswald–Ferrie Link Made by Ex-Cabbie." *Fort Worth Star-Telegram*, March 10, 1967.

"Oswald Friend Labeled CIA Informant in Memo." *Dallas Times Herald*, July 27, 1978.

"Oswald Grave Now Battle Site." *Fort Worth Star-Telegram*, October 19, 1979.

"Oswald Pictures Released by FBI." *Dallas Morning News*, August 7, 1978.

Oswald, Robert L. (with Land, Myrick, and Land, Barbara). *Lee: A Portrait of Lee Harvey Oswald*. New York: Coward-McCann, 1967.

"Oswald's Camera Disappeared During FBI Investigation." *Dallas Morning News*, June 15, 1978.

"Oswald's Mother Asks Exhumation." *Fort Worth Star Telegram*, November 17, 1967.

"Oswald's Prints Revealed on Rifle Killing Kennedy." *Dallas Times Herald*, November 25, 1963.

O'Toole, George. *The Assassination Tapes*. New York: Penthouse Press, 1975.

"Overwhelming Evidence Oswald Was Assassin." *U.S. News & World Report*, October 10, 1966.

Oxford, Edward. "Destiny in Dallas." *American History Illustrated*, November 1988.

"Panel's Finding Pleases Mother of Lee Oswald." *Fort Worth Star-Telegram*, December 31, 1978.

"Paper Shows Oswald Eyed." *Fort Worth Star-Telegram*, October 1, 1976.

"Papers Link Ruby, Oswald." *Dallas Morning News*, March 28, 1976.

"Papers Reveal Justice Ended Kennedy, King Death Probes." *Dallas Times Herald*, September 4, 1988.

"Permindex: Britain's International Assassination Bureau." *Executive Intelligence Review*, November 14, 1981.

Phelan, James R. "The Assassination That Will Not Die." *New York Times Magazine*, November 23, 1975, p. 110.

Podhoretz, Norman. "The Warren Commission: An Editorial." *Commentary*, January 1964.

Phinney, Kevin. "JFK Expert: Rather Twisted Facts." *Hollywood Reporter*, April 20, 1992, p. 4.

Polikoff, Jerry. "Investigations That Were Bound to Fail." *Gallery*, July 1979.

————. "The Media and the Murder of John Kennedy." *New Times*, August 8, 1975.

Polikoff, Jerry, and Malone, William Scott. "A Great Show, A Lousy Investigation." *New Times*. September 4, 1978. An overview of the HSCA.

Popkin, Richard. *The Second Oswald*. New York: Avon, 1966.

Poster, Tom. "JFK Doc: Head Shot Wasn't Oswald's." *New York Daily News*, March 31, 1992.

————. "JFK Doc Hits Claim by Colleague." *New York Daily News*, April 14, 1992.

Pound, Jay. "Who Told the TRUTH about JFK? A Review of the Research." *Critique: A Journal of Conspiracies and Metaphysics*. Spring/Summer 1986, vol. 6, nos. 1, 2.

"President Dead, Connally Shot." *Dallas Times Herald*, November 22, 1963.

"President Names Board to Probe JFK's Slaying." *Dallas Morning News*, November 30, 1963.

Prouty, L. Fletcher. *J.F.K.: The CIA, Vietnam and the Plot to Assassinate John F. Kennedy*. New York: Birch Lane Press, 1992.

———. "The Betrayal of JFK Kept Fidel Castro in Power." *Gallery*, February 1978.

———. "An Introduction to the Assassination Business." *Gallery*, September 1975.

———. "The Guns of Dallas." *Gallery*, October, 1975.

———. *The Secret Team: The CIA and Its Allies in Control of the United States and the World*. New York: Prentice-Hall, 1973.

Rand, Michael, with Loxton, Howard, and Deighton, Len. *The Assassination of President Kennedy*. London: Jonathan Cape, 1967.

"Rapid Bang of Gun Changes History's Course." *Dallas Times Herald*, November 23, 1963.

Rawls, Wendell, Jr. "Assassination Panel Is Given Right to Bypass House." *New York Times*, October 17, 1977, p. 15.

———. "Cornell Professor Is Named as Assassination Panel Counsel." *New York Times*, June 21, 1977, p. 21.

———. "Ex-Castro Soldier Balks at House Inquiry on Kennedy." *New York Times*, June 8, 1977. Story about Loran Hall.

———. "House Inquiry Reported Fruitless on Kennedy-King Assassinations." *New York Times*, June 6, 1977, p. 1.

"Reporter Recalls the Day Camelot Died in Dallas." *Dallas Morning News*, April 5, 1981.

"Return to Dealey Plaza." *Hollywood Reporter*, February 6, 1992. Associated Press interview with Dan Rather.

Roberts, Charles. *The Truth About the Assassination*. New York: Grosset & Dunlap, Inc., 1967.

Roberts, Gene. "Arrests in Kennedy Case Delayed for Months, New Orleans Prosecutor Says." *New York Times*, February 21, 1967, p. 20.

———. "Businessmen Aid Inquiry on Plot." *New York Times*, February 25, 1967, p. 56. Reveals that Jim Garrison's assassination probe is being privately funded.

———. "Figure in Oswald Inquiry Is Dead in New Orleans." *New York Times*, February 23, 1967, p. 22. Report on the death of David Ferrie.

———. "Investigator Quits Garrison's Staff and Assails Inquiry into Plot." *New York Times*, June 27, 1967, p. 25.

———. "Louisiana ACLU Scores Garrison." *New York Times*, March 7, 1967, p. 21.

———. "Suspect in 'Plot' Linked to Oswald." *New York Times*, March 3, 1967, p. 22.

Roffman, Howard. *Presumed Guilty*. Cranbury, N.J.: Fairleigh Dickinson Press, 1975.

Rogers, Warren. "The Persecution of Clay Shaw." *Look*, August 26, 1969, pp. 53–60.

Rose, Jerry D. "The Epileptic Seizure." *Continuing Inquiry*, February 22, 1984.

Rosen, James. "Book Claims Agent Fired 3d JFK Shot." *New York Daily News*, February 23, 1992.

———. "Tex. JFK File Offers Clues." *New York Daily News*, February 14, 1992.

Rosenbaum, Ron. "Taking a Darker View." *Time*, January 13, 1992.

Ross, Barbara. "JFK Whodunit: Puzzle Pieces Missing." *New York Daily News*, January 21, 1992.

"Ruby Murder Trial Postponed." *Dallas Times Herald*, December 3, 1963.

"Ruby-Oswald Link Cited by Witness." *Fort Worth Star-Telegram*, July 18, 1976.

Russell, Dick. "Loran Hall and the Politics of Assassination." *Village Voice*, October 3, 1977.

——— with Navard, Dave. "The Man Who Had a Contract to Kill Lee Harvey Oswald Before the Assassination of President John F. Kennedy." *Gallery*, March 1981.

———. *The Man Who Knew Too Much*. New York: Carroll & Graf, 1992.

Salandria, Vincent. "The Head Wounds of President Kennedy." *Liberation*, March 1965.

———. "The Impossible Tasks of One Assassination Bullet." *Minority of One*, 1966.

———. "A Philadelphia Lawyer Analyzes the President's Back and Neck Wounds." *Liberation*, March 1965.

———. "The Warren Report?" *Liberation*, March 1965.

"Salesman Insists FBI Discounted Facts on Oswald." *Dallas Morning News*, May 8, 1977.

Sauvage, Leo. *The Oswald Affair*. Cleveland: World Publishing Co., 1966.

Scheer, Robert. "Oliver Stone's Conspiracy Theory." *Newsday*, December 15, 1991.

Scheim, David. *Contract on America: The Mafia Murder of President John F. Kennedy*. New York: Shapolsky Publishers, 1988.

Schorr, Daniel. "The Assassins." *New York Review of Books*, October 13, 1977.

"Schweiker Predicts Collapse of Warren Report on Kennedy." *New York Times*, October 16, 1975, p. 28.

Sciolino, Elaine. "K.G.B. Telltale Is Telling, But Is He Telling U.S. All?" *New York Times*, January 20, 1992.

Scott, Peter Dale. *Crime and Cover-Up*. Berkeley, Cal.: Westworks, 1977.

———. *The Dallas Conspiracy*. Unpublished document.

——— with Hoch, Paul and Stetler, Russell. *The Assassinations: Dallas and Beyond*. New York: Random House, 1976.

Semple, Robert B., Jr. "Clark Discounts Shaw Conspiracy." *New York Times*, March 3, 1967, p. 22.

"Seven Shared Emergency Room With JFK." *Dallas Morning News*, November 22, 1973.

"Seven Shots Believed Fired at Kennedy." *Fort Worth Star-Telegram*, September 1, 1977.

Shaw, J. Gary, and Harris, Larry R. *Cover-up: The Governmental Conspiracy to Conceal the Facts About the Public Execution of John Kennedy.* Cleburne, Tex.: self-published, 1976; Austin, Tex.: Collector's Editions, 1992.

———. "The Dallas Mystery Man." *Continuing Inquiry*, August 1979.

———. "Is the FBI Shielding a JFK Assassin?" *Continuing Inquiry*, November 22, 1977.

Sheatsley, Paul B., and Feldman, Jacob J. "The Assassination of President Kennedy." *Public Opinion Quarterly*, Summer 1964.

Sheehy, Maura. "The Searchers." *Details*, January 1992. Story about assassination researchers.

Shuster, Mike. "George DeMohrenschildt." *Seven Days*, May 9, 1977.

"Silence Not Golden, Probers Say." *New Orleans Times-Picayune*, January 19, 1992.

Sisk, Richard. "'JFK' Tramps, FBI Says, Were Just Vagrants." *New York Daily News*, March 4, 1992.

Sloan, Bill, with Hill, Jean. *JFK: The Last Dissenting Witness.* Gretna, La.: Pelican, 1992. Book about the experiences of a.w. Jean Hill.

Smith, Nancy, "Acoustics Experts Reenact '63 Kennedy Assassination in Dallas." *Washington Post*, August 21, 1978, p. A3.

Sparrow, John. *After the Assassination: A Positive Appraisal of the Warren Report.* New York: Chilmark Press, 1968.

Sprague, Richard E. "The Assassination of President John F. Kennedy: The Application of the Photographic Evidence." *Computers and Automation*, May 1970.

———. "The Assignment of G. Robert Blakey." *Continuing Inquiry*, March 1981.

———. *The Taking of America 1-2-3.* Self-published, 1976.

"SS 'Imposters' Spotted by JFK Witnesses." *Dallas Morning News*, August 27, 1978.

Stafford, Jean. *A Mother in History.* New York: Farrar, Straus, 1965. Book about Marguerite Oswald.

Standora, Leo. "Cronkite: LBJ Doubted Warren Report." *New York Post*, February 6, 1992.

———. "Hobo Bares Latest JFK-Slay Twist." *New York Post*, February 25, 1992.

Steele, Jonathan. "Ford Kept FBI Briefed on Kennedy Inquiry." *Guardian*, January 20, 1978.

Stolley, Richard B. "Shots Seen Around the World." *Entertainment Weekly*, January 17, 1992.

Strausbaugh, John. "Making Book." *New York Press*, vol. 4, no. 25, June 19–25, 1991, pp. 8–9.

"Study to Belittle Assassination Data." *Dallas Morning News*, July 9, 1981.

Summers, Anthony. *Conspiracy.* New York: McGraw-Hill, 1981.

———. "The Dark Side of Camelot." *New York Daily News*, October 6, 1991.

————. "The Mob Seeks Revenge." *New York Daily News*, October 7, 1991.

"Surveyor: More Than One Man Shot Kennedy." *Fort Worth Star-Telegram*, April 14, 1978.

Sutton, Larry, "Author Expresses Doubts about Latest JFK Theory." *New York Daily News*, January 20, 1992.

Szulc, Ted. "The Warren Commission in Its Own Words." *New Republic*, September 27, 1975.

Thompson, George. *The Quest for Truth.* Glendale, Cal.: G. C. Thompson Engineering Company, 1964.

Thompson, Josiah. "The Crossfire That Killed President Kennedy." *Look*, December 2, 1967.

————. *Six Seconds in Dallas.* New York: Bernard Geis Associates, 1967.

Thompson, Robert E. *The Trial of Lee Harvey Oswald.* New York: Ace Books, 1977.

Thornley, Kerry W. *Oswald.* Chicago: New Classics, 1965.

"Three Patients at Parkland." *Texas State Journal of Medicine*, January 1964.

"Time Gives Back Identity." *Dallas Times Herald*, November 21, 1971. Story about Billy Lovelady.

Tolbert, Frank X. "The Odd Fate of Oswald's Other Victims." *Saturday Evening Post*, August 29, 1964.

Torbitt, William. *Nomenclature of an Assassin Cabal.* Self-published, 1970.

The Torch Is Passed: The Associated Press Story of the Death of a President. New York: Associated Press, 1963.

"Towson Gunsmith Tells Panel JFK Was Killed Accidentally by Secret Service Agent." *Baltimore Sun*, July 13, 1977, p. 15.

"The Truth About the Kennedy Assassination." *U.S. News and World Report*, October 10, 1966.

Turner, William. "The Garrison Commission on the Assassination of President Kennedy." *Ramparts*, January 1968.

Vidal, Gore. "The Art and Arts of Howard Hunt." *New York Review of Books*, December 13, 1973.

Viorst, Milton. "The Mafia, the CIA and the Kennedy Assassination." *Washingtonian*, 1975.

"Wade Calls Killing a 'Dastardly Act.'" *Dallas Morning News*, November 23, 1963.

Wainwright, Loudon. "Warren Report Is Not Enough." *Life*, October 7, 1966.

Waldron, Martin. "FBI Chiefs Linked to Oswald File Loss." *New York Times*, September 14, 1975, p. 1.

————. "Garrison Charges CIA and FBI Conceal Evidence on Oswald." *New York Times*, May 10, 1967, p. 27.

————. "Schweiker Joins Attack on Warren Report as Clamor for New Inquiry Rises." *New York Times*, October 20, 1975, p. 16.

Ward, E. Graham. *Transcripts 1: An Interview With Marguerite Oswald.* Boston: Houghton Mifflin, 1973.

"Warren Report Held Unbelievable." *Fort Worth Star-Telegram*, June 24, 1976.

Wecht, Cyril, M.D. "JFK Assassination: A Prolonged and Willful Cover-Up." *Modern Medicine*, October 28, 1974.

_____. "A Pathologist's View of the JFK Autopsy: An Unsolved Case." *Modern Medicine*, November 27, 1972.

_____. "Why Is the Rockefeller Commission So Single-Minded About a Lone Assassin in the Kennedy Case?" *Journal of Legal Medicine*, July/August 1975.

Weisberg, Harold. *Oswald in New Orleans*, New York: Canyon Books, 1967.

_____. *Photographic Whitewash—Suppressed Kennedy Assassination Pictures.* Frederick, Md.: self-published, 1967, 1976.

_____. *Whitewash*, 4 vols. Hyattstown, Md.: self-published, 1965, 1966, 1967, 1974.

_____. *Post-Mortem*. Frederick, M.D.: self-published, 1975.

Whalen, Richard J. "The Kennedy Assassination." *Saturday Evening Post*, January 14, 1967.

The White House Transcripts, New York: Viking Press, 1973.

White, Jack, "Can a Photograph Lie?" *Continuing Inquiry*, October 1979.

White, Stephen. *Should We Now Believe the Warren Report?* New York: Macmillan, 1968.

Wicker, Tom. "Does 'J.F.K.' Conspire Against Reason?" *New York Times*, December 15, 1991.

_____. "Wicker Describes That Day in Dallas." *Times Talk*, December 1963.

Wills, Gary, and Demaris, Ovid. *Jack Ruby*. New York: New American Library, 1967.

Wise, Dan, with Maxfield, Marietta. *The Day Kennedy Died*. San Antonio, Tex.: Naylor, 1964.

"Witness from the News Describes Assassination." *Dallas Morning News*, November 23, 1963.

"Witnesses Overlooked in JFK Probe." *Dallas Morning News*, December 19, 1978.

"World Leaders Voice Sympathy and Shock." *New York Times*, November 23, 1963.

Wright, David. "LBJ Killed Kennedy!" *National Enquirer*, December 10, 1991.

Zirbel, Craig I. *The Texas Connection*. Scottsdale, Ariz.: Texas Connection Company, 1991.

Zoglin, Richard. "More Shots in Dealey Plaza." *Time*, June 10, 1991, pp. 64, 66. About Oliver Stone's *JFK*.